An Index of "In Brief" Boxes

WRITING

A COLLEGE HANDBOOK

FOURTH EDITION

WRITING

A COLLEGE HANDBOOK

JAMES A.W. HEFFERNAN
Dartmouth College

JOHN E. LINCOLN

FOURTH EDITION

W.W. Norton & Company
New York   London

Contents

GLOSSARIES

APPENDICES

Preface to the Fourth Edition

The first three editions of this book set out to demonstrate that good writing is not simply the absence of grammatical error but the presence of rhetorical power. This remains our leading aim. We have tightened many sections and added a few new ones, but our basic approach remains unchanged. While identifying the mistakes commonly made in student writing and showing how to correct them, we emphasize what student writers *can* do rather than what they can't or shouldn't do. Above all, we try to show them how to generate the kind of writing that informs, excites, delights, and persuades the readers for whom it is written. This positive, empowering approach is at the core of *Writing: A College Handbook*.

Since many teachers like to start by introducing students to the writing process as a whole, Part 1, "Writing Essays," begins with a five-chapter overview of that process. Users of the third edition will see that we continue to illustrate the writing process with various examples of student writing-in-progress and with successive versions of one student essay as it evolves from pre-writing to final draft. But we have made a number of needed changes. Besides adding many new examples of student writing, we explain more fully how to formulate an effective thesis (section 2.3), how to consider the needs and expectations of the reader (section 3.1), and how to write an effective introduction (section 3.4B). In addition, we have added a new guide to peer reviewing of student drafts (section 4.1A); we now illustrate revision by showing a draft with instructor's comments plus a revised version on facing pages; and to illustrate editing, we now use hand-edited sentences wherever possible throughout the book. Hand-edited sentences let students see again and again that writing is a process, sometimes a messy process, and that they not only can but *should* mark up their drafts.

We have also strengthened chapters 6 through 10. Chapter 6 now highlights the role of authorial choice at every stage of the writing process. Chapter 7 shows more clearly how logic helps to make an argument credible, gives more weight to the often neglected role of emotional appeal in the making of arguments, and includes a new section on rhetorical questions (7.7). Chapter 8 uses more examples of student writing to show how a paragraph can be organized. Chapter 9 ("Choosing Words") includes a new five-part exercise on using the dictionary as well as a new section (9.12) on choosing words respectful of the diverse groups and individuals that make up our society. Finally, as a prelude to its treatment of reading as a source of writing, chapter 10 begins with a new set of basic guidelines on critical reading (section 10.1).

Part 2, "Writing Sentences," now works better as a reference source because it offers more "In Brief" boxes with short tips on specific features of sentence construction. For students needing detailed guidance on this topic, Part 2 keeps its basically positive approach by repeatedly stressing the rhetorical impact of a partic-ular construction when it is correctly and effectively used. Before we attack the misplaced modifier, for instance, we show what a well-placed modifier can do; and before we identify the wrong ways of joining independent clauses (the run-on sentence and the comma splice), we show what coordination can do. Using lively examples from student essays as well as from the work of leading writers, we consistently aim to show students how they can exploit the rich, vital, and inexhaustible resources of the English language. Our chief aim in the whole of Part 2, in fact, is summed up by the title of chapter 25: "Invigorating Your Style."

The emphasis on rhetorical effect in Part 2 is reinforced by the exercises. Instead of merely calling for the correction of errors, many of them ask for short sentences to be combined in more than one way so that students can see what rhetorical effects they can achieve with various constructions. Also, nearly all of the exercises consist of consecutive sentences that work together to tell a story, build a description, or develop a point.

Part 3, "Punctuation and Mechanics," is a reference source that we have strengthened by trimming it in some parts and by adding to other parts new examples and new consecutive-sentence exercises.

Part 4, "The Research Paper," now takes four chapters (not five) to explain the preparation, writing, and documentation of an argumentative research paper. Besides incorporating a new sample paper on sexual harassment in the workplace, we have clarified and expanded the sections on choosing a topic (33.1), taking notes with a word processor (33.10C), outlining the paper (34.2), avoiding plagiarism (34.3), and using the MLA style of parenthetical citation (section 34.4B and chapter 35).

Part 4 ends with two more chapters—one from the previous edition, the other wholly new. "Writing and Research across the Curriculum" (chapter 38) treats the various ways in which humanists, social scientists, and natural scientists approach their subjects, write about them, and cite their sources. The new chapter 37 ("Writing about Literature") explains how to study poetry, fiction, and drama; how to find a fertile topic and generate an incisive thesis; how to distinguish between plot summary and critical analysis; how to develop an interpretation by quoting and citing sources; and how to enrich the study of literature by linking it to history. Also included are two student essays—one (with secondary sources) on a poem, the other (without secondary sources) on a short story.

Two glossaries—one on usage and the other on grammatical terms—are followed by two appendices. As in previous editions, appendix 2 moves "Beyond Freshman English" to show how good writing can serve a variety of practical purposes both inside and outside the world of college. The new appendix 1 aims to help ESL students—students of English as a second language—learn the kinds of skills that native speakers acquire without conscious effort, such as when and how to use *the, a,* and *an* and how to choose between gerunds and infinitives.

SUPPLEMENTARY MATERIALS

Writing: A College Handbook, Fourth Edition, is supported by a complete instructional package.

For the student, *Writing: A College Workbook,* Fourth Edition, is a basic textbook on the writing of sentences and the handling of punctuation and mechanics. It parallels and supplements Parts 2 and 3 of the *Handbook* and includes basic instruction on sentence structure as well as over one hundred exercises—ranging from recognition and error correction to sentence-combining to revising and editing complete paragraphs and essays—printed on tear-out pages that can be assigned as classwork or homework. It also includes the *Handbook*'s appendix for ESL students and adds to the appendix exercises especially designed for the *Workbook.* An answer pamphlet for the *Workbook* as a whole is available to instructors on request. New to the Fourth Edition, *Grammar Workouts,* an interactive exercise disk for IBMs and compatibles, contains more than ninety sets of multiple-choice exercises that build sentence-writing skills. It is available packaged with the *Workbook* for a low additional cost.

Norton Textra Writer 2.5 combines a powerful word processor and spell checker with a concise on-line version of *Writing: A College Handbook.* At a keystroke students can find grammatical and rhetorical advice in keeping with the positive approach of the *Handbook,* as well as cross-references to the book itself. *Norton Textra Writer 2.5* is available for IBMs and compatibles.

For the instructor, the *Annotated Instructor's Edition,* new with the fourth edition, combines the full text of the *Handbook* with marginalia containing chapter overviews, teaching tips, ESL notes, suggestions for peer work, backgrounds and bibliographies, quotations, and answers to exercises.

Also available are *Instructor's Resource Materials* including *Interactive Transparency Masters,* which provide more than thirty-five ready-made classroom activities; the *Norton Textra/Connect Assignment Disk,* writing assignments and activities for use in networked classrooms; and *Diagnostic Tests* in print or on disk for Macintosh and IBM and compatible computers.

James A. W. Heffernan
John E. Lincoln

Acknowledgments

We have incurred many debts in the preparation of this book, and we are happy to acknowledge them here. It began as *The Dartmouth Guide to Writing,* by John E. Lincoln—a book of lessons and exercises issued by Dartmouth College for its students under a grant from the Lilly Foundation.

For help with the fourth edition, we are grateful, first of all, to the teachers who acted as on-going consultants on the entire manuscript: Mimi Dixon, Wittenberg College; Kristine Hansen, Brigham Young University; Alexandra Rowe Henry, University of South Carolina; Donald Hettinga, Calvin College; Kary Smout, Washington and Lee University.

We are also indebted to many others for various kinds of help: to William Cook, Charles Culver, Robert Fogelin, Ronald Green, Michael Kubersky, and Thomas Roos, all of Dartmouth College; Lynn Dianne Beene, University of New Mexico; Harry Brent, Rutgers University, Camden College of Arts and Sciences; Barry E. Brown, Missouri Southern State College; Jean Brunk, Oregon State University—Corvallis; Alma G. Bryant, University of South Florida; Michael Cartwright, California State College—Bakersfield; Lynne Constantine, James Madison University; the late Gregory Cowan, Texas A & M University; Diana DeLuca, University of Hawaii at Manoa; Hubert M. English, Jr., University of Michigan; Judith Ferstser, North Carolina State University; John J. Fenstermaker, Florida State University; Jennifer Ginn; Barbara Munson Goff, Cook College of Rutgers University; S. J. Hanna, Mary Washington College; James Hartman, University of Kansas; Joan E. Hartman, College of Staten Island,

City University of New York; Francis Hubbard, University of Wisconsin—Milwaukee; Naomi Jacobs, University of Missouri—Columbia; Craig Johnson, Hillsborough Community College—Ybor City Campus; Richard Johnson, Mount Holyoke College; Mildred A. Kalish, Suffolk County Community College; C. H. Knoblauch, Columbia University; James MacKillop, Onondaga Community College; Stephen R. Mandell, Drexel University; John C. Mellon, University of Illinois, Chicago Circle Campus; Susan Miller, University of Wisconsin—Milwaukee; James Murphy, California State University—Hayward; Karen Ogden, University of Manitoba; James F. O'Neil, Edison Community College; Andrew Parkin, University of British Columbia; Diana Pingatore, Lake Superior State College; Kenneth Roe, Shasta College; Ann Sharp, Furman University; Craig B. Snow, University of Arizona; Ken M. Symes, Western Washington State College; Keith A. Tandy, Moorehead State University; Mary Thysell, University of Waterloo; Barbara Weaver, Anderson College; Harvey S. Wiener, La Guardia Community College; and Wendy Wood, Florida International University. We thank George Savvides, Charles Rice, Donald Murray, Charles Moran of the University of Massachusetts, and Ron Fortune, Illinois State University.

We must record here, too, our indebtedness to the many students who have contributed examples of what they do in their writing—in particular Mitch Arion, Barbara Clark, Sarah Watson, Robin Martinez, Erica Berl, Lisa Miles, James Mann, Timothy Boyle, Ken Oshima, Qiao Xing, David Lenrow, Sherri Hughes, Rick Kurihara, Daphne Bien, Scott Jaynes, Adam Usadi, Steven Arkowitz, David Leitao, Neil Okun, Jonathan Kulas, Vanessa Bernstein, Gary Pappas, Cirri Washington, Julie Cusick, Arturo Garcia, Rick Harris, Leonard Chang, Samantha Bauni, Gino Fernandez, Osamu Yagasaki, Ruben Hequilein, Carlos Martinez, Juan Carlos Manosalvas, Maglio Montiel, Valeria Bijos, Chih-Li-Len, and Dora Shyan-mei Wang. Thanks are due as well to Francis X. Oscadal and Lois Krieger, who gave us their expert advice on the use of library resources for research, and also to those who generously supplied us with material for appendix 2: Frances R. Hall of Dartmouth Medical School, Robert Sokol and Kenneth Shewmaker of Dartmouth College, and Andrew Vouras of the New England Telephone Company. We also thank Kathy Harp and Barbara Cunningham of the Dartmouth College English Department, who kindly helped us with the photocopying of material for this edition.

In addition, we wish to thank present and former members of our publisher's staff for their signal contributions. Ethelbert Nevin II and John E. Neill each played a part in persuading us to write the first edition of the book. John W. N. Francis and the late John Benedict gave superb editorial guidance for the first two editions, and Julia Reidhead has done outstanding work on the third and fourth editions. In addition, we owe special thanks to Jay Davis, who did extensive research for us and contributed a number of exercises; to Marian Johnson, whose many fine suggestions went far above and beyond her duties as a manuscript editor; to Carol Hollar-Zwick, who ably coordinated and edited the ancillaries. We also thank Ann Tappert for her assistance and Susan Brekka, our permissions editor; Margaret Wagner, our designer; Diane O'Connor, who supervised the production of the book; Peter Simon, marketing associate; and Nancy Palmquist and Ben Gamit, who created much of the art.

We also wish to acknowledge our debt to the following books and articles: Chris Anderson, *Free/Style: A Direct Approach to Writing* (Boston: Houghton Mifflin, 1992); Charles Bazerman, *Shaping Written Knowledge: The Genre and Activity of the Experimental Article in Science* (Madison, Wisconsin: U of Wisconsin P, 1988); Monroe Beardsley, *Thinking Straight,* 4th ed. (New York: Prentice-Hall, 1975); Fredric V. Bogel and Katherine K. Gottschalk, eds., *Teaching Prose* (New York: Norton, 1984); Richard Braddock, "The Frequency and Placement of Topic Sentences in Expository Prose," *Research in the Teaching of English* 8 (1974): 287–302; Kenneth Bruffee, *A Short Course in Writing* (Glenview, IL: Scott, Foresman, 1990); P. Carrell, "The Effects of Rhetorical Organization on ESL Readers," TESOL *Quarterly* 18 (1984): 441–69; N. R. Cattell, *The New English Grammar* (Cambridge, MA: MIT Press, 1969); Elaine Chaika, "Grammars and Teaching," *College English* 39 (March 1978): 770–83; Francis Christensen, "A Generative Rhetoric of the Sentence," "Notes toward a

New Rhetoric," and "A Generative Rhetoric of the Paragraph," in *The Sentence and the Paragraph* (Urbana, IL: NCTE, 1966); Harry H. Crosby and George F. Estey, *College Writing: The Rhetorical Imperative* (New York: Harper & Row, 1968); George O. Curme, *English Grammar* (New York: Barnes and Noble, 1968); Peter Elbow, *Writing without Teachers* (New York: Oxford UP, 1973) and *Writing with Power: Techniques for Mastering the Writing Process* (New York: Oxford UP, 1981); Bergen and Cornelia Evans, *A Dictionary of Contemporary American Usage* (New York: Random House, 1957); Charles Fillmore, "The Case for Case," in *Universals in Linguistic Theory,* ed. Emmon Bach and Robert T. Harms (New York: Holt, 1968); Linda S. Flower, *Problem Solving Strategies for Writing* (New York: Harcourt Brace, 1981); W. Nelson Francis, *The Structure of American English* (New York: Ronald, 1958); John Gage, *The Shape of Reason: Argumentative Writing in College,* 2nd ed. (New York: Macmillan, 1991); Robert J. Geist, *An Introduction to Transformational Grammar* (New York: Macmillan, 1971); William E. Gruber, " 'Servile Copying' and the Teaching of English Composition," *College English* 39 (December 1977): 491–97; Alexandra Henry, *Second Language Rhetorics in Process: A Comparison of Arabic, Chinese, and Spanish* (New York: Lang, 1993); Anne J. Herrington and Deborah Cadman, "Peer Review and Revising in an Anthropology Course: Lessons for Learning," *College Composition and Communication* 42 (1991): 184–99; A. S. Hornby, *A Guide to Patterns and Usage in English* (London: Oxford UP, 1954); Darrell Huff, *How to Lie with Statistics* (New York: Norton, 1954); Roderick A. Jacobs and Peter S. Rosenbaum, *English Transformational Grammar* (Waltham, MA: Blaisdell, 1968); Otto Jespersen, *Essentials of English Grammar* (London: George Allen & Unwin, 1959); David Kelley, *The Art of Reasoning* (New York: Norton, 1994); James L. Kinneavy, *A Theory of Discourse* (New York: Norton, 1980); Henriette Ann Klausen, *Writing on Both Sides of the Brain* (San Francisco: Harper & Row, 1987): Catherine Lamb, "Beyond Argument in Feminist Composition," *College Composition and Communication* 42 (1991): 11–24; Susan Peck MacDonald, "Problem Definition in Academic Writing," *College English* 49 (1987), 315–31; Elaine P. Maimon et al., *Writing in the Arts and Sciences* (Cambridge, MA:

Winthrop, 1981): John C. Mellon, *Transformational Sentence Combining* (Urbana, IL: NCTE, 1969); Donald Murray, *A Writer Teaches Writing: A Practical Method of Teaching Composition* (Boston: Houghton Mifflin, 1968), *Write to Learn,* 3rd ed. (Fort Worth: Holt, 1990), and also various essays and lectures; Frank O'Hare, *Sentence Combining* (Urbana, IL: NCTE, 1973), and *Sentencecraft* (Lexington, MA: Ginn, 1975); Gabriele Lusser Rico, *Writing the Natural Way* (Los Angeles: Tarcher, 1983); Mina Shaughnessy, *Errors and Expectations: A Guide for the Teacher of Basic Writing* (New York: Oxford UP, 1977); Harry Shaw, *Errors in English and Ways to Correct Them* (New York: Barnes and Noble, 1970); R. Spack, "Invention Strategies and the ESL College Student," *TESOL Quarterly* 18 (1984): 649–68; Stephen Toulmin, *The Uses of Argument* (Cambridge: Cambridge UP, 1958); Joseph Williams, *Style: Ten Lessons in Clarity and Grace* (Glenview, IL: Scott, Foresman, 1981); the *MLA Handbook for Writers of Research Papers,* 3rd ed. (New York: MLA, 1988); and the *Publication Manual of the American Psychological Association,* 3rd ed. (Washington, DC: APA, 1983).

Lastly, we thank our spouses, Nancy Heffernan and Mary Lincoln, who contributed to the preparation of this book in ways too various to mention, and we thank our children—Andrew and Virginia Heffernan, and Chris, Peter, and Brian Lincoln—for supplying both vivid examples of their own writing and their own special brand of encouragement.

WRITING

A COLLEGE HANDBOOK

FOURTH EDITION

Introduction

TALKING AND WRITING

Talking is something most of us seem to do naturally. We learn to talk almost automatically, first imitating the words we hear and then imitating the ways in which people around us put them together. Well before we learn how to put words on paper, we unconsciously learn how to use them in speech.

But no one learns to write automatically. You cannot write even a single letter of the alphabet without a conscious effort of mind and hand, and to get beyond the single letter, you must be shown how to form words, how to put words together into sentences, and how to punctuate those sentences.

Writing, then, is a means of communication you must consciously learn. And part of what makes it hard to learn is that written words usually have to express your meaning in your absence, have to "speak" all by themselves. When you speak face to face with a listener, you can communicate in many different ways. You can raise or lower the pitch or volume of your voice to emphasize a point; you can grin, frown, wink, or shrug; you can use your hands to shape a meaning when you don't quite have the words to do it; you can even make your silence mean something. But in writing you have to communicate without facial expressions, gestures, or body English of any kind. You have to speak with words and punctuation alone.

Furthermore, writing is a solitary act. When you talk, you

normally talk to someone who talks back, who raises questions, who lets you know whether or not you are making yourself clear. But when you write, you work alone. Even if you are writing a letter to a friend, he or she will not suddenly materialize to prod or prompt you into speech, to help you fill in the gaps that so often occur when you try to tell a story or give an explanation off the top of your head. To write well, you have to anticipate the reactions of a reader you cannot see or hear.

But writing does have one big advantage over speaking. It gives you time to think, to try out your ideas on paper, to choose your words, to read what you have written, to rethink, revise, and rearrange it, and most important, to consider its effect on a reader. Writing gives you time to find the best possible way of stating what you mean. And the more you study the craft of writing, the better you will use your writing time.

STANDARD ENGLISH, OTHER DIALECTS, AND DISCOURSE COMMUNITIES

This book aims to help you write effectively in English. But since there are many kinds of English, you should know which kind this book teaches—and why.

The language called "English" is used in many parts of the world. It is spoken not only in England but also in the British West Indies and in countries that were once British colonies— such as Canada, the United States, Australia, India, and Nigeria. These are all "English-speaking" countries, but they have different ways of using English. Sometimes, for instance, they have different words for the same thing:

> truck [U.S.] = lorry [Great Britain]
> pond [U.S.] = billabong [Australia]

Sometimes they have different ways of spelling or pronouncing the same word:

> labor [U.S.] = labour [Great Britain and Canada]
> recognize [U.S.] = recognise [Great Britain and Canada]
> laugh: pronounced "laff" in the U.S., "lahff" in Great Britain

paint: pronounced "paynt" in the U.S., "pint" in Australia
check [U.S.] = cheque [Great Britain and Canada]

Sometimes they use different grammatical forms:

The jury has reached a verdict. [U.S.]
The jury have reached a verdict. [all other English-speaking
    countries]

Probably you have already noticed differences such as these.
Even if you have never traveled abroad, you have probably heard
British or Australian speech. When you did, you could undoubtedly tell after just a few words that what you were hearing was
different from any kind of English commonly spoken in North
America. The reason for the difference is that a living language
never stands still. Like the people who speak it and the world
they speak it in, it changes. And if English-speaking peoples live
far enough apart, the English they use will change in divergent
ways. That is why English sounds different in different parts of
the world.

Just as English varies from one country to another, it also
varies from one region of a country to another, and from one
cultural or ethnic group to another. Consider these statements:

She says I be crazy.
She says I am crazy.

They ain't got no ponies; they got big horses: I rode one, real
big uns.
They don't have any ponies; they have big horses. I rode one,
a really big one.

I have three brother and two sister.
I have three brothers and two sisters.

These statements illustrate four dialects—four kinds of English
used in North America. The first statement in each pair illustrates a regional or ethnic dialect; the second illustrates Standard
English. Each of these dialects has its own distinctive character
and rules. But of them all, Standard English is the only one normally taught in schools and colleges, the only one normally
required in business and the professions, and the only one widely

used in writing—especially in print. Why does Standard English enjoy this privilege? Is it always better than any other kind? And if you were raised to speak an ethnic or regional dialect, must you stop speaking that dialect in order to learn the Standard one?

There is no easy answer to the first of these three questions. But the answer to the second one is no. Standard English is not always better than any other kind. In a spoken exchange, it can sometimes be less expressive—and therefore less effective—than a regional or ethnic dialect. Compare, for instance, the original version of a regional proverb with the Standard version:

> Them as has, gets; them as ain't, gets took.
> Those who have, get; those who do not have, get taken.

These two statements strike the ear in different ways. While the first has the expressive vitality of regional speech, the second— the Standard version—sounds comparatively stiff.

Part of what makes the original version so effective is the tradition that stands behind it. Because of that tradition, the answer to the third question we raised is also no. A regional or ethnic dialect is not just a way of speaking; it is the living record of a shared heritage and shared concerns. For this reason, no one who speaks such a dialect should be forced to give it up.

The same is true for anyone who speaks a kind of English peculiar to a *discourse community:* a group that defines itself largely by the way it speaks or writes a language used by others in different ways. A magazine called *Volume,* for instance, is written entirely in hip-hop, the speech of urban rappers: a kind of English in which "hood" is used for "neighborhood," "chillin' " for "cool," "chillun' " for "children," and "yo' " for "your."

But just as many people can learn how to read both *Volume* and *The New York Times,* most people can learn how to speak and write more than one dialect. Standard English is what you will normally be expected to use in your writing. During college, it is what teachers will expect you to use in essays, exams, reports, and research papers. After college, it is what others will expect you to use in anything you write for business or professional purposes. For all of these reasons, Standard English is what this book aims to help you learn.

GRAMMAR AND RHETORIC

The grammar of a language is the set of rules by which its sentences are made. You started learning the rules of English grammar as soon as you started to talk. Well before you learned how to write, you could have said which of these two statements made sense:

> *Eggs breakfast fried I two for had.
> I had two fried eggs for breakfast.

The words in each statement are the same, but you can readily see that only the second arrangement makes sense. What you know about the English language tells you that some ways of arranging the seven words are acceptable and others are not. You may not be able to say just why the word order in the first arrangement is wrong, but you know that it is.

Good writing requires a working knowledge of grammar, a basic command of the rules that govern the forming of a sentence. But good writing is more than the act of obeying grammatical rules. It is also the art of using rhetoric—of arranging words, phrases, sentences, and paragraphs in such a way as to engage and sustain the reader's attention.

The power of rhetoric can sometimes be felt in a single sentence. Virginia Woolf wrote, "Women have burnt like beacons in all the works of all the poets from the beginning of time." General George S. Patton said to his troops after a battle, "You have been baptized in fire and blood and have come out steel." Martin Luther King, Jr., said to a crowd of civil-rights demonstrators, "I have a dream." Good sentences like these not only take their place in a paragraph but also make a place for themselves, striking the reader with their own special clarity and force. One aim of this book, therefore, is to help you maximize the rhetorical impact of every sentence you write.

Yet you do not normally write single sentences in isolation. You write them in sequence, and rhetoric is the art of making

---

*From this point on, nonstandard constructions in this book generally are marked with a star. We also use asterisks to mark misspelled words in drafts of student essays.

that sequence effective—of moving from one sentence to another in a paragraph, and from one paragraph to another in an essay. It is the art of sustaining continuity while continually moving ahead, of developing a description, a narrative, an explanation, or an argument in such a way as to take the reader with you from beginning to end. The ultimate aim of this book, therefore, is to explain the rhetoric of the writing process as a whole.

USING THIS BOOK

If you are using this book in a composition course, your teacher may assign certain chapters to the whole class or, after seeing your work, may refer you individually to the sections you need. Either way, it will help you to know what the book offers.

The book has four main parts. Part 1, "Writing Essays," surveys the whole writing process from pre-writing to proofreading a final draft. Then it treats different kinds of writing, such as exposition and persuasion, and specific parts of the writing process, such as paragraphing and choosing words. Part 2, "Writing Sentences," shows you how to make sentence structure work for you. We explain things you should not do, such as misplacing modifiers and misusing the passive voice. But we stress the things you can and should do, such as highlighting the main point of each sentence and varying your sentence patterns to invigorate your style.† Part 3, "Punctuation and Mechanics," treats punctuation, spelling, and the use of mechanical conventions such as capitals and italics. Part 4, "The Research Paper," tells how to prepare, write, and document a library research paper. It also explains how to write about literature as well as about other subjects in the curriculum: the sciences, the social sciences, and the humanities.

At the end of the book are two alphabetical glossaries. The Glossary of Usage explains many of the words or phrases that

---

† To illustrate various constructions, we often quote other writers, and we often italicize certain words in their sentences to stress particular points. In all such cases, the italics are ours, not the writers'.

writers find troublesome or confusing; the Glossary of Grammatical Terms defines words and phrases commonly used in discussions of sentence construction.

Finally, the book includes two appendices. Appendix 1 is a compact reference guide for students of English as a second language; if you're an ESL student, this appendix will help you solve the special grammatical problems you commonly face. Appendix 2 explains writing in the world "Beyond Freshman English," where you will have to compose such things as essay exams, personal statements for applications to professional schools, and covering letters for job applications.

The book is designed for ready reference. To find what you need, see the index at the back, scan the table of contents at the front, or check the summary on the back endpapers, which gives you a chart of the entire *Handbook*.

Most teachers assign specific sections of the book by using numbers, such as 14.4, which refers to chapter 14, section 4, "Editing Faulty Parallelism." But if your teacher writes on your paper an abbreviation such as "frag" or a symbol such as $(\!/\!/)$, look for it on the front endpaper lists, where you'll find that "frag" means "sentence fragment" (section 17.2) and $(\!/\!/)$ means faulty parallelism (section 14.4).

1

WRITING ESSAYS

1

Pre-Writing

Where does writing begin? Where do writers find within themselves the energy and desire to generate words, to compose sentences, and to build paragraphs? How do essays originate?

To these questions we have no simple answer. But since writing originates somewhere in the mind, your first task is to find a way into your mind and then out again so that you can bring back the news locked up inside you, waiting to be broadcast and published. **Pre-writing,** then, is the process of discovering your own ideas.

To help you discover them, this chapter offers a variety of suggestions. If any one of them leads you to a promising idea for an essay, you may not need all of the others, and you certainly don't need to take them all in order. Feel free to experiment with different methods of getting started, and jump ahead to any method that you think will help you.

1.1 BRANCHING

Branching is an alternative to outlining (section 3.3)—to the vertical listing of points under headings and subheadings. Unless you already know how your essay will develop its points, you can't very well list them in sequential order. What you can do, however, is put them on branches radiating from a single idea and make the branches sprout more ideas. You can thus generate a picture of the ideas in your mind, a pattern of connections to see.

Branching starts with a single word or phrase and grows from there by a process of association—but not free association. Since all main branches radiate from one key term, branching is a process of exploring its implications, of seeing the range and variety of thoughts it can evoke, of moving from the general to the specific. Branching allows the mind to wander to the detailed ends of an idea—the slenderest twigs of the tree—and then return to the source to develop a new main branch. So branching is a way of organizing as well as discovering your ideas—a way of brainstorming and patterning at the same time.

To develop such a picture of your ideas is to use what some psychologists call the right brain—that is, the right half of the brain. According to their theory, the two halves of the brain do different jobs. While the left brain is verbal, analytical, logical, and systematic, taking things one step at a time, the right brain is visual, imaginative, intuitive, and synthesizing, making one big picture from many details.

The best equipment for branching is a sheet of unlined paper and a pen or pencil. To start, write a word or phrase in the middle of the sheet and circle it. Then add a main branch for each idea that grows directly from the circled term, a smaller branch for each idea that sprouts from a main branch, and so on. You will soon find that you have to turn the sheet around as you work. On the following page, for instance, is a branching diagram that grew from the term "writer's block."

Paradoxically, the very act of thinking about writer's block can unblock a writer willing to think with the right brain, to make patterns and pictures such as the one of the locked door. The locked door may be a picture of the way you sometimes feel when you sit down to write: frustrated, balked, unable to penetrate your own mind. But as this diagram shows, branching can open the door of your mind and let you explore its passageways, let you see how one leads to another and how the return to the main idea stimulates you further.

This periodic return to the main idea is known as **looping**. Looping prefigures what an essay does, which is to create from a collection of various points a pattern of meaning organized around a central point. So in returning to the center of the

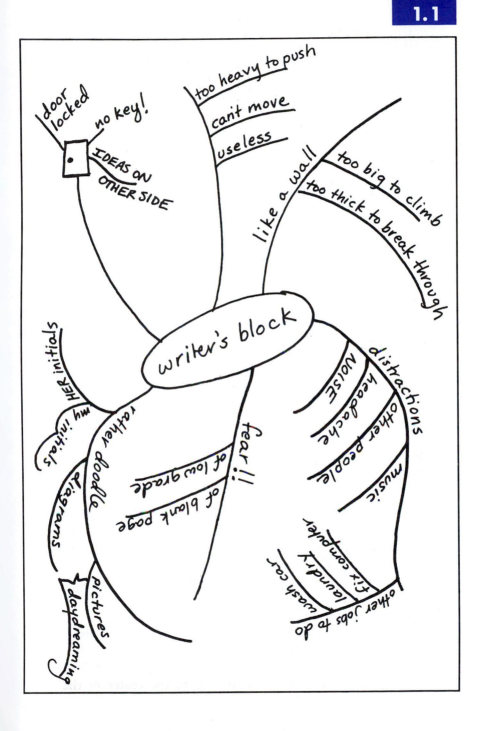

branching diagram when you have thought your way to the end of a particular branch, you are actually beginning the work of organizing an essay.

Now try the following exercise to see what your right brain can do.

> **EXERCISE 1 BRANCHING**
>
> Construct a branching diagram from a term of your choice or from any one of the following terms. See how many branches you can generate in ten minutes. (In later exercises we'll ask you to use this diagram.)
>
> smoking
> music videos
> computers
> AIDS
> graffiti
> pollution

1.2 CHOOSING A TOPIC

Branching will help you discover and organize your ideas on any topic. But if you're asked to **choose a topic** of your own and you have trouble doing so, here are five ways to find a good one:

1. Use your expertise. Help others learn how to do something you do well. You may be an expert photographer, carpenter, guitar player, computer operator, cartoonist, salesclerk, or actor. What advice could you give others who would like to acquire your skill? What should they be prepared to do and sacrifice? What characteristics do they need to have? What obstacles will confront them? What kind of regimen should they follow?

2. Explore a conflict. Since the richest moments of experience are often born out of conflict, suppose you recall a time when you were made or asked to do something you did not want to do. When and where did it happen? How did you feel about having to act against your will? How did you feel about the

person who asked you to do so? What did you learn from the episode? Raising questions like these—and trying to answer them—will help you think more about the experience until you discover the point you want to explore in depth.

Alternatively, you can imagine a conflict of ideas—a debate about a question of current importance: Should limits be placed on the number of terms that members of Congress may serve? Should public schools teach Hispanic children in Spanish? Should any one course be required of all college students? Should handguns be federally regulated? Questions like these can provoke sharp dispute. If you picture the dispute as an argument between two people, you can write a dialogue, and thus generate the material for an essay.

3. Spy on people. Have you noticed the way some people (including you, perhaps) behave at rock concerts, at movies, in shopping malls, in supermarkets, in classrooms, in restaurants, on sidewalks, on beaches, at parties? Does anything they do, say, or wear strike you as funny or strange or irritating? If so, why? And if you had the power to change their behavior, what would you do?

4. Remember a moment that powerfully moved you. Was it the first time you gave a speech? Was it the day you broke your arm? Was it the first night you appeared in a play? Was it a funeral? If you search your memory, you can find at least one moment that is branded there forever by the sheer power of joy, grief, fear, guilt, or pain. Use your right brain to picture that moment again.

5. Choose a topic you want to know more about. Tap your curiosity. Investigate a subject that interests you. Go to the reference room of your college library and see what an encyclopedia can tell you about submarines, balloon flight, volcanoes, or the women's suffrage movement in the United States. As you learn about your topic, you will probably want to tell others about it—especially if the subject is one you have wondered about for some time. Look for the unexpected. Surprises will interest your readers as much as they interest you. (For more on reading in order to write, see section 1.11.)

EXERCISE 2 CHOOSING A TOPIC AND BRANCHING

Use any one of the approaches explained above to find a topic, and then use branching to discover and organize your ideas about it.

EXERCISE 3 NONSTOP WRITING

Using your branching diagram from exercise 1 or exercise 2 as a source of ideas, write nonstop for ten minutes. Don't worry about spelling, punctuation, or grammar; just keep following the points made on each of the branches (adding more points as they come to mind) and looping back to the main point. After ten minutes, read what you have just written, and underline anything that you discovered or remembered in the process of writing.

1.3 MAKING AN ASSIGNED TOPIC YOUR OWN

If you are asked to write a paper on an **assigned topic,** one good way of getting started is to consider how you might connect the topic to your own interests and experience. Even though the paper itself may be chiefly impersonal and analytical, you can stimulate your thinking about the topic by considering it in personal terms. Suppose you are asked to write about the free enterprise system for a course in economics. Your first thought may be of huge corporations: DuPont, IBM, General Motors, Chrysler, AT&T. But big firms like these are far outnumbered by small ones such as pizza parlors, taxicab companies, barbershops, hairdressing salons, and drugstores. If you've ever had a job, you've had the chance to see how someone else runs a business. If you've participated in Junior Achievement, you've helped to run a company yourself. And if you've ever sold anything of your own, whether goods or services (such as lawnmowing or babysitting), then you know what it means to run your own business, however small. Finally, if at different times you've worked for someone else and for yourself, you have firsthand experience of the difference between the predictability of a set wage and the unpredictability of profit, between security and risk, between earnings that are guaranteed but limited and earnings that are unguaranteed but limitless. Personal experience, then, can help you to find your way into a topic even when the paper you're writing goes beyond such experience.

> EXERCISE 4 MAKING A TOPIC YOUR OWN
>
> Describe a personal experience that you might use to make a point about any one of the following topics:
>
> | | | |
> |---|---|---|
> | cellular phones | banks | politics |
> | families | violence | poverty |
> | education | sports | transportation |
> | farming | housing | drugs |

1.4 NARROWING THE TOPIC

One of the biggest obstacles to the success of a short essay is an overly broad topic. If you try to write eight hundred words on the free enterprise system, you will probably find that you have room for only commonplace generalizations about it: big businesses don't pay their fair share of taxes; company executives are overpaid; workers are underpaid; the whole system takes from the many and gives to the fortunate few. When you fill up your paper with generalizations like these, you offer no fresh insights of your own.

If you can link a particular topic to your own experience, you have already begun reducing it to manageable size. But whether or not you personalize the topic, try to make it as precise and specific as possible, like one of these:

GENERAL	SPECIFIC	MORE SPECIFIC
schools	inner city public schools	inner city Chicago public schools
cars	Volvos	my twenty-five-year-old Volvo 144
working women	working mothers	working mothers with small children

GENERAL	SPECIFIC	MORE SPECIFIC
national elections	role of TV in national elections	role of TV in presidential campaign of 1992
nuclear wastes	disposal of nuclear waste	burying nuclear waste vs. dumping it in the ocean
television commercials	women in TV commercials	changing roles of women in TV commercials
pollution	acid rain	effects of acid rain on trees
immigration	illegal aliens	employment of illegal aliens
drugs	drug testing	drug testing of professional athletes
drugs	steroids	side effects of steroids
schools	public schools	inner-city public schools

> **EXERCISE 5 NARROWING THE TOPIC**
>
> Take any one of the topics listed in exercise 4 and make it as specific as possible.
>
> **EXAMPLE**
> crime   shoplifting   punishment of shoplifters

1.5 TRIPLE-VIEWING THE TOPIC: PARTICLE, WAVE, AND FIELD

Once you have chosen a topic, you can discover its possibilities by viewing it in three different ways:

> - as a **particle:** something isolated from everything else
> - as a **wave:** something flowing from what precedes it as a cause to what follows it as an effect
> - as **part of a field:** something related to what surrounds it

1. To view a topic as a particle is to view it all by itself, isolated from anything else. Suppose your topic is the rioting that erupted in south-central Los Angeles in the spring of 1992. To

write about the rioting alone, you would need to pursue questions such as these: How long did the rioting last? Who were the rioters? How many people did they injure or kill? How many buildings did they burn? How much did they steal? What did the police do? What did firefighters do? How did local politicians respond? How was the rioting covered by the news media?

2. To view a topic as a <u>wave</u> is to see it as part of a process, to ask what caused it and what it produced, or may produce. Was the Los Angeles rioting solely caused by the acquittal of four white police officers who had been videotaped beating a black suspect? If not, what else might have led people to riot? And what effects did the rioting have? Besides causing enormous loss and pain, has it led to any new ways of helping the poor and the jobless in Los Angeles?

3. To view the topic as <u>part of a field</u> is to consider its relation to other topics that surround it, so to speak, in space. Is police brutality a widespread phenomenon in the United States? Do police often treat black suspects more harshly than white ones? What, if anything, distinguishes the Los Angeles rioting from the kinds of violence that commonly occur elsewhere in this country? And how much does the Los Angeles rioting represent or typify the lives and feelings of those who live in the poorest parts of other U.S. cities?

> EXERCISE 6 TRIPLE-VIEWING THE TOPIC
>
> Consider your topic first as a particle, then as a wave, then as part of a field. For each way of viewing the topic, write as many questions as possible and put a parenthesized R (R) after any question that would have to be answered from reading in relevant source material.

1.6 DRAMATIZING THE TOPIC WITH QUESTIONS

Another way of generating ideas about a topic is to dramatize it with six basic questions:

- **What** happened? (the action)
- **Who** was involved? (agents, spectators, and anyone else affected by it)
- **When and where** did it happen? (the setting)
- **How** did it happen? (the method)
- **Why** did it happen? (the cause or motive)
- **What effect** did it have? (the consequence)

To see how this dramatizing method works in practice, suppose your topic is the effect of acid rain on trees. You can investigate it with questions like these:

What does acid rain do to trees? What happens to their leaves? What do their roots do? What happens to the bark and branches?

Who is responsible for acid rain? If it comes from the burning of high-sulfur industrial fuels, which industries are burning them? Who runs those industries? And who is affected by the damage that acid rain does to trees?

When and where does acid rain affect trees? What parts of the world or the country are most affected? How does a forest appear after an acid rainfall? How often does acid rain fall?

How does acid rain develop? How does the acid get to the clouds? How do the clouds carry the acid to the forests?

Why does acid rain occur? Is it because we are burning too much fuel? Is it because we are using the wrong kind of fuel? Is it because we care more about promoting industry than protecting the environment?

What effect does the damage to trees have? How does it affect the timber supply? What does it do to birds and other wildlife? How does it affect people living near forests or elsewhere? Does acid rain reduce the capacity of trees to absorb carbon dioxide? If so, how much more global warming will result?

To answer all of these questions, you would need to do some reading and research—something we introduce in section 1.11.

But when you dramatize your topic with questions, you are decisively beginning to investigate it.

> **EXERCISE 7** ASKING QUESTIONS TO DRAMATIZE YOUR
> TOPIC
>
> Using each of the six categories illustrated by the example given above, ask at least twelve questions about your topic.

1.7 CHOOSING A BASIC QUESTION TO DEFINE A PROBLEM OR CONFLICT

All of the questions you ask can help you generate material, and a good deal of this material may find its way into your essay. But just as you need to define your topic as specifically as possible, you also need a **basic question** to help identify the problem, puzzle, or conflict you will try to resolve. For a student named Gary Pappas, who chose to write about his experience in a high school play, the key question was *Why?* Why did he love acting so much?

To focus on one basic question is also to see its relation to others. When Gary decided to concentrate on why he loved acting, he knew that he would also have to answer other questions: to say something about what he actually did on stage, the other actors, the audience, the set, his method of acting, and the effect of the play on all the people involved in its performance. But he decided to make all these other points secondary, to use them in answering the question *Why?* (We show what Gary did with his basic question in section 2.3.)

Questions can bring out the conflicts inherent in any topic worth writing about. Take, for instance, one of the *Why* questions asked about acid rain: Does acid rain occur because we care more about promoting industry than protecting the environment? This question clearly identifies a conflict between the value of our natural surroundings and the value of industry. Besides holding water, retaining soil, giving us beauty and shade, and absorbing carbon dioxide, trees furnish wood, pulp, resins, and many other products. But the industries that make rain acidic furnish jobs as well as goods and services, and all three may be threatened by the cost of environmental regulations. So we might ask the question another way: Should we regulate and penalize industry in order to protect our trees? Here is at once a question to be answered and a problem to be solved—the kind of problem that can generate an essay.

Once you've chosen a basic question, you can choose other questions that will help you pursue it. The first set of questions on acid rain—the *What* questions—concern the damage that acid rain does. To ask about the damage is to raise further questions about the cost of acid rain: what it costs us not just in beauty, shade, and water retention but also in all the raw materials that come from trees. The first set of questions, therefore, would help you to pursue the basic question, "Should we regulate and penalize industry in order to protect our trees?" This question cannot be answered without some reference to the costs of not protecting them.

> EXERCISE 8 CHOOSING A BASIC QUESTION
>
> Choose one of the questions you wrote for exercise 7 and briefly explain what conflict or problem it raises. Then make a list of other questions that could help you pursue the basic question.

1.8 GETTING REACTIONS TO YOUR QUESTION

One of the hardest things about writing is that you normally have to do it alone. Before you begin to write, therefore, find someone you can talk to about the basic question you plan to explore. If you already have some idea of how you might answer the question, your listener may give you a different answer. Hearing it will make you more sensitive to the complexity of your subject, more skillful in anticipating possible misunderstandings or objections to your point of view, and therefore more effective in explaining or defending it.

> **EXERCISE 9** GETTING RESPONSES
>
> Explain to someone else the basic question you hope to explore and also—if you can—your own ideas about how to answer it. Then (1) record his or her response in writing and (2) comment on the response.

1.9 USING ANALOGIES

An **analogy** is a comparison of something abstract or strange with something concrete and familiar. An analogy answers the kind of question we almost always ask about anything new to us: "What's it like?" Because analogies let you translate abstract ideas or feelings into concrete terms, they can open your eyes to a whole new way of looking at your topic. A freshman wrote recently that college first appeared to him as "a new mountain to be climbed." Think of the questions this picture generates: Is he ready for this mountain? Can he see the summit? Is he going to slip and fall? What trail will he take? How much guidance will he have? Good analogies turn thoughts into pictures. In the branching diagram on p. 15, writer's block is literally pictured as a locked door, which could mean either one of two things: the writer's imagination is locked in, unable to break out and express itself, or the writer's conscious mind is locked out, unable to enter the world of imagination. But analogy is one of the keys that can open the door, for analogy is a way of picturing your subject in words. Put your right brain to work for a moment on acid rain. Picture yourself taking a shower in full-strength bleach. What would that do to your skin? How would it make you feel? If you can answer those questions, you can begin to describe vividly what acid rain does to trees.

> **EXERCISE 10** USING ANALOGIES
>
> Use an analogy to picture at least one aspect of the basic question you chose in exercise 8. Then write three questions about your picture.

1.10 WORKING WITH A NUGGET

As you think about your topic, do you find yourself struck by a single word, phrase, image, idea, or example connected with it? If so, that may be your golden nugget, a rich source of further ideas. When Gary Pappas began to think about acting, he remembered first of all what he saw in the *mirror* just before he went on stage. That vivid image of another self—a stage self—became the point of departure for his essay on the magic of acting.

A rich nugget—like a good analogy—usually calls up a picture. Once you have the picture in your mind's eye, you can use questions to discover what it means.

> **EXERCISE 11 WORKING WITH A NUGGET**
>
> Circle or underline the most evocative word or phrase you can find in what you have written so far about your topic. Then use this item to generate a branching diagram.

1.11 ACTIVE READING

Readable words surround us. They compete for our attention on all sides—from magazines and newspapers, from cereal boxes, from billboards, bumper stickers, TV screens, letters, and notes. Even the graffiti that are scrawled, scratched, or spray-painted on public walls demand to be read, and—some of the time at least—they make us think. Any word you read may feed your writing. "If guns are outlawed," says one bumper sticker, "only outlaws will have guns." Is that true—or just a catchy slogan? Has anyone seriously proposed making all guns illegal? Would any form of gun regulation take all guns away from law-abiding citizens? The words of the bumper sticker prompt the kinds of questions that could generate a thoughtful essay.

Besides reading for stimulation, hard facts, and provocative opinions that you can cite in your writing, you will often be asked in college to write *about* a piece of assigned reading—such as a published essay. To prepare yourself for this kind of writing, you should first get your own copy of the reading matter and then read it with a pen or pencil in your hand. (A colored marker is also handy for highlighting important passages.) As you read, you should make the text your own by marking it up. Underline or highlight whatever seems important, and use the margin for annotations—questions or comments. Here's how a student named Sheila annotated a passage about the value of children's play:

A four-year-old girl reacted to her mother's pregnancy by regressing. Although she had been well trained, she began to wet again, insisted on being fed only from a baby bottle, and reverted to crawling on the floor. All this greatly distressed her mother, who, anticipating the demands of a new infant, had counted on her daughter's relative maturity. Fortunately, she did not try to prevent her daughter's regressions. After a few months of this behavior, the girl replaced it with much more mature play. She now played "good mother." She became extremely caring for her baby doll, ministering to it much more seriously than ever before. Having in the regressed stage identified with the coming infant, she now identified with her mother. By the time her sibling was born, the girl had done much of the work needed for her to cope with the change in the family and her position in it, and her adjustment to the new baby was easier than her mother had expected.

What's this?

Ok—it means turning yourself into a baby again

So play is a serious business for kids—a way of adjusting. But is all regression good? Is there any other way of adjusting?

In retrospect it can be seen that the child, on learning that a new baby was to join the family, must have been afraid that the baby would deprive her of her infantile gratifications, and therefore tried to provide herself with them. She may have thought that if her mother wanted an infant, then she herself would again be an infant. There would be no need for her mother to acquire another, and she might give up on the idea.

pleasures?

fantasy

Permitted to act on notions like these, the girl must have realized after a while that wetting herself was not as pleasant as she might have imagined; that being able to eat a wide variety of foods had definite advantages when compared with drinking only from the bottle; and that walking and running brought many more satisfactions than did crawling. From this

key idea experience she convinced herself that being grown up is preferable to being a baby. So she gave up pretending that she was a baby and instead decided to be like her mother: in play to be like her right now, in imagination to become at some future time a real mother. Play provided the child and her mother

right with a happy solution to what otherwise might have resulted in an impasse.

—Bruno Bettelheim, "The Importance of Play"

The questions, comments, and underlinings here signify **active reading.** Finding in the very first sentence a word she doesn't recognize, Sheila circles it, and then discovers its meaning in the second sentence—without even checking her dictionary. More

PRE-WRITING: IN BRIEF

- Use branching (1.1) to discover your ideas on any topic.

- To choose a topic (1.2)—
  use your expertise;
  explore a conflict;
  spy on people;
  recall a moment of intense feeling;
  pick a subject you want to know more about.

- Make an assigned topic your own. (1.3)

- Make the topic as specific as you can. (1.4)

- View the topic as particle, wave, and field. (1.5)

- Dramatize the topic with questions. (1.6)

- Choose a basic question to define a problem or conflict. (1.7)

- Get reactions to your question. (1.8)

- Use analogies. (1.9)

- Work with a nugget—something richly suggestive. (1.10)

- Read actively. (1.11)

important than learning new words, however, is learning what the passage has to teach. By underlining, commenting on, and asking questions about the author's most important points, the reader has learned something new and vital about the importance of play in growing up. She can now begin to think about how she would explore the author's ideas in an essay of her own, about the kinds of questions she would pursue. Is play a means of moving from fantasy (such as persuading her mother to give up pregnancy) to reality? Do older children and adults indulge in regression? If so, do they also use play to readjust to their responsibilities? And should kids be allowed to regress as often and as much as they want?

Active reading is so important to writing that we discuss it at length in chapter 10, "Reading in Order to Write." But for now, exercise 12 will get you started on reading with an eye to your own writing.

EXERCISE 12 ACTIVE READING

Read the following passages, annotating each with questions and comments and underlining any points that seem important. Then write three questions about each passage—questions you could explore in an essay.

1. BEIJING—They are China's pampered darlings.

Eight years after the world's most populous nation put its controversial family planning program into effect, limiting most couples to one child, one of the most conspicuous results has been the rise of a generation of "little emperors," which in the West would be known as spoiled brats.

The official press is full of stories about such children. Last year, the newspaper *China Youth News* published a 12-part series entitled "The Little Suns in Our Lives" that painted some disturbing portraits.

The parents of one third-grade boy, for example, bought him whatever he wanted. He dined on meat pies; his parents ate porridge. He spurned clothing that had been worn once. After his grandfather spanked him for starting a fight in school, the youngster took a pair of scissors and threatened to kill himself until the grandfather apologized and bought him a new toy.

A 7-year-old girl was asked by her parents to empty the chamber pot, but only emptied half because she said she was not the only one who had used it.

"What will be the outcome if parents allow this willfulness to continue?" the newspaper asked.

China has 337 million children under age 14. Of those, about 9 percent, or 30.5 million, are children without siblings, most of them concentrated at the younger grades, family planning officials said. Eight of every 10 first-graders come from single-child families. With the recent renewed emphasis on the one-couple, one-child policy, that ratio is likely to increase to 90 percent over the next five years, according to Liu Bin, vice minister of the State Education Commission.

Many only children are so doted upon by their families that they become timid, overbearing, lazy, self-indulgent or contemptuous of physical labor, officials said. Most only children have "weak points, such as (the) low ability to care for themselves, selfishness, willfulness and arrogance," Liu said.

"The only-children issue has caused social problems," said Zhou Huayin, a Beijing education official. Spoiled by their parents, these children often become "hot-tempered and pay little respect to parents and older generations," he said.

—Lena H. Sun, "China's One-Child Policy Produces
Spoiled 'Little Emperors' "

2. Each sex has the same capacity to experience the pleasures and pains of romantic love. Women and men describe being in love in similar terms. This is surely as we would expect, since the deep impulses that give rise to love and the capacity to synthesize those impulses derive from our human nature; the potential for exaltation, transcendence, and transformation is not fundamentally altered by the accident of gender. In love we are more alike than different. Still, there are some important differences between women's and men's experiences of romantic love, particularly in the incidence of the different distortions to which love is prone.

The tapestry of an individual's love chronicles, his need for love, capacity for it, and specific vulnerabilities, is always woven of a complex mixture of social and psychological imperatives, penchants, and possibilities. Many of these are contingent on gender, and gender issues in turn have social and psychological, as well as biological, components. Although men and women face the same existential problems in life—death, aloneness, insufficiency, imperfection—they attempt to solve these problems in different ways and utilize love differently. Why? First, because there is a strong cultural component to love, and there are different cultural imperatives for the sexes. Second, the psychological development of each sex preordains different central problems and different strategies for resolving them. And finally, the ongoing cultural context locks in the pre-existing tendencies toward difference.

Because they are socialized in different ways, men and women tend to have different passionate quests—the passionate quest being that which constitutes the central psychological theme of a person's life. This passionate quest supplies the context for one's pursuit of self-realization, adventure, excitement, and, ultimately, transformation and even transcendence. The passionate quest is always a romance in the larger meaning of the word, but it is not always a quest for romantic love per se.

For women the passionate quest has usually been interpersonal, and has generally involved romantic love; for men it has more often been heroic, the pursuit of achievement or power. One might say that men tend to favor power over love and that women tend to achieve power through love. Socialization seems to be one of the factors that create the different dreams through which each sex shapes its narrative life.

—Ethel S. Person, "The Passionate Quest"

Finding Your Aim

2

If you have tried all or even some of the methods explained in the previous chapter, you are probably ready to start writing. But two things may hold you back. One is the feeling that you don't yet know what you **aim** to do in your essay besides somehow getting it written. The other is the feeling that you aren't yet sure how to **organize** your thoughts—how to introduce your main point, develop it, and write a conclusion.

These problems should be faced one at a time. If you aren't yet sure how to organize your thoughts, don't worry. Organization will come in chapter 3. In this chapter we focus on the first problem—finding your aim.

2.1 THINKING ABOUT YOUR AIM

You can think of your aim in two ways: specific and general. Once you have written your essay, your **specific aim** is your **thesis**—the main point you express, explain, or try to prove. If you think you know now what your thesis is going to be, you can turn at once to section 2.3, which can help you to formulate it. But not every essay includes an explicit statement of its thesis, and not even published writers always know what the thesis of an essay will be when they start writing it. What they do know is what you should try to decide at this point: your **general aim.**

Everything you write involves you, your reader, and the world around you both. Your general aim depends on which of these three elements is most important:

1. If you are writing chiefly about yourself and your own experience, your aim is <u>self-expression.</u> You seek not so much to
affect the reader or to explain the outside world to him or her
as to express your personal thoughts, feelings, experiences, and
recollections:

> One of the reasons that I got along so well with boys when I
> was younger was that I didn't know that I wasn't expected to.
> I didn't realize that the other girls in my grade spent their
> time playing with makeup and dolls because they thought that
> boys were hideous creatures from another planet. I believed
> that a friend was someone that you had fun with, and my idea
> of fun was similar to that of a boy: playing tackle football,
> riding a dirt bike off a jump in the woods, and playing 45
> scatter. Because no one seemed to care that my two best friends
> were boys, I never realized such friendships were uncom-
> mon.   —College student

2. If your writing focuses chiefly on the outside world, your
aim is <u>exposition.</u> You set out to explain something that,
you assume, your reader does not yet know or fully understand:

> Laughter comes in assorted shapes and forms. The nervous
> giggle, the cackle, the chuckle, and the guffaw are just a few
> of its many and strange variations. One friend of mine is
> known for a laugh that convulses anyone who hears it. Another
> friend laughs without making a sound, but her whole body
> shakes and heaves so violently that I sometimes wonder if she'll
> come out of the laugh alive. Still another friend laughs so hard
> that his face wrinkles up like a raisin, his eyes squinch shut,
> and tears well out of the corners and trickle down his face.
> Why, I wonder, should laughter lead to tears? Why do we
> speak of "laughing to death"?   —College student

See chapter 6 for extended guidance on the various methods of
developing an explanation.

3. If your writing seeks primarily to influence the reader,
your aim is <u>persuasion.</u> You hope to lead the reader to do something or to believe something without being compelled to do
so:

I believe that maturity is not an outgrowing, but a growing up: that an adult is not a dead child, but a child who survived. I believe that all the best faculties of a mature human being exist in the child, and that if these faculties are encouraged in youth they will act well and wisely in the adult, but if they are repressed and denied in the child they will stunt and cripple the adult personality. And finally, I believe that one of the most deeply human, and humane, of these faculties is the power of imagination: so that it is our pleasant duty, as librarians, or teachers, or parents, or writers, or simply as grownups, to encourage that faculty of imagination in our children, to encourage it to grow freely, to flourish like the green bay tree, by giving it the best, absolutely the best and purest, nourishment that it can absorb. And never, under any circumstances, to squelch it, or sneer at it, or imply that it is childish, or unmanly, or untrue.

—Ursula Le Guin,
"Why Are Americans Afraid of Dragons?"

If you can decide on your general aim, you are on your way to shaping your essay. But suppose you do not yet know what your thesis—your main point—is going to be. You may be able to discover your main point by freewriting—as we explain next.

2.2 DIRECTED FREEWRITING

Directed freewriting is writing guided by a general aim—to express yourself, to explain something, or to persuade—and by the urge to **pursue** a basic question. In freewriting, you don't have to worry about an introduction or conclusion, about paragraphing, spelling, or completing all your sentences. Just go to work on your basic question—as Gary did with the question "Why do I love acting so much?"

Acting excites me tremendously—but why? Is it working closely with other people? Is it knowing that a whole lot of people are out there watching you? Last time I snuck a look through the folds of the curtain just before it went up. Felt butterflies just seeing all those people. Is it the big round of applause—anyway you hope's it's big—that comes at curtain call? And all the good things people say to you afterwards, sometimes for days or even weeks. And the pats on the back. Or maybe it's something else. Last spring I was in *Ah, Wilderness!*, by O'Neill—a school production. I played Nat Miller—a 50-year-old businessman. I remember checking my makeup in the mirror just before I went on. Like—who is this guy? I thought. Well of course I knew, I'd been rehearsing the part two hours a day for eight weeks. Publishes a small town newspaper, father of four kids. But it was *wierd looking in the mirror at that strange face. And maybe it's just that feeling, the feeling that makes acting so *differant from anything else. Acting sort of takes you away from yourself. Like sitting down and having breakfast in the opening scene. An imaginary family. We were all together, all the actors, creating the family group. I had to put myself in the family, figure out where I fit. How I related to all the others, Nat's wife, a bustling matron. Her prim sister. Their kids. Kids, yes—children. Maybe acting is like going back to childhood and playing games—let's-pretend games—like the day I ran down the street dressed up as Batman. Acting is like that—getting away from yourself. Like taking a vacation from yourself. Maybe that's the magic of it.

This passage shows what you can do with directed freewriting. Free from the need to worry about spelling, grammar, punctuation, paragraphing, or organization, Gary simply tried to find on paper the answer to his basic question: why did he love acting so much? In the process of writing, he discovered the answer: acting is like taking a vacation from yourself.

For one more example of what you can do with directed freewriting, here is a passage freewritten by a student named Andrea Lyle:

> Looking back, I guess it was pretty stupid. No climbing experience and nothing to climb with but a thin clothesline rope, and yet there we were in the middle of the old abandoned copper mine crawling and sliding our way down to the bottom

---

* Misspelled words in writing samples are marked with asterisks.

which Ellie had heard somewhere was over a hundred feet down. For a while a great adventure, a colossal marvelous cave. Outcroppings like gargoyles all over the walls. But after about three hours, we were dirty and cut up from a few minor falls, and the muscles in our fingers and hands and arms all ached from climbing, so we decided to go back up. Then it hit us. On the way down we'd sort of slid rather than climbed our way down a fifteen-foot almost sheer *precepice and nobody thought to leave a rope hanging there so we could climb back up. Now we tried again and again to scramble up the *precepice but *niether of us could do it. It was scary. We looked up to the top of the mine where the light was but it seemed so far away—not much bigger than a single star in a coal-black sky. We felt trapped. But we weren't giving up. Not yet. We tried to find a way around the *precepice and couldn't. Then we tried throwing the rope up to catch it somehow on the top of the *precepice but that didn't work either. Finally on the bottom of the mine I found two old rusty pipes. They were only about seven feet long, but Ellie noticed that the ends of each pipe were threaded, so we screwed the pipes together to make a long pole. Bracing the pole on the ground beside the *precepice, we helped each other climb the pole and get out of the cave.

As I think back on this whole thing I'm not sure why we both felt so proud. We hadn't really done anything spectacular, and when we got home, nobody was surprised to see us. There was no celebration and no story in the paper. But maybe it was just that by working together, we figured our own way out of that place. We rescued each other. We had a problem that might have gotten really serious and we found a solution. Working together, depending on each other—there was nobody else—we found out what it means to be independent.

Once again, freewriting leads the writer to her main point. As Andrea tells her story and tries to discover its significance, the memory of fear gives way to the memory of pride, and this memory in turn prompts her to ask why she felt proud. The answer is a point already implied by the story, but not made explicit until the end: in finding their way out of the cave, Andrea and her friend discovered what it means to be dependent and independent at the same time.

Using any of the methods described in sections 1.6 and 1.7, choose a basic question you might ask about the meaning of any personal experience you can vividly recall. Then do a half hour of freewriting to find the answer to this question.

2.3 FORMULATING A THESIS

A **statement of thesis** expresses the main point of your essay by making a precise, specific assertion *about* the topic. Whether you aim to write about yourself, to explain something in the outside world, or to influence the reader, you should be able to state your main point in one sentence. An effective thesis is more than a vague generalization. It should be specific, pointed, and provocative: the kind of statement that promises to reveal something new.

The following examples show how you can use a question to help turn a vague generalization into an effective thesis:

TOPIC: Scoring goals in hockey

GENERAL AIM: Self-expression

VAGUE GENERALIZATION: I love scoring goals in hockey. (Why?)

EFFECTIVE THESIS: I love scoring goals in hockey because it momentarily gives me a sense of power.

TOPIC: Groups and individuals in Japanese society

GENERAL AIM: Exposition

VAGUE GENERALIZATION: In Japanese society, individuals depend on groups. (How?)

EFFECTIVE THESIS: In Japanese society, individuals identify themselves with groups that mark them as insiders and thus separate them from outsiders.

TOPIC: Baseball players' salaries

GENERAL AIM: Persuasion

VAGUE GENERALIZATION: Baseball players' salaries are too high. (What should be done about them?)

EFFECTIVE THESIS: To keep baseball players' salaries from overburdening teams, team owners should recalculate the value of each player every year.

As shown above in section 2.2, a thesis is often something discovered *in the writing process*—not something formulated before the writing begins. Also, not every essay makes its thesis explicit; sometimes the thesis is merely implied. But whether or not the final version of your essay includes an explicit statement of your thesis, you will do well to write the thesis out for your own guidance. This is what Gary did as soon as he finished freewriting.

When Gary read over his freewritten material, he found his most important point at the end, which is always a good place to look for discoveries. From this point he formulated his first try at a thesis:

> I love acting because it gives me a vacation from myself.

This is a good start. But looking at this statement, Gary realized that it prompted a question: just what is it about acting that gives me a vacation from myself? Gary's answer to this question made his thesis more effective:

> I love acting because playing someone else gives me a vacation from myself.

This is better. But with the help of his teacher, Gary saw that a further question remained. What other reasons make people like acting? Some reference to these other reasons would help him to highlight the unique importance of *his* reason. He supplied the needed reference by starting off with *Though:*

> *Though* some people may be drawn to acting by the prospect of winning applause and acclaim, or working closely with others, I love it because playing someone else gives me a vacation from myself.

This kind of statement serves as a blueprint for the essay to come, in which Gary will fully explain his main reason for loving to act. As a complex sentence, it **subordinates** two lesser points to the main point (see chapter 15) and thus begins the work of organizing the essay. For this reason, a complex sentence usually makes a more effective thesis than a simple sentence, which states a single idea, or a compound sentence, which puts two ideas on the same level of importance. A complex sentence indicates which of two ideas is more important. Thus it gives the writer a sense of direction.

As Gary's experience shows, a fully effective thesis seldom comes quickly. Formulating it usually takes a good deal of thinking and more than one try. The following examples—all from the work of student writers—show what can result from a succession of tries:

1. TOPIC: My twenty-five-year-old Volvo 144
   A. FIRST TRY: My old car has great character.
   B. SECOND TRY: Compared with the cars driven by some of the other students in my class, mine has a special character.
   C. FINAL VERSION: Compared with the old cars driven by some of the other students in my class, my twenty-five-year-old Volvo 144 takes the prize in all major categories: age, ugliness, and lack of power.

2. TOPIC: Male-female relationships
   A. FIRST TRY: Male-female relationships these days are very confusing.
   B. SECOND TRY: As a little girl I felt perfectly free to play with boys; now it's different.
   C. FINAL VERSION: Though I felt perfectly free to play with boys when I was a little girl, now I can't have a male friend without making everyone think I'm in love with him.

3. TOPIC: Women in TV commercials
   A. FIRST TRY: TV commercials often focus on housewives, unlike TV shows, which tend to glamorize women.
   B. SECOND TRY: Though TV shows often glamorize women, TV commercials typically present them as housewives—often in distress.
   C. FINAL VERSION: Though TV shows often glamorize women, TV commercials typically present them as housewives in distress so they can be rescued by the sponsor's product.

4. TOPIC: Escaping from a mine
   A. FIRST TRY: Escaping from a mine taught me something about myself.

B. SECOND TRY: Escaping from a mine with my friend Ellie showed me how two friends can help each other out of a tight spot.

C. FINAL VERSION: Escaping from a mine with my friend Ellie showed me how mutual dependence can lead to independence.

5. TOPIC: Social competition in a small community

A. FIRST TRY: The Shinnecook Indians are often divided among themselves, but they can stand together when threatened from the outside.

B. SECOND TRY: Though the five clans of the Shinnecook Indian tribe sometimes don't get along, they stand together against outsiders.

C. FINAL VERSION: Though the five clans of the Shinnecook Indian tribe sometimes envy and resent each other, they stand together because they know that unity alone will keep their land from being lost.

EXERCISE 2 FORMULATING A THESIS FROM
FREEWRITTEN MATERIAL

First, underline the most important point you discovered about your topic in the process of freewriting. Second, using this point, write at least three versions of a sentence that could serve as a statement of thesis for the essay you plan to write. Third, say which version you think is best—and why.

EXERCISE 3 FORMULATING A THESIS FROM
A BASIC QUESTION

Returning to the basic question you asked in exercise 1 (p. 37), write an answer to the question. Then rewrite the answer to make it as precise and specific as possible.

2.4 FINDING YOUR TONE

The human voice always carries a **tone**. Imagine, for instance, how these two questions would sound if spoken aloud:

Would you mind putting out that cigarette?

Would you *mind* putting out that cigarette?

The words of both questions are exactly the same. Only the tone is different. The first question is polite; the second is insistent.

Though it is harder to hear the tone of a written word than the tone of a spoken one, the writer's attitude toward the reader and the topic determines the tone of an essay. Gary's thesis, for instance, catches the personal tone of his freewritten material. He sounds open, candid, and sincere about what he has learned from his own experience in acting. As you formulate your own thesis, you should try to choose your tone. Will you sound earnest or playful? Calm or impassioned? Authoritative or tentative?

Tone depends partly on your sense of the audience you aim to reach (see section 3.1) and partly on the content of your essay. To sound authoritative, you must be writing about what you know, and to sound convincingly impassioned, you must be writing about a subject of importance. But whatever your subject, you can strongly affect the tone of your writing by deciding (1) whether you want to sound *personal* or *impersonal,* and (2) whether you want to be *straightforward* or *ironic.*

2.4A SOUNDING PERSONAL

Generally, writing sounds **personal** when the author is *I* speaking to the reader as *you.* When you write with a personal tone, you accentuate the fact that you are expressing your own feelings, opinions, observations, or beliefs. But a personal tone can be used in essays that serve any one of the three general aims. In section 2.1 above, writer 1 uses *I* to state her personal feelings in a self-expressive essay, but writer 2 uses *I* to stress the personal quality of her observations in an expository essay, and Ursula Le Guin uses *I* to stress the personal quality of her convictions in a persuasive essay.

A personal tone can enhance the effect of an essay by making your readers feel that you are talking directly to them. Nevertheless, you should use the personal tone with restraint. When overused in explanatory writing, it can make you sound impressionistic and self-absorbed—not a reliable guide to your subject. When overused in persuasive writing, it can make you sound merely self-assertive—not persuasive. For these reasons, you should know what the alternatives are.

2.4B SOUNDING IMPERSONAL

Your writing sounds **impersonal** when you make no reference to
yourself or the reader, but focus on something distinct from you
both:

> Whenever two friends meet after a long separation, they
> go through a special Greeting Ritual. During the first
> moments of the reunion they amplify their friendly signals to
> superfriendly signals. They smile and touch, often embrace
> and kiss, and generally behave more intimately and expan-
> sively than usual. They do this because they have to make up
> for lost time—lost friendship time. While they have been
> apart it has been impossible for them to send the hundreds of
> small, minute-by-minute friendly signals to each other that
> their relationship requires, and they have, so to speak, built
> up a backlog of these signals.
>
> This backlog amounts to a gestural debt that must be
> repaid without delay, as an assurance that the bond of friend-
> ship has not waned but has survived the passage of time spent
> apart—hence the gushing ceremonies of the reunion scene,
> which must try to pay off this debt in a single outburst of
> activity.   —Desmond Morris, "Salutation Displays"

Like the student author of the passage on laughter just above
(p. 33), Desmond Morris reports on human behavior. But unlike
the student, he makes no reference to himself as an observer.
Morris writes not about *his* friends but about friendly behavior in
general, using the third person "they" and such generalizing
terms as the "Greeting Ritual" and "the reunion scene." His
impersonal tone makes the writing sound factual, objective, and
reliable.

A consistently impersonal tone suits lab reports and scientific
articles written for specialists. But most good writing strikes a
chord that combines the personal and the impersonal, that har-
monizes "it is" with "I feel." Generally, therefore, you can
enhance your writing by making some use of a personal tone,
which simply reminds the reader that your essay has been written
by a human being.

2.4C SOUNDING STRAIGHTFORWARD

Straightforward writing sounds honest, direct, and sincere. Its tone can range from cool to impassioned, as you can see by comparing Desmond Morris's passage with this one by Dorothea Morefield:

> Anyone who knows that my husband Richard was one of the 53 American hostages in Iran for 444 days wouldn't be surprised to know that I still have nightmares.
>
> But my nightmares aren't over what might have happened in Iran.
>
> My nightmares are over what did happen four years earlier—right here in America—in a fast-food restaurant in Annandale, Va., where our 19-year-old son, Richard Jr., worked part time.
>
> One Friday night in March he didn't come home from work. That was unlike Rick. He was a happy and responsible young man. He loved his family, told us wherever he was going and never gave us reason to worry.
>
> The next morning, I went to the restaurant. I was told by police that my oldest son, my firstborn, had been murdered, shot in the back of the head, executed, blown away.
>
> A robber had hidden in the restroom past closing time. He was given all the available cash without resistance, but then he herded all four remaining employees of the Roy Rogers Family Restaurant (and one of their relatives) into the back freezer and made them all lie face down on the floor. They offered no resistance. None. But he emptied his handgun into the back of their heads. In case that wasn't enough, he reloaded and did it again. And then a third time.
>
> —Dorothea Morefield, "Gun Control California Style:
> A Victim Fights"

By itself, the subject matter here is shocking and brutal. But the writer conveys a passionate tone by repeating the word "nightmares" and by firing a volley of synonyms for the killing itself: "murdered, shot in the back of the head, executed, blown away." The passionate tone serves a persuasive aim: to argue for gun control.

2.4D BEING IRONIC

Irony emerges from a split between tone and content. Your writing is ironic when you pretend to sound sincere and earnest while condemning something that is obviously good, or recommending something that is obviously bad:

> Sitting down on our family's lop-sided sofa, I turned on the TV by remote control. After clicking my way through sitcoms, commercials, and movies, I settled on the 24-hour cable news channel, where the topic of the hour was the question of what America could do with its nuclear waste. I soon switched channels again, but the question lurked in the back of my brain as I watched two *Mission: Impossible* reruns and the first half of a *Roseanne* episode. All at once, during a commercial break in *Roseanne,* the answer came to me: marketing! To solve the problem of nuclear waste, the government should turn it into souvenir gift items and sell them to the American public.
>
> For purposes of marketing, nuclear waste could assume any number of forms. It could be molded, for instance, into the shapes of the fifty states, or put into bottles with labels such as "100% Pure Nuclear Waste from Oklahoma." Made into shavings, it could be placed into a transparent plastic bubble filled with water and containing a miniature city. When the bubble was shaken, an atomic snowfall would rain down upon the tiny city. This would make a great novelty item and, in addition, the water would help filter out some of the more harmful gamma rays.
>
> Of course it would take massive sales to reduce the vast amount of radioactive by-products now sitting in various dumps around the nation. But if a talented advertising agency took on the account, I believe it could start a run on nuclear gifts that would rival the Cabbage Patch Doll craze of 1983. Furthermore, because the supply of nuclear waste may be limited, advertisers could legitimately claim that nuclear souvenirs would someday become collectors' items. It's quite possible, in fact, that a radioactive bubble on the living room coffee table would become the ultimate status symbol.
>
> —College student

The irony here makes the writer's explicit thesis merely a disguise for his implicit one. While he pretends to recommend the conversion of nuclear waste into souvenir gift items, he is actually arguing that present methods of dealing with nuclear waste make no more sense than the method he proposes: a method based on the assumption that Americans can be persuaded to buy anything.

Irony can be hard to achieve and sustain because you must continually find ways to indicate that you mean something different from what you seem to be saying. But because irony prompts the reader to share your outrage or to laugh with you at whatever you find absurd, it can be a highly effective means of persuasion. (For more on how to catch the tone in what you read and also how to detect irony, see section 10.3A.)

> EXERCISE 4 FINDING YOUR TONE
>
> a. If you have done exercise 1, do as follows with the freewritten material you produced: (1) describe the prevailing tone of the material; (2) indicate what features of the writing convey this tone; (3) explain how this tone will help you realize your thesis.
>
> b. If you have *not* done exercise 1, describe the tone you will use to develop your thesis and explain why you are choosing this tone.

3

Organizing Your Essay

If you have managed by now to formulate a statement of thesis that satisfies you, you have already started to **organize** your essay. You have given yourself a sense of direction by identifying your most important point. With this point firmly in mind, you can draw other points from the material you have produced in the pre-writing and freewriting stages and arrange those points in such a way as to support and develop your thesis.

Moving from pre-writing or freewriting to organization doesn't mean stopping the flow of new material. Even now you may turn back to rethink your original idea, which is why writing is sometimes called a *recursive* process—a process of periodically recurring (running back) to your starting point. In thus returning, you may discover new ideas at any point, right up to the production of the final draft. But to make your essay effective, you must know how to shape, reshape, and refine your ideas so that your readers can grasp them.

A well-organized essay is usually a series of answers to the most basic questions a reader might ask:

What are you talking about?	Introduction
What point are you trying to make?	Statement of thesis (sometimes deferred or merely implied)
Can you explain that?	Development
What's it all add up to?	Conclusion

In this chapter we explain how to organize an essay that answers these questions. But to answer them effectively, you first need to know something about your readers.

3.1 THINKING ABOUT YOUR READERS

Who are they? The obvious answer is that your readers are your teachers, or *the* teacher of the course for which you are writing an essay. But in a writing course, your **audience** may include your fellow students as well, who are commonly asked to read and discuss what you have written. In any case, writing well means learning how to write for different kinds of readers. For this reason, teachers of writing courses will sometimes assign not only a topic but an audience. You may be asked to explain a lab experiment to readers who know nothing about science, to re-create a personal experience for readers who know nothing about you, or to persuade a banker that you deserve a loan so that you can start a business. In assignments of this kind, the teacher is not so much your reader as your coach—helping you to reach the specified audience.

You can learn how to reach a specified audience by considering the following questions:

1. How much do your readers know about the topic? If you underestimate their knowledge, you will bore them by telling them things they already know; if you overestimate their knowledge, you may confuse them with unfamiliar terms or incomplete explanations. Try to tell your readers only as much as they need to know in order to understand you.

How much do they need to know? This depends on both your topic and your audience. If you are writing a lab report for your chemistry professor, you can assume that he or she already knows the meaning of technical terms such as *fractionation.* But for readers unfamiliar with chemistry, you would have to explain such terms. (For more on this point, see section 38.3, "Writing on Specialized Topics for Nonspecialists.") The same is true for any specialized terms that you cannot reasonably expect your readers to know.

2. How do your readers feel about the topic? Are they likely to feel any desire to read about it? If you're writing about terrorism, abortion, or smoking, you can assume that most readers will be interested in what you have to say. But if you're writing about chess for readers who may never have played the game, you can't assume much interest. You will have to stimulate it by explaining what makes chess so interesting—even fascinating—to you.

If you *can* assume that your readers are interested in your topic, do they all feel the same way about it? And how strongly do they hold their views? If you want to write about smoking restrictions for an audience of fellow students, you have to realize that their attitudes toward smoking probably range from strong aversion to strong attachment.

3. What is your readers' relation to you? Are you a student writing for other students? Are you a job-hunter writing to a prospective employer? Are you a specialist (in any particular sport or hobby) writing for nonspecialists? The better you grasp your relation to your readers, the better you will communicate.

4. Do your readers differ from you in race, class, gender, or nationality? If so, you can hardly assume that their experience and points of view will match yours. In the first draft of his essay on acting (see below, section 4.6), which was written to be read by the other students in his class of nine men and eleven women, Gary made the mistake of assuming that *all* his readers could remember playing boys' games and dressing up as male heroes. A similar mistake would be made by any upper-class writer who assumed that all her readers could remember their prep school days, or any white writer who assumed that all her readers could remember being tanned or sunburned. Whenever you generalize from your own experience, you must think carefully about the experience of your readers. (To see how Gary corrected his mistake, see below, section 5.7; and for advice on using language that is respectful of women and ethnic minorities, see sections 9.11 and 9.12.)

5. Do your readers differ from you in religious beliefs or political attitudes? If so, their view of your topic may differ drasti-

cally from your own. If, for instance, you intend to argue that all U.S. health care services should be federally regulated, you would need to recognize that many Americans regard federal regulation as federal interference with their lives. Likewise, if you wish to argue that capital punishment may be justified in some circumstances, you need to know that some religious groups believe it wrong under any circumstances.

6. How do your readers expect you to treat the topic? Sometimes this question is answered by the terms of an assignment. Professional writers—especially journalists—often work under instructions from editors who tell them not only what to write but also how to treat it. When you get a writing assignment, therefore, you should learn as much as you can about the approach you are expected to take.

In part that approach will depend on the rules of the game, the conditions under which you are writing. If your chemistry professor asks for a lab report, you are expected to record what the experiment showed, not what you felt when you performed it. But if your English teacher asks for an account of a personal experience and you decide to describe your first lab experiment, you will include your feelings, since for this assignment you are expected to describe what you felt. (For further guidance on what is expected in essays written for specialized fields in the humanities, sciences, and social sciences, see chapter 38.)

7. How long is the finished essay supposed to be? You already know that teachers often specify a minimum or maximum number of words for the essays they require in their courses. Outside the classroom, length requirements are regularly imposed on contestants in writing contests and on everyone who writes for newspapers, magazines, and other publications. Whatever you write for such a publication—an essay, a story, or a letter to the editor—you should know what sort of length is expected if you hope to see your words in print.

But don't be afraid of writing too much or too little on your first draft. Aim first of all to get all of your thoughts about the topic down on paper. If you end up with too many words, you can tighten your sentences and cut out redundant points when you revise. If you end up with too few words, you can identify points that need further development.

REACHING YOUR AUDIENCE: IN BRIEF

- How much do your readers know about the topic?
- How do they feel about the topic?
- What is their relation to you?
- Do they differ from you in race, class, gender, or nationality?
- Do they differ from you in religious beliefs or political attitudes?
- How do they expect you to treat the topic?
- How long is the finished essay supposed to be?

EXERCISE 1   THINKING ABOUT YOUR READERS

1. Suppose you are either *proposing* or *opposing* a Congressional bill that would ban smoking in all public places throughout the United States. Choose just one position, and then briefly explain how you would present it to each of the following: (a) smokers, (b) nonsmokers, (c) tobacco company executives.

2. Suppose you are explaining why a particular sport, hobby, or subject fascinates you. Write two sample paragraphs of explanation: one for readers who share your interest and knowledge, and one for those who don't. Also, make a list of any specialized terms that you are defining for the reader.

3. Write a letter to the faculty of your college or university explaining why you should be made its president.

4. Write a letter to all shareholders of General Motors explaining why the salary of the chairman of its board should not exceed twenty-five times the salary of the lowest-paid GM worker. (It is now well over a hundred times greater than the lowest salary.)

5. Write a letter to H. Ross Perot (the Texas billionaire) explaining why he should give you a million dollars.

6. Addressing a group of readers who differ from you in gender, write an essay defending, attacking, or modifying the proposition that women serving in the armed services should be allowed to play combat roles.

7. Addressing a group of readers who differ from you in race, write an essay attacking or defending the proposition that all colleges should reserve a minimum percentage of places for members of racial minorities.

3.2 ARRANGING YOUR MAJOR POINTS

Once you have considered the readers you will be writing for, you can **select** and **arrange** your major points. To do so, you should first make a list of all the points you have identified up to now. Gary did this simply by rereading his freewritten material and then jotting down the various points that he connected with acting:

1. excitement of acting
2. working with others
3. drawing crowds
4. getting applause
5. winning compliments
6. playing Nat Miller in *Ah, Wilderness!*
7. seeing myself in mirror as someone else
8. sitting at breakfast table for opening scene
9. creating an imaginary family
10. relating to every other character
11. acting and children's make-believe games
12. acting as vacation from myself

This, of course, is just a random list. But the advantage of making such a list before you make your outline is that it puts before you all of the points you have thought up so far. You can then do what Gary did: underline the most important ones:

7. seeing myself in mirror as someone else
9. creating an imaginary family
12. acting as vacation from myself

Your next task is to decide on the **order** or **arrangement** of your major points. To decide that, you must know what arrangements are possible and which are better than others for your particular topic, aim, and audience. In other words, the choice of order depends on your rhetorical strategy, on what you plan to do in your essay. Following are some of the arrangements you might use—alone or in combination:

1. Chronological Order. This arrangement follows the order of events in time, and therefore works well in essays written to explain a procedure, such as pitching a tent, or a natural process, such as the migration of birds. (On explaining procedures and processes, see section 6.9.) It is also commonly used in narrative (section 6.2), as well as in essays that use narrative.

2. Spatial Order. Spatial arrangement follows the order of objects in space and therefore works well in descriptive writing (section 6.1). Spatial order typically follows the movements of an imaginary eye surveying a scene—moving around a room, or across a landscape from left to right, or from foreground to background. It can also shift in scale, as when it moves from a comprehensive view to a close-up.

3. Cause and Effect Order. Cause and effect order allows you to explain one point as the reason for or as the result of another. In an essay on why women long to be thin (pp. 127–29), the writer starts with the fact that many American women are obsessed with losing weight. Then she explains the reasons for this development. Likewise, in the first part of her freewriting on the cave, Andrea briefly presents the girls' predicament as a result of the way they came down (sliding and leaving no rope). In the final version of her essay, Andrea emphasizes causal order by starting with the girls at the bottom of the cave (see p. 59), and then backing up to explain how they got there. Thus she modifies chronological order with causal order.

4. Climactic Order. When you order your writing climactically, you arrange points in order of ascending importance, rising from least important to most important. Climactic order sometimes corresponds to chronological order. But in the passage

from Dorothea Morefield's essay (p. 43), the most important point is what came first in time—the death of her son. To prepare us for the impact of this point, she puts it *after* her explanation of how—on the morning after his death—she set out to learn what had happened to him.

5. Oppositional Order. This arrangement opposes one point to another. It often works well at the start of a persuasive essay written for readers who are likely to resist the thesis. You can also use oppositional order to compare and contrast two things, as shown in section 6.6, or just to highlight their differences.

6. Categorical Order. This order helps you to explain one large group as a collection of subgroups. The student author of an essay on Brooklyn teenagers, for instance, divided them into two groups: a minority of drug-free "ducks" who go to school every day, and a majority of drug-taking "hard rocks" who regularly skip school and beat up the ducks. He put the ducks first because he was writing for a group of students who would be called "ducks" if they lived in Brooklyn. Then he turned to the hard rocks, who live by a code that most of his readers would find strange. Thus he presented the two groups in an order that suited his topic and his audience. (For more on this method of arrangement, see section 6.8.)

To see how you might use and combine some of these arrangements, consider what Gary did. Since he was writing for the other students in his class, he decided to start with common reasons for wanting to act, including items 2–5. Then, taking an oppositional stance, he would shift to his special reasons. These he would treat in climactic order, moving from "creating an imaginary family" to "vacationing from myself."

> **EXERCISE 2 ARRANGING YOUR MAJOR POINTS**
>
> Rereading your freewritten material and any other notes from the pre-writing process, make a random list of all the points you have so far accumulated for your essay-in-progress. Then underline the most important points, arrange them as well as you can, and identify the order(s) you have used.

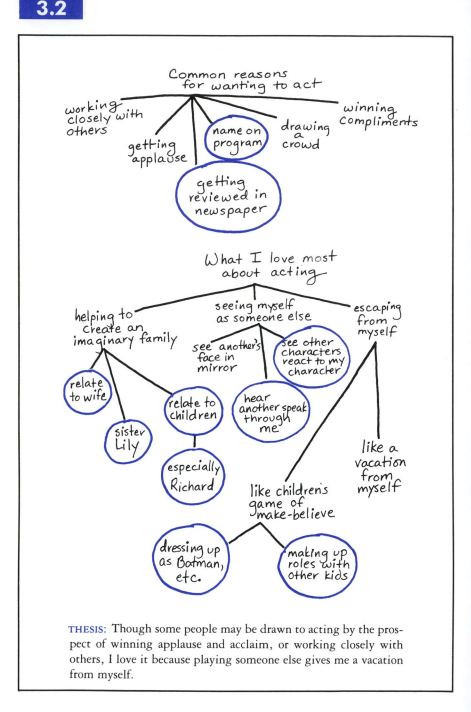

THESIS: Though some people may be drawn to acting by the prospect of winning applause and acclaim, or working closely with others, I love it because playing someone else gives me a vacation from myself.

3.3 MAKING AN OUTLINE

After deciding how to arrange your major points, you must decide how to connect your minor points to the major ones. The best way to plan your connections is to make an **outline,** which may be either a tree diagram or a vertical list. But whichever you choose, you should think of an outline as a *tentative* plan for your essay, not a rigid scheme. If new ideas or new questions come to mind while you are writing, feel free to revise your outline or even to scrap it altogether and make a new one.

3.3A OUTLINING WITH A TREE DIAGRAM

A **tree diagram** is a regulated version of a branching diagram. Its branches are arranged to be read from left to right, and they spread out in one direction only—down from the thesis like the branches of a tree reflected in water. Because the tree is open-ended, it leaves space for you to visualize more branches. So once you have drawn the tree to organize all your major and minor points, you can make it grow by adding more points as they come to mind.

The tree diagram Gary drew (p. 54) illustrates this kind of growth. The items we've circled in color are not among the list of points he originally took from his freewritten material; the circled items came to him as he was laying out the branches of the tree. Thus the tree diagram served not just as a record of his thoughts, but as a means of discovering new ones.

3.3B OUTLINING WITH A VERTICAL LIST

After you have produced some freewritten material, making a **vertical outline** of it is a good way to check the organization of your material—to see where the sequence and development are good, and also to spot any gaps where more information is needed. To outline your material vertically, write your thesis at the head of the page and then use headings and indented sub-headings:

THESIS: Though some people may be drawn to acting by the prospect of winning applause and acclaim, or working closely with others, I love it because playing someone else gives me a vacation from myself.

I. Common reasons for wanting to act
   A. Working closely with others
   B. Getting name on program
   C. Getting applause
   D. Drawing a crowd
   E. Winning compliments
II. What I love most about acting
   A. Seeing myself as someone else
      1. Seeing another's face in the mirror
      2. Hearing another speak through me
      3. Seeing other characters react to my character
   B. Helping create an imaginary family
      1. Relating to wife
      2. Relating to children
   C. Vacationing from myself
      1. Like children's games of make-believe
         a. Dressing up as Batman, etc.
         b. Making up roles with other kids
      2. Like traveling

Besides listing points in order of rising importance, this outline groups them under headings that show their relation to each other and to the thesis. Points that were at first jotted down in a random list have now become the skeleton of an essay.

3.3C USING YOUR OUTLINE AND MAKING IT GROW

The best way to use an outline is to follow it as a guide, not a dictator. Just because you've made an outline doesn't mean that you can't ever remake it or depart from it as you write. Writing is a *recursive* process, which means that at any stage it may turn back or run back (recur) to its first stage: back to pre-writing techniques, back to searching for new ideas.

So what do you do with a brand-new idea that comes to you in the middle of writing? If it obviously supports the point you're developing in a particular paragraph, you can take it up right away. If it doesn't, see whether the new idea can be grafted onto a branch of your tree diagram or tucked into your vertical outline for use later on. You can thus make your outline grow even as you follow its guidance.

> **EXERCISE 3** OUTLINING WITH A TREE DIAGRAM
>
> Following the example shown on p. 54, use a tree diagram to arrange all of your points. Then add whatever new branches you think are needed.
>
> **EXERCISE 4** OUTLINING WITH A VERTICAL LIST
>
> Using a vertical list with headings and subheadings, arrange your points in such a way as to clarify their relation to your thesis and to each other, and put them in an order that you think will best support the thesis.

3.4 INTRODUCING YOUR ESSAY

3.4A COMPOSING A TITLE

Every essay needs a **title**. It should be short but sharply focused on the main point of the essay. Compare the titles on the left with those on the right:

College	Where College Fails Us
Lawyers	When Lawyers Help Villains
The Mine	Escaping from a Mine
First-Year Students	How First-Year Students Manage Money
College	Why Returning to College Beats Arriving
Acting	Why I Love to Act

While the titles on the left merely identify a general topic, those on the right make the topic specific and tell the reader what to expect. Also, if you can think of a good working title as you outline your essay, it can guide you through the writing of the essay itself. When you finish writing, you can reword the title if necessary to make it more precise.

3.4B WRITING THE INTRODUCTION

The **introduction** comes first for the reader, but not necessarily first for the writer. Since you can't write a good introduction until you know what you're introducing, you may want to plunge immediately into the middle of your draft, write your way to a conclusion, and only then write your introduction. But whenever you write it, this section may help you to make it effective.

To see the difference between a weak introduction and a strong one, consider these two versions of an introductory paragraph written by a college freshman:

ORIGINAL

Professional athletes, in return for entertaining millions of people, get paid enormous amounts of money. All sports, from basketball to hockey to boxing, offer lucrative salaries and endorsement opportunities to their elite participants. Athletes' multimillion-dollar salaries can be somewhat rationalized if one accepts the reasoning that anyone at the pinnacle of a profession ought to be paid accordingly. However, some sports appropriate money more responsibly than others. Professional baseball players get too much, especially when compared to professional golfers.

REVISED

As I watched the Atlanta Braves and the Minnesota Twins do battle in the 1991 World Series, I was reminded of just how gripping baseball can be. But shortly after the series ended, the spoiled stars of both major leagues were once again competing for the salary crown. Led by Bobby Bonilla, who made over five million with the Pittsburgh Pirates in 1991 and has since then moved to the New York Mets, they have been leaving smaller clubs for bigger and richer ones. This race for millions drives ticket prices up beyond the reach of working-class fans and pushes most televised games off free channels. It's time to stop this drain on team budgets and fans' pockets. To get players' salaries under control, team owners should recalculate the value of each player every year and pay no more than three million a year to any player.

The original introduction sprawls all over professional sports, mentioning baseball only at the end and leaving the reader confused about what the writer plans to do. The revised version focuses sharply and consistently on the salaries of baseball players, and by the time we finish this paragraph, we know exactly what the writer plans to do.

You don't always need to end your opening paragraph with a perfect preview of your essay, a complete statement of what it will show. To excite curiosity, you may end with a question, or with a point that stops well short of the one you will eventually make. The only thing a good introduction must do is to forecast what will follow, and it can do this in a virtually endless number of ways. Here are some of them:

1. Lead up to an explicit statement of your thesis:

THE TOWN DUMP

The town dump of Whitemud, Saskatchewan, could only have been a few years old when I knew it, for the village was born in 1913 and I left there in 1919. But I remember the dump better than I remember most things in that town, better than I remember most of the people. I spent more time with it, for one thing; it had more poetry and excitement in it than people did.
—Wallace Stegner

2. Define a conflict, problem, or question you aim to resolve:

ESCAPING FROM A MINE

A slow, forbidding breeze chilled me as I watched Ellie struggling to get a grip on a rock wall that must have been at least fifteen feet high. She cursed. The breeze passed, but the chill on my face remained as I looked around again at where we were. The four rudely cut walls that had held so much mystery and excitement for us a few hours ago now loomed threateningly over our heads. One hundred feet up was our salvation—the opening to the copper mine, looking not much bigger than a single star in a coal-black sky. The sharp overhangings and gargoylelike outcroppings jutted harshly from the sides of the massive cave, ominously reminding us that we had climbed in, and now we had to climb out. But we couldn't. For at least an hour we tried to scale that one section of the mine wall, and couldn't see how to do it.

—Andrea Lyle

3. Tell a story that illustrates the main point you will go on to make:

DOUBLE VISION

When I was a little girl, my mother told me to wait for the light to turn green before I crossed the street and to cross always at the corner. This I did. Indeed, I was positive as a very young child that I would get mashed like a potato if I even so much as stepped a foot off the sidewalk while the light burned red. I followed my mother's advice until I realized that she herself jaywalked constantly, dodging in and out of moving traffic—and pulling me with her. So after a while I followed her example and not her advice. —Lynn Minton

Minton tells a personal story to introduce the main point of her essay, which is that adults are hypocritical.

4. Move from a generalization to a specific case:

COLLEGE: DEPAUW

American families differ greatly in their expectations about what going to college will mean in their children's lives. In the intellectual community to which my parents belonged, college was as necessary as learning to read. It was an intellectual experience and the gateway to the rest of life. All my life I expected to go to college, and I was prepared to enjoy it.

—Margaret Mead

5. Indicate the method of your essay:

HOW FAMILIES CREATE CULTURE IN EAST AND WEST

Sociologists study the family because it is the basic unit of society. As a Chinese student who lived with an American family for six months, I had the opportunity to compare this family with my own in China. In so doing, I learned that the differences between the two countries are mainly created within the family. Though I was raised to tell my parents everything and to depend on others, each member of the American family had a private life, and the children were trained to be independent, to refuse help even when they needed it. The differences between my family and the American one help to explain why Eastern and Western cultures have such different attitudes toward privacy, dependence, and independence. —College student

6. Challenge a widespread assumption or stereotype:

WHERE COLLEGE FAILS US

The case *for* college has been accepted without question for more than a generation. All high school graduates ought to go, says Conventional Wisdom and statistical evidence, because college will help them earn more money, become "better" people, and learn to be more responsible citizens than those who don't go.

But college has never been able to work its magic for everyone. And now that close to half our high school graduates are attending, those who don't fit the pattern are becoming more numerous, and more obvious. College graduates are selling shoes and driving taxis; college students sabotage each other's experiments and forge letters of recommendation in the intense competition for admission to graduate school. Others find no stimulation in their studies, and drop out—often encouraged by college administrators. —Caroline Bird

7. Establish a historical context for your topic:

THE CASE FOR TORTURE

It is generally assumed that torture is impermissible, a throwback to a more brutal age. Enlightened societies reject it outright, and regimes suspected of using it risk the wrath of the United States.

I believe this attitude is unwise. There are situations in which torture is not merely permissible but morally mandatory. Moreover, these situations are moving from the realm of imagination to fact. —Michael Levin

8. To accommodate readers who may not agree with you, explain the position you aim to oppose:

THE CASE FOR TEST-TUBE BABIES

The mere mention of "test-tube babies" triggers instant repugnance in most of us. Visions arise, from Aldous Huxley's *Brave New World,* of moving assembly lines of glassware out of which babies are decanted at each terminus by a detached and impersonal technician. Procreation thus becomes reproduction in the full factory-like connotation of that word. And as we conjure up the distasteful (at the least) scene, words like *mechanization* and *dehumanization* reverberate through our neuronal networks.

Nevertheless, despite the offense to our sensibilities provoked by even the thought of artificial wombs, there is a valid case to be made for test-tube babies in the full Huxleyan image—not mass-produced on an assembly line, perhaps, but nevertheless wholly and "artificially" grown in a scientifically monitored environment without ever being carried in the uterus of a human mother. Such a case can be made (which does not mean that I personally advocate it) on the basis not merely of bizarre and exotic speculations but of purely humane, down-to-earth considerations having to do with the health of individual babies.   —Albert Rosenfeld

---

INTRODUCING YOUR ESSAY: IN BRIEF

- Lead up to an explicit statement of your thesis.

- Define a conflict, problem, or question you aim to resolve.

- Tell a story that illustrates the main point you will go on to make.

- Move from a generalization to a specific case.

- Indicate the method of your essay.

- Challenge a widespread assumption or stereotype.

- Establish a historical context for your topic.

- Explain the position you aim to oppose.

> **EXERCISE 5 COMPOSING A TITLE AND WRITING AN INTRODUCTION**
>
> After reviewing section 3.4A, compose a title for your essay. Then, using any one of the methods explained above, write an introduction.

3.5 SHAPING THE MIDDLE PARAGRAPHS

If you have made an outline or drawn a tree diagram, you have already clustered certain points under each of several headings and you have seen how the mere act of arranging points can lead to your thinking of new points. Now you can use each of the headings in your outline as the **topic of a paragraph.** For instance, the branch labeled "Helping to create an imaginary family" in the tree diagram shown on p. 54 led Gary to write these two paragraphs:

> In becoming Nat Miller, I entered the world of an imaginary family living in a small town at the beginning of this century. I helped to create this family. During eight weeks of rehearsal I came to know every member of it well. Nat's sister Lily, a shy, bespectacled, old maid schoolteacher who lives with Nat and his family, is yearning to marry his irresponsible, *alcaholic brother-in-law Sid, but never will as long as Sid drinks. Nat's bustling, matronly wife Essie is constantly over-anxious about their children: Arthur, the college boy home for the summer; Tommy, a chubby, impish eleven-year-old; Mildred, a lively fifteen; and Richard, one year older, a shy, rebellious, bookish dreamer in love with a girl named Muriel.
>
> Richard's notes to Muriel are a source of trouble. They include some rather "warm" lines quoted from a love poem by Swinburne. They infuriate Muriel's dried-up tyrannical father, and they make Nat nervous enough to give Richard a lecture on sex. The lecture is comically roundabout and vague. I was just sixteen when I appeared in the play. So I had to imagine myself the father of a boy my own age, trying to tell him how to control his sexual drives.

Since this is only the first draft, it is not yet all it should be, and Gary has some revisions to make. But this paragraph shows what he did with one group of items in his tree diagram. Notice that he feels no need to give all items the same space. Though "Especially Richard" was almost an afterthought in the tree diagram, Gary realized while writing the paragraph—and remembering the play—that he had more to say about his relation to Richard than about anyone else in his imaginary family. So he created a new paragraph focusing on his special relation to Richard and opening up the question of what it feels like to play the parent of someone your own age.

> **EXERCISE 6 DRAFTING THE MIDDLE**
>
> Using your outline or tree diagram as a guide, write one paragraph for each of its headings. If you find that a particular heading generates more or less than one paragraph, feel free to modify the outline or tree diagram. Remember that this is only a first draft.

3.6 ENDING YOUR ESSAY

To **end** an essay effectively, ask yourself what final impression you want to make on your reader. You can leave a strong impression by any one of the following means:

1. Make the implications of your thesis explicit:

> We have found that violence on prime-time network TV cultivates exaggerated assumptions about the threat of danger in the real world. Fear is a universal emotion, and easy to exploit. The exaggerated sense of risk and insecurity may lead to increasing demands for protection, and to increasing pressure for the use of force by established authority. Instead of threatening the social order, television may have become our chief instrument of social control.
>
> —George Gerbner and Larry Gross,
> "The Scary World of TV's Heavy Viewer"

2. Echo your introduction in terms that widen its significance:

> Poetry is seldom useful, but always memorable. I think I learned more from the town dump than I learned from school: more about people, more about how life is lived, not elsewhere but here, not in other times but now. If I were a sociologist anxious to study in detail the life of any community, I would go very early to its refuse piles. For a community may be as well judged by what it throws away—what it has to throw away and what it chooses to—as by any other evidence. For whole civilizations we have sometimes no more of the poetry and little more of the history than this.
>
> —Wallace Stegner, "The Town Dump"

3. Recommend a specific course of action:

> The physically handicapped have the liabilities of a minority group. Shouldn't they be given the rights of a minority group? The answer is affirmative. It is time the action was also. —Nancy Weinberg, "Disability Isn't Beautiful"

4. Answer a question posed by the introduction:

> What, then, can we conclude about mathematics and sex? If math anxiety is in part the result of math avoidance, why not require girls to take as much math as they can possibly master? If being the only girl in "trig" is the reason so many women drop math at the end of high school, why not provide psychological counseling and support for those young women who wish to go on? Since ability in mathematics is considered by many to be unfeminine, perhaps fear of success, more than any bodily or mental dysfunction, may interfere with girls' ability to learn math.
>
> —Sheila Tobias, "Who's Afraid of Math, and Why?"

5. Reflect on the experience that the essay records:

> We hadn't done anything spectacular, and when we got home, no one was surprised to see us. There was no celebration and no story in the paper. Yet looking back on our escape from the mine, I realize now why we both felt something more than relief. We felt proud that we had not panicked or simply given up and waited for help. We had faced a problem together, and

we had finally found a solution. Paradoxically, by depending on each other—there was no one else—we discovered what it means to be independent. In a sense, we rescued each other.　　　　　　　　—Andrea Lyle, "Escaping from a Mine"

6. <u>Reaffirm your thesis with a final telling example.</u> To end an essay on the amount of garbage produced by New York City, Katie Kelley tells what she saw and heard at Fresh Kills, a Staten Island dumping site:

> "It sure has changed out here," one worker, who has been at Fresh Kills for years, told me. "Why, there used to be fresh natural springs over there." He gestured out over the hundreds of acres of garbage. Natural crab beds once flourished in the area. Now they, too, are gone, buried under tons of garbage.
>
> 　　　　　　　　　　　　　　　　　　　　—"Garbage"

ENDING YOUR ESSAY: IN BRIEF

- Make the implications of your thesis explicit.
- Echo your introduction in terms that widen its significance.
- Recommend a specific course of action.
- Answer a question posed by the introduction.
- Reflect on the experience that the essay records.
- Reaffirm your thesis with a telling example.

EXERCISE 7 ENDING AN ESSAY

First, turn to p. 118 and put a card or small sheet of paper over paragraph 6. Then turn to pp. 116–18 and read the first five paragraphs of the essay titled "Why Videotapes Won't Kill Movie Theatres." Finally—without looking at paragraph 6—furnish your own concluding paragraph for this essay.

EXERCISE 8 COMPARING ENDINGS

Read paragraph 6 on p. 118 and compare it with your own concluding paragraph. Then explain what each ending does and how well it works.

EXERCISE 9 ENDING YOUR OWN ESSAY

Write a paragraph to conclude the essay you have been writing in this chapter.

4

Revising Your Essay

Revising literally means "looking again." To look at your essay again, the first thing you need is a copy of it on paper. If you have it only on a computer disk, you cannot see it as a whole. So anything you write with a word processor should be printed before you try to revise it. After you have marked it up by hand, you can make your changes on your disk.

Why do you need to revise—to look again at what you have written? The main reason is that to produce an effective essay, you must *put yourself in the place of the reader.* You must see what the essay presents to a reader and check its effect against your aims. Since a first draft seldom if ever realizes the writer's aims perfectly, you must consider what it needs.

It will usually need more than tinkering: more than small corrections in spelling, grammar, punctuation, or usage. That is what we call **editing,** and it is treated in chapter 5. This chapter deals with revising, which means looking again at the whole of your essay: its tone, the development of its main point, and its appeal to the readers for whom it is written. The key to effective revision is this: *try to make big changes before turning to little ones.* If you try to do both at the same time, you may find yourself laboring over a particular sentence and then deciding to rewrite or cut out altogether the whole paragraph that contains it. So we suggest you revise and edit your essay in two stages. That is why we treat revising in this chapter and editing in the next.

Revising works best when you have set your draft aside for two or three days so that you can read it with fresh eyes, as if it had been written by someone else. In addition, you may need some guidance from your instructor, your fellow students, or both. The following section explains the kind of comments you may get from another student as well as the kind of comments you may be asked to make on another student's paper.

4.1 MAKING AND GETTING WRITTEN COMMENTS ON A DRAFT

Written comments made by one or more readers of your draft can be genuinely helpful. As you read comments made on your draft by your teacher or another student, don't think of them simply as a list of complaints or commands. Look for recognition of the strengths of the draft, insight into its weaknesses, and suggestions for improvement. These comments come from your first readers. If you're not reaching them effectively, their comments can help you see why.

4.1A PEER COMMENTS: REVIEWING ANOTHER STUDENT'S DRAFT

If you are asked to comment on another student's draft, you may be expected to answer a set of questions such as those in the box below. Note that *none* of the questions involves grammar, punctuation, or spelling. All those things should be considered later—in the editing phase.

In reviewing another student's draft, give credit wherever it is due. If a word seems particularly well chosen, or if a phrase or sentence seems notably well crafted, mark it as a **hit**. Be considerate in expressing your criticism. If you spot a weakness or a problem, you should certainly identify it, but rather than saying what the writer has failed to do, try to say what you missed—or what you need—as a reader: "This point left me confused" or "I felt the need for more detail here." Bear in mind that your comments should *help* the writer to revise.

Besides serving for peer review, the following questions can also be applied to a draft of your own. But they will work best on your own draft if you have set it aside for a few days after writing it.

PEER REVIEW QUESTIONNAIRE

1. What did you like best about this essay?

2. Where did you find *hits:* well-chosen words, well-crafted phrases, or strikingly good sentences?

3. Can you state the main point of the essay in a single sentence?

4. If not, why not?

5. Where do you feel the need for more information or development?

6. Where did you find the essay confusing or hard to follow, and why?

7. Did the author write with full respect for readers of different sexes, classes, races, and nationalities?

Following is a set of answers to these questions made by Alicia Ramirez, a student who was asked to comment on the first draft of Gary's paper. (For the paper itself, together with the teacher's comments on it, see section 4.6.)

1. I liked the opening image of the mirror and the sense of seeing himself as someone else. Also the idea of playing the father of a boy his own age.

2. HIT SENTENCE: "As I worked my way through a speech full of sputterings, sudden halts, and evasive phrases, I felt the pain of Nat's embarrassment but also the force of his love for a son that he was struggling to communicate with." HIT PHRASE: "living inside me" (par. 5).

3. "Acting is like taking a vacation from yourself."

4. Pass on this one.

5. In the first par. I'd like to see more about what the mirror showed—how he actually looked. Also, who wrote the play?

6. I got confused at the beginning of par. 3. I didn't get the point of the move from the idea of the team at the end of par. 2 to the idea of the family. Is the family supposed to be a team, or what?

7. As a woman reader, I felt respected until I got to the paragraph where he talks about how "we all" played cowboys and Indians, or cops and robbers. Well, I didn't. Who is this "we," anyway?

4.2 RECONSIDERING YOUR GENERAL AIM

As we said in section 2.1, you can think about the aim of an essay in two ways—specific and general. Once the essay is written, its specific aim is to express, to explain, or to prove its main point—its thesis. Whether your thesis is explicit or implicit, you should now be able to say what it is and to see how well your essay develops it. But as you think about your thesis, ask yourself again about your general aim. Do you chiefly want to express your own feelings, to explain something outside yourself, or to persuade your reader?

You may decide to **modify your general aim,** as Gary did. In his first draft, he aimed simply to express himself, to say what *he* loved most about acting. So the thesis he formulated is purely personal. But while pondering his instructor's comments on his draft (see below, section 4.6), Gary decided to change his aim. What he learned about acting from his own experience, he realized, might be made to serve an expository aim, to explain what all (or most) actors find most appealing about their work. So he revised his thesis this way:

> ORIGINAL VERSION: Though some people may be drawn to acting by the prospect of winning applause and acclaim, or working closely with others, I love it because playing someone else gives me a vacation from myself.

> REVISED: Though some people may be drawn to acting by the prospect of winning applause and acclaim, or working closely with others, I believe they love it most because playing someone else gives them a vacation from themselves.

The full statement of the revised thesis appears nowhere in the essay itself. Gary used the full statement to guide him in revising his essay, but he did not use it in his introductory paragraph or his conclusion. Instead, he took his instructor's suggestion. From a question about acting he worked toward the gradual discovery of an answer that becomes perfectly clear—without a full statement of it—in the final paragraph.

> **EXERCISE 1   RECONSIDERING YOUR AIM**
>
> Do three things: (1) state the thesis of your essay in its present form; (2) state the general aim you have decided to pursue— whether self-expression, explanation, or persuasion; (3) if necessary, rewrite the thesis to make it fit the aim.

4.3 RECONSIDERING YOUR TONE

The best way to hear the **tone** of your first draft is to read it aloud to yourself, or ask someone to read it aloud to you. As you listen, consider these questions: Does the writing sound too personal for your topic and aim, or too impersonal? Is the tone consistent? Does it help you develop your thesis and realize your aim? To see how you might answer such questions, consider this opening paragraph of a student's first draft:

> Going to college for most people means the onset of new freedoms and many responsibilities. The acquisition of these new responsibilities helps to develop values and maturity in an individual. This makes the prospect of going to college appealing. Upon returning home for the Christmas holidays, I experienced new freedoms and respect from my parents.

The final sentence of this paragraph leads to a statement of thesis. But the detached, impersonal tone of the opening sentences, which refer to "most people" and "an individual," hardly prepares us for the personal tone of the final sentence. To bridge the gap between the two, the student made the middle sentences sound personal, so that the paragraph read this way:

> For most people, going to college means the onset of new freedoms and many responsibilities. In my first semester of college, new responsibilities helped me to develop values and maturity. This opportunity to mature is what drew me to col-

lege in the first place, and I especially felt the change in myself when the semester ended. Upon returning home for the Christmas holidays, I experienced new freedoms and respect from my parents.

Now the paragraph moves from the impersonal tone of the opening generalization to a personal tone in the middle sentences, which lead the way to the distinctly personal statement of thesis. Thus the tone of the paragraph enhances its most important point. (For more on tone, see or review section 2.4.)

EXERCISE 2 RECONSIDERING TONE

Read the passage below and then say whether or not the tone is consistent. If not, identify the inconsistencies, and then revise the passage to make its tone consistent.

As Patrick Henry once delivered fiery speeches that roused American colonists to revolution in the 1770s, so Martin Luther King, Jr., inspired many Americans during the 1960s. Many people in this period struggled to bring blacks and whites together, but no one expressed the ideal of integration   5 more movingly than King when he stood in front of the Lincoln Memorial and declared to the thousands of people gathered there, "I have a dream." King spoke straight from the heart. He didn't hide his feelings, as politicians often do. Of course the reason they hide their feelings is that they can't get   10 elected any other way. That's the problem with straightforward speaking; it doesn't win elections. But I still like to hear an honest speech now and then. It's refreshing.

4.4 RECONSIDERING YOUR STRUCTURE

To see how well your essay is constructed, consider the following questions:

1. Can you state the thesis of your essay? A well-structured essay is unified by its emphasis on one main point, the thesis of the essay as a whole. Whether stated or merely implied, a thesis should emerge from every essay you write. Even a personal nar-

rative should strive to answer a basic question such as "What did I learn from this experience?" If you can't state the thesis of your essay, you should rethink the relation between or among the points it makes, decide which point you want to stress most, and subordinate the other points to that one.

2. Does your introduction announce or forecast your thesis?

3. Can you state the main point or identify the most important image in each paragraph? If you can't do either, the paragraph must be split up, reconstructed, or both. (For more on this topic, see section 8.4.)

4. Does each paragraph help to develop the thesis? If the main point of any paragraph departs from or works against the thesis, you should cut the paragraph, find a way to make it work for the development of the thesis, or revise the thesis. In the first draft of Gary's essay, the opening sentence of paragraph 2— "There are lots of reasons to love acting"—seems to depart from the thesis just stated, which forecasts a special reason to love acting. In the revised version, a new closing sentence for paragraph 1 indicates that the writer is *seeking* a special reason. To develop this point, the opening sentence of paragraph 2 forecasts a narrowing of the search.

5. After the first paragraph, is each new paragraph linked to the one before it? Readers look for a chain of connections as they move through an essay. The chain breaks when the opening sentence of a new paragraph has no connection to the closing sentence of the one before it, or begins by simply saying, "Another point to consider is X."

You can forge a link between two paragraphs by repeating a key word or phrase from the first one in the opening sentence of the second, or by opening the second with a transitional word or phrase (see section 8.6). To see how Gary used transitional sentences to strengthen the connections of his essay, see section 4.6.

6. Does each new paragraph reveal something new about the topic? Besides continuity, readers expect to see progression. If a new paragraph mainly repeats the point made by the one before, you should either cut the paragraph altogether or find a way to stress whatever is new in it.

7. Does the ending reaffirm, reflect upon, or extend the main point of the essay?

RECONSIDERING YOUR STRUCTURE: IN BRIEF

- Can you state your thesis?
- Does your introduction state or forecast your thesis?
- Can you state the main point of each paragraph?
- Does each paragraph help develop the thesis?
- Are the paragraphs linked to each other?
- Does each new paragraph reveal something new?
- Does the ending reaffirm, reflect upon, or extend the main point of the essay?

4.5 DEVELOPING TEXTURE

You can develop **texture** by interweaving general ideas with specific details. Writing that lacks specific detail will seem abstract, colorless, and vacant, like a big empty windowless room with cinder-block walls. Writing that lacks any generalizations will seem dense and confusing, like a newspaper without headlines. To develop your texture, do two things:

1. Add specifics to make generalizations (in italics) vivid and tangible:

> *Laughter takes many different forms.* The nervous giggle, the cackle, the chuckle, and the guffaw are just a few of its variations.

> *In his first year as a rock musician, he had a hard time.* He could not afford heat or hot water in his apartment, so he slept under a pile of heavy blankets and washed and shaved each morning in the men's room at McDonald's.

2. Add generalizations to show the significance of specific details:

> FIRST DRAFT: Getting dressed in the locker room, we said nothing to each other beyond "What's your name?" and "Where are you from?" We dressed quickly, finishing the job while running onto the field. Each of us wanted to get there first. One guy spoke my thoughts. Leaning my way, he said in a low voice, "These guys are massive. I don't stand a chance of playing."

> REVISED (additions shown in italics): *On the first day of practice, competitiveness made us all tense and wary.* Getting dressed in the locker room, we said nothing to each other beyond "What's your name?" and "Where are you from?" We dressed quickly, finishing the job while running onto the field. Each of us wanted to get there first. *Everyone seemed to be checking over the rest of the team, measuring himself against the others.* One guy spoke my thoughts. Leaning my way, he said in a low voice, "These guys are massive. I don't stand a chance of playing."

EXERCISE 3 RECOGNIZING GENERALIZATIONS AND SPECIFICS

Identify the shifts between generalizations and specifics in the following passage:

WALLS AND BARRIERS

My father's reaction to the bank building at 43rd Street and Fifth Avenue in New York City was immediate and definite: "You won't catch me putting my money in *there!*" he declared. "Not in that glass box!"

Of course, my father is a gentleman of the old school, a   5
member of the generation to whom a good deal of modern architecture is unnerving; but I suspect—I more than suspect, I am convinced—that his negative response was not so much to the architecture as to a violation of his concept of the nature of money.   10

In his generation money was thought of as a tangible commodity—bullion, bank notes, coins—that could be hefted, carried, or stolen. Consequently, to attract the custom of a sensible man, a bank had to have heavy walls, barred windows, and bronze doors, to affirm the fact, however untrue, that 15 money would be safe inside. If a building's design made it appear impregnable, the institution was necessarily sound, and the meaning of the heavy wall as an architectural symbol dwelt in the prevailing attitude toward money, rather than in any aesthetic theory.   —Eugene Raskin

EXERCISE 4 FURNISHING SPECIFICS

Add specific details or examples to each of the following generalizations:

1. The sudden cry of "Fire!" panicked everyone in the restaurant.
2. The closing of the shoe factory drained the life out of the town.
3. College students face many different kinds of pressure.

EXERCISE 5 FURNISHING GENERALIZATIONS

Suppose you are writing a booklet to be used in recruiting young people for the U.S. Army. What attractive generalization about the army could you make on the basis of the following details?

After completing basic training in obedience, privates are assigned to an advanced training unit, where they learn a particular specialty such as mechanics, radio operation, or infantry tactics. Privates who learn their specialties exceptionally well have the chance to become noncommissioned officers (NCOs) after training in leadership and supervisory skills.

EXERCISE 6 REVISING WITH SPECIFICS

Add specific details or examples to any passage in your first draft that leans too heavily on generalizations.

EXERCISE 7 REVISING WITH GENERALIZATIONS

Add one or more generalizations to any passage in your first draft that is not sufficiently clear in its overall significance.

4.6 SAMPLE STUDENT ESSAY: DRAFT AND REVISION

The left-hand pages show the first draft of Gary's essay with the instructor's comments. The right-hand pages show Gary's revi-

DRAFT

Why I Love to Act [First Draft]

(1) Recently I appeared in Ah, *?author*
time
Wilderness! I played Nat Miller, a respected *period*
?
fifty-year-old businessman. Strangely

enough, one of the things I remember best

about the performance was what happened just

before I went on the stage for the opening

scene. *When I took a final look at myself in *mirror*
image
the mirror and saw that I was someone else. *good—why*
not just
I was startled to see that other face looking *start with*
this image
back at me, and I remember feeling startled *+ give*
details of
again when I took one last look in the mirror *what you*
saw? then
before wiping off my makeup and changing back *mention*
the
into my own clothes. As I looked in the *play —*

mirror, I wondered again what made acting so

magical. Eventually I realized that its

magic came from this sense of being someone

else--of losing myself in another character.

Though some people may be drawn to acting by

the prospect of winning applause and acclaim,

thesis fine, or working closely with others, I love it
but could
you simply because playing someone else gives me a
end with
the idea vacation from myself.
of
wondering about the mirrored face? then
work your way toward the answer.

sion, with the large-scale changes he made before improving the style of individual sentences and correcting errors in grammar, punctuation, and spelling.

REVISION

Why I Love to Act [Unedited Revision]

Standing alone in a small changing room behind the auditorium, I looked at myself in the mirror. Looking back at me was a fifty-year-old man dressed for his job as a newspaper publisher: gray flannel suit, white shirt, maroon tie. His hair was flecked with spots of gray, and his face was creased with wrinkles. I knew very well that his name was Nat Miller, for I was about to play him in <u>Ah, Wilderness!</u>, a comedy by Eugene O'Neill that is set in the year 1906. Yet even though I had come to know him well during eight weeks of rehearsal, I was startled and gripped by the sight of his face in the mirror. As I thought about this moment later, I began to wonder whether it could help me understand just what makes acting so magical.

I can't explain its magic simply by citing its social rewards. We all know that acting brings recognition: your name in a program, the roar of applause, the flutter of compliments, and perhaps even praise in a newspaper review. *Also the excitement of working closely with other people toward a common goal, a fixed and definite purpose.

DRAFT

Transition weak — can you connect these other reasons with the idea of vacationing from yourself?

(2) There are lots of reasons to love acting. We all know that it brings recognition: your name in a program, the roar of applause, the flutter of compliments, and perhaps even praise in a newspaper review. *Also the excitement of working closely with other people toward a common goal, a fixed and *definate purpose. But none of these things is peculiar to acting. In general, athletes enjoy just as much recognition as actors do, and any group of people that makes up a team works toward a common goal.

(3) In becoming Nat Miller, I entered the world of an imaginary family living in a small town at the beginning of this century. I helped to create this family. During eight weeks of rehearsal I came to know each of them intimately. Nat's sister Lily, a shy, bespectacled, old maid schoolteacher who lives with the Millers, is yearning to marry Nat's irresponsible, *alcaholic brother-in-law Sid, but never will as long as he drinks. Nat's bustling, matronly wife, Essie, is constantly overanxious about their children: Arthur, the college boy home for the summer; Tommy, a chubby, impish eleven-year-old; Mildred, a lively fifteen; and Richard, one

Transition weak — where's the argument headed at this point?

Great! Rich detail here —

But none of these things is peculiar to acting. In general, athletes get just as much recognition as actors do, and any group of people that makes up a team works toward a common goal.

What then makes acting different? I can answer this question only from my own experience. In becoming Nat Miller, I entered another world: the world of an imaginary family that I helped to create. During eight weeks of rehearsal I came to know this family as well as my own. Nat's sister Lily, a shy, bespectacled, old maid schoolteacher who lives with the Millers, is yearning to marry Nat's irresponsible, *alcaholic brother-in-law Sid, but never will as long as he drinks. Nat's bustling, matronly wife, Essie, is constantly overanxious about their children: Arthur, the college boy home for the summer; Tommy, a chubby, impish eleven-year-old; Mildred, a lively fifteen; and Richard, one year older, a shy, rebellious, bookish dreamer in love with a girl named Muriel.

Richard's notes to Muriel are a source of trouble. They include some rather "warm" lines quoted from a love poem by Swinburne, so they infuriate her dried-up tyrannical father and make Nat worried enough to give Richard a lecture on sex. The lecture is comically vague and roundabout. I was just sixteen when I appeared in the play. So I had

year older, a shy *rebelious, bookish dreamer
in love with a girl named Muriel.

(4) Richard's notes to Muriel are a
source of trouble. They include some rather
"warm" lines quoted from a love poem by
Swinburne. They infuriate Muriel's dried-up
tyrannical father, and they make Nat nervous
enough to give Richard a lecture on sex. The
lecture is comically roundabout and vague. I
was sixteen when I appeared in the play. So
I had to imagine myself the father of a boy
my own age, trying to tell him how to control
his sexual drives.

TERRIFIC point!

(5) At moments like that, I could feel
Nat Miller living inside me, speaking through
me to the other characters in the play. As I
worked my way through a speech full of
sputterings, sudden halts, and evasive
phrases, I felt the pain of Nat's
embarrassment but also the force of his love
for a son that he was struggling to
communicate with. Richard's response to my
speech--his resentment of what Nat had to
say--made me feel even more sharply that I
was Nat, and I had the same feeling whenever
my character's words sparked a conflict with
another character. In the first act, for

Great transition— here you really connect the "moment" of the lecture with what follows

to imagine myself the father of a boy my own age, trying to tell him how to control his sexual drives.

At moments like that, I could feel Nat Miller living inside me, speaking through me to the other characters in the play. As I worked my way through a speech full of sputterings, sudden halts, and evasive phrases, I felt the pain of Nat's embarrassment but also the force of his love for a son that he was struggling to communicate with. Richard's resentful answer made me feel even more sharply that I was Nat, and I had the same feeling whenever Nat's words sparked a conflict with another character. In the first act, for instance, Muriel's father comes to Nat's house and accuses Richard of trying to corrupt her with his lewd notes. Nat calls the man a liar, tells him to go to hell, and almost bodily throws him out. I could feel all of Nat's rage as I spoke his words.

Playing an angry man or acting out any other role on stage is like reverting to childhood. As children, we all liked to dress up in costumes or at least pretend we were someone else. We played cowboys and Indians, or queens and princesses, or made believe we were comic book heroes like Batman or Wonder Woman. As we grew older, we left these fantasy roles behind for real-life roles in school and the workplace. But acting revives the pleasure

instance, Muriel's father comes to the Miller household and accuses Richard of trying to corrupt Muriel with his lewd notes. Nat calls the man a liar, tells him to go to hell, and almost literally throws him out. I could feel all of Nat's rage as I spoke his words.

Weak transition again — how do we get from Nat's rage to kids' make-believe?

(6) As children, we all liked to dress up in costumes or at least pretend we were someone else. We played cowboys and Indians, or cops and robbers, or made believe we were comic book heroes like Spiderman, or movie heroes like Indiana Jones. As we grow older, we leave these fantasy roles behind for real-life roles, such as jobs. But acting revives the pleasure of childhood make-believe. I love acting for much the same reason that I loved to run down the street dressed up as Batman when I was eight years old.

Who's "we" here? Where does a female reader find herself in this all-male fantasy?

(7) Whether or not we yearn to revive such childhood fantasies, we all need an occasional release of some kind. *A change from the regularity of our lives. Acting is like taking a vacation from yourself. At its best, acting is leaving one identity for another, losing yourself in the character you create. That is what makes it magical.

of childhood make-believe. It makes actors feel
something like what I remember feeling at the age of
eight, when I ran down the street one day in a Batman
mask and cape.

Whether or not we yearn to revive such childhood
fantasies, we all need an occasional release of some
kind. *A change from the regularity of our lives.
Some people revive themselves by traveling. After
heading off to Hawaii or the Grand Canyon or Banff or
just driving somewhere for a few days, they come home
refreshed. Acting is mental traveling; it's like
taking a vacation from yourself. At its best, acting
is leaving one identity for another, losing yourself
in the character you create. That is what makes
acting magical.

EXERCISE 8   REVISING YOUR ESSAY

Following the suggestions made in this chapter and illustrated in section 4.6, reexamine the aim, structure, tone, and texture of your essay and revise it where necessary. Do not worry now about correcting errors in spelling, grammar, or punctuation. Those can wait.

Editing Your Essay

Editing is the final stage of writing, the final chance to ensure that your essay makes the best possible impression on your reader. While revising treats the substance and structure of an essay as a whole, editing concentrates on the energy and construction of individual sentences, on punctuation, grammar, spelling, and word choice. These things make up the face of your essay. No matter how well organized an essay may be, small errors can foul its clarity and mar its credibility, and awkward sentences can weaken its rhetorical impact. Good editing helps you to win the good opinion of your reader, and with it your reader's willingness to see things your way.

What follows is a series of brief suggestions designed to guide you through the editing process. To learn more about any point listed here, see the section noted in parentheses.

5.1 MAKING YOUR SENTENCES RHETORICALLY EFFECTIVE

Good writing is made of sentences that are not just grammatically correct but also **rhetorically effective:** vigorous, concise, emphatic, well-balanced, and varied. To achieve these effects with your own sentences, consider the following suggestions:

87

1. Use subordination to break the monotony of short, simple sentences and to stress your main points (see chapter 15):

▶ ~~One~~ *When one* clown took a roundhouse swing at the other~~,~~ *and* ~~He~~ wound up punching himself in the nose~~,~~ *, the* ~~The~~ children roared.

2. Vary the length and structure of your sentences (see section 25.1):

▶ Ultimately, it is not for our teams, our schools, or our coaches that we love to score~~,~~ *. It is* ~~but~~ for ourselves.

3. Use verbs of action (see section 25.2). Wherever possible, replace forms of the verb *be*—forms such as *is, are, was, were, has been,* and *had been*—with verbs denoting action:

▶ Nat's bustling, matronly wife, Essie, ~~is~~ constantly ~~overanxious~~ *frets* about their children.

▶ Richard's notes to Muriel ~~are a source of~~ *cause* trouble.

▶ [or] Richard's notes to Muriel ~~are a source of trouble.~~ *kick up dust.*

4. Change passive-voice verbs to the active whenever no good reason justifies the passive (section 22.3):

▶ In Japanese families, all of the husband's salary ~~is taken by the wife,~~ *the wife takes* and all household expenditures ~~are managed by her.~~ *manages*

5. Use parallel construction to enhance the coordination of two or more items (chapter 14):

▶ To score a goal is for one shining moment to conquer all frustration~~,~~ *, to banish anxiety,* ~~Anxiety has been banished,~~ and ~~we~~ *to* rule the world.

6. Cut words you don't really need to deliver your meaning (see section 9.13):

> Many
> ► ~~There are many~~ things ~~that~~ make me laugh.

7. If a sentence is too tangled to be understood on the first reading, break it up and reorganize it (section 16.2):

> Due to the progress in military weaponry over the years, there has been an increased passivity in mankind that such advancements bring as wars are easier to fight resulting in a total loss of honor in fighting.

> EDITED: Since progress in military weaponry over the years has made mankind more passive and wars easier to fight, fighting has lost all honor.

5.2 CHECKING YOUR CHOICE OF WORDS

1. Replace words too high or low for the level of diction prevailing around them (section 9.1):

> ► After debating it for more than an hour and considering various amendments, the faculty finally ~~blew off~~ *rejected* the proposal.

2. Replace words or phrases that are misused:

> ► Fortunately, the earthquake had no ~~a~~*e*ffect on the city.

You may need help from your teacher to spot misused words or phrases. See sections 9.2–9.4 and the Glossary of Usage.

3. Replace vague abstractions with concrete, specific, or figurative terms (sections 9.5–9.6):

> ► Going to college ~~involves learning many new things.~~ *is like exploring a big city for the first time.*

4. Replace <u>pretentious verbiage and jargon</u> (section 9.10) <u>with words that plainly deliver your meaning:</u>

> *Ambitious*
> ▶ ~~Upwardly mobile~~ young lawyers and doctors often work ~~in~~
> *more than*
> ^
> ~~excess of~~ seventy hours a week.
> ^

5. Replace clichés (section 9.8):

> *worked steadily*
> ▶ I ~~was busy as a bee~~ all week long.
> ^

5.3 CHECKING YOUR GRAMMAR

Watch for the following errors, which are explained in the designated section or chapter of part 2.

1. <u>The sentence fragment</u> (chapter 17)

> ▶ Strangely enough, one of the things I remember best about the
>   performance was what happened just before I went on the stage
>   , *w*
>   for the opening scene_^ _^When I took a final look at myself in
>   the mirror and saw that I was someone else.

> ▶ We all know that it brings recognition: your name in a pro-
>   gram, the roar of applause, the flutter of compliments, and
>   *You also feel*
>   perhaps even praise in a newspaper review. ~~Also~~ the excite-
>   ^
>   ment of working closely with other people toward a common
>   , *a*
>   goal_^ _^fixed and definite purpose.

2. <u>The dangling modifier</u> (section 12.18)

> *we took*
> ▶ After exercising a swim ~~was taken.~~
>   ^   ^

3. <u>The misplaced modifier</u> (section 12.15)

   While sitting in the tub,
   ▶ I thought about the speech I had to give in French class ~~while~~
   ∧

   ~~sitting in the tub.~~

4. <u>The run-on (fused) sentence</u> (section 13.7)

   , and
   ▶ The quake struck without warning in minutes it leveled half
   ∧

   the town.

5. <u>Unclear reference of pronouns</u> (section 18.4)

   the manager
   ▶ When I took the Walkman back to the store, ~~they~~ told me I
   ∧

   couldn't get a refund.

6. <u>Faulty shifts in pronoun reference</u> (section 18.8)

   its
   ▶ When a college requires drug testing of ~~their~~ athletes, does
   ∧

   the testing violate their rights?

7. <u>Incorrect pronoun case forms</u> (sections 18.9–18.12)

   He
   ▶ ~~Him~~ and I always disagreed.
   ∧

8. <u>Faulty agreement of subject and verb</u> (chapter 19)

   knows
   ▶ Anyone with small children ~~know~~ how demanding they are.
   ∧

9. <u>Faulty tense shifts</u> (section 21.5)

   recognized
   ▶ As soon as I saw the coat, I ~~recognize~~ it.
   ∧

5.4 CHECKING YOUR PUNCTUATION

For guidance on punctuation, see part 3. Make a list of any punctuation errors that your teacher notes in your writing so that you can learn to spot them for yourself. Watch especially for the following comma errors:

1. The comma splice (section 13.6)

   ▶ Temperatures dropped below zero, the big pond froze for the
   and
   first time in ten years.

2. Commas misused with restrictive elements (section 26.6)

   ▶ Cars/ equipped with airbags/ can save the lives of drivers/ who fail to wear safety belts.

3. Comma after a conjunction (section 26.2)

   ▶ We walked all over town, but/ we couldn't find the store.

4. Comma separating the basic parts of a sentence (section 26.13)

   ▶ Poisonous gas from a pesticide factory in India/ killed more than two thousand people in 1984.

5.5 CHECKING YOUR SPELLING, CAPITALIZATION, AND APOSTROPHES

Check the following:

1. Your own spelling demons. These are the words you have trouble spelling correctly. If you're using a word processor and

a spell-checker program (see section 31.1), you can catch your spelling demons that way. Otherwise you may need your teacher to identify them for you:

```
Lily is yearning to marry Nat's irresponsable,

alcoholic brother Sid, but never will as long as he

drinks.  Nat's bustling, matronly wife, Essie, is
```

To find the correct spelling of the word marked *sp.*, look it up in a dictionary. Then analyze the misspelling as explained in section 31.2, and correct it:

```
irresponsible
```

2. <u>Apostrophes needed or misused</u> (sections 31.9–31.10)

▶ The towns police force consisted of the sheriff and his dog/s.

3. <u>Capitalization needed or misused</u> (section 32.1)

▶ Theodore Roosevelt became president of the United states when William McKinley was assassinated in 1901.

5.6 PROOFREADING YOUR ESSAY

Technically, proofreading is the reading of proof sheets—what the printer submits for the author's final corrections before a piece of writing is published. As you read your own essay once more, imagine that it is going to be published. Reread every word carefully, watching particularly for errors in grammar, spelling, and punctuation. If you make more than five corrections on a page, retype or reprint the page.

EDITING CHECKLIST

SENTENCE RHETORIC (5.1)

Do you use subordination to stress your main point?

Do your sentences vary in length and structure?

Do you frequently use verbs of action and the active voice?

Do you use parallel construction whenever possible?

Have you cut all words you don't really need to deliver your meaning?

Is any sentence tangled?

WORD CHOICE (5.2)

Is any word too high or too low for your level of diction?

Is any word or phrase misused?

Do you see vague abstractions that could be replaced with concrete terms?

Do you see pretentious words that could be replaced with plain ones?

Do you find any clichés?

SENTENCE GRAMMAR (5.3)

Does any sentence sound incomplete?

Does any part of a sentence seem out of place?

Is the reference of each pronoun clear?

Does the form of each verb agree with its subject?

PUNCTUATION AND MECHANICS (5.4, 5.5)

Have you used commas where they belong, and only where they belong?

Are you sure that each word is correctly spelled?

Have you fixed all typographical errors?

EXERCISE 1 PROOFREADING

We have deliberately mutilated this passage from Mark Twain's "Advice to Youth" so that it contains three misspellings, a sentence fragment, and a comma splice. Find the errors and correct them.

You want to be very careful about lying, otherwise you are nearly sure to get caught. Once caught, you can never again be, in the eyes of the good and the pure, what you were before. Many a young person has injured himself pernamently through a single clumsy and ill-finished lie. The result of care- 5
lessness born of incomplete training. Some authorities hold that the young ought not to lie at all. That, of course, is put- ing it rather stronger than necessary; still, while I cannot go quite so far as that, I do maintane, and I believe I am right, that the young ought to be temperate in the use of this great 10
art until practice and experience shall give them that confi- dence, elegance, and precision which alone can make the accomplishment graceful and profitable.

EXERCISE 2 PROOFREADING

Following is a paragraph from the next-to-last version of the essay by Andrea Lyle cited in earlier chapters. Correct any errors you find.

For over half an hour we tried to snag the rope on an overhanging rock. We never did make it. We tried other, longer routes, giving each other boosts with our hands, but the top layre of copper sediment was so thick. That what we thought was a firm handhold would often crumble in our 5
grasp. So we couldnt trust the climbing surface. We even explored old mine shafts in hopes that they would lead us out, they only led us deeper into the mine. As we explored one shaft, however, we stumbled over an eight-foot iron rod and then a six-foot metal tube. With some dificulty, we found a 10
way to fit the rod into the tube, forming a crude but relativly sturdy pole of about thirteen feet. Bracing the pole to the ground next to the precipece, we climbed it and made our way out of the cave.

5.7 PREPARING AND SUBMITTING YOUR FINAL COPY *ms*

The final copy of Gary's paper on pp. 99–102 illustrates a format commonly used in the final copy of essays. Your teacher will tell you whether or not to use a separate title page. Type or print your text on one side only of standard-size (8½-by-11) white sheets. If you use fanfold computer paper, separate the sheets and remove the perforated strips.

FORMAT WITH TITLE ON FIRST PAGE OF TEXT

½"

Pappas 1

1"

Gary Pappas

Professor Ignacio

1" English 101

16 November 1993

5-space indentation

What Makes Acting Magical? — Double-space

Standing alone in a small changing room behind

the auditorium, I looked at myself in the mirror.

Looking back at me was a fifty-year-old man dressed

for his job as a newspaper publisher: gray flannel — 1"

suit, white shirt, maroon tie. Gray spots flecked his

hair, and wrinkles creased his face. I knew very well

that his name was Nat Miller, for I was about to play

him in <u>Ah, Wilderness!</u>, a comedy by Eugene O'Neill

that is set in the year 1906. Yet even though I had

come to know him well during eight weeks of

rehearsal, I was startled and gripped by the sight of

his face in the mirror. As I thought about this

moment later, I began to realize just what makes

FORMAT WITH SEPARATE TITLE PAGE

4″

What Makes Acting Magical?

Gary Pappas   *Quadruple-space*

Professor Ignacio

English 101   *Double-space*

16 November 1993

FIRST PAGE OF TEXT FOLLOWING SEPARATE TITLE PAGE—NOTE REPEATING TITLE

2"

What Makes Acting Magical?

Quadruple-space

    Standing alone in a small changing room behind

1" the auditorium, I looked at myself in the mirror. 1"

Looking back at me was a fifty-year-old man dressed

for his job as a newspaper publisher: gray flannel

suit, white shirt, maroon tie. Gray spots flecked his

hair, and wrinkles creased his face. I knew very well

that his name was Nat Miller, for I was about to play

him in Ah, Wilderness!, a comedy by Eugene O'Neill

that is set in the year 1906. Yet even though I had

SECOND AND SUCCEEDING PAGES OF TEXT

½"

1"   Pappas 2

½"

an imaginary family that I helped to create. During

1" eight weeks of rehearsal I came to know this family 1"

as well as my own. Nat's sister Lily, a shy,

bespectacled, old maid schoolteacher who lives with

the Millers, yearns to marry Nat's irresponsible,

alcoholic brother-in-law Sid, but never will as long

What Makes Acting Magical?

Standing alone in a small changing room behind the auditorium, I looked at myself in the mirror. Looking back at me was a fifty-year-old man dressed for his job as a newspaper publisher: gray flannel suit, white shirt, maroon tie. Gray spots flecked his hair, and wrinkles creased his face. I knew very well that his name was Nat Miller, for I was about to play him in <u>Ah, Wilderness!</u>, a comedy by Eugene O'Neill that is set in the year 1906. Yet even though I had come to know him well during eight weeks of rehearsal, I was startled and gripped by the sight of his face in the mirror. As I thought about this moment later, I began to realize just what makes acting so magical.

Its magic cannot be explained simply by its social rewards. We all know that acting brings recognition: your name in a program, the roar of applause, the flutter of compliments, and perhaps even praise in a newspaper review. You also feel the excitement of working closely with other people toward a common goal, a fixed and definite purpose. But none of these things is peculiar to acting. In

Pappas 2

general, athletes get just as much recognition as actors do, and any group of people that makes up a team works toward a common goal.

What then makes acting different? I can answer this question only from my own experience. In becoming Nat Miller, I entered another world: the world of an imaginary family that I helped to create. During eight weeks of rehearsal I came to know this family as well as my own. Nat's sister Lily, a shy, bespectacled, old maid schoolteacher who lives with the Millers, yearns to marry Nat's irresponsible, alcoholic brother-in-law Sid, but never will as long as he drinks. Nat's bustling, matronly wife, Essie, constantly frets about their children. They have four: Arthur, the college boy home for the summer; Tommy, a chubby, impish eleven-year-old; Mildred, a lively fifteen; and Richard, one year older, a shy, rebellious, bookish dreamer in love with a girl named Muriel.

Richard's notes to Muriel kick up dust. Because they include some rather "warm" lines quoted from a love poem by Swinburne, they infuriate her dried-up, tyrannical father and make Nat worried enough to give Richard a comically vague, roundabout lecture on sex. Since I was just sixteen when I appeared in the play, I had to imagine myself as the father of a boy my own age, trying to tell him how to control his sexual drives.

At moments like that, I could feel Nat Miller living inside me, speaking through me to the other characters in the play. As I worked my way through a speech full of sputterings, sudden halts, and evasive phrases, I felt the pain of Nat's embarrassment but also the force of his love for a son that he was struggling to communicate with. Richard's resentful answer made me feel even more sharply that I was Nat, and I had the same feeling whenever Nat's words sparked a conflict with another character. In the first act, for instance, Muriel's father comes to Nat's house and accuses Richard of trying to corrupt her with his notes. Nat calls the man a liar, tells him to go to hell, and almost bodily throws him out. I could feel all of Nat's rage as I spoke his words.

Playing an angry man or acting out any other role on stage is like reverting to childhood. As children, we all liked to dress up in costumes or at least pretend we were someone else. We played cowboys and Indians, or queens and princesses, or made believe we were comic book heroes like Batman or Wonder Woman. As we grew older, we left these fantasy roles behind for real-life roles in school and the workplace. But acting revives the pleasure of

Pappas 4

childhood make-believe. It makes actors feel something like what I remember feeling at the age of eight, when I ran down the street one day in a Batman mask and cape.

Whether or not we yearn to revive such childhood fantasies, we all need an occasional release of some kind, a change from the regularity of our lives. Some people revive themselves by traveling. After heading off to Hawaii or the Grand Canyon or Banff or just driving somewhere for a few days, they come home refreshed. Acting is mental traveling; it's like taking a vacation from yourself. At its best, acting is leaving one identity for another, losing yourself in the character you create. That is what makes acting magical.

Methods of Development

6

A **method of development** is a way of achieving your writing aim: a way of expressing your feelings, of explaining something in the world outside yourself, or of persuading the reader to accept your opinion.

Some methods of development—such as description and narration—may become ends in themselves. You may simply aim to describe a particular object or to tell a particular story. But a method of development commonly serves as a means to a further end. To explain pole vaulting, for instance, you would need to describe the kind of pole used in it, and to help persuade readers that a corporation-sponsored daycare center is a good investment, you might well tell a story of how such a center has changed the life of one working parent.

This chapter presents various methods of development and shows how they can be used for exposition—for explaining something. (Since persuasion often requires special techniques of argumentation, we treat it mainly in chapter 7.)

6.1 USING DESCRIPTION

Description is writing about the way things appear, the way they are constructed, or the way they act. Like every other method of development, description calls for some choices. You must decide which details to identify, how to arrange them, and how to use the description in the essay as a whole. But as you make your choices, you may find it helpful to know that description usually takes one of three forms: external, analytical, or evocative.

6.1A EXTERNAL DESCRIPTION

An **external description** enables the reader to visualize and recognize the object described:

> At first glance, Harry—my 1968 Volvo 144—is ugly. The dirty cream paint is badly chipped, rust covers the hood and the big dent in the rear left side, and the wheel wells sag dangerously close to the rear tires. The only snappy feature of its exterior is the glint of forest green on the windshield wiper blades.
> —College student

> **EXERCISE 1** EXTERNAL DESCRIPTION
>
> Briefly describe the appearance of any structure—building, statue, sculpture, store, bar, restaurant, whatever—that is on or near your college grounds. Don't name it; see if other students can recognize it from your description.

6.1B ANALYTICAL OR TECHNICAL DESCRIPTION

An **analytical or technical description** enables the reader to understand the structure of an object:

> The panda's "thumb" is not, anatomically, a finger at all. It is constructed from a bone called the radial sesamoid, normally a small component of the wrist. In pandas, the radial sesamoid is greatly enlarged and elongated until it almost equals the metapoidal bones of the true digits in length. The radial sesamoid underlies a pad on the panda's forepaw; the five digits form the framework of another pad, the palmar. A shallow furrow separates the two pads and serves as a channelway for bamboo stalks. —Stephen Jay Gould, *The Panda's Thumb*

Gould's language is precise, objective, technical (*radial sesamoid, metapoidal bones*), and above all analytical. He focuses not on the furry surface of the panda's paw but on the framework of "thumb" and finger bones that underlie it. This analytical description serves an argumentative aim. Gould wants to show that the panda—which long ago had nothing but five fingers in its paw—gradually developed its radial sesamoid to do the work of an opposable thumb, to operate like a human thumb in grasping the bamboo stalks that pandas love to eat. Analytically described, the panda's paw helps Gould to substantiate the theory of evolution.

> **Exercise 2 Analytical or Technical Description**
>
> Describe in a paragraph any one of the following in such a way that the reader can understand its structure, design, or function:
>
> | | |
> |---|---|
> | a bicycle | a tire jack |
> | a surfboard | the human foot |
> | a solar house | the keystone arch |
> | a rifle | the human hand |
> | a trumpet | a pine tree |
> | a skateboard | a peony |

6.1C Evocative Description

Evocative description re-creates the impression made by an object:

> The coyote is a long, slim, sick, and sorry-looking skeleton, with a grey wolf-skin stretched over it, a tolerably bushy tail that forever sags down with a despairing expression of forsakenness and misery, a furtive and evil eye, and a long, sharp face, with slightly lifted lip and exposed teeth. —Mark Twain

Evocative description can appeal not just to the eye but to all the other senses:

> The heat of summer was mellow and produced sweet scents which lay in the air so damp and rich you could almost taste them. Mornings smelled of purple wisteria, afternoons of the wild roses which tumbled over stone fences, and evenings of honeysuckle. . . .
>
> In the heat of mid-afternoon the women would draw the blinds, spread blankets on the floor for coolness and nap, while in the fields the cattle herded together in the shade of spreading trees to escape the sun. Afternoons were absolutely still, yet filled with sounds.

Bees buzzed in the clover. Far away over the fields the chug of an ancient steam-powered threshing machine could be faintly heard. Birds rustled under the tin of the porch roof.

—Russell Baker, *Growing Up*

EXERCISE 3 EXPLAINING EVOCATIVE DESCRIPTION

Compare the following two descriptions and explain what makes the second more evocative than the first:

1. I couldn't stand Palatka. It was poor, seedy, smelly, and ugly, and the weather was always bad. I couldn't relate to the people either. My stay there was a nightmare.

2. Situated on the banks of the St. Johns River, Palatka was surrounded by dense tropical foliage in limitless swamps. It was always hot, and it rained daily. The town's main street, made of bricks, was called Lemon Street. Weeds grew out of the spaces between the bricks and out of the cracks in the sidewalks and at the bottom of the concrete buildings, so that to a stranger the vegetation appeared to be strangling the town. There was a paper mill in town. It supplied most of the blacks and poorer whites with employment. Each morning at six they were summoned to work by a whistle that woke the entire area. Shortly thereafter Palatka was blanketed by a lavender haze and filled with a terrible stench.   —Pat Jordan, *A False Spring*

EXERCISE 4 WRITING EVOCATIVE DESCRIPTION

Using Russell Baker's paragraphs as a model, write an evocative description of the place in which you grew up, or (if you moved around during childhood) of the place you remember most vividly. Assume that the reader has never seen this place, and describe as many sights, sounds, and smells as possible.

6.2 USING NARRATION

Narration is telling or writing about a sequence of events. Like description, narration calls for authorial choice at every stage. Stories do not tell themselves; a sequence of events becomes a story only when a writer has chosen, arranged, and linked them. Also, besides deciding how to begin and end the sequence, the author is free to follow or not follow chronological order. Here we treat both of these alternatives.

6.2A CHRONOLOGICAL NARRATION

Narration or storytelling is writing about a succession of events. The simplest kind of narration follows **chronological order:** the order in which the narrated events actually occurred or could have occurred. Consider this account of an incident that helped to provoke the Boston Massacre in 1770:

> On Friday, March 2, a Boston ropemaker named William Green, busy with his fellows braiding fibers on an outdoor "ropewalk" or ropemaking machine, called to Patrick Walker, a soldier of the Twenty-ninth [Regiment] who was passing by, and asked if he wanted work. "Yes," Walker replied. "Then go and clean my shithouse," was Green's response. The soldier answered him in similar terms, and when Green threatened him, he departed, swearing to return with some of his regimental mates. Return he did with no less than forty soldiers, led by a big Negro drummer.
> —Page Smith, *A New Age Now Begins*

Here the writer reports events as they followed one another in time, and his use of dialogue—of Green's actual words—makes a moment in American history come vividly alive.

A short narrative or anecdote can readily serve an explanatory aim. The story above helps to explain the relations between American colonists and the British army in the years before the outbreak of the American Revolution. The following anecdote helps to explain how Harry Houdini used the police to publicize his prowess:

> When he arrived in London in 1900 the twenty-six-year-old magician did not have a single booking. His news clippings eventually inspired an English agent, who had Houdini manacled to a pillar in Scotland Yard. Seeing that Houdini was securely fastened, Superintendent Melville of the Criminal Investigation Department said he would return in a couple of hours, when the escapist had worn himself out. By the time

Melville got to the door, the magician was free to open it for him.

The publicity surrounding his escape from the most prestigious police force in the world opened up many another door for him. . . .

—Daniel Mark Epstein, "The Case of Harry Houdini"

EXERCISE 5 NARRATING TO EXPLAIN PERSONALITY

Write a short chronological narrative or anecdote that helps to explain the personality of anyone you know, including yourself.

EXERCISE 6 NARRATING A FIGHT

Using chronological order, give a brief narration of a fight or quarrel you have seen or been involved in. Concentrate on how the fight or quarrel got started.

6.2B NONCHRONOLOGICAL NARRATION

A short narrative can often follow chronological order with good results. But strict adherence to chronological order in an extended narrative can lead to a boring succession of "and thens." To keep the story lively and to clarify its meaning, the writer may need to depart from chronological order, moving backward to explain the cause of a particular event or jumping forward to identify its ultimate effect:

Writer begins story of what happened in 1964.

In June 1964 . . . two Italian fishing boats, working in tandem with a crew of 18, were dragging their nets along the bottom of the Adriatic. Toward dawn, as they pulled up the nets after a long trawl, the fishermen realized their catch was unusually heavy. . . . When they finally swung the nets inboard they saw an ungainly, prehistoric-looking figure missing both feet. It was, in fact, a 500-pound Greek statue covered with nearly 2,000 years of sea encrustations.

Writer flashes forward to 1977.

In November 1977, this life-size bronze fetched the highest known price ever paid for a statue—$3.9 million. The work is attributed to the fourth century B.C. Greek artist Lysippus. . . . Professor Paolo Moreno of Rome University, author of two books on Lysippus, identifies the statue as the portrait of a young athlete after victory and suggests that it may have been plundered by ancient Romans from Mount Olympus. The ship bearing the statue was probably sunk in a storm and there may well have been other treasures on board. Pliny the Elder tells us Lysippus made more than 1,500 works, all of them bronze, but it was doubted that any of the originals had survived—until this one surfaced.

Writer flashes back to ancient times.

The fishermen stealthily unloaded the barnacle-covered masterpiece in Fano, near Rimini, and took it to the captain's house, where it was put on a kitchen table and propped up against a wall. —Bryan Rosten, "Smuggled!"

Writer resumes story of what happened in 1964.

EXERCISE 7 USING FLASHBACKS AND FLASH-FORWARDS

Using at least one flashback and one flash-forward, tell the story of one of the following:

your first day on a full-time job

your first day in college

your first meeting with someone who later became important in your life

the first time you felt that you were doing something wrong

6.3 COMBINING DESCRIPTION AND NARRATION

Description and narration commonly go hand in hand:

Everyone knows that a night relief is among the most difficult of infantry maneuvers. But we didn't know it, and in our innocence we expected it to go according to plan. We and the company we were replacing were cleverly and severely shelled: it was as if the Germans a few hundred feet away could see us in the dark and through the thick pine growth. When the shelling finally stopped, at about midnight, we realized that, although near the place we were supposed to be, until daylight we would remain hopelessly lost. The order came down to stop where we were, lie down among the trees, and get some sleep. We would finish the relief at first light. Scattered over several hundred yards, the two hundred and fifty of us in F Company lay down in a darkness so thick we could see nothing at all. Despite the terror of our first shelling (and several people had been hit), we slept as soundly as babes. At dawn I awoke, and what I saw all around were numerous objects I'd miraculously not tripped over in the dark. These objects were dozens of dead German boys in greenish-gray uniforms, killed a day or two before by the company we were relieving. If darkness had hidden them from us, dawn disclosed them with open eyes and greenish-white faces like marble, still clutching their rifles and machine-pistols in their seventeen-year-old hands, fixed where they had fallen. . . . My adolescent illusions, largely intact to that moment, fell away all at once, and I suddenly knew I was not and never would be in a world that was reasonable or just.

—Paul Fussell, "My War"

This story of a night on the battlefield includes a vivid description of German corpses, and as the last sentence indicates, the author tells the story to express his personal feelings.

> **EXERCISE 8** NARRATING EVENTS IN AND OUT OF CHRONOLOGICAL ORDER
>
> This exercise has two parts. First, tell in strict chronological order the story of the most memorable trip you have taken. Then retell the story in nonchronological order, starting not with the beginning but with the part of the trip you remember best. Then work backward and forward from that point.

> **EXERCISE 9** USING DESCRIPTION IN NARRATION
>
> Use as much description as possible to expand the narrative you wrote for exercise 5.

> **EXERCISE 10** USING A STORY TO MAKE A POINT
>
> Tell a story about anyone you know that could be used to illustrate a general point about the experience of growing up. Or tell a story about your experience of a conflict—a story that could be used to illustrate a general point about relationships between people. Whichever story you tell, state its point at the end.

6.4 USING EXAMPLES

You can develop almost any point by using examples. The author
of the following paragraphs uses a series of them to show how
law-abiding Canadians are:

> When the great cattle drives of the American Midwest
> flowed north to railheads in Canada, cowboys adjusted to the
> shock of being asked to surrender their guns to the single
> policeman who met them at the border. One Mountie rode
> into Sitting Bull's camp a few days after the Battle at Little
> Big Horn, noted fresh American scalps and horses with U.S.
> cavalry brands, and advised Sitting Bull to obey Canadian laws
> or he, the Mountie, would deport the whole tribe. And Sitting
> Bull nodded.
>
> During the Klondike gold rush of the nineties, the Amer-
> ican town of Skagway in the Alaskan panhandle was run by a
> ruthless American gangster and gunfights in the streets were
> common. Across the border in Canada, Yukon mining towns
> were so law-abiding that a miner safely could leave his poke of
> gold in an unlocked cabin.
>
> —June Callwood, "Portrait of Canada"

**EXERCISE 11 STATING THE POINT MADE BY
EXAMPLES**

Each of the following passages offers one or more examples to
explain or illustrate a point. State the point in a single short
sentence, and briefly explain how the examples support it.

1. A hockey player rushing up ice travels at more than twenty-
   five miles an hour; a slap shot hurls a frozen rubber disc
   toward a goalie at one hundred miles an hour. Everything
   that happens in hockey—passing, stickhandling, checking,
   shooting—happens fast.

   —Jeff Greenfield, "The Iceman Arriveth"

2. Curiosity is as clear and definite as any of our urges. We
   wonder what is in a sealed telegram or in a letter in which
   someone else is absorbed, or what is being said in the telephone booth or in low conversation.

   —James Harvey Robinson, *The Mind in the Making*

3. Anyone who reads [ancient Greek stories] with attention discovers that even the most nonsensical take place in a world which is essentially rational and matter-of-fact. Hercules, whose life was one long combat against preposterous monsters, is always said to have had his home in the city of Thebes. The exact spot where Aphrodite was born of the foam could be visited by any ancient tourist; it was just offshore from the island of Cythera. The winged steed Pegasus, after skimming the air all day, went every night to a comfortable stable in Corinth. A familiar local habitation gave reality to all the mythical beings.

—Edith Hamilton, *Mythology*

EXERCISE 12 USING EXAMPLES

Develop the following point by adding a series of short examples to illustrate it:

Some of the most important things we need to know have to be learned outside a classroom.

6.5 USING ANALOGY

The first question we commonly ask about anything new and strange is "What's it like?" We ask the question because the only way we can understand what we don't know is by seeing its relation to what we do know. An **analogy** helps the reader to understand something vast, remote, abstract, or specialized by comparing it to something compact, familiar, concrete, or ordinary. Though a single analogy seldom extends to the length of a whole essay, it can be developed beyond a single sentence. Here are three examples:

1. The surface of the earth is like the skin of an orange, which cannot be spread out flat unless it is torn into strips. That is why flat maps of the whole earth always distort its appearance.

2. Starting college was like being a child in the middle of a candy store. Everywhere I turned I found an exotic treat, something I wanted to taste. But I couldn't taste everything, much less

consume it all. A child who eats too much candy develops a stomach ache. A college student who joins too many clubs has too little time for course work, and must eventually suffer the pain of low grades. So I had to learn how to resist the sweet temptations of college life.

3. Since the lattice-work molecular structure of metal normally vibrates, sending electrons through a copper wire by ordinary conduction is like shooting a bunch of pellets through a chain-link fence in the middle of an earthquake. Because the fence is shaking, some of the pellets hit the links or bounce off each other instead of passing through. But superconduction occurs when supercooling stops the vibration of the conductor. Super-conduction, therefore, is like firing pellets through the fence when the earthquake is over. Because the fence stands still, all the pellets get through.

You can use analogy not just to explain, but to argue:

> Defenders of so-called "passive" euthanasia distinguish between killing a patient and letting one die. But whether euthanasia is morally right or wrong under any circumstances, allowing a preventable death to occur is morally no better than causing it. The practitioner of "passive" euthanasia is like a lifeguard allowing a man to drown. Suppose that the man is depressed or even suffering from an incurable disease, that he has asked the lifeguard to hold him under, and that the life-guard has refused. If the lifeguard's duty is to save the lives of swimmers, letting the man sink to his death in deep water is not morally different from drowning him. Likewise, if a doc-tor's duty is to prolong the lives of patients, letting any one of them die is not morally different from giving a fatal injection.

Arguing by analogy takes special care. If the two things being compared don't correspond in essential ways, the argument will be misleading, unconvincing, or both. (For more on this point, see "False Analogy," section 7.4E.)

EXERCISE 13 **USING ANALOGY**

The federal government estimates that more than 26 million American adults are functionally illiterate, unable to read such things as recipes, warning labels, and want ads. Construct an analogy that begins, "To be functionally illiterate in our society is like . . ."

EXERCISE 14 USING ANALOGY

In the presidential campaign of 1988, one candidate proposed that no one should be granted a driver's license unless he or she had been tested for drugs. Construct an analogy that could be used to argue for or against this proposal.

6.6 USING COMPARISON AND CONTRAST

While analogy links two things that we normally put in different categories, such as an orange and the whole earth, **comparison and contrast** operates on two things that we normally put in the same category: two cities, two schools, two board games, two means of transportation. Typically, writers compare and contrast two things in order to show how they differ, and often to show that one of them is better than the other.

Besides working on two things in the same category, comparison and contrast usually focuses on corresponding features: New York traffic and Montreal traffic, class size in public schools and class size in private schools, and so on. The following passage on cars and motorcycles treats just one feature: what they allow us to experience of the passing world.

> You see things vacationing on a motorcycle in a way that is completely different from any other. In a car you're always in a compartment, and because you're used to it you don't realize that through that car window everything you see is just more TV. You're a passive observer and it is all moving by you boringly in a frame.
>
> On a cycle the frame is gone. You're completely in contact with it all. You're *in* the scene, not just watching it anymore, and the sense of presence is overwhelming. That concrete whizzing by five inches below your foot is the real thing, the same stuff you walk on, it's right there, so blurred you can't focus on it, yet you can put your foot down and touch it any-

time, and the whole thing, the whole experience, is never removed from immediate consciousness.

—Robert Pirsig, *Zen and the Art of Motorcycle Maintenance*

This is clearly more than a neutral account of contrasting features. Pirsig uses comparison and contrast not just to bring out differences, but to serve a persuasive aim: to show the reader— "you"—why riding a motorcycle is more stimulating than driving a car.

6.6A BLOCK STRUCTURE AND ALTERNATING STRUCTURE

You can organize a comparison and contrast in either of two ways: in **blocks** or in **regular alternation.** In a block-structured comparison and contrast, each of the two things considered gets a block of sentences or an entire paragraph to itself. Pirsig, for instance, devotes most of his first paragraph to traveling by car and all of his second to traveling by motorcycle. But you can also compare and contrast two things by alternating back and forth between them:

Videotaped films offer many advantages over the celluloid kind. For one thing, they are often cheaper. If three or more people want to see a movie, they can usually rent a cassette version and a videotape machine for less than it would cost them all to go to a theater. Second, movie theaters offer nothing like the range of choice that videotapes provide. While the moviegoer has to take whatever the local theater happens to be playing, the videotape viewer can choose from hundreds of films, including foreign or X-rated items that will probably never find their way onto a local screen. Third, while movies are shown only at fixed times, videotapes can be seen whenever the viewer wants to see them, and just as often as he or she likes. Finally, videotapes allow the viewer a kind of privacy and comfort that no public movie theater can possibly furnish. The videotape viewer need not strain to hear a film over the buzz of the talkers sitting behind or to see it over the heads of the people sitting in front. Instead, he or she can enjoy it with just a few close friends at home.

Corresponding features

Cost

Range of choice

Timing

Viewing conditions

Here the writer moves back and forth between the two things while also moving down a list of corresponding features. But once again the writer is not simply listing differences. Comparison and contrast serve to explain the special attraction of videotape cassettes.

6.6B Writing an Essay of Comparison and Contrast

Because alternating structure continually reminds the reader that two things are being compared and contrasted, it can work well for the length of a paragraph. But steady alternation can become monotonous. For this reason, an essay that makes extensive use of comparison and contrast should combine alternation with block structure:

WHY VIDEOTAPES WON'T KILL MOVIE THEATERS

[1] In the late forties and early fifties, when television first invaded American homes, self-appointed prophets grimly predicted the death of the movie theater. How could it possibly compete with TV? Why would people go out and pay to see what they could get for nothing in their own homes? In recent years, the same kind of questions have been asked about videotape cassettes. Can movie theaters survive them? Can they compete with the more than five thousand commercial-free movies now available for home-viewing on videotape? The answer is yes, decisively. New movies continue to earn millions of dollars, and the most popular new ones earn hundreds of millions. The question, then, is not *whether* movie theaters can survive this latest threat, but *why* they are doing so.

Basic question of essay

[2] To see what they are up against, consider the advantages of videotape. First, it's frequently cheaper. If three or more people want to see a movie, they can usually rent a videocassette and recorder for less than it would cost them all to go to a theater, and if they happen to own a VCR, they can rent a cassette for less than the price of a single admission. Second, movie theaters offer nothing like the range of choice that videotapes provide. While the moviegoer has to take whatever the local theater happens to be showing, the videotape viewer can choose from hundreds of films, including foreign or X-rated items that will probably never find their way onto a local screen. Third, while movies are shown at fixed times only, videotapes can be seen whenever the viewer wants

Alternating structure shows advantages of videotape.

to see them, and just as often as he or she likes. Finally, videotapes allow the viewer a kind of privacy and comfort that no public movie theater can possibly furnish. The videotape viewer need not strain to hear a film over the buzz of the talkers sitting behind or to see it over the heads of the people sitting in front. Instead, he or she can enjoy it alone or with just a few close friends at home.

[3] Given all these advantages, why haven't videotapes already put movie theaters out of business? Why are theaters selling more tickets than ever before? Part of the answer is restlessness. Movie theaters offer us what no form of home entertainment—no matter how technologically sophisticated—will ever be able to provide: a chance to get out of the house, to get away from the kids, to leave behind the crumb-speckled carpet and the peeling wallpaper and the dirty dishes piled up in the sink. The fact that most people can make delicious dinners in the privacy of their own kitchens has not yet killed the restaurant business. Whatever we can eat, do, or see at home, all of us need an occasional night out. *Block structure shows advantages of movie-going.*

[4] Movie theaters give us not only a night out but also a social experience. By forsaking the privacy of home, we escape its isolation. We go out to the movies in order to laugh, cry, and cheer with other people. Not every movie is like *The Rocky Horror Picture Show*, which invites us to dress up and act out the film ourselves, but all movies shown in theaters do invite and excite a communal response. They make us feel part of a group.

[5] Besides getting us out of the house and into the company of others, movie theaters provide a visual experience far surpassing what videocassettes now offer. To the eye, a videotaped movie has two major drawbacks: scan lines and severe reduction. Television makes a video image by breaking down the subject into thousands of bits which are then transmitted across the screen in horizontal scan lines. These are always visible, especially at close range, and enlarging the screen simply enlarges the lines. The other thing that videotaped movies suffer from is contraction. Though older movies were made for near-square screens that are roughly proportional to those of television sets, the big, spectacular, wide-screen movies of recent years simply cannot fit on a TV screen. Lopping tops of heads and bottoms of legs, reducing long shots to medium *Block structure shows disadvantages of videotape.*

shots and close-ups, cutting away material on either side of the central image, the videocassette literally shows only part of the movie. It cannot duplicate the original.

Conclusion summarizes advantages of movie-going and thus completes answer to basic question.

[6] For all of these reasons, I believe that movie theaters will survive the impact of videocassettes and video machines just as well as they have survived the impact of television. Nothing to be seen now on any television screen—no matter how big—equals the clarity, magnitude, and breadth of detail to be seen on the wide screen of a movie theaters showing a good 35-millimeter print. Combined with the purely social attraction of moviegoing, this visual advantage will—for the time being anyway—keep movie theaters very much alive.

—Tony Walsh

EXERCISE 15   COMPARING AND CONTRASTING WITH BLOCK STRUCTURE

Taking as a model the two paragraphs by Pirsig given on p. 114, use block structure to compare and contrast the two items in any one of the following pairs:

surfing / sailing

good teaching / bad teaching

crime / terrorism

law / custom

typing / writing with a word processor

living with one's parents / living on one's own

grunge rock / heavy metal

EXERCISE 16   COMPARING AND CONTRASTING WITH ALTERNATING STRUCTURE

Taking as a model the example in section 6.6A (p. 115), use alternating structure to compare and contrast the two items in any one of the following pairs:

jogging / walking

eating at home / eating in a restaurant

any small town / any large city

watching a movie / seeing a play

cycling / motorcycling

painting / photography

astronomy / astrology

rollerblades / roller skates

**EXERCISE 17 USING COMPARISON AND CONTRAST TO
EXPLAIN A POINT**

Using comparison and contrast, write an essay that explains
any one of the following:

1. why custom is sometimes more powerful than law

2. why growing up in a small town is better than growing up
   in a city, or vice versa

3. why video games are better than board games, or vice versa

4. why living on one's own is better than living with one's
   parents, or vice versa

5. why plays are more lifelike than movies, or vice versa

6. why running one's own business is better than working for
   someone else, or vice versa

6.7 USING DEFINITIONS

Definition is a way of enhancing the clarity of your writing.
Whatever you aim to do in your essay, you cannot reach your
readers unless they can readily understand your words. Whenever
you use a term that your readers are unlikely to know, or whenever you use a common word in a specialized sense, you can use
definition to help the reader grasp its meaning.

The most common and also least effective way to define a
word or phrase is to quote the dictionary ("*Webster's* defines *freedom* as . . ."). Instead of quoting the dictionary, use one or more
of these methods:

1. Defining by synonym

> *Apathetic* means "indifferent."
>
> *Prevaricate* means "lie."
>
> *Clandestinely* means "secretly."

The form of the synonym should correspond to the form of the word being defined. *Apathetic* doesn't mean "indifference," but "indifferent."

2. Defining by comparison, contrast, or analogy

The *plover* is a bird that lives on the shore, like the sandpiper. But the plover is usually fatter, and unlike the sandpiper, it has a short, hard-tipped bill.

While burglary is the stealing of property from a place, *robbery* is the stealing of property from a person.

A *lien* on a piece of property is like a leash on a dog. It's a way of legally attaching the property to someone who has a claim against the property owner.

3. Defining by function

An *orthopedist* treats bone diseases.

An *ombudsman* defends an individual in a conflict with an institution.

4. Defining by classification. You can define a word by naming the class of the person or thing it denotes and then giving one or more distinctive features:

	CLASS	FEATURE
An *orthopedist* is	a doctor	who specializes in bones.
A *plover* is	a bird	that lives on the shore.
A *skylight* is	a window	set in the roof of a building.

5. Defining by example. You can define a word by giving examples after classifying the person or thing it denotes:

A *crustacean* is a shelled creature such as a lobster, a shrimp, or a crab.

A *planet* is a heavenly sphere such as Jupiter, Mercury, Mars, or Earth.

6. Defining by etymology. Etymology is the study of the roots of words. You can sometimes define a word by giving its root meaning and thus showing where it came from:

Intuition comes from the Latin words *in* (meaning "in" or "into") and *tueri* (meaning "look" or "gaze"). Literally, therefore, it means a "looking inward."

6.7A COMBINING METHODS OF DEFINITION

A single definition may combine two or more methods:

> Interferon is a large hormone-like protein produced by the cells of all vertebrate animals. It was discovered in 1957 in Britain by virologists Alick Isaacs and Jean Lindenmann during their investigation of a curious phenomenon: people are almost never infected by more than one virus at a time. Seeking an explanation, the researchers infected cells from chick embryos with influenza virus. What they found was a substance that protected chick cells from both the flu and other viruses. Because it interfered with the infection process, it was dubbed interferon. —*Time*, November 6, 1978

This definition combines classification with comparison and with etymology of a sort—a little digging into the origin of the word. Interferon is a protein; that is its class. It is compared to hormones—described as "hormone-like"—and its name is said to have come from the word *interfere*.

> **EXERCISE 18** **DEFINING**
>
> Using at least two of the methods just described, define one of the following words:
>
> | | |
> |---|---|
> | conservative | racism |
> | suburbanite | rape |
> | bigotry | sexism |
> | feminist | holograph |
> | ecology | neurotic |
> | terrorist | gringo |
> | hypocrite | amoeba |
> | technology | poverty |

6.8 EXPLAINING BY ANALYZING: CLASSIFICATION AND DIVISION

Analyzing means looking closely at the parts of an object or group. To analyze a *single* object, such as the human body, you **divide** it into its parts, such as the heart, the brain, the stomach, and the liver. To analyze a *group* of objects or persons, you divide and **classify** them, cutting one group into two or more smaller groups. To analyze the American people, for instance, you could divide and classify them in political categories such as voters and nonvoters, in ethnic groups such as Italian, Hispanic, and African American, or in regional groups such as Northerners and Southerners. In so doing, you would be using classification and division.

Classification is a way of ordering the world around us. It's the arrangement of objects, people, or ideas into classes or groups. Whenever you speak of professors, sophomores, women, men, joggers, jocks, or grinds, you are grouping individuals together as a class because of one or more things they have in common. You can do the same with individual objects or ideas. You can classify motorcycles, cars, and trucks as "motor vehicles"; apples, pears, and oranges as "fruits"; monarchy, democracy, and plutocracy as "political systems."

Classification usually goes hand in hand with **division**. If, for instance, you divide "fruit juices" into fresh, frozen, canned, and powdered, you have identified four different forms of juice. But instead of dividing the juices according to their forms, you could divide them according to their flavors: apple, orange, grapefruit, lemon, and so on. How you divide and classify depends on your purpose. When you come home with a bag of groceries, you commonly divide and classify them at first into just two groups: those that need refrigeration and those that don't.

In everyday living, then, everyone has to classify and divide in order to cope with a world of individual objects and people. And what is true in everyday living is also true in writing. Whenever you write about a group of people, objects, or ideas, you need a system of classifying and dividing them. Consider how the student author of this essay uses classification and division to explain Japanese society.

INSIDERS AND OUTSIDERS IN JAPANESE SOCIETY

[1] Many things about Japanese society puzzle Americans. But hardest of all for Americans to understand is the Japanese devotion to groups. Unlike Americans, the Japanese do not

usually think of themselves as independent individuals. They act as members of a community, of a company, or at the very least of a family, which is the minimum social unit. Whatever the group, its very existence depends on the basic difference between insiders and outsiders. Understanding that difference is the key to understanding Japanese society as a whole, and the Japanese family in particular.

[2] The first thing to be understood about *insiders* and *outsiders* is that these are relative terms. Japanese society cannot be imagined as a tight little circle of insiders surrounded by a great big ring of outsiders. It is rather a world of bubbles. In each bubble is a group of people who think of each other as insiders and who look upon all the other people in all the other bubbles as outsiders. No one can be absolutely classified as either an insider or an outsider. To be inside one bubble is, inevitably, to be outside all the others.

[3] The system is complicated because one big bubble may sometimes contain many small ones. A big company, for instance, may include many departments or sections, and each of those sections is a bubble of insiders who work together closely, see each other often, and think of all other company workers as outsiders. Yet as soon as the insiders of a particular section think of their whole company in relation to a competitor, everyone who works for the company becomes an insider, and the outsiders are those who work for the competition.

[4] The opposition between insiders and outsiders becomes still more evident when we turn from Japanese companies to Japanese families. The Japanese family does not merge with other families, or with society at large. While American families often entertain large numbers of casual acquaintances, Japanese families seldom open their doors to anyone but insiders: family members or relatives. On the rare occasions when a close friend of the family is invited, he or she thereby becomes an insider—in effect, one of the family. Everyone else remains an outsider, and is literally kept outside the family home.

[5] The opposition between insiders and outsiders also explains why the actual structure of the Japanese family differs so much from the way it appears to the outside world, especially to Americans. Most Americans think the typical Japanese family is totally ruled by the husband, with the wife no

more than a servant. In fact, the modern Japanese family is ruled by the wife. It is she who takes all of her husband's salary, oversees all household repairs and expenditures, and supervises the education of the children. Inside the family, she has absolute authority.

[6] Yet as soon as the family confronts an outsider, the husband plays the ruler. A perfect example of this switch is what happens when a Japanese family goes out to eat. Before the family leaves the house, the wife gives the husband enough cash to pay the bill. When the family members sit down in the restaurant, the wife decides what the children will eat and often what her husband will eat as well, overruling him if she finds his choices too expensive. But as soon as the waiter arrives, the husband orders for the entire family as if he had made all the choices himself. In so doing, he represents the family for the eyes of an outsider, and so long as those eyes are watching, he is in charge. When he finishes paying the check with the money that his wife has allowed him, she and the children bow to him and say, "Thank you for a good meal, Father."

[7] To understand Japanese society, then, one must understand both the power of the group and the distinction between insiders and outsiders. Since all members of a group are insiders, they can act as individuals among themselves, arguing with each other until they agree or until one of them—the wife in the case of a family group—decides for all. But to outsiders they present a united front. Once they turn from confronting each other to confronting the outside world, insiders cease to be individuals and become part of a group which determines what their public roles will be.

—Rick Kurihara

Throughout this essay, the writer uses classification and division to explain Japanese society. The basic distinction between insiders and outsiders allows him to divide and classify all individuals in relation to groups, and thus to explain how group mentality in Japan governs individual action.

This essay also shows how different means of exposition can work together. For more on this topic, see section 6.11, "Combining Methods of Development."

6.9 EXPLAINING A PROCESS

A **process** is a sequence of actions that lead or should lead to a
predictable result. The way you explain a process depends on your
purpose—on whether you want to teach the process or simply
help your reader understand it.

6.9A TEACHING A PROCESS

To teach a process so that your readers can carry it out, you must
explain every thing and every step it requires, as in this explanation of how to replace spark plugs:

> To replace worn plugs, you need three tools that you can
> buy at any automotive parts store: a ratchet wrench with a
> short extension handle, a spark plug socket, and a spark plug
> gauge.
> The most important thing to know about spark plugs is
> that you have to remove and replace them *one at a time*. If you
> take them all out at once, you will have to disconnect all of
> their wires at the same time, and you will probably not
> remember which plugs they came from. Since each plug has
> its own wire and since the car will not run if the wires are
> mixed up, you should never have more than one wire discon-
> nected at any one time.
> The owner's manual for your car will tell you where the
> spark plugs are. Once you have located them, you must do five
> things with each plug in turn. First, disconnect the wire
> attached to it. Second, with the spark plug socket placed over
> the plug and the ratchet wrench in the socket, remove the plug

by turning the wrench counterclockwise. Third, use the spark plug gauge to measure the size of the little gap in the electrode—the small open square of metal that sticks up out of the threaded tube at one end of the spark plug. If the gap is too big, the electrode is worn, and the plug must be replaced. Fourth, insert the old plug or a new one by turning it clockwise with your fingers until it sticks, and then using the wrench to turn it a quarter of a circle more. Fifth, reconnect the wire that belongs to that particular plug.   —Jim Robb

6.9B REPORTING A PROCESS

If you aim to help your readers understand a process rather than teaching them to carry it out, just report its chief stages:

> In contact with the proper food on leaving the egg, the caterpillar begins to eat immediately and continues until it has increased its weight hundreds of times. On each of the first three segments of the body is a pair of short legs ending in a sharp claw. These legs correspond to the six legs of the adult insect. In addition, the caterpillar has up to ten short, fleshy feet called prolegs, which are shed before it changes form. The insect passes its pupal stage incased in comparatively rigid integuments [layers] that form a chrysalis.
>
> Most butterfly chrysalides remain naked, unlike those of the moth, which have a protective cocoon. Breathing goes on through an air opening while the complete adult, or imago, develops. Wings, legs, proboscis, even the pigment in the scales, form in the tight prison of the chrysalis.
>
> At maturity, the chrysalis splits its covering and wriggles out as an imago, or perfect insect. Hanging from a leaf or rock, it forces blood, or haemolymph, into the veins of its wet wings, straightening them to their normal span. Soon the wings are dry, and the insect flies into a life of nectar drinking and courtship.   —"Butterfly," *Funk & Wagnalls New Encyclopedia*

This is a reporting explanation. The writer describes the stages through which the insect passes, but does not explain everything about its transformation. The writer is trying to help us understand an overall process—not teach us how to become butterflies ourselves.

EXERCISE 20   TEACHING A PROCESS

Write a teaching explanation of any simple process that you
know well and that can be taught in writing—such as changing a tire, making a bed, frying an egg, or getting from one
place to another. When you have finished, see if someone else
can actually perform the process by following your instructions.

EXERCISE 21   REPORTING A PROCESS

Write a reporting explanation of any process you know well,
such as climbing a cliff, painting a picture, making a clay pot,
taking or developing a good photograph. If you use any specialized terms, be sure to define them as you go along.

6.10 EXPLAINING CAUSE AND EFFECT

Since any situation or event can provoke questions about its
causes, its **effects,** or both, one good way of explaining anything
is to raise such questions. You can ask about causes, for instance.
Why are more than 26 million adult Americans functionally illiterate? What caused the Los Angeles riots of 1992? Alternatively,
or in addition, you can ask about effects. How does functional
illiteracy affect an adult's life? What will happen if the "greenhouse effect" really is raising the temperature of the earth?

In the physical sciences, questions about causes and effects
sometimes have simple, straightforward answers. Scientists
know, for instance, that heat makes gases expand, that salt raises
the boiling point of water, that chlorine disrupts ozone mole-
cules, and so on. But inside as well as outside science, many
questions about causes and effects elicit no single answer. For a
particular situation or event there may be several causes, several
effects, or both. Consider the following essay:

WHY DO WOMEN LONG TO BE THIN?

[1] "I've just *got* to lose ten pounds by the end of the
month," said Karen. Sitting opposite me at a little square
white table in the North Campus cafeteria, she was doggedly

crunching her way through a salad of iceberg lettuce and sliced cucumbers, trying hard not to look at the mountain of chocolate sauce, vanilla ice cream, whipped cream, and chopped walnuts that had just been served to some junk food addict at the next table. Karen is not fat, but she'll never be thin enough to eat anything she wants without feeling guilty. As I looked at her while dutifully sipping my own Diet Coke, I asked myself why nearly all young women in America yearn to lose weight.

Situation to be explained

[2] Part of the reason can be found in magazines like *Seventeen* and *Glamour*, which are cunningly designed to reach teenage girls in their most impressionable years. The articles and ads in these magazines all preach the gospel of thinness. The typical ad shows a skinny model like Christy Brinkley along with some gorgeous guy who is gazing at her with enraptured eyes. The typical article reveals a new diet, a new kind of exercise, or just some new piece of evidence for the argument that thinner is better.

First cause: magazine ads and articles

[3] An article about the lead singer in the group called Wilson Phillips, for instance, reported that she was always put in the back when pictures were taken for their albums. When she asked why, she was told that the image of her fat body might scare album buyers away. So she determined to lose weight and did. As a result, she now stands in the front of the album pictures, and her story exemplifies what young women are endlessly told: while fatness pushes you out of the picture, thinness brings you popularity and self-confidence.

[4] Television tells us much the same. To dramatize the message "Keep the muscle—lose the fat," the Kellogg's Special K ad uses a model filmed from the neck down so that we are made to see how perfectly trim she is. Fat women seldom appear in TV commercials except to show what they looked like before the sponsor's product slimmed them down. In TV programs, fat women are just as scarce. With a few exceptions such as Roseanne Barr and Oprah Winfrey, the women we see in TV programs are thin. Any actress who gets fat may suffer the fate of Delta Burke. After years of work in the series called *Designing Women*, she was fired after gaining weight. Though the show's producers claimed she was fired for not doing a good job, I suspect the real reason is that she dared to be fat.

Second cause: TV ads and programs

[5] Besides the messages about fat that we get from mag-

azines and television, books feed us a steady diet of advice on how to lose weight, be fit, and stay fit. Often these books are gobbled up because they are written or promoted by famous women with beautifully slim figures. Jane Fonda is no authority on nutrition, but when the diving board scene of *On Golden Pond* showed how thin she could be even in her forties, her book on fitness became a best-seller.

Third cause: books on fitness and dieting by slim female celebrities

[6] In a variety of ways, then, magazines, television, and books relentlessly preach the message that women must be thin. While fatness, we are told, leads to neglect, unemployment, and loneliness, thinness makes a woman desirable, successful, and perhaps even glamorous, like Jane Fonda or Cher. But we hear far too much about the bad effects of being fat and the good effects of being thin. We hear far too little about the bad effects of the yearning to be thin. This yearning turns some women into anorexics, who starve themselves to death, and others into bulimics, who ravage their stomachs by gorging and disgorging food. Even those who try to lose weight by ordinary dieting—like my friend Karen—too often allow the quest for thinness to become an obsession that rules their lives.

Effects of thinness and fatness, effects of yearning for thinness

[7] What would happen, I wonder, if American women decided to shuck this obsession? Well, for one thing, the people who make billions of dollars every year by selling diet pills and fitness plans would find themselves out of business. At the same time, instead of letting magazines and TV shows tell them how to look, instead of basing their self-esteem on the size or shape of their bodies, women could restart the business of running their own lives.   —René Cardle

Effects of breaking the obses-sion with thinness

EXERCISE 22 EXPLAINING CAUSE AND EFFECT

1. Identify what you believe are the causes of littering, and then explain how we could use our understanding of those causes to combat it.

2. Discuss the effects of unemployment on any community you know.

3. Explain the causes or effects of any event or condition that you know about.

4. The "greenhouse effect" is a global warming. It will occur when the sun's infrared radiation is trapped by increased

levels of carbon dioxide in the atmosphere—an increase caused by the burning of fossil fuels. If the global warming occurs, the chart below outlines what it will probably do to the Southeastern United States. Using this chart as a guide and stimulus, explain the effects of global warming in at least three of the six categories shown. Write one paragraph for each category discussed.

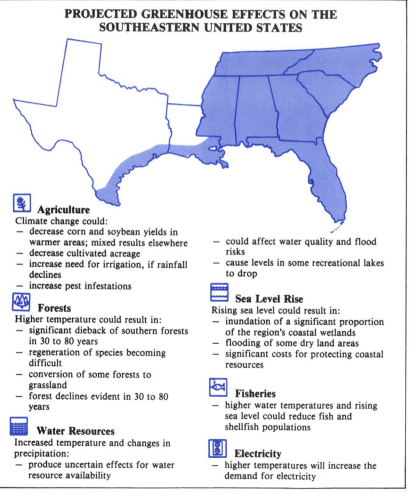

PROJECTED GREENHOUSE EFFECTS ON THE SOUTHEASTERN UNITED STATES

Agriculture

Climate change could:
— decrease corn and soybean yields in warmer areas; mixed results elsewhere
— decrease cultivated acreage
— increase need for irrigation, if rainfall declines
— increase pest infestations

Forests

Higher temperature could result in:
— significant dieback of southern forests in 30 to 80 years
— regeneration of species becoming difficult
— conversion of some forests to grassland
— forest declines evident in 30 to 80 years

Water Resources

Increased temperature and changes in precipitation:
— produce uncertain effects for water resource availability
— could affect water quality and flood risks
— cause levels in some recreational lakes to drop

Sea Level Rise

Rising sea level could result in:
— inundation of a significant proportion of the region's coastal wetlands
— flooding of some dry land areas
— significant costs for protecting coastal resources

Fisheries
— higher water temperatures and rising sea level could reduce fish and shellfish populations

Electricity
— higher temperatures will increase the demand for electricity

—Bill McKibben, "Is the World Getting Hotter?"
New York Review of Books, December 9, 1988

METHODS OF DEVELOPMENT: IN BRIEF

Description
External: re-creates in words the appearance of an object
Analytical or technical: explains the structure of an object
Evocative: re-creates the impression of an object on the senses

Narration
Chronological: records a sequence of events in the order in which they occurred or could have occurred
Nonchronological: uses flashbacks and flash-forwards to clarify the meaning of a sequence of events

Example: illustrates or supports a point

Analogy: explains something unfamiliar by likening it to something familiar

Comparison and Contrast: explains how two things in the same category differ, usually in ways that make one of them seem better

Definition: explains a word or phrase by
  synonym
  comparison, contrast, or analogy
  function
  class and distinctive feature
  example
  etymology

Analysis: divides a whole into parts or classifies a group of items

Explaining a Process: teaches someone else to take every step *or* reports its chief stages to make it understandable

Explaining Cause and Effect: shows the causal link between one or more events or conditions

6.11 COMBINING METHODS OF DEVELOPMENT

Good essays often combine two or more methods of development. The essay on insiders and outsiders in Japanese society (pp. 122–24), for instance, not only classifies and divides; it also compares and contrasts Japanese society with American society (paragraphs 1 and 4), constructs the analogy of bubbles (paragraphs 2 and 3), and uses an example to illustrate Japanese family life (paragraph 6).

> EXERCISE 23 COMBINING METHODS OF DEVELOPMENT
>
> Using at least three of the methods of development that we have discussed in this chapter, write an essay in which you explain to a high school senior the operation of any team, club, or organization at your college.

7

Persuasion and Argument

Persuasion is the art of leading people to do something or to believe something without compelling them to do so. It is an art practiced with pictures and gestures as well as with spoken and written words, and it is practiced all around us. Persuasive appeals spring from billboards, magazines, newspapers, television, radio, and even our own telephones whenever we lift the receiver to hear the voice of a salesperson. To survive and succeed in this world, we must be able to recognize persuasion, to judge it, and to use it ourselves.

Persuasion never occurs in a vacuum. It always rests on a base of shared assumptions. Suppose, for instance, that the zoning board of Amityville has been asked to approve a request that a house on Elm Street be used as a residence for people recovering from mental illness, who would live there under the supervision of a nurse. If Jane E. Homeowner, who now lives on Elm Street, doesn't like this idea, she might say to the zoning board that the presence of such patients on her street would reduce the value of her property. If that point persuaded the zoning board to vote against the request, she and a majority of its members must have shared one assumption: maintaining property values is more important than helping the recovering mentally ill readjust to living in a normal environment.

Occasionally, persuasion may also be fueled by some form of power. Suppose that one member of the zoning board mentioned above is the automobile dealer from whom Jane Homeowner normally buys her cars. While considering her point about property values, he knows very well what this good customer might do if he votes to approve the new residence. She doesn't even have to remind him of the power she holds.

Just as persuasion may be fueled by some form of power, it is commonly lubricated by an appeal to the feelings—especially in selling and advertising. Over a big color picture of a farming family gathered around a tractor, a recent insurance ad proclaims:

> **There are people more famous we insure.**
> **But none more important.**

Under the picture the ad continues:

> For over a hundred years, we've tried to keep personal insurance from becoming too impersonal.
> When you do business with _____, it's with one of our independent agents. So when you have a question about auto, health, home or life insurance, you deal with someone who is close to you and your situation.
> You can easily find an independent _____ agent in the Yellow Pages.
> _____ is one of the world's largest insurance companies, a size that doesn't diminish our big concern for the individual.

As in many ads, picture and text together seek to persuade readers that the advertiser cares about each of them. The means of persuasion are essentially emotional. With the family picture reinforcing the point, the reader is told that the company deals in "personal insurance," that the company agent will be "someone who is close to you and your situation." The tone is warm and reassuring; the statement is the verbal equivalent of a friendly handshake.

Since feelings play a part in the formation of almost every opinion, you need to understand as well as you can the feelings of your readers. But you can seldom persuade an audience by appealing to their feelings alone. If you respect the intelligence of your readers, you will also appeal to their minds. And to do that successfully, you must construct an argument.

7.1 WHAT IS AN ARGUMENT?

We commonly think of an **argument** as a quarrel—a shouting match in which tempers flare and necks turn red. But the word *argument* can also mean "a rational way of persuading." It differs from exposition because it seeks to convince, not just to explain, and it differs from emotional persuasion because it seeks to convince by appealing to the mind. To see these differences more clearly, consider the following three passages:

1. The bear population of Maine is 7,000 to 10,000 animals, and the annual "harvest," or kill, averages 930. State wildlife biologists estimate that the number killed falls short by 120 of the "allowable harvest," i.e., "the harvest level that takes only the annual increase and does not affect the population size."
   —Jonathan Evan Maslow, "Stalking the Black Bear"

   Exposition

2. Every year, bloodthirsty hunters go into the Maine woods and ruthlessly shoot to death hundreds of bears. The hunters care nothing for the suffering they cause, for the blood they spill, or for the harm they do to creatures who have done no harm to them. Hunters kill for a thrill, and that is all they care about. No one seems to care anything for the bears.

   Emotional appeal

3. Though some people may think hunting is nothing more than wholesale and wanton destruction of living creatures, hunters actually help to ensure the health and survival of wildlife. Take bear-hunting in Maine as a case in point. Out of the 7,000 to 10,000 bears that roam the Maine woods, hunters kill an average of 930 a year. State wildlife biologists estimate that this is 120 fewer than the annual population increase. If the bear population were allowed to grow unchecked, it would increase well over 1,000 a year, and the food available for any one bear would correspondingly decrease. By killing an average of 930 bears a year, hunters keep the annual increase down, and therefore help to ensure an adequate food supply for the bear population as a whole.

   Argument

These three passages treat the same topic in fundamentally different ways. The first calmly explains the relation between the number of bears born and the number killed in Maine each year. The second tries to make the reader feel outrage at hunters and pity for bears. The third tries to prove that hunting is beneficial to wildlife.

Note the difference between passage 2 and passage 3. Passage 2 relies on words like *bloodthirsty* to stir the reader's feelings; passage 3 relies on facts, figures, and authoritative estimates to gain the reader's agreement. Purely emotive words may appeal to a reader who already tends to feel the way the writer does, but they are unlikely to change an opponent's mind. On the other hand, the argument of passage 3 is thought-provoking. It won't persuade all readers, but it will give even fervent conservationists something to think about. To combat such an argument effectively, conservationists would have to challenge its facts, figures, and estimates in a manner such as this:

4. Hunting advocates try to justify the killing of bears by arguing that it limits the annual increase in the bear population and thereby helps to ensure an adequate food supply for the bears that remain. But this argument rests on the assumption that wildlife biologists can reliably estimate the size of the population increase, which is said to be 120 more than the number of bears killed each year. Can we be sure it is? If estimates of the bear population range from 7,000 to 10,000, how can we accurately calculate the annual increase in that population? Do we even know how many bears die each year of natural causes? If we don't know that, we cannot determine what the net annual increase in the bear population would be in the absence of hunters. And even if we knew this figure exactly, it would not tell us just how well an unregulated bear population would manage to feed itself. Without hunters threatening them, bears might well become more venturesome and thus more successful in their quest for food. We can hardly be certain, therefore, that bears are better off with hunters than they would be without them.

Like passage 2, this passage aims to convince the reader that bear-hunting is unjustified. But unlike passage 2, it does not try to stir pity for bears or outrage at hunters. Instead, it calmly exposes the weaknesses in the prohunting argument, and thus appeals to the reader's mind.

Just as argument differs from emotional persuasion, so also does it differ from exposition. In exposition, every statement is offered as a matter of accepted fact. In argument, only some statements are offered as matters of fact, and these are given as reasons to make us believe assertions or claims. For example, the assertion in passage 3 that "hunters actually help to ensure the health and survival of wildlife" is disputable and needs defending. Instead of assuming that we will believe it, the writer must give us reasons for doing so.

> ### BASIC ELEMENTS OF AN ARGUMENT: IN BRIEF
>
> • **Claim:** statement that needs defending
>
> • **Evidence:** statements of fact made to support the claim
>
> • **Assumption:** belief or principle (often unstated) that the writer takes for granted.

An effective argument is the product of an imaginary conversation between the writer and a skeptical, questioning reader. The conversation starts with a claim, which is a statement of what the writer intends to prove:

1. CLAIM: Hunters help to ensure the health and survival of bears.
   QUESTION: How?
2. EVIDENCE: They limit the growth of the bear population.
   QUESTION: But how does that help the bears?
3. ASSUMPTION: Fewer bears means more food per bear.

The **evidence** for a claim includes the specific facts or data on which the claim rests. But statements of fact can often be challenged, as passage 4 shows, especially when they depend on estimates rather than precise measurement. To build an effective argument, therefore, you must be sure that your statements of fact are true.

Besides evidence, most arguments include one or more **assumptions,** which are beliefs or principles—often unstated— that the writer takes for granted. An assumption binds the evidence to the claim. To prove that hunters help ensure the health and survival of bears, it's not enough to say that hunters limit population growth among bears; you must also ask readers to assume that fewer bears means more food per bear. To argue effectively, therefore, you should know what your assumptions are and whether or not your readers are likely to share them.

7.2 SUPPORTING CLAIMS WITH EVIDENCE

Effective arguments support general claims with specific evidence. Giving evidence means doing one or more of the following things.

7.2A GIVING STATEMENTS OF FACT AND EXAMPLES

A **statement of fact** is a statement of what the writer takes for certain because it is well known ("George Washington was the first president of the United States"), readily verifiable by experiment ("Heat makes gases expand"), or set down in public record ("Martin Luther King, Jr., won the Nobel Peace Prize in 1963").

An **example** is a particular object, event, or condition that is said to represent something larger than itself. Statements of fact often serve as examples. The statement about Martin Luther King, Jr., could readily serve as an example of the international recognition he achieved. But not all examples are statements of fact. On p. 133 above, to show how persuasion depends on shared assumptions, we offered an imaginary example. We asked you to *suppose* a set of circumstances.

The persuasive force of an imaginary example depends on its plausibility—that is, on whether or not the reader can imagine that it could be true or that something like it could actually happen. The persuasive force of a factual example depends in part on its plausibility (you would not readily accept the statement that a tribe of pygmies has been discovered living underwater), but also on its specificity, and sometimes (as explained in section 7.2C) on the sources or authorities that are said to stand behind it.

To see how an argument may be strengthened by examples and statements of fact, which we'll simply call *facts* from now on, compare these two passages written by first-term college freshmen:

My feeling is that all people are equal. Neither sex is superior to the other. In the times of today, men and women both have an equal opportunity for education. They can pursue any career that they are qualified for. Schools are now getting away from trying to make certain things for boys and vice versa. Children are growing up as equals.

Claim supported only by broad generalizations

There are differences between men and women, but none that make either sex inferior. Athletic performance is a case in point. A major study by a West German doctor has shown that because of different skeletal leverage in men and women, muscles of identical strength will produce about 5 percent greater apparent strength in men. In sports such as running and mountaineering, however, women show greater endurance and resistance to stress. Several years ago, when I assisted a friend running the Boston Marathon, I noticed that although many of the male runners were literally collapsing at the finish or at least in need of help, the women rarely needed any help at all.

Claim supported by specific facts and examples

The persuasive force of an argument generally grows with the weight of evidence presented. See how the following argument gathers power as it gathers facts and examples to support its opening claim:

Nuclear power plants are fundamentally unsafe. The history of nuclear power is a list of major accidents and near catastrophes. At Windscale, England, in 1957, a fire and a partial meltdown of a nuclear core spread radioactivity across miles of pastureland, and thousands of gallons of contaminated cows' milk had to be dumped. In 1966 another partial meltdown occurred at Unit One of the Fermi plant near Detroit. In 1970 fifty thousand gallons of radioactive water and steam escaped from the reactor vessel of the huge Commonwealth Edison plant near Chicago. At Browns Ferry, Alabama, in 1975, a single candle started a fire at a nuclear power plant that burned for seven hours, caused 150 million dollars' worth of damage and loss to the plant, and—according to some experts—very nearly caused a catastrophic release of radiation. Even after the Rasmussen report supposedly analyzed everything that could go wrong with a nuclear reactor, a malfunctioning water gauge led to yet another near meltdown at Three Mile Island, Pennsylvania, in 1979. Finally, in April 1986, an explosion and fire in the graphite core of a nuclear reactor at Chernobyl in the Soviet Ukraine caused more than 25 fatalities, spread radioactive dust over much of Europe, contaminated food supplies in Scandinavia, and may lead to more than 30,000 cancer-related deaths over the next 70 years. Taken together, all of these accidents show that the risks we run in operating nuclear power plants are intolerably high.

Statements of established fact ("Heat makes gases expand") or of public record (like the statements of fact made in the passage above) can usually stand by themselves. But for some other kinds of evidence, you must cite your sources, as explained below in section 7.2C.

7.2B CITING STATISTICS

Statistics help to make an argument persuasive by providing what appears to be "hard" evidence. If, for instance, you want to argue that hunters help bears, you can strengthen your case by stating that hunters hold the net growth of the bear population to 120 each year. If you want to argue that American highways have grown steadily more dangerous in the past forty-five years, you can state that auto fatalities in 1989 were 18,000 higher than they were in 1945.

But figures and statistics alone will not make your argument for you. If the figures on the bear population are only an estimate, this "hard" piece of evidence turns soft. If the number of automobile fatalities has risen since 1945, what about the number of cars and drivers on the road? If they've risen also—and they have—the number of fatalities doesn't tell the whole story. Other figures tell a different story: the *rate* of fatalities per 100 million vehicle miles actually *fell* after 1945, from 9.8 in 1946 to 2.25 in 1989. The meaning of the number of fatalities at Chernobyl must likewise be interpreted. If more than 25 persons were killed by the Chernobyl explosion, does this mean that every nuclear power plant is a disaster waiting to happen? Not necessarily, since (as a matter of fact) the design of the Chernobyl reactor is fundamentally different from the design of most commercial reactors in the West.

To make figures and statistics serve as evidence, then, you must clearly explain what they mean and you may also have to establish their reliability by citing their source.

7.2C CITING SOURCES AND AUTHORITIES

Cite **sources** for statistics and **authorities** for estimates and opinions.

1. Statistics are not matters of fact. They are products of calculation. Their reliability depends on who calculated them, how they were calculated, and for what purpose. So you should cite your source for any statistics you use, and you can do so in one of two ways:

> Source cited in passing:

> According to the U.S. Bureau of Census, the proportion of working women who are mothers of children under 6 rose from 11.9 percent in 1950 to 56.8 percent in 1987.

> Source cited in parentheses:

> The rate of fatalities per 100 million vehicle miles fell from 9.8 in 1946 to 4.24 in 1973 (National Safety Council).

These are both *informal* ways of citing sources. For detailed guidance on *formally* citing a source, see chapter 35.

2. The value of an estimate or opinion is only as good as the authority who stands behind it. Before citing an authority, ask yourself the following questions:

a. Who is the authority? Is he or she an unnamed "expert" or a named, established specialist in a particular field? A "major study" of anatomical differences between men and women made "by a West German doctor" carries less weight than "a thorough study of nuclear power plants made at a cost of four million dollars under the supervision of Norman Rasmussen, professor of nuclear engineering at M.I.T."

b. Is the authority speaking on a topic in his or her field of expertise? If a specialist in the study of alcohol says that a driver with a blood alcohol content of .05 percent is twice as likely to have an accident as a driver who is perfectly sober, that statement carries the weight of special authority. But if the alcohol expert says that teenagers should not be allowed to drive until they are eighteen, he or she no longer speaks with special authority, because the topic has changed.

c. <u>Given the facts available on a particular question, can any expert answer it with certainty?</u> Predictions are notoriously unreliable, and experts on some subjects—the stock market, for instance—frequently miscalculate what will happen. No amount of authority can give to a prediction or an estimate the weight of an established fact.

d. <u>Does any other authority agree with the one you cite?</u> Experts often disagree. If the expert you cite is alone in his or her testimony, it will carry less weight than testimony backed by other experts.

EVIDENCE: IN BRIEF

• Use statements of fact that are reliable and relevant to your claim.

• Cite statistics that are reliable and meaningful.

• Cite sources for statistics.

• Cite authorities for estimates and opinions after considering these questions:
  Who is the authority?
  Is he or she an expert on the topic?
  Given the available facts on this topic, can any expert give a wholly reliable opinion on it?
  Does any other authority agree with the one you are citing?

7.3 DEDUCTION AND INDUCTION

Successful argumentation requires a basic understanding of **logic**, which is the art of drawing **inferences** or **conclusions**. Whether you realize it or not, you make inferences every day. If, for instance, you accidentally slide your finger along the edge of a piece of paper and then discover a thin line of dark red on the fingertip, you will probably infer that you have cut yourself. That is a logical inference because it is based on a credible set of **assumptions** (the edge of a paper can be sharp enough to cut; a dark red line on the fingertip is more likely to be blood than anything else) and a known **fact** (you have indeed run that fingertip along the paper's edge).

If we all make inferences every day, why do we need logic? Why do we need rules of inference? We need them because it is all too easy to make mistakes in drawing inferences, and arguments based on mistaken inferences are like buildings resting on cracked foundations. At best they will totter; at worst they will fall.

Without logic to rein us in, we commonly jump to conclusions. How often have you heard two or three people complain about a proposal and then concluded that *everyone* dislikes it? How often have you seen a member of a particular group do something odd or offensive and then concluded, "That's the way they all are"? If you are sensible enough to avoid such obvious mistakes in inference as those, you may nonetheless fall into more subtle traps. Suppose you were with the police at Berkeley in 1964 when they entered the office of President Emeritus Robert Gordon Sproul to remove student demonstrators who had broken into it during the Free Speech Movement. After the demonstrators were taken out, police found papers strewn all over the floor of Sproul's office. Surely, they thought, this was the work of the demonstrators. But in fact it wasn't. The papers had been strewn about by Sproul himself, who often liked to do his work on the floor.

To avoid subtle as well as obvious traps in the construction of your own arguments, you need to know something about inference—the process of drawing conclusions from assumptions and evidence. It commonly takes one of two forms—deduction or induction.

7.3A DEDUCTION AND VALIDITY

Deduction applies a general principle to a specific case. In formal logic, deduction is sometimes illustrated by a **syllogism**, a set of categorical statements that looks like this:

MAJOR PREMISE (ASSUMPTION): All those who limit the growth of the bear population help bears.

MINOR PREMISE (EVIDENCE): Bear hunters limit the growth of the bear population.

CONCLUSION (CLAIM): Bear hunters help bears.

In a syllogism, the claim supported by an argument appears last, as a conclusion. The conclusion is deduced or inferred from the major premise (a general principle the writer assumes), and the minor premise (normally evidence—a statement of fact). When a deduction is **valid,** the conclusion follows *necessarily* from the premises. The above syllogism is valid because the minor premise puts bear hunters within the category of "all those who limit the growth of the bear population." Since what applies to all members of this category must apply to every group within it, the conclusion is validly drawn. But if this syllogism were to conclude that bear hunters help all animals, the conclusion would be invalidly drawn, for it would then have strayed outside the category established by the premises.

7.3B MAKING DEDUCTIVE ARGUMENTS PERSUASIVE

Validity alone will not make an argument persuasive. The persuasiveness of an argument depends on the **credibility** of its assumptions.

Take, for instance, the assumption (major premise) made by the syllogism above. If we don't know how many bears die each year from natural causes, how do we know that anyone who limits the growth of their population is helping them? So long as the assumption can be questioned in this way, any conclusion drawn from it will be questionable also. A conclusion validly drawn from premises that are questionable or false is like a route carefully followed in strict obedience to a faulty compass. The route is only as good as the compass that determines it, and the argument is only as credible as the assumption that stands behind it.

Consider the assumption made by this deductive argument:

> In spite of the widespread fear and resistance they often generate, nuclear power plants are fundamentally safe. From 1972 to 1975, a thorough study of nuclear power plants was made at a cost of four million dollars under the supervision of Norman Rasmussen, professor of nuclear engineering at M.I.T. Given the time, money, and expertise devoted to this study, its results must be reliable. And in fact they are not only reliable; they are also reassuring. After examining, identifying, and—with computer analysis—establishing the risk of every possible accident that could release radiation from a nuclear power plant, the Rasmussen study concluded that in any given year the odds against a single death from a nuclear plant accident are five billion to one. Obviously, therefore, nuclear power plants are at least as safe as anything on earth can be.

This argument rests on an assumption about authority: any prolonged, expensive study supervised by a recognized expert in the field being studied must be reliable. Since the Rasmussen study fits these requirements, the conclusion ("its results must be reliable") is validly drawn. But the conclusion is credible only if the assumption is credible. Can anyone—no matter how authoritative—reliably calculate the odds against a nuclear plant fatality? And even apart from accidents, what about the dangers caused by radioactive wastes?

To make such an argument persuasive, you would have to reformulate the assumption on which it is based. Try this one: any enterprise that has functioned for more than thirty years without causing a single death or injury is fundamentally safe. If that assumption is credible—and it is certainly more credible than the assumption about authority—it could help to build a persuasive argument for the safety of nuclear power plants in the United States. (Such an argument would not have to explain the fatalities caused by the Chernobyl explosion, which occurred outside the United States—and after the Rasmussen study was made.)

7.3C INDUCTION AND PROBABLE CONCLUSIONS

While deductive arguments draw **necessary** conclusions, as explained above (section 7.3A), inductive arguments draw **probable** conclusions, which are commonly generalizations based on specific examples. Thus, to support the claim that nuclear power plants are unsafe, the author of the argument on p. 139 cites six major accidents that have occurred at such plants since 1957. These examples do not prove that all nuclear power plants are unsafe, but they could help to make this general claim seem probable.

7.3D MAKING INDUCTIVE ARGUMENTS

The chief advantage of an inductive argument lies in the cumulative impact of successive examples. Because of this impact, an inductive argument can sometimes feel strongly persuasive, and the argument against nuclear power plants (above, p. 139) may feel that way to you. But would the argument bring any new supporters to the no-nuke side, or merely bolster the morale of the old ones? To answer questions like these, you must not only weigh the impact of the examples but also consider the unstated assumption linking them to the claim that nuclear power plants are fundamentally unsafe.

Consider first the number of examples cited. Given all the nuclear power plants throughout the world, does a record of six accidents in thirty years justify this claim? Behind the imposing facade of examples lurks an unstated and shaky assumption: if six nuclear power plants have suffered major accidents, all such plants are unsafe. Is this any better than assuming that six defective washing machines prove all washing machines to be defective?

Whether or not the writer states the assumption that stands behind an argument, he or she should know what the assumption is and how well it binds the evidence to the general claim. Is a fatal disaster at Chernobyl relevant to a general claim about the safety of nuclear power plants? Prior to the Chernobyl disaster, no one had been killed or injured in any of the accidents cited, and the Chernobyl accident was caused (as we have already noted) by a reactor fundamentally different from those in the United States. Given that difference, and given also the absence of any nuclear fatalities in the West, the unstated assumption does not adequately bind the evidence to the general claim.

To make an inductive argument persuasive, state your claim with caution, and be sure that your evidence can be linked to the claim by a credible assumption. The inductive argument about nuclear power plants, for instance, would be more persuasive like this:

> CLAIM: It is probably impossible to guarantee the safety of nuclear power plants.
>
> EVIDENCE: Six nuclear power plants have suffered major accidents in the past thirty years.
>
> ASSUMPTION: If major accidents have repeatedly occurred at nuclear power plants, it is probably impossible to guarantee that no more accidents will occur.

7.3E COMBINING INDUCTION AND DEDUCTION

By itself, a deductive argument will seldom persuade your reader. Here, for instance, is a purely deductive version of an argument that Martin Luther King, Jr., made for the rights of African Americans in 1963:

> MAJOR PREMISE (ASSUMPTION): A people repeatedly abused and humiliated should not be required to wait any longer for their rights.
>
> MINOR PREMISE (FACT): African Americans are repeatedly abused and humiliated.
>
> CONCLUSION: African Americans should not be required to wait any longer for their rights.

What King actually wrote implies the above assumption and uses induction—generalization drawn from a set of examples—to prove the minor premise (fact) stated above. The combination of induction and deduction makes a highly persuasive argument:

> Perhaps it is easy for those who have never felt the stinging darts of segregation to say, "Wait." But when you have seen vicious mobs lynch your mothers and fathers at will and drown

your sisters and brothers at whim; when you have seen hate-filled policemen curse, kick, and even kill your black brothers and sisters; when you see the vast majority of your twenty million Negro brothers smothering in an airtight cage of poverty in the midst of an affluent society; when you suddenly find your tongue twisted and your speech stammering as you seek to explain to your six-year-old daughter why she can't go to the public amusement park that has just been advertised on television, and see tears welling up in her eyes when she is told that Funtown is closed to colored children, and see ominous clouds of inferiority beginning to form in her little mental sky, and see her beginning to distort her personality by developing an unconscious bitterness toward white people; when you have to concoct an answer for a five-year-old son who is asking, "Daddy, why do white people treat colored people so mean?"; when you take a cross-country drive and find it necessary to sleep night after night in the uncomfortable corners of your automobile because no motel will accept you; when you are humiliated day in and day out by nagging signs reading "white" and "colored"; when your first name becomes "nigger," your middle name becomes "boy" (however old you are) and your last name becomes "John," and your wife and mother are never given the respected title "Mrs."; when you are harried by day and haunted by night by the fact that you are a Negro, living constantly at tiptoe stance, never quite knowing what to expect next, and are plagued with inner fears and outer resentments; when you are forever fighting a degenerating sense of "nobodiness"—then you will understand why we find it difficult to wait. There comes a time when the cup of endurance runs over, and men are no longer willing to be plunged into the abyss of despair. I hope, sirs, you can understand our legitimate and unavoidable impatience.

—"Letter from Birmingham Jail"

King's examples help to persuade us not only because of their number but also because of their appeal to our feelings, as in the pictures of the weeping child and of black men "smothering in an airtight cage of poverty." For more on appealing to the feelings, see 7.6.

EXERCISE 1 SPOTTING ASSUMPTIONS

Identify the assumptions made by each of the following arguments, and say how credible the assumptions are:

1. A woman's career threatens a marriage because it makes the woman financially independent of her husband. When a married woman depends on her husband for support, she is strongly motivated to stay with him. She knows that divorce would probably lead to a sharp reduction in her allowance and style of living, that she might have to move into smaller living quarters and give up many of the comforts and benefits she enjoys while married. But if she has her own career, she can comfortably support herself, so she has no need for her husband. A two-career marriage, therefore, is far more likely to end in divorce than a marriage in which only the husband works.

2. Infants born with severe handicaps should be allowed to die rather than forced to endure lives of pain, privation, and constant dependence. An infant born with spina bifida, for instance, has a lesion in the spinal column that usually causes an accumulation of spinal fluid within the brain and thereby leads to mental retardation. In addition, some doctors predict that children born with spina bifida will never walk and will suffer gradually worsening problems of the bowels and bladder. In at least one well-publicized case—that of Baby Jane Doe on Long Island—the doctor in charge also predicted that the child would have a life of constant pain. For all these reasons, infants born with handicaps such as spina bifida should be allowed to die.

EXERCISE 2 USING DEDUCTION

This exercise has three steps: (1) formulate an assumption that could be used in a deductive argument that supports or attacks one of the following propositions; (2) write a syllogism containing the assumption; (3) write a short deductive argument based on the syllogism.

1. All college students should be required to study at least one foreign language.

2. No one convicted of a nonviolent crime should be sent to prison.

3. No animals should be used in laboratory experiments for any reason.

4. The U.S. government should never subsidize a work of art that might be offensive to any member of the country's population.

EXERCISE 3   USING INDUCTION

This exercise has four steps: (1) make a general claim about any one of the topics listed below; (2) make a list of facts that could be used to establish the probability of the claim; (3) explain what assumption links the facts to the claim; (4) use this material to write a brief inductive argument.

abortion	cigarettes
Japanese cars	computers
American cars	part-time jobs
female politicians	unemployment
sexual harrassment	financing a college education

EXERCISE 4   COMBINING INDUCTION AND DEDUCTION

Use induction to strengthen the deductive argument you made in exercise 2.

7.4 AVOIDING FALLACIES   *fal*

Fallacies are mistakes in reasoning. Here are the most common of them.

7.4A ARGUING BY ASSOCIATION

According to Senator Blank, all parents of school-age children should be given vouchers that may be used at any school of their choice. Leading conservatives also support the voucher system. Obviously, therefore, Senator Blank is a conservative.

The fact that Senator Blank shares *one* opinion with leading conservatives does not mean that she shares any other opinions with them. She may disagree with conservatives on every other issue.

7.4B SHIFTING THE MEANING OF A KEY TERM

> Criminals do everything possible to avoid and obstruct arrest, prosecution, and conviction. Likewise, liberal lawyers try in every possible way to obstruct the work of police. They are the ones responsible for things like the Miranda rule, which says that the police can't even interrogate anyone they've arrested until they tell the person what his or her rights are, and if they forget to do so, the case can be thrown out of court. Obviously, then, liberal lawyers are no better than criminals themselves.

This argument uses the word *obstruct* in two different senses. Criminals obstruct the police by hiding out, resisting arrest, or refusing to answer questions. Lawyers obstruct the police only insofar as they demand respect for the constitutional rights of the suspect, who—under the U.S. system of justice—must be presumed innocent until proven guilty. Since the writer uses the word *obstruct* to identify what lawyers and criminals have in common, the shift in the meaning of this key term invalidates the argument.

7.4C BEGGING THE QUESTION (CIRCULAR ARGUMENT)

> Anyone who cannot afford to pay for basic medical care should be treated at government expense, because it's the government's responsibility to see that poor people get the medical help they need.

The second part of this sentence (starting with *because*) is offered as a reason for us to accept the first, but this would-be "reason" is just another way of saying what the writer is trying to prove—which is stated in the first part of the sentence. Rather than proving this point by means of other points, the writer circles back to it in different words. Thus the writer begs us—not persuades us—to accept it.

7.4D FALSE ALTERNATIVE

> If guns are outlawed, only outlaws will have guns.

This slogan assumes that the disarming of all law-abiding citizens—including the police—is the only alternative to allowing everyone to own a gun. But of course there are many other alternatives.

7.4E FALSE ANALOGY

> A college has no right to fire a popular teacher. To do so is like throwing out of office a public official who has just been reelected by a majority of voters. Colleges that fire popular teachers violate the basic principles of democracy.

But a college is not a democracy. While teachers and college administrators like to know what students think of teachers—just as public officials like to know what voters think of them—teaching is not an elective office.

We said earlier in this book that analogy may be used to explain. If you wanted to *explain* what teachers do, you might well compare them to public officials because both groups must be able to speak effectively to various audiences. But you cannot use analogy to argue unless the two things compared are essentially similar. (For more on this point, see section 6.5.)

7.4F PERSONAL ATTACK

> When former president Richard M. Nixon argues that we should increase our trade with China, we must remember that Nixon ended his presidency in disgrace.

This line of would-be reasoning tries to divert our attention from the substance of an argument to the character of the person making it. (Technically, this is arguing *ad hominem*—"to the person.") But there is no necessary connection between the two.

7.4G FALSE CAUSE

> To protect the habitat of the northern spotted owl, a federal judge last month ordered a stop to all logging in old-growth national forests. Now, just one month later, the price of

wholesale lumber is up 30 percent. Is saving the owl worth that much?

This kind of argument equates sequence with causality: because event A (the judge's order) was followed by event B (the price increase), the first caused the second. (Technically, this fallacy is called *post hoc, ergo propter hoc*—"after this, therefore because of it.") But sequence and causality are two different things. By itself, the fact that one event follows another proves nothing at all about a causal link between them.

7.4H IRRELEVANT CONCLUSION

> As everyone knows, the U.S. Constitution gives all American citizens the right to bear arms. Furthermore, there is far too much crime in the streets and subways of our major cities. So anyone faced with a mugger should have the right to kill the mugger on the spot.

After stating a fact and then a common opinion, this writer lurches to an irrelevant conclusion. Neither the right to bear arms nor crime in the streets gives anyone the right to shoot anyone else. To make a persuasive case for the right to retaliate against muggers, the writer should focus on life-threatening situations, which would allow him to introduce the highly relevant topic of self-defense.

7.4I HASTY GENERALIZATION

> Keating won by a landslide, so it is obvious that everyone in the state supports his plan to reduce the deficit in the state budget. Regardless of complaints about what his plan will do to housing for the elderly and other state-supported welfare programs, Keating's plan is clearly what the people want.

In politics, winning by a "landslide" means winning by a decisive majority of the votes cast. Yet this writer tries to identify Keating's supporters with "everyone"—not just with all of the voters, but with all of "the people" in the state, whether or not they voted at all (and whether or not they may be hurt by this plan). This argument would be more persuasive with a restricted claim based on specific evidence, such as the claim that Keating's plan is supported by 58 percent of voters polled about his deficit-reduction plan.

FALLACIES: IN BRIEF

- Arguing by association (if A and B each have the attribute C, A is B) 7.4A

- Shifting the meaning of a key term (7.4B)

- Begging the question (taking for granted what is to be proved) 7.4C

- False alternative (the *only* alternative to A is B) 7.4D

- False analogy (A is like B in some ways, so A is like B in every way) 7.4E

- Personal attack (the argument is bad because the arguer is bad) 7.4F

- False cause (B followed A; therefore, A caused B) 7.4G

- Irrelevant conclusion (7.4H)

- Hasty generalization (7.4I)

EXERCISE 5 SPOTTING, EXPLAINING, AND ELIMINATING FALLACIES

Identify and explain the fallacy in each of the following statements. Then, if you can, eliminate the fallacy by revising the statement. If you can't salvage the argument, say so.

EXAMPLE

Since 1968, when a federal gun control act made it illegal to order a handgun by mail, the crime rate has risen substantially. So any attempt to regulate guns simply aggravates crime.

FALLACY: False cause.

EXPLANATION: This statement does not prove that the gun control act *caused* the increase in the crime rate, even though the increase followed the act. What the first sentence does show is that gun control laws are sometimes ineffectual. So a more workable version of the statement would look as follows:

REVISION: Since 1968, when a federal gun control act made it illegal to order a handgun by mail, the crime rate has risen substantially. Gun control laws, therefore, do not necessarily reduce crime.

1. The U.S. Supreme Court ruled recently that no state could penalize anyone for expressing opinions offensive to members of a particular religion or race. This decision has been applauded by racist organizations such as the American Nazi Party and the Ku Klux Klan. Obviously, therefore, the Supreme Court is racist.

2. "If divorce becomes legal in Ireland, it will spread through the country like the radiation that started at Chernobyl and then covered all of Europe." —Archbishop of Dublin

3. On December 7, 1941, shortly after the United States government received Japanese envoys who had come to discuss peace, the Japanese bombed the U.S. naval base in Pearl Harbor. That event plainly shows that a willingness to discuss peace simply encourages the enemy to attack.

4. The only way to make the tax law truly fair is to cancel all deductions and exemptions. Everyone knows that the government squanders billions of our tax dollars on expensive and unnecessary trips for legislators and their spouses, on lavish official parties, and on military equipment for which the Pentagon is grossly overcharged. Something must be done to stop the waste in government spending.

5. Since we know that cigarette smoking has caused cancer in some cases, it is clearly dangerous to the health of the nation and should be banned altogether.

7.5 TREATING THE OPPOSITION WITH RESPECT

Persuasive writing never appears in a vacuum. It springs not only from the desire to defend a particular belief, but also from the recognition that others hold a contrary belief, that conflicting claims compete for public support—like rival products in the marketplace or rival candidates in a political campaign. If there is no room for disagreement, there is no need for persuasion.

How do you deal with the **opposition** in a persuasive essay? To ignore it entirely is to risk antagonizing the reader or provoking objections that may undermine your argument. To argue effectively, you must first reckon with the opposition, and thereby anticipate objections. You can do one of two things: make concessions or fairly explain the position you plan to oppose.

7.5A MAKING CONCESSIONS

A **concession** is a point granted to the other side: an expression of concern for the feelings of those who may disagree with you, of respect for the reasons that prompt them to do so, or of positive agreement with them on one or more aspects of the topic in dispute. Starting with concession is a good way to overcome the reader's resistance to an unpopular argument and gain a hearing for even the most controversial point of view. Compare these two ways of arguing that everyone applying to college should be interviewed by an admissions officer:

No concessions:

No one should be admitted to college without a personal interview. What can admissions people tell from a piece of paper? They can't really tell anything. Only when they see a student face to face can they decide what kind of a person he or she is.

With concessions:

Admissions officers can tell some things from a piece of paper. They can tell how well a person writes and what he or she is interested in, factors which go a long way toward determining if a student is capable of using the college resources to the fullest extent possible. However, there are things that an application cannot bring forth, things that can only be seen in a personal meeting. The way a person talks, answers questions on the spot, and reacts to certain pieces of information are all important signs of personality which cannot be found on a written piece of paper.

In the second paragraph, the transitional word *However* marks the shift from concession to contrasting assertion. (For another good example of the concessive opening, see page 61, item 6; on transitional words in the paragraph, see section 8.2B.)

7.5B DEFINING THE POSITION YOU WILL OPPOSE

To begin with a concession is to express sympathetic concern for those you plan to disagree with, or even partial agreement with them. But if you see no reason for sympathetic concern or partial agreement, you can nonetheless begin your essay by fairly defining the position you aim to oppose, by letting the reader know that you understand and respect the views of your adversaries. Here is the opening paragraph of an essay written to defend the high salaries of corporate executives:

> Ralph Nader stands at the end of a long line of critics who assail the high incomes of top corporate executives. Nader and his associates suggest that "in the absence of judicial limitations, excessive remuneration has become the norm." They observe that the average top executive in each of the fifty largest industrial corporations earns more salary in a year than many of the corporate employees earn in a lifetime. Salaries are only part (albeit the major part) of the compensation the top executives receive. Bonuses, lavish retirements, stock options, and stock ownership combine to swell the incomes of corporate chief executives by another 50 to 75 percent of the executives' direct remunerations. Nader and his associates conclude that the top corporate executives receive "staggeringly large salaries and stock options."
>
> —Robert Thomas, "Is Corporate Executive Compensation
> Excessive?"

By respectfully defining his adversary's position, Thomas earns the right to a respectful hearing for his own.

You will seldom persuade anyone by simply expressing contempt for the position you oppose:

> Logic, common sense and public opinion are on the side of gun control, but America's firearms fanatics are insufferably relentless. Now, for pete's sake, they want their own political party.
> With their own blind, the gun lovers can offer us candi-

dates promising not a chicken in every pot, but a pistol in every pocket. And carnage in every home. Someone else to vote against.

—Richard J. Roth, "Despite Evidence and Reason, Pro-Gun Talk Won't Go Away"

To describe the opponents of gun control as "firearms fanatics" who promise "a pistol in every pocket" and "carnage in every home" is to antagonize any reader who is not already on the writer's side. This is not persuasive writing; it is a slapdash mix of invective and gross exaggeration. It will rouse the antigun faithful, but it is unlikely to make any converts.

Exercise 6 Making Concessions

Rewrite each of the following arguments in one of two ways: (1) support the writer's point of view but add one or more concessive sentences at the beginning, or (2) argue against the writer's point of view by first making a concession to it and then defending the other side. Whichever you choose to do, be sure to use a transitional word between your concession and the main point you are making.

1. Regional expressions are a hindrance to communication. Each part of the country has adopted many which cannot be found anywhere else. For instance, New England is the only part of the U.S. where you can order a "frappe" in a drugstore or ice cream parlor. Try ordering a frappe in Nebraska and see what kind of reaction you will get. The purpose of language is to make communication possible. By separating regions of the country from each other, nonstandardized forms of expression defeat this purpose.

   —College freshman

2. American restaurants should abolish tipping and do what European restaurants do: add a service charge of 10 to 15 percent to every bill. The service charge would eliminate the worrying and wondering that goes into tipping: the customer worrying about how much to leave, and the waiter or waitress wondering how much is going to be left. Since the tip is always left at the end of the meal, not before, it can't really affect the quality of service provided, and shouldn't be left to chance.

EXERCISE 7 DEFINING A POSITION YOU OPPOSE

Choose from a newspaper, magazine, or any other printed
source an essay written to defend a position that you oppose.
Then, using Thomas's introduction (p. 157) as a guide, write
a paragraph defining this position.

7.6 APPEALING TO THE EMOTIONS

A working knowledge of argumentative technique is indispensable for the writer who wants to persuade. But readers are seldom
persuaded by rational arguments alone. For this reason the writer
should try to understand the reader's feelings and appeal to them.
Though excessive or exclusive appeal to the reader's feelings
weakens an argument, the combination of **emotional appeal** and
rational support can be powerfully persuasive.

Consider the final paragraphs of Stephen Jay Gould's *Mismea-
sure of Man*. In the book as a whole, Gould demonstrates that
biological determination has no basis in fact, that no characteristics of anyone's parents can determine what he or she will
become, and therefore that laws requiring the sterilization of
children born to allegedly feebleminded parents are scientifically
unjustified. After making this argument by strictly rational
means, Gould ends his book by citing the case of Doris Buck,
whose fifty-two-year-old mother had been judged to have a mental age of seven, and who was sterilized under a Virginia law in
1928. Gould writes:

> She later married Matthew Figgins, a plumber. But Doris
> Buck was never informed. "They told me," she recalled, "that
> the operation was for an appendix and rupture." So she and
> Matthew Figgins tried to conceive a child. They consulted
> physicians at three hospitals throughout her child-bearing
> years; no one recognized that her Fallopian tubes had been
> severed. Last year [1979], Doris Buck Figgins discovered the
> cause of her lifelong sadness.
>
> One might invoke an unfeeling calculus and say that
> Doris Buck's disappointment ranks as nothing compared with
> millions of dead in wars to support the designs of madmen or
> the conceits of rulers. But can one measure the pain of a single

dream unfulfilled, the hope of a defenseless woman snatched by public power in the name of an ideology advanced to purify a race? May Doris Buck's simple and eloquent testimony stand for millions of deaths and disappointments and help us to remember that the Sabbath was made for man, not man for the Sabbath: "I broke down and cried. My husband and me wanted children desperately. We were crazy about them. I never knew what they'd done to me."

Given at the very end of a strictly rational, analytic, and mathematically supported argument, the story and the words of Doris Buck powerfully appeal to our emotions. They move us to see that biological determinism is not just scientifically unjustified, but unconscionably cruel.

> **EXERCISE 8 USING EMOTIONAL APPEAL**
>
> From your own experience or the experience of anyone you know, tell a story or describe a situation that could lend emotional appeal to an argument made for or against any one of the following:
>
> 1. company-sponsored daycare centers
> 2. drug testing
> 3. TV commercials aimed at children
> 4. preferential treatment of women or racial minorities in hiring, granting of contracts, or offers of admission
> 5. preferential treatment of athletes applying for admission to college
> 6. the Scholastic Aptitude Test

7.7 USING RHETORICAL QUESTIONS

A rhetorical question is a question asked not to get information but to stir the reader. Typically, a rhetorical question prompts the reader to answer yes or no and thus draws the reader to side with the writer:

Can any goal truly justify the torturing of animals?

Should a woman's self-esteem depend wholly on the size and shape of her body?

With air pollution rising every year, especially in large cities, isn't it high time we started driving electric cars?

But can one measure the pain of a single dream unfulfilled, the hope of a defenseless woman snatched by public power in the name of an ideology advanced to purify a race?

—Stephen Jay Gould

As these examples show, rhetorical questions may appeal to the mind, the feelings, or both. Their chief advantage lies in their provocative impact; they challenge the reader to think or feel in a particular way. But rhetorical questions are not a foolproof means of persuasion because the writer cannot guarantee how the reader will answer them. The question about animals, for instance, is clearly meant to be answered no, but some readers might answer it "Yes, the goal of combating disease in humans." To use a rhetorical question effectively, therefore, you should consider the possibility of more than one answer, and be willing to explain—in statements—why your answer is the right one.

> **EXERCISE 9 USING RHETORICAL QUESTIONS**
>
> Formulate a rhetorical question on a topic of your choice.

7.8 CONSTRUCTING AN ARGUMENTATIVE ESSAY

To see how various methods of argumentation can work together, consider this essay:

SAVING THE CULTURAL ENVIRONMENT

[1] The Earth Summit in Rio de Janeiro that begins this week is a response to the piercing of the ozone layer, the despoiling of rain forests, the polluting of oceans and rivers, the endangering of species from the whales to the spotted owl. But a complete environmentalist should be concerned with more than damage to our natural habitat. Just as vulnerable as nature to a noxious environment are the artifacts of civilization.

Introduction leads up to statement of thesis (claim) in last sentence.

*Conces-
sion:
danger to
Earth itself
seems
more
important
than
danger to
monuments.*

[2] A few years ago the plight of Venice attracted attention, because of the prospect of an enchanting city's being swallowed up by the waters over which it was so ingeniously constructed. But except for Venice, the apocalyptic scenarios that make the headlines tend to deal less with the risk to cultural monuments than with primal threats to the very existence of the Earth.

[3] As the 100 or so world leaders gathered in Rio work out their so-called Agenda 21, the issues of sheer survival must take priority. What is the eroding nose of the Sphinx compared to the greenhouse effect? Yet the havoc wreaked on cherished and irreplaceable masterworks by the vandalism of a polluted environment should not be ignored. The great expressions of culture are themselves integral parts of humankind's moral and spiritual environment.

*Emotional
appeal:
cherished
master-
works
being van-
dalized.*

[4] June, the month of the Earth Summit, is also the month when tourists by the millions begin their pilgrimages to cultural shrines, from medieval cathedrals to Stonehenge, from the Acropolis to the Pyramids. But how many of those who visit Chartres know that Europe's medieval stained-glass windows are turning opaque and slowly disintegrating because they are susceptible to the gases from automobile exhausts and coal-burning factories? Of the 6,000 tourists a day who gaze in awe at the Parthenon, how many are aware of the vandalism committed upon it by the smog rising from Athens, known by the Greeks as "the Cloud"? In Cairo, where the Sphinx crumbles, scholars estimate that up to 90 percent of the historic structures in the city should be classified as in desperate need of restoration—some undermined by sewage leaks, some shaken by the vibration from new construction.

*Evidence
(three
examples),
rhetorical
questions,
and
authorita-
tive esti-
mate cited.*

*Claim
restated as
conclusion,
with final
emotional
appeal in
"precious
treasures."*

[5] Nature knows nothing of national boundaries. A poisoned environment affects all living things on the planet. This is the theme at Rio. Art—built upon the power of symbolism—can and should reinforce the theme, illustrating by every deteriorating work of expression that the toxic byproducts of civilization assault not only nature, but also the precious treasures of civilization itself.

—Editorial, *Christian Science Monitor,*
June 2, 1992

This essay states its claim in the first paragraph and restates it as a conclusion in the final paragraph: our toxic wastes damage masterworks of civilization as much as they damage nature.

Recognizing the opposition that this claim might provoke, the essay makes a concession: combating environmental damage to the Earth itself "must take priority" over combating damage to cultural monuments. But the plight of the monuments is stressed by an emotional appeal on behalf of these "irreplaceable master-works" that are parts of our "moral and spiritual environment."

After making this emotional appeal, the essay presents its evidence: environmental pollution is now seriously damaging three major cultural monuments in different parts of the world. These examples are presented with the aid of two rhetorical questions and an authoritative estimate.

So the basic argumentative strategy here is induction, with an implied deduction standing behind it:

> IMPLIED ASSUMPTION: If pollution is damaging major monu-ments in different parts of the world, then it threatens not only nature but also the masterworks of civilization, which are essential to our moral and spiritual environment.

> EVIDENCE: Pollution is damaging the medieval stained-glass windows of Europe, the Parthenon in Athens, and the Sphinx in Cairo.

> CONCLUSION: Pollution threatens not only nature but also the masterworks of civilization, which are essential to our moral and spiritual environment.

Since the implied assumption is credible, and since the evidence is both reliable and relevant to the conclusion, the argument is plausible. Together with the emotional appeal made in the third paragraph, the final appeal to our feelings helps to make this essay persuasive.

EXERCISE 10 COMPOSING AN ARGUMENTATIVE ESSAY

Using at least ten of the following items plus any others that you can gather from printed sources, compose an argumentative essay that defends or attacks the need for more gun-control laws. The argument should be chiefly based on evidence and assumptions, but you may reinforce it with one or more emotional appeals, and you should reckon with the opposition before introducing your claim.

When you have written the essay, identify as well as you can the assumptions it makes—both explicit and implicit.

1. Lincoln, McKinley, and John F. Kennedy were all killed by guns. No American president has ever been stabbed or clubbed to death.

2. Article II of the United States Bill of Rights says, "A well-regulated militia being necessary to the security of a free state, the right of the people to keep and bear arms shall not be infringed."

3. There are now almost 200 million guns in the United States, and 50 million of those are handguns.

4. According to a report released in March 1993 by the National Center for Health Statistics, the rate at which American teens (aged 15–19) were killed by guns nearly doubled from 1985 to 1990, rising from 13.3 per 100,000 to 23.5 per 100,000.

5. Rifle and shotgun barrels can be sawed off with a fifty-nine-cent hacksaw blade, and the resulting weapons are more lethal than most handguns.

6. John F. Kennedy, assassinated by rifle shots in 1963, was a member of the National Rifle Association who strongly believed in the citizens' right to bear arms.

7. Theodore Roosevelt, who was wounded by a pistol shot in the chest while making a speech, recovered from the wound and afterward joined the National Rifle Association, which he staunchly supported.

8. Guns are used in 250,000 crimes each year, and 20,000 of those are homicides.

9. A 1968 report by the National Commission on the Causes and Prevention of Violence said that for every burglar stopped by a gun, four gun owners or members of their families are killed in firearm accidents.

10. Hunters kill an estimated 200 million birds and 50 million other animals each year.

11. Public opinion polls show that 70 percent of Americans favor gun registration and slightly over 50 percent favor an absolute ban.

12. The worst mass murder on record in the city of Buffalo during this century was committed with a knife and hatchet.

13. According to the Uniform Crime Reports issued by the FBI in August 1992, the number of juveniles (aged 10–17) committing murder with guns increased by 79 percent from 1980 to 1990. In 1990, almost 75 percent of youthful murderers used a firearm.

14. The National Rifle Association claims that legislation designed to restrict criminals' access to firearms will also curtail the rights of law-abiding citizens.

15. Together with the federal gun control act of 1968, many state laws already regulate ownership of handguns. In the states of New York and Massachusetts, for instance, persons convicted of carrying unlicensed handguns—regardless of what they are carried for—must go to jail for a year.

16. Statistics indicate that 995 of 1,000 handgun owners are safe, responsible, law-abiding citizens.

17. On February 25, 1993, the Virginia General Assembly passed a bill that restricts the purchase of handguns to one gun per person per month.

18. Former President Reagan, a lifelong member of the NRA and himself wounded by gunfire in an attempted assassination, favored a bill that would have imposed a national seven-day waiting period on all handgun purchases. This would allow local police to investigate the buyer.

19. In 1987, there were 166 times more handgun murders in the United States than in Canada, where the purchase and carrying of handguns are severely restricted.

20. In January 1989, a psychopath wielding an imitation AK-47 assault rifle killed five schoolchildren in Stockton, California.

21. High-powered semiautomatic rifles can fire thirty rounds in a clip. About 50,000 of these weapons in the United States are privately owned.

22. In the year 1990 in Texas, deaths from firearms were 20

per 100,000 people. That exceeded the number of people killed in auto accidents.

23. In October 1991, a crazed gunman in Killeen, Texas, murdered twenty-two people with a Glock 9-millimeter semiautomatic pistol and a Ruger P89.

24. In 1991, gunshots killed 74 people in Japan—67 of them with ties to organized crime. In the same year, according to the FBI, gunshots killed 24,000 in the United States, which has roughly twice the population of Japan.

25. In October 1992, a sixteen-year-old Japanese exchange student was shot to death by a Louisiana homeowner when the student was mistaken for an intruder after ringing the doorbell. In May 1993, a Baton Rouge jury acquitted the homeowner of murder.

26. In March 1993, in the face of intense lobbying by the National Rifle Association, the New Jersey Senate voted 26 to 0 to sustain Governor Jim Florio's veto of a measure that would have weakened the state's ban on semi-automatic assault weapons. Passed in 1990, the ban is considered the toughest gun-control law in the United States.

27. In November 1993 Congress passed the Brady Bill, which requires a five-day waiting period for the purchase of handguns. The National Rifle Association strongly opposes this waiting period and lobbied against the bill.

28. According to a study published in the October 7, 1993, issue of the *New England Journal of Medicine,* homicides are more likely to occur in households that have guns than in households that don't. Rather than protecting families from intruders, guns increase the chances that one family member or acquaintance will kill another.

29. A 1993 survey conducted by criminologist Gary Kleck of Florida State University showed that guns of all types are used defensively in the United States between 850,000 and 2.5 million times a year. Most of the guns used defensively are handguns, and rather than being fired, they are simply brandished to scare away an attacker.

30. In a recent study of incarcerated felons made by the National Institute of Justice, 38 percent said that they had decided not to commit a particular crime because they were afraid the potential victim might be armed.

8

Writing Paragraphs

A **paragraph** is usually a block of sentences set off by spacing or indentation at the beginning. Though commonly part of an essay, it can and sometimes does serve as an essay in its own right, and the writing of one-paragraph essays will give you small-scale practice in organization. For that reason, much of this chapter deals with the single paragraph as a self-contained unit.

But just as you learn how to relate the separate sentences of a paragraph, you should learn also how to relate the separate paragraphs of an essay, and how to move from one paragraph to another. So this chapter shows you how to do both—after first explaining why writers use paragraphs and then how to organize them.

8.1 WHY USE PARAGRAPHS?

Part of the answer to this question is that an essay is like a long stairway. Unless it is interrupted now and then as if by a landing, a place to stop before continuing, the reader may simply get tired or bored. Have you ever turned the page of a book or an article to find nothing but a solid block of print? Did you heave a little sigh, or a big one? That's because you expect to *see* paragraph breaks at regular intervals, especially where the writer's thought turns. Compare these two ways of presenting the same passage:

Movement of tribes

1. [At one time the migrants] had set forth in tribes. They wandered across the steppe or edged out of the forests down to the plains with wives and children and cattle in the long columns of all their possessions. Home was where they were and movement did not disrupt the usual order of their ways. It was quite otherwise in human experience when some among the Europeans of the sixteenth and seventeenth centuries migrated. Often it was a man alone, an individual, who went, one who in going left home, that is, cut himself apart from the associations and attachments that until then had given meaning to his life. Some inner restlessness or external compulsion sent such wanderers away solitary on a personal quest to which they gave various names, such as fortune or salvation.

No break marks shift in focus

Movement of individuals

2. [At one time the migrants] had set forth in tribes. They wandered across the steppe or edged out of the forests down to the plains with wives and children and cattle in the long columns of all their possessions. Home was where they were and movement did not disrupt the usual order of their ways.

New paragraph marks shift in focus

It was quite otherwise in human experience when some among the Europeans of the sixteenth and seventeenth centuries migrated. Often it was a man alone, an individual, who went, one who in going left home, that is, cut himself apart from the associations and attachments that until then had given meaning to his life. Some inner restlessness or external compulsion sent such wanderers away solitary on a personal quest to which they gave various names, such as fortune or salvation.   —Oscar Handlin, *Nationality in American Life*

EXERCISE 1 DIVIDING A PASSAGE INTO PARAGRAPHS

In the following passage from Loren Eiseley's "Man of the Future," we have deliberately run the author's original three paragraphs into one. Divide the passage into what you think were Eiseley's original three paragraphs, and state the main point of each.

There are days when I find myself unduly pessimistic about the future of man. Indeed, I will confess that there have been occasions when I swore I would never again make the study of time a profession. My walls are lined with books expounding its mysteries; my hands have been split and rubbed raw with   5 grubbing into the quicklime of its waste bins and hidden crevices. I have stared so much at death that I can recognize the lingering personalities in the faces of skulls and feel accompanying affinities and repulsions. One such skull lies in the lockers of a great metropolitan museum. It is labeled simply: 10 Strandlooper, South Africa. I have never looked longer into any human face than I have upon the features of that skull. I come there often, drawn in spite of myself. It is a face that would lend reality to the fantastic tales of our childhood. There is a hint of Wells' *Time Machine* folk in it—those 15 pathetic, childlike people whom Wells pictures as haunting earth's autumnal cities in the far future of the dying planet. Yet this skull has not been spirited back to us through future eras by a time machine. It is a thing, instead, of the millennial past. It is a caricature of modern man, not by reason of its 20 primitiveness but, startlingly, because of a modernity outreaching his own. It constitutes, in fact, a mysterious prophecy and warning. For at the very moment in which students of humanity have been sketching their concept of the man of the future, that being has already come, and lived, and passed 25 away.

EXERCISE 2 BUILDING PARAGRAPHS

In the following passage from a student's essay about a character in a short story, some of the paragraphs are too short. Combine them so that each new paragraph marks a turn in the writer's thought.

Humble Jewett reveals his love of natural beauty in several ways.

When he and Amarantha reach the crest of the hill, he kneels down and prays to the Creator. He is moved to worship by the sight of the sunlight lining the distant treetops.

He has a similar reaction later in the story as he is walking to Wyker's house. He is so awestruck by the splendor of the sunset that he doesn't notice the wound in his leg.

The sight of human beauty also casts a spell. He wants to kiss Amarantha, yet he holds back, restrained by her loveliness. It's as if he chooses to keep such radiant beauty pure, within his sight but beyond his reach.

8.2 DIRECTION ¶ *d*

A **well-directed paragraph** guides the reader from beginning to end. It follows the lead of its opening sentence and turns from that lead only after giving a clear signal. To write a well-directed paragraph, therefore, **forecast your main point** and **signal your turns.**

8.2A FORECASTING YOUR MAIN POINT

To forecast the main point of a paragraph, start with a **lead sentence**—a sentence that tells the reader where you are headed. The lead sentence is sometimes the **topic sentence** of the paragraph, the sentence that states its main point. But not every good paragraph begins with a topic sentence, and in some paragraphs the main point is merely implied. So a lead sentence can do its forecasting in any one of the following ways:

1. Stating the main point

> *Ellie and I had come to the mine earlier that day for adventure.* When we got there, the sun was shining on the remote dunes, stained red with copper sediment. An old, chillingly frank sign warned us "Danger: Keep Out!" Undaunted, I peered into the mine. The walls bulged as if they were going to fall down, blocking my view of the bottom. Ellie, who had been to the mine several times before, said she thought it was over a hundred feet deep. Carefully we worked our way down into the chasm, lowering ourselves inch by inch until we finally reached the bottom. We spent hours scaling the walls, exploring the caves, and marveling at the vastness of the mine.
>
> —Andrea Lyle

2. Stating the topic

> *I have grown fond of semicolons in recent years.* The semicolon tells you that there is still some question about the preceding full sentence; something needs to be added; it reminds you sometimes of Greek usage. It is almost always a greater pleasure to come across a semicolon than a period. The period tells you that that is that; if you didn't get all the meaning you wanted or expected, anyway you got all the writer intended to

parcel out and now you have to move along. But with a semicolon there you get a pleasant little feeling of expectancy; there
is more to come; read on; it will get clearer.
                    —Lewis Thomas, "Notes on Punctuation"

The lead sentence announces the topic (semicolons) and thus leads
up to the main point, which comes at the end.

3. Asking a question

Can you remember tying on your shoes this morning? Could you
give the rules for when it is proper to call another person by
his first name? Could you describe the gestures you make in
conversation? These examples illustrate how much of our
behavior is "out of awareness," and how easy it is to get into
trouble in another culture.
                    —Edward T. Hall, "The Anthropology of Manners"

The opening question initiates a series of questions that lead to
the main point, which (once again) appears at the end.

4. Setting a new direction

. . . When my father sent love letters to my mother, my
grandmother would open and hide them, and when my
mother told her parents she was going to marry this man, my
grandmother said if that happened, it would kill her.
Not likely, of course. My grandmother is a woman who used
to crack Brazil nuts open with her teeth, a woman who once
lifted a car off the ground, when there was an accident and it
had to be moved. She has been representing her death as imminent ever since I've known her—twenty-five years—and has
discussed, at length, the distribution of her possessions and
her lamb coat. Every time we said goodbye, after our annual
visit to Winnipeg, she'd weep and say she'd never see us again.
But in the meantime, while every relative of her generation,
and a good many of the younger ones, has died (usually nursed
by her), she has kept making knishes, shopping for bargains,
tending the healthiest plants I've ever seen.
                    —Joyce Maynard, "Four Generations"

Here the lead sentence forecasts the main point of the paragraph
simply by setting a new direction. The main point of the para-

graph is nowhere stated in a topic sentence but is nonetheless clearly implied: my grandmother knows how to survive.

8.2B Signaling Turns: Transitions within the Paragraph
trans/wp

Transitional words and phrases guide readers through a paragraph by signaling turns in thought, shifts in viewpoint, or movement from one point to another. Use transitional words and phrases for

1. Marking time

> Technology makes life easier for everyone. *A hundred years ago* a man would have to take a horse-drawn carriage to deliver his produce to market. *Now* he can drive a truck.
>
> —College freshman

2. Marking addition

> Different as they were—in background, in personality, in underlying aspiration—[Grant and Lee] had much in common. Under everything else, they were marvelous fighters. *Furthermore,* their fighting qualities were really very much alike. —Bruce Catton, *A Stillness at Appomattox*

3. Pointing up conflict or contrast

> At many universities across the country, more than half the students in each entering class plan on entering med school. *But* there just aren't enough spaces for them.
>
> —College freshman

You can also point up contrast by sharp variation of any kind:

> Most Americans have never had to live with terror. *I had to live with it all my life*—the psychological terror of segregation, in which there was a special set of laws governing your movements. —Mary Mebane, "The Back of the Bus"

4. Marking the shift from cause to effect

> The world of religion and philosophy was shocked recently when Henry P. Van Dusen and his wife ended their

lives by their own hands. Dr. Van Dusen had been president of Union Theological Seminary; for more than a quarter-century he had been one of the luminous names in Protestant theology. He enjoyed world status as a spiritual leader. News of the self-inflicted deaths of the Van Dusens, *therefore,* was profoundly disturbing to all those who attach a moral stigma to suicide and regard it as a violation of God's laws.

—Norman Cousins, "The Right to Die"

5. Marking likeness (comparing)

Geniuses have an uncanny power to defy physical handicaps and create masterpieces in the face of obstacles that might overwhelm the rest of us. John Milton was blind when he wrote the greatest of English epics, *Paradise Lost. Likewise,* Beethoven was deaf when he composed some of his greatest symphonies.

6. Marking numerical order

Churchill had many reasons for cooperating with Stalin during the Second World War. *For one,* Stalin was battling the Germans on the Eastern front and thus reducing German pressure on England. *Second,* Russia had power, and in the face of German aggression, England needed powerful allies. *Finally,* Churchill's hatred of Hitler consumed all other feelings. Though Stalin made him uneasy, Churchill said once that to destroy Hitler, he would have made a pact with the devil himself.

Use numerical markers sparingly. A succession of numbered sentences soon becomes boring.

7. Marking spatial order

The once-a-year sale had apparently drawn just about everyone in town to Gerry's department store. *To the left* of the main entrance, the three-acre parking lot was jammed with bicycles, cars, motorcycles, and pickup trucks. *To the right,* a line of people stretched down East Main Street for six blocks, making it almost impossible for everyone else to negotiate the narrow sidewalk.

TRANSITIONAL WORDS AND PHRASES: A SELECTIVE LIST

TO MARK A SHIFT IN TIME

a few weeks ago
two years ago
previously
earlier
in the past
before
at present
now
nowadays
meanwhile
in the future
later
eventually

TO MARK A SHIFT FROM CAUSE TO EFFECT

therefore
hence
as a result
consequently
accordingly

TO MARK SPATIAL ORDER

nearby
in the distance
below
above
in front
in back
to the right
to the left

TO MARK ADDITION

besides
moreover
in addition
furthermore

TO SIGNAL CONFLICT OR CONTRAST

but
nevertheless
however
conversely
on the other hand
still
otherwise
in contrast
unfortunately
instead

TO COMPARE

likewise
similarly

TO MARK NUMERICAL ORDER

first, second, etc.
in the first place
secondly, thirdly, etc.
to begin with, next, finally

EXERCISE 3 FORECASTING YOUR MAIN POINT

In the following passage by a college freshman, we have deleted the opening sentence of paragraph 3. Write a sentence that forecasts its main point.

[1] Going to college for most people means the onset of new freedoms and many responsibilities. In my first semester of college, new responsibilities helped me to develop values and maturity. This opportunity to mature is what drew me to college in the first place, and I especially felt the change in myself when the semester ended. Upon returning home for the Christmas holidays, I experienced new freedoms and respect from my parents.

[2] Before I went to college, I lived under their watchful eyes. My father pried me from the TV set whenever he knew I had homework to do, and my mother made sure I ate something besides hamburgers and pizza at least once a day. They also took turns reminding me to wear whatever I needed to keep me warm and dry whenever it was wet or cold. Most important of all, they never let me out of the house at night without asking where I was bound and setting a time for my return.

[3] Since no one checked me in or out, I could stay up all night if I chose. I could eat pizza till I looked like one, and I could watch TV till my eyes glazed over. Starting college, in fact, was like being a child in the middle of a candy store. Everywhere I turned I found an exotic treat, something I wanted to taste. But I couldn't taste everything, much less consume it all. To get any work done, I had to learn how to say no to myself.

EXERCISE 4 SIGNALING TURNS WITHIN THE PARAGRAPH

At one or more points in each of the following passages a transitional word or phrase is missing. Find the points and insert suitable transitions.

1. The group that led the campaign against gay rights in Florida held the belief that homosexuality is immoral and that, once allowed in an area, it would lead to a breakdown of the values of a society. Homosexuality has existed throughout the past. Some of the world's greatest geniuses have professed to be homosexuals. These men have made great contributions to society. Whether one agrees that their practices were immoral or not, one must respect the contributions of men such as Michelangelo and Tchaikovsky.

—College student

2. Higher education in America has hit a new low. In liberal-arts colleges, the abolition of many or even all specific requirements for graduation has left students to find their own way, which is often a closed alley. Allowed to take any courses they want, many students concentrate on just one subject or specialized skill. They graduate with narrow minds.

3. Revolution and moderation seldom go hand in hand. In the early years of the French Revolution, the moderate Girondists were outmaneuvered by the bloodthirsty Jacobins, who launched a reign of terror. Within months after the moderate Mensheviks launched the Russian Revolution of 1917, the radical Bolsheviks seized power and established a government of ruthless repression.

4. In the seventeenth century, a voyage across the Atlantic took more than two months. A supersonic plane does the trip in three hours.

8.3 COHERENCE   ¶ *coh*

Coherence is the verbal thread that binds one sentence to another. When a paragraph is coherent, the reader can see a continuous line of thought passing from one sentence to the next. When a paragraph is incoherent, the sentences are discontinuous, and readers may lose their way. You can strengthen the coherence of a paragraph by using list structure or chain structure.

8.3A USING LIST STRUCTURE

List structure uses a sequence of sentences with the same basic pattern to develop a general point, which is usually stated in the first sentence. Each sentence is a new item in a list of examples:

They were a diverse group. *There were* priests *who* had brooded over the problem of a world in eternity and made the startling discovery that a holy mission summoned them away. *There were* noblemen in the great courts *who* stared out beyond the formal lines of the garden and saw the vision of new empires to be won. *There were* young men without places *who* depended on daring and their swords and were willing to soldier for their fortunes. *There were* clerks in the countinghouses, impatient of the endless rows of digits, *who* thought why should they not reach out for the wealth that set their masters high? *There were* journeymen without employment and servants without situations and peasants without land and many others whom war or pestilence displaced *who* dreamed in desperation of an alternative to home. Through the eighteenth century their numbers grew and, even more, through the nineteenth. —Oscar Handlin, *Race and Nationality in American Life*

EXERCISE 5 USING LIST STRUCTURE

Develop the following paragraph by adding to it at least three more examples in sentences that repeat the italicized words:

As I jogged along the highway early this morning, *I thought* of all the different roads my friends from high school were starting on. *I thought* of Ruth, *who* was headed for Syracuse to major in broadcast journalism.

8.3B USING CHAIN STRUCTURE

Another way of ensuring coherence in your paragraphs is to make your sentences form a **chain.** As long as each new sentence is linked in meaning to the sentence before it, the reader can readily follow your line of thought:

The process of learning is essential to our lives. All higher animals seek it deliberately. They are inquisitive and they experiment. An experiment is a sort of harmless trial run of some action which we shall have to make in the real world; and this, whether it is made in the laboratory by scientists or by fox-cubs outside their earth. The scientist experiments and the cub plays; both are learning to correct their errors of judgment in a setting in which errors are not fatal. Perhaps this is what gives them both their air of happiness and freedom in these activities. —Jacob Bronowski, *The Common Sense of Science*

The sentences in this paragraph are connected like the links in a chain:

LEAD SENTENCE: The process of learning is essential to our lives.
A. All higher animals seek it deliberately.
B. They are inquisitive and they experiment.
C. An experiment is a sort of harmless trial run of some action which we shall have to make in the real world; and this, whether it is made in the laboratory by scientists or by fox-cubs outside their earth.
D. The scientist experiments and the cub plays; both are learning to correct their errors of judgment in a setting in which errors are not fatal.
E. Perhaps this is what gives them both their air of happiness and freedom in these activities.

Only the second sentence is directly linked to the lead sentence; each of the others is linked in meaning to the sentence just before it.

For the writer, the advantage of chain structure is that each sentence tends to suggest or generate the next sentence. The idea of the process of learning leads to the idea of learners (*All higher animals*); *animals* leads to a comment on what they do (*experiment*); *experiment* leads to a definition of that term (*An experiment is a sort . . .*), and so on. When you use chain structure, you are not free to forget about the topic sentence entirely, but you are free to experiment, to pursue the trail opened up by your own sentences, and even to discover something you did not foresee when you wrote the topic sentence. When Jacob Bronowski started this paragraph with a sentence about the process of learning, did he expect to end the paragraph with a sentence about happiness and freedom?

EXERCISE 6 USING CHAIN STRUCTURE

Using chain structure, develop one of the following paragraphs by adding at least three more sentences to it. Be sure that each new sentence is linked to the one before it.

1. LEAD SENTENCE: In recent years, letter writing has been dramatically changed by the fax machine.

A. A fax machine can send a letter to its destination in a tiny fraction of the time required for delivery by mail.

2. LEAD SENTENCE: The federal government estimates that approximately 28 million American adults are functionally illiterate.

A. A person who is functionally illiterate cannot understand such ordinary pieces of writing as recipes, labels on medicine bottles, instructions for the use of an appliance, and applications.

8.3C COMBINING LIST STRUCTURE AND CHAIN STRUCTURE

The following paragraph by a college freshman shows how list structure and chain structure can work together:

> Going home for the Christmas vacation gave me the chance to see my life at college in a new light. At home, relatives and friends asked me how I liked the school and my classmates. I answered most of their questions with one-word responses, but I also questioned myself. Had I made any real friends? Did I like the campus atmosphere? Did I enjoy my courses as well as learn from them? As I thought about these questions, I realized that every one of them had a two-sided answer. I had picked up many acquaintances, but I could not yet call anyone my friend. I liked the general atmosphere of the campus, but disliked its conservative air. I enjoyed my courses, but felt many self-doubts. I had to admit to myself that I had no settled opinion about anything at college. I was still finding my way.
> —Adam Usadi

Basically, this paragraph uses a chain structure with two lists attached to it—a list of questions and a list of answers:

LEAD SENTENCE: Going ⌐home⌐ for the Christmas vacation gave me the chance to see my life at college in a new light.

A. At ⌐home,⌐ relatives and friends ⌐asked⌐ me how I liked the school and my classmates.

  B. I answered most of their ⌐questions⌐ with one-word responses, but I also questioned myself.

    1. Had I made any real friends?

    2. Did I like the campus atmosphere?

    3. Did I enjoy my courses as well as learn from them?

      C. As I thought about these questions, I realized that every one of them had a two-sided ⌐answer.⌐

        1. I had picked up many acquaintances, but I could not yet call anyone my friend.

        2. I liked the general atmosphere of the campus, but disliked its conservative air.

        3. I enjoyed my courses, but I felt many ⌐self-doubts.⌐

          D. I had to admit to myself that I had ⌐no settled opinion⌐ about anything at college.

          E. I was ⌐still finding my way.⌐

EXERCISE 7 USING LIST AND CHAIN STRUCTURE TOGETHER

Expand the following paragraph by using a combination of list and chain structure to add supporting points. (Doing this exercise may require some reading.)

LEAD SENTENCE: The strongest weapon we can use in the war against AIDS is knowledge of the way it spreads.

A. For one thing, it can spread from a mother to her unborn child.

  1. If a woman is infected, her child has a 50 percent chance of inheriting the virus.

  2. So any woman who thinks that she could be infected should be tested for the virus before she considers having a child.

B. Secondly, it can spread from a drug needle.

8.3D STRENGTHENING WEAK CONNECTIONS

Separately or together, list structure and chain structure can help you develop a paragraph as well as hold it together. Most important, practice with each kind of structure can help you gain a sense of coherence—the ability to see at once whether or not a set of sentences makes continuous sense. Consider this set:

> I enjoy watching my son grow up. Children are a tremendous challenge. I read to him and try to let him be as creative as possible.

This passage is perfectly coherent until we reach the third sentence. To understand what *him* refers to, we have to leap back over *Children* in the second sentence to *my son* in the first. How can the gap be closed? One way is to rearrange the sentences:

> Children are a tremendous challenge. I enjoy watching my son grow up. I read to him and try to let him be as creative as possible.

Now we can see at once what *him* refers to. But since *watching* is hardly a tremendous challenge, the link between the first two sentences is weak, and it cannot be repaired by any further rearrangement. In this case, the writer must remove the sentence about watching her son grow up (she might use it elsewhere in her essay) and replace that sentence with one explaining the challenge:

> Children are a tremendous challenge. I try to answer all the questions my son asks. I read to him and encourage his creativity as much as possible.

Whenever you can't repair a link by simply rearranging sentences, add whatever new material is needed to make your points cohere.

8.4 EMPHASIZING YOUR MAIN POINT

You can emphasize the **main point** of a paragraph by repeating key words or by placing the main point at the beginning or end.

8.4A REPEATING KEY WORDS OR PHRASES

You may have been told that you should never repeat a word or phrase when you write, that you should scour your brain or your thesaurus for synonyms to avoid using a word or phrase again. That is nonsense. If repetition gets out of control, it will soon become monotonous and boring. But selective repetition keeps the eye of the reader on your main point. Compare these two paragraphs:

Uncontrolled repetition

As a student begins her last year of high school, she may start to wonder what college or university is right for her. She will usually apply to several schools for *admission*. At _____ College, the student actually *exchanges* information on herself through her *application* and other forms and interviews for information about the school. It is through a *fair admissions process* that _____ College and its candidates for entrance learn a lot about each other. This *fair exchange* of ideas and insight in the *admissions process* can be seen through the college's *application* for *admission,* the guidance counselor forms, and the alumni *interview*. —College freshman

Selective repetition

To me the *interview* comes as close as possible to being the quintessence of proper admissions procedure. It is a well-known secret (to use a paradox) that one can study for the achievement tests and the S.A.T. From personal experience I also know that schools "pad" grades and that students can receive marvelous grades without one iota of knowledge in a subject. One cannot, however, "fudge" an *interview*. One can buy a new suit and put on false airs, but 999 times out of 1,000 the *interviewer* can easily unmask the fraud and can thus reveal the true person. —College freshman

8.4B PLACING THE MAIN POINT

You can emphasize a point by putting it at the beginning or the end of a paragraph, or in both places—provided you don't simply repeat it. The last sentence of this paragraph, for instance, not only recalls the meaning of the first one but adds something new:

It seems to me that the safest and most prudent of bets to lay money on is surprise. There is a very high probability that whatever astonishes us in biology today will turn out to be usable, and useful, tomorrow. This, I think, is the established record of science itself, over the past two hundred years, and we ought to have more confidence in the process. It worked this way for the beginnings of chemistry; we obtained electricity in this manner; using surprise as a guide, we progressed from Newtonian physics to electro-magnetism, to quantum mechanics and contemporary geophysics and cosmology. In biology, evolution and genetics were the earliest big astonishments, but what has been going on in the past quarter century is simply flabbergasting. For medicine, the greatest surprises lie still ahead of us, but they are there, waiting to be discovered or stumbled over, sooner or later.

—Lewis Thomas, "Medical Lessons from History"

8.5 PARAGRAPHING IN ACTION: REARRANGING SENTENCES

Now that you have seen how good paragraphs are put together, consider a passage that badly needs paragraph structure:

[1] My life has been a very satisfying one so far. [2] I've faced many challenges and attained some of the goals I've set. [3] I am one of five children. [4] I have two older sisters and two younger brothers. [5] My father was a successful chef. [6] He had a college degree in electrical engineering, but chose to study cooking instead. [7] He traveled in Europe and worked with many different chefs. [8] He had a great influence on all of our lives. [9] He showed me what determination and hard work could do for a person. [10] My mother was a good mother. [11] She guided me in a very practical way. [12] I was able to learn and grow under their supervision. [13] At times, it's hard to attain confidence in some situations, but I think of my parents and continue on. [14] I enjoy knitting and making things for others and I also love to cook. [15] Preparing economical meals is a constant challenge. [16] I like to read a lot. [17] I also enjoy watching my son grow up. [18] Children are a tremendous challenge. [19] I read to him and try to let him be as creative as possible. [20] I have also helped my husband go through his last year of college. [21] It was a

proud moment for me to watch him walk up and get his degree. [22] I enjoyed working with him and learning as he did. [23] You really get a good feeling when you've helped someone. [24] Your rewards are twofold. [25] Helping others is my main goal in life. [26] I enjoy people. [27] So far, my life has been satisfactory to me. [28] I've got future goals set to attain. [29] I've got lots of hard work ahead of me. [30] I just look forward to going day by day and getting further toward my one goal of a college education with a challenging job.

The only thing that makes this set of sentences a "paragraph" is the indentation at the beginning. Every sentence here makes sense in itself, but reading these sentences one after the other is like trying to keep up with a kangaroo. The writer moves in short, sudden leaps, and the reader never knows where she will land next. She goes from challenges and goals to sisters and brothers, from parents to knitting and cooking, from helping others to helping herself. What point is she trying to make? She herself seems unsure. To reorganize a jumble like this, she must think about the connections and the differences between her sentences, and she must decide what her main point is. Only then can she write a paragraph that makes sense.

Rereading these sentences in the light of what you know about paragraph structure, you may see that there is matter here for at least two paragraphs: one on the writer's childhood and the influence of her parents, the other on her life and goals as a wife, mother, and college student. This division in the material becomes obvious if you examine the links between the sentences. The first sentence looks like a lead sentence, and the second is connected to it, but the third sentence has nothing to do with *challenges* and *goals,* and not until sentence 15 does either of those words appear again. Sentences 3–13 are really a detour from the road that the first two sentences open up, and therefore need to be taken out and reorganized under a topic sentence of their own.

Sentences 3–13 can be used to make a paragraph because they all concern the same topic—the writer's childhood and her parents. But to develop a paragraph from these sentences, the writer will first have to identify one of them as a lead sentence, a sentence that can state or forecast the main point of the whole group. A likely candidate is sentence 12: *I was able to learn and grow under their supervision.* To make this sentence work at the beginning of the paragraph, the writer will have to change *their* to *my parents'.* She will then have the start of a paragraph:

I was able to learn and grow under my parents' supervision.

Now see how this lead sentence can help the writer organize the other sentences in the 3–13 group:

LEAD SENTENCE: I was able to learn and grow under my parents' supervision.

3. I am one of five children.
4. I have two older sisters and two younger brothers.
5. My father was a successful chef.
6. He had a college degree in electrical engineering, but chose to study cooking instead.
7. He traveled in Europe and worked with many different chefs.
8. He had a great influence on all of our lives.
9. He showed me what determination and hard work could do for a person.
10. My mother was a good mother.
11. She guided me in a very practical way.
13. At times, it's hard to attain confidence in some situations, but I think of my parents and continue on.

There are still some problems here. The lead sentence forecasts a discussion of the writer's parents, but sentences 3 and 4 concern her brothers and sisters. Though the brothers and sisters are obviously related to the writer's parents, they are not connected with her parents' supervision of her, or—except in the phrase *our lives* (sentence 8)—with their influence on her. When sentences 3 and 4 are cut out, you actually begin to see a paragraph taking shape:

I was able to learn and grow under my parents' supervision.
5. My father was a successful chef.

The writer now has a definite link between the topic sentence and the one that follows it. In fact, she has the beginnings of a paragraph combining list structure and chain structure:

LEAD SENTENCE: I was able to learn and grow under my parents' supervision. [formerly sentence 12]

1. A. My father had a great influence on my life. [8, with *all of our lives* changed to *my life*]
   B. He showed me what determination and hard work could do for a person. [9]
   C. He had a college degree in electrical engineering, but chose to study cooking instead. [6]
   D. He traveled in Europe and worked with many different chefs. [7]
   E. He was a successful chef. [5]
2. A. My mother was a good mother. [10]
   B. She guided me in a very practical way. [11]

CONCLUDING SENTENCE: At times, it's hard to attain confidence in some situations, but I think of my parents and continue on. [13]

With the basic structure of the paragraph established, the writer can improve it further by adding transitional words and combining some of the sentences:

LEAD SENTENCE: I was able to learn and grow under my parents' supervision.

1. A. My father had a great influence on me *because* he showed me what determination and hard work could do for a person.
   B. He had a college degree in electrical engineering, but chose to study cooking instead, traveling in Europe and working with many different chefs.
   C. He *thus became* a successful chef *himself*.
2. A. My mother was a good mother *who* guided me in a very practical way.

CONCLUDING SENTENCE: At times, it's hard to attain confidence in some situations, but I think of my parents and continue on.

There is still room for development in this paragraph. To balance the chain of sentences about the father, the writer should say more about the mother, explaining how she gave guidance and what she taught. Specific statements here would enrich the paragraph and clarify the meaning of the topic sentence.

Shaping the rest of the original passage into paragraph form is harder. For one thing, there is no obvious lead sentence. Nearly all of the other sentences concern the writer's challenges and goals, but no one sentence on this subject forecasts the rest in the way that sentence 12 forecasts sentences 5–13. The writer speaks of past goals in sentences 1–2, 20–24, and 27, of present challenges and satisfactions in sentences 14–19 and 26, and of future goals in sentences 28–30. Most revealingly, she does not seem to know whether her main goal is helping others (sentence 25) or helping herself (sentence 30), or what the relation between these goals might be. Before she can write a coherent paragraph on her goals, she will have to do some more thinking and decide just what they are.

EXERCISE 8 EXPANDING A PARAGRAPH

Expand the final version of the paragraph given above by inserting at least two sentences about the mother after sentence 2.A.

EXERCISE 9 FORMING A PARAGRAPH

Choose a lead sentence from the following list and rearrange the remaining sentences to complete a paragraph, combining them and adding words where necessary:

1. The announcement of this principle led scientists in the United States and Great Britain to test and prove it by various devices.

2. The zoetrope was a cylinder covered with images.

3. According to this principle, the human eye retains an image for a fraction of a second longer than the image is present.

4. The principle was announced in 1824 by a British scholar named Peter Mark Roget.

5. One of these was a toy known as a zoetrope.

6. These simple applications of Roget's principle eventually led to the development of the motion picture.

7. Motion pictures originated from the discovery of the principle known as the persistence of vision.

8. Another device was a small book of drawings that seemed to move when flipped by the thumb.

9. The motion picture is actually a rapid succession of still pictures put together by the persistence of vision in the eye.

10. The images merged into a single picture when the cylinder was rapidly spun.

8.6 LINKING AND TURNING: TRANSITIONS BETWEEN PARAGRAPHS   *trans/bp*

A good essay is more than a collection of separate paragraphs. It is made up of paragraphs linked to each other not only by the substance of what they say but also by the transitions between them. We have already explained how to signal turns and transitions within the paragraph (section 8.2B). Likewise, there are various ways to link one paragraph with another, or to signal a turn as you begin the new one. Here are three ways to do so:

1. Use a transitional word or phrase:

> As a young girl I could say anything to my two male friends, and they would know exactly what I meant. My words were never misunderstood. If I asked Shawn to go skating with me, we both knew that it was only a friendly gesture. When I asked Mark to spend the night at our house, there was nothing romantic implied. We slept quietly in the same room with nothing but occasional snoring to wake one of us up.
>
> Now, *however,* I have to be very careful of what I say to male friends.   —College student

For a selective list of transitional words and phrases, see p. 174.

2. Start a new paragraph by answering one or more questions raised in the one before:

> . . . What should we talk about in order to make the right impression, or not to make the wrong one?
>
> The *answer* has to be something more important than the weather, something that allows us to learn what serious interests we share. —College student

3. Start a new paragraph by asking a question about a point you have just made:

> . . . One has not only a legal but a moral responsibility to obey just laws. Conversely, one has a moral responsibility to disobey unjust laws. I would agree with St. Augustine that "an unjust law is no law at all."
>
> Now, what is the difference between the two? How does one determine whether a law is just or unjust?
>
> —Martin Luther King, Jr., "Letter from Birmingham Jail"

4. Start a new paragraph by echoing a key word or recalling a key idea from the one before:

> . . . My peers look at my rattletrap and think I am a cursed child, with no hope of ever being popular. They are quite wrong, though. Once you get to know him, Harry is the American dream car.
>
> He's far from a dream at first glance. He is ugly. . . .
>
> Harry also complicates my life because of his faulty fuel gauge. Thirty miles after I fill him with gas, the needle falls directly from full to empty, so I have to depend on the odometer to tell me how much gas I've got left. Unfortunately, Harry's mileage per gallon drops drastically from summer to winter, as I discovered one night last December. While I was driving to a jumping meet in fifteen-degree weather, Harry sucked the last drop of unleaded gasoline from his tank and stopped. I had to decide whether to hunt for gas and miss the jumping meet or abandon Harry for two hours. I chose the latter.
>
> This sort of thing would never happen to the driver of a late-model car. —College freshman

WRITING PARAGRAPHS: IN BRIEF

TO DIRECT EACH PARAGRAPH

Forecast your main point with a lead sentence that tells the reader where you are headed.

Signal each turn of your thought with an apt word or phrase.

TO ENSURE COHERENCE

Use a sequence of sentences with the same basic pattern (list structure).

OR

Link each new sentence to the sentence before it (chain structure).

OR

Use a combination of list and chain structures.

TO EMPHASIZE THE MAIN POINT

Repeat key words or phrases.

OR

Place the main point at the beginning or end.

TO LINK EACH NEW PARAGRAPH TO THE ONE BEFORE

Start with a transitional word or phrase.

OR

Start by answering questions raised in the previous paragraph.

OR

Start by echoing a key word or recalling a key idea from the previous paragraph.

EXERCISE 10 MAKING TRANSITIONS BETWEEN PARAGRAPHS

1. In the following passage, one or more words at the beginning of the second paragraph have been deleted. Use a transitional word or phrase to clarify the shift between the two paragraphs.

As children growing up in a small town, my brother and I were the only ones whose father was "different." He couldn't sing the national anthem or remember the words of the Pledge of Allegiance and found it difficult to comprehend the intricacies of football and baseball.

. . . he was a very special parent. On rainy days he was always waiting for us at the school door, rubbers in hand; if we were ill he was there to take us home. He worked in town and was available to take us to music and dancing lessons or on little drives. When I was a small child he planted beside my window a beautiful oak tree that grew to be taller than our home. —Janet Heller, "About Morris Heller"

2. In the following passage, we have deleted the first sentence of the second paragraph and the first two sentences of the third. For each of those paragraphs write one or two opening sentences to clarify the transition from one paragraph to the next.

Outside, in our childhood summers—the war. The summers of 1939 to '45. I was six and finally twelve; and the war was three thousand miles to the right where London, Warsaw, Cologne crouched huge, immortal under nights of bombs or, farther, to the left where our men (among them three cousins of mine) crawled over dead friends from foxhole to foxhole towards Tokyo or, terribly, where there were children (our age, our size) starving, fleeing, trapped, stripped, abandoned.

. . . A shot would ring in the midst of our play, freezing us in the knowledge that here at last were the first Storm Troopers till we thought and looked—Mrs. Hightower's Ford. And any plane passing overhead after dark seemed pregnant with black chutes ready to blossom. There were hints that war was nearer than it seemed—swastikaed subs off Hatteras or the German sailor's tattered corpse washed up at Virginia Beach with a Norfolk movie ticket in his pocket.

. . . Our deadly threats were polio, being hit by a car, drowning in pure chlorine if we swam after eating. No shot was fired for a hundred miles. (Fort Bragg—a hundred miles.) We had excess food to shame us at every meal, excess clothes to fling about us in the heat of play.

—Reynolds Price, *Permanent Errors*

Choosing Words

To speak or write is to choose words. You choose them not just to express your meaning but also to suit your audience in a particular situation. Referring to an adult male, for instance, you might use the word *dude* in talking to a friend at a party and *man* in talking to a prospective employer in her office.

In speaking and in the early stages of writing, you often choose words unconsciously. But to write effectively, you must think about the words you use, their shades of meaning, and their effect on your readers. These are the things that this chapter aims to help you do.

9.1 CHOOSING YOUR LEVEL OF DICTION

Diction consists of the words you choose. The choices you make establish your **level of diction**—that is, your level of formality. This may be high, low, in the middle, or mixed.

9.1A MIDDLE LEVEL

To see how the **middle level of diction** is set and maintained, consider the following passage from an essay written for a college course:

> Fears based on ignorance can sometimes be conquered by scientific fact. In 1938 a radio program called *War of the Worlds* actually terrified large numbers of Americans by pretending to report that the earth was being invaded by people from Mars. But as we now know from instrumental explora-

tion of Mars itself, the idea that "Martians" could invade the
earth is ———.

As is right for a piece on a serious subject aimed at an intelligent
and somewhat critical audience (the instructor), this passage is
neither casual nor highly formal in tone. Words such as *conquered,
invaded,* and *exploration* establish a level of diction that is clearly
above the colloquial. But the diction is not highly formal. It is
written at the middle level of diction, the normal level for most
college and professional writing, the level consistent with Standard English (as defined on pp. 4–6).

What, then, should the last word be? Here are some words
that would fit the meaning of the passage. Choose one:

insupportable	silly
preposterous	false
incredible	crazy
ludicrous	loony
groundless	bull
absurd	

A quick glance down the list should make you see that these
eleven words descend through several levels of diction, from the
high formality of *insupportable* through the informality of *crazy* to
the outright slanginess of *bull.* If you chose a word from the
middle of the list—*ludicrous, groundless, absurd, silly,* or *false*—
you chose sensibly, for these words are all at the middle level of
diction, and can fit into most contexts without seeming either
coarse or pretentious, too low or too high. Slang words like *loony*
and *bull* may be all right in conversation, but they do not suit a
formal discussion of human fears, and the odds are they will not
suit the audience either. So why not *insupportable,* from the top of
the list? This word is impressively long, but its very length
makes it carry more weight than most sentences can bear, and
seasoned writers do not use long words just to impress their readers. In this case, the meaning of *insupportable* can readily be con-
veyed by a shorter word such as *groundless.*

Whether you actually choose *groundless* or another word from
the middle group depends on the shade of meaning you want, as
explained in section 9.3.

9.1B HIGHLY FORMAL LEVEL

Some occasions call for **highly formal diction:**

> I feel that this award was not made to me as a man but to my work—a life's work in the agony and sweat of the human spirit, not for glory and least of all for profit, but to create out of the materials of the human spirit something which did not exist before. So this award is only mine in trust. It will not be difficult to find a dedication for the money part of it commensurate with the purpose and significance of its origin. But I would like to do the same with the acclaim too, by using this moment as a pinnacle from which I might be listened to by the young men and women already dedicated to the same anguish and travail, among whom is already that one who will some day stand here where I am standing.
> —William Faulkner, Nobel Prize acceptance speech

Faulkner is delivering a speech of acknowledgment on a ceremonial occasion. Such a speech requires language of high formality—stately words like *dedication, commensurate, pinnacle,* and *travail.*

9.1C INFORMAL OR LOW LEVEL: COLLOQUIALISMS AND SLANG

Colloquialisms and **slang** are words commonly used in conversation and sometimes in writing. They often appear, for instance, in sports reporting:

> Baker led off the ninth with a scorcher into the rightfield corner, and took second when Bailey bobbled the ball. Muzio caught Lehmann looking at a slider on the outside corner, but Tetrazzini clouted the next delivery into the upper deck. In the bottom of the inning Tom Stewart retired the Sox in order to ice the win.

Strictly speaking, slang is one step lower than colloquial diction. While "led off" is colloquial, "ice the win" has the racy flavor of slang. (Dictionaries use the word *informal* to designate colloquialisms alone, and put slang in a separate category: see below, section 9.2.)

9.1D MIXED LEVELS: PRO AND CON

Even when you are choosing most of your words from the middle level of diction, you may occasionally need a highly formal word, or—on the other hand—a piece of slang:

> In Moulmein, in Lower Burma, I was hated by large numbers of people—the only time in my life that I have been important enough for this to happen to me. I was sub-divisional police officer of the town, and in an aimless, petty kind of way anti-European feeling was very bitter. No one had the guts to raise a riot, but if a European woman went through the bazaars alone somebody would probably spit betel juice over her dress. —George Orwell, "Shooting an Elephant"

Since Orwell is writing about violent feelings, the slang word *guts* belongs here. Together with *spit,* it illustrates and vivifies the abstract phrase *anti-European feeling.*

Orwell's slang is effective because he uses it sparingly and purposefully. When overused, slang loses its bite:

> When I got out of high school, I figured I wouldn't start college right off because books were giving me really bad vibes at the time and I wanted to get my head together before I hit the books again.

Just as bad is a sentence that suddenly lurches into slang with no good reason for doing so:

> When I finished high school, I decided not to enter college immediately because academic work was giving me really bad vibes.

In formal writing, therefore, use slang sparingly, or not at all:

> When I finished high school, I decided not to enter college immediately because I just couldn't stomach any more academic work.

The verb *stomach* has plenty of force; you could also use *swallow* or simply *take.* The more you write, the more you will find variety and power within the middle range of diction. You will know when to use formal words or slang.

EXERCISE 1 MAKING DICTION CONSISTENT

Revise the following passage to eliminate any unjustified slang
or excessive formality in its diction:

While I'm complaining, let me mention another gripe about
New York. It's impossible to get a haircut here! When I
inhabited a house in the town of Rye, I had a terrific barber, a
person who, every month or so, would give me a straightforward trim for $8.50, a price which was reasonable in my opin-   5
ion. He always cut my tresses exactly as I wanted him to, and
he never suggested that a different style would be more beneficial. I like simple haircuts but have yet to get one in the five
months I've been attending Columbia University, which is
right here in New York City. It is my considered opinion that   10
all of the barbers left town years ago, to be replaced by hair
stylists, as they label themselves, men who use scissors on a
man's locks in the way bad sculptors use their mitts to put soft
clay into some kind of shape. If I present a request for a simple
trim, these bums spray my head with water, comb my hair in   15
every direction but the right one, grab tufts, and start hack-
ing. They try to layer it in ways only a high-priced fashion
model could ever want; and they leave the sideburns raw,
claiming that's how men of taste want them. Then they plug
in their damned hair dryers and blow up the mess they've   20
made. In conclusion, they have the effrontery to submit a bill
for a monetary sum in excess of $15. You can't win.

9.2 USING THE DICTIONARY

A good dictionary is the indispensable tool of a good writer. This
sample entry from *The American Heritage Dictionary* shows you
what a dictionary can tell you about a single word—even a word
you use often:

1. Spelling, syllable division, pronunciation. You already know
how to spell and pronounce a one-syllable word like *cool,* but
what about a longer word, such as *government?* The definition of
this word begins "**gov-ern-ment** (gŭv'ərn-mənt)." With the
word broken into three syllables, you can tell where to divide it

Spelling

Pronunciation

Definition as adjective

General usage

Slang usage

Verb forms

Definition as noun

History of the word

Related forms

Comparative and superlative forms

Definition as verb

Definition as intransitive verb

Informal or colloquial usage

Distinctions in meaning between the word and others like it

cool (kōol) *adj.* **cooler, coolest.** **1.** Moderately cold; neither warm nor very cold. **2.** Reducing discomfort in hot weather; allowing a feeling of coolness: *a cool blouse.* **3.** Not excited; calm; controlled. **4.** Showing dislike, disdain, or indifference; unenthusiastic; not cordial; *a cool greeting.* **5.** Calmly audacious or bold; impudent. **6.** Designating or characteristic of colors, such as blue and green, that produce the impression of coolness. **7.** *Slang.* Having a quiet, indifferent, and aloof attitude. **8.** *Slang.* Excellent; first-rate; superior. **9.** *Informal.* Without exaggeration; entire; full: *He lost a cool million.* —*v.* **cooled, cooling, cools.** —*tr.* **1.** To make less warm. **2.** To make less ardent, intense, or zealous. —*intr.* **1.** To become less warm. **2.** To become calm. —**cool it.** *Slang.* To calm down, slow down, or relax. —**cool one's heels.** *Informal.* To be kept waiting for a long time. —*n.* **1.** Anything that is cool or moderately cold; *the cool of early morning.* **2.** The state or quality of being cool. **3.** *Slang.* Composure; *recover one's cool.* [Middle English *col,* Old English *cōl.* See **gel-**[3] in Appendix.*] —**cool'ly** *adv.* —**cool'ness** *n.*

Synonyms: *cool, composed, collected, unruffled, nonchalant, imperturbable, detached.* These adjectives apply to persons to indicate calmness, especially in time of stress. *Cool* has the widest application. Usually it implies merely a high degree of self-control, though it may also indicate aloofness. *Composed* and *collected* more strongly imply conscious display of self-discipline and absence of agitation. *Composed* also often suggests serenity or sedateness, and *collected,* mental concentration. *Unruffled* emphasizes calmness in the face of severe provocation that may have produced agitation in others present. *Nonchalant* describes a casual exterior manner that suggests, sometimes misleadingly, a lack of interest or concern. *Imperturbable* stresses unshakable calmness considered usually as an inherent trait rather than as a product of self-discipline. *Detached* implies aloofness and either lack of active concern or resistance to emotional involvement.

when you need to hyphenate it at the end of a line. The phonetic spelling in parentheses tells you to pronounce it with the accent on the first syllable (gŭv'). The pronunciation key at the beginning of the dictionary (and at the bottom of each page) explains that *ŭ* sounds like the *u* in *cut* and *ə* sounds like the *e* in *item.*

2. Parts of speech. Like many other words, *cool* can be used in various ways. The abbreviation *adj.* tells you that it is being defined first as an adjective; the entry then goes on to explain what it means when used as a verb (—*v.*) and as a noun (—*n.*).

3. Forms. For certain parts of speech several forms of the word are given. For example, *adj.* is followed by *cooler* and *coolest.*

4. Definitions. When a word can function in various ways (as adjective or verb, for instance), a separate set of numbered definitions is given for each. Some dictionaries begin with the earliest meaning of the word and then proceed in order to the latest

ones, but most dictionaries—like the *American Heritage*—simply begin with the central, commonest meaning.

5. <u>Usage labels.</u> These identify words or uses of words that are not part of current Standard English.

WORD	LABEL	MEANING
cool	Informal *or* Colloquial	entire, full
cool	Slang	composure
yclept	Archaic *or* Obsolete	named, called
calculate	Regional *or* Dialect	think, suppose
nowheres	Nonstandard	nowhere

The level of diction is often set by the sense in which a word is used. *Cool* is informal when used to mean "full" ("a cool million"), and slang when used to mean "composure" ("Don't blow your cool").

You will also find labels indicating words that are specialized and will therefore have to be explained for most readers:

WORD	LABEL	MEANING
ganef	Yiddish	thief, rascal
gamophylous	Botany	having united leaves

6. <u>Transitive and intransitive use of the verb.</u> A verb may be transitive *(tr.)*, intransitive *(intr.)*, or both. After —*tr.* in the sample entry are definitions for *cool* as a transitive verb, one that acts on a direct object (as in "The icy stream cooled the beer"). Under —*intr.* are definitions of *cool* as an intransitive verb, a verb without a direct object (as in "The beer cooled slowly"). Sometimes the abbreviations *v.t.* and *v.i.* are used instead.

7. <u>Etymology.</u> The etymology of the word being defined—its history or derivation—is given in brackets: [ ]. Some dictionaries put it at the beginning of the entry. In our sample it comes near the end of the first part; there we learn that *cool* can be traced to the Old English word *cōl*. "See **gel-**[3] in Appendix" means that under the heading **gel-**[3] in the Appendix you can find still older roots for the word *cool* in a prehistoric group of languages known as Indo-European. You can also find other

words that come from the same roots (including *chill, cold, congeal, jelly,* and *glacier*). Sometimes you can find definitions of word roots. If you look up *calculate,* for instance, you will find that it comes from the Latin word *calculus,* which means "a small stone." (The ancient Romans used small stones for reckoning.)

8. Related forms. A related form is a variation on the form of the word being defined. For *cool,* the related forms include the adverb *coolly* (note the spelling) and the noun *coolness.* Sometimes these related forms have separate entries of their own.

9. Synonyms. In a standard dictionary, entries for some words include definitions of synonyms. These can help you choose the exact word for your meaning. (A thesaurus provides lists of synonyms, but does not usually define them.)

> **EXERCISE 2   USING A DICTIONARY**
>
> This is a five-part exercise.
>
> 1. From any piece or pieces of writing you have read recently, choose five words that you don't recognize or that you aren't sure you understand.
> 2. Write out the sentence in which each word appears, citing its author in parentheses.
> 3. Using the sentences to guide you, define each word as well as you can.
> 4. Look up each word in your dictionary, and write out the definition you find there. Give the name of the dictionary in parentheses.
> 5. Use each word in a sentence of your own.
>
> **EXAMPLE**
>
> 1. perfunctory
> 2. Some beavers, especially young or solitary old ones, are sloppy and perfunctory builders. (David Rains Wallace)
> 3. sort of careless, I think
> 4. "done or acting routinely and with little interest or care"
> 5. Not even looking at me, she mumbled a perfunctory "thanks" and walked away.

9.3 CHOOSING WORDS FOR THEIR DENOTATION

The **denotation** of a word is its explicit meaning. To write precisely is to choose the word that means exactly what you want to say. Consider again this uncompleted sentence:

> But as we now know from instrumental exploration of Mars itself, the idea that "Martians" could invade the earth is ____.

To fill in the blank, you might first consult a thesaurus, a book that gives you a cluster of synonyms for each of the words it alphabetically lists. Some computer programs now include an on-line thesaurus that will give you a list of synonyms on your screen.

Suppose you're looking for a word that means something like *crazy* but is somewhat more formal, to suit the context. A thesaurus might give you as synonyms *ludicrous, groundless, absurd, silly,* and *false.* Any one of these words would make sense in the blank, and all of them come from the middle level of diction. But to choose the word that best fits your meaning, you need to know exactly what each one means. A good dictionary will tell the following:

Ludicrous means "worthy of scornful laughter."

Groundless means "unsupported by evidence." A *groundless* belief is not necessarily *silly, absurd,* or *ludicrous,* or even *false.* It simply has no basis in what is known.

Absurd means "irrational" or "nonsensical" but not "frivolous"; deadly serious people can sometimes have completely absurd ideas.

Silly means "frivolous," "foolish," or "thoughtless."

False means "not true." A statement may be *false* without being either *silly, ludicrous,* or *absurd.* It would be *absurd* to say that the first president of the United States was King George III, but merely *false* to say that the first president was Thomas Jefferson.

Learning what every word denotes is not easy. But if you read extensively and use your dictionary often, you will come to know the shades of difference between words with similar meanings. This knowledge, in turn, will help you express more precisely your *own* opinion of an idea—such as the idea that Martians could invade the earth. No one else can fill in the blank for you.

> EXERCISE 3 CHOOSING WORDS FOR THEIR DENOTATION
>
> Using a good dictionary where necessary, answer each of the following questions.
>
> EXAMPLE
> Should you use *fatal* or *deadly* to describe a weapon that can kill?
> ANSWER: deadly
>
> 1. If your meaning is "annoy continually," should you use *bother* or *harass?*
> 2. If your meaning is "defy," should you use *flaunt* or *flout?*
> 3. Should you use *toady* or *flatterer* to mean "someone who lavishly praises another for material gain"?
> 4. Is an impartial judge *uninterested* or *disinterested* in the case brought before her?
> 5. If your meaning is "express strong disapproval of," should you use *criticize* or *denounce?*

9.4 CHOOSING WORDS FOR THEIR CONNOTATION

The **connotation** of a word is its implicit meaning: the feeling, attitude, or set of associations it implies.

Take *house* and *home.* Both denote a dwelling place or residence. But their connotations differ sharply. *House* connotes little more than it denotes—a place where people can live—while *home* normally connotes family affection, memories of childhood, and a reassuring sense of welcome.

Precisely because they involve feelings, the connotations of a word are sometimes too personal and variable to be defined. The connotations of *steak,* for instance, will be different for a vegetarian and for a Texas cattleman. Yet many words do have widely accepted connotations, and these determine the electrical charge of a word—positive or negative, favorable or unfavorable, generous or harsh.

Compare the adjectives in each of the following sentences:

> Ray is ambitious; Ralph is pushy.
> Ray is tough-minded; Ralph is ruthless.
> Ray is foresighted; Ralph is calculating.
> Ray is firm; Ralph is stubborn.

Each pair of adjectives in these sentences is joined by denotation but split by connotation. While the words describing Ray are generous, the words applied to Ralph are loaded with negative connotations. Loaded language appeals only to readers who themselves are already loaded with the prejudices of the writer. If you want to persuade readers who have various views, you should try to choose words with connotations that are fair to your subject. This does not mean that you must never describe anyone in terms like *pushy, stubborn, calculating,* or *ruthless;* it means only that before you use such words, you must be sure that you mean them.

EXERCISE 4 **RECOGNIZING CONNOTATIONS**

Following are groups of three words alike in denotation but unlike in connotations. Arrange the words so that the one with the most favorable connotation is first and the one with the least favorable connotation is last. If you have trouble arranging them, your dictionary may help you.

EXAMPLE
pushy   ambitious   aggressive
ambitious, aggressive, pushy

1. frugal	stingy	thrifty
2. scent	stench	odor
3. call	scream	yell
4. firmly	harshly	sternly
5. prejudiced	partial	bigoted
6. slender	emaciated	skinny
7. retreat	flee	depart
8. mistake	blunder	error
9. dull	stupid	unintelligent
10. question	interrogate	ask

EXERCISE 5 **CHOOSING WORDS BY CONNOTATION**

Replace the italicized word in each sentence with a word of similar denotation but more favorable connotation.

EXAMPLE

> After I showed him my receipt, the store owner admitted
> his ~~blunder.~~ mistake.

1. Ramona's skydiving reflects her *foolhardy* nature.
2. Felipe thinks she should be more *timid*.
3. In return, she *ridicules* him.
4. They make an *eccentric* couple.
5. Whenever they go out together, he wears a coat and tie, and she dresses *sloppily*.

9.5 CHOOSING GENERAL AND SPECIFIC WORDS

Words range in meaning from the most **general** to the most **specific.** If you want to identify something named Fido that runs, barks, and wags its tail, you can call it a *creature,* an *animal,* a *dog,* a *hound,* or a *basset.* Each of the words in this series is more specific than the one before, and each of them has its use:

> Fido is the most lovable *creature* I know.
> Fido is the first *animal* I ever liked.
> Fido is one of our three *dogs.*
> Fido is the fastest *hound* I've ever seen.
> We have three hounds: a dachshund named Willy, a greyhound named Mick, and a *basset* named Fido.

Almost everything can be classified in several different ways, with words ranging from the very general to the very specific. If someone moves, for instance, you can write that she *moves,* or more specifically that she *walks,* or still more specifically that she *struts.*

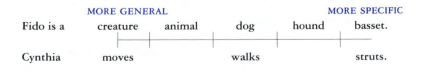

	MORE GENERAL				MORE SPECIFIC
Fido is a	creature	animal	dog	hound	basset.
Cynthia	moves		walks		struts.

A **concrete** or specific word names something you can see, touch, taste, smell, or hear. Examples are *fingernail, strawberry, sandpaper, smoke, whisper,* or *scream.* An **abstract** or general word names a feeling *(love),* a state of being *(misery),* an idea *(democracy),* a theory *(evolution),* a field of study *(biology),* or a class of things too broad to be visualized *(creature, plant, organism).* Abstract words can be used to categorize or contain a collection of items, as in "She went to Mexico and returned with a vanload of *souvenirs.*"

But too many abstract words turn writing into fog. Good writing combines the abstract and the concrete, the general and the specific:

> The cartilage in my ankle ripped painfully when I hit the icy sidewalk. As I lay on my back, cursing myself for jogging in subzero weather, the chill of the morning wind made me shiver. I tried to raise my body, but my ankle would not move, and all I could do was fall back on my concrete bed. I felt nothing but pain, cold, and dismay.   —College freshman

Dismay is an abstract word, but it perfectly sums up all the concrete details that come before it.

Exercise 6 Recognizing General and Specific Words

Following are groups of three words. Arrange the words in order, from the most abstract or general to the most specific or concrete.

EXAMPLE

walk   go   strut
go, walk, strut

1. sofa   property   furniture
2. poodle   animal   dog
3. whale   creature   mammal
4. dwelling   shelter   cottage
5. pitcher   athlete   ballplayer
6. automobile   Chevrolet   vehicle

7. run	move	spring
8. meat	pork	food
9. literature	novel	book
10. pain	problem	toothache
11. maple	plant	tree

EXERCISE 7 USING ABSTRACT WORDS

Use one abstract noun to sum up each of the following sets of three specific words.

EXAMPLE
kiss, smile, hug
affection

1. snarl, spit, scream
2. wheezing, stumbling, aching
3. pale, rigid, breathless
4. diamonds, marble, gold
5. laughter, singing, dancing

EXERCISE 8 USING SPECIFIC AND CONCRETE WORDS

Replace the italicized words with words or phrases that are more specific or concrete.

EXAMPLE
    whispered
    Janet ~~spoke~~ to Tom.

1. During the road race there were three *accidents*.
2. *Defects* in the pavement made driving hazardous.
3. Also, the *weather* made visibility poor.
4. One car *went* off the road and *made contact with an object*.
5. A second *moved* into a *cavity* by the side of the road.
6. A third *got* out of control when its right front tire *malfunctioned*.
7. The driver of one car suffered an *injury*.

9.6 USING WORDS FIGURATIVELY: SIMILE AND METAPHOR

Figurative language helps to make the writer's meaning vividly clear. While ordinary comparisons bring together two things of the same kind, figurative words and phrases bring together two things of a different kind, comparing something abstract or unfamiliar with something concrete, familiar, or both.

Ordinary comparison:

Boston is like Philadelphia; it lives on its past.

Figurative comparison:

Sending one police officer to stop a riot is like shooting a squirt gun at a forest fire.

A figurative word or phrase can be a **simile** or a **metaphor**.

1. In a simile, the writer says or implies that one thing is *like* another:

> After the mole devoured its prey, it sank into the earth *as a submarine sinks into the water.* —Konrad Z. Lorenz, adapted

> Her eyes were *like two hard, cold pebbles from the ocean.*
> —College student

> The guide shooed his charges back along the gravel path *as if they were chickens,* which was what they sounded like.
> —Margaret Atwood

> He stumbled out into the hall *as if his legs were tied together with rope.* —College student

2. In a metaphor, which is a compressed or intensified version of the simile, the writer says or implies that one thing *is* another:

> An angry man *is a raging bull.*

> What does education often do? It makes a straight-cut ditch of a free, meandering brook. —Henry David Thoreau

> Every muscle in my body ached and cried for mercy.
> —College student

> EXERCISE 9 USING FIGURATIVE LANGUAGE
>
> In each of the following sentences, an abstract word or phrase is italicized. Make it concrete or specific by changing it to a simile or metaphor.
>
> EXAMPLE
>
> Life is *something to be organized.*
>
> REVISED: Life is like a lump of clay; it is our task to mold it.
>
> 1. Travel books are *descriptions* of far-off places.
> 2. Entering a roomful of strange people is *frightening.*
> 3. The first week of college is *confusing.*
> 4. The fat man *moved awkwardly* across the street.
> 5. The child accepted the story *trustingly.*

9.7 AVOIDING MIXED METAPHOR *mix met*

A mixed metaphor is a set of two or more metaphors that do not mesh:

> * When the proposal was made, he smelled a rat, and he set out to nip it in the bud.
>
> * If we cannot get the deficit under control, the ship of state may soon come to the end of the road.

In the first example, a rat turns into a bud; in the second, a ship travels a road. To correct a mixed metaphor, make your metaphors consistent:

> EDITED: When the proposal was made, he smelled a rat, and he set out to trap it.
>
> EDITED: If we cannot get the deficit under control, the ship of state may soon capsize.

9.8 CONTROLLING CLICHÉS *cli*

Clichés are the old coins of language: phrases that once made a striking impression but have since been rubbed smooth by repeated handling. (The mixed metaphors above, for instance, are all clichés.) We use clichés because they come readily to mind, because they can quickly fill up or fill out a sentence, and because many of them are figures of speech and therefore seem colorful or catchy. But overuse of clichés leads to passages like this:

> *At this point in time,* we should *let bygones be bygones, bury the hatchet,* and *put our shoulders to the wheel.* We cannot *stand idly by;* we must *make hay while the sun shines. In the final analysis,* if we fail, we will have *only ourselves to blame.*

When you spot a cliché in your writing, you can sometimes give it a new twist, as in *Halfway up the ladder of success, she found several rungs missing.* But if you can't give it a new twist, replace the cliché with a carefully chosen word or phrase. Compare the original version of each sentence given below with the edited version:

▶ ~~At this point in time, we~~ **We** cannot get a loan. **now**

▶ In rural areas doctors are ~~few and far between~~ **scarce.**

▶ ~~Busy as a bee, the~~ **The industrious** cobbler worked from dawn to sundown.

▶ Jerry's proposal ~~hit the nail on the head~~ **solved the problem.**

EXERCISE 10 REPLACING CLICHÉS

Replace every cliché in the following sentences with a well-chosen word or phrase.

EXAMPLE

We ~~chewed the fat~~ **talked** until the ~~wee~~ **early** hours of the morning.

1. The Dean's recent report sent shock waves through the entire college.

2. It revealed that only half the students were putting their shoulders to the wheel.

3. The rest were just having a ball and painting the town red every night.

4. The president of the college said that all these students should be made to straighten up and fly right.

5. But she and the faculty couldn't see eye to eye on how to get this proposal off the ground.

EXERCISE 11 REPLACING YOUR OWN CLICHÉS

Using as many clichés as possible, write a paragraph arguing that all thin persons in the United States should immediately go on a junk-food binge. Then rewrite the paragraph and see if you can squeeze every one of those clichés out of it.

9.9 USING IDIOMS

An **idiom** is a combination of words that is peculiar to a specific language but follows no known rule. No rule, for instance, explains why speakers of British English say "Let's have *a* coffee," while speakers of American English say "Let's have coffee." In American English, some idioms combine an adjective or participle with a preposition (dependent *on,* bored *with,* superior *to*); others combine a verb with one or more *particles*—prepositions serving as adverbs (look *into,* look *down on*). Here is a partial list of such idioms:

according *to*

abide *by* (a rule, regulation, or agreement)

able *to*

agree *with* (a person)

bored *with*

capable *of*

compare *to* or *with* (see Glossary of Usage)

complain *to* (a person)

complain *about* (a thing)

comply *with*

conform *to*

cooperate *with*

dependent *on*

desirous *of*

differ *with* (meaning *disagree with*)

differ *from* (meaning *is different from*, as in "Body building differs from weight lifting.")

different *from*

disgust / disgusted *with*

independent *of*

inferior *to*

preferable *to*

prior *to*

responsible / responsibility *for*

superior *to*

sure *to*

waiting *for* (expecting)

waiting *on* (serving)

For an extended list of multiword verbs (verb-particle combinations), with sample sentences and brief definitions, see appendix 1.

EXERCISE 12 CHOOSING PREPOSITIONS

Fill each blank with an appropriate preposition.

EXAMPLE

Some people always complain _____ the weather _____ anyone who will listen.

ANSWER: about, to

1. Crane's disgust _____ her country's special racial policies and her hatred _____ its rulers drove her _____ self-imposed exile.

2. She had no confidence _____ the government's promises _____ gradual reform.

3. She could no longer silently cooperate _____ its demeaning laws.

4. Only _____ exile could she speak and write freely _____ them.

5. But she longed _____ the day when she could return _____ a country that would at last be free _____ oppression.

9.10 AVOIDING JARGON, PRETENTIOUS WORDS, AND EUPHEMISMS

Jargon, pretentious words, and euphemisms can muffle the impact of a sentence or choke the flow of its meaning. For this reason, you should generally avoid all three.

9.10A JARGON   *jarg*

Jargon is technical terminology. Technical terms belong in writing on a specialized subject, but they seldom suit essays on subjects of general interest, especially when ordinary words can be used in their place:

> ▶ When I asked my parents if I could use the car, the ~~feedback~~ *answer* was ~~negative.~~ *no.*

> ▶ [or] When I asked my parents if I could use the car, ~~the feedback was negative.~~ *they said no.*

> ▶ ~~Upwardly mobile~~ *Ambitious* lawyers often work seventy hours a week.

If you are writing on a specialized subject for general readers, make sure you explain any technical terms as you go along. You can often do so with a parenthesized word or phrase:

> She fractured her tibia (shinbone) in three places.

9.10B PRETENTIOUS WORDS   *pret*

Pretentious words and phrases are too long and high-flown for the meaning they actually deliver. Substitute simpler words wherever possible:

> ▶ Were it not for the ~~lucrative financial rewards,~~ *money,* she would have ~~tendered her resignation.~~ *quit.*

> ▶ ~~Large-size passenger vehicles utilize excessive quantities of fuel.~~ *Big cars use too much gas.*

▶ Years of research have ~~impacted positively on~~ our understand-
_{improved}

ing of cancer.

9.10C EUPHEMISMS   *euph*

A **euphemism** is a word or expression that takes the sting out of
an unpleasant reality. A euphemism for *dead* is *departed;* euphemisms for *kill* include *eliminate* and *harvest*. Since euphemisms
veil the truth instead of stating it openly, you should use them
only when plainer words would needlessly hurt the feelings of
those you are writing for or about.

But euphemisms should never be used to hide the truth or
spare the feelings of those who have done wrong. George Orwell
gives a telling example:

> Defenseless villagers are bombarded from the air, the
> inhabitants driven out into the countryside, the cattle
> machine-gunned, the huts set on fire with incendiary bullets:
> this is called *pacification*.

EXERCISE 13 CHANGING JARGON, PRETENTIOUS WORDS, AND EUPHEMISMS INTO PLAIN ENGLISH

The following sentences are disfigured by jargon, euphemisms, or pretentious words. Using your dictionary if necessary, rewrite each sentence in plain English.

EXAMPLE

The very thought of flying ~~made her paranoid.~~
_{frightened her.}

1. Young children need positive feedback from their parents
   and teachers regularly.
2. Nonsupportive articulations impact negatively on their
   development.
3. While interacting with them, therefore, grownups should
   utilize encouraging words as much as possible.
4. Also, children should be urged to verbalize their feelings,
   especially when they are sad.
5. A child whose mother or father has passed on, for instance,
   needs a sympathetic listener.

9.11 USING GENDER-INCLUSIVE (NONSEXIST) LANGUAGE   *sxl*

Sexist language is language demeaning to either sex. It includes not just such obviously insulting terms as *stud* and *bimbo* but also any words and phrases that are condescending to women, that mark women as inferior to men or restrict them because of their gender. To make your writing fair to both genders, you should use language that includes both of them unless you have good reason for excluding one.

1. Use **gender-inclusive** terms to designate any job or position that can be held by a member of either sex:

▶ Beverly Pepper is an American ~~sculptress.~~ sculptor.

▶ The ~~stewardess~~ flight attendant checked her list of passengers.

▶ U.S. ~~Congressmen~~ representatives are elected for two-year terms.

▶ The ~~chairman~~ chair ruled the motion out of order.

In words like those just above, you can change the *-man* ending to *-person,* as in *Congresspersons* and *chairperson.* But since the *-person* ending is awkward, use alternatives whenever possible: *letter carriers* (for mailmen), *business executives* or *business owners* (for businessmen), *meteorologists* (for weathermen), *fire fighter* (for fireman), and so on. A few gendered word forms, however—words such as *actress* and *waitress,* for instance—remain acceptable to most readers.

2. Whenever *man* or a *man*-word refers to both sexes, replace it with a **genderless alternative** such as *person, human,* or *people:*

▶ Modern ~~man~~ people takes electricity for granted.

▶ ~~Mankind~~ Human beings as we know ~~it~~ them first appeared about 40,000 years ago.

▶ Voters seldom get the chance to choose the best ~~man~~ person available.

3. When a pronoun refers to a word of unspecified gender, try to do one of the following:

a. Make the word and the pronoun plural:

> ▶ ~~A doctor~~ Doctors ~~needs~~ need years of training before ~~he is~~ they are ready to operate.

> ▶ ~~Any student~~ Students who ~~thinks~~ think that ~~he~~ they can easily pass organic chemistry ~~is~~ are deceiving ~~himself~~ themselves.

b. Use a feminine pronoun to balance the use of a masculine one:

> ▶ What a doctor expects from his patients is not quite the same as what a lawyer expects from ~~his~~ her clients.

> **EXERCISE 14 USING GENDER-INCLUSIVE LANGUAGE**
>
> Following is the opening paragraph of an essay published in 1949. Revise any words or phrases that unjustifiably fail to include women. If you make any singular pronouns plural, be sure to make their antecedents (section 18.1) plural also.
>
> The American is optimistic, self-confident, and self-satisfied. He takes for granted that his is the best of all countries, the happiest and most virtuous of all societies, the richest and most bounteous of all economies. He knows that Providence has favored him in the past and he takes for granted that he   5 will continue to be the object of special dispensation. Collectively he has never known defeat, or prolonged misery, and only colored Americans*—who are usually left out of calculations—have known oppression. He is not indifferent to the past, as long as it is American, and is inclined to believe that   10 history began in 1607 or—if he is a Yankee—in 1620. Mostly, however, he lives in the present or the future. Although less sure of progress than his fathers or grandfathers, he is confident that if there is progress, it will be under American leadership and bear the American imprint. Accustomed   15 to seeing his boldest plans and most sanguine anticipations

---

*Persons once called "colored" in the United States now generally prefer to be known as "African Americans" or persons "of color." See section 9.12.

realized, he believes that they will continue to be fulfilled—
but with that belief goes a suspicion that in these matters he
is no longer the free agent he was during the period of relative
immunity from European affairs.

—Henry Steele Commager, "Portrait of the American" (1949)

9.12 RESPECTING OTHERS

To reach the widest possible audience, to attract and persuade
readers of different ethnic backgrounds, religious affiliations,
physical conditions, or sexual orientations, and to show consideration for people in general, you should use terms respectful of
any group you write about. Generally, these are the terms that
members of groups use to describe themselves.

These terms often change. Americans of African descent, for
instance, once called themselves *colored*—a word still prominent
in the name of the National Association for the Advancement of
Colored People (NAACP). But in the past forty years, they have
called themselves *Negro,* then (since the 1960s) *black,* then *Afro-
American,* and now, more and more, *African American.* Alternatively, some Americans of African descent now wish to be known
as persons "of color."

Similarly, the people who for long were called *American Indians* keep this name alive in the name of one of their own organizations, the American Indian Movement. But many now prefer
to be called *Native Americans.*

Groups deserving of respect include not just races, religious
organizations, and ethnic minorities, but also other minorities
such as homosexuals and those commonly called *elderly, handicapped,* or *overweight.* Some of these groups have established names
for themselves, such as *gay* for homosexual. Others—those who
weigh more than average, for instance—may prefer not to be
singled out by any name at all.

Since the terms that groups apply to themselves are so difficult to fix, and since members of particular groups do not always
agree on what they wish to be called, we cannot offer here any
list of preferred terms. All we can offer is a single piece of advice:
before writing about any group—whether singled out by age,

physical condition, socio-economic class, race, religion, or ethnic category—try to learn what its members wish to be called.

> **EXERCISE 15 RESPECTING OTHERS**
>
> This is a five-part exercise.
>
> 1. Name the ethnic, racial, or religious group(s) to which you belong, and for each group named give the term you prefer to be called.
>
> 2. List three persons you know who belong to ethnic, racial, or religious groups distinct from your own.
>
> 3. Ask each of the three persons to say what name you should use for the group(s) to which he or she belongs.
>
> 4. Consult a recent dictionary—such as the 1991 edition of the *Random House Webster's College Dictionary*—to see what terms it recommends for each of their groups and for your own group(s).
>
> 5. Compare the terms recommended by the dictionary with the terms that you and your acquaintances prefer for your groups.

9.13 AVOIDING WORDINESS

Wordiness is an excess of words: more words than you need for the meaning you aim to deliver. To help you eliminate wordiness, here is one general technique and several specific ones:

9.13A IDENTIFYING THE MOST IMPORTANT WORDS

If you can't figure out how to improve a sentence that sounds wordy, underline the most important words and make a sentence out of them, using a minimum of linking words:

1. It is a matter of the gravest possible importance to the health of anyone with a history of a problem with disease of the heart that he or she should avoid the sort of foods with a high percentage of saturated fats.

2. Anyone with a history of heart disease should avoid saturated fats.

9.13B AVOIDING SPECIFIC SOURCES OF WORDINESS

1. Avoid repeating a word unless you need it again for clarity or emphasis:

> ▶ Of all the different topics of controversy, from politics to reli-
> ~~the environment,~~
> gion to ~~environmental questions,~~ nothing appears to get peo-
> ~~the topic of~~
> ple so inflamed as ~~those questions dealing with~~ sex.

For clarity, *topic* is repeated just once, at the end of the sentence. See also section 8.4A, "Repeating Key Words or Phrases."

2. Avoid redundancy—using two or more words that mean essentially the same thing:

> ▶ The defendant was accused of six ~~illegal~~ crimes.

> ▶ This ~~particular~~ problem has been ignored.

3. In general, avoid starting sentences with phrases such as *There is* and *It is:*

> Many
> ▶ ~~There are many~~ women ~~who~~ have to work.
> This
> ▶ ~~It is this that~~ makes cities flourish.

Occasionally, however, *There is, There are,* or *There were* can be used with good effect to open a paragraph ("There are two reasons for acting now"), to line up the sentences in a list-structure paragraph (see p. 176), or to serve as a placeholder when the subject is too long to go easily before the verb ("There were two reasons for the breakdown in essential services").

4. Wherever possible, turn nouns into verbs:

> encountered
> ▶ The crew ~~had an encounter with~~ an emergency.

▶ ~~The reason for his decision~~ to visit Spain ~~was his desire~~ to see
    He decided   *because he wanted*

a bullfight.

▶ [or] ~~The reason for his decision to visit~~ Spain ~~was his desire~~ to
    He went to

see a bullfight.

5. Wherever possible, get rid of adjective clauses like *who are,*
which was, and *that had been:*

▶ Students ~~who are~~ in the band have to practice twice a week.

6. Wherever possible, replace prepositional phrases with single
words:

▶ She spoke ~~in regard to~~ water pollution.
    about

▶ We ~~are in~~ need ~~of~~ players ~~with intelligence.~~
    intelligent

▶ They were ~~in a state of~~ noticeab*l**y** ~~confusion.~~ *confused.*

7. Avoid the verb *to be* in sentences like the following:

▶ Shakespeare is considered ~~to be~~ the greatest of all English

playwrights.

▶ Loss of memory may ~~be indicative of~~ Alzheimer's disease.
    indicate

8. When possible, avoid *the fact that:*

▶ ~~The fact that Redford appeared~~ nearly caused a riot.
    Redford's appearance

▶ ~~Due to the fact that~~ my paper was wordy, I had to rewrite it.
    Because

For more on *due to,* see the Glossary of Usage.

9. <u>Avoid verbal detours</u>:

► When we try to understand what God is, our first problem is
     we cannot see him.
that ~~of nonencounter at the level of vision.~~
   ^

EXERCISE 16 Making Sentences Concise

The following sentences are wordy. Without dropping anything essential to their meaning, make each of them more concise.

EXAMPLE

    The chipmunk ~~who was~~ hiding in the stone wall put its
        warily.
head out ~~in a wary fashion.~~
   ^

1. Photographers who worked in the nineteenth century
   faced many hardships and perils.

2. In their quest for pictures that would be perfect, some fell
   off mountains or buildings.

3. While engaged in photographing wildlife, they were
   attacked by elephants, rhinoceroses, lions, tigers, and, in
   addition, wild dogs.

4. But they were just as likely to die in the darkroom as they
   were to die in a jungle.

5. Darkrooms were dangerous due to the fact that the chemicals that were required for film processing in the nineteenth century were highly poisonous.

6. It is a fact that photographers had to breathe for several
   hours each day an atmosphere that was filled with noxious
   fumes.

7. In 1852 one photographer nearly experienced death from
   inhalation of mercury fumes.

8. Furthermore, there were some poisonous substances which
   penetrated the skin.

9. Worst of all were the hazards of consuming anything of a
   liquid nature in the darkroom.

10. In 1891, a Baltimore photographer who was well known mistook a solution of pyrogallic acid for a glass of whiskey and water.

11. As a resulting consequence, he died in three days' time.

12. For all these reasons, photography in the nineteenth century was considered to be an unhealthy occupation.

CHOOSING THE RIGHT WORDS: IN BRIEF

- Is your level of diction suitable for your subject and audience? Is it consistent? If not, is every shift in level justified? (9.1)

- Have you checked the dictionary for any word you're not quite sure how to use? (9.2)

- Do your words denote exactly the meaning you want to express? (9.3)

- Do your words connote what you want them to? (9.4)

- Does your writing combine general and specific words, the abstract and the concrete? (9.5)

- Have you enlivened your writing with figurative language? (9.6)

- Have you avoided mixed metaphors? (9.7)

- Have you avoided clichés (9.8), jargon, pretentious words, and euphemisms? (9.10)

- Have you used idioms correctly? (9.9)

- Is your language gender-inclusive? (9.11)

- Are your terms respectful of others? (9.12)

- Have you cut all words that you don't really need to deliver your meaning? (9.13)

EXERCISE 17 EDITING A DRAFT

The following passage illustrates weaknesses of wording common in many drafts. Improve the wording as best you can.

A LIFE OF RESISTANCE

Black Boy is an autobiographical account of the childhood
of Richard Wright. In the autobiography Wright describes
how all the odds were stacked against him from his birth until
the day many years later when he headed north to Chicago.
The book portrays his struggle for success against these seem-   5
ingly insurmountable odds, and the story illustrates in particular how his strong sense of justice allowed him to succeed.
This sense of justice is shown partly in the way he responded
when others tried to control his actions and behavior. Whenever someone tried to control him, his response depended on   10
how he assessed the fairness of what they wanted him to do.

Richard would not agree to submit to a punishment he
felt he did not deserve. Richard had encounters with this kind
of punishment while he was living with his grandmother and
one of his aunts. Her name was Aunt Addie, and she was mean   15
to Richard, and she was a teacher at a church school. His aunt
was continually trying to prove to the other students that she
didn't favor Richard, who was her nephew. She tried to prove
this by constantly punishing Richard for things he had not
done. Finally she pushed him to the limit when she started   20
attempting to punish him at home for things he had not even
done at school. Richard assured her that he had not done the
things she was accusing him of doing. This assurance only
made her furious, angry. She threatened him and warned him
she would beat him physically. Then Richard grabbed a   25
kitchen knife to defend himself. He told Aunt Addie that he
was not guilty of doing the things she said he had done. He
said he would not accept her abusiveness just because she
wanted to prove something to the other kids at school.

When Aunt Addie saw the knife, she became even more   30
angry, and she told Richard he was crazy. However, from that
point in time onward, she stopped accusing Richard of every
little thing, and, in fact, she started ignoring him totally. She
said he was a lost cause. Richard found that being on his aunt's
lost cause list was quite enjoyable, and he was glad that he had   35
defied her by not accepting the punishment that he felt, with
his sense of justice, he did not deserve.

10

Reading in Order to Write

Reading generates writing in many ways: by stimulating you to a subjective response, by prompting you to analyze what you have read, or by inspiring you to imitate it. But since most academic writing depends on your ability to read critically, this chapter begins with a brief set of guidelines on that.

10.1 GUIDELINES FOR CRITICAL READING

Critical reading means systematically investigating a text. We suggest you do this as follows:

1. Consider your purpose. Are you studying for a test? Are you preparing for a class? Are you seeking information for an essay? Are you gathering material for a research paper? In short, what do you hope to get from your reading?

2. Find out the author's qualifications. At the beginning or end of books and essays (or sometimes on the back cover of a paperback book), you can often find a short biographical note that will tell you something of the author's qualifications to write on the given topic—and perhaps something of his or her biases. For instance, if you were reading S. I. Hayakawa's "Sex Is Not a Spectator Sport" in one recent collection of essays by various hands, you could learn from a note on the author in the back of the book that Hayakawa was president of San Francisco State

College, and that during his tenure—marked by student pro-
tests—he asserted "a firm belief in authority, traditional values,
and the rule of law and order."

3. Consider what the title and subtitle (if any) tell you. By
itself, the title of Gail Sheehy's *Passages* doesn't tell you much,
but you can learn a good deal about the book from its subtitle:
Predictable Crises of Adult Life. And sometimes the title gives you
the author's thesis. From "Sex Is Not a Spectator Sport" you can
foresee the main point of Hayakawa's essay.

4. Note the date of publication. Everything you read is written
at a particular time, and to some extent at least, all writing is
time-bound. If you read Lewis Thomas's essay on the health care
system (pp. 229–32), for instance, you may be surprised to find
that he makes no mention of AIDS unless you note that his
essay was published in 1979, well before AIDS was generally
known—even to doctors—in the United States.

5. Preview a book by scanning its table of contents and index.
Together, these two things can give you a quick idea of what
the book contains. If your topic is quite specific, the index will
tell you where to find immediately what you need.

6. Then read the preface or introduction to learn the book's
scope, aim, and audience. Aside from checking the table of contents and index, the best way to learn quickly what a book
offers is to read the preface, introduction, or both. Here you can
learn what topics the book covers, what it chiefly aims to show,
and the audience for whom it was written.

7. Get ready to take notes. The least you need for critical reading is a pen or pencil. If you don't own the text you're reading,
prepare to make your notes on separate sheets or in a notebook,
or sit yourself down with a typewriter or word processor. (For
more on taking notes with a word processor, see section
33.10C.)

8. Read actively, talking back to the author by making notes
and comments. In the margins of your text—or on a separate
sheet if the text is not your own—talk back to the author by

making your own notes and comments on whatever provokes, surprises, puzzles, or in any way interests you. (For more on active reading, see section 1.11.)

9. <u>Read analytically, looking for main points, supporting points, and assumptions.</u> Evaluate the work's main points in light of its supporting points, and identify as well as you can the author's assumptions—both stated and unstated. Do you agree with those assumptions?

For more on how to read in preparation for the writing of a research paper, see chapter 33.

CRITICAL READING: IN BRIEF

- Consider your purpose.
- Find out the author's qualifications.
- Consider what the title and subtitle (if any) tell you.
- Note the date of publication.
- Preview a book by scanning the table of contents and index.
- Then read the preface or introduction to learn the book's scope, aim, and audience.
- Get ready to take notes.
- Read actively, talking back to the author by making notes and comments. (1.11)
- Read analytically, looking for main points, supporting points, and assumptions. (10.3A–E)

  On reading for a research paper, see chapter 33.

10.2 SUBJECTIVE RESPONSE

One way to get started writing about anything you read is to write about the way it feels to *you*. Do you like or dislike it? Why? Is it easy to understand or hard? Does it answer a question you've sometimes wondered about or tell you something you've never thought about before? Does it leave you with further questions? And how do you feel about the author?

These are all questions that call for personal, subjective answers. Besides taking notes, you can express your personal response in a piece of freewriting. Here, for instance, is a short passage from Carl L. Becker's *Modern History,* followed by one student's freewritten response:

> Students often say to me: "I don't know any history; I think it would be a good thing to learn some." What they seem to mean is that they have never had a "course" in history, or have never read Gibbon's *Decline and Fall of the Roman Empire,* or Mr. Rhodes's *History of the United States from the Compromise of 1850,* or other books similar to these. But they are greatly mistaken if they think they "don't know any history." Every man, woman, and child knows some history, enough at least to stumble along in the world.
>
> Suppose, for example, that you had awakened this morning totally unable to remember anything—all your other faculties working properly, but memory entirely gone. You would be in a bad way indeed! You wouldn't know who you were, or where; what you had done yesterday, or what you intended or other people expected you to do today. What could you do in that case? Wander about helplessly, seeing and hearing things, taking them in as altogether new, not at all knowing what they might mean in relation either to the past or the future. You would have to discover your little world all over again, much as you discovered it in childhood; you would have to "re-orient" yourself and get a new running start. In short, you would be a lost soul because you had ceased to have any knowledge of history, the history of your personal doings and associations in the past.
>
> For history is no more than things said and done in the past. It is as simple as that; and we might as well omit the word "past," since everything said and done is already in the past as soon as it is said or done. Done, but not done *with.* We have to remember many things said and done in order to live our lives intelligently; and so far as we remember things said and done we have a knowledge of history, for that is what historical knowledge is—*memory of things said and done.* Thus

everyone has some knowledge of history, and it is quite essential that everyone should have, since it is only by remembering something of the past that we can anticipate something of the future. Please note that I do not say *predict* the future. We cannot predict the future, but we can *anticipate* it—we can look forward to it and in some sense prepare for it. Now if memory of some things said and done is necessary, it seems that memory of more things ought to be better. The more we remember of things said and done (if they be the right things for our purpose), the better we can manage our affairs today, and the more intelligently we can prepare for what is coming to us tomorrow and next year and all our lives.

Student response:

OK, OK. Knowledge and understanding of history is helpful and important. But not all *that* important. True it would be hard living every day without knowing what was said and done in the past but this could be an advantage.

We've learned a great deal socially through history that has proved beneficial but at times it seems history has not proved helpful. So maybe *no* knowledge of history could be an advantage. If we suddenly awakened and had no memory at all I believe many problems could be solved in social relations. We wouldn't have knowledge of some of the evil or great things one minority had done, and so we wouldn't look at any one group above or below the others. We would have no knowledge of the feuds and wars that may have existed and possibly still exist between nations and minorities. Present and past discrimination and prejudice would be forgotten. Now I'm not saying this would make the world one giant, laughing, and incredibly happy place but I believe it would make the value of life much greater. Doubtless people would still become angered with each other, but it would be for a reason of their own, not because of some hate he or his ancestors may have for that person's minority. The world would now not be divided among nations and minorities but by the quality of the people.

Something exciting happens here. Carl Becker's argument that we cannot live without history has prompted this student to take the opposite view: that we could live better without it

because we would then be free of the prejudices and racial hostil-
ities that our knowledge of the past gives us. The student does
not have the whole truth, but neither does Becker. The point is
that a few minutes of reading, and perhaps fifteen minutes of
writing, have given the student a topic to think further about.
Reading Becker has put him in touch with his own ideas.

If he wants to state those ideas for others, of course, he will
need to do more thinking. Does he really want to say that *all*
history is better forgotten? Or does he believe that we should not
let our knowledge of the past tie our hands as we try to shape the
future? Can he find examples to support his belief? Thinking
about his point may bring him to a more persuasive as well as
more polished formulation of it.

But polishing a personal response does not mean depersonal-
izing it. Here is the first part of a published essay in which the
writer states her response to a book:

> There's a book out called *Is There Life after High School?*
> It's a fairly silly book, maybe because the subject matter is the
> kind that only hurts when you think. Its thesis—that most
> people never get over the social triumphs or humiliations of
> high school—is not novel. Still, I read it with the respectful
> attention a serious hypochondriac accords the lowliest "dear
> doctor" column. I don't know about most people, but for me,
> forgiving my parents for real and imagined derelictions has
> been easy compared to forgiving myself for being a teenage
> reject.
>
> Victims of high school trauma—which seems to have
> afflicted a disproportionate number of writers, including
> Ralph Keyes, the author of this book—tend to embrace the
> ugly duckling myth of adolescent social relations: the "innies"
> (Keyes's term) are good-looking, athletic mediocrities who
> will never amount to much, while the "outies" are intelligent,
> sensitive, creative individuals who will do great things in an
> effort to make up for their early defeats. . . . In contrast, the
> ex-prom queens and kings he interviews slink through life,
> hiding their pasts lest someone call them "dumb jock" or
> "cheerleader type," perpetually wondering what to do for an
> encore.
>
> If only it were that simple. There may really be high

schools where life approximates an Archie comic, but even in the Fifties, my large (5000 students), semisuburban (Queens, New York), heterogeneous high school was not one of them. The students' social life was fragmented along ethnic and class lines; there was no universally recognized, schoolwide social hierarchy. Being an athlete or a cheerleader or a student officer didn't mean much. Belonging to an illegal sorority or fraternity meant more, at least in some circles, but many socially active students chose not to join. The most popular kids were not necessarily the best looking or the best dressed or the most snobbish or the least studious. In retrospect, it seems to me that they were popular for much more honorable reasons. They were attuned to other people, aware of subtle social nuances. They projected an inviting sexual warmth. Far from being slavish followers of fashion, they were self-confident enough to set fashions. They suggested, initiated, led. Above all—this was their main appeal for me—they knew how to have a good time.   —Ellen Willis, "Memoirs of a Non-Prom Queen"

This writer's account of a book she has read is both objective and subjective. Objectively, she mentions its thesis—its main point—in her first paragraph, and she goes on in the next one to describe its contents. But the rest of her discussion is personal.

Another way of turning a subjective response into a finished essay is to begin with a personal experience that *introduces* one of the basic themes in the book you are writing about. Here, for instance, are the opening paragraphs of a student essay on the theme of solitude in Thoreau's *Walden:*

The whirling snow and howling wind seemed determined to destroy me for trespassing on the sacred heights of Mount Washington in the middle of the winter. Spindrift poured down the Northern Gully like water from a faucet, but the screaming blasts of bone-chilling wind took my mind off the snow. With a cloud cover sitting on the mountaintop like a mother hen on her egg, I could see hardly anything of the steep, huge, icy headwall on which I perched. As I pressed upward, my modern steel ice tools seemed no more than thumbtacks. My arms felt like enormous sponges—full and heavy, yet also powerless. My calves burned, my feet froze, and my legs trembled like a mouse before a lion. The climb seemed endless. No rope bound me to anyone else; my climbing partner had turned back hours ago. There was only me and a wild, white, screaming world of perils. I have never in my life felt such solitude, and at the same time such freedom from loneliness.

To experience this kind of solitude is to understand one of the most important things that Thoreau discovered at Walden Pond. In *Walden,* Thoreau observes that many people fear or dislike solitude, that they cannot understand how he could bear to live alone for two years. To answer this question, Thoreau reveals in his book the difference between solitude and loneliness. While these two states may seem inseparable, Thoreau shows that they can be entirely independent.

This student's personal experience provides him with a way into Thoreau's book. It leads him to a thesis—a statement about the meaning of the book—and thus to the germ of an essay about it.

EXERCISE 1   EXPRESSING A SUBJECTIVE RESPONSE

This exercise has three parts: (1) read the following essay and record your immediate personal reaction to it—without worrying about sentence structure or form; (2) compare Thomas's description of American health care to your experience of it; (3) use your experience of health care to introduce a statement of thesis about the meaning or value of the author's comments.

THE HEALTH-CARE SYSTEM

The health-care system of this country is a staggering enterprise, in any sense of the adjective. Whatever the failures of distribution and lack of coordination, it is the gigantic scale and scope of the total collective effort that first catches the breath, and its cost. The dollar figures are almost beyond   5
grasping. They vary from year to year, always upward, ranging from something like $10 billion in 1950 to an estimated $140 billion in 1978, with much more to come in the years just ahead, whenever a national health-insurance program is installed. The official guess is that we are now investing a   10
round 8 percent of the GNP in Health; it could soon rise to 10 or 12 percent.

Those are the official numbers, and only for the dollars

that flow in an authorized way—for hospital charges, physician's fees, prescribed drugs, insurance premiums, the construction of facilities, research, and the like.

But these dollars are only part of it. Why limit the estimates to the strictly professional costs? There is another huge marketplace, in which vast sums are exchanged for items designed for the improvement of Health.

The television and radio industry, no small part of the national economy, feeds on Health, or, more precisely, on disease, for a large part of its sustenance. Not just the primarily medical dramas and the illness or surgical episodes threaded through many of the nonmedical stories, in which the central human dilemma is illness; almost all the commercial announcements, in an average evening, are pitches for items to restore failed health: things for stomach gas, constipation, headaches, nervousness, sleeplessness or sleepiness, arthritis, anemia, disquiet, and the despair of malodorousness, sweat, yellowed teeth, dandruff, furuncles, piles. The food industry plays the role of surrogate physician, advertising breakfast cereals as though they were tonics, vitamins, restoratives; they are now out-hawked by the specialized Health-food industry itself, with its nonpolluted, organic, "naturally" vitalizing products. Chewing gum is sold as a tooth cleanser. Vitamins have taken the place of prayer.

The publishing industry, hardcover, paperbacks, magazines, and all, seems to be kept alive by Health, new techniques for achieving mental health, cures for arthritis, and diets mostly for the improvement of everything.

The transformation of our environment has itself become an immense industry, costing rather more than the moon, in aid of Health. Pollution is supposed to be primarily a medical problem; when the television weatherman tells whether New York's air is "acceptable" or not that day, he is talking about human lungs, he believes. Pollutants which may be impairing photosynthesis by algae in the world's oceans, or destroying all the life in topsoil, or killing all the birds are being worried about lest they cause cancer in us, for heaven's sake.

Tennis has become more than the national sport; it is a rigorous discipline, a form of collective physiotherapy. Jogging is done by swarms of people, out onto the streets each day in underpants, moving in a stolid sort of rapid trudge, hoping by this to stay alive. Bicycles are cures. Meditation may be good for the soul but it is even better for the blood pressure.

As a people, we have become obsessed with Health.

There is something fundamentally, radically unhealthy about all this. We do not seem to be seeking more exuberance 60 in living as much as staving off failure, putting off dying. We have lost all confidence in the human body.

The new consensus is that we are badly designed, intrinsically fallible, vulnerable to a host of hostile influences inside and around us, and only precariously alive. We live in danger 65 of falling apart at any moment, and are therefore always in need of surveillance and propping up. Without the professional attention of a health-care system, we would fall in our tracks.

This is a new way of looking at things, and perhaps it can 70 only be accounted for as a manifestation of spontaneous, undirected, societal *propaganda*. We keep telling each other this sort of thing, and back it comes on television or in the weekly newsmagazines, confirming all the fears, instructing us, as in the usual final paragraph of the personal-advice columns in the 75 daily paper, to "seek professional help." Get a checkup. Go on a diet. Meditate. Jog. Have some surgery. Take two tablets, with water. *Spring* water. If pain persists, if anomie persists, if boredom persists, see your doctor.

It is extraordinary that we have just now become con- 80 vinced of our bad health, our constant jeopardy of disease and death, at the very time when the facts should be telling us the opposite. In a more rational world, you'd think we would be staging bicentennial ceremonies for the celebration of our general good shape. In the year 1976, out of a population of 85 around 220 million, only 1.9 million died, or just under 1 percent, not at all a discouraging record once you accept the fact of mortality itself. The life expectancy for the whole population rose to seventy-two years, the longest stretch ever achieved in this country. Despite the persisting roster of still- 90 unsolved major diseases—cancer, heart disease, stroke, arthritis, and the rest—most of us have a clear, unimpeded run at a longer and healthier lifetime than could have been foreseen by any earlier generation. The illnesses that plague us the most, when you count up the numbers in the U.S. Vital Statistics 95 reports, are respiratory and gastrointestinal infections, which are, by and large, transient, reversible affairs needing not much more than Grandmother's advice for getting through safely. Thanks in great part to the improved sanitary engineering, nutrition, and housing of the past century, and in real but less part to contemporary immunization and antibiotics, we are free of the great infectious diseases, especially tuberculosis and lobar pneumonia, which used to cut us down long before our time. We are even beginning to make progress in our understanding of the mechanisms underlying the chronic illnesses still with us, and sooner or later, depending on the quality and energy of biomedical research, we will learn to cope effectively with most of these, maybe all. We will still age away and die, but the aging, and even the dying, can become a healthy process. On balance, we ought to be more pleased with ourselves than we are, and more optimistic for the future.

The trouble is, we are being taken in by the propaganda, and it is bad not only for the spirit of society; it will make any health-care system, no matter how large and efficient, unworkable. If people are educated to believe that they are fundamentally fragile, always on the verge of mortal disease, perpetually in need of support by health-care professionals at every side, always dependent on an imagined discipline of "preventive" medicine, there can be no limit to the numbers of doctors' offices, clinics, and hospitals required to meet the demand. In the end, we would all become doctors, spending our days screening each other for disease.

We are, in real life, a reasonably healthy people. Far from being ineptly put together, we are amazingly tough, durable organisms, full of health, ready for most contingencies. The new danger to our well-being, if we continue to listen to all the talk, is in becoming a nation of healthy hypochondriacs, living gingerly, worrying ourselves half to death.

And we do not have time for this sort of thing anymore, nor can we afford such a distraction from our other, considerably more urgent problems. Indeed, we should be worrying that our preoccupation with personal health may be a symptom of copping out, an excuse for running upstairs to recline on a couch, sniffing the air for contaminants, spraying the room with deodorants, while just outside, the whole of society is coming undone.

—Lewis Thomas, from *The Medusa and the Snail* (1979)

10.3 ANALYTICAL RESPONSE

To **analyze** a piece of writing is to take it apart in order to show how it works: to identify its components so that you can explain their relation to each other and to the chief point the writer is trying to make.

Effective analysis begins with study of the writer's tone, then moves to his or her main and supporting points.

10.3A CATCHING THE TONE

Earlier we explained how you can convey a particular tone of voice in your own writing (see section 2.4). But tone is also part of what you experience when you read the writing of someone else. It affects the way you "take" what you read—the way you feel about it and hence the way you interpret it. When Carl Becker writes "Students often say to me," he reveals that he is probably a teacher, as we might also guess from his lecture-room tone: "Please note that I do not say *predict* the future." Politely but firmly, he is treating us as students, carefully guiding us through his explanation. The tone tells us that he straightforwardly means what he says, so that we can take his words at face value.

Now consider the opening paragraphs of an essay:

WHY I WANT A WIFE

I belong to that classification of people known as wives. I am A Wife. And, not altogether incidentally, I am a mother.

Not too long ago a male friend of mine appeared on the scene fresh from a recent divorce. He had one child, who is, of course, with his ex-wife. He is looking for another wife. As I thought about him while I was ironing one evening, it suddenly occurred to me that I, too, would like to have a wife. Why do I want a wife?

I would like to go back to school so that I can become economically independent, support myself, and, if need be, support those dependent upon me. I want a wife who will work and send me to school. And while I am going to school I want a wife to take care of my children. I want a wife to keep track of the children's doctor and dentist appointments. And to keep track of mine, too. I want a wife to make sure my children eat properly and are kept clean. I want a wife who is a good nurturant attendant to my children, who arranges for their schooling, makes sure that they have an adequate social life with their peers, takes them to the park, the zoo, etc. I want a wife who takes care of the children when they are sick, a wife who arranges to be around when the children need special care, because, of course, I cannot miss classes at school. My wife must arrange to lose time at work and not lose the job. It may mean a small cut in my wife's income from time to time, but I guess I can tolerate that. Needless to say, my wife will arrange and pay for the care of the children while my wife is working.

—Judy Syfers

On the surface, the writer's tone is direct and decisive. Starting with the title, Syfers leaves no doubt about what she wants. Yet the conclusion of the second paragraph tells us that we can't take this essay at face value. A writer who calls herself "A Wife" and who also declares that she *wants* a wife must be playing some kind of game.

We soon discover that Syfers is masquerading as a wife-hunting man: the kind of man who expects his wife to hold a job and put him through school, satisfy all of his needs, serve him and his children in every possible way, and demand nothing in return. The purpose of the masquerade becomes obvious when we consider the sheer extravagance of these clearly stated requirements. What the writer actually wants to do is expose the egotism and insensitivity of men who think of wives as all-purpose servants.

The gap between tone and content here signals **irony**. If a writer sounds direct, decisive, and reasonable in stating demands that are grossly inconsiderate, or earnest and sincere in proposing something crazy, silly, or wildly inconsistent, you can be fairly certain that he or she is being *ironic*.

Now consider the tone in this passage:

Home for Christmas my first year in college, I spoke to my best friend from high school. Elizabeth and I stayed on the phone for 45 minutes, but we had nothing very much to say to each other. After the conversation, I was upset. I remember wanting to tell my mother, who asked what the matter was, about the weirdness of discovering that this woman and I, who had talked every school day for five years, no longer had anything in common. All I could do was cry.

Except for a brief, awkward visit to my house a month later when my father died, a church wedding where Elizabeth married a man I'd gone out with in seventh grade, and two short stopovers in southern New Jersey, I don't remember ever seeing or speaking to her again.

We used to spend hours talking about our relationships with boys. We never discussed our relationship with each other. Except for the few minutes with my mother, who told me she thought Elizabeth and I never had anything in common, and my once making a distinction between acquaintances and friends, I'd never spoken about what I considered a real friendship.

Many people have expressed agreement with Cicero that "friendship can only exist between good men." I'm not one of them. As a 30-year-old woman who has had friends since grade school, I have been very concerned with those friendships. Yet only in the last few years have such relationships been acknowledged as being as important as they've always been.

It was always commonplace for girls in my high school to spend a great deal of time together. It was also commonplace for a girl to spend Saturdays with another girl listening to Johnny Mathis albums, trying on clothes to find something that fit right, or babysitting and then having the evening that was planned together usurped by some boy calling up for a date. When this happened to me, I felt betrayed. I never said anything. It didn't occur to me that this wasn't the natural order of things. I didn't know anyone who complained, nor do I remember anyone who ever turned down a boy because she'd already made plans with a girl.

—Susan Lee, "Friendship, Feminism, and Betrayal"

Here the tone is neither didactic nor ironically assertive. The writer is neither telling us plainly what we ought to think ("Please note . . .") nor pretending to say the opposite of what she really means. Instead, her tone is confiding.

Exercise 2 Recognizing Tone

Read the following passage and then briefly describe (1) the author's tone and (2) his intention.

Being told I would be expected to talk here, I inquired what sort of talk I ought to make. They said it should be something suitable to youth—something didactic, instructive, or something in the nature of good advice. Very well. I have a few things in my mind which I have often longed to say 5 for the instruction of the young; for it is in one's tender early years that such things will best take root and be most enduring and most valuable. First, then, I will say to you, my young friends—and I say it beseechingly, urgingly—

Always obey your parents, when they are present. This is 10 the best policy in the long run, because if you don't they will make you. Most parents think they know better than you do, and you can generally make more by humoring that superstition than you can by acting on your own better judgment.

Be respectful to your superiors, if you have any, also to 15 strangers, and sometimes to others. If a person offends you, and you are in doubt as to whether it was intentional or not, do not resort to extreme measures; simply watch your chance and hit him with a brick. That will be sufficient. If you shall find that he had not intended any offense, come out frankly 20 and confess yourself in the wrong when you struck him; acknowledge it like a man and say you didn't mean to. Yes, always avoid violence; in this age of charity and kindliness, the time has gone by for such things. Leave dynamite to the low and unrefined. —Mark Twain, "Advice to Youth"

10.3B Finding the Writer's Main Point

To find the writer's **main point,** you can do one or more of the following.

1. <u>Use the title as a guide.</u> "Where College Fails Us," the title of an essay by Caroline Bird (see p. 61), clearly forecasts her main point and thus enables us to recognize this point when it appears in the first sentence of her second paragraph: "But college has never been able to work its magic for everyone."

2. Look for the main point in the first sentence of the opening paragraph:

> *People feel safer behind some kind of physical barrier.* If a social situation is in any way threatening, then there is an immediate urge to set up such a barricade. For a tiny child faced with a stranger, the problem is usually solved by hiding behind its mother's body and peeping out at the intruder to see what he or she will do next. If the mother's body is not available, then a chair or some other piece of solid furniture will do. If the stranger insists on coming closer, then the peeping face must be hidden too. If the insensitive intruder continues to approach despite these obvious signals of fear, then there is nothing for it but to scream or flee.
>
> —Desmond Morris, *Manwatching: A Field Guide to Human Behavior*

3. Look for the main point in the last sentence of the opening paragraph:

> In her stunning memoir of bicultural girlhood, *The Woman Warrior,* Maxine Hong Kingston writes, "There is a Chinese word for the female *I*—which is 'slave.' Break the women with their own tongues!" English contains no such dramatic instance of the ways in which language shapes women's reality. We can, after all, use the same "I" as men do. We can, but we're not supposed to, at least not often. *In myriad ways the rules of polite discourse in this country serve, among other purposes, not to enslave but certainly to silence women and thus to prevent them from uttering the truth about their lives.*
>
> —Nancy Mairs, "Who Are You?"

4. Watch for the main point to be implied:

> I once choked a chicken to death. It was my only barefaced, not to say barehanded, confrontation with death and the killer in me and happened on my grandparents' farm. I couldn't have been more than nine or ten and no firearms were included or necessary. I was on my knees and the chicken fluttered its outstretched wings with the last of the outraged protest. I gripped, beyond release, above its swollen crop, its beak gaping, translucent eyelids sliding up and down. . . . My grandfather, who was widely traveled and world-wise, in his eighties then, and had just started using a cane from earlier

times, came tapping at that moment around the corner of the chicken coop and saw what I was doing and started gagging at the hideousness of it, did a quick assisted spin away and never again, hours later nor for the rest of his life, for that matter, ever mentioned the homicidal incident to me. Keeping his silence, he seemed to understand; and yet whenever I'm invaded by the incident, the point of it seems to be his turning away from me. —Larry Woiwode, "Guns"

The last sentence states the would-be point of the incident but merely implies the main point of the paragraph: the grandfather's turning away made the writer recognize himself as a killer.

5. Watch for the main point to emerge. In Caroline Bird's "Where College Fails Us" (p. 61), the main point emerges in the second paragraph. In Eugene Raskin's "Walls and Barriers," an essay whose opening paragraphs appear in chapter 4, exercise 3, p. 76, the main point takes longer to surface. After first introducing his topic (banks), the author takes three paragraphs to develop the point that banks have changed: since tangible money (coins and bills) has been largely replaced by credit, the banker now offers not a heavy-walled safe, but a bright, open, inviting service. In the fifth paragraph, the point about bank design gives way to a more general point. Raskin uses the contrast between old banks and new ones to illustrate the contrast between traditional and modern architecture as a whole. In turn, that contrast supports the main point of the essay: architecture reflects the way we think about our relation to the outside world.

> **EXERCISE 3** IDENTIFYING THE MAIN POINT
>
> In each of the following passages, one sentence expresses the main point. Identify that sentence.
>
> 1. The history of Florida is measured in freezes. Severe ones, for example, occurred in 1747, 1766, and 1774. The freeze of February, 1835, was probably the worst one in the state's history. But, because more growers were affected, the Great Freeze of 1895 seems to enjoy the same sort of status in 5 Florida that the Blizzard of '88 once held in the North.

Temperatures on the Ridge on February 8, 1895, went into
the teens for much of the night. It is said that some orange
growers, on being told what was happening out in the
groves, got up from their dinner tables and left the state. 10
In the morning, it was apparent that the Florida citrus
industry had been virtually wiped out.

—John McPhee, *Oranges*

2. In early human history a Stone Age, a Bronze Age, or an
   Iron Age came into unhurried gestation and endured for
   centuries or even millennia; and as one technology gradually displaced or merged with another, the changes
   wrought in any single lifetime were easily absorbed, if 5
   noticed at all. But a transformation has come about in our
   own time. A centenarian born in 1879 has seen, in the years
   of his own life, scientific and technological advances more
   sweeping and radical than those that took place in all the
   accumulated past. He has witnessed—and felt the personal 10
   impact of—the Age of Electricity, the Automobile Age,
   the Aviation Age, the Electronic Age, the Atomic Age, the
   Space Age, and the Computer Age, to name but a few of
   the "ages" that have been crowding in upon us at such an
   unprecedented rate, sometimes arriving virtually side by 15
   side. Let us use the shortcut designation the "Age of Science" to encompass them all.

—Albert Rosenfeld,
"How Anxious Should Science Make Us?"

EXERCISE 4 IDENTIFYING THE MAIN POINT

Reread the essay given in exercise 1, pp. 229–32, and identify
its main point.

10.3C SUMMARIZING

Summarizing a piece of writing is a good way to test and demonstrate your understanding of it. The **summary** of an essay
should begin by stating its main point and then proceed to the
chief supporting points. Here, for instance, is a summary of
Eugene Raskin's "Walls and Barriers" (opening paragraphs
above, p. 76):

> Architecture reveals the way we think about our relation to the outside world. While the heavy walls of traditional architecture express a fear of that world, the glass walls of modern architecture express confidence that human beings can master the outside world and eventually solve all of its problems.

This summary begins with the main point of the whole essay, and the second sentence states the chief supporting point. Most of the summary is drawn from the final paragraph, which clearly states the essay's main point and is often the best place to look for such a statement:

> To repeat, it is not our advanced technology, but our changing conceptions of ourselves in relation to the world that determine how we shall build our walls. The glass wall expresses man's conviction that he can and does master nature and society. The "open plan" and the unobstructed view are consistent with his faith in the eventual solution of all problems through the expanding efforts of science. This is perhaps why it is the most "advanced" and "forward-looking" among us who live and work in glass houses. Even the fear of the cast stone has been analyzed out of us.

The summary of a narrative or drama is usually called a **plot summary**. A plot summary may be **sequential** or **comprehensive**:

1. A sequential plot summary follows the order in which a narrative or drama presents its main events:

> Discontented with his life on land, a young schoolteacher who calls himself Ishmael decides to go to sea on a whaling ship. He travels to New Bedford, where he meets and strikes up a friendship with a harpooner named Queequeg. Then the two men go to Nantucket and sign on board a ship named the *Pequod*. . . .

2. A comprehensive plot summary starts with an overall statement about the chief action of the narrative or drama and then gives the chain of events that make up that action:

> *Moby-Dick* is the story of Ahab's relentless quest for revenge against a great white whale that has taken his leg and

that eventually takes his life. Ahab is the captain of a whaling ship named the *Pequod,* and the story of his quest is told by one of the seamen who serves on his ship—a man who calls himself Ishmael. Discontented with his life on land, Ishmael decides to go to sea on a whaling voyage, so he signs on the *Pequod* along with a newfound friend named Queequeg. Shortly after the ship embarks, Ahab announces that the sole purpose of the voyage is to catch and kill Moby-Dick. . . .

While a sequential plot summary recounts one event after another without saying which is the most important, a comprehensive plot summary identifies the central action to which all other actions must be referred.

For advice on summarizing and paraphrasing material in the writing of a research paper, see section 34.6.

EXERCISE 5 SUMMARIZING

Summarize the essay given in exercise 1, pp. 229–32.

10.3D PARAPHRASING

Paraphrasing is restating a short passage in your own words. Besides demonstrating your understanding of what you read, paraphrasing enables you to discuss texts without quoting every word of them. If you plan to analyze a particular passage in detail, you should quote it in full. But if you simply want to convey the essential point of the passage, you can paraphrase all or part of it:

QUOTATION: According to Thoreau, the legendary Kouroo artist spent hundreds of years making a perfect staff because, "having considered that in an imperfect work time is an ingredient, but into a perfect work time does not enter, he said to himself, 'It shall be perfect in all respects, though I should do nothing else in my life.' "

PARAPHRASE: According to Thoreau, the legendary Kouroo artist spent hundreds of years making a perfect staff because he believed that time had nothing to do with perfection, and he was willing to spend his whole life pursuing it.

While the quotation makes an awkward bulge in the writer's sentence, the paraphrase fits nicely. Slightly compressing the original, it clearly expresses Thoreau's essential point. (When paraphrasing, be sure to acknowledge your source. If you don't, you will be guilty of plagiarism, as explained in section 34.3.)

EXERCISE 6 PARAPHRASING

Restate each of the following passages in one sentence, using your own words:

1. "Most people who bother with the matter at all would admit that the English language is in a bad way, but it is generally assumed that we cannot by conscious action do anything about it."
                                                        —George Orwell

2. "A good city street neighborhood achieves a marvel of balance between its people's determination to have essential privacy and their simultaneous wishes for differing degrees of contact, enjoyment, or help from people around."
                                                        —Jane Jacobs

10.3E JUDGING THE SUPPORTING POINTS IN AN ESSAY

To summarize an essay, you must be able to identify its main point and its chief supporting points. To analyze an essay, you must also be able to judge the relevance and strength of each **supporting point.** You should therefore try to answer these questions:

1. Are the supporting points statements of fact or opinions? A statement of fact can be indisputably verified. An opinion is a statement that may be impossible to verify but can be supported by facts—and usually needs such support to make an impression on the reader.

Since an opinion cannot stand on its own feet, you should take a hard look at what is said to support it. Sometimes there is no supporting statement at all, and sometimes the supporting statement turns out to be nothing but another opinion. When a writer says that "young people no longer work seriously" to persuade us that the nation is declining, the supporting statement is mere opinion. It cannot be verified until we know who the "young people" are, what their "work" is, and how to measure their seriousness.

Between a statement of fact and an opinion stands another kind of statement: the assertion made with a number. Suppose you read that there are eight million rats in New York City. This looks like a statement that can be checked and verified—a fact. But who can actually count the number of rats in New York? Contrary to popular belief, numbers have no special authority over words. The figures a writer cites are only as reliable as the methods used to get them or the source from which they come.

In general, therefore, you should read with a question mark between you and the page. Be on the watch for deceptive exaggeration, "figures" that come out of thin air, and editorial opinion masquerading as reportorial fact. Life is too short for you to check out every unsupported claim or surprising new "fact" for yourself; usually you must trust the writer. But you can reasonably ask that a writer earn your trust—by respecting the difference between statements of fact and opinions.

2. Are there enough supporting points? In the paragraph on barriers (p. 237), Desmond Morris's main point is that "people feel safer behind some kind of physical barrier," and he supports this point by describing what a child does when confronted by a stranger. But Morris's paragraph on the child is merely the opening of a chapter in which he describes the barrier signals that grownups use, the subtle movements and postures with which adults continue to shield themselves in unfamiliar company. By citing specific examples of adult as well as child behavior, Morris convincingly supports his point in the chapter as a whole.

3. Are the supporting points relevant to the main point? A main point "supported" by irrelevant points is like a house trying to rest on a foundation that is laid beside it. If, for instance, a writer wants to show that women should not be allowed to engage in combat, the fact that many women do not want to serve in the armed forces at all is irrelevant. The question is whether the women who *do* want to fight should be allowed to do so.

4. Has the writer considered opposing points? To be wholly convincing, an argument must recognize the major points that can be set against it. (See section 7.5, "Reckoning with the Opposition.") When you read a completely one-sided essay on a subject you know has at least two sides, you may be sure that the argument is slanted.

5. Are there any fallacies in the writer's argument? Fallacies are mistakes in reasoning. (See section 7.4, "Avoiding Fallacies.")

READING ANALYTICALLY: IN BRIEF

TONE (10.3A)

What is the writer's attitude toward the subject?

Can the writing be taken at face value, or is it ironic?

MAIN POINT (10.3B)

What is the writer's main point?

Where is it stated or how is it implied?

SUPPORTING POINTS (10.3E)

Are the supporting points facts or opinions?

Are there enough supporting points?

Are they relevant to the main point?

Has the writer considered opposing points of view?

Are there any fallacies in the writer's argument?

EXERCISE 7 ANALYZING A PARAGRAPH

Read the following paragraph and answer these questions: (1) What is the main point? (2) What are the supporting points? (3) Are any of the supporting points not strictly relevant to the main point? (4) Which sentences are statements of fact and which are opinions?

[1] No wild animal has been a greater incitement to the discovery of new worlds than the beaver. [2] North America

was largely explored by men seeking to profit from an insatia-
ble European market for felt hats made from shorn and pressed
beaver fur. [3] The Hudson's Bay Company, established in   5
1669 to trade with the Indians for beaver pelts, was the effective government of most of Canada from the French and Indian
War until the mid-nineteenth century. [4] American beaver
traders such as Jedediah Smith preceded gold miners and set-
tlers to the West Coast by several decades. [5] During the   10
height of the beaver trade, after the steel trap began to be
produced industrially and before new felt-making processes
depressed the price of a beaver pelt by some 80 percent, a
beaver trapper could average a daily income estimated at
thirty-two times that of a farm laborer. [6] It's no wonder that   15
mountain men explored every watershed from Santa Fe to Van-
couver in the 1820s. [7] Even after beaver prices fell in the
1840s, an estimated 500,000 beavers were being killed every
year, primarily for their fur, which was (and is) used to make
coats and collars.   20

—David Rains Wallace,
"The Mind of the Beaver" (1986)

Exercise 8 Analyzing and Judging an Argument

Analyze and judge Lewis Thomas's argument about the health-
care system (exercise 1, pp. 229–32).

Exercise 9 Using Facts in an Argument

Explain whether or not the facts stated in the essay by Lewis
Thomas (pp. 229–32) could be used to support a positive conclusion about the state of American health care.

10.3F Writing an Interpretive Essay

To **interpret** a piece of writing is to explain what it means.
Though interpretation calls for many of the analytical skills discussed above, it commonly aims not so much to judge as to elu-
cidate: to show what the writer has to teach us. Essentially, an
interpretive essay constructs an argument *about* the writer's meaning. Here is an example:

THOREAU'S TREATMENT OF TIME IN *WALDEN*

Introduction: topic leads to question; question leads to statement of thesis.

Henry David Thoreau's *Walden* is an account of the author's attempt to remove himself from society and live a life of self-sufficiency at Walden Pond. Yet strangely enough, Thoreau seems highly preoccupied with one of the very things that dominate the society he has left behind: time. If he is truly independent of society, if he has really forsaken the world of clock-watching business managers and wage-earners, why is he so concerned with measuring time? Why does he have so much to say about it? The answer, I think, is that Thoreau measures his life at Walden not by clock time but by nature's time: not in hours and minutes but in mornings, evenings, seasons, deaths, and births.

Supporting point #1: story of Kouroo artist shows the ideal of freedom from time.

Thoreau is sufficiently free from conventional notions of time that he can imagine a life without any time at all. He illustrates such a life with the story of the Kouroo artist who set out to make the perfect staff, and who devoted hundreds of years to the project because he believed that time had nothing to do with perfection, and he was willing to spend his whole life pursuing it. "As he made no compromise with Time," says Thoreau, "Time kept out of his way, and only sighed at a distance because he [Time] could not overcome him" (218). This story represents the ideal state that Thoreau would like to achieve. For him, the ultimate achievement would be to make time stand still.

Supporting point #2: Thoreau was reborn each morning and in the spring.

But Thoreau knows that time cannot be stopped. At Walden, therefore, he decides to regulate his life not by the clock time that mechanically runs society but by the natural cycles that govern every living thing on earth, and even the earth itself. The morning of each new day at Walden marks the beginning of a new life, just as spring marks the awakening of the pond from its long winter's death. Thoreau measures his life at Walden by these natural patterns of cyclic renewal. Though he actually spent two years at Walden Pond, he compresses the story of his sojourn into just one complete cycle that begins with the building of his house in the spring and ends—after summer and fall and the chill of winter—with the glorious return of spring. "As every season seems best to us in its turn," he writes, "so the coming in of spring is like the creation of Cosmos out of Chaos and the realization of the

Golden Age" (209). The calendar might say that he was one or two years older, but Thoreau feels reborn when spring returns.

In Thoreau's concept of time, hours and minutes give way to the immeasurable rhythms of nature and life itself. He ends *Walden* with the story of the bug that suddenly emerged from the wood of a table. Many years before, its egg had been deposited in the tree from which the table was made; one day it gnawed its way out, "hatched perchance by the heat of an urn" (222). With no knowledge of how many years it had been buried and no desire to find out, it simply appeared because it had reached at last the peak of its life-cycle.

Supporting point #3: story of bug illustrates triumph over time.

In *Walden*, then, Thoreau urges us to disregard the years in which we have imprisoned ourselves and to stop measuring our existence by the clock and calendar. Instead, he shows us how to measure existence by the number of times we experience a renewal of our lives.

Conclusion

WORKS CITED

Thoreau, Henry D. *Walden*. Ed. William Rossi. 2nd ed. New York: Norton, 1992.

This analysis of *Walden* illustrates a good way of organizing an interpretive essay. The author (a college freshman) begins with a specific topic (Thoreau's concept of time), defines a problem (the conflict between a desire for freedom and a preoccupation with time), and then proposes a solution in the form of a thesis (Thoreau measures life at Walden not by clock time but by nature's time). To develop the thesis, he writes three paragraphs on three specific things from the text: the story of the Kouroo artist, the passage on spring, and the story of the bug. In each of these paragraphs he quotes from *Walden* but only enough to make his points. He uses paraphrase to keep down the amount of material quoted and thus to keep the reader's eye on the line of interpretation he develops.

For further advice on writing about works of literature, see chapter 37 and section 38.2A. For guidance on writing research papers about literary topics, see chapter 37 and sections 38.4–38.5.

EXERCISE 10 INTRODUCING AN INTERPRETIVE ESSAY

Following the model shown above, write the introductory paragraph for an interpretive essay on any work chosen by you or your teacher. Your paragraph should (1) identify a topic, (2) define a problem, and (3) propose a solution in the form of a thesis to be developed.

EXERCISE 11 WRITING AN INTERPRETIVE ESSAY

Using the thesis generated for the previous exercise, write an interpretive essay in which you specifically refer to at least three passages from the work you have chosen. Include at least three quotations from the work, but be careful to limit the length of each one.

10.4 IMITATIVE RESPONSE: READING FOR STYLE

The **style** of a piece of writing is the total effect made by such things as the writer's sentence structure, choice of words, and figures of speech. Ernest Hemingway creates his understated style, for instance, by using chiefly short, simple words and a loose string of coordinate clauses: "In the fall the war was always there, but we did not go to it any more. It was cold in the fall in Milan and the dark came very early." James Baldwin, on the other hand, creates a powerfully ornate style by frequently using long words and a tight structure of subordinate clauses: "The black man insists, by whatever means he finds at his disposal, that the white man cease to regard him as an exotic rarity and recognize him as a human being." Maya Angelou, who is a poet as well as a writer of prose, often enlivens her sentences with figures of speech: "The man's dead words fell like bricks around the auditorium and too many settled in my belly."

In writing, as in any other art, you learn by studying and imitating styles you admire. If you read a sentence or a paragraph that excites you, write it down or memorize it. Then quote it when you get the chance, or imitate its style in a sentence of your own.

Conscious and formal imitation of a writer with a distinctive style can be an excellent exercise. Start by reading aloud to yourself this passage from Mark Twain's *Autobiography:*

> As I have said, I spent some part of every year at the farm until I was twelve or thirteen years old. The life which I led there with my cousins was full of charm and so is the memory of it yet. I can call back the solemn twilight and the mystery of the deep woods, the earthy smells, the faint odors of the wild flowers, the sheen of rain-washed foliage, the rattling clatter of drops when the wind shook the trees, the far-off hammering of woodpeckers and the muffled drumming of wood-pheasants in the remoteness of the forest, the snapshot glimpses of disturbed wild creatures scurrying through the grass—I can call it all back and make it as real as it ever was, and as blessed. I can call back the prairie, and its loneliness and peace, and a vast hawk hanging motionless in the sky with his wings spread wide and the blue of the vault showing through the fringe of their end-feathers. I can see the woods in their autumn dress, the oaks purple, the hickories washed with gold, the maples and the sumachs luminous with crimson fires, and I can hear the rustle made by the fallen leaves as we plowed through them. I can see the blue clusters of wild grapes hanging amongst the foliage of the saplings and I remember the taste of them and the smell. I know how the wild blackberries looked and how they tasted; and the same with the pawpaws, the hazelnuts, and the persimmons; and I can feel the thumping rain upon my head of hickory-nuts and walnuts when we were out in the frosty dawn to scramble for them with the pigs, and the gusts of wind loosed them and sent them down.

You may not think you could ever write like this. But you can—right now. In your own descriptive writing you can immediately use the two simple techniques illustrated here: starting with a memory statement *(I can call back, I can see),* and filling each sentence with specific memories—sights, sounds, smells, and feelings.

Here, for instance, is a description of working on an asparagus farm written by a student who was deliberately imitating Twain:

I can still remember changing pipe in nothing but gym shorts and tennis shoes, with swarms of bees humming all around me in the fern and never once was I stung. I remember disturbing countless quail and pheasants, and once in a while catching a brief glimpse of a coyote or jackrabbit. I remember freezing hands in early spring, when frost covered the pipes in the early morning, and burning hands in late summer, when a line had lain in the hot sun for a day or so. I know the sweet taste of grapes liberated from the next field, and the bitter taste of raw potato from another neighboring unit. I know how to grab a handful of wheat and rub off the chaff, leaving only the crunchy grain, and how good it tastes after a hard day's work. I can call back the ringing in my ears after driving a tractor all day, nonstop, and how good it would have felt to have had some earplugs. I remember the shimmering sun baking us to a golden brown as we lay snoozing on the ground after the pipes were changed, and how once in a while the boss would find us in that position. He never appreciated our attitude toward work.

Though you can easily recognize Twain's two basic techniques, you can also see that this is creative imitation. The student does not copy Twain's words. Rather he uses Twain's techniques to summon up personal memories, to generate a description of his own experience.

A passage of any length can be a model for you to imitate. Here, for instance, is a short paragraph:

When we are children, growing up in our parents' care, we await the spark from the outside world. Sometimes our parents provide it—if we are lucky—sometimes it comes from another source far from home. We sit, paralyzed, surrounded by our anxiety and dread, hoping we will not have to grow up into the narrow world and ways we see about us. We are hungry for a life that turns us on; we yearn for a knowledge of living that will save us from our innocuous lives that resemble death. We look for signs in every strange event; we search for heroes in every unknown face.

—Alice Walker, "The Civil Rights Movement:
What Good Was It?"

With the main part of the first sentence—*we await the spark from the outside world*—Walker establishes the pattern that dominates the style of this paragraph. Repeatedly starting sentences with *we*, she builds a list of parallels that gather force as she proceeds: *we await, we sit, we are hungry, we yearn, we look for signs, we search for heroes*. (On list-structure paragraphing, see section 8.3A.)

EXERCISE 12 IMITATING STYLE

1. Drawing on your own memories of a specific period or experience in your life, write an imitation of Twain's passage. Begin at least one of your sentences with *I can still see*, at least one with *I can still hear*, and at least one with *I can still feel*.

2. Using Walker's paragraph as a model, explain what your own hopes and expectations are right now.

EXERCISE 13 EXPLAINING AND IMITATING THE STYLE OF A PASSAGE

Copy out a brief passage by any writer whose work you admire, and then (1) explain why you admire its style, and (2) imitate its style in a passage of your own.

2

WRITING SENTENCES

11

The Simple Sentence

The **sentence** is a fundamentally human creation. Like the human beings who write them, sentences come in a seemingly endless variety of shapes and sizes: some stretch out for line upon line; others stop short after two or three words. Yet for all its variety, the sentence has a definable structure.

How much do you need to know about this structure to write well? If you can speak and write English, you already know a good deal about the structure of the English sentence. But to make your sentences both grammatically correct and rhetorically effective, you may need to know more about the basic parts.

11.1 THE SUBJECT AND THE PREDICATE

A sentence consists of at least one clause—a word group with a subject and a predicate. The **subject** identifies a person, place, or thing. The **predicate** tells what the subject does or is, where it is, what it has, or what is done to it. In statements the subject often comes first:

SUBJECT	PREDICATE
Economists	study the production and consumption of goods and services.
The American economic system	is a form of capitalism.
Control of production	is private.
Consumers	have a variety of choices.
Prices of goods and services	are largely determined by supply and demand.

In this chapter we consider the basic parts of the one-clause sentence (the **simple sentence**) because all other sentences are based on this structure.

11.2 VERBS AND VERB PHRASES

The predicate always includes a **verb,** which may be one word or a phrase:

> The comet *is* visible now.
> A solar eclipse *will be* visible in October.
>
> Napoleon's victory *revived* his dream of political domination.
> Dreams *can revive* old memories.
>
> Over 80 percent of the first inhabitants *perished* in 1607.
> All of the early settlers *would have perished* without help from the natives.
>
> *Is* the ceremony a humane one?
> *Do* the initiation rites *include* bloodletting?
>
> *Are* interest rates *falling?*
> The recession *has* not *ended* yet.

Every **verb phrase** consists of a base verb and at least one "helping" verb or auxiliary. Auxiliaries include forms of *be* (*is, are, was, were*), *have, has, had, do, does, may, might, can, could, will, shall, would,* and *should.*

11.3 TYPES OF VERBS

Verbs may be linking, intransitive, or transitive.

11.3A LINKING VERBS

A **linking verb** connects the subject to a word or phrase that identifies, classifies, or describes it:

John Marshall *was* the fourth chief justice of the United States.

Pyrite *is* a mineral chiefly used as a source of sulfur.

The primaries *are* testing grounds for the candidates of political parties.

Primary campaigns soon *become* expensive.

The most widely used linking verb is a form of *be,* such as *am, is, are, was,* or *were.* Other linking verbs include *seem, become, feel, sound,* and *taste.*

The word or phrase that follows a linking verb is called a **subject complement.** If the word is a noun, such as *mineral,* it is called a **predicate noun.** If the word is an adjective, such as *expensive,* it is called a **predicate adjective.**

11.3B INTRANSITIVE VERB

An **intransitive verb** names an action that has no direct impact on anyone or anything named in the predicate:

The earth *turns* on its axis.

All symptoms of the disease *vanished.*

The volcano *could erupt* at any time.

As the examples show, intransitive verbs do not have objects. Compare them with transitive verbs, shown in the next section.

11.3C TRANSITIVE VERBS

A **transitive verb** names an action that directly affects a person or thing mentioned in the predicate. The word or phrase naming this person or thing is called the **direct object** (DO):

DO

An enthusiastic crowd *greeted* the president at the airport.

DO

Gamblers *lose* money.

DO

A fungus *has been threatening* maples in the region.

Some verbs take an **indirect object** (IO), which may go before or after the direct object:

> IO   DO
> The president *gave* his staff a stern warning.

You could also write:

> DO   IO
> The president *gave* a stern warning to his staff.

Other verbs that give you this option include *make, send, offer, show, write,* and *tell.* But whatever the verb, you must put the direct object first whenever both objects are pronouns:

> DO   IO
> Ellen offered it to them.

Another kind of transitive verb takes an **object complement** (OC), a word or phrase that follows the direct object and classifies or describes it:

> DO   OC
> Many scientists *considered* the experiment a disaster.

> DO   OC
> Unfair accusations *make* most people angry.

> DO   OC
> The jury *found* the defendant guilty of treason.

Other verbs of this kind include *name, elect, appoint, think, judge,* and *prove.*

You can use a transitive verb in either the active or the passive voice. When the subject performs the action named by the verb, the verb is **active**:

> Farmers *plow* fields.
> Vandals *defaced* the queen's portrait.

When the subject undergoes, receives, or suffers the action named by the verb, the verb is **passive**:

> Fields *are plowed* by farmers.
> The queen's portrait *was defaced* by vandals.

For a full discussion of voice, see chapter 22.

TYPES OF VERBS: IN BRIEF

A **linking verb** connects the subject to a word or phrase that identifies, classifies, or describes it:

> Lima *is* the capital of Peru.
> Some professional athletes *become* wealthy.

An **intransitive verb** names an action that has no effect on a person or thing mentioned in the predicate:

> Children *giggle*.
> Palm trees *were swaying* in the moonlight.

A **transitive verb** in the **active voice** names an action performed by the subject and affecting a person or thing mentioned in the predicate:

> Winston Churchill *inspired* the people of Great Britain during World War II.
> Traffic jams *inhibit* the flow of goods and services.

A **transitive verb** in the **passive voice** names an action affecting the subject. The person or thing performing the action may be mentioned in the predicate after the word *by*, or left unmentioned:

> During World War II the people of Great Britain *were inspired* by Winston Churchill.
> The flow of goods and services *is inhibited* by traffic jams.
> Traces of mercury *were found* in the water.

11.4 WRITING THE SUBJECT

The **subject** of a simple sentence can be a noun, a noun phrase, a pronoun, or a verbal noun.

1. A **noun** is a word naming one or more persons, creatures, places, things, activities, conditions, or ideas:

SUBJECT	PREDICATE
Children	thrive on loving care.
Freedom	entails responsibility.
Dinosaurs	became extinct some sixty-five million years ago.

2. **A noun phrase** is a group of words, consisting of a main noun (MN) and the words that describe, limit, or qualify it:

SUBJECT (NOUN PHRASE)	PREDICATE
MN The price of gold	has dropped sharply.
MN Long-standing labor disputes	can be difficult to settle.
MN The sound of snoring in the audience	distracted the performers.

3. **A pronoun** (PR) takes the place of a noun (N):

SUBJECT	PREDICATE
N Investors	have become cautious
PR They	fear a recession.
N Traffic	moved briskly at first.
PR It	soon slowed to a crawl.

For a full discussion of pronouns, see chapter 18.

4. **A verbal noun** is a word or phrase formed from a verb and used as a noun. It can function as the subject in a sentence:

SUBJECT	PREDICATE
To err	is human.
Splitting logs	takes muscle.
Verifying the testimony of witnesses to an accident	can be a time-consuming process.

Verbal nouns enable you to treat actions as things, and thus to get more action into your sentences. There are two types: the **gerund,** which ends in *-ing,* and the **infinitive,** which is usually marked by *to.* A verbal noun may also serve

a. as a predicate noun (PN) after a linking verb:

> PN
>
> Their aim is *to obstruct justice.*

> PN
>
> The most common mishap of all is *breaking a test tube.*

b. as the direct object (DO) of a transitive verb:

> DO
>
> Gourmands love *to eat.*

> DO
>
> Few enjoy *my singing of the national anthem.*

WRITING THE SUBJECT: IN BRIEF

The subject of a simple sentence may be—

- a noun:

    Children thrive on loving care.

- a noun phrase:

    All the children of the world thrive on loving care.

- a pronoun:

    They need our help.

- a verbal noun:

    To work is to pray.
    Seeing is believing.

11.5 PUTTING THE SUBJECT AFTER THE VERB

The subject of a declarative sentence—a sentence that makes a statement—usually precedes the verb. But the subject follows the verb in sentences like these:

There were *riots* in the occupied territories.

It is hard to *read small print*.

In these sentences *There* and *It* are introductory words or **expletives**. They are not part of either the subject or the predicate.

The subject also follows the verb when the word order is inverted:

In the center of the painting stands *a white unicorn with a golden horn*.

The inversion of subject-verb order gives special prominence to the subject, so you should use inversion sparingly—and only when you want this special effect.

In most questions the subject (S) follows a verb so that the predicate (P) is divided:

P	S	P
Can	we	find a cure for AIDS?
Have	we	the will and the means?

11.6 OMITTING THE SUBJECT

A sentence that gives a command or makes a request often omits the subject, which is understood to be *you:*

Keep off the grass.

Please don't litter.

Submit your application before June 1.

For more on this type of sentence, which is called **imperative,** see section 23.3.

11.7 USING MODIFIERS

The complete subject and the complete predicate of a sentence normally include modifiers. A **modifier** is a word, phrase, or clause that describes, limits, or qualifies another word or word group. The italicized words are all modifiers in this sentence:

SUBJECT PREDICATE
The price *of gold* had dropped *sharply.*

The words modifying *price* form part of the subject; the word modifying *has dropped* forms part of the predicate. Here are further examples:

S P
A *negligent* workman spilled lye *over the oriental rug.*

S P
The equivocal statements of the *prime minister* are sending
mixed signals *to the opposition.*

S
The brightly painted masks *used in the hunting rituals*

P
are sacred objects *representing tribal ancestors.*

S P
Grandfather sat *in his rocker, watching the children.*

For a full discussion of modifiers, see chapter 12.

EXERCISE 1 RECOGNIZING SUBJECTS AND PREDICATES

In each of the following sentences, identify the subject and the predicate, using brackets around the complete subject and parentheses around each part of the predicate.

EXAMPLE

[A fool's brain] (digests philosophy into folly, science into superstition, and art into pedantry) —G. B. Shaw

1. The hills across the valley of the Ebro were long and white. —Ernest Hemingway
2. At once a black fin slit the pink cloud on the water, shearing it in two. —Annie Dillard
3. Florence Nightingale shrieked aloud in her agony. —Virginia Woolf

4. Outside literature, the main motive for writing is to describe the world.
—Northrop Frye

5. It is not worth the while to go round the earth to count the cats in Zanzibar.
—Henry David Thoreau

6. A work of art expresses a conception of life, emotion, inward reality.
—Susanne K. Langer

7. There is nothing so exhilarating as to be shot at without effect.
—Winston Churchill

8. Who will compute the lonely nights made less lonely by your songs, or the empty pots made less tragic by your tales?
—Maya Angelou

11.8 USING COMPOUND PHRASES

Compound phrases help to turn short, meager sentences into longer, meatier ones. A **compound phrase** joins words or phrases to show one of the following things:

1. Addition

Presidential election campaigns have become long.

Presidential election campaigns have become expensive.

COMBINED: Presidential campaigns have become *long and expensive.*

The dancer was lean.

The dancer was acrobatic.

The dancer was bold.

COMBINED: The dancer was *lean, acrobatic, and bold.*

Ants crawled over the floor.

They crawled up the wall.

They crawled onto the counter.

They crawled into the honey pot.

COMBINED: Ants crawled *over the floor, up the wall, onto the counter, and into the honey pot.*

The witness blushed.

He cleared his throat.

He began to speak in a halting manner.

COMBINED: The witness *blushed, cleared his throat, and began to speak in a halting manner.*

2. Contrast

Marketing U.S. products in Japan is difficult.

But it is not impossible.

COMBINED: Marketing U.S. products in Japan is *difficult but not impossible.*

3. Choice

The government must reduce its spending.

Or it must raise taxes.

COMBINED: The government must *either reduce its spending or raise taxes.*

The senator had not anticipated the setback.

Her staff had not anticipated the setback.

COMBINED: *Neither the senator nor her staff* had anticipated the setback.

For advice on punctuating the items in a compound phrase, see sections 26.7–26.8.

EXERCISE 2 SENTENCE COMBINING AND COMPOUND PHRASES

Combine the sentences in each of the following sets by using compound phrases.

EXAMPLE

Proud nations have gradually fallen into dust.

Great civilizations have gradually fallen into dust.

COMBINED: Proud nations and great civilizations have gradually fallen into dust.

1. The painting was savage.
   The painting was sensuous.
   The painting was brilliant.

2. It cost the artist hundreds of hours.
   It demanded all of her skill.
   It left her exhausted.
   It left her elated.

3. She had feared the demands on her strength.
   She could not spare herself.

4. She devoted the summer to sketching.
   She devoted the fall to painting.
   She devoted the winter to repainting.

5. An artist must use her powers.
   Otherwise she must lose them.

11.9 EDITING MIXED CONSTRUCTIONS   *mixed*

A mixed construction is a combination of word groups that do not fit together grammatically or meaningfully:

   MODIFIER MISUSED AS SUBJECT
1. *Fearful of the dark

   PREDICATE
   kept the boy awake all night.

To correct a sentence like this, you can do one of two things:

a. Turn the modifier into a noun:

   SUBJECT   PREDICATE
   EDITED: Fear of the dark / kept the boy awake all night.

b. Furnish a noun as the subject:

   MODIFIER   SUBJECT   PREDICATE
   EDITED: Fearful of the dark, the boy / lay awake all night.

2. *The head of the shipbuilding company congratulated the achievement of the workers.

An *achievement* cannot be congratulated; only people can be. To correct the error, change the verb or the object so that the two things fit together:

EDITED: The head of the shipbuilding company congratulated the workers on their achievement. [or] The head of the shipbuilding company praised the achievement of the workers.

3. *Of the two hundred persons questioned, no correct answer was given.

The first part of this sentence leads us to expect that the second part will say something about the *persons questioned*. Since the second part says nothing about them, it leaves us confused:

EDITED: Of the two hundred persons questioned, none answered correctly.

EXERCISE 3   EDITING MIXED CONSTRUCTIONS

In each of the following a word or phrase is misused in relation to other parts of the sentence. Edit the wording to produce an acceptable sentence.

EXAMPLE
*Raised in Wyoming has made Polly love the West.
EDITED: Raised in Wyoming, Polly loves the West.

1. By climbing with sneakers in subzero weather nearly froze my toes.

2. Numbed with the cold often made me stumble.

3. But on reaching a heated cabin before sundown restored circulation to my feet.

4. Loaned a pair of insulated boots helped me get back down the mountain safely the next day.

5. Out of all the trips in my experience, I was challenged the most.

11.10 EDITING FAULTY PREDICATION   *pred*

Faulty predication is following a linking verb with words that are not compatible with the subject:

1. *Another kind of flying is a glider.

The sentence classifies an activity (*flying*) as an object (*a glider*). But an activity is not an object. To correct the sentence, make the verb link two activities or two objects:

> EDITED: Another type of flying is gliding. (two activities)
> [or] Another type of aircraft is a glider. (two objects)

> 2. *According to the senator, his greatest achievement was when he persuaded the president not to seek reelection.

An achievement is not a time, a *when.* It is an act:

> EDITED: According to the senator, his greatest achievement was persuading the president not to seek reelection. (two acts)

> 3. *The reason for the evacuation of the building was because a bomb threat had been made.

This sentence equates *reason* with *because.* Those two words are related but not equivalent. *Reason* is a noun, and *because* is not.

> EDITED: The reason for the evacuation of the building was that a bomb threat had been made. (noun plus noun equivalent)
> [or] The building was evacuated because a bomb threat had been made.

This sentence contains an adverb clause; for more on adverb clauses, see section 15.8.

EXERCISE 4 EDITING FAULTY PREDICATION

Rewrite each of the following sentences to make the words after the linking verb compatible with the subject. If the sentence is correct as it stands, write *Correct.*

EXAMPLE
* A picnic is when you eat outdoors.
EDITED: A picnic is an outdoor meal.

1. Successful campaigning is where you attract a wide range of voters.

2. The main fault of Claghorn's speeches was how they offended votes over sixty.

3. Claghorn's worst mistake was when he recommended large cuts in Social Security payments.

4. The reason for the proposal was because he wanted to balance the federal budget.

5. Another cause of his unpopularity with older voters was his endorsement of mandatory retirement at age sixty.

11.11 ADDING THE POSSESSIVE BEFORE A GERUND
poss/g

Normally a noun or pronoun used before a gerund should be in the possessive case:

▶ Jake winning surprised everyone.

▶ Everyone was surprised by him winning.

The possessive shows that what concerns you is not the person but the action—the winning. When the gerund is followed by a noun, you can use *of* to clarify the meaning:

> Jake's winning of the marathon surprised everyone.
> Everyone was surprised by his winning of the marathon.

For more on the apostrophe, see sections 31.9–31.10. For more on the possessive case of pronouns, see section 18.10C.

EXERCISE 5 ADDING THE POSSESSIVE BEFORE A GERUND

Revise each of the following sentences in which the writer fails to use the possessive case with a noun or pronoun followed by a gerund. If a sentence is correct as it stands, write *Correct*.

EXAMPLE
Helen shouting startled me.
EDITED: Helen's shouting startled me.

1. Davy Crockett defending the Alamo is one of the great heroic feats in American history.

2. Along with approximately 180 Texans, he chose to fight to the death against an army numbering in the thousands.

3. There was no chance of Davy emerging from the battle alive.

4. With the defenders refusing to raise the white flag, Santa Anna's soldiers would take no prisoners.

5. Since that fateful day in 1836, Americans faced with overwhelming odds have been inspired to hold firm by someone shouting, "Remember the Alamo!"

Modifiers

12.1 WHAT MODIFIERS DO

A **modifier** is a word or word group that describes, limits, or qualifies another word or word group. Consider this sentence:

> The stag leapt.

This is a **bare-bones sentence.** It has a subject *(stag)* and a predicate *(leapt),* but no modifiers (except *The*), no words to tell us what the stag looked like or how he leapt. Modifiers can show the reader the size, color, and shape of a thing, or the way an action is performed. Thus they can help to make a sentence vivid, specific, emphatic, and lively:

> *Startled and terrified,* the stag leapt *suddenly from a high rock, bounding and crashing through the dense green woods.*

Modifiers also let you add information without adding more sentences. If you had to start a new sentence for every new piece of detail, you would begin to sound monotonous:

> The stag *leapt.*
> He was *startled.*
> He leapt *suddenly.*
> He leapt *from a rock.*
> The rock was *high.*

Instead of serving up information in bite-size pieces like these, you can arrange the pieces in one simple sentence, putting each piece where it belongs:

> The *startled* stag leapt *suddenly from a high rock.*

12.2 USING ADJECTIVES AND ADJECTIVE PHRASES

Adjectives modify nouns, specifying such things as what kind and which ones:

Complex problems require *careful* study.

Investors were *jubilant.*

The prosecutor, *intense and aggressive,* jabbed her forefinger at the witness.

Adjective phrases begin with a preposition—a word like *with, under, by, in, of,* or *at:*

History books *for children* are thus more contemporary than any

other form *of history.* —Frances Fitzgerald

The city was *in debt.*

It was Seymour, *with a big bottle of champagne in his hand, a mile-wide grin on his fat, jolly face, and a triumphant gleam in his eye.*

12.3 OVERUSING NOUNS AS ADJECTIVES

A noun used before another noun often serves as an adjective:

Cars may not travel in the *bus* lane.
A *stone* wall surrounded the *dairy* farm.
An orthopedist is a *bone* doctor.

But the overuse of nouns as adjectives makes a sentence confusing:

The *fund drive completion target date* postponement gave the finance committee *extension contact* time to increase *area business* contributions.

In this sentence, too many nouns are lined up, and the reader is left to figure out how they relate to one another. To clarify the statement, turn some of the nouns into ordinary adjectives, and use prepositional phrases:

> Postponement of the final date of the fund drive gave the finance committee additional time to increase contributions. from local businesses.

12.4 USING ADVERBS AND ADVERB PHRASES

An **adverb** tells such things as how, when, where, why, and for what purpose:

> The delegates cheered *loudly.* (adverb modifying verb)
>
> Two bolts were *dangerously* loose. (adverb modifying adjective)
>
> Light travels *amazingly* fast. (adverb modifying another adverb)
>
> *Unfortunately,* acid rain has damaged many forests. (adverb modifying entire clause)

To form most adverbs, you add *-ly* to an adjective. Thus *quick* becomes *quickly,* and *gruff* becomes *gruffly.* Exceptions are as follows:

1. A few words (such as *fast, far, well,* and *little*) keep the same form when they turn from adjectives into adverbs:

> We made a *fast* stop. (adjective)
> We stopped *fast.* (adverb)

2. Adjectives ending in *-y* must be made to end in *-ily* when they become adverbs:

> A *lucky* guess saved me. (adjective)
> *Luckily,* I knew the answer. (adverb)

3. Adjectives ending in *-ly* do not change their endings when they become adverbs:

> A *deadly* blow struck him. (adjective)
> He looked *deadly* pale. (adverb)

4. Some adverbs—such as *never, soon,* and *always*—are not based on adjectives at all and have their own special forms:

> The injured child *never* cried.
>
> She will *soon* be walking again.

An **adverb phrase** begins with a preposition—a word such as *at, with, in,* or *like*—and works like an adverb, telling how, when, or where:

> *In 1885* a severe drought forced some farmers to increase their mortgages.
>
> The production of machine tools has fallen *behind schedule.*
>
> Tyson used his right fist *like a sledgehammer.*

12.5 MISUSING ADJECTIVES AS ADVERBS

When the adjective form differs from the adverb form, do not use the first in place of the second. In conversation you might say that a car *stopped quick* or that its driver *talked gruff,* but formal writing requires *stopped quickly* and *talked gruffly.* Most adverbs require the *-ly* ending. On *good* and *well, bad* and *badly, poor* and *poorly,* see the Glossary of Usage.

12.6 FORMING AND USING COMPARATIVES AND SUPERLATIVES

The **comparative** lets you compare one person or thing with another; the **superlative** lets you compare one person or thing with all others in a group of three or more:

> Jake is *tall.*
>
> Jake is *taller* than Steve. (comparative)
>
> Jake is the *tallest* man on the team. (superlative)

12.6A COMPARATIVES

A **comparative adjective** starts a comparison that normally must be completed by *than* plus a noun or noun equivalent:

Dolphins are *smarter* than sharks.

To form a comparative adjective, add *-er* to most short adjectives. To form the comparative of adjectives ending in *-y*, such as *risky*, change the *-y* to *i* before adding *-er:*

Skiing is *riskier* than skating.

With a long adjective, form the comparative by using *more* rather than *-er:*

Are women *more observant* than men?

Use *less* with an adjective of any length:

Are the Iraquis any *less hostile* now than they were when they occupied Kuwait?

To form a **comparative adverb,** use *more* before an adverb ending in *-ly;* otherwise, add *-er.* Use *less* before any adverb:

The north star shines *more brightly* than any other star.

Does anything move *faster* than light?

Roberts campaigned *less effectively* than Johnson did.

12.6B SUPERLATIVES

To form a **superlative adjective,** add *-est* to most short adjectives:

St. Augustine, Florida, is the *oldest* city in the United States.

The blue whale is the *largest* of all living creatures.

With a long adjective, form the superlative by using *most* rather than *-est:*

Forest Lawn Meadow Memorial Park in Los Angeles has been called "the *most cheerful* graveyard in the world."

Use *least* with an adjective of any length:

According to the *Guinness Book of World Records,* the *least successful* author in the world is William A. Gold, who in eighteen years of writing earned only fifty cents.

Use *most* or *least* to form a **superlative adverb:**

The *most lavishly* decorated float in the parade came last.

Of all grammatical forms, the superlative adverb is perhaps the one *least commonly* used.

12.6C SPECIAL FORMS

Some modifiers have special forms for the comparative and superlative:

	POSITIVE	COMPARATIVE	SUPERLATIVE
good well	[adjective] [adverb] }	better	best
bad badly	[adjective] [adverb] }	worse	worst
little	[adjective and adverb, for quantity]	less	least
much	[adjective and adverb]	more	most
far	[adjective and adverb]	farther	farthest

12.7 MISUSING COMPARATIVES AND SUPERLATIVES

Do nor use *-er* and *more* or *-est* and *most* at the same time:

▶ Anthracite is ~~more~~ harder than bituminous coal.

▶ Mount Everest is the ~~most~~ highest peak in the world.

FORMING COMPARATIVES AND SUPERLATIVES: IN BRIEF

POSITIVE	COMPARATIVE	SUPERLATIVE
high	higher	highest
confident	more confident	most confident
anxious	less anxious	least anxious
carefully	more carefully	most carefully
commonly	less commonly	least commonly

12.8 DOUBLE NEGATIVES   *d neg*

A **double negative** occurs when the writer uses two negative words to make one negative statement:

> * The patient didn't want no sleeping pills.

To correct a double negative, remove or change one of the negative words:

> EDITED: The patient did not want any sleeping pills. [or] The patient wanted no sleeping pills.

Negative words include *not (n't), never, hardly, scarcely, barely, none, nothing, no one, no, neither,* and *nor.* Here are further examples of the double negative, with corrections:

> ► People sitting in the back couldn't hardly hear the speaker.
>
> ► The foreman ~~didn't give~~ ^{gave} me nothing but grief.
>
> ► [or] The foreman didn't give me ~~nothing~~ ^{anything} but grief.
>
> ► The other team didn't follow the rules ~~neither.~~ ^{either.}

For advice on * *could care less,* see the Glossary of Usage.

12.9 USING APPOSITIVES

An **appositive** is a noun or noun phrase that identifies another noun phrase or a pronoun:

> Graduation, *the hush-hush magic time of frills and gifts and congratulations and diplomas,* was finished for me before my name was called.   —Maya Angelou

> Could I, *a knock-kneed beginner,* ever hope to ski down that icy slope without breaking a leg?

An appositive is usually placed right after the word or phrase it identifies. But it may sometimes come just before:

> A *chronic complainer*, he was never satisfied.

Most appositives are set off by commas, as in all of the examples above. But you can set off an appositive with dashes if you want to emphasize it, and you should use dashes if the appositive consists of three or more nouns in a series:

> Ninety-foot statues of three Confederate leaders—Jefferson Davis, Robert E. Lee, and Stonewall Jackson—have been carved in the face of Stone Mountain in Georgia.

Use no commas when the appositive identifies the noun just before it and the noun is not preceded by *a* or *the:*

> Reporters questioned city employee *Frank Roberts* about the fire. (COMPARE: Reporters questioned a city employee, Frank Roberts, about the fire.)

> Film producer *Brenda Budget* is making a movie about the last woman on earth.

12.10 USING PARTICIPLES AND PARTICIPLE PHRASES

A **participle** is a word formed from a verb and used to modify a noun; it can enrich any sentence with descriptive detail:

> The *sobbing* child stared at the *broken* toy.

A **participle phrase** is a group of words based on a participle:

> Her father, *taking her in his arms*, promised to fix it.

Participles may be present, past, or perfect:

1. The **present participle,** formed by the addition of *-ing* to the bare form of the verb, describes a noun as *acting:*

> Athletes from fifty nations entered the stadium with *flaming torches*.
>
> *Building* contractors watch for *falling* interest rates.

Present participles can be expanded into phrases:

Planning every minute of the journey, she studied maps and tourist guides.

The prospector stared in disbelief at the gold dust *shining brightly in his palm.*

2. The past participle, commonly formed by the addition of *-d* or *-ed* to the bare form of the verb, describes a noun as *acted upon:*

A *sculpted* figure graced the entrance to the museum.

Past participles can be expanded into phrases:

Politicians *influenced by flattery* talk of victory at receptions *given by self-serving backers.*

In the last sentence, the past participle *given* ends in *-n* because it is formed from an irregular verb, *give.* The past participles of other irregular verbs have various other forms, such as *seen, bought, flung,* and *bred.* (For the past participles of commonly used irregular verbs, see the list on pp. 392–95.)

3. The perfect participle, formed with *having* plus a past participle, describes the noun as *having acted*—having completed some action:

Having struck a reef, the supertanker dumped over ten million gallons of oil into the waters of Prince William Sound.

12.10A PUNCTUATING PARTICIPLES

Punctuate participles and participle phrases as follows:

1. Normally, use one or more commas to set off a participle or participle phrase from the word or phrase it modifies:

Stalking her prey noiselessly, the cat crept up to the mouse.
The mouse, *frightened by a shadow,* darted off into a hole.
The cat squealed, *clawing the hole in vain.*

2. Don't use commas to set off a single participle when it is part of a noun phrase or when it immediately follows a verb:

The *exhausted* fighter sank to his knees.

Let *sleeping* dogs lie.

Steve walked *muttering* out of the room.

3. Don't use commas to set off a participle phrase when it restricts—limits—the meaning of the word or phrase it modifies:

Students *majoring in economics* must take one course in statistics.

For more on restrictive modifiers, see sections 15.6 and 26.6.

12.11 MISFORMING THE PAST PARTICIPLE

The past participle is misformed in these sentences:

* For lunch I ate nothing but yogurt and *toss* salad.
* *Prejudice* persons see no difference between one Chicano and another.

If you write this way, it may be because you speak this way, not pronouncing the final *-d* or *-ed* when they are needed. To hear the difference those endings make, see if you can make them audible as you read the following sentences aloud:

EDITED: For lunch I ate nothing but yogurt and *tossed* salad.

EDITED: *Prejudiced* persons see no difference between one Chicano and another.

PARTICIPLES: IN BRIEF

Present participle:	planning
Present participle phrase:	planning every minute of the journey
Past participle:	influenced
Past participle phrase:	influenced by flattery
Perfect participle:	having lost
Perfect participle phrase:	having lost the election

EXERCISE 1 SENTENCE COMBINING WITH MODIFIERS

Combine the sentences in each of the following sets by using the first sentence as a base and adding modifiers from the others. Some modifiers may have to be combined with each other before they can be joined to the base sentence. Combine the sentences of each set in at least two different ways. Then, if you prefer one of the combinations, put a check next to it.

EXAMPLE

The bird sailed.
He did so for hours.
He was searching the grasses.
The grasses were blanched.
The grasses were below him.
He was searching with his eyes.
The eyes were telescopic.
He was gaining height.
He was gaining it against the wind.
He was descending in swoops.
The swoops were mile-long.
The swoops were gently declining.

—Deliberately altered from a sentence
by Walter Van Tilburg Clark

COMBINATION 1: The bird sailed for hours, searching the blanched grasses below him with his telescopic eyes, gaining height against the wind, descending in mile-long, gently declining swoops.   —Walter Van Tilburg Clark

COMBINATION 2: Searching the blanched grasses below him with his telescopic eyes, gaining height against the wind, descending in mile-long, gently declining swoops, the bird sailed for hours.

1. Wally sang.
   He was soulful.
   He was swaying.
   He was sensuous.
   He was dressed in a skinsuit.
   The skinsuit was glittering.
   The skinsuit was white.
   The skinsuit was satin.

He was stroking his guitar.
The guitar was blue.
The guitar was electric.
He stroked with fingers.
The fingers were long.
The fingers were pink.
The fingers were nimble.

2. The spotlight illuminated his form.
The spotlight was dim.
His form was slender.
The illumination was faint.
The spotlight drew him out of the darkness.
He looked like an apparition.
The darkness was clammy.

3. He sang about a woman.
The woman was young.
She had red hair.
She was dressed in a raincoat.
The raincoat was shiny.
The raincoat was black.
She was standing on a street corner.
The street corner was in New York.
The street corner was crowded.
She was waiting for a bus.

4. She waited in a certain mood.
Her mood was restless.
She clutched a suitcase.
It was big.
It was vinyl.
It was white.
Stickers covered it.
They were marked "Broadway or Bust."

5. She had just arrived from a town.
The town was little.
It was in Oregon.
It was in the eastern part.
She was filled with ambition.
She was dreaming of a career.
The career would be great.
It would be in the theater.

EXERCISE 2 SENTENCE EXPANDING WITH MODIFIERS

Expand five of the following sentences by adding as many modifiers as possible. Let your imagination go.

1. The gorilla roared.
2. The flames crackled.
3. The clown danced.
4. The rock-climber slipped.
5. The building shook.
6. The waiter stumbled.
7. The piñata cracked.
8. The boy cried.
9. The dog growled.
10. The curtain rose.

12.12 USING INFINITIVES AND INFINITIVE PHRASES

The **infinitive** (usually made by placing *to* before the bare form of the verb) can be used to modify various parts of a sentence:

Civilization has never eradicated the urge *to hunt.*
My favorite time *to run* is early in the morning.
Determined *to succeed,* she redoubled her efforts.
In every situation Chester plays *to win.*

Infinitives can form phrases:

To write grammatically, you must know something about sentence structure.
On August 27, 1966, Sir Francis Chichester set out *to sail a 53-foot boat singlehandedly around the world.*

Infinitives with *have* and *have been* plus a participle identify an action or condition completed before another one:

The work to be done that morning seemed enormous. Sandra was glad *to have slept* a full eight hours the night before. But she was annoyed *to have been told* nothing of this work earlier.

EXERCISE 3   SUPPLYING INFINITIVES

Complete each of the following sentences with a suitable infinitive or infinitive phrase.

EXAMPLE
The sheer will _____ brought him through the operation.
to live

1. Throughout history a compelling desire _____ the unknown has led men and women _____.

2. Almost eight hundred years ago Vikings sailed west _____.

3. In recent years adventurous explorers like Jacques Cousteau have developed special underwater equipment _____.

4. The wish _____ has taken astronauts to the moon, and may someday take others beyond the solar system.

5. In medicine, doctors needing _____ regularly use x-ray machines and other technological devices.

6. Even the tiny atom has been yielding its secrets to scientists determined _____.

12.13   AVOIDING THE SPLIT INFINITIVE   *si*

When one or more adverbs are wedged between *to* and a verb form, the infinitive is **split**:

Detectives needed special equipment to *thoroughly and accurately* investigate the mystery.

This sentence is weakened by the cumbersome splitting. The adverbs should go at the end of the infinitive phrase:

EDITED: Detectives needed special equipment to investigate the mystery *thoroughly and accurately.*

Sometimes an infinitive may be split by a one-word modifier that would be awkward in any other position:

The mayors convened in order to *fully* explore and discuss the problems of managing large cities.

A construction of this type is acceptable nowadays to most readers. But unless you are sure there is no other suitable place in the sentence for the adverb or adverb phrase, do not split an infinitive with it.

> **EXERCISE 4 EDITING SPLIT INFINITIVES**
>
> Each of the following contains a split infinitive. If you find the split awkward, revise the word order to get rid of it. If you find the split necessary, write *Acceptable*.
>
> **EXAMPLE**
>
> He was sorry to have ~~rudely~~ answered. *rudely.*
>
> 1. The nurse took a deep breath before starting to gently remove the bandage from the child's stomach.
> 2. The child, in turn, began to with strong determination resist her.
> 3. He exercised all of his cunning to quickly distract her attention from the task.
> 4. Then, after running out of distractions, he decided to at the last moment grab her hands and bite them.
> 5. To fully control this ferocious little animal in the shape of a boy, she had to strap him down.

12.14 USING ABSOLUTE PHRASES

An **absolute phrase** usually consists of a noun or noun phrase followed by a participle. It can modify a noun, a pronoun, or an entire clause:

> Donna laughed, *her eyes flashing with mischief.*
> *Its fuel line blocked,* the engine sputtered to a halt.

The participle may sometimes be omitted:

> *Head down,* the bull charged straight at the matador.
> *Nose in the air,* she walked right past me.

You can form compounds with absolute phrases, and you can use them in succession anywhere in a sentence:

> *Its freshly painted walls gleaming in the sunlight and dazzling the beholder,* the factory symbolized economic progress.

> The village was silent, *its shops closed, the streets deserted.*

> The skaters are quick-silvering around the frosty rink, *the girls gliding and spinning, the boys swooping, their arms flailing like wings.* —College student

EXERCISE 5   SENTENCE COMBINING WITH ABSOLUTE PHRASES

Combine the sentences in each of the following sets by using the first sentence as a base and turning the others into absolute phrases.

EXAMPLE
Finch dozed.
His chin was resting on his chest.
COMBINED: Finch dozed, his chin resting on his chest.

1. Janet rode the big wave.
   Her shoulders were hunched.
   Her hair was streaming in the wind.
   Her toes were curled over the edge of the board.

2. The board sped forward.
   Its slender frame was propelled by surging water.

3. Janet yelled with delight.
   Her heart was pounding.
   Her eyes were sparkling with excitement.

4. Meanwhile the lifeguard gripped the arms of his chair.
   His knuckles were white.
   His hair was standing on end.
   His stomach was heaving.

12.15 PLACING MODIFIERS

One of the hardest things about writing an effective sentence is that unless you can plan it out completely in your head beforehand, you may not know at once the best way to arrange all of its parts. You know by habit, of course, that an adjective usually comes before the noun it modifies. You don't write *leaves green* or *fumes smelly* or *brass hot;* you write *green leaves, smelly fumes,* and *hot brass.* But the placing of other modifiers—especially modifying phrases—may call for some thought. Often, in fact, you will not be able to decide where to put a particular modifier until *after* you have written out the whole sentence in which it appears.

While you are writing a sentence, therefore, don't worry right away about where to place the modifiers. You can often start with the base sentence and put the modifiers at the end, using one modifier to lead you to another. See how this sentence grows:

Mary traveled.

Where from?

Mary traveled *from Denver.*

Where to?

Mary traveled *from Denver to San Francisco.*

How?

Mary traveled *from Denver to San Francisco by hitchhiking.*

Did she hitchhike all the way?

Mary traveled *from Denver to San Francisco by hitchhiking to the house of a friend in Salt Lake City.*

And how did she finish the trip?

Mary traveled *from Denver to San Francisco by hitchhiking to the house of a friend in Salt Lake City and then borrowing his motorcycle to make the rest of the trip.*

Now, having written your base sentence and added as many modifiers as you want, you can think about where to place those modifiers. You may decide, for instance, that you want to put most of them up front instead of at the end. In that case, bracket the words you want to move and use an arrow to show where they are to go:

Mary traveled from Denver to San Francisco [by hitchhiking to the house of a friend in Salt Lake City and then borrowing his motorcycle to make the rest of the trip.]

When you rewrite the sentence, it will look like this:

By hitchhiking to the house of a friend in Salt Lake City and then borrowing his motorcycle to make the rest of the trip, Mary traveled from Denver to San Francisco.

Do you like this version better than the other? That's the kind of question you will have to answer for yourself. If you want to state a simple point and then develop it, you will lead with that point and then put the modifiers after it. But if you want to create suspense, you will put all or most of your modifiers first. In that position they signal that the main point is coming at the end, where it gets special emphasis. (For more discussion of how to emphasize your main point, see sections 15.1 and 15.10.)

Placing a modifier well means connecting the modifier to its **headword**—the word or phrase it modifies. If the modifier doesn't clearly point to its headword, the modifier is **misplaced**; if the headword is missing from the sentence, the modifier **dangles.**

12.16 EDITING MISPLACED MODIFIERS   *mm*

A **misplaced modifier** does not point clearly to its headword—the word or phrase it modifies:

1. *I asked her for the time while waiting for the bus to start a conversation.

The sentence seems to say that the bus was ready to start a conversation. To get the meaning straight, put the modifying phrase right before its headword—*I:*

EDITED: To start a conversation, I asked her for the time while waiting for the bus.

2. *The College Librarian announced that all fines on overdue books will be doubled yesterday.

The sentence puts the future into yesterday, or yesterday into the future. Either way it makes no sense:

> EDITED: The College Librarian announced yesterday that all fines on overdue books will be doubled.

12.16A EDITING SQUINTING MODIFIERS   *sm*

A **squinting modifier** is one placed where it could modify either of two possible headwords:

> *The street vendor she saw on her way to school occasionally sold wild mushrooms.

Did she see the vendor occasionally, or did he sell wild mushrooms occasionally?

> EDITED: The street vendor she occasionally saw on her way to school sold wild mushrooms. [or] The street vendor she saw on her way to school sold wild mushrooms occasionally.

12.16B EDITING MISPLACED RESTRICTERS   *mr*

A **restricter** is a one-word modifier that limits the meaning of another word or a group of words. Restricters include *almost, only, merely, nearly, scarcely, simply, even, exactly, just,* and *hardly.* Usually a restricter modifies the word or phrase that immediately follows it:

> 1. *Only* the Fabulous Fork serves brunch on Sundays.
>
> 2. The Fabulous Fork serves *only* brunch on Sundays.
>
> 3. The Fabulous Fork serves brunch *only* on Sundays.

A restricter placed at the end of a sentence modifies the word or phrase just before it:

> 4. The Fabulous Fork serves brunch on Sundays *only.*

If you place *only* carelessly, you will confuse your reader:

> *The Fabulous Fork only serves brunch on Sundays.

Is brunch the only meal it serves on Sundays, or is Sunday the only day on which it serves brunch? The meaning becomes plain

only when *only* stands right next to *brunch* or *on Sundays,* as shown above in sentences 2, 3, and 4.

EXERCISE 6 EDITING MISPLACED MODIFIERS

Revise each of the following sentences that includes one or more misplaced modifiers, squinting modifiers, or misplaced restricters. If a sentence is correct, write *Correct.*

EXAMPLE

in Time magazine

An article describes the way skunks eat ~~in Time magazine.~~

1. Alvin Toffler states that young Americans are becoming consumers of disposable goods in a recently published essay.

2. After just keeping an item for a few months, children want to throw it out and get something new.

3. I have learned that this practice marks a change from conversations with my grandparents.

4. In their childhood, a girl only played with one doll for years.

5. Then, wrapped in tissue paper, she would put it away against the day when she would present it to a daughter or a niece with fond memories.

6. Likewise a boy would keep his electric train so that he could one day give it to his children carefully boxed.

7. There are several reasons why children no longer keep toys in this way according to Toffler.

8. One is the impact of industrialization and in particular of mass production.

9. Most toys were made by craftsmen who devoted years to just mastering their trade and hours to carefully shaping each product by hand until the late 1800s.

10. Toys were expensive and hard to get as a result; but each was a treasure, a unique creation.

11. Today large machines make toys in seconds, and each looks just like all the others of its kind.

12. Most of these mass-produced toys only captivate children for a short time and then wind up in the trash.

13. Another reason why modern toys soon lose their appeal is that they are made of plastic commonly.

14. Plastic almost costs nothing to make; and when painted in bright, vivid colors, it can seem shiny and desirable.

15. But unlike such materials as leather and wood, plastic does not mellow with age.

16. Finally, children are pressured to be habitual disposers and consumers by advertising.

17. With TV and catalogues continually showing them new toys, how can they learn to cherish their old ones?

12.17 EDITING DANGLING MODIFIERS *dg*

A modifier **dangles** when its headword is missing. Since a modifier always needs a headword, it will attach itself to a false one if the true one is not in the sentence.

*After doing my homework, the dog was fed.

And any dog that can do your homework for you certainly deserves his food! But unless the dog is unusually clever, this sentence contains a dangling modifier. You can eliminate it by saying who actually did the homework:

EDITED: After I did my homework, the dog was fed.

But this version still doesn't tell us who fed the dog. It fails to do so because *The dog was fed* is in the passive voice and does not mention the agent—the one *by whom* the dog was fed. That agent should be named:

The dog was fed by me.

Once you've named the agent, you can turn this sentence from the passive to the active voice (chapter 22):

I fed the dog.

Now you can write:

> After I did my homework, I fed the dog.

Or you can drop the first *I* and change *did* to *doing:*

> After doing my homework, I fed the dog.

Here is one more example:

> *Based on the gradual decline in College Board scores over the past twenty years, American high school education is less effective than it used to be.

There is a miscombination of two sentences:

> American high school education is less effective than it used to be. This conclusion is based on the gradual decline of College Board scores over the past twenty years.

So how can you combine these two sentences and not leave *Based* dangling? We suggest you kick the *Based* habit altogether. To combine sentences like these, use *shows that, indicates that,* or *leads to the conclusion that:*

> EDITED: The gradual decline of College Board scores over the past twenty years indicates that American high school education is less effective than it used to be.

SPOTTING MISUSED MODIFIERS: IN BRIEF

Misplaced modifier (12.16):

> *I asked her for the time while waiting for the bus *to start a conversation.*

Squinting modifier (12.16A):

> *The street vendor she saw on her way to school *occasionally* sold wild mushrooms.

Misplaced restricter (12.16B):

> *The Fabulous Fork *only* serves brunch on Sundays.

Dangling modifier (12.17):

> *After doing my homework, the dog was fed.*

EXERCISE 7 EDITING DANGLING MODIFIERS

Revise each of the following sentences that includes a dangling modifier. Either supply a suitable headword as best you can, or reconstruct the whole sentence. If a sentence is correct as it stands, write *Correct*.

EXAMPLE

After checking the figures, the new budget was rejected.

EDITED: After checking the figures, the voters rejected the new budget.

1. At six each morning, the ringing of my alarm clock stirs me from a sound sleep.

2. Crawling from my bed, my black wool cycling shorts are put on, along with my green-and-black shirt.

3. I grope my way into the kitchen and unlock the back door onto the breezeway connecting the house to the garage.

4. As I face the early morning light, my breath is visible, chilled by the cold air.

5. Hastily pulling on my shoes and tightening my helmet strap, no help from my brain seems to be needed by my hands.

6. My legs begin to wake up wheeling the bicycle out of the garage.

7. Once peddling along the road, my circulation quickens, and I no longer feel cold.

8. Turning left at Bank Street and beginning the rapid descent to River Road, the air rushes through my helmet and causes my eyes to water uncontrollably.

9. My senses are fully awakened, and I hear the swishing sound made by the tires speeding over the pavement.

10. Exhilarated, my bike is pushed forward, eager to outrace the sun.

11. Sixty minutes later I am becoming tired, straining to push myself up every hill.

12. Reaching the top of a long rise, a short break is taken before turning back and heading home.

13. The morning sun has won the race, just as it always does when pedaling to the point of exhaustion.

EXERCISE 8 EDITING MISUSED MODIFIERS

Edit the following passage by correcting all misused modifiers:

The *New York Times Magazine* publishes often striking advertisements. One example is an ad for Movado watches, which are made in Switzerland from a recent issue of the magazine. Standing in the center of a ten-by-fifteen-inch page, with pitch-black fur, the ad shows a cat focusing its bright golden eyes on a fishbowl filled with sand, water, and white coral. But the fishbowl contains no fish. Resting among the pieces of coral, it only contains two Movado watches. Below the fishbowl are a brief description of the watches and the words "Movado, a century of Swiss Watchcraft" printed in large white letters.

The ad designer has created an eerie effect by almost covering half the page in black, hiding the body of the cat in darkness, and only showing its head in a dim glow of light. Looking down at the fishbowl, the watches are being eyed by the cat as if they were fish. But the watches also look like the cat. Set in a gold case, one has a black face, while the other has a gold face set in a black case. Thus both watches match the colors of the cat's eyes and fur.

The ad succeeds because it catches the reader's attention. Leafing through the magazine, the mysterious-looking cat will strike the average reader, and, submerged in a fishbowl, he or she will certainly examine the watches. The combination of gold and black under water will make them look like treasures discovered at the bottom of the sea.

5

10

15

20

25

Coordination

MAKING COMPOUND SENTENCES

To **coordinate** two or more parts of a sentence is to give them the same rank and role by making them grammatically alike. As we noted in section 11.8, you can coordinate words or phrases to make a compound phrase. In this chapter we show how you can coordinate simple sentences to make a compound sentence.

13.1 MAKING COMPOUND SENTENCES

A **compound sentence** consists of two or more independent clauses joined by conjunctions, semicolons, or conjunctive adverbs. Each clause is called **independent** because each could stand by itself as a complete sentence:

COMPOUND SENTENCE

IC	JOINED TO	IC	JOINED BY
They acquired horses	and	their ancient nomadic spirit was suddenly free of the ground. —N. Scott Momaday	*Conjunction*
History does not stutter	;	it rhymes.	*Semicolon*
The average age for women to marry in Ireland is 26;	in contrast,	women of India marry at an average age of 14.	*Conjunctive adverb*

13.2 COMPOUNDING WITH CONJUNCTIONS

Conjunctions include the set of words commonly known as "A. B. Fonsy": *and, but, for, or, nor, so,* and *yet.* They show the following relations:

1. Simple addition

> The economists considered budget cuts, *and* the politicians thought of votes.

2. Addition of a negative point

> Many of the settlers had never farmed before, *nor* were they ready for the brutal Saskatchewan winters.

3. Contrast

> We are all in the gutter, *but* some of us are looking at the stars.   —Oscar Wilde

> All of the candidates claim to understand Europeans, *yet* none has ever lived in Europe.

4. Logical consequence

> My father never attended the military parades in the city, *for* he hated war.

> During World War II, Americans of Japanese descent were unjustly suspected of disloyalty, *so* they were placed in detention camps.

For introduces a reason; *so* introduces a consequence.

5. Choice

> Nelson could keep his ships near England, *or* he could order them to attack the French in Egypt.

13.2A PUNCTUATION WITH CONJUNCTIONS

A conjunction used between independent clauses normally needs a comma just before it, as shown by all of the examples above. But there are two exceptions.

1. You can omit the comma when the clauses are short:

> Many are called but few are chosen.

2. You can replace the comma with a semicolon when there are commas elsewhere in the sentence:

> On the morning of June 28, 1969, the weather finally cleared; but the climbers, wearied by their efforts of the previous days, could not attempt the summit.

You can use a comma without a conjunction when there are more than two clauses, but you should normally use a conjunction between the last two:

> The sun shone, a stiff breeze ruffled the bay, the sails bellied out, and the bow cut the water like a knife.

13.3 OVERUSING *AND*

Use *and* sparingly in compound sentences. A series of clauses strung together by *and* can become boring:

> I was born in Illinois, and the first big city I ever saw was Chicago, and was I ever excited! I went there with my father and mother, and we stayed in a big hotel in the Loop, and I saw lots of interesting sights. We spent a whole day just walking around the city, and I got a stiff neck from looking up at the skyscrapers, and my feet got sore too from walking down so many streets. I was glad to go back to the hotel and take a long soak in the Jacuzzi.

To break the monotony of compounding with *and,* substitute other linking words—or other constructions:

> Since I was born in Illinois, the first big city I ever saw was Chicago. Was I ever excited! My father and mother took me to a big hotel in the Loop. On the day after our arrival, we spent eight hours just walking around the city to see the sights. It was exhausting. In fact, I got a stiff neck from looking up at all the skyscrapers, and sore feet from walking down so many streets. I couldn't wait to take a long soak in the Jacuzzi at our hotel.

For alternatives to the overuse of *and* constructions, see chapter 15.

13.4 COMPOUNDING WITH THE SEMICOLON

A semicolon alone can join two independent clauses when the relationship between them is obvious:

<table>
<tr><td>Some books are undeserv-
edly forgotten</td><td>;</td><td>none are undeservedly
remembered
—W. H. Auden</td></tr>
<tr><td>Too much, perhaps, has
been said of his silence</td><td>;</td><td>too much stress has been
laid upon his reserve.
—Virginia Woolf</td></tr>
</table>

13.5 COMPOUNDING WITH CONJUNCTIVE ADVERBS

A **conjunctive adverb**—sometimes called a **sentence adverb**—is a word or phrase that shows a relation between the clauses it joins, as a conjunction does. But a conjunctive adverb is usually weightier and more emphatic than a conjunction:

The Iron Duke had complete confidence in his soldiers' training and valor; *furthermore,* he considered his battle plan a work of genius.

Conjunctive adverbs indicate the following relations between one clause and another:

1. Addition (*besides, furthermore, moreover, in addition*):

Some economists oppose legislation restricting foreign trade; *in addition,* they attack proposals to increase corporate taxes.

2. Likeness (*likewise, similarly, in the same way*):

Many young Englishmen condemned the English war against France in the 1790s; *likewise,* many young Americans condemned the American war against North Vietnam in the 1960s.

3. Contrast (*however, nevertheless, still, nonetheless, conversely, otherwise, instead, in contrast, on the other hand*):

> Einstein's theory of relativity was largely the product of speculation; experiments made within the past fifty years, *however*, have confirmed many of its basic points.

4. Cause and effect (*accordingly, consequently, hence, therefore, as a result, for this reason*):

> Chamberlain made an ill-considered peace treaty with Hitler after the German invasion of Czechoslovakia; *as a result*, England was unprepared for the German invasion of Poland.

5. A means-and-end relation (*thus, thereby, by this means, in this manner*):

> Florence Nightingale organized a unit of thirty-eight nurses for the Crimean War in the 1850s; *thus* she became a legend.

6. Reinforcement (*for example, for instance, in fact, in particular, indeed*):

> Public transportation will also be vastly improved; a high-speed train, *for instance*, will take passengers from Montreal to Toronto in less than two hours.

7. Time (*meanwhile, then, subsequently, afterward, earlier, later*):

> At first, members of the audience were overtly hostile to the speaker; *later*, they cheered her as one of their own.

As items 3 and 6 show, you may use a conjunctive adverb *within* a clause, not just before its subject.

13.5A Punctuation with Conjunctive Adverbs

A conjunctive adverb normally takes punctuation on either side of it. The punctuation depends on where the conjunctive adverb is used:

1. When used *between* two independent clauses, the conjunctive adverb is normally preceded by a semicolon and followed by a comma:

Townspeople consider the covered bridge a link to a golden age; *as a result,* they have voted funds for its restoration.

2. Some conjunctive adverbs (including *thus, then, still, otherwise,* and *hence*) may begin a clause with no comma after them:

The rise of the dollar against foreign currencies drives up the price of our exports; *thus* we lose customers abroad.

3. When used *within* the second clause, the conjunctive adverb is normally set off by commas:

Jackson did not get the nomination; he managed, *however,* to win the votes of over one thousand delegates.

EXCEPTION: Some conjunctive adverbs, including *therefore, nevertheless, nonetheless, instead,* and those mentioned above in entry 2, may be used without commas when they are placed just before the main verb:

The hole in the ozone layer is steadily growing; we must therefore stop sending fluorocarbons into the atmosphere.

JOINING INDEPENDENT CLAUSES: IN BRIEF

The independent clauses (IC) of a compound sentence are normally joined in one of the following three ways:

1. ___IC___ ; ___IC___ when the relation between clauses is obvious.

2. ___IC___ , conjunction ___IC___ to make the relation explicit.

3. ___IC___ ; conjunctive adverb, ___IC___ to make the relation emphatic. (Placement of the conjunctive adverb is optional)

EXERCISE 1 SENTENCE COMBINING TO MAKE COMPOUND SENTENCES

Using a semicolon, a conjunction, or a conjunctive adverb, combine the sentences in each of the following sets into a single sentence. Whenever you use a conjunction or conjunctive adverb, state in parentheses the relationship it shows.

EXAMPLE
We are all in the gutter.
Some of us are looking at the stars.
COMBINED: We are all in the gutter, but some of us are looking at the stars. (contrast)

1. In sixteenth-century England women with literary talent undoubtedly wrote.
   None was encouraged to publish her work.

2. In the nineteenth century, Jane Austen earned little acclaim for her novels.
   Today they are considered masterpieces.

3. Some writers gain fame with their first major work.
   Others win fame later or possibly never.

4. Harriet Beecher Stowe became widely known with the publication of *Uncle Tom's Cabin* in 1852.
   Emily Dickinson remained unacclaimed until fifty years after her death.

5. James Joyce was a painstaking writer.
   He once spent half a day on the composition of a single sentence.

6. Ernest Hemingway would have sympathized with Joyce.
   Hemingway rewrote the last page of *A Farewell to Arms* thirty-nine times.

7. In his later years John O'Hara is said to have disregarded revision altogether.
   He typed his pages and mailed them untouched to his publisher.

8. Fictions become reality for some writers.
   Balzac's characters walked about on his desk, speaking, striving, suffering.

9. Georges Simenon used to impersonate his main characters before writing about them.
   His wife had to cope with a series of strangers.

10. Joseph Conrad's native language was Polish.
    He wrote his novels and short stories in English.

13.6 EDITING COMMA SPLICES   *cs*

The **comma splice** is the error of joining two independent clauses—two possible sentences—with nothing but a comma:

> * One of the runners suffered from heat exhaustion, she collapsed two miles from the finish.

When you use the comma to join or splice two distinct statements, you are probably trying to keep two related points together in one sentence. But the comma alone cannot do that for you. You should therefore do one of four things:

1. Put a conjunction after the comma:

> EDITED: One of the runners suffered from heat exhaustion, so she collapsed two miles from the finish.

2. Replace the comma with a semicolon:

> EDITED: One of the runners suffered from heat exhaustion; she collapsed two miles from the finish.

3. Replace the comma with a semicolon and a conjunctive adverb:

> EDITED: One of the runners suffered from heat exhaustion; as a result, she collapsed two miles from the finish.

4. Replace the comma with a period, making two sentences:

> EDITED: One of the runners suffered from heat exhaustion. She collapsed two miles from the finish.

Sometimes a comma splice occurs when the second clause in a sentence begins with a conjunctive adverb:

> * Most working people get at least one raise a year, nevertheless, inflation often leaves them with no increase in buying power.

A conjunctive adverb used between two clauses must be preceded by a semicolon:

> EDITED: Most working people get at least one raise a year; nevertheless, inflation often leaves them with no increase in buying power.

Alternatively, you can use a period, making two sentences:

EDITED: Most working people get at least one raise a year. Nevertheless, inflation often leaves them with no increase in buying power.

EXERCISE 2 EDITING COMMA SPLICES

Some of the following entries contain a comma splice. If you find one, correct it. If the punctuation is correct, write *Correct*.

EXAMPLE

The chemicals lodge in soil/they also enter streams and ponds.

1. The sculpture represents Don Quixote and his horse Rocinante, the Don is the most famous knight in Spanish literature.

2. The knight looks ready for adventure, perhaps he has spotted giants disguised as windmills.

3. His left hand is grasping a shield, his right hand holds a sturdy lance.

4. The appeal of the small work lies in its materials, they could have been the contents of a mechanic's trash can.

5. The sculptor has used bolts, screws, washers, and scraps of sheet metal, they are all painted a flat black.

6. Rocinante's head, neck, and muzzle are a single unit made from a small elbow joint; and her body is an L-shaped allen wrench, with the smaller part forming a tail.

7. Welded to the body are four legs, they are made from socket head cap screws.

8. Slanting outward and to the rear, they give an impression of movement.

9. The Don's body is a threaded carriage bolt, one end is welded to the back of Rocinante.

10. The top of the bolt is rounded, and it represents a Spanish sombrero.

11. The Don's arms are made from two allen wrenches, in fact, they curve around his back to create the image of shoulders.

12. Two more allen wrenches form legs. Bent at the knees, they end in small globs of welding rods, the rods are molded to resemble boots with tiny spurs.

13. The knight's shield is a thin metal plate, its rough edges and solder marks give it a battle-scarred look.

14. The lance is not particularly long, nonetheless, it looks like a potent weapon.

15. Supporting both the horse and the man is a hefty looking washer, the base of the piece.

13.7 EDITING RUN-ON (FUSED) SENTENCES
run-on

A **run-on sentence,** sometimes called a **fused sentence,** joins two independent clauses—two possible sentences—with no punctuation or conjunction between them:

> * Emily listened to the lobster boats chugging out to sea from the cove she watched the gulls sailing overhead.

Here the first independent clause simply pushes into the second one. We cannot tell for sure where the first one ends. Is its last word *sea* or *cove?*

You make this error when your thoughts come in a rush, outrunning your hand. You are most likely to find the error by reading your sentences aloud, listening for the drop in your voice to tell you where one statement (or independent clause) ends and another begins. When you find that point and see no punctuation to mark it, do one of four things:

1. Use a comma and a conjunction between the clauses:

> EDITED: Emily listened to the lobster boats chugging out to sea from the cove, and she watched the gulls sailing overhead.

2. Use a semicolon between the clauses:

> EDITED: Emily listened to the lobster boats chugging out to sea from the cove; she watched the gulls sailing overhead.

3. Use a semicolon and a conjunctive adverb between the clauses:

> EDITED: Emily listened to the lobster boats chugging out to sea from the cove; then she watched the gulls sailing overhead.

4. Use a period at the end of the first clause. You will then have two sentences:

> EDITED: Emily listened to the lobster boats chugging out to sea from the cove. She watched the gulls sailing overhead.

> **EXERCISE 3** **EDITING COMMA SPLICES AND RUN-ON (FUSED) SENTENCES**
>
> In some of the following, the punctuation is faulty. Correct any mistakes you find, adding words where necessary. If a sentence is correct as it stands, write *Correct*.
>
> **EXAMPLE**
>
> Cloudy days tend to make us gloomy; sunny days, in contrast, make us cheerful.
>
> 1. On the coast of Maine is the small town of Pirates Cove it resembles the old New England seaports depicted in paintings hanging in country inns and seafood restaurants.
> 2. The narrow streets are paved with irregularly shaped bricks these make walking an adventure.
> 3. Most of the buildings have a weathered look the shingles are gray and the blue of the shutters is faded from exposure to the salt air.
> 4. At the harbor picturesque rock formations glisten in the sunlight, and the hulls of freshly painted fishing boats bob in the waves.

5. Completing the scene is a welcome touch of wildness large white gulls swoop over the boats and various clam shells lie on the sand.

6. Walking on the beach I collect the shells, they slide and rattle in my bucket as I step over rocks.

Parallel
Construction

14.1 WHY CHOOSE PARALLELISM?

Parallel construction, also called **parallelism,** shows that two or more ideas are equally important by stating them in grammatically parallel form: noun lined up with noun, verb with verb, phrase with phrase. Parallelism can lend clarity, elegance, and symmetry to what you say:

> I *came;*
> I *saw;*
> I *conquered.*
>
> —Julius Caesar

Using three simple verbs to list the things he did, Caesar makes coming, seeing, and conquering all equal in importance. He also implies that for him, conquering was as easy as coming and seeing.

> In many ways writing is the act *of saying I,*
>   *of imposing* oneself upon
>   other people,
>   *of saying listen* to me,
>   *see* it my way,
>   *change* your
>   mind.
>
> —Joan Didion

Didion gives equal importance to saying *I,* imposing oneself, and voicing certain commands. Furthermore, she builds one parallel construction into another. Using a series of imperative verbs, she puts equal weight on *listen, see,* and *change.* The result is a rhetorically commanding definition of the act of writing.

> We look for signs in every strange event; we search for heroes in every unknown face.
>
> —Alice Walker

Walker stresses our searching by making the second half of this sentence exactly parallel with the first.

14.2 WRITING PARALLEL CONSTRUCTIONS

To write parallel constructions, put two or more coordinate items into the same grammatical form:

> I have nothing to offer but *blood, toil, tears,* and *sweat.*
>
> —Winston Churchill

Churchill uses four nouns to identify what he offers the British people in wartime.

> . . . and that government *of the people, by the people, for the people* shall not perish from the earth.
>
> —Abraham Lincoln

Lincoln uses three prepositional phrases to describe the essential characteristics of American democracy.

> On all these shores there are echoes *of past and future: of the flow of time, obliterating* yet *containing* all that has gone before.
>
> —Rachel Carson

Carson uses two prepositional phrases about time, and then a pair of participles to contrast its effects.

> *We must indeed all hang together,* or most assuredly *we shall all hang separately.*
>
> —Benjamin Franklin

Franklin uses two parallel clauses to stress the difference between two equally pressing alternatives.

> A *living dog* is better than *a dead lion.*
>
> —Ecclesiastes

The likeness in form between the two phrases lets us clearly see how much they differ in meaning.

14.3 USING CORRELATIVES WITH PARALLELISM

Correlatives are words or phrases used in pairs to join words, phrases, or clauses. The principal correlatives are *both . . . and. not only . . . but also, either . . . or, neither . . . nor.* and *whether . . . or.* When using correlatives to highlight a parallel construction, be sure that the word or word group following the first member of the pair is parallel with the word or word group following the second:

> Before the Polish strikes of 1980, *both* the Hungarians *and* the Czechs tried in vain to defy Soviet authority.
>
> His speech *not only* outraged his opponents, *but (also) cost* him the support of his own party. (*Also* is optional here.)
>
> Near the end of the story Daniel Webster threatens to wrestle with the devil *either* on earth *or* in hell.
>
> In the nineteenth century, tuberculosis spared *neither* the wealthy *nor* the poor.

EXERCISE 1 RECOGNIZING PARALLEL ELEMENTS

Each of the following sentences contains one or more parallel constructions. Write down the parallel elements.

EXAMPLE

Crawling down a mountain is often harder than climbing up.
Crawling down, climbing up

1. The cosmic ulcer comes not from great concerns but from little irritations. —John Steinbeck

2. She was impervious to lies or foolish excuses or the insufferable plea of not knowing any better. —Eudora Welty

3. I went to the woods because I wished to live deliberately, to front only the essential facts of life. . . . —Henry David Thoreau

4. I open my eyes and I see dark, muscled forms curl out of water, with flapping gills and flattened eyes. —Annie Dillard

5. What is written without effort is in general read without pleasure. —Samuel Johnson

14.4 EDITING FAULTY PARALLELISM   ⓛⓛ

When two or more parts of a sentence are parallel in meaning, you should coordinate them fully by making them parallel in form. If you don't, the **faulty parallelism** may jar your reader:

> ► The Allies decided to invade Italy and then ~~that they would~~ **to**
>
> launch a massive assault on the Normandy coast.

Here are further examples:

> ► I like swimming, skiing, and ~~to hike~~ **hiking** in the mountains.
>
> ► [or] I like ~~swimming, skiing,~~ **to swim, ski,** and ~~to~~ hike in the mountains.
>
> ► Either we must make nuclear power safe **, we must** or stop using it.
>
> ► [or] ~~Either~~ **W** ~~w~~e **either** must make nuclear power safe or stop using it.
>
> ► The more I see of men, I find dogs ~~more likable~~ **the more likable**   —Madame de Staël

> ► My idea of heaven is a great big baked potato**,** and ~~I would like~~ someone to share it with.   –Oprah Winfrey

In sentences made with correlatives, each correlative goes just before one of the parallel items.

> ► They fought in the streets, **in** the fields, and in the woods.

In a series of phrases beginning with a word such as *to* or *in*, repeat the word before each phrase or don't repeat it at all after the first one (*in the streets, the fields, and the woods*).

EXERCISE 2 EDITING FAULTY PARALLELISM

Revise each of the following sentences that is marred by faulty parallelism. If a sentence is correct as it stands, write *Correct*.

EXAMPLE

You can improve your performance ~~if you master~~ **by mastering** the fundamentals and by training daily.

1. Ancient Greek myths often describe the exploits of heroes confronting threats from violent men, evil monsters, and the gods sometimes menace them as well.

2. The heroes seek undying fame, not to become wealthy or live peacefully.

3. They generally display their remarkable prowess at an early age both by performing difficult tasks and they show bravery in the face of danger.

4. The infant Hercules, for example, strangles not only two venomous serpents in his crib but laughs without fear at the menace.

5. Young Theseus enters the dreaded labyrinth on Crete determined either to slay the Minotaur or he will die in the attempt.

6. Besides demonstrating bravery and strength in fighting deadly foes of many kinds, heroes often undertake dangerous journeys.

7. A companion travels with the hero, and sometimes the companion is not mortal but a god.

8. Athene, in perhaps the most famous story of all, guides young Telemachos not only during a voyage from Ithaca to Pylos, the home of Nestor, but also helps him to win the regard of kings.

9. Even for heroes, meeting a challenge can be as dangerous as to play Russian roulette.

10. In a major test of strength and courage, Jason has to yoke a pair of fire-breathing bulls, seed a field with dragons' teeth, and there is a climactic battle to be won against armed men sprouting from the seeds.

EXERCISE 3 SENTENCE COMBINING

Combine the sentences in each of the following sets into a single compound sentence, using parallel construction where possible.

EXAMPLE

Much of the land was arid.

The presence of many rocks was another feature.

To the Moabites the land was beautiful.

They loved it passionately.

They fought to keep it.

COMBINED: Much of the land was both arid and rocky; nonetheless, the Moabites found it beautiful, loved it passionately, and fought to keep it.

1. Most tarantulas live in the tropics.
   The temperate zone, however, is home to some species of them. A few species commonly occur in the southern United States.

2. Some tarantulas have large bodies.
   Their fangs are powerful.
   They can bite hard.
   They can cause deep wounds.
   But they don't attack human beings.
   Their bite harms only certain small creatures.
   These include insects.
   Mice can be harmed by their bite too.

3. Tarantulas come out of their burrows at dusk.
   Dawn is the time of their return to their burrows.
   At night the mature males look for females.
   Sometimes they become intruders in people's homes.

4. A fertilized female tarantula lays several hundred eggs at one time.
   Her next act is to weave a cocoon of silk to enclose them.
   She does nothing more for her young.

5. When hatched, the young walk away.
   They live alone.
   They are unlike ants in this respect.
   They also differ from bees.
   They do not live in colonies.

Subordination

COMPLEX SENTENCES

15.1 WHAT SUBORDINATION DOES

Subordination lets you show the relative importance of the parts of a sentence. Suppose you want to describe what a dog did on a particular night, and you want your description to include the following points:

> The dog lived next door.
> The dog was scrawny.
> The dog barked.
> The dog was old.
> The dog howled.
> The dog kept me awake.
> I was awake all night.

What is the best way to arrange these isolated facts in a sentence? Part of the answer is to coordinate facts that are equally important to the point you want to make:

> The dog was scrawny and old, and he lived next door; he barked and howled and kept me awake all night.

This sentence puts all the facts together, but it fails to show which fact is most important to the writer—to you.

Which *is* the most important? That depends on the topic of your essay. If you're writing about yourself, for instance, the most important fact about the dog is that it kept you awake all night. To highlight that fact, you could rewrite the sentence like this:

> The scrawny old dog next door kept me awake all night by barking and howling.

This sentence emphasizes just one statement: the dog kept me awake. By turning all the other statements into modifiers of *dog* or *kept me awake,* it subordinates them to the point that is most important to you. You can stress this point even more by placing it at the end of the sentence—the stress position:

> By barking and howling, the scrawny old dog next door kept me awake all night.

Alternatively, you can subordinate all the other facts about the dog to the fact that it lived next door:

> The dog *that kept me awake all night with its barking and howling* lived next door.

The entire group of italicized words modifies *dog.* So all the other facts about the dog are now subordinated to the fact that it lived next door.

Finally, suppose you want to subordinate all of these facts about the dog to a brand-new fact. Suppose you mainly want to tell what happened to you *as a result* of that sleepless night. Then you might write a sentence like this:

> Because the barking and howling of the scrawny old dog next door had kept me awake all night, I fell asleep in the middle of the chemistry final.

Subordination helps to make a sentence fit its context. Consider these paragraphs:

> For me, the one big problem with dogs is noise. On the night before I had to take a final exam in chemistry, "man's best friend" turned out to be my worst enemy. I got to bed at eleven, but I didn't sleep a wink. *What kept me awake all night was the barking and howling of the scrawny old dog next door.*

The Bible tells us all to love our neighbors, but I have always had trouble even liking most of mine. When I was about six years old, I climbed over the fence in our backyard, wandered into Mr. O'Reilly's flower garden, and sat down in the middle of some big yellow daffodils. Mr. O'Reilly came up from behind and whacked me so hard I can still feel it now. We've moved a few times since then, but I have yet to find neighbors that I love. On the contrary, many of the things I don't love seem to come from across a fence. In El Paso, for instance, *a scrawny old dog that kept me awake all night with its barking and howling lived next door.*

In the chemistry course I managed to do just about everything wrong. To begin with, I bought a used textbook at a bargain price, and then found out that I was supposed to buy the new edition. Trying to get along instead with the old one, I almost always wound up reading the wrong pages for the assignment and giving the wrong answers to quiz questions. I did no better with beakers and test tubes; the only thing my experiments showed is that I could have blown up the lab. But the worst came last. *Because the barking and howling of the scrawny old dog next door had kept me awake all night, I fell asleep in the middle of the final.*

The sentence about the dog is written three different ways to emphasize three different things: the noise it made, the fact that it lived next door, and the fact that something happened because of its noise. In each case, the methods of subordination make the sentence fit the particular paragraph for which it is written. The three ways of writing the sentence also illustrate three different kinds of subordinate clauses. We consider these in the next sections.

15.2 WHAT SUBORDINATE CLAUSES ARE

A **subordinate clause** (SC), also called a **dependent clause,** is a group of words that has its own subject and predicate but cannot stand alone as a simple sentence. It must be included in or connected to an **independent clause** (IC)—one that can stand by itself as a sentence:

SC	IC
Before she spoke to reporters,	she conferred with her advisers.

IC	SC
Medical researchers have long been seeking a cure for a disease	that takes thousands of lives each year.

IC	SC	SC
Pavarotti was cheered	as he finished the beautiful aria	in which Rodolfo declares his love to Mimi.

A sentence containing one independent clause and at least one subordinate clause is called **complex.** Complex sentences are made with various kinds of subordinate clauses, as explained below.

15.3   USING ADJECTIVE (RELATIVE) CLAUSES

An **adjective clause,** sometimes called a **relative clause,** normally begins with a **relative pronoun**—*which, that, who, whom,* or *whose.* The relative pronoun refers to a noun or noun phrase that is called its **antecedent.** The adjective clause modifies this antecedent, which usually appears just before the relative pronoun:

> The dog *that* kept me awake all night lived next door.

An adjective clause can say more about its antecedent than a single adjective does. Compare these two sentences:

> Medical researchers have long been seeking a cure for a *fatal* disease.

> Medical researchers have long been seeking a cure for a disease *that takes thousands of lives every year.*

An adjective clause also enables you to subordinate one set of facts to another set. See how these two sentences can be combined:

> Amelia Earhart disappeared in 1937 during a round-the-world trip. She set new speed records for long-distance flying in the 1930s.
>
> COMBINATION 1: Amelia Earhart, *who set new speed records for long-distance flying in the 1930s,* disappeared in 1937 during a round-the-world trip.
>
> COMBINATION 2: Amelia Earhart, *who disappeared in 1937 during a round-the-world trip,* set new speed records for long-distance flying in the 1930s.

Combination 1 subordinates Earhart's record-setting to her disappearance; combination 2 subordinates her disappearance to her record-setting. Which combination the writer chooses depends on which fact the writer wants to emphasize in a particular context.

15.4 CHOOSING RELATIVE PRONOUNS

The relative pronoun you choose depends chiefly on the antecedent—the noun or pronoun the clause modifies.

1. Use *who, whom, whose,* or *that* when the antecedent is one or more persons:

> A cynic is a man *who* knows the price of everything and the value of nothing.
> —Oscar Wilde
>
> Millard Fillmore, *whom* almost nobody remembers, was president of the United States from 1848 to 1852.
>
> Never trust a doctor whose office plants have died.
> —Erma Bombeck
>
> Pedestrians *that* ignore traffic lights are living dangerously.

The case endings of *who, whom,* and *whose* depend on what the pronoun does in the clause it introduces. (For a full discussion of case endings, see section 18.11.)

2. Use *which* or *that* when the antecedent is one or more things:

> A mind *that* is stretched to a new idea never returns to its original dimensions. —Oliver Wendell Holmes

> A team of shipwreck hunters recently found the wreck of the S.S. *Leopoldville, which* was sunk by a German torpedo on Christmas Eve 1944.

> We must preserve the freedoms for *which* our ancestors fought.

3. Use *which* when the antecedent is an entire clause—but only when nothing else can be mistaken for the antecedent:

> Tim cackled maliciously, *which* infuriated Paul.

> The accident could have been avoided, *which* made it all the harder to bear.

For more on this use of *which,* see section 18.4B.

4. Do not use *that* when the antecedent is a proper name, a clearly identified person, or a clearly identified thing:

▶ The world's greatest jumpers include Carl Lewis, ~~that~~ **who** has cleared nearly twenty-nine feet.

▶ The Verrazano-Narrows Bridge, ~~that~~ **which** links Brooklyn to Staten Island, has the longest suspension span in the world.

▶ Passengers on Flight 89 commended the pilot, ~~that~~ **who** had guided the plane to safety despite the blizzard.

▶ The town's library, ~~that~~ **which** was built in 1850, holds over 100,000 volumes.

5. You may use *whose* with any antecedent to avoid writing *of which:*

> The children worked in a schoolroom *whose* windows were never opened. (**COMPARE:** The children worked in a schoolroom *of which* the windows were never opened.)

> She landed a helicopter *whose* pilot had collapsed over the controls.

6. You may use *where* or *when* as a relative pronoun when the antecedent is a place or a time:

> That morning we drove to the town of Appomattox Court House, Virginia, *where* Lee surrendered to Grant at the end of the Civil War.
>
> Her favorite season was spring, *when* the earth seemed born again.
>
> She felt a chill as she stood on the very spot *where* the murderer had been hanged.

15.5 PLACING THE ADJECTIVE CLAUSE

Place the adjective clause so that the reader can clearly see its connection to the antecedent of the relative pronoun. Observe the following guidelines:

1. Whenever possible, place the adjective clause immediately after the antecedent of the relative pronoun:

> Students *who cheat* poison the atmosphere of the college.
> Newhouse made a proposal *that nobody else liked.*
> The police shot a raccoon *that appeared to be rabid.*

2. If an adjective phrase gets between the relative pronoun and its antecedent, you can sometimes turn the phrase into another adjective clause:

> **and who have small children**
> ▶ Mothers ~~of small children~~ who work must juggle conflicting
> responsibilities.

Alternatively, you can reconstruct the sentence:

> Working mothers of small children must juggle conflicting responsibilities.

For more on the placement of modifying phrases, see sections 12.14–12.18.

3. If the adjective clause is long, you can move the antecedent (in bold print here) to the end of the main clause:

> **Leonardo da Vinci,** *whose knowledge of sculpture, painting, architecture, engineering, and science made him the intellectual wonder of his time,* painted the *Mona Lisa* in Florence about 1504.

> EDITED: The *Mona Lisa* was painted in Florence about 1504 by **Leonardo da Vinci,** *whose knowledge of sculpture, painting, architecture, engineering, and science made him the intellectual wonder of his time.*

The second version keeps both parts of the main clause together.

EXERCISE 1 PLACING ADJECTIVE CLAUSES

To each of the sentences add the adjective clause written within parentheses. Reword the sentence and add punctuation as necessary so as to connect the clause clearly to the italicized item.

EXAMPLE
Psychologists have been studying the mental effects of prolonged weightlessness. (who work for NASA)
NEW SENTENCE: Psychologists who work for NASA have been studying the mental effects of prolonged weightlessness.

1. Workers are busy cleaning a *statue* in Cedar Park. (that was designed by Phidias Gold in 1953)

2. The *statue* has been discolored by pollutants emitted by motor vehicles and nearby cement factories. (which represents the American farmer)

3. City officials want to honor *Gold* with a parade and a banquet on Labor Day. (whose works have earned him a reputation for bold designs)

4. The sculptor recently described a *memorial* in an interview with reporters. (that will honor the astronauts killed in the explosion of the space shuttle *Challenger*)

5. The *Challenger* blew up within minutes of its launching on January 28, 1986. (whose crew included the first schoolteacher ever sent into space)

15.6 PUNCTUATING ADJECTIVE CLAUSES

1. Use commas to set off an adjective clause only when it is **nonrestrictive**—that is, not needed to identify the antecedent.

A nonrestrictive adjective clause has a well-identified noun as its antecedent:

> Linda Watson, *who earned a cumulative grade-point average of 3.8,* was graduated with highest honors.

This adjective clause is not needed to identify the antecedent because she is already identified by name. Without the adjective clause, some details would be lacking, but the essential information would remain:

> Linda Watson was graduated with highest honors.

Well-identified nouns include not only names of persons but also names of things, job titles, and any other phrases that plainly identify one of a kind:

> The Lincoln Memorial, *which was dedicated in 1922,* attracts visitors from all over the world.
>
> We attended a reception for the Dean of the Business School, *who will retire in June.*
>
> My youngest brother, *who seldom opened a book as a teenager,* has just been appointed head librarian of Wakefield University.

In all of these examples, the adjective clauses are nonrestrictive. They give information about the antecedents but do not identify them.

EXCEPTION: When the antecedent is the proper name of a group, the clause may restrict its meaning to certain members of the group and would therefore require no commas:

> Most Canadians *who speak French* live in the province of Quebec.

2. Do not use commas to set off a **restrictive** adjective clause— one that *does* identify the antecedent:

> Students *who earn a cumulative grade point average of 3.7 or more* will be graduated with highest honors.

This adjective clause restricts the meaning of the antecedent, specifying which students are eligible for highest honors. Without the clause the sentence would say something quite different:

> Students will be graduated with highest honors.

Since a restrictive clause is essential to the meaning of the antecedent and of the sentence as a whole, it must not be set off from the antecedent by commas. Here is one more example:

> Tree surgeons may have to remove the oak *that towers over the new greenhouse.*

15.7 OVERUSING ADJECTIVE CLAUSES

Do not use adjective clauses starting with phrases like *who is* and *which are* when you don't need them. Cut the excess words:

▶ Some of the compact cars ~~that are~~ sold by American companies are manufactured in Japan.

▶ Joseph P. Kennedy, ~~who was the~~ father of President John F. Kennedy, made a fortune in banking and real estate.

> **EXERCISE 2 SENTENCE COMBINING WITH ADJECTIVE CLAUSES**
>
> Combine the sentences in each of the following pairs by turning one sentence into an adjective clause and using it in the other. Then underline the adjective clause and in parentheses state whether it is restrictive or nonrestrictive.
>
> **EXAMPLE**
> Employees of a certain kind will be fired.
> Those employees arrive late.
> **COMBINED:** Employees *who arrive late* will be fired. (restrictive)
>
> 1. On Interstate 70 in Colorado, a stretch offers tourists many attractive sights.
>   The stretch extends from Idaho Springs to Glenwood Springs.

2. At Idaho Springs the countryside is dotted with the entrances to old silver mines.
   One hundred years ago, the mines were making people rich.

3. Farther along, the highway enters Vail.
   Vail draws thousands of skiers to its beautiful trails every winter.

4. Glenwood Canyon is another rewarding place.
   Its colorful walls rise steeply above a winding river.

5. Here, in the spring, men and women ride the rapids in rubber rafts.
   The men and women relish adventure and spectacular scenery.

EXERCISE 3 SENTENCE COMBINING WITH ADJECTIVE
                CLAUSES

Combine the sentences in each of the following sets by using one or more adjective clauses.

EXAMPLE

Ronald Reagan governed the state of California from 1967 to 1975.
Six years later, he became president of the United States.
He first made his name in the movies.
COMBINED: Ronald Reagan, who governed the state of California from 1967 to 1975 and became president of the United States six years later, first made his name in the movies.

1. Susan B. Anthony was arrested on a certain day in 1872.
   On that day she led a group of women to the polls in Rochester, New York.
   Women owe their voting rights to early feminists like Susan B. Anthony.

2. Feminism in the nineteenth century was also strongly promoted by Elizabeth Cady Stanton.
   She organized the first U.S. women's rights convention in 1848.
   She presided over the National American Woman Suffrage Association from 1890 to 1892.

3. In the early twentieth century, Carrie Chapman Catt led the fight for women's rights.
   She became president of the National American Woman Suffrage Association in 1900.

4. She achieved her goal in 1920.
   At that time Congress passed the Nineteenth Amendment.
   That amendment gave women the right to vote.

5. Since the 1960s, the spirit of feminism has been revived by the National Organization for Women.
   This organization has demanded for women certain rights and opportunities.
   Those rights and opportunities have been traditionally granted only to men.

15.8 USING ADVERB CLAUSES

An **adverb clause** begins with a subordinator—a word like *when, because, if,* and *although.* Modifying a word, phrase, or clause, an adverb clause tells such things as why, when, how, and under what conditions. Normally it gives more information than a simple adverb does:

ADVERB
Then I hit the brakes.

ADVERB CLAUSE
As the deer leaped onto the road, I hit the brakes.

An adverb clause also enables you to subordinate one point to another:

As he was being tackled, he threw the ball.

This sentence highlights the throwing of the ball and is designed to fit into a paragraph like this:

The line wavered, and Keene knew it would break in seconds. But he dropped back, dancing around until he spotted a receiver. *As he was being tackled, he threw the ball.* Polanski made a leaping catch at the twenty-five-yard line, came down running, zigzagged past the Iowa safety, and crossed the goal line. The crowd went wild.

On the other hand, if the most important thing is not the pass but the tackle, the sentence should emphasize that:

> Keene looked desperately for a receiver, sensing the seconds ticking away. Suddenly his blocking broke down, and he was surrounded. *As he threw the ball, he was being tackled.* The pass went nearly straight up, then fell to earth behind him. The game was over.

In each version of the italicized sentence, the adverb clause lets you indicate which of two points is more important.

15.9 CHOOSING SUBORDINATORS

A **subordinator** is a word or phrase that subordinates the clause to whatever it modifies. Subordinators signal a variety of relations:

1. Time

> The factory closed *when* the owner died.
>
> *Until* the power lines were restored, we had to read at night by candlelight.
>
> *While* Marian sang, Zachary played the piano.

2. Causality

> Kate was happy *because* she had just won her first case.
>
> *Since* I had no money, I walked all the way home.

3. Concession and contrast

> Money cannot make you happy, *though* it can keep you comfortable.
>
> *Though* money cannot make you happy, it can keep you comfortable.
>
> *Although* the mosquitoes were out in force, we spent an enjoyable hour fishing before sundown.
>
> In my new car, I am averaging over thirty-five miles per gallon of gas, *whereas* I got only twenty in my old one.
>
> *While* Finnegan himself never ran for any office, he ran many successful campaigns.

4. Condition

If battery-powered cars become popular, the price of gas will drop.

He ran *as if* he had a broken leg.

5. Purpose

I worked in a department store for a year *so that* I could earn money for college.

RELATIONS SIGNALED BY SUBORDINATORS

TIME

after
as
as long as
as soon as
before
ever since
until
when
whenever
while

CONDITION

as if
as though
if
provided that
unless

PLACE

whence
where
wherever

CAUSALITY

because
since

CONCESSION AND CONTRAST

although
even though
though
whereas
while

PURPOSE

in order that
lest
so that

RESULT

so that
that

COMPARISON

than

RANGE OF POSSIBILITIES

however   whichever
whatever   whoever

6. Place

> *Where* federal funds go, federal regulations go with them.

7. Result

> We are *so* accustomed to adopting a mask before others *that* we
> end by being unable to recognize ourselves. —William Hazlitt
> She fixed the clock *so that* it worked.

8. Range of possibilities

> *Whatever* the president wants, Congress has a will of its own.

You can also signal general possibility with *whenever, wherever,
whoever, whichever,* and *however:*

> I can't pronounce the name *however* it is spelled.

9. Comparison

> The river is cleaner now *than* it was two years ago.

15.10 PLACING ADVERB CLAUSES

An adverb clause of result and comparison normally follows the
main clause. But most other adverb clauses are movable. So
where do you put them?

To be clear-cut and straightforward, lead with your main
clause and let the adverb clause follow:

> The colonel ordered an investigation as soon as he heard the
> complaint of the enlisted men.
> I worked in a department store for a year so that I could earn
> money for college.

This kind of order has a brisk, no-nonsense effect, and you will
seldom go wrong with it. But it is not always the best order. To
create suspense, or to build up to your main point, put the adverb
clause at the beginning and save the main clause for the end.
Consider these two versions of a sentence spoken by Winston
Churchill in 1941, when the Germans had occupied most of
Europe and were threatening to invade England:

We shall not flag or fail even though large tracts of Europe and many old and famous states have fallen or may fall into the grip of the Gestapo and all the odious apparatus of Nazi rule.

Even though large tracts of Europe and many old and famous states have fallen or may fall into the grip of the Gestapo and all the odious apparatus of Nazi rule, we shall not flag or fail.

There is nothing grammatically wrong with the first sentence, which starts with a main clause and finishes with a long adverb clause. But this sentence has all the fire of a wet match. Because the crucial words *we shall not flag or fail* come first, they are virtually smothered by what follows them. By the time we reach the end of the sentence we may even have forgotten its main point. The arrangement of the second sentence—the one Churchill actually wrote—guarantees that we will remember. Precisely because we are made to wait until the end of the sentence for the main clause, it strikes with telling effect.

15.11 PUNCTUATING ADVERB CLAUSES

Introductory adverb clauses are followed by a comma:

Even though I knocked loudly on the door, the storekeeper would not open it.
When the gate opened, the bull charged into the ring.

Ordinarily, an adverb clause coming at the end of a sentence is not preceded by a comma:

The bull charged into the ring *when the gate opened.*
A wall collapsed *because the foundation was poorly constructed.*

If the adverb clause at the end of a sentence is nonrestrictive—not essential to the meaning of the sentence—a comma may precede it:

We planted the trees in the fall of 1984, *just after we bought the house.*

EXERCISE 4 SENTENCE COMBINING WITH ADVERB CLAUSES

Combine the sentences in each of the following pairs by turning one sentence into an adverb clause and attaching it to the other. Be sure to begin the adverb clause with a suitable subordinator, and in parentheses state the relation that the subordinator shows.

EXAMPLE
I see roses.
Then my nose starts to itch.
COMBINED: Whenever I see roses, my nose starts to itch. (time)

1. Assume that commercial airlines will offer regular flights to the moon by the year 2000.
   The moon may become the new playground of the super-rich.

2. This prospect is unlikely.
   But scientists may eventually establish some kind of observatory on the moon.

3. The moon has no atmosphere.
   Therefore it affords a perfectly clear view of the stars.

4. Even without a lunar observatory, we may be able to put a telescope in a permanently orbiting space station.
   As a result, we will get an equally clear view.

5. We will be able to study the stars without the least interference from atmospheric disturbance.
   Then our understanding of them will dramatically increase.

15.12 MAKING ADVERB CLAUSES COMPLETE: AVOIDING FAULTY COMPARISONS *comp*

1. Do not use an incomplete adverb clause when a complete one is needed to make a comparison clear:

▶ The river is as clean now as **it was** two years ago.

The original sentence seems to compare the river with *two years*.

2. Do not skip any word that is essential to a comparison:

▶ Roger moves faster than any other player on the team ~~does.~~

If Roger himself is a player on the team, the original sentence seems to compare him with himself as well as others.

▶ Tokyo's population is larger than New York's is.

The original seems to compare a population with a city. Another way of correcting the sentence is this:

Tokyo's population is larger *than that of New York.*

3. You may skip any words in a comparison that can be easily supplied by the reader:

The exhaust system emits less sulphur dioxide *than the original system (did).*

Some writers think more about plot *than (they do) about characters.*

Ever since I began swimming every day, I have felt better *(than I did before I began swimming).*

Roger moves faster than any other player on the team *(does).*

Tokyo's population is larger than New York's *(is).*

EXERCISE 5 **CORRECTING FAULTY COMPARISONS**

Each of the following sentences makes a comparison. Revise any sentence in which the comparison is not clear and complete. If a sentence is correct as it stands, write *Correct.*

EXAMPLE

The Federal Reserve Bank in New York City holds more gold than any other bank in the United States.

1. The old house on the bay at St. Anthony's Island looks just as good as twenty years ago.

2. At that time, however, the sand was much whiter.

3. Also, the water in the bay was clearer than any bay in the islands.

4. Now the bay gets more sewage than any septic system on St. Anthony's.

5. And fishermen are not catching nearly as many cod and haddock as twenty years ago.

15.13 USING NOUN CLAUSES

A **noun clause** is a clause used as a noun within a sentence. Normally it gives more information than a simple noun can. Compare the following:

> Government officials did not anticipate the *problem.*

> Government officials did not anticipate *that protestors would occupy the presidential palace.*

A noun clause can serve as subject, object, or predicate noun.

1. Noun clause as subject

> *What Sylvia did* amazed me.
> *Whoever wins the nomination* will be running against a popular incumbent.

2. Noun clause as object

> I feared *(that) we would never get out alive.* (*That* is optional.)
> The police have not discovered *how the prisoner escaped.*
> No one knew *whether or not interest rates would rise.*
> We will plug the leaks with *whatever is handy.*
> Alexandra wondered *what marriage would do to her.*

3. Noun clause as predicate noun

> The main reason for the change is *that all in the company will benefit.*
> A computer with the brain of a genius is *what I need right now.*
> The most puzzling mystery of all is *why she abdicated at the height of her power.*

SUBORDINATE CLAUSES: IN BRIEF

The **adjective (relative) clause** begins with a relative pronoun—*which, that, who, whom,* or *whose.* The relative pronoun refers to its antecedent, the noun or noun phrase that normally appears just before it:

> All *that glitters* is not gold.

The **adverb clause** begins with a subordinator—a word like *when, because,* or *although*—and tells such things as why, when, or how something happened:

> I missed class *because I had to go out of town for a job interview.*

The **noun clause** is used as a noun within a sentence:

> Many people want *what they cannot afford.*

Noun clauses may begin with—

> a pronoun: No one knows exactly *who* built Stonehenge.
> an adverb: Astronomers can explain *how* stars are born.
> *that:* Many workers fear *that* they will lose their jobs.

That may be omitted if the meaning is clear without it:

> Many workers fear they will lose their jobs.

EXERCISE 6 USING NOUN CLAUSES

Underline the noun clause(s) in the following sentences. Then write a sentence that resembles the form of the original one.

EXAMPLE

I have sometimes wondered <u>how automatic elevators respond to conflicting signals.</u>
Children often ask how bears survive winter.

1. Whoever tries to resolve a conflict soon learns that nothing pleases everybody.

2. What solves one problem often causes another.

3. No one knows whether gains will be greater than losses.

4. It soon becomes evident that progress is elusive.

5. Who can explain why negotiations sometimes take months?

EXERCISE 7 SENTENCE COMBINING: REVIEW OF
SUBORDINATION

Combine the sentences in each of the following sets by using at least two of the three different kinds of subordinate clauses—noun clauses, adjective clauses, and adverb clauses.

EXAMPLE
Frank Waters was a powerful man.
He could not lift the big stove.
It weighed over four hundred pounds.
COMBINED: Though Frank Waters was a powerful man, he could not lift the big stove, which weighed over four hundred pounds.

1. The Sioux Indians settled down near the Black Hills in 1867.
   Soon after, the Black Hills were invaded by white men.
   The white men were searching for gold.

2. A U.S. treaty forbade white men to enter the Black Hills.
   Army cavalrymen entered the Black Hills in 1874 under General George Custer.
   Custer had led the slaughter of the Southern Cheyenne in 1868.

3. Red Cloud led the Sioux.
   Red Cloud denounced Custer's invasion.
   The invasion violated the treaty.

4. This violation led to disaster in 1876 at Little Bighorn River.
   At that time the Sioux attacked Custer ferociously.
   As a result, he and all his men were killed.

5. Custer's extraordinary exploits in the Civil War made him the youngest general in the Union Army.
   But most people know only one thing about Custer.
   He was the central figure in "Custer's last stand."

16

Coordination and Subordination

16.1 USING COORDINATION AND SUBORDINATION TOGETHER

Using coordination and subordination together, you can arrange all the parts of a sentence according to their relative importance and the desired emphasis. For example:

1. No one had the guts to raise a riot.

2. But suppose a European woman went through the bazaars alone.

3. Somebody would probably spit betel juice over her dress.
COMBINED: No one had the guts to raise a riot, but if a European woman went through the bazaars alone somebody would probably spit betel juice over her dress.   —George Orwell

In the combined sentence, both sentence 1 and sentence 3 remain independent clauses, though they are now joined by *but*. The result is a compound sentence. Within it, sentence 2 becomes a subordinate clause introduced by *if*. Here is another example:

When Matthew heard about the accident, he molded his face into a mask as he had seen actors do, and he holed up in his bedroom, where he unplugged his stereo and tried to cry.

—College student

EXERCISE 1 SENTENCE COMBINING

Using coordination and subordination together, make one sentence from each of the following sets of sentences. Include all the information given, but feel free to change the wording or arrangement of the sentences. Combine the sentences of each set in at least two different ways. Then, if you prefer one of the combinations, put a check next to it.

EXAMPLE

The snow melts in the spring.
The dirt roads in the region turn into muddy streams.
Certain people live in isolated houses.
Those people use old footpaths to reach Bridgeton.
Bridgeton has two grocery stores.
It has one gas pump.

COMBINATION 1: The snow melts in the spring, so the dirt roads in the region turn into muddy streams; certain people live in isolated houses, and those people use old footpaths to reach Bridgeton, which has two grocery stores and one gas pump.

COMBINATION 2: When the snow melts in the spring, the dirt roads in the region turn into muddy streams, so people who live in isolated houses use old footpaths to reach Bridgeton, which has two grocery stores and one gas pump.

1. According to some, the source of evil lies in society's institutions.
   These are said to nurture evil behavior in otherwise good people.
   According to others, evil springs directly from human nature.
   This is said to be inherently corrupt.

2. William Golding states his opinion in a novel.
   The novel is called *Lord of the Flies.*
   He nowhere states his opinion directly.
   But the setting, plot, and characters of his novel clearly reveal it.

3. The action is set on a beautiful South Pacific island.
   It has a bountiful supply of fruit trees.
   It has springs of fresh water.
   It has wild pigs.
   They run freely through the thick vegetation.

4. The only human inhabitants are a group of British school-children.
   The children survived the crash of a plane.
   The plane was shot down during World War II.

5. Ralph is the leader of the boys.
   Ralph summons them to meetings in a certain way.
   He uses a large shell.
   The shell makes a loud noise at a certain time.
   He blows into it at that time.
   The boys respond to the sound for a certain reason.
   The shell is a symbol of authority.
   It is also a symbol of order.

6. At first the older boys follow Ralph's lead.
   They agree to perform certain tasks.
   One task is to build shelters.
   Another task is to care for the youngest.
   A third is to keep a fire burning.
   The fire burns on a hilltop.
   Its purpose is to serve as an SOS signal for crews of passing ships.

7. But trouble develops shortly.
   Ralph's leadership is challenged by Jack.
   Jack has been a leader of choirboys.
   He wants to be the chief again.
   Then he can give orders.
   He will not take them.

8. Jack forms his own band of followers.
   They walk out on Ralph.
   They want to stop working on the signal fire.
   They want to hunt wild pigs.
   They like the excitement of the chase.
   They like the excitement of the kill.
   They stab the squealing pig with a wooden spear.

9. Jack's followers attack Ralph's group one night.
   They take Piggy's glasses.
   They want the lenses for a purpose.
   They will use the lenses.
   The lenses will concentrate the sun's rays on firewood.
   The lenses will make a fire.
   The fire will cook the pig meat.

10. In the end, the boys are discovered by a strong naval officer.
    The naval officer scolds the boys.
    The boys look like savages.
    The boys have been fighting among themselves.
    Yet he has been fighting too.
    He has come ashore from a warship.
    The warship aims to sink enemy warships and their crews.

EXERCISE 2 WRITING ONE-SENTENCE SUMMARIES

Using coordination, subordination, or both, write a one-sentence summary of each of the following passages.

EXAMPLE

More than ever before in American politics, language is used not as an instrument for forming and expressing thought. It is used to prevent, confuse, and conceal thinking. Members of each branch and agency of government at every level, representing every hue of political opinion, habitually speak a language of nonresponsibility.

—Richard Gambino, "Through the Dark, Glassily"

ONE-SENTENCE SUMMARY: More than ever before, American politicians and government workers use language not to express thought but to prevent, confuse, and conceal it; they speak a language of nonresponsibility.

1. The average person has many worries, but there is one thing he does not generally worry about. He does not worry that somewhere, without his knowledge, a secret tribunal is about to order him seized, drugged, and imprisoned without the right of appeal. Indeed, anyone who worries overmuch about such a thing, and expresses that worry repeatedly and forcefully enough, would probably be classified as a paranoid schizophrenic.

   —Hendrik Hertzberg and David C. K. McClelland, "Paranoia"

2. Every grown up person expects to pay a price for his pleasures, but seldom is the price as vast as the one endured "however happily" by most mothers. We have mentioned the literal cost factor. But what does that mean? For middle-class American women, it means a life style with severe and usually unimagined limitations; i.e., life in the

suburbs, because who can afford three bedrooms in the city? And what do suburbs mean? For women, suburbs mean other women and children and leftover peanut-butter sandwiches and car pools and seldom seen husbands.

—Betty Rollin, "Motherhood: Who Needs It?"

3. Historically, clutter is a modern phenomenon, born of the industrial revolution. There was a time when goods were limited; and the rich and fashionable were few in number and objects were precious and hard to come by. Clutter is a 19th century esthetic; it came with the abundance of products combined with the rise of purchasing power, and the shifts in society that required manifestations of status and style.

—Ada Louise Huxtable, "Modern-Life Battle: Conquering Clutter"

4. I have described imagination as the ability to make images and to move them about inside one's head in new arrangements. This is the faculty that is specifically human, and it is the common root from which science and literature both spring and grow and flourish together.

—Jacob Bronowski, "The Reach of Imagination"

5. To lie habitually, as a way of life, is to lose contact with the unconscious. It is like taking sleeping pills, which confer sleep but blot out dreaming. The unconscious wants truth. It ceases to speak to those who want something else more than truth.

—Adrienne Rich, "Women and Honor: Some Notes on Lying"

16.2 UNTANGLING SENTENCES   *tgl*

It is sometimes hard to put several ideas into a single sentence without getting them tangled up in the process. Consider this sentence:

* Due to the progress in military weaponry over the years, there has been an increased passivity in mankind that such advancements bring as wars are easier to fight resulting in a total loss of honor in fighting.

If you come across such a sentence in your own writing, you should first of all break it up into single ideas:

1. There has been progress in military weaponry over the years.
2. There has been increased passivity in mankind.
3. Such advancements bring passivity.
4. The passivity is due to the progress.
5. Wars are easier to fight.
6. This results in a total loss of honor in fighting.

Once you have broken up the sentence into single ideas, you can use coordination, and subordination to put them back together clearly:

> Since progress in military weaponry over the years has made mankind more passive and wars easier to fight, there has been a total loss of honor in fighting.

> [or] Since progress in military weaponry over the years has made mankind more passive and wars easier to fight, fighting has lost all honor.

EXERCISE 3 SENTENCE UNTANGLING—A CHALLENGE

This may well be the toughest exercise in the book. All of the following sentences were written by students who had a lot to say but who got into a tangle when they tried to say it. So you will probably have trouble even figuring out what the writers meant. But we're asking you to do just that—and more. We're asking you to untangle each sentence in the same way we untangled the sentence about weaponry in the preceding discussion. First, cut up each tangled sentence into a series of short, simple sentences; second, using coordination, subordination, or both, recombine these into one long sentence that makes sense.

1. Thoreau spent much of his time outdoors in nature, which he loved, so he saw no reason to keep it out of his cabin, and he symbolized a doormat as the mistake of avoiding natural things like dirt and leaves like his neighbors.

2. The bean field made him self-sufficient, which was one of his beliefs, and he could also see it as an extension of himself, through the bean field, into nature in returning to a natural state.

3. The author of "The Cold Equations" is saying, in effect, that the main difference of life on the frontier for people living there after living in settled communities is that their lives are now ruled by the laws of nature instead of people making the laws.

4. For fifty years the people prospered under his rule; then, feeling a personal responsibility for the welfare of his subjects and their safety, the old king fought another monster which he was severely injured and soon died.

17

Sentence Fragments

Complete sentences help the writer to sound well organized and the reader to grasp the writer's point. Sentence fragments often do just the opposite. Unless skillfully used, they give the impression that the writer's thoughts are incomplete or disorganized, and they may confuse the reader.

17.1 USING AND MISUSING SENTENCE FRAGMENTS

A **sentence fragment** is part of a sentence punctuated as if it were a whole one:

> A new mountain to be climbed.

In conversation we often use fragments that make perfectly good sense:

> "When is she leaving?"
> "Tomorrow."
> "Really?"
> "No question about it."
> "Rats!"

Occasionally, sentence fragments also occur in writing:

> For so many years college had seemed far-off, but all of a sudden it was there, staring me in the face. A new mountain to be climbed.
> —College student

This passage ends with a sentence fragment whose meaning is perfectly clear in its context. In fact, the fragment highlights a point that might not have been made so effectively with a complete sentence.

But sentence fragments must be handled with care. If you don't know how to use them sparingly and strategically, your writing will look disorganized:

> In conclusion I feel Falstaff proves to be a most likable and interesting character. Showing an ability to think quickly in tight spots. But above all he lends a comical light to the play. Which I feel makes it all the more enjoyable.
>
> —College student

This passage includes two fragments—one after the first sentence and one at the end. Alternating with sentences of about equal length, they seem improvised and arbitrary, as if the writer could only now and then form a complete thought.

If you know how to use fragments effectively, do so. If you don't, or if your instructor will not accept any fragments at all, make sure all of your sentences are complete.

17.2 SPOTTING AND EDITING SENTENCE FRAGMENTS *frag*

How can you tell whether a particular word group is a sentence fragment? Here are some useful questions to ask if you aren't sure.

1. Does the "sentence" start with a subordinator or a relative pronoun? A clause that starts with a subordinator or a relative pronoun and stands by itself is a fragment. It should be attached to an independent clause:

a. On Halloween night some years ago, a full-grown man with a sick sense of humor disguised himself as a ghost. *So that he could terrify little children. (fragment starting with subordinator)

EDITED: On Halloween night some years ago, a full-grown man with a sick sense of humor disguised himself as a ghost so that he could terrify little children.

b. The British and French developed a supersonic plane called the Concorde. *Which can fly from New York to London in three hours. (fragment starting with relative pronoun)

EDITED: The British and French developed a supersonic plane called the Concorde, which can fly from New York to London in three hours.

2. Does the "sentence" lack a subject?

Lancelot won fame as a knight because of his prowess in battle. *Defeated the other great warriors in the kingdom.

EDITED: He defeated the other great warriors in the kingdom.

3. Does the "sentence" lack a predicate?

*The common cold. It strikes everyone at least once a year.

This fragment should be combined with the sentence following it:

EDITED: The common cold strikes everyone at least once a year.

4. Is the "sentence" merely a modifying phrase?

They went to a ski lodge. *With a view of the Rockies.

This fragment should be combined with the sentence preceding it:

EDITED: They went to a ski lodge with a view of the Rockies.

SPOTTING SENTENCE FRAGMENTS: IN BRIEF

Word group starting with a subordinator:

*So that he could terrify little children.

Word group starting with a relative pronoun:

*Which can fly from New York to London in three hours.

Word group missing a subject:

*Defeated the other great warriors.

Word group missing a predicate:

*The common cold.

Word group that is merely a modifying phrase:

*With a panoramic view of the Rockies.

EXERCISE ELIMINATING SENTENCE FRAGMENTS

Each of the following passages includes several sentence fragments. Make whatever changes are necessary to remove them.

EXAMPLE
line 2: assumption that mentally

1. The directors of social programs like Special Olympics
   make the accurate assumption. That mentally and physically disabled kids need to develop self-confidence. If they
   are going to function in society. According to Evelyn West,
   handicapped children need "to develop a strong, realistic   5
   sense of self." Society hinders this development. Children
   tease handicapped classmates. Separate facilities and special
   education classes are all clues to the handicapped. That they
   are different. Because they cannot succeed in regular classrooms or gyms. They feel incompetent. Now any child who   10
   feels incompetent is not ready to compete. This is where
   competitive programs fail. Wanting to foster confidence,
   Special Olympics demands it of the contestants. Who are
   already sure they are going to lose out. Because they lack a
   vital prerequisite for any competition. Confidence.   15

   The kids' lack of confidence is, ironically, nurtured by
   Saturday morning practices. For which the kids are
   unequally skilled. The qualifications for enrollment in Special Olympics are nebulous at best. Supposedly, only children with a ninety or lower on an I.Q. test are considered   20
   eligible. Few, however, are actually tested, and no one is
   turned away. Consequently, many mothers with several
   children send all of their brood to Saturday practices. For
   the free, supervised care. Some of these kids are barely
   handicapped. So that their competing with the severely dis-   25
   abled clearly loads the dice. With unfortunate consequences
   for all. The least handicapped kids—the winners—gain a
   feeling of superiority. Based on a false measure of their
   skills. The severely handicapped—the losers—feel shunned
   again. This time in their own program. None emerges with   30
   the sense of pride and respect for others. That the program's
   founders hoped to instill.

2. Most of the people who eat at a fast-food restaurant like McDonald's fall into one of four subgroups. The regulars, the families, the groups of kids, and the travelers.

   Unlike all the others. Regulars actually enjoy the restaurant. They talk to the servers about personal matters. While waiting for their meals. They eat carefully. Placing french fries one by one into their mouths. And sipping their drinks slowly. Their meals are an opportunity. To relax after a strenuous day on the job.

   Groups of kids often come to celebrate a birthday. Under the supervision of a mother. Who leaves them at a table. While she orders identical meals. For all of them. The kids play with straws. As they wait. Blowing them through the air and shooting the wrappers at each other. When the food comes to the table, they argue over who gets what. Even though all their meals are the same. During the meal they talk loudly. Despite the mother's efforts to control the volume. They also stare at nearby adults. Who wish the kids were sitting someplace else.

Using Pronouns

A **pronoun** is a word that commonly takes the place of a noun or noun phrase:

> Brenda thought that *she* had lost the dog, but *it* had followed *her.*

She and *her* take the place of *Brenda,* a noun; *it* takes the place of *the dog,* a noun phrase. Pronouns thus eliminate the need for awkward repetition.

18.1 USING PRONOUNS WITH ANTECEDENTS

The word or word group that a pronoun refers to is called its **antecedent.** "Antecedent" means "going before," and this term is used because the antecedent usually goes before the pronoun that refers to it:

1. The old man smiled as he listened to the marching band.

   Its spirited playing made him feel young again.

2. To build city districts that are custom-made for crime is

   idiotic. Yet that is what we do.   —Jane Jacobs

In the second example, the antecedent of the first *that* is *city districts.* The antecedent of the second *that* is a whole word group: *To build city districts that are custom-made for crime.*

346

The antecedent sometimes follows the pronoun that refers to it:

By the time he was three, Coleridge could read a chapter of the Bible.

18.2 USING PRONOUNS WITHOUT ANTECEDENTS

Some pronouns have no antecedent, and others may sometimes be used without one.

1. Indefinite pronouns have no antecedents. Compare these two sentences:

Ellen said that *she* wanted privacy.

Everyone needs some privacy.

She is a **definite** pronoun. It refers to a particular person, and its meaning is clear only if its antecedent has been provided—that is, if the person has already been identified. But *Everyone* is an **indefinite** pronoun. Because it refers to no one in particular, it has no antecedent. Other widely used indefinite pronouns include *everybody, one, no one, each, many,* and *some.*

2. The pronouns *I* and *you* have no antecedent because they are understood to refer to the writer and the reader or to the speaker and the listener.

3. The pronoun *we* sometimes appears without an antecedent—for example, in newspaper editorials, where the writer clearly speaks for a group of people.

18.3 USING PRONOUNS CLEARLY

The meaning of a definite pronoun is clear when readers can identify the antecedent with certainty:

People who saw the Tall Ships sail up the Hudson River in 1976 will long remember the experience. It gave them a handsome image of a bygone era.

The antecedent of each pronoun is obvious. *Who* clearly refers to *People; It* refers to *the experience; them* refers to *People who saw the Tall Ships.*

18.4 AVOIDING UNCLEAR PRONOUN REFERENCE
pr ref

The meaning of a definite pronoun is unclear when readers cannot identify the antecedent with certainty. The chief obstacles to clear reference are as follows.

18.4A AMBIGUITY

A pronoun is **ambiguous** when it has more than one possible antecedent:

> *Whenever Mike met Dan, he felt nervous.

Does *he* refer to *Mike* or to *Dan?* The reader cannot tell. The simplest way to eliminate the ambiguity is to replace the pronoun with a noun:

> EDITED: Whenever Mike met Dan, Mike felt nervous.

To avoid repeating the noun, you can put the pronoun before it:

> EDITED: Whenever he met Dan, Mike felt nervous.

18.4B BROAD REFERENCE

Pronoun reference is **broad** when *that, this, which,* or *it* refers to a whole statement containing one or more possible antecedents within it:

> *The senator supports the bottle bill, which rankles many of his constituents.

Are they rankled by the bill or by the senator's support for it?

> EDITED: The senator's support for the bottle bill rankles many of his constituents.

> *Some people insist that a woman should have a career, while others say that she belongs in the home. This is unfair.

What is unfair? *This* could refer to the whole sentence that precedes it, to the first half, or to the second:

> EDITED: This contradictory set of demands is unfair.

18.4C MUFFLED REFERENCE

Pronoun reference is **muffled** when the pronoun refers to something merely implied by what precedes it:

> A recent editorial contained an attack on the medical profession. *The writer accused them of charging excessively high fees.

Who is meant by *them?* Before using *them,* the writer should clearly establish its antecedent:

> EDITED: A recent editorial contained an attack on hospital administrators and doctors. The writers accused them of charging excessively high fees.
>
> *Lincoln spoke immortal words at Gettysburg, but most of the large crowd gathered there couldn't hear it.

The writer is thinking of Lincoln's address, of course, but the word *address* is missing. It must be inserted:

> EDITED: Lincoln gave an immortal address at Gettysburg, but most of the large crowd gathered there couldn't hear it.
> [or] Lincoln spoke immortal words at Gettysburg, but most of the large crowd gathered there couldn't hear his address.
> [or] . . . couldn't hear them.

The last way of editing the sentence changes the *number* of the pronoun to match the number of its antecedent; see section 18.6.

18.4D FREE-FLOATING *THEY* AND *IT*

They and *it* are **free-floating** when they are used as pronouns but have no definite antecedents:

> *In the first part of the movie, it shows clouds billowing like waves.

What shows clouds? The pronoun *it* has no antecedent. The writer is probably thinking of the *it* that simply fills out a sentence, such as *It was cloudy,* meaning *There were clouds.* That kind *of it* (called an expletive) needs no antecedent. But the pronoun *it* does. If you can't readily figure out a way to furnish one, reconstruct the sentence:

> EDITED: The first part of the movie shows clouds billowing like waves.
>
> Traveling in Eastern Europe used to be difficult. *At some checkpoints they held foreigners for questioning.

The word *they* needs an antecedent:

> EDITED: Traveling in Eastern Europe used to be difficult because of the *security police.* At some checkpoints they held foreigners for questioning.

Alternatively, you can replace the pronoun with a noun:

> EDITED: At some checkpoints the security police held foreigners for questioning.

Or you can use the passive voice:

> EDITED: At some checkpoints foreigners were held for questioning.

18.4E INDEFINITE *YOU* AND *YOUR*

You and *your* are **indefinite** when used to mean anything but the reader. Though writers sometimes use *you* to mean "people in general," you will increase the precision of your sentences if you use *you* and *your* for your reader alone.

> *You didn't have microphones in Lincoln's day.
>
> EDITED: There were no microphones in Lincoln's day.

> One of Orwell's contradictions is the unperson, a man who existed once, but doesn't anymore, so he never existed. *But by defining someone as an unperson, you are saying that he once existed.
>
> EDITED: But to define someone as an unperson is to say that he once existed.

18.4F REMOTE REFERENCE

Pronoun reference is **remote** when the pronoun is so far from the antecedent that readers cannot find their way from one to the other:

> Bankers have said that another increase in the prime lending rate during the current quarter would seriously hurt their major customers: homeowners, small business personnel, and self-employed contractors using heavy equipment. *It would keep all of these borrowers from getting needed capital.
>
> Such an increase would keep all of these borrowers from getting needed capital.

OBSTACLES TO CLEAR PRONOUN REFERENCE: IN BRIEF

Ambiguity (18.4A):

> *Whenever Mike met Dan, *he* felt nervous.

Broad reference (18.4B):

> *The senator supports the bottle bill, *which* rankles many of his constituents.

Muffled reference (18.4C):

> A recent editorial contained an attack on the medical profession. *The writer accused *them* of charging excessively high fees.

Free-floating *they* and *it* (18.4D):

> *In the first part of the movie, *it* shows clouds billowing like waves.
>
> *Traveling in Eastern Europe used to be difficult. *At some checkpoints *they* held foreigners for questioning.

Indefinite *you* and *your* (18.4E):

> *You* didn't have microphones in Lincoln's day.

Remote reference (18.4F)

Exercise 1   Editing Unclear Pronouns

In some of the following sentences, the italicized pronoun has been used confusingly. Briefly diagnose what is wrong and then clarify the sentence. If the sentence is correct as it stands, write *Correct*.

EXAMPLE

The boy and the old man both knew that *he* had not much longer to live.

DIAGNOSIS: *He* is ambiguous; it can refer to either the boy or the old man.

CURE: The boy and the old man both knew that the old man had not much longer to live.

1. Archimedes discovered the principle of displacement while he was taking a bath. *It* made him leap out of the water with excitement.

2. Shouting "Eureka!" over and over, he ran naked through the streets of Syracuse. *They* must have been amazed to see him—or at least amused.

3. But in any case, Archimedes had found the solution to a problem assigned to him by King Hieron II. *He* would surely be pleased.

4. Hieron wanted Archimedes to investigate a crown that had been recently made for the king from an ingot of gold. The king wanted to know if *it* was pure gold.

5. The weight of the crown exactly matched the weight of the original ingot, *which* pleased the king.

6. But the goldsmith could have taken some of the gold for himself and added copper in *its* place.

7. Since the resulting alloy would look just like pure gold and weigh as much as the original ingot, *you* couldn't tell by appearance or weight what the goldsmith had done.

8. Gold, however, is denser than copper. So any given weight of pure gold takes up less space than the same weight of copper, or of gold mixed with *it*.

9. To learn whether or not the crown was pure gold, therefore, *they* had to see whether its volume matched the volume of a pure gold ingot that weighed the same.

10. But the crown was so intricately shaped that no way of measuring known in Archimedes' time could establish *it.*

11. Only when Archimedes got into the tub did a solution strike *him.*

12. By measuring the water displaced by the crown, and then measuring the water displaced by the ingot, he could easily tell whether or not *they* matched in volume, and thus whether or not the crown was pure gold.

18.5 MAKING ANTECEDENTS AND PRONOUNS AGREE IN GENDER *pr agr/g*

In some languages, many words change in form to indicate **gender.** In French, for instance, the word for *the* is *le* when used of a male (as in *le garçon,* the boy) and *la* when used of a female (as in *la femme,* the woman).

In English, gender affects only personal pronouns referring to a single thing in the third person. (*I* and *we* are first-person pronouns; *you* is the second-person pronoun; third-person pronouns include *he, she, it,* and *they.*) The gender of a personal pronoun in the third-person singular depends on the gender of its antecedent.

> When Marie Curie outlined the first steps of the award-winning research to *her* husband, *he* encouraged *her* to complete *it.* Though *he himself* was an eminent chemist, *he* wanted *her* to gain credit for *it.*

When the antecedent is a word of unspecified gender such as *doctor* or *lawyer,* you should use something other than a singular masculine pronoun. See section 9.11, "Using Gender-Inclusive (Nonsexist) Language."

18.6 MAKING ANTECEDENTS AND PRONOUNS AGREE IN NUMBER

An antecedent is singular if it refers to one person or thing, and plural if it refers to more than one. A singular antecedent calls for a singular pronoun; a plural antecedent calls for a plural pronoun:

The boy saw that he had cut his hand.

The Edmonton Oilers believed that they could win the Stanley Cup in 1988, and they did.

18.7 RESOLVING PROBLEMS IN NUMBER *pr agr/n*

Some antecedents can be hard to classify as either singular or plural. Here are guidelines:

1. Two or more nouns or pronouns joined by *and* are usually plural:

Orville and Wilbur Wright are best known for *their* invention of the airplane.

Nouns joined by *and* are singular only if they refer to one person or thing:

The chief cook and bottle washer demanded *his* pay.

2. When two nouns are joined by *or* or *nor,* the pronoun agrees with the second noun:

Neither Pierre LaCroix nor his boldest followers wanted to expose *themselves* to danger.

3. A noun or pronoun followed by a prepositional phrase is treated as if it stood by itself:

In 1980 Canada, together with the United States and several other countries, kept *its* athletes from participating in the Moscow Olympics.

The antecedent of *its* is *Canada.* Unlike the conjunction *and,* a phrase like *together with* or *along with* does not make a compound antecedent.

The leader of the strikers said that *he* would get them a new package of benefits.

The pronoun *he* agrees with *leader*. The antecedent of *them* is *strikers*.

4. Collective nouns can be either singular or plural, depending on the context:

> The team chooses *its* captain in the spring.

Since the captain is a symbol of unity, the writer treats *The team* as singular, using the singular pronoun *its*.

> The audience shouted and stamped *their* feet.

Since each person in the audience was acting independently, the writer treats *The audience* as plural, using the plural pronoun *their*.

5. Some indefinite pronouns are singular, some are plural, and some can be either singular or plural:

ALWAYS SINGULAR

anybody	either	one
anyone	neither	another
anything		
each	nobody	somebody
each one	none	someone
	no one	something
everybody	nothing	
everyone		whatever
everything		whichever
		whoever

ALWAYS PLURAL

both	few	others	several

**SOMETIMES SINGULAR
AND SOMETIMES PLURAL**

all	many	some
any	most	

As this list indicates, *each* by itself is always singular:

> Each of the men brought *his* own tools.

But *each* does not change the number of a plural subject that it follows:

> The men each brought *their* own tools.

Though some writers treat *everybody* and *everyone* as plural, *we* suggest you treat them as singular or simply avoid using them as antecedents:

> Everyone in the cast had to furnish *his* or *her* own costume.
>
> All cast members had to furnish *their* own costumes.

The number of a pronoun in the third group depends on the number of the word or phrase to which it refers:

> Some of the salad dressing left *its* mark on my shirt.
>
> Some of the students earn *their* tuition by working part-time.
>
> Many of the customers do not pay *their* bills on time.
>
> Many a man learns to appreciate *his* father only after *he* has become one *himself*.

6. The number of a relative pronoun depends on the number of the antecedent:

> Mark is one of those independent carpenters who *want* to work for *themselves*.
>
> Marilyn is the only one of the gymnasts who *wants* to compete in the Olympics.

EXERCISE 2 RECOGNIZING AGREEMENT IN NUMBER

Each of the following consists of two sentences. In one sentence the number of the pronoun matches that of its antecedent; in the other it doesn't. Say which sentence is correct—and why.

EXAMPLE

(a) Twenty years ago, a woman who kept her own name after marriage was hardly considered married at all.

(b) Twenty years ago, a woman who kept their own name after marriage was hardly considered married at all.

Sentence (a) is correct because the singular pronoun *her* matches the singular antecedent *woman*.

1. (a) On the first day of summer, the members of the Smith family found a rude surprise behind its house.

   (b) On the first day of summer, the members of the Smith family found a rude surprise behind their house.

2. (a) A raccoon or the neighbor's dogs had left their tracks on the freshly painted deck in the backyard.

   (b) A raccoon or the neighbor's dogs had left its tracks on the freshly painted deck in the backyard.

3. (a) Every one of the boards showed their trace of the intruders.

   (b) Every one of the boards showed its trace of the intruders.

4. (a) Ordinarily Mr. Smith is one of those stoical types who can control his temper.

   (b) Ordinarily Mr. Smith is one of those stoical types who can control their temper.

5. (a) But this time, he, along with his wife and two daughters, vented his rage.

   (b) But this time, he, along with his wife and two daughters, vented their rage.

6. (a) Everyone in the neighborhood has their own version of the uproar that followed.

   (b) Everyone in the neighborhood has his or her own version of the uproar that followed.

7. (a) But every animal within shouting distance of the Smiths' house was put in terror of losing its life.

   (b) But every animal within shouting distance of the Smiths' house was put in terror of losing their lives.

8. (a) For weeks, in fact, neither of the neighbor's two dogs would show its head.

   (b) For weeks, in fact, neither of the neighbor's two dogs would show their head.

18.8 AVOIDING FAULTY SHIFTS IN PRONOUN REFERENCE *pr shift*

To make sure pronouns fit their antecedents, do as follows:

1. Avoid using *they, them,* or *their* with a singular antecedent:

                              he or she does

▶ No one should be forced into a career that ~~they do~~ not want to pursue.

2. Avoid shifting the reference of a pronoun from one grammatical person to another:

> *When one [third person] is alone, one is free to do whatever you [second person] want.

> EDITED: When one is alone, one is free to do whatever one wants. [or] When you are alone, you are free to do whatever you want.

For the correct use of *you*, see section 18.4E.

EXERCISE 3　REVISING A PASSAGE WITH INCONSISTENT PRONOUN USAGE

Each of the following passages is marred by shifts in the number and person of pronouns referring to the same antecedent. Make these pronouns consistent in number and person.

1. The job of being a counselor in a girls' summer camp is not an easy one. You have to meet your responsibilities twenty-four hours a day, and they may include such things as making sure her girls attend all the camp meetings, overseeing the cleaning of your cabin, and giving our campers archery lessons. Because of the demands on us, we sometimes become tired and even cross. At these times everybody wants a break—a chance to go someplace else and relax. In a well-run camp you can do this; the director gives everybody a day off. After that we resume our duties with a cheerful, positive attitude.

2. Our body language often expresses our emotions. Through gestures, postures, facial expressions, and other visible signs, we indicate our feelings. If you are elated, for example, you tend to speak with more tonal fluctuations and with more arm movement than when a person is depressed. In a good mood, our eyes sparkle, our posture is erect, and you smile a lot. When someone is angry, their body language tells the tale. Our faces scowl, our jaws are clenched, one's gestures look aggressive, and sparks flash from your eyes. When you are sad, the feeling shows in your downcast eyes, limp shoulders, and shuffling walk.

18.9 PRONOUN CASE FORMS

The form of a pronoun referring to a person depends partly on its case—that is, on the role it plays in a sentence. Consider this passage:

> The Kiowas are a summer people; *they* abide the cold and keep to themselves, but when the season turns and the land becomes warm and vital *they* cannot hold still; an old love of going returns upon *them.* The aged visitors who came to my grandmother's house when I was a child were made of lean and leather, and they bore *themselves* upright. *They* wore great black hats and bright ample shirts that shook in the wind. *They* rubbed fat upon *their* hair and wound *their* braids with strips of colored cloth.
>
> —N. Scott Momaday, *The Way to Rainy Mountain*

They, them, themselves, and *their* all have the same antecedent, *Kiowas.* But these four pronouns differ in form because they play different roles: subject (*they* abide), object (upon *them*), reflexive object (bore *themselves*), and possessive (*their* braids). Because each form signifies a different case, the difference between one case form and another helps this writer show exactly what his pronouns mean.

CASE FORMS OF PRONOUNS
PERSONAL PRONOUNS

	I	*He*	*She*	*It*	*We*	*You*	*They*
SUBJECT CASE	I	he	she	it	we	you	they
OBJECT CASE	me	him	her	it	us	you	them
POSSESSIVE CASE	my, mine	his	her, hers	it	our, ours	your, yours	their theirs
REFLEXIVE/ EMPHATIC CASE	myself	him- self	her- self	itself	our- selves	yourself, yourselves	them- selves

PRONOUNS USED IN QUESTIONS AND ADJECTIVE CLAUSES

	Who	*Whoever*
SUBJECT CASE	who	whoever
OBJECT CASE	whom	whomever
POSSESSIVE CASE	whose	

18.10 USING PRONOUN CASE

18.10A SUBJECT CASE

Use the subject case when the pronoun is the subject of a verb:

> When Adam and Eve were accused of eating the forbidden fruit, *they* each excused themselves; *he* blamed Eve for tempting him, and *she* blamed the serpent for tempting her.

18.10B OBJECT CASE

1. Use the object case when the pronoun is the object of a verb:

> We heard birds but could not see *them*.

2. Use the object case when the pronoun is the object of a gerund, infinitive, or participle:

> GERUND   INFINITIVE
> Hearing *them* made us eager to see *them*.
>
> PARTICIPLE
> Seeing *them*, we could hardly believe our eyes.

3. Use the object case when the pronoun is the object of a preposition:

> I hate to spread rumors, but what else can one do with *them?*
> —Amanda Lear

4. Use the object case when the pronoun comes immediately before an infinitive:

> A sentry ordered *us* to leave the area.

18.10C POSSESSIVE CASE

1. Use the possessive case of the pronoun—with *no* apostrophe—to indicate ownership of an object or close connection to it:

> *My* car has a dent in *its* right rear door.
> The car with the new paint job is *hers*.

2. Use the possessive case of the pronoun before a gerund—an *-ing* word used as the name of an action:

> Joan hoped that *her* leaving the class early would not be noticed.

For more on this point, see section 11.11.

18.10D REFLEXIVE/EMPHATIC CASE

Use the reflexive/emphatic case of the pronoun when

1. the object of a verb or preposition is a pronoun referring to the subject:

> He gazed at *himself* in the mirror as she dressed *herself*.

2. you want to stress the antecedent of the pronoun:

> The governor *herself* conceived the new plan.

EXERCISE 4 CHOOSING CASE FORMS

Choose the correct form for the pronoun or pronouns in each of the following sentences, and explain each choice.

EXAMPLE
The coach watched Rosenberg and (I, me) run.
Me (object case) is correct because the pronoun is the direct object of the verb *watched*.

1. (Me, My) brother Frank and (him, his) wife, Rhonda, love to play poker; it's (them, their) favorite pastime.
2. (My, Mine) is pool.
3. Frank and (I, me) sometimes argue about which of the two is more interesting.
4. Since Frank and (me, I) seldom agree on anything, I don't expect (we, us) to settle this question soon—if ever.
5. Frank (him, himself) realizes that (him, his) arguing will never convince (I, me) and that the dispute between (we, us) may continue indefinitely.
6. But Frank and Rhonda don't realize what (them, they) are missing.

7. While poker takes only a good head, pool takes good hands as well. Every shot depends on (their, them) steadiness.

8. Though Frank will admit this, Rhonda always objects to (me, my) saying that poker is mainly a game of luck.

9. In reply, I point out to (they, them) that pool is a game of nothing but skill.

10. But that statement is never the last word. In fact, we would talk (us, ourselves) to exhaustion on this subject if Rhonda did not finally tell Frank and (I, me) to stop.

18.11 USING *WHO, WHOM, WHOSE, WHOEVER,* AND *WHOMEVER*

The form you need depends on which role the pronoun plays in the sentence or clause that contains it. Observe the following guidelines:

1. Use *who* or *whoever* whenever the pronoun is a subject:

> Some people *who* attended the concert were lucky.
> Tickets were given away to *whoever* wanted them.

2. Use *whom* or *whomever* when the pronoun is an object:

> To *whom* can we turn?
> Some voters will support *whomever* their party nominates.
> They back a candidate *whom* others have selected.

A sentence like this last one can be tightened by the omission of *whom:*

> They back a candidate others have selected.

And if you find *whomever* stiff, you can replace it with *anyone:*

> Some voters will support *anyone* their party nominates.

3. Use *whose* whenever the pronoun is a possessor:

> The colt *whose* picked skeleton lay out there was mine.
>
> —Wallace Stegner

18.12 MISUSING PRONOUN CASE FORMS *pr ca*

To avoid misusing the case forms of pronouns, observe the following guidelines:

1. Use the same case forms for pronouns linked by *and:*

a. *Her and I went swimming every day.

Her is in the object case; *I* is in the subject case. Since they are linked by *and,* both should be in the same case. To see which case that should be, test each pronoun by itself:

TEST: Her went swimming every day.

I went swimming every day.

EDITED: She and I went swimming every day.

b. *He and myself took turns driving.

TEST: He took turns driving

Myself took turns driving.

EDITED: He and I took turns driving.

c. *There was little to choose between them and we.

TEST: There was little to choose between them.

There was little to choose between we.

EDITED: There was little to choose between them and us.

2. Avoid using *me, him, myself, himself, herself,* or *themselves* as the subject of a verb:

*Me and Sally waited three hours for a bus.

TEST: Me waited three hours for a bus.

Sally waited three hours.

EDITED: Sally and I waited three hours for a bus.

3. Avoid using a *-self* pronoun as the object of a verb unless the pronoun refers to the subject:

▶ The director chose Laura and ~~myself~~ **me** for two minor parts, and

then cast herself in the leading role.

4. Avoid using a *-self* pronoun as the object of a preposition:

▶ The letter was addressed to ~~myself.~~
  me.

▶ The director had to choose between Laura and ~~myself.~~
  me.

EXCEPTION: A *-self* pronoun may be the object of *by:*

Diana organized the exhibition by herself.

5. Avoid using the forms * *hisself,* * *theirself,* or * *theirselves* under any conditions in Standard English.

6. Avoid using *I, he, she, we,* or *they* as the object of a verb or preposition:

▶ My uncle always brought presents for my sister and ~~I.~~
  me.

▶ We rarely gave anything to my aunt or ~~he.~~
  him.

7. When a pronoun after *than* or *as* is compared with a subject, use the subject case:

▶ Pete [subject] dribbles faster than ~~me.~~
  I.

8. Use the object case after *than* or *as* when the pronoun is compared to an object:

> *The manager pays a veteran like Bob [object] more than I [subject case].
> EDITED: The manager pays a veteran like Bob more than he pays me.

9. Avoid confusing *its* and *it's;* or *their, there,* and *they're;* or *whose and who's.* For help distinguishing between these words, see the Glossary of Usage.

EXERCISE 5 EDITING MISTAKES IN CASE

Each of the following sentences may contain one or more mistakes in case. Correct every mistake you find by writing the correct form of the pronoun. If a sentence contains a compound, test it as shown in section 18.12. If a sentence is correct as it stands, write *Correct*.

EXAMPLE

         me
  The argument between Paul and I is unimportant.
            ^

1. Every spring my Aunt Mary and me go fishing in the mountains.

2. We put two sets of camping gear in the truck—mine and her.

3. Sometimes a forest ranger shows us where to look for trout.

4. The rangers theirselves have never fished with us; they just want to help ourselves get our quota.

5. Once my cousin Roger asked if he could go fishing with Aunt Mary and I.

6. Aunt Mary had to decide who to take—him or myself.

7. There wasn't room for we two in the truck, and neither him nor me had a car.

8. That spring her and Roger caught the biggest trout she had ever seen.

9. I heard all about it when Roger arrived home; nobody talks more than him.

10. He can hardly wait until Aunt Mary and him go fishing again.

Subject-Verb Agreement

19.1 WHAT IS AGREEMENT?

To say that a verb **agrees** in form with its subject is to say that a verb has more than one form and that each form matches up with a particular kind of subject. Here are three parallel sets of examples:

	STANDARD ENGLISH	FRENCH	SPANISH
SINGULAR	I live	je vis	(yo)† vivo
	you live	tu vis	(tú) vives
	he lives	il vit	(él) vive
	she lives	elle vit	(ella) vive
PLURAL	we live	nous vivons	vivimos
	you live	vous vivez	vivís
	they live	ils vivent	(ellos) viven
		[masc.]	[masc.]
		elles vivent	(ellas) viven
		[fem.]	[fem.]

In this example, Spanish has six different verb forms, French has five, and Standard English has just two: *live* and *lives*.

---

† In Spanish, when the subject is a pronoun, it is sometimes omitted.

To write Standard English correctly, you need to know which form goes with each type of subject, where to find the subject in a clause, and whether the subject is singular or plural.

19.2 MAKING VERBS AGREE WITH SUBJECTS   *sv agr*

In most cases, the subject affects the form of the verb only when the verb is in the present tense. Except for the verb *be* (see section 19.3) and for subjunctive verb forms (see sections 23.4 and 23.5), the rules of agreement in the present tense are as follows.

1. With third-person singular subjects, add *-s* or *-es* to the bare form of the verb:

> Peggy *wants* to study economics.
> She *works* at the bank.
> It *serves* over two thousand depositors.
> Each of them *holds* a passbook.
> Marvin Megabucks *owns* the bank.
> He *polishes* his Jaguar once a week.

EXCEPTION: The verb *have* becomes *has:*

> Everyone *has* moments of self-doubt.
> Uncertainty *has* gripped all of us.

2. With all other subjects, use the bare form of the verb:

> Economists *study* the stock market.
> They *evaluate* the fluctuation of prices.
> Like the experts, we *want* to make profitable investments.
> My brother and his wife both *work* on Wall Street.
> I *do* other things.

3. Whatever the subject, use the bare form of any verb that follows an auxiliary, such as *does, can,* or *may:*

> Does she *play* the sax?
> She can *sing.*
> She may *become* famous.

19.3 MAKING THE VERB *BE* AGREE WITH SUBJECTS

1. When *be* is a main verb, its forms are as follows:

PRESENT TENSE		PAST TENSE	
I *am* cold.		I *was* busy.	
You *are* cold.		You *were* busy.	
She		She	
He		He	
It	*is* cold.	It	*was* busy.
Everyone		Everyone	
The student		The student	
We		We	
You		You	
They	*are* cold.	They	*were* busy.
Many		Many	
The students		The students	

2. When *be* is an auxiliary, its form depends on the subject, just as when *be* is a main verb:

> I *am annoyed* by most tax forms.
>
> The current one *is written* in incomprehensible language.
>
> The pages *are covered* with small print and confusing diagrams.
>
> What *were* the experts *thinking* of when they designed the form?

19.4 AVOIDING DIALECTAL MISTAKES IN AGREEMENT

The rules of agreement in Standard English differ from the rules of agreement in regional and ethnic dialects. To write Standard English correctly, observe the following guidelines.

1. If you're writing about what anyone or anything does now, make sure you add *-s* or *-es* to the verb:

> ▶ My brother work for the post office.

> ▶ He live with a couple of his friends.

2. If you're writing about what you or they (any group of two or more) do now, use only the bare form of the verb:

▶ I needs a job.

▶ Politicians loves to make promises.

▶ They wants votes.

3. The only verb to use between *I* and a verb with *-ing* added is *am* or *have been:*

▶ I ~~be~~ taking calculus this semester.
   am

4. If you're writing about what anyone or anything is at present, use *is:*

▶ Veronica ~~be~~ my best friend.
      is

▶ Chain-smoking ~~be~~ risky.
        is

5. If you're writing about what two or more persons or things are, use *are:*

▶ Banks ~~be~~ closed on holidays.
   are

6. Use *has* after any one person or thing:

▶ My sister ~~have~~ a new apartment.
     has

▶ It ~~have~~ two bedrooms.
   has

7. Use *have* after *I, you,* or any words naming more than one:

▶ I ~~has~~ a lot of bills to pay.
  have

▶ My feet ~~has~~ been hurting.
   have

8. Before *been,* always use *has, have,* or *had:*

> *has*
> ▶ Everyone been hurt by the layoffs.

> *have   ∧*
> ▶ I been studying chemistry

> *∧ had*
> ▶ I ~~done~~ been watching the news when the phone rang.
> *∧*

For more on the differences between Standard English and other dialects, see the Introduction.

EXERCISE 1   USING CORRECT VERB FORMS

For each verb in parentheses, write down a verb form that agrees with the subject. The correct form will sometimes be the same as the one in parentheses. Use the present tense.

EXAMPLE
A cold drink (taste) good on a hot day when you (be) working outside.

tastes, are

1. In Charles Dickens' well-known tale *A Christmas Carol,* Scrooge (be) a coldhearted miser.

2. He (drive) a hard bargain in business and (spend) less on food, lodging, and clothing than any other inhabitant of London (do).

3. The needs of others (do) not concern him; in his opinion, the poor and the homeless may (find) shelter in the public workhouses or prisons.

4. Or they can (die) and thereby help to reduce the surplus population.

5. It (be) not surprising, therefore, that no one (like) to visit with him.

6. Nor (do) he enjoy the company of others; to his way of thinking, all their socializing (have) no value whatsoever.

7. Any moment lost from money-making, he thinks, (be) misspent: nobody (get) rich if he or she (devote) even one moment in the day to speaking with friends, helping the needy, or caring for families.

8. Scrooge's outlook (be) vividly illustrated by his behavior on Christmas Eve.

9. He (make) his underpaid clerk work until dark; he (do) not contribute a penny to a subscription for the poor; he (chase) a caroler from the office; and he cannot (speak) a civil word to his only nephew, who (invite) Scrooge to spend Christmas Day with his family.

10. To the miser, all talk of a happy holiday (be) "humbug," and people (be) fools not to spend the hours making money.

19.5 FINDING THE SUBJECT

You can find the subject easily when it comes right before the verb:

     s

Alan Paton / has written movingly about life in South Africa.

     s

Many readers / consider *Cry, the Beloved Country* a classic.

But the subject follows the verb in sentences of the following kinds:

1. Sentences starting with *There* or *Here* plus a form of the verb *be:*

                    s

There was once / a thriving civilization in the jungles of the
                                      Yucatán.

         s

Here is / a translation of *Popol Vuh,* the Mayan book about
                              the dawn of life.

2. Sentences with inverted word order:

                                        s

Visible near Monte Alban in southern / massive pyramids
                  Mexico are   constructed over
                                  two thousand
                                    years ago.

3. Some questions:

> s
> Have / archeologists / identified the builders of the pyramids?

> s
> Are / you / going to Egypt this year?

> s
> Will / the travel agent / book you on a
> charter flight?

19.6 Recognizing the Number of the Subject

To make a verb agree with the subject, you must know whether
the subject is singular or plural. Observe the following guidelines
for various kinds of subjects.

19.6A Nouns Meaning One Thing

A noun meaning one thing is always singular, even if it ends in
-s:

> The *lens* was cracked.
> According to some critics, *The Grapes of Wrath* is John Stein-
> beck's greatest novel.
> *Gas* is cheaper this summer than it was last fall.

19.6B Nouns Meaning More Than One Thing

A noun meaning more than one thing is always plural:

> The *lenses* were cracked.
> His *teeth* are crooked.
> *Women* deserve to be paid as much as *men* are.
> The new *data* require study.
> *Mice* like cheese.
> *Cats* like mice.

19.6C PRONOUNS FIXED IN NUMBER

Most pronouns are fixed in number. They include the following:

ALWAYS SINGULAR

he	each	one
she	each one	another
it		
	everybody	somebody
this	everyone	someone
that	everything	something
anybody	either	whatever
anyone	neither	whichever
anything		whoever
	nobody	
	none	
	no one	
	nothing	

ALWAYS PLURAL

we	these	both	few
they	those	others	several

19.6D PRONOUNS VARIABLE IN NUMBER

The pronouns *all, any, many, more, most, some, who, that,* and *which* are variable in number. The number of such a pronoun depends on the number of the word or phrase to which it refers:

Most of the sand *is* washed by the tide.

Most of the sandpipers *are* white.

Some of the oil *has* been cleaned up.

Some of the problems *have* been solved.

Titan is one of the fifteen known satellites that *revolve* around Saturn.

Titan is the only one of the satellites that *has* an atmosphere.

Many is singular only when used with *a* or *an:*

Many of the artists *visit* Florence.

Many an artist *visits* Florence.

Other pronouns are not affected in number by the phrases that modify them; see section 19.G below.

19.6E VERBAL NOUNS AND NOUN CLAUSES

Verbal nouns are always singular:

Reassembling the broken pieces of a china bowl is difficult.
To fit the fragments together takes considerable patience.

Noun clauses are always singular too:

What one also needs is steady hands.

19.6F NOUNS FOLLOWED BY A FORM OF THE VERB *BE*

The verb agrees with what comes before it, no matter what comes after it:

Newspapers are his business.
His *business* is newspapers.

19.6G MODIFIED NOUNS AND PRONOUNS

Except for pronouns variable in number (see 19.6D), the number of a modified noun or pronoun depends on the noun (N) or pronoun (PR) itself—not on any of the modifiers (M) attached to it:

M N   M
A ship carrying hundreds of tourists enters the narrow harbor every Friday.

PR   M
Each of the tourists has a credit card, traveler checks, and the phone number of the local consulate.

M   M   N   M

Any gold ornament, together with silver bracelets and earrings, always attracts a crowd.

19.6H COMPOUNDS MADE WITH *AND*

1. Compound subjects made with *and* are plural when they are used before the verb and refer to more than one thing:

> *The lion and the tiger* belong to the cat family.
>
> *Bach and Beethoven* are among the greatest composers of all time.

2. When a compound subject made with *and* follows the verb, and the first item in the compound is singular, the verb may agree with that:

> There was *a desk and three chairs* in the room.

Strictly speaking, the verb should agree with both items: There *were* a desk and three chairs in the room. But since *There were a desk* sounds odd, no matter what follows *desk,* the verb may agree with *desk* alone—the first item. If the first item is plural, the verb always agrees with it:

> At the entrance stand *two marble pillars and a statue of Napoleon.*

3. A compound subject that is made with *and* and refers to only one thing is always singular:

> *The founder and first president of the college* was Eleazor Wheelock.

19.6I ITEMS JOINED BY *OR, EITHER. . . OR,* ETC.

When items are joined by *or, either . . . or, neither . . . nor, not . . . but,* or *not only . . . but also,* the verb agrees with the item just before it:

> *Neither steel nor glass* cuts a diamond.
>
> Not *a new machine but new workers* are needed for the job.

19.6J NOUNS SPELLED THE SAME WAY IN SINGULAR AND PLURAL

A noun spelled the same way in the singular and the plural depends for its number on the way it is used:

> A *deer* was nibbling the lettuce.
>
> *Two deer* were standing in the middle of the road.
>
> *One means* of campaigning is direct mail.
>
> *Two other means* are TV advertising and mass rallies.

19.6K COLLECTIVE NOUNS AND NOUNS OF MEASUREMENT

Collective nouns and nouns of measurement are singular when they refer to a unit, and plural when they refer to the individuals or elements of a unit:

> *Half of the cake* was eaten.
>
> *Half of the jewels* were stolen.
>
> *Statistics* is the study and analysis of numerical information about the world.
>
> *Recent statistics* show a marked decline in the U.S. birthrate during the past twenty years.
>
> *Fifty dollars* is a lot to ask for a cap.

19.6L SUBJECTS BEGINNING WITH *EVERY*

A subject beginning with *every* is normally singular:

> *Every cat and dog in the neighborhood* was fighting.

But if the subject includes plural items, treat it as plural:

> *Every cat and two of the dogs* were fighting.

19.6M THE WORD *NUMBER* AS SUBJECT

The word *number* is singular when it follows *the,* plural when it follows *a:*

> *The number of applications* was huge.
>
> *A number of teenagers* now hold full-time jobs.

19.6N FOREIGN WORDS AND EXPRESSIONS

When the subject is a foreign word or expression, use a dictionary to find out whether it is singular or plural:

The *coup d'etat* has caught diplomats by surprise.

The *Carbonari* of the early nineteenth century were members of a secret political organization in Italy.

TROUBLE SPOTS IN AGREEMENT: IN BRIEF

Singular nouns ending in -*s* (19.6A):

The *lens* needs to be polished.

Plurals not ending in -*s* (19.6B):

The new *data* require study.

Pronouns variable in number (19.6D):

Hospital patients like doctors *who* listen.
My aunt has a doctor *who* listens.

Modified nouns and pronouns (19.6G):

Each of the chairs is an antique.

Subjects joined by *either . . . or, not only . . . but also,* etc. (19.6I):

Not only the managers but also the umpire was at fault.
Neither the pitcher nor his teammates were responsible.

Collective nouns and nouns of measurement (19.6K):

The *jury* has a private room.
The *jury* are unable to agree on a verdict.

Modified nouns and pronouns (19.6G):

One-third of the seniors are planning to study medicine.
Each of them has applied to medical school.

The word *number* as subject (19.6M):

A number of women have applied for the job.
The number of applications has exceeded expectations.

EXERCISE 2 CORRECTING FAULTY AGREEMENT

In some of the following sentences the verb does not agree with
its subject. Correct every verb you consider wrong and then
explain the correction. If a sentence is correct as it stands,
explain why.

EXAMPLE
One of the insurance agents are a graduate of my university.
The verb should be *is* because the subject is *One*, a singular
pronoun.

1. Members of the city's transportation department is seeking a solution to the traffic problem on Main Street.
2. There has been many complaints from merchants and
   shoppers.
3. An attorney representing five store owners are preparing
   to sue the city for negligence and economic harassment.
4. Each of the five companies have lost money in the last ten
   months.
5. A number of shoppers is circulating a petition calling for
   the resignation of the mayor.
6. She, along with the heads of the transportation department, are feeling the heat.
7. Three-quarters of the gripes is justified.
8. Thirty minutes are too long for any motorist to drive two
   blocks.
9. No one with important errands wants to spend most of a
   lunch hour looking for a parking space.
10. A new and improved means of traffic control need to be
    found.

EXERCISE 3 CORRECTING FAULTY AGREEMENT

This exercise will give you practice in dealing with subject-
verb agreement in an extended passage. In the following paragraphs from Juanita H. Williams's *Psychology of Women*, we
have deliberately inserted some errors in agreement. We hope
you can spot and correct them.

EXAMPLE

lines 4–5: efficiency and level . . . are usually measured

Cognition is the process by which the individual acquires knowledge about an object or an event. It includes perceiving, recognizing, judging, and sensing—the ways of knowing. The efficiency and level of the acquisition of knowledge is usually measured in older children and adults by the use of tests which 5 requires language. Studies of infant cognition, of what and how babies "know," have begun to appear only in the last decade, with the development of new techniques which provides insights into what and how babies learn.

In spite of the persistent belief that babies differ along sex 10 lines—for example, that girl babies vocalize more and boy babies are more active—sex differences in cognitive functions in the first two years of life has not been demonstrated (Maccoby and Jacklin, 1974). Measurements of intellectual ability, learning, and memory does not differ on the average for boys 15 and girls. However, patterns of performances are different for the two sexes, as are the consistency (thus the predictability) of the measures as the infants get older. A longitudinal study of 180 white, first-born infants, 91 boys and 89 girls, each of whom were tested in the laboratory at four, eight, thirteen, 20 and twenty-seven months, offers some evidence concerning these patterns (Kagan, 1971). One of the behaviors for which different patterns were observed for boys and girls were vocalization, the infant's response when aroused or excited by an unusual or discrepant stimulus. 25

Verbs

TENSE

If English is your native language, you probably have a good working knowledge of tenses. You know how to describe what someone or something did in the past, is doing in the present, or will do in the future. But you may not know just how to describe an action that doesn't fall neatly into one time slot. For instance, how do you describe the action of a character in a novel or a play? How do you describe an action that started in the past but is still going on now? How do you write about an action that will be completed at some time in the future? This chapter is chiefly meant to answer questions like these.

The chapter is limited to verbs in the indicative mood (the mood of fact or matters close to fact) and in the active voice (in which the subject performs the action, as in "Whales eat plankton"). For a full discussion of mood, see chapter 23; for a full discussion of voice, see chapter 22.

20.1 TENSE AND TIME

The **tense** of a verb helps to indicate the time of an action or condition:

PAST: The sun *rose* at 6:03 this morning.

PRESENT: As I *write* these words, the sun *is setting*.

FUTURE: The sun *will rise* tomorrow at 6:04.

But tense is not the same as time. A verb in the present tense, for instance, may be used in a statement about the future:

> The bus leaves tomorrow at 7:30 A.M.

The time of an action or state is often indicated by a word or phrase like *tomorrow*, *next week*, or *last month*.

20.2 FORMING THE TENSES   *tf*

The tenses of all but a few verbs are made from the four **principal parts.** The principal parts of regular verbs are formed by the addition of *-ing* or *-ed* to the bare form, as shown here:

PRESENT (BARE FORM)	PRESENT PARTICIPLE	PAST	PAST PARTICIPLE
cook	cook*ing*	cook*ed*	cook*ed*
lift	lift*ing*	lift*ed*	lift*ed*
polish	polish*ing*	polish*ed*	polish*ed*

Verbs with some principal parts formed in other ways are called **irregular:**

eat	eating	ate	eaten
write	writing	wrote	written
go	going	went	gone
speak	speaking	spoke	spoken

For the principal parts of other commonly used irregular verbs, see section 20.11.

20.2A FORMING THE PRESENT

With most subjects, the form of a verb in the present tense is simply the bare form:

> Seasoned traders *drive* hard bargains.
> I *polish* my shoes every day.

But after a singular noun or a third-person singular pronoun, such as *she, it, this, each,* or *everyone,* you must add *-s* or *-es* to the bare form of the verb:

> Helen *drives* a cab.
> She *polishes* it once a week.

For more on this point, see sections 19.1–19.4.

20.2B Forming the Past

The past tense of regular verbs is formed by the addition of *-d* or *-ed* to the bare form:

> Helen *liked* her work.
> She *polished* her cab regularly.

For the past tense of commonly used irregular verbs, see section 20.11.

20.2C Forming Tenses with Auxiliaries

Besides the present and the past, there are four other tenses. You form these by using certain auxiliary verbs, such as *will, has,* and *had:*

	REGULAR VERB	IRREGULAR VERB
FUTURE	She will work.	She will speak.
PRESENT PERFECT	She has worked.	She has spoken.
PAST PERFECT	She had worked.	She had spoken.
FUTURE PERFECT	She will have worked.	She will have spoken.

20.2D Using the Common and Progressive Forms

The **common** forms shown above indicate an action viewed as momentary, habitual, completed, or expected. The **progressive** forms indicate that the action named by the verb is viewed as continuing. Either form may be used with each tense:

> PRESENT
>
> COMMON: Coluntuano *runs* two miles every morning.
>
> PROGRESSIVE: Coluntuano *is running* for mayor.

PAST

COMMON: Charles Dickens *wrote* many novels.

PROGRESSIVE: Charles Dickens *was writing* a mystery novel when he died.

FUTURE

COMMON: In the years ahead, many cars *will run* on batteries.

PROGRESSIVE: Many of us *will be driving* electric cars.

EXERCISE 1 WRITING PRINCIPAL PARTS

For each of the following sentences write out the principal parts of the italicized verb, listing in sequence the present, the present participle, the past, and the past participle. Whenever you are unsure of a form, refer to your dictionary or to the list of irregular verbs in section 20.11.

EXAMPLE
The concert *begins* at 8 P.M.
begin, beginning, began, begun

1. In 1927 Charles A. Lindbergh *flew* nonstop from New York to Paris.
2. On his return New Yorkers *gave* him a hero's welcome.
3. Some spectators *had slept* on the sidewalk in order not to miss the parade.
4. No one who *witnessed* the triumphant procession ever *forgot* the spectacle.
5. The young American *had laid* to rest the fear of crossing the Atlantic in a plane. (For a full discussion of the verbs *lay* and *lie,* see the Glossary of Usage.)
6. He *had broken* a barrier with his record flight.

0.3 USING THE PRESENT

1. Use the <u>common present</u>:

a. To report what happens regularly:

Concert pianists usually *practice* every day.
Leaves *change* color in autumn.

b. To state a fact or widely held belief:

Water *freezes* at 32°F.
Opposites *attract*.

c. To describe characters, events, or other matters in an aesthetic work, such as a painting, a piece of music, a work of literature, a movie, or a television show:

In *Jaws,* a vicious shark *attacks* and *terrifies* swimmers until it is finally killed.
In the first chapter of *Far from the Madding Crowd,* Gabriel *sees* the beautiful Bathsheba, but she *does* not *see* him.

d. To say what a writer or a creative artist does in his or her work:

Many of Georgia O'Keefe's paintings *convey* the stark contrasts of the harsh and beautiful desert.
In *The Wealth of Nations* (1776), Adam Smith *argues* that an "invisible hand" regulates individual enterprise for the good of society as a whole.
In his famous Fifth Symphony, Beethoven *reveals* the power and fury of his imagination.

e. To describe an opinion or idea:

In the Marxist vision of history, the ruling classes ceaselessly *oppress* the working class.

f. To indicate that a condition or situation is likely to last:

My sister *loves* chocolate ice cream.

g. To describe a future action that is definitely predictable:

The fair *opens* on Wednesday.

h. To report a statement of lasting significance:

"All art," *says* Oscar Wilde, "is quite useless."

2. Use the present progressive:

a. To indicate that an action or state is occurring at the time of the writing:

The sun *is setting* now, and the birches *are bending* in the wind.

b. To indicate a gradual process that need not be taking place at the exact moment of the writing:

> Suburban life *is losing* its appeal. Many young couples *are moving* out of the suburbs and into the cities.

20.4 USING THE PRESENT PERFECT

1. Use the common present perfect:

a. To report a past action or state that touches in some way on the present:

> I *have* just *finished* reading *Gone with the Wind.*
>
> A presidential commission *has* already *investigated* the causes of one nuclear accident.

The words *just* and *already* are often used with the present perfect.

b. To report an action or state begun in the past but extending into the present:

> Engineers *have begun* to explore the possibility of harnessing the tides.
>
> Since the invention of the automobile, traffic accidents *have taken* many thousands of lives.

c. To report an action performed at some unspecified time in the past:

> I *have seen* the Statue of Liberty.

2. Use the progressive form of the present perfect when you want to emphasize both the continuity of an action from the past into the present and the likelihood of its continuing into the future:

> Some instrumental satellites *have been traveling* through space for years.
>
> The cost of routine medical care *has been growing* at a staggering rate.

20.5 USING THE PAST

1. Use the <u>common past</u>:

a. To report an action or state that was definitely completed in the past:

> Thomas Edison *invented* the phonograph in 1877.
> The city *became* calm after the cease-fire.

b. To report actions repeated in the past but no longer occurring at the time of the writing:

> The family always *went* to church on Sundays.

2. Use the <u>past progressive</u>:

a. To emphasize the continuity of a past action:

> His insults *were becoming* unbearable.

b. To state that one action was being performed when another occurred:

> I *was pouring* a glass of water when the pitcher suddenly cracked.

20.6 USING THE PAST PERFECT

1. Use the <u>common past perfect</u>:

a. To state that an action or state was completed by a specified time in the past:

> By noon we *had gathered* three hundred bushels.

b. To indicate that one past action or state was completed by the time another occurred:

> By the time Hitler sent reinforcements, the Allies *had* already *taken* much of France.
> I suddenly realized that I *had left* my keys at home.
> By the age of thirty, she *had already had* seven children.

c. To report an unfulfilled hope or intention:

> Mary *had planned* to travel as far as Denver, but her money ran out while she was still in Chicago.

2. Use the progressive form of the past perfect to indicate that the first of two past actions or states went on until the second occurred:

> Before Gloria entered Mark's life, he *had been spending* most of his time with books.

20.7 USING THE FUTURE

1. Use the common future:

a. To report a future event or state that will occur regardless of human intent:

> The sun *will rise* at 6:35 tomorrow morning.
> I *will be* nineteen on my next birthday.

b. To indicate willingness or determination to do something:

> The president has declared that he *will veto* the bill.

c. To report what will happen under certain conditions:

> If you get up early enough, you *will see* the sunrise.

d. To indicate future probability:

> The cost of a college education *will increase*.

In the preceding examples, the auxiliary *will* is used. Years ago, *will* generally went with *you, they, he, she, it*, and noun subjects, and *shall* was used with *I* and *we* to express the simple future. When *will* was used with *I* and *we*, it signified the speaker's (or writer's) determination: "We will stop the enemy." The use of *shall* with *you, they, he, she, it*, or a noun subject had the same function: "You shall pay the tax." But in current usage *shall* and *will* mean about the same thing, and most writers use *will* with all subjects to express the simple future. Some writers substitute *shall,* again with all subjects, to express determination or certainty: "We shall overcome."

2. Use the future progressive:

a. To say that an action or state will be continuing for a period of time in the future:

> Twenty years from now, many Americans *will be driving* electric cars..
>
> In doing so, they *will be helping* to reduce our consumption of fuel and our pollution of the air.

b. To say what the subject will be doing at a given time in the future:

> Next semester I *will be taking* Sociology 101.
>
> Also, I *will be auditing* two other social science classes.

20.8 USING THE FUTURE PERFECT

1. Use the common future perfect:

a. To say that an action or state will be completed by a specified time in the future:

> At the rate I'm living, I *will have spent* all my summer earnings by the end of October.

b. To say that an action or state will be completed by the time something else happens:

> By the time an efficient engine is produced, we *will have exhausted* our supplies of fuel.

2. Use the progressive form of the future perfect to say that an activity or state will continue until a specified time in the future:

> By 2000 the *Pioneer 10* probe *will have been traveling* through space for more than twenty-five years.
>
> No one *will have been tracking* its progress longer than Dr. Stellar.

PICTURING THE TENSES: IN BRIEF

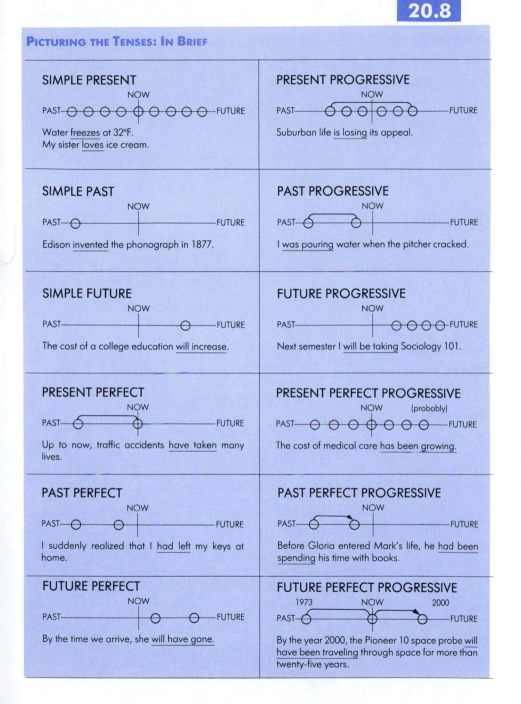

SIMPLE PRESENT

Water freezes at 32°F.
My sister loves ice cream.

PRESENT PROGRESSIVE

Suburban life is losing its appeal.

SIMPLE PAST

Edison invented the phonograph in 1877.

PAST PROGRESSIVE

I was pouring water when the pitcher cracked.

SIMPLE FUTURE

The cost of a college education will increase.

FUTURE PROGRESSIVE

Next semester I will be taking Sociology 101.

PRESENT PERFECT

Up to now, traffic accidents have taken many lives.

PRESENT PERFECT PROGRESSIVE

The cost of medical care has been growing.

PAST PERFECT

I suddenly realized that I had left my keys at home.

PAST PERFECT PROGRESSIVE

Before Gloria entered Mark's life, he had been spending his time with books.

FUTURE PERFECT

By the time we arrive, she will have gone.

FUTURE PERFECT PROGRESSIVE

By the year 2000, the Pioneer 10 space probe will have been traveling through space for more than twenty-five years.

20.9 MISUSING TENSES *m t*

1. Use the common present—not the present progressive—to report what happens regularly:

> Usually my day ~~is starting~~ **starts** at 7:00 A.M.

2. Use the past perfect—not the simple past—for action completed by the time something else happened:

> By the time the game ended, many of the spectators **had** left.

3. Use the present perfect—not the past—for action continuing into the present:

> Ever since the steel plant closed, the town **has** suffered.

20.10 MANAGING TENSE AND TIME WITH PARTICIPLES AND INFINITIVES

Participles and infinitives have two tenses: the present and the perfect:

	PRESENT	PERFECT
INFINITIVE	to dance	to have danced
PARTICIPLE	dancing	having danced

1. Use the present tense when the action or state named by the participle or infinitive occurs at or after the time of the main verb:

> We spend hours in conference with individual students, hours *meeting* together and with counselors, *trying to teach* ourselves how *to teach* and *asking* ourselves what we ought *to be teaching*. —Adrienne Rich

2. Use the perfect tense when the action or state named by the participle or infinitive occurred before the time of the main verb:

Having lost his cargo during the hurricane, the captain faced bankruptcy when his vessel finally reached port.

Several reporters are sorry *to have missed* the president's impromptu press conference.

> **EXERCISE 2 USING TENSES**
>
> In the following passage from Daniel Mark Epstein's essay "The Case of Harry Houdini," we have replaced nearly every verb with a blank and put the bare form of the verb in parentheses. Write out the passage with the appropriate tense of each verb.
>
> **EXAMPLE**
> When he _____ (arrive) in London in 1900, the twenty-six-year-old magician _____ (do) not have a single booking.
> arrived, did
>
> In 1901, when Houdini _____ (take) on the Imperial Police, he _____ (is) not _____ (whistle) in the dark. By the time he _____ (leave) America at the end of the nineteenth century he _____ (dissect) every kind of lock he _____ (can) find in the New World, and whatever he _____ (can) import from the old one. Arriving in London, Houdini _____ (can) write that there _____ (are) only a few kinds of British handcuffs, "seven or eight at the utmost," and these _____ (are) some of the simplest he _____ (have) ever _____ (see). He _____ (search) the markets, antique shops, and locksmiths, buying up all the European locks he _____ (can) find so he _____ (can) dismantle and study them.

20.11 FORMING THE PRINCIPLE PARTS OF COMMONLY USED IRREGULAR VERBS

Following is a selected list of irregular verbs—those with special forms for the past, the past participle, or both. When more than one form for a principal part is shown, the first is more commonly used (except for *was* and *were,* which are used with equal frequency). For verbs not listed here, see your dictionary.

PRESENT (BARE FORM)	PRESENT PARTICIPLE	PAST	PAST PARTICIPLE
arise	arising	arose	arisen
awake	awaking	awoke, awaked	awoke, awaked, awoken
be †	being	was / were	been
bear [bring forth]	bearing	bore	born, borne
bear [carry]	bearing	bore	borne
beat	beating	beat	beaten, beat
begin	beginning	began	begun
bid [command]	bidding	bade	bid, bidden
bid [offer to pay]	bidding	bid	bid
bite	biting	bit	bitten
bleed	bleeding	bled	bled
blend	blending	blended, blent	blended, blent
blow	blowing	blew	blown
break	breaking	broke	broken
bring	bringing	brought	brought
buy	buying	bought	bought
catch	catching	caught	caught
choose	choosing	chose	chosen
clothe	clothing	clothed, clad	clothed, clad
come	coming	came	come
cost	costing	cost	cost
creep	creeping	crept	crept
dig	digging	dug	dug
dive	diving	dived, dove	dived
do	doing	did	done
draw	drawing	drew	drawn
drink	drinking	drank	drunk, drunken
drive	driving	drove	driven

† In this case the bare form *(be)* is not the same as the present *(am, is, are).*

PRESENT (BARE FORM)	PRESENT PARTICIPLE	PAST	PAST PARTICIPLE
eat	eating	ate	eaten
fall	falling	fell	fallen
feel	feeling	felt	felt
fight	fighting	fought	fought
find	finding	found	found
fly	flying	flew	flown
forbid	forbidding	forbade, forbad	forbidden, forbid
forget	forgetting	forgot	forgotten, forgot
freeze	freezing	froze	frozen
get	getting	got	got, gotten
give	giving	gave	given
go	going	went	gone
grow	growing	grew	grown
hang [execute]	hanging	hanged	hanged
hang [suspend]	hanging	hung	hung
have	having	had	had
hear	hearing	heard	heard
hide	hiding	hid	hidden, hid
hit	hitting	hit	hit
hold	holding	held	held
keep	keeping	kept	kept
know	knowing	knew	known
lay	laying	laid	laid
lead	leading	led	led
learn	learning	learned, learnt	learned, learnt
leave	leaving	left	left
let	letting	let	let
lie [recline]	lying	lay	lain
lie [tell a false- hood]	lying	lied	lied
lose	losing	lost	lost

PRESENT (BARE FORM)	PRESENT PARTICIPLE	PAST	PAST PARTICIPLE
make	making	made	made
pay	paying	paid	paid
prove	proving	proved	proved, proven
ride	riding	rode	ridden
ring	ringing	rang	rung
rise	rising	rose	risen
run	running	ran	run
saw	sawing	sawed	sawed, sawn
see	seeing	saw	seen
seek	seeking	sought	sought
shake	shaking	shook	shaken
shine	shining	shone	shone
show	showing	showed	shown, showed
shrink	shrinking	shrank, shrunk	shrunk, shrunken
sing	singing	sang	sung
sink	sinking	sank, sunk	sunk, sunken
slay	slaying	slew	slain
sleep	sleeping	slept	slept
smell	smelling	smelled, smelt	smelled, smelt
speak	speaking	spoke	spoken
spin	spinning	spun, span	spun
spring	springing	sprang	sprung
steal	stealing	stole	stolen
stride	striding	strode	stridden
strike	striking	struck	struck, stricken
strive	striving	strove	striven
swear	swearing	swore	sworn
sweep	sweeping	swept	swept
swim	swimming	swam	swum
take	taking	took	taken
teach	teaching	taught	taught

PRESENT (BARE FORM)	PRESENT PARTICIPLE	PAST	PAST PARTICIPLE
tear	tearing	tore	torn
throw	throwing	threw	thrown
tread	treading	trod	trodden, trod
wake	waking	woke, waked	woke, waked, woken
wear	wearing	wore	worn
weave	weaving	wove	woven
wed	wedding	wed, wedded	wed, wedded
weep	weeping	wept	wept
wind	winding	wound	wound
work	working	worked, wrought	worked, wrought
write	writing	wrote	written

21

Verbs

SEQUENCE OF TENSES

21.1 UNDERSTANDING SEQUENCE OF TENSES

When a passage has more than one verb, the relation between the tenses of the verbs is called the **sequence of tenses.** Various sequences are possible.

When all the verbs in a sentence describe actions or states that occur at or about the same time, their tenses should be the same:

Whenever the alarm clock *rings,* I *yawn, stretch,* and *roll* over for another fifteen minutes of sleep. (all present tense)

The prima donna *opened* her arms to the audience, *smiled,* and *bowed* deeply. (all past tense)

On the other hand, a sentence may describe actions that happen at different times. It will then have verbs in different tenses:

Beth *had been working* on the research project for almost three years before she *made* the first discovery. (past perfect and past)

Recently the largest bank in the area *lowered* its interest rate on loans; the directors *want* to stimulate borrowing. (past and present)

21.2 SEQUENCES IN COMPOUND SENTENCES

A **compound sentence** consists of two or more independent clauses. Since the clauses are independent, the tenses of the verbs may be independent of each other:

In the past, most Americans *wanted* big cars, but now many *drive* small ones. (past and present)

The number of finback whales *is decreasing;* as a result, they *will be added* to the list of endangered species. (present and future)

I *wanted* a big raise, but I *will be getting* a small one. (past and future)

21.3 SEQUENCES IN COMPLEX SENTENCES

A **complex sentence** consists of one independent clause and at least one subordinate clause (see chapter 15). In this kind of sentence, which often deals with two different times, many sequences are possible. The sequence chiefly depends on the tense of the main verb.

21.3A MAIN VERB IN THE PRESENT

MAIN VERB	SUBORDINATE VERB
[verb of independent clause]	[verb of subordinate clause]
Some Americans *are* so poor	that they *suffer* from malnutrition. (present)
Most children *learn* to talk	after they *have learned* to walk. (present perfect)
Greg *likes* to boast about the marlin	that he *caught* last summer. (past)
Astronomers *predict*	that the sun *will die* in about ten billion years. (future)

21.3B MAIN VERB IN THE PRESENT PERFECT

MAIN VERB	SUBORDINATE VERB
Scientists *have studied* the rings of Saturn	ever since Galileo *discovered* them. (past)

SUBORDINATE VERB	MAIN VERB
Although drivers *have complained* about the heavy traffic, (present perfect)	the police *have done* nothing to alleviate the problem.

21.3C MAIN VERB IN THE PAST

MAIN VERB	SUBORDINATE VERB
Centuries ago most people *believed*	that the sun *revolved* around the earth. (past)
Copernicus *discovered*	that the earth *revolves* around the sun. (present, for statements of timeless truth)
Recently archaeologists working in Egypt *opened* a tomb	that *had been sealed* in about 2500 B.C. (past perfect)

SUBORDINATE VERB	MAIN VERB
When the crewmen *saw* land, (past)	they cheered.

21.3D MAIN VERB IN THE PAST PERFECT

SUBORDINATE VERB	MAIN VERB
By the time Columbus *sighted* land, (past)	most of his crew *had lost* all hope of survival.

21.3E MAIN VERB INDICATING FUTURE

MAIN VERB	SUBORDINATE VERB
People *will buy* new homes	when interest rates *are* (or *have been*) *lowered*. (present or present perfect)
Students *will get* their diplomas	only after they *pay* (or *have paid*) their library fines. (present or present perfect)
I *start* my summer job	just as soon as I *take* (or *have taken*) my exams. (present or present perfect)

As the examples show, the subordinate verb in this kind of sequence is never future in form:

▶ The building will be demolished when the school year ~~will~~ **ends.**
~~end.~~
∧

▶ [or] The building will be demolished when the school year ~~will~~ **has**
ended.
~~end.~~   ∧
∧

21.3F MAIN VERB IN THE FUTURE PERFECT

MAIN VERB	SUBORDINATE VERB
Workmen *will have completed* repairs	by the time the airport *reopens*. (present)

On the sequence of tenses in the indirect reporting of discourse, see section 24.2B.

EXERCISE 1 TRANSFORMING TENSES

In each of the following, change the italicized verb to the past tense if it is in the present, and to the presnt tense if it is in the past. Then, if necessary, change the tense of the subordinate verb.

EXAMPLE

           wanted   **started**

We ~~want~~ to take a walk before it ~~starts~~ raining.
      ∧   ∧

1. On April 9, 1865, when Lee's Army of Northern Virginia has already been defeated, Ulysses S. Grant *meets* Robert E. Lee at Appomattox Court House, Virginia.

2. Historians *believed* that this meeting ended the Civil War.

3. The Confederate government *struggles* to survive for a short time even after Lee formally surrenders to Grant.

4. But Grant and Lee both *know* that the war is over.

5. They *realize* that the time for peace has come.

21.4 USING SEQUENCES IN PARAGRAPHS

A paragraph normally includes many verbs and often several different tenses. But you should **shift tenses** in a paragraph only when you have good reason for doing so.

A well-written paragraph is usually dominated by just one tense. Consider the following example:

Before I *set* my world record, I *was* a great fan of *The Guinness Book of World Records* and *read* each new edition from cover to cover. I *liked* knowing and being able to tell others that the world's chug-a-lug champ *consumed* 2.58 pints of beer in 10 seconds, that the world's lightest adult person *weighed* only 13 pounds, that the largest vocabulary for a talking bird *was* 531 words, spoken by a brown-beaked budgerigar named Sparky. There *is*, of course, only a fine line between admiration and envy, and for awhile I *had been* secretly *desiring* to be in that book myself—to astonish others just as I *had been astonished*. But it *seemed* hopeless. How could a nervous college sopho-more, an anonymous bookworm, perform any of those won-derful feats? The open-throat technique necessary for chug-a-lugging *was* incomprehensible to my trachea—and I *thought* my head alone must weigh close to 13 pounds.

—William Allen, "How to Set a World Record"

The author is describing a past condition, so the dominant tense here is the simple past, as in *was, read, liked, consumed, weighed,* and *seemed*. Midway through the paragraph the author shifts out of the simple past, to express a general truth in the present tense (there *is* a fine line) and two conditions that existed before the simple past (*had been desiring, had been astonished*). Then the author returns to the simple past with *seemed, was,* and *thought*.

Now consider this paragraph:

February 2, 1975. Wasps *begin* to appear in country houses about now, and even in some suburban houses. One *sees* them dart uncertainly about, *hears* them buzz and bang on window panes, and one *wonders* where they *came* from. They probably *came* from the attic, where they *spent* the early part of the win-ter hibernating. *Now* with longer hours of daylight, the wasps *begin* to rouse and *start* exploring.

—Hal Borland, "Those Attic Wasps"

This passage describes not a past condition but a recurrent one—something that happens every year. The dominant tense of the verbs, therefore, is the present: *begin, sees, hears, wonders, begin, start*. Since the presence of the wasps calls for some explanation, the writer shifts tense in the middle of the paragraph to tell us where they *came* from and where they *spent* the early part of the winter. But in the final sentence, *Now* brings us back to the present, and the verbs of this sentence, *begin* and *start*, are in the present tense.

21.5 CORRECTING FAULTY TENSE SHIFTS IN SENTENCES *t shift*

The shift of tenses in a sentence is faulty when the tense of any verb differs without good reason from the tense of the one before it, or when the tense of a subordinate verb is inconsistent with the tense of the main verb:

▶ The novel describes the adventures of two immigrant families who enter the United States at New York, withstand the stresses of culture shock, and ~~traveled~~ **travel** to the Dakota Territory to make their fortune.

▶ Marthe likes to display the miniature spoons she ~~had~~ **has** collected since her marriage to an antique dealer.

> **EXERCISE 2 CORRECTING FAULTY TENSE SHIFTS IN A SENTENCE**
>
> In some of the following sentences, the tense of one or more verbs does not properly correspond to the tense of the italicized verb. Correct those sentences. If a sentence is correct as it stands, write *Correct*.
>
> **EXAMPLE**
>
> A roll of thunder *announced* the coming of the storm; then drops of rain ~~begin~~ **began** to pelt the earth.
>
> 1. Filters *are being installed* in water systems that had been threatened by pollutants from industrial wastes.
> 2. The pollutants *were* first *discovered* last July when inspectors from the city's water department have checked the systems.
> 3. At that time, inspectors *found* that pollutants have already made the water unsafe to drink.

4. The water *will be* drinkable after the filters had been installed.

5. But until the installation was complete, residents *will drink* bottled water.

21.6 CORRECTING FAULTY TENSE SHIFTS IN PARAGRAPHS   *t shift*

The shift of tenses in a paragraph is faulty when the tense of a verb differs without good reason from the dominant tense of the paragraph. Consider two examples, the first a commentary on *Green Mansions,* a novel by W. H. Hudson:

> [1] On his return to the once peaceful woods, Abel *is horrified* to learn that his beloved Rima *has been slain* by savages. [2] Rage and grief *swell* within him as Kua-kó *tells* how Rima *was forced* to seek refuge in a tree and how the tree *became* a trap when the savages *sent* searing flames and choking smoke high into the branches. [3] As Abel *hears* of her final cry—"Abel! Abel!"—and fatal plunge to earth, he *fought* against a wild impulse to leap upon the Indian and tear his heart out.

Since the present tense is normally used in the summary of a literary work (see 20.3), the dominant tense is the present *(swell, tells,* and *hears).* There is one shift to the present perfect *(has been slain* in sentence 1) and four shifts to the past *(was forced, became, sent* in sentence 2; *fought* in sentence 3). The shifts in sentences 1 and 2 are correct; the shift in sentence 3 is not. In sentence 1, *has been slain* tells what has just happened before Abel is horrified to learn about it. In sentence 2, the past-tense verbs describe what happened well before Kua-kó *tells* about it. But in sentence 3, the verb *fought* tells what Abel does when he *hears* of Rima's death. *Fought* should be *fights.*

> [1] To understand Marx, we *need* to know something about the times in which he *lived.* [2] The period *was characterized* by revolutionary pressures against the ruling classes. [3] In most of the countries of Europe, there *was* little democracy, as we *know* it. [4] The masses *participated* little, if at all, in the world of political affairs, and very fully in the world of drudgery. [5] For example, at one factory in Manchester, England, in 1862,

people *work* an average of 80 hours per week. [6] For these long hours of toil, the workers generally *receive* small wages. [7] They often *can do* little more than feed and clothe themselves. [8] Given these circumstances, it *is* little wonder that revolutionary pressures *were* manifest.

—Deliberately altered from Edwin Mansfield, *Economics*

In sentence 1 the writer correctly shifts from the present tense (*need*), which signifies the writer's time, to the past tense (*lived*), which signifies Marx's time. In the last part of sentence 3, he correctly returns to the present tense (*know*) to signify his own time, and then shifts back to Marx's time with the past tense (*participated*). But in sentences 5, 6, and 7, the shifts to the present tense (*work, receive, can do*) are wrong because the verbs refer to past actions; they should be *worked, received,* and *could do.* In sentence 8 both tenses are correct. The present tense *is* signifies the writer's time, while the past tense *were* signifies Marx's time.

AVOIDING FAULTY TENSE SHIFTS: IN BRIEF

In discussing literary works, use the common present—not the past—as the dominant tense (20.3 and 21.6):

As Macbeth *ponders* the prophecies, a desire to be king *rises*
envisions **imagines**
within him. He ~~envisioned~~ the crown upon his head and ~~imag-~~
^ **will** ^
~~ined~~ how the Scots ~~would~~ cheer when he *sits* upon the throne.
^

In writing about past events from the vantage point of the present, use the past tense for what applies to the past, and the present tense for what applies to the present (21.6):

Today many Democrats *like* to swap stories about Harry Truman, who *was* noted for his plain speech. He *is* especially
threatened
remembered for what he ~~threatens~~ to do after he *reads* a harsh
^
review of a concert given by his daughter.

EXERCISE 3 CORRECTING FAULTY TENSE SHIFTS IN A
PARAGRAPH

Each of the following paragraphs is a rewritten version of a
paragraph from the source cited after it. Into each paragraph,
we have deliberately introduced one or more faulty shifts in
tense. Correct them.

EXAMPLE
line 3: manfully thrashes

1. However violent his acts, Kong remains a gentleman.
Whenever a fresh boa constrictor threatens Fay, Kong first sees
that the lady is safely parked, then manfully thrashed her
attacker. (And she, the ingrate, runs away every time his back
was turned.) Atop the Empire State Building, ignoring his   5
pursuers, Kong places Fay on a ledge as tenderly as if she were
a dozen eggs. He fondled her, then turned to face the Army
Air Force. And Kong is perhaps the most disinterested lover
since Cyrano: his attentions to the lady were utterly without
hope of reward. After all, between a five-foot blonde and a   10
fifty-foot ape, love can hardly be more than an intellectual
flirtation. His forced exit from his jungle, in chains, results
directly from his single-minded pursuit of Fay. He smashes a
Broadway theater when the notion entered his dull brain that
the flashbulbs of photographers somehow endanger the lady.   15
His perilous shinnying up a skyscraper to have plucked Fay
from her boudoir is an act of the kindliest of hearts. He was
impossible to discourage even though the love of his life can't
lay eyes on him without shrieking murder.

—Deliberately altered from X. J. Kennedy,
"Who Killed King Kong?"

2. Since graduating from college, Susan has held a variety of
political jobs. Her warm, friendly manner, together with her
capacity for hard work, makes her an ideal employee. Three
years ago, she managed the reelection campaign of a New
England governor. She has to talk with people in all parts of   5
the state, trying to build support. Soon after the election,
which turns out successfully for the governor, Susan goes to
Washington, D.C., to work for a senator. She had a high-
paying position; but, being more interested in working cre-

atively than in making money, she soon resigned, proclaim- 10
ing, "Never have so many people done so little work for so
much money." Because she has had so much experience, finding a new job was easy. She becomes an adviser to the New
England Governors' Conference on Energy.

—Deliberately altered from Mark Bartlett,
"A Political Woman"

22

Verbs

ACTIVE AND PASSIVE VOICE

22.1 WHAT VOICE IS

The **voice** of a verb depends on the relation between the verb and its subject. When the subject of a verb *acts,* the verb is in the **active voice;** when the subject is *acted upon,* the verb is in the **passive voice.**

The active voice stresses the activity of the subject and helps to make a sentence direct, concise, and vigorous:

The old woman *threatened* me with her umbrella.
The tornado *flattened* entire houses.
Each man *kills* the thing he *loves.*   —Oscar Wilde

The passive voice presents the subject as the target of an action:

Entire houses *were flattened* by the tornado.
The barn *was struck* by a bolt of lightning.
In Moulmein, in Lower Burma, I *was hated* by large numbers of people—the only time in my life that I have been important enough for this to happen to me.   —George Orwell

In passive constructions, the performer of the action is called an **agent.** In the examples above, *a bolt of lightning* and *large numbers of people* are agents.

22.2 FORMING THE ACTIVE AND THE PASSIVE VOICE

Verbs in the active voice can take many forms: the bare form, the past-tense form, the *-ing* form with *be,* and the form with *have:*

> My sisters often *chop* logs for exercise.
> Last week they *stacked* firewood for the stove.
> But today they *are lifting* weights.
> They *have done* wonders.

Verbs in the passive voice are formed from their past participle and some tense of *be:*

> The burglar alarms *were chosen* by a security guard.
> They *will be installed* next week.
> They *will be tested* every month.

22.2A CHANGING FROM ACTIVE TO PASSIVE

You can change a verb from active to passive only if it has a direct object (DO):

>   S   ACTIVE   DO
> Heavy waves pounded *the seacoast.*
>
>   S   PASSIVE   AGENT
> *The seacoast* was pounded by heavy waves.

If the performer of an action is not important to your point, you don't need to mention the agent:

>   S   ACTIVE   DO
> Workmen installed burglar alarms.
>
>   S   PASSIVE   AGENT OMITTED
> Burglar alarms were installed.

22.2B CHANGING FROM PASSIVE TO ACTIVE

To change a verb from the passive to the active voice, turn the subject of the passive verb into the direct object of the active one:

If the passive version does not include the agent, you must either keep the passive or supply the agent itself before changing to the active:

> The city of Washington was planned in 1791. (passive, no agent)

> The city of Washington was planned in 1791 by Pierre Charles L'Enfant. (passive, agent supplied)

> Pierre Charles L'Enfant planned the city of Washington in 1791. (active)

22.2C PASSIVE VOICE VERSUS PROGRESSIVE FORM

Passive-voice verbs look something like verbs in the progressive form, because both types of verbs include a form of *be.* But don't confuse the types. The passive voice includes a form of *be* and the *past* participle, which usually ends in *-ed;* the progressive form includes a form of *be* and the *present* participle, which always ends in *-ing.* The progressive form is never used in the passive and often used in the active:

> PROGRESSIVE FORM
> ACTIVE VOICE
> Ellen *was washing* her dog when I arrived.

> PASSIVE VOICE
> The dog *was washed* as I watched.

22.3 CHOOSING THE ACTIVE VOICE

To make your writing forceful, direct, and concise, you should use the active voice frequently. Compare these sentences:

> Through her studies of child-rearing and culture, world fame was achieved by Margaret Mead. (passive)

> Through her studies of child-rearing and culture, Margaret Mead achieved world fame. (active)

The active version ditches the excess verbal baggage—*was* and *by*—and highlights the action of the subject. To a great extent, the life and energy of your writing will depend on what the subjects of your sentences do.

22.4 CHOOSING THE PASSIVE

Forceful as the active voice is, you should know when to use the passive.

1. Use the passive when you want to keep the focus on someone or something that is acted upon:

> On August 13, 1927, while driving on the Promenade des Anglais at Nice, Isadora Duncan met her death. She *was strangled* by her colored shawl, which became tangled in the wheel of the automobile. —Janet Flanner

> Frederick Douglass learned to read while he *was owned* by Mr. and Mrs. Ault of Baltimore.

> If our heads swim occasionally, if we grow giddy with change, is it any wonder? We *are urged* to take our rightful place in the world of affairs. We *are* also *commanded* to stay at home and mind the hearth. We *are lauded* for our stamina and *pitied* for our lack of it. If we run to large families, we *are told* we are overpopulating the earth. If we are childless, we *are damned* for not fulfilling our functions. We *are goaded* into jobs and careers, then warned that our competition with men is unsettling both sexes.
>
> —Phyllis McGinley,
> "The Honor of Being a Woman"

2. Use the passive when the agent is unknown or unimportant to your point:

> Traces of the oil spill *were found* as far away as Newfoundland.

3. Use the passive when you want to put the agent at the end of a clause, where you can easily attach a long modifier:

> A secret mission to help thousands of starving Cambodians was organized in the summer of 1979 by *Father Robert I. Charles-*

bois, a forty-eight-year-old Catholic priest from Gary, Indiana, with twelve years of experience in the Vietnam war zone.

> ### ACTIVE VOICE AND PASSIVE VOICE: IN BRIEF
>
> In active-voice constructions, the subject of the verb *acts*:
>
> > Wolfe *defeated* Montcalm on the Plains of Abraham in 1759.
>
> In passive-voice constructions, the subject of the verb is *acted upon*:
>
> > Montcalm *was defeated* by Wolfe on the Plains of Abraham in 1759.
>
> Use the active voice to make your writing direct, forceful, and concise:
>
> > Marie Curie *won* the Nobel Prize for Chemistry in 1911.
>
> Use the passive voice to keep the focus on someone or something that is acted upon:
>
> > She *was honored* for her discovery of polonium and radium.

22.5 MISUSING THE PASSIVE *pass*

Avoid switching from active to passive when you have no particular reason to do so:

> Usually I run two miles in the morning, but that morning it *was decided* that a four-mile run *should be taken*.

Who made the decision?

> EDITED: Usually I run two miles in the morning, but that morning I decided to run four.

The active voice snaps the sentence into shape and keeps the focus on the one who is acting. Switch to the passive only to gain a special advantage—such as keeping the focus on someone who is acted upon:

> Usually I run two miles in the morning, but that morning I *was kept* in bed by the flu.

EXERCISE 1   ELIMINATING THE PASSIVE

Rewrite any of the following sentences in which you find the passive voice misused. If the passive voice is justified, write *Acceptable.*

EXAMPLE

Every year we cut a Christmas tree in the woods, and ~~it is~~

decorated ~~by us~~ on December 24.

1. A terrible conflict between a doctor and a child is dramatized by William Carlos Williams's short story "The Use of Force."

2. At the start of the story, the doctor enters the house of a blue-collar family knowing that a throat culture has to be obtained from a frightened girl.

3. No one in the family, however, gives him the cooperation that is needed by him.

4. His initial efforts to examine the girl are thwarted when his glasses are knocked to the floor by her.

5. The mother is visibly disturbed by the child's screams and lack of cooperation.

6. In addition, ambivalence over the examination is displayed by the father when his hold on his daughter's arms is first tightened and then loosened.

7. With no support from the family, the doctor wonders whether his visit should be ended.

8. He is troubled by a growing fear that he may lose his temper.

9. The idea of leaving is rejected, however, as his better judgment is overruled by his increasing anger and wounded pride.

10. The child must be defeated; her resistance must be overcome.

11. An attack is launched with the aid of a metal spoon that is jammed between her teeth and pressed down hard like a lever.

EXERCISE 2   GAINING VIGOR AND COHERENCE WITH THE
ACTIVE VOICE

Passive verbs predominate in the following passage, and since
almost every sentence has a different subject, the writing is
not only tedious but unfocused. Wherever you find the passive
voice unjustified, make the verb active.

At the sound of a bell, the huge red building was entered
by me along with hundreds of others. Just inside the entrance,
instructions were being yelled at us by a mean-looking old
lady. My lunchbox was clutched, and a crowd of six-year-olds
was followed down a long hallway, up some steps, and down   5
another corridor. Mrs. Nearing's room was being looked for
by us. I knew our destination had been reached when I was
greeted loudly by a tall, black-haired woman. I was asked my
name by her. Then it was printed by her on a sticky tag, and
the tag was pressed to my chest. Inside the room several other   10
six-year-olds could be seen, some of them big. Finally the
classroom door was closed by Mrs. Nearing, and a loud bang
was made in the process. The small pane of glass near the top
was kept from shattering by a network of wires. To my imagination, the wires looked like the bars in a prison. I was back   15
in school.

EXERCISE 3   USING ACTIVE AND PASSIVE EFFECTIVELY
TOGETHER

Following is a group of simple sentences, some with verbs in
the active voice, others with verbs in the passive. Make one
continuous passage out of these sentences by combining some
of them and changing the voice of the verbs whenever such a
change will tighten a sentence or improve its focus. Underline
all changes in voice.

EXAMPLE

1. As a prime minister of England from 1940 to 1945, Churchill led his country through World War II.

2. But immediately after the war people voted him out of
   office.

3. Later his position as prime minister was regained by him.

4. That office was left by him in 1955.

5. Great popularity for the rest of his life was enjoyed by him.

6. He died in 1965.

7. People acclaimed him as a national hero.

COMBINED: As prime minister of England from 1940 to 1945, Churchill led his country through World War II, but immediately after the war he <u>was voted</u> out of office. Later he <u>regained</u> his position as prime minister. After he <u>left</u> that office <u>in 1955</u>, he <u>enjoyed</u> great popularity for the rest of his life, and when he <u>died in 1965</u>, he <u>was acclaimed</u> as a national hero.

1. The political structure of modern China was largely created by Mao Zedong.

2. Mao led the Chinese Communist revolution.

3. The theory behind it was formulated by him.

4. China was virtually ruled by him from 1949 to his death in 1976.

5. Mao worked for revolution throughout much of his early life.

6. In 1911 the Nationalist armed forces of Hunan Province were joined by him in their revolt against the Manchu dynasty.

7. He was then eighteen.

8. In 1921 he helped to found the Chinese Communist party.

9. In the spring of 1928, the Fourth Chinese Red Army was organized by him and a fellow revolutionary named Zhu De.

10. In 1934–35, he and Zhu De led a six-thousand-mile march of Chinese Communist forces to northwest China.

11. There a new base of operations was established by the two leaders.

12. The new base was established against the Kuomintang.

13. That was the Nationalist political organization.

14. Generalissimo Chiang Kai-shek headed it.

15. Mao and Chiang joined forces during World War II to fight their common enemy, the Japanese.

16. But in the summer of 1946 a full-scale civil war against the Nationalists was resumed by Mao.

17. Mao's forces won the war in three years.

18. On September 21, 1949, the establishment of the People's Republic of China was proclaimed by Mao.

19. A succession of increasingly powerful posts was then assumed by him.

20. The posts included chairmanship of the Government Council, chairmanship of the Republic, and, most important, chairmanship of the Chinese Communist party.

21. In effect, China was ruled by Mao for nearly thirty years.

22. For better or worse, a lasting change in that country was made by Mao.

23. People will long remember him as one of the most important revolutionaries of the twentieth century.

Verbs

MOOD

23.1 WHAT MOOD IS

The **mood** of a verb or verb phrase indicates your attitude toward a particular statement as you are making it. Do you think of it as a statement of fact? Then you will use the **indicative** mood. Do you think of it as a command? Then you will use the **imperative**. Do you think of it as a wish, a recommendation, or an imaginary condition? Then you will use the **subjunctive**.

23.2 USING THE INDICATIVE

The **indicative** mood is for statements of actuality or strong probability:

> The spine-tailed swift *flies* faster than any other bird in the world.
> The Missouri and Mississippi Rivers *rose* to record highs in the summer of 1993.
> Midwesterners *will remember* the flooding for many years to come.

Use *do, does,* or *did* with the indicative for emphasis.

23.3 USING THE IMPERATIVE

The **imperative** mood is for commands and requests made directly.

1. Use the bare form of the verb for commands addressed entirely to others:

> *Vote* for change.
> *Fight* pollution.
> *Be* yourself.
> Kindly *send* me your latest catalog.

2. When a command or suggestion includes yourself as well as others, use *let us* or *let's* before the bare form of the verb:

> *Let us negotiate* our differences in a spirit of mutual trust and respect.
> *Let's cooperate.*

23.4 USING THE SUBJUNCTIVE: MODAL AUXILIARIES

The **subjunctive** mood is for statements of hypothetical conditions or of wishes, recommendations, requirements, or suggestions. To express the subjunctive, you often need one of the modal auxiliaries, which include *can, could, may, might, must, ought, should,* and *would.* Use them as follows:

1. Use <u>can</u> to express

> CAPABILITY: *Can* the Israelis and the Palestinians ever make peace?
>
> PERMISSION: Why *can't* Americans visit Cuba?

In formal writing, permission is normally signified by *may* rather than *can,* which is reserved for capability. But *can* may be used informally to express permission and is actually better than *may* in requests for permission involving the negative. The only alternative to *can't* in such questions is the awkward term *mayn't.*

2. Use <u>could</u> to express

THE OBJECT OF A WISH: I wish I *could* climb Mount Everest.

A CONDITION: If all countries of the world *could* set aside their antagonism once every four years, the Olympics would be truly international.

A DISTINCT POSSIBILITY: A major earthquake *could* strike California within the next ten years.

On the distinction between *would* and *could* in statements of wishing, see number 8 below.

3. Use <u>may</u> to express

A MILD POSSIBILITY: The next president of the United States *may* be a woman.

PERMISSION: Students who cannot afford tuition *may* apply for loans.

4. Use <u>might</u> to express

A REMOTE POSSIBILITY: Biogenetic experiments *might* produce some horribly dangerous new form of life.

THE RESULT OF A CONTRARY-TO-FACT CONDITION: If I had driven all night, I *might* have fallen asleep at the wheel.

5. Use <u>ought</u> to express

STRONG RECOMMENDATION: The Pentagon *ought* to eliminate waste in defense spending.

LIKELIHOOD: The new museum *ought* to be ready by next fall.

Ought is normally followed by the infinitive.

6. Use <u>must</u> to express

AN ABSOLUTE OBLIGATION: Firefighters *must* be ready for action at any hour of the day or night.

A FIRM CONCLUSION: William Bligh, who sailed a small boat nearly four thousand miles, *must* have been an extraordinary seaman.

7. Use <u>should</u> to express

ADVICE: Students who hope to get into medical school *should* take biology.

EXPECTATION: By the year 2025, the population of the world *should* exceed eight billion.

8. Use <u>would</u> to express

THE RESULT OF A CONDITION OR EVENT: If a one-kiloton neutron bomb were exploded a few hundred feet over the earth, it *would* kill everyone within a radius of three hundred yards.

THE OBJECT OF A WISH: Some people wish the federal government *would* support them for the rest of their lives.

Both *would* and *could* may be used to express the object of a wish. But "I wish you could go" means "I wish you were able to go"; "I wish you would go" means "I wish you were willing to go."

23.4A MISUSING MODAL AUXILIARIES

Avoid putting two or more modal auxiliaries together:

▶ I might ~~could~~ move to Calgary.

▶ [or] I ~~might~~ could move to Calgary.

EXERCISE 1 SUPPLYING MODAL AUXILIARIES

Complete the following sentences with suitable modal auxiliaries. Identify in parentheses their meanings.

EXAMPLE
Students hoping to attend medical school _____ take biology.
Students hoping to attend medical school <u>should</u> take biology.
(advice)

1. Helen _____ leave the hospital for the weekend; the doctor has just given her permission.

2. She _____, however, avoid going up or down stairs.

3. And she _____ limit her walking to ten steps every two hours.

4. She _____ eat whatever she likes, provided she limits the size of the portions.

5. Although complications _____ develop, she _____ be strong enough to spend Thanksgiving at home.

23.5 Using the Subjunctive: Special Verb Forms

The **subjunctive** mood is sometimes indicated by a special verb form instead of by a modal auxiliary.

1. The present subjunctive is the same in form as the bare form (infinitive form) of the verb, and it is the same with every subject. Use the present subjunctive to express a hope, a requirement, a recommendation, a demand, a request, or a suggestion:

INDICATIVE	SUBJUNCTIVE
God *has* mercy on us.	God *have* mercy on us!
The queen *lives.*	Long *live* the queen!
A premed student normally *takes* biology.	The college requires that every student *take* freshman English.
The toxic dump *is* still open	Protesters demand that the dump *be* closed.
The trustees' meetings *are* closed.	The students demand that those meetings *be* open.

The present subjunctive of the verb *be* is *be* with every subject (dump *be* closed; meetings *be* open).

2. The past subjunctive is the same in form as the common past, except that the past subjunctive of *be* is *were* with every subject. Use the past subjunctive to express a wish for something in the present:

INDICATIVE (FACT)	SUBJUNCTIVE (WISH)
I *have* five dollars.	I wish (that) I *had* a hundred dollars.
I *am* a pauper.	I wish (that) I *were* a millionaire.
I *am taking* Math 36.	I wish (that) I *were taking* Math 23.
I *live* in Ottawa.	I wish (that) I *lived* in Vancouver.
I *am* in New York.	I wish (that) I *were* in Texas.
It *is* summer.	I wish (that) it *were* winter.

3. The past perfect subjunctive is the same in form as the common past perfect. Use it to express a wish for something in the past:

INDICATIVE (FACT)	SUBJUNCTIVE (WISH)
I *saw* the second half of the game.	I wish (that) I *had seen* the first. [or] I wished (that) I *had seen* the first.
I *was* there for the second half.	I wish (that) I *had been* there for the first.
I *had* no binoculars with me.	I wish (that) I *had had* them.

23.6 FORMING AND USING CONDITIONAL SENTENCES

A **conditional sentence** normally consists of an *if* clause, which states a condition, and a result clause, which states the result of that condition. The mood of the verb in the *if* clause depends on the likelihood of the condition.

23.6A THE POSSIBLE CONDITION

If the condition is likely or even barely possible, the mood is indicative:

[condition] If electric cars *replace* gas-powered cars in our cities, [result] urban air will be much cleaner than it is now.

23.6B THE IMPOSSIBLE OR CONTRARY-TO-FACT CONDITION

If the condition is impossible or contrary to fact, the mood of the verb in the *if* clause is subjunctive, and the result clause usually includes a modal auxiliary, such as *would* or *might*. The tense of the verb in the *if* clause depends on the tense of the condition.

1. A condition contrary to present fact should be stated in the past subjunctive:

If the federal government *spent* no more than it collected, interest rates would plunge.

If I *were* a millionaire, I would buy an airplane.

The new clerk acts as if he *were* the owner.

The expression *as if* always signals a condition contrary to fact. Some writers now use *was* instead of *were* in sentences like the second and third, but in formal writing you should use *were*.

2. A <u>condition contrary to past fact</u> should be stated in the past perfect subjunctive:

> After the fight, the former champion looked as if he *had been put* through a meat grinder.
>
> If Montcalm *had defeated* Wolfe in 1759, the Canadian province of Quebec might now belong to France.

23.6C MISUSING *WOULD HAVE* IN CONDITIONAL CLAUSES

Avoid using *would have* to express a condition of any kind:

> * If I *would have* attended the meeting, I would have attacked the proposal.

Use *would have* only to express the *result* of a condition:

> EDITED: If I had attended the meeting, I *would have* attacked the proposal.

EXERCISE 2 SUPPLYING VERBS IN CONDITIONAL SENTENCES

Using the facts in brackets as a guide, complete each of the following sentences by supplying a suitable verb or verb phrase.

EXAMPLE

If Ross Perot _____ the presidency in 1992, he would have fundamentally altered the two-party sustem. [Ross Perot did not win the presidency in 1992.]

had won

1. If high-speed trains _____ all major cities in the United States, Americans could travel much more often without their cars. [High-speed trains serve hardly any cities in the United States.]

2. If my father _____ five hundred shares of Microsoft in 1980, he would be a millionaire today. [Alas, my father never bought any shares of Microsoft.]

3. If the prime rate _____ unemployment may go up also. [The prime rate goes up and down regularly.]

4. After winning the match, Joan felt as if she _____ the world. [She did not actually conquer the world.]

5. If the Continental Army _____ to the British at Yorktown, George Washington might never have become president of the United States. [The Continental Army did not lose to the British at Yorktown.]

EXERCISE 3 **SUPPLYING VERBS IN A PARAGRAPH**

For each of the blanks in the following passage, supply a suitable verb or verb phrase.

EXAMPLE
line 1: were

Many students wish that the Thanksgiving recess _____ one week long, or that the fall term _____ completely before Thanksgiving, so that they could stay home between Thanksgiving and Christmas. But the students have not asked for either of those things. They have asked only that the Thanks- 5
giving recess _____ on the Wednesday before Thanksgiving. If the recess _____ on Wednesday, students would have one full day to travel home before Thanksgiving Day itself. Many students need that time. If every student _____ rich, he or she could fly home in an hour or two. But most students are not 10 rich.

Direct and Indirect Reporting of Discourse

Any statement, whether spoken or written, can be reported directly—by quotation of the actual words. Or it can be reported indirectly—by a paraphrase of those words. In this chapter we explain when and how to use each method of reporting discourse. (For special instruction in how to quote or paraphrase source material in a research paper, see sections 34.5 and 34.6.)

24.1 DIRECT REPORTING

Use **direct reporting** when the exact words of the original statement are memorable or otherwise important. Enclose the words in quotation marks:

> "The vilest abortionist," writes Shaw, "is he who attempts to mould a child's character."
> Frost puts four stresses in his opening line: "The well was dry beside the door."

For a full discussion of how to punctuate quotations, see chapter 29.

24.1A USING TENSES IN TAGS

Since no statement can be reported until after it has been made, you should normally use the past tense for the verb in the accompanying tag:

> "No child should be homeless," *said* the nurse.
>
> "I agree with you completely," *answered* the orderly.
>
> In 1782 Thomas Jefferson *wrote:* "There must doubtless be an unhappy influence on the manners of our people produced by the existence of slavery among us."

But use the present when you are quoting an undated statement of lasting significance or a statement made by a character in a work of literature:

> "In every work of genius," *observes* Emerson, "we recognize our own rejected thoughts."
>
> In the first chapter of *Huckleberry Finn,* Huck *says,* "I don't take no stock in dead people."

24.1B QUOTING EXTENDED DIALOGUE

In reporting an exchange between two speakers, you should first indicate clearly who is speaking and in what order. You can then omit tags until the dialogue ends or is interrupted:

> "Our market surveys indicate," Hurts said, "that there are also a lot of kids who claim their parents don't listen to them. If they could rent a gun, they feel they could arrive at an understanding with their folks in no time."
>
> "There's no end to the business," I said. "How would you charge for Hurts Rent-A-Gun?"
>
> "There would be hourly rates, day rates, and weekly rates, plus ten cents for each bullet fired. Our guns would be the latest models, and we would guarantee clean barrels and the latest safety devices. If a gun malfunctions through no fault of the user, we will give him another gun absolutely free. . . ."
>
> "Why didn't you start this before?"
>
> "We wanted to see what happened with the gun-control legislation. . . ." —Art Buchwald, "Hurts Rent-A-Gun"

Paragraph indentations mark the shift from one speaker to another.

24.1C QUOTING SEVERAL LINES OF PROSE OR POETRY

When you quote more than four lines of prose or three lines of poetry, you should indent instead of using quotation marks, as described in sections 29.4 and 29.5.

24.2 INDIRECT REPORTING OF STATEMENTS

Use **indirect reporting** when the exact words of a statement are less important than their content:

> During the campaign, the senator said that she favored federal subsidizing of day care.

Form indirect statements as shown here:

> ORIGINAL STATEMENT: I want you to play the lead.
>
> DIRECT REPORT (QUOTATION): The director said, "I want you to play the lead."
>
> INDIRECT REPORT: The director said that she wanted me to play the lead.

As this example shows, an indirect report does the following:

1. It refers to the speaker or writer.

2. It uses no quotation marks.

3. It often puts *that* just before the reported statement. But *that* may be omitted:

> The director said she wanted me to play the lead.

4. It changes the pronouns in the reported statement where necessary. In this example, *I* becomes *she,* and *you* becomes *me.*

5. It may change the tense of the verb in the original statement so that it matches the tense of the introductory verb. Thus *want* in the original statement becomes *wanted* in the indirect report. But if the original statement has continuing force at the time it is reported, the indirect report may keep the original tense:

> The director said that she wants me to play the lead.

Generalizations may be reported with the present tense for both verbs:

> Farmers say that rain before seven means sun by eleven.
>
> They also say that when cows lie down, a storm is coming.

EXERCISE 1 TRANSFORMING REPORTS OF STATEMENTS

Each of the following consists of a statement, with the speaker and (in two cases) the listener identified in brackets. Write a direct and an indirect report of the statement. Then put a check next to the version you think is more suitable, and say why you prefer it.

EXAMPLE

You will have to take a breath test. [*Speaker:* policeman; *listener:* me]

DIRECT: "You will have to take a breath test," said the policeman to me.

√ INDIRECT: The policeman told me that I would have to take a breath test.

(Since the content is more important than the exact words, the indirect version is preferable.)

1. You will have to earn your own spending money. [*Speaker:* my father; *listener,* me]

2. I do not mind lying, but I hate inaccuracy. [*Writer:* Samuel Butler]

3. I will pay you $3.50 an hour. [*Speaker:* manager; *listener:* me]

4. You have been baptized in fire and blood and have come out steel. [*Speaker:* General Patton; *listeners:* battle survivors]

5. Nothing in education is so astonishing as the amount of ignorance it accumulates in the form of inert facts. [*Writer:* Henry Adams]

6. Fanaticism consists in redoubling your efforts when you have forgotten your aim. [*Writer:* George Santayana]

24.3 DIRECT REPORTING OF QUESTIONS

To report a question directly, you normally use a verb of asking (such as *ask, request,* or *inquire*) in the past tense:

> The Sphinx asked, "What walks on four legs in the morning, two legs at noon, and three legs in the evening?"
>
> "Have you thought about college?" my father inquired.
>
> "When did the plane leave?" I asked.

Use the present tense when you are reporting a question of standing importance or a question asked by a literary character:

> The consumer advocate asks, "How can we have safe and effective products without government regulations?"
>
> The business owner asks, "How can we have free enterprise with government interference?"
>
> When Tom Sawyer proposes to form a gang that will rob and kill people, Huck says, "Must we always kill the people?"

24.4 INDIRECT REPORTING OF QUESTIONS

To report a question indirectly, you normally introduce it with a verb of asking and a word like *who, what, whether, how, when, where, why,* or *if:*

> ORIGINAL QUESTION: Why do birds migrate each year?
>
> INDIRECT REPORT: The teacher asked why birds migrate each year.

The indirect report drops the auxiliary verb *do,* which is commonly used in questions. Also, the question mark becomes a period.

Use the present tense for the introductory verb when reporting a question of continuing importance or a question asked by a literary character:

> The consumer advocate asks how we can have safe and effective products without government regulation.
>
> When Tom Sawyer proposes to form a gang that will rob and kill people, Huck asks whether they must always kill the people.

After a past-tense verb of asking, you must normally use the past tense in the reported question:

> The interviewer asked me what I knew about programming.
> She also asked if I had an advanced degree.

But you may use the present tense if the reported question is essentially timeless:

> The utilitarian asks what practical purpose poetry serves.
> The romantic asks how we could live without it.

24.5 CONFUSING THE DIRECT AND INDIRECT REPORTING OF QUESTIONS *quest*

1. Do not use a question mark to punctuate the indirect report of a question:

> * The customer sat down at the counter and asked did we have any scruples?

The **direct report** of a question repeats its actual words and ends in a question mark:

> EDITED: The customer sat down at the counter and asked, "Do you have any scruples?"

The **indirect report** of a question states that a question has been asked. It must end with a period:

> EDITED: The customer sat down at the counter and asked if we had any scruples.

2. When reporting a question indirectly, do not use interrogative word order:

> * The policeman asked when was the car stolen.

The direct report of a question preserves its word order, putting the auxiliary verb before the subject:

> EDITED: The policeman asked, "When was the car stolen?"

The indirect report uses declarative word order, putting the subject first:

> EDITED: The policeman asked when the car was stolen.

24.6 FITTING QUOTATIONS INTO YOUR OWN PROSE

The combination of your own prose and a quotation should always make a complete, coherent sentence:

> According to Phyllis Rose, "We shop to cheer ourselves up."
>
> Ambrose Bierce defines achievement as "the death of endeavor and the birth of disgust."
>
> Barbara Garson writes: "The crime of modern industry is not forcing us to work, but denying us real work."

24.6A MISFITTED QUOTATIONS *mq*

A quotation is misfitted when it fails to combine with your own prose to make a complete, coherent sentence:

> * According to Orwell, "When there is a gap between one's real and one's declared aims."

This sentence fragment lacks a main clause, and it leaves the reader guessing about what happens "when there is a gap." To correct the error, do one of the following:

1. Quote a complete sentence:

> EDITED: According to Orwell, "When there is a gap between one's real and one's declared aims, one turns as it were instinctively to long words and exhausted idioms, like a cuttle fish squirting out ink."

2. Make the quoted matter part of a complete sentence:

> EDITED: According to Orwell, one resorts to obscure language "when there is a gap between one's real and one's declared aims."

EXERCISE 2 FITTING QUOTATIONS INTO YOUR OWN PROSE

Take a sentence from any printed source and do three things:
(1) copy it out and put the author's name in parentheses after
it; (2) write a sentence in which you quote it all; (3) write a
sentence in which you quote part of it.

EXAMPLE

1. Taught from infancy that beauty is woman's sceptre, the
   mind shapes itself to the body, and roaming around its gilt
   cage, only seeks to adorn its prison. (Mary Wollstonecraft)

2. Mary Wollstonecraft writes: "Taught from infancy that
   beauty is woman's sceptre, the mind shapes itself to the
   body, and roaming around its gilt cage, only seeks to adorn
   its prison."

3. When a woman has been conditioned to worry constantly
   about her appearance, her mind, says Mary Wollstonecraft,
   "shapes itself to the body, and roaming around its gilt cage,
   only seeks to adorn its prison."

Invigorating Your Style

Nearly all of the chapters in parts 2 and 3 of this book aim to help you improve your **style:** to write not just correctly but cogently, to shape your sentences with coordination and subordination, to enhance them with parallel structure, to enrich them with modifiers, and to perfect them with well-chosen words. In this chapter, we focus specifically on what you can do to invigorate your style.

Good writing exudes vitality. It not only sidesteps awkwardness, obscurity, and grammatical error; it also expresses a mind continually at work, a mind seeking, discovering, wondering, prodding, provoking, asserting. Whatever else it does, good writing keeps the reader awake.

Unfortunately, much of what gets written seems designed to put readers to sleep. Too many people write the way they jog, never changing the pace or skipping a beat, never leaping, zigzagging, or stopping to scratch the reader's mind. In most college writing you are expected to sound thoughtful and judicious. But no reader wants you to sound dull. To enliven your writing on any subject, here are five specific things you can do.

25.1 VARY YOUR SENTENCES

Take a hard look at one of your paragraphs—or at a whole essay. Do all of your sentences sound about the same? If most are short and simple, combine some of them to make longer ones. If most are lengthened out with modifiers and dependent clauses, break some of them up. Be bold. Be surprising. Use a short sentence to set off a long one, a simple structure to set off a complicated one. Though you need some consistency in order to keep the reader with you (did you notice that all of our last five sentences are imperatives?), you can and should eschew the monotony of assembly-line sentences.

To see what you can do with a variety of sentences, consider this example:

> Someone is always at my elbow reminding me that I am the granddaughter of slaves. It fails to register depression with me. Slavery is sixty years in the past. The operation was successful and the patient is doing well, thank you. The terrible struggle that made me an American out of a potential slave said "On the line!" The Reconstruction said "Get set!"; and the generation before said "Go!" I am off to a flying start and I must not halt in the stretch to look behind and weep. Slavery is the price I paid for civilization, and the choice was not with me. It is a bully adventure and worth all that I have paid through my ancestors for it. —Zora Neale Hurston

Among the many things that invigorate the style of this passage is the variety of sentence types that Hurston uses—simple, compound, complex, and compound with a subordinate clause:

SIMPLE: It fails to register depression with me.
Slavery is sixty years in the past.

COMPOUND: The operation was successful *and* the patient is doing well, thank you.
I am off to a flying start *and* I must not halt in the stretch to look behind and weep.

COMPLEX: Someone is always at my elbow reminding me *that I am the granddaughter of slaves.*
It is a bully adventure and worth all *that I have paid through my ancestors for it.*

COMPOUND WITH SUBORDINATE CLAUSE: Slavery is the price *that I paid for civilization,* and the choice was not with me.

Now consider this passage:

> This looking business is risky. Once I stood on nearby Purgatory Mountain, watching through binoculars the great autumn hawk migration below, until I discovered that I was in danger of joining the hawks on a vertical migration of my own. I was used to binoculars, but not, apparently, to balancing on humped rocks while looking through them. I reeled. —Annie Dillard, *Pilgrim at Tinker Creek*

Dillard varies both the structure and the length of her sentences. She moves from five to thirty-five words, then down to just two at the end. When a very short sentence follows one or more long ones, it can strike like a dart.

25.2 USE VERBS OF ACTION INSTEAD OF *BE*

Verbs of action show the subject not just *being* something but *doing* something. At times, of course, you need to say what your subject *is* or *was* or *has been,* and these words can speak strongly when used to express equality or identity, as in *Beauty is truth.* But verbs of action can often replace verbs of being:

▶ Sheila ~~was the winner of~~ the nomination. [won]

▶ Frederick's desire to learn reading would have ~~been a shock to~~ other slaveholders. [shocked]

▶ Mr. Ault believed that learning would ~~be the~~ ruin ~~of~~ Frederick as a slave.

25.3 USE THE ACTIVE VOICE MORE OFTEN THAN THE PASSIVE

Use the active voice as much as possible. Verbs that tell of a subject acting usually express more vitality than verbs that tell of a subject acted upon:

PASSIVE: After a big hole was dug and sprinkled with fertilizer, the tree *was planted*.

ACTIVE: After digging a big hole and sprinkling it with fertilizer, I *planted* the tree.

While some sentences work better in the passive voice, overuse of the passive can paralyze your writing. This is a problem *to be seriously considered by anyone who has ever been asked* to write an essay in which a subject of some sort is *to be analyzed, to be explained, or to be commented upon by him or her*. That sentence shows what overuse of the passive will do to your sentences: it will make them wordy, stagnant, boring, dead. Whenever you start to use the passive, ask yourself whether the sentence might sound better in the active. Often it will (For a full discussion of the active and passive voice, see chapter 22.)

25.4 ASK QUESTIONS

Break the forward march of your statements with an occasional question:

> He falls back upon the bed awkwardly. His stumps, unweighted by legs and feet, rise in the air, presenting themselves. I unwrap the bandages from the stumps, and begin to cut away the black scabs and the dead, glazed fat with scissors and forceps. A shard of white bone comes loose. I pick it away. I wash the wounds with disinfectant and redress the stumps. All this while, he does not speak. What is he thinking behind those lids that do not blink? Is he remembering a time when he was whole? Does he dream of feet?
>
> —Richard Selzer, "The Discus Thrower"

Questions like these can draw the reader into the very heart of your subject. And questions can do more than advertise your curiosity. They can also voice your conviction. In conversation you sometimes ask a question that assumes a particular answer—don't you? Such a question is called **rhetorical,** and you can use it in writing as well as in speech. It will challenge your readers, prompting them either to agree with you or to explain to themselves why they do not. And why shouldn't you challenge your readers now and then?

25.5 CUT ANY WORDS YOU DON'T NEED

Cut out all needless repetition and strive to be concise (see section 9.13):

▶ During their tour of Ottawa, they saw the Parliament buildings, and ~~they saw~~ the National Art Center.

▶ ~~The reason for his decision~~ *He decided* to ~~make a~~ visit ~~to~~ Spain ~~was his~~ *because he wanted* ~~desire~~ to see a bullfight.

▶ [or] ~~The reason for his decision to make a visit~~ *He went* to Spain ~~was his desire~~ to see a bullfight.

INVIGORATING YOUR STYLE: IN BRIEF

Vary the length and structure of your sentences (25.1):

> I was used to binoculars but not, apparently, to balancing on humped rocks while looking through them.
> I reeled.
> —Annie Dillard

Use verbs of action instead of *be* (25.2):

> Sheila won the nomination.

Use the active voice as much as possible (25.3).

Ask questions (25.4):

> What on earth is *our* common goal? How did we ever get mixed up in a place like this?
> —Lewis Thomas

Cut any words you don't need (25.5):

> ~~The reason for his decision to make a visit~~ *He went* to Spain ~~was his desire~~ to see a bullfight.

EXERCISE REWRITING TO INVIGORATE STYLE

Using verbs of action and the active voice as much as possible, asking at least one question, cutting all unneeded words, and varying the length and structure of your sentences, rewrite each of the following paragraphs to invigorate its style.

1. Mr. and Mrs. Ault were once the owners of Frederick Douglass. They were residents of Baltimore. At this time Frederick learned to read. He asked Mrs. Ault to help him learn. He felt safe in doing so. She thought of him more as a child than as a slave. Those of course were not the only 5 alternatives. She could have seen him as a man. But at least he was more in her eyes than a piece of property. His request would have been a shock to other slaveholders. He would have been thrashed just for making it. But Mrs. Ault was not shocked by it. She was willing to help. Under her 10 care the alphabet was learned by Frederick. He began to read simple verses in the Bible. Then there was intervention by Mr. Ault. He forbade his wife to continue the lessons. He believed that learning would be the ruin of Frederick as a slave. But fortunately Frederick had learned enough to 15 teach himself more. Soon he became an excellent reader.

2. The French culture is greatly respected by the French. No other culture, in their opinion, is even close to theirs in value, worth, or overall quality. And they want to keep things that way. Strenuous efforts are made to be sure there is protection against a loss of excellence from contamina- 5 tion. One of the greatest fears is the fear of words which are a threat to come into the country from American English. According to the defenders of French culture, it is a fact that a purity of the French language will be tainted if words used by the uncouth speakers of the American tongue are 10 uttered by French men and women. Since 1945 many important electronic machines have been made by Ameri-cans, and given American English names. The computer is one such machine, and *computer* has become an important, widely used word in American society along with many 15 other related words. Among the French, however, there has been no willingness to use these American words, so French words have been created. A computer is called an *ordinateur,*

software is called *le logiciel,* and data processing is called *l'informatique.* For the guardians of French culture, there must be a French sound to the words that are spoken and written by them.

3. Critics of detective stories have three complaints. First, there is too much senseless violence. Lots of characters are killed. Others are badly beaten. In *The Lonely Silver Rain* by John D. MacDonald over twenty people are killed. The violence and deaths are not "senseless," however. A purpose is served by them. Clues are furnished to the detective. Second, detective stories are said to be filled with old, lifeless plots. The age of the plots is a problem, but a youthful vitality is usually imparted to them by writing which is conducive to a dramatic effect with regard to both places and characters. Interiors are described in vivid detail by Rex Stout. In the dialogues of Ed McBain, the words spoken by his characters sound just like the words of real people. This vitality is ignored by critics. They have a third complaint. The detectives, they say, are cardboard cutouts. The characters are likened to wooden statues. In reality, fictional detectives are like real human beings. There are real problems in their lives. Agatha Christie's Hercule Poirot is faced with the problem of being an old man. A failed marriage is a haunting memory in the mind of Ross MacDonald's Lew Archer. There is almost no end to the examples. So it may be asked whether the critics ever read the stories they criticize.

4. In the modern city there is no safety for decent people. They are in a situation of continual exposure to crime. But it is my belief that a solution to this problem is attainable. The solution may sound strange, even crazy. New ideas often sound that way. Here is my proposal. Criminals and law-abiding city dwellers must switch places—literally. Criminals should be released from prison. They will live in the perilous freedom of our cities. They will become victims of their own robberies, muggings, and killings. Eventually self-destruction will result. Meanwhile the prisons will be remodeled for all decent people. A cell will be allotted to each single person. Families will be housed in multicell units. With regard to those who prefer to live in

solitude, applications for solitary confinement may be sub-
mitted on a first-come, first-served basis. Food and medical 15
services will be available for the inmates. Educational pro-
grams will be broadcast to large TV screens in every cell.
For entertainment there will be block parties. There will be
games for children to play. Dances for adults will be
arranged. At the end a movie will be shown. It will be 20
about the bad old days. It will be a reminder of the dangers
before the big switch.

5. In "The American Scholar" the wise use of books is dis-
cussed by Emerson. Unwise uses are also considered. The
use is unwise, Emerson says, when the contents of books
are taken as final truth by readers. They are deficient in
their ability to see something. Truth in one period of time 5
is not necessarily truth at a later time. There is another
problem. Mistakes are made by authors. What is said in a
book may be false to begin with. There is another unwise
use. Some readers become bookworms. They enter the
paper and binding of a book. No thought is given to its 10
contents. But the behavior of wise readers is different.
Emerson says that books can be studied by the wise reader
for knowledge of history. They are also a source of scientific
facts that can be absorbed. There is an additional good use.
Inspiration can be gained from books. If books are used 15
properly, they can be wonderful instruments for readers.

3

PUNCTUATION AND MECHANICS

The Comma

26.1 USING COMMAS WITH CONJUNCTIONS

1. Use a comma before a conjunction (*and, but, for, or, nor, so, yet*) linking two independent clauses:

> Canadians watch America closely, *but* most Americans know little about Canada.
>
> The prospectors hoped to find gold on the rocky slopes of the Sierra Madre, *so* they set out eagerly.
>
> Cowards never started on the long trek west, *and* the weak died along the way.

2. Use a comma before a conjunction linking the last two items in a series:

> She loved life, liberty, and the happiness of being pursued.

For more on conjunctions, see sections 13.2 and 13.3. For more on punctuating items in a series, see section 26.7.

26.2 MISUSING COMMAS WITH CONJUNCTIONS ⊙ *conj*

1. Do not use a comma before a conjunction within a series of just two items:

▶ The manager was genial⁄ but shrewd.

▶ She checked my weekly sales⁄ and asked to speak with me.

EXCEPTION: You may use a comma to set off a contrasting phrase:

> She liked running her own business, but not working on week-ends.

2. Do not use a comma after a conjunction:

▶ The speaker coughed, studied his notes, and, frowned.

▶ He was scheduled to discuss Rembrandt. But, the notes treated the etchings of Picasso.

EXCEPTION: Use a pair of commas after a conjunction to set off a word, phrase, or clause:

> But, he sadly realized, the notes treated the etchings of Picasso.

26.3 MISUSING COMMAS BETWEEN INDEPENDENT CLAUSES: THE COMMA SPLICE (,) *cs*

Do not use a comma alone between two independent clauses:

▶ The beams have rotted, they can no longer support the roof.

▶ [or] The beams have rotted, they can no longer support the roof.

▶ [or] The beams have rotted, they can no longer support the roof.

For a full discussion of the comma splice, see section 13.6.

> ### EXERCISE 1 USING COMMAS WITH CONJUNCTIONS
>
> Each of the following may require the addition or removal or moving of a comma. Make any changes necessary. If an entry is correct as it stands, write *Correct*.
>
> EXAMPLE
>
> We can stop for the night in Moose Jaw, or we can push on.

1. Odysseus longs to return to his home on the island of Ithaca but he does not reach it for ten years.

2. He blinds the son of the sea-god Poseidon so, he must endure Poseidon's avenging wrath.

3. Poseidon's son is a one-eyed giant named Polyphemus and he lives alone in a cave with herds of sheep, and goats.

4. Odysseus enters the cave with his men one day, for, he expects to find hospitality there.

5. Instead the giant blocks the exit with a massive stone, eats two of Odysseus's men, and threatens to devour the rest.

6. Odysseus and his men seem doomed but, Odysseus blinds the giant, and escapes with his men.

7. They escape by hiding under the bellies of rams for the giant does not see the men when he lets his herds out of the cave.

8. Odysseus then recklessly shouts his name to the giant so, the giant asks Poseidon to make Odysseus's homecoming as painful as possible.

26.4 USING COMMAS AFTER INTRODUCTORY ELEMENTS

1. Use a comma after an introductory clause, phrase, or word:

Whenever it rains hard, the roof leaks.

To stop the leak, we have been replacing old shingles with new ones.

Unfortunately, last night's thunderstorm showed us that we still have more work to do.

2. Use a comma after a conjunctive adverb at the beginning of a sentence or clause:

The kitchen was drenched; *in fact,* an inch of water covered the floor.

Nevertheless, the living room remained dry.

For more on conjunctive adverbs, see sections 13.5, 13.5A, and 13.5B.

26.4

EXCEPTION: To accelerate the pace of their sentences, writers sometimes skip the comma after an introductory adverb or short introductory phrase:

> Today students protest individually rather than in concert.
>
> —Caroline Bird

> Throughout the 1930s the number of addicts remained about the same in both England and the United States.
>
> —Edward Bunker

EXERCISE 2 USING COMMAS AFTER INTRODUCTORY ELEMENTS

Each of the following may require a comma after an introductory element. Add a comma if needed. If the sentence is correct as it stands, write *Correct*.

EXAMPLE

Furthermore⌃ an increase in property taxes would severely limit the number of young adults who could live here.

1. After Odysseus and his men escape from the giant's cave they sail to the island of Aeolus, god of winds.
2. From Aeolus Odysseus gets a bag of winds that is supposed to ensure his safe return to Ithaca.
3. Having sailed for nine days Odysseus and his men actually catch sight of Ithaca; nevertheless they are swept away by a storm when the men foolishly open the bag.
4. As a result they must sail on to further adventures.
5. On the island of Aiaia they find an enchantress named Circe.
6. When a group of Odysseus's men go to see her she turns them into pigs.
7. On learning of their fate Odysseus decides to see her for himself.
8. His remaining companions are terrified; in fact they fear that he will never return.

9. Fortunately he obtains a magic potion from Hermes.

10. With the aid of that, he withstands Circe's magic and persuades her to change the pigs back into men.

26.5   USING COMMAS WITH NONRESTRICTIVE ELEMENTS

Use a comma or a pair of commas to set off **nonrestrictive** elements: words, phrases, and clauses that are not essential to the meaning of the sentences in which they appear. Compare these two sentences:

Anyone *who publishes a book at the age of six* must be remarkable. (restrictive)

Dorothy Straight of Washington, D.C., *who published her first book at the age of six,* was a remarkable child. (nonrestrictive)

In the first sentence, the *who* clause is essential to the meaning of the sentence because it restricts the meaning of *Anyone* to a certain person. The clause tells *which one* is remarkable. In the second sentence, the *who* clause is nonrestrictive and nonessential because it does not identify *Dorothy Straight*. She has already been identified by her name.

Now compare these two sentences:

At the microphone stood a man *wearing a green suit.* (restrictive)

At the microphone stood the master of ceremonies, *wearing a green suit.* (nonrestrictive)

In the first sentence, the italicized phrase is restrictive because it identifies *a man*. In the second sentence, the italicized phrase is nonrestrictive because the man has already been identified by his title. The italicized phrase just adds further information about him.

The distinction between restrictive and nonrestrictive is commonly applied to adjective clauses, such as *who publishes a book at the age of six,* and participle phrases, such as *wearing a green suit.* Broadly speaking, however, nonrestrictive elements include any-

thing that supplements the basic meaning of the sentence, anything not essential to that meaning. Here are further examples:

> The surgeon, *her hands moving deftly,* probed the wound.
> Fearful, *not confident,* he embarked on his journey.
> At midnight, *long after the final out of the game,* the losing man-
> ager was still shaking his head in disbelief.
> In October of 1987, *however,* stock prices plummeted.

A single comma sets off a nonrestrictive element that comes at
the end of the sentence:

> The tour includes three days in Toronto, *which must be one of
> the cleanest cities in the world.*
> Celia stood in the wings, *waiting for her cue.*

26.6 MISUSING COMMAS WITH RESTRICTIVE ELEMENTS   ⊙ *res*

Do not use commas with restrictive elements: with words,
phrases, or clauses essential to the meaning of the sentences in
which they appear:

> ► All entries⁄ postmarked later than July 1⁄ will be discounted.

> ► Plants⁄ that aren't watered⁄ will die.

(Adjective clauses starting with *that* are always restrictive.)

> ► No one⁄ without a ticket⁄ will be admitted.

> ► Film director⁄ François Truffaut⁄ died of cancer in 1984.

A name that follows a common noun or noun phrase is
restrictive and should not be set off by commas. But when the
name comes first, the common noun that follows it is nonrestrictive and should be set off by commas:

> François Truffaut, *the film director,* died of cancer in 1984.

EXERCISE 3 PUNCTUATING RESTRICTIVE AND
NONRESTRICTIVE ELEMENTS

Decide whether each of the italicized elements is restrictive or
nonrestrictive, and add or remove commas where necessary. If
a sentence is correct as it stands, write *Correct*.

EXAMPLE

All motorists, *who drive recklessly,* should have their licenses
suspended for six months.
DECISION: restrictive.
EDITED: All motorists who drive recklessly should have their
licenses suspended for six months.

1. My brother's car *a 1979 Ford Fiesta* looks like a gooey red
   marshmallow.

2. The interior *which has never been cleaned* is sticky with
   grime.

3. Nobody could close the front ashtray *which is stuffed with
   bottle caps, Kleenex tissues, and wads of chewing gum.*

4. The dashboard, another disaster area, has all but disap-
   peared beneath the dust *that has built up over the months.*

5. The speedometer is barely visible, and it's impossible for
   anyone, *with normal vision,* to read the fuel gauge.

6. The driver's seat *which is covered with a piece of worn vinyl*
   smells like a loaf of moldy bread.

7. The exterior *with its layers of grime, rust spots, and dents*
   looks no better than the inside.

8. The rear window *lacking a windshield wiper* looks like one
   of those gray boards, that *collect dust in the corners of old
   barns.*

9. The front windshield *on the other hand* has a clear spot,
   made by an ice scraper.

10. For the past month, my brother has been looking for a
    used-car dealer, *who will take the car off his hands without
    charging him.*

11. He's not sure, though, whether he'll find a dealer who
    wants a car, *that stands little chance of ever being sold.*

26.7 USING COMMAS WITH COORDINATE ITEMS IN A SERIES

1. Use commas to separate three or more coordinate items in a series:

> Maples, oaks, and sycamores have been afflicted.
> The leaves shrivel, wither, and fall to the ground before autumn.
> Scientists are seeking to learn what is causing the blight, how it enters the trees, and whether it can be halted.

2. Use commas to separate two or more coordinate adjectives modifying the same noun:

> A big, old, dilapidated house stood on the corner.
> Its owner always spoke in a low, husky voice.

For more help with punctuating items in a series, see section 26.1, item 2.

26.8 MISUSING COMMAS WITH COORDINATE ITEMS IN A SERIES   ⟨ , ⟩ *ser*

1. Do not use a comma to separate adjectives when they are not coordinate—that is, when they do not modify the same word:

> ▶ His deep̸ blue eyes stared at me.

Deep modifies *blue; blue* modifies *eyes.* Coordinate adjectives can be reversed. A *low, husky* voice can become a *husky, low* voice. But *deep blue* eyes cannot become *blue deep* eyes.

2. Do not use a comma before a conjunction when there are just two items:

> ▶ Her hair was black̸ and long.

(For an exception, see section 26.2, item 1.)

EXERCISE 4   USING COMMAS WITH ITEMS IN A SERIES

Each of the following may require the addition or removal of a comma or commas. Make the necessary changes. If an entry is correct as it stands, write *Correct*.

EXAMPLE

Under the circumstances, only an intelligent, discreet, and experienced official should be assigned to the case.

1. Last summer my brother, my father, and, I visited a busy, logging camp in a rugged, picturesque, largely uninhabited part of Maine.

2. From dawn to dusk, hardy skilled lumberjacks felled trees, cut them into logs, and cleared the thick, green underbrush.

3. Our guide was a slow-moving infirm old man with dark brown eyes; but he could still repair broken, or sputtering chain saws.

4. Dressed in his bright, red, flannel jacket, he had a sturdy, workbench in a pleasant, shaded area next to the large, equipment shed.

5. Inside the shed were various things, including coils of thick heavy rope, stacks of wooden, axe handles, and bright, yellow, slickers for rainy days.

6. Our guide's worn, carpenter's chest contained pliers, screwdrivers with hard, rubber handles, a set of galvanized, steel, wrenches, two copper oil cans, and bolts of many different sizes.

7. Carefully expertly, and patiently he worked on each, broken chain saw until its motor coughed, wheezed, and sputtered into life.

8. Then, with a deft, and clever adjustment of the carburetor, he would soon have the motor purring like a cat stretched out before a warm cozy fire.

9. My father, my brother and I wondered how many kinds of discarded appliances might be thus revived, and saved from the trash can, and the dump.

26.10

26.9 USING COMMAS TO PREVENT A MISREADING

Use a comma when you need one to prevent a misreading of your sentence:

▶ On the left, walls of sheer ice rose over five thousand feet into the clouds.

26.10 USING COMMAS WITH DATES, ADDRESSES, GREETINGS, NAMES, AND LARGE NUMBERS

1. Use commas to set off parts of dates and addresses that appear within a sentence:

On the afternoon of July 1, 1963, the fighting began.
The return address on the letter was 23 Hockey Street, Lexington, Kentucky 40502.

EXCEPTION: Use no comma to separate parts of a date that begins with the day:

The atomic bomb was first dropped on 6 August 1945.

2. Use commas to set off the names of someone directly addressed in a sentence:

A few weeks ago, Mr. Taplow, I spoke to you on the telephone about the possibility of a summer job.

3. Use a comma after the greeting in a friendly or informal letter, and after the closing in a letter of any kind:

Dear Mary,   Sincerely,
Dear Uncle Paul,   Yours truly,

4. Use commas to set off titles or degrees after a person's name:

Barbara Kane, M.D., delivered the commencement address.

But *Jr., Sr.,* and *III* may be written without commas:

Sammy Davis Jr. started his singing career at age four.

5. Use a comma after the last part of a proper name when the last part comes first:

> Lunt, George D.

6. Use commas to mark groups of three digits in large numbers, counting from the right:

> Antarctica is 5,400,000 square miles of ice-covered land.

26.11 MISUSING COMMAS WITH DATES AND ADDRESSES (,) d/a

1. Do not use a comma to separate the name of the month from the day:

> ▶ October/ 22   ▶ 15/ May

2. Do not use a comma to separate the name of the month from the year:

> ▶ January/ 1988   ▶ 22 April/ 1939

3. Do not use a comma to separate a street number from the name of the street:

> ▶ 15/ Amsterdam Avenue

4. Do not use a comma before a zip code or anywhere else in an address that is written out on an envelope:

> ▶ 24 Mechanic Street   ▶ 35 Rosemount Avenue
>
>   Lebanon/ NH/ 03766   Montreal/ Que./ H3Y3G6
>
>   Canada

(On the abbreviations used here, see section 32.4.)

26.12 USING COMMAS WITH QUOTATION MARKS

For a full discussion of how to use commas with quotation marks, see section 29.3.

USING COMMAS: IN BRIEF

Generally, use a comma before a conjunction linking independent clauses (26.1):

> Canadians watch America closely, *but* most Americans know little about Canada.

Generally, do not use a comma after a conjunction (26.2):

> The speaker coughed, studied his notes, and / frowned.

Do not use a comma alone between two independent clauses (26.3):

> The beams have rotted / they can no longer support the roof.

Generally, use commas after an introductory item (26.4):

> Whenever it rains hard, the roof leaks.
> Unfortunately, we haven't yet fixed it.

Use commas with nonrestrictive elements (26.5):

> Dorothy Straight of Washington, D.C., *who published her first book at the age of six,* was a remarkable child.

Do not use commas with restrictive elements (26.6):

> Anyone, / who publishes a book at the age of six, / must be remarkable.

Generally, use commas to separate three or more coordinate items in a series (26.7):

> We played cards, told stories, and sang old songs.

26.13   MISUSING THE COMMA BETWEEN BASIC PARTS OF A SENTENCE   ⊙ *bp*

1. Do not use a comma between a subject and its predicate:

▶ In August, all the members of the Johnson clan/ gathered for

their annual picnic.

EXCEPTION: Use a *pair* of commas to set off a phrase or clause that comes between the subject and the predicate:

> In August, all the members of the Johnson clan, from little Susie to ancient Winona, gathered for their annual picnic.

2. Do not use a comma between a verb and its object:

▶ Altogether we ate/ forty hamburgers and six big watermelons.

▶ I don't know/ how many ears of corn we consumed.

EXERCISE 5   EDITING COMMAS—A REVIEW

In the following passage from Peter M. Lincoln's "Documentary Wallpapers," we have deliberately introduced some errors in punctuation. Remove all misused commas, add any that are needed, and leave any that are correctly used.

Many early American homes, were decorated with block-printed wallpapers. Imported from England, and France, the papers made the arrival of ships from abroad an exciting event for Colonial homemakers. Merchants, looking for sales, advertised that papering was cheaper than whitewashing, and, they   5
urged would-be customers to examine the endless variety of brightly colored patterns. Indeed by today's standards the colors in many Colonial papers seem vibrant, intense, and, even gaudy. One wonders whether the citizens of Boston Massachusetts and Providence Rhode Island, yearned for bright reds,   10
greens, and, blues because of the grey, New England winters.
     The process of reproducing historic wallpapers, requires

the finesse of a craftsman. To establish a particular paper's full pattern, the expert may have to fit together the fragments of surviving samples, that he finds in museums in the attics of old houses and even under layers of other papers. He determines the original hue of the colors in various ways: he runs chemical tests, or, he matches a fragment to a fresh original in some museum, even then he must be careful before proceeding to the next step printing the design. As a final precaution therefore he makes, a blacklight examination knowing it may reveal otherwise indistinguishable elements of the pattern.

One of the leading experts in America is Dorothy Waterhouse cofounder of Waterhouse Hangings. She first became interested in historic wallpapers in 1932 when she was restoring, an old house on Cape Cod Massachusetts. While stripping the walls in one room she got down to the eighth, and bottom layer of paper. She became very excited, she knew it had to be over 140 years old. That discovery was the first of many. Today she has a collection of some three hundred historic wallpapers, all carefully stored in her Boston home.

The Semicolon and the Colon

27.1 USING THE SEMICOLON ;

1. You may use a semicolon to join two independent clauses that are closely related in meaning:

> Insist on yourself; never imitate.   —Ralph Waldo Emerson

2. You may use a semicolon to join two independent clauses when the second begins with or includes a conjunctive adverb:

> Shakespeare's plays are four hundred years old; nevertheless, they still speak to us.
>
> Many of his characters resemble people we encounter or read about daily; a few, in fact, remind us of ourselves.

For more on semicolons and conjunctive adverbs, see section 13.5.

3. You may use a semicolon before a conjunction to join two independent clauses that contain commas:

> By laughing at our faults, we can learn to acknowledge them graciously; and we can try to overcome them in a positive, even cheerful way, not grimly and disagreeably.

4. Use semicolons to emphasize the division between items that include commas:

> There were three new delegates at the meeting: Ms. Barbara Smith from Boulder, Colorado; Ms. Beth Waters from Omaha, Nebraska; and Mr. James Papson from Greenwood, Arkansas.

27.2 MISUSING THE SEMICOLON   (;)

1. Do not use a semicolon between a phrase and the clause to which it belongs:

▶ The climbers carried an extra nylon rope, to ensure their safe descent from the cliff.

2. Do not use a semicolon between a subordinate clause and the main clause:

▶ Most of the crowd had left, before the concert ended.

▶ Although the hall was almost empty, she came out for a second bow.

▶ Ticket sales had been good, which made both her agent and her manager happy.

3. Do not use a semicolon to introduce a list. Use a colon:

▶ The prophets denounced three types of wrongdoing: idolatry, injustice, and neglect of the needy.

For more on colons, see the next section.

EXERCISE 1 USING SEMICOLONS

Each of the following requires the addition or removal of one or more semicolons. Make any necessary changes, adding other punctuation if necessary.

EXAMPLE

Some people give**;** others take.

1. The Gateway Arch in St. Louis symbolizes opportunity, in particular, it represents the soaring aspirations of America's pioneers; who ventured into unknown lands throughout the nineteenth century.
2. The pioneers consisted of many subgroups: New England farmers seeking richer soil, immigrants fleeing a nation's slums, shy trappers from the north; lusty mountain men, failed merchants, and adventurers with an eye for danger.
3. For all of these people St. Louis was a gateway, it was the entrance to a new and prosperous life somewhere beyond the Mississippi River.
4. Few of the pioneers realized how difficult their new lives would be, on the contrary, they thought of the west as a vast land flowing with milk and honey.
5. They would live high on the hog they would live like kings and queens.

27.3 USING THE COLON   :

1. Use a colon after an independent clause to introduce a list:

   Success depends on three things: talent, determination, and luck.

2. Use a colon to introduce an example or an explanation related to something just mentioned:

   The animals have a good many of our practical skills: some insects make pretty fair architects, and beavers know quite a lot about engineering.   —Northrop Frye

27.4

3. Use a colon to introduce one or more complete sentences quoted from formal speech or writing:

> In the opening sentence of his novel *Scaramouche,* Rafael Sabatini says of his hero: "He was born with the gift of laughter, and a sense that the world was mad."

4. Use a colon to follow the salutation in a formal letter:

> Dear Mr. Mayor:
> Dear Ms. Watson:
> To Whom It May Concern:

5. Use a colon to separate hours from minutes when the time of day is shown in numerals:

> 8:40   6:30   11:15

27.4 Misusing the Colon

1. Do not use a colon after *such as, including,* or a form of the verb *be:*

▶ On rainy days at camp, we played board games such as:/ Monopoly, Scrabble, and Trivial Pursuit.

▶ One morning I woke up to find that someone had taken all of my valuables, including:/ my watch, my camera, and my money.

▶ Still in my locker were:/ my toilet kit, my flashlight, and my wallet—now empty.

2. Do not use a colon between a verb and its object or between a preposition and its object:

▶ Before heading home, we stopped at:/ the supermarket, the hardware store, and the gas station.

▶ We needed:/ pasta, a window screen, and a tank of gasoline.

EXERCISE 2 USING SEMICOLONS AND COLONS

In the following passage from Ismene Phylactopoulou's "Greek Easter," we have deliberately removed some of the author's punctuation. Add a semicolon or a colon wherever necessary.

EXAMPLE
line 1: 10:00

The events on Good Friday are tragic. At 10 00 a grim-looking priest conducts a solemn service Christ is removed from the Cross and placed in a tomb. All work ceases flags fly at half mast. Soldiers carry their rifles reversed as they do during funeral processions. Offices and shops close everyone goes to church. The church bells will toll all day long. After the service the young girls of the parish perform a bitter-sweet task they decorate the bier of Jesus with flowers from 11 00 to 1 00. By that time it is a mass of flowers.

Lunch consists of simple fare boiled lentils, which represent the tears of the Virgin, and vinegar, which represents the vinegar given to Christ on the Cross.

On Friday evening the church is filled to overflowing. All in the city are present old men and women, officials, husbands and wives, children. The songs of mourning are lovely in their sadness for example, in one of them Mary refers to her dead son as a child who was as sweet as spring. After the service, which usually ends at 9 00, a kind of funeral procession takes place. It follows a definite order first comes a band playing a funeral march next comes a priest carrying the Cross then comes the bier accompanied by girls in white, the Boy Scouts, and a detachment of soldiers then come the other priests. The people follow, each one carrying a brown candle. The gathering has spiritual meaning. It is also deeply human.

End Marks

28.1 USING THE PERIOD

1. Use a period to mark the end of a declarative sentence, a mild command, or an indirect question:

> The days are growing shorter, and the nights are becoming cool.
>
> On some mornings a hint of frost chills the air.
>
> Nature is proceeding at her accustomed pace.
>
> Note her ways closely.
>
> I wonder what she will do next.

When typing, skip two spaces after the period before beginning the next sentence.

2. Use a period to mark the end of some abbreviations:

> Dr. Boyle
> 500 Fifth Ave.
> Kate Fansler, Ph.D.
> Mr. G. H. Johnson
> Mrs. L. S. Allingham
> Ms. N. A. Stephens
> 3:28 P.M.
> 350 B.C.

Generally, you don't need periods with acronyms (words formed from the initials of a multiword title), with capital-letter abbre-

viations of technical terms, or with abbreviated names of states, agencies, and organizations:

CBS	ROTC	IBM
NATO	TVA	IQ
FM	ID	KP
NY	CIA	VISTA

But you do need periods with abbreviations standing for the names of political entities:

U.S.A.   U.K.   C.I.S.

For guidance, see your dictionary.

3. Use a period to mark letters or numerals used in vertical lists:

> Woven into the history of the human race is the history of its four great religions:
>   1. Buddhism
>   2. Judaism
>   3. Christianity
>   4. Islam

If you give the information in a sentence, enclose the letters or numbers within parentheses and omit the periods:

> Woven into the history of the world is the history of its four great religions: (1) Buddhism, (2) Judaism, (3) Christianity, and (4) Islam.

28.2 MISUSING THE PERIOD

1. In formal writing, do not use a period to separate the different parts of a sentence. If you do, you will create a sentence fragment:

▶ Customers should be treated courteously, ~~Even~~ *even* if they are extremely rude.

For more on sentence fragments, see chapter 17.

2. Do not use a period after another period or other end mark:

▶ To please our customers, we have ordered scarce materials from Home Supplies Company, Inc./

▶ We don't want customers saying, "Why don't you have what I want?"/

28.3 USING THE QUESTION MARK   ?

Use a question mark—

1. To mark the end of a direct question:

> Must the problems of farmers be ignored?
> To what agency can they go for legal aid?

2. To indicate uncertainty within a statement:

> Some exotic dish—pheasant under glass?—was served at the banquet.
> The host must have paid a lot of money (fifty dollars?) for each meal.

28.4 MISUSING THE QUESTION MARK   ⑦

Do not use a question mark at the end of a question reported indirectly:

▶ I wonder who wrote this song?/.

▶ She asked if I wanted more cheese?/.

For more on this topic, see section 24.4.

28.5 USING THE EXCLAMATION POINT   !

Use the exclamation point to mark an expression of strong feeling:

What a spectacular view!
Impossible!

Because exclamation points make a special appeal to the reader, you should use them sparingly.

> **EXERCISE** USING PERIODS AND QUESTION MARKS
>
> Improve the punctuation in the following paragraph by adding a period or question mark wherever necessary; also make any accompanying change in capitalization that may be required. As you make these corrections, write out the entire paragraph.
>
> How do historians rate the contributions of General Gordon to his country their opinions differ some consider him a military genius, one of the greatest soldiers in British history others criticize him severely in their opinion General C G Gordon, or "Chinese" Gordon as he was popularly known, acted   5
> impulsively he was rash he was dangerous he was not fit to hold a command did he seek death on January 26, 1885 historians give conflicting answers

Quotation Marks and Quoting

29.1 QUOTING WORDS, PHRASES, AND SHORT PASSAGES OF PROSE

Use double quotation marks (" ") to enclose any words, phrases, or short passages quoted from speech, writing, or printed matter:

> After the murder of the old king in Shakespeare's *Macbeth*, Lady Macbeth imagines there is blood on her hand and cries, "Out, damned spot!"
>
> "Look before you leap" is particularly good advice for divers.
>
> "An agnostic," writes Clarence Darrow, "is a doubter."

Quoted passages must normally be accompanied by tags identifying the speaker or writer; see sections 24.1A and B.

29.2 USING DOUBLE AND SINGLE QUOTATION MARKS

1. Use double quotation marks to enclose the words of speakers engaged in dialogue (conversation), and start a new paragraph each time the speaker changes:

> "How did the interview go?" Bob asked.
>
> "It's hard to say," said Helen. "At first I was nervous. Then I relaxed and spoke clearly. I began to enjoy myself."
>
> "Well, it sounds as if you might get the job. If you do, let's celebrate."

2. Use single quotation marks (' ') to enclose a quotation within a quotation:

> At the beginning of the class, the teacher asked, "Where does Thoreau speak of 'quiet desperation,' and what does he mean by this phrase?"

29.3 USING QUOTATION MARKS WITH OTHER PUNCTUATION

1. To introduce a quoted sentence with a phrase, use a comma:

> According to G. B. Shaw, "Economy is the art of making the most of life."

2. To introduce a quoted sentence with a clause, use a comma or colon:

> Winston Churchill said, "To jaw-jaw is always better than to war-war."

> In his first Inaugural Address, Lincoln asked: "Why should there not be a patient confidence in the ultimate justice of the people?"

> June Callwood writes, "Canadians are not Americans who live in a colder climate; they are different people."

Some writers use a comma after a short introductory clause and a colon after a long one. Other writers use a comma before quoting informal speech and a colon before quoting formal speech or writing.

3. Use quotation marks alone to introduce a quoted word or phrase or any quoted words introduced by *that:*

> According to Jung, the "something greater" is the unconscious, which he defines as "a natural phenomenon producing symbols that prove to be meaningful."

> The professor said Jung's theories have been "seminal."

> Margaret Atwood writes that "in fact, a character in a book who is consistently well-behaved probably spells disaster for the book."

4. To end a quoted statement that is followed by a tag, use a comma:

"It's time for you to leave," said Mimi.

But do not use the comma if the quoted sentence ends in a question mark or an exclamation point:

"What's your problem?" John asked.
"Get out!" she yelled.

The tag begins with a lowercase letter unless its first word is a proper name.

5. To set off an interruptive tag, use a pair of commas:

"Ideas," writes Carl Jung, "spring from something greater than the personal human being."

The word "spring" is lower-cased because it simply continues the quoted sentence.

6. To end a quoted statement that ends a sentence, use a period:

The governor stated, "I will not seek reelection."

7. A closing comma or period goes inside the closing quotation mark:

"High school," writes Ellen Willis, "permanently damaged my self-esteem."

8. A closing semicolon or colon goes outside the closing quotation mark:

The head of the union announced, "The new contract is a good one for management and labor"; then she left the room. Later she told reporters that the new contract "has major benefits for women": payment for overtime, maternity leave, and seniority privileges.

9. A quotation mark or an exclamation point that belongs to the quotation goes inside the closing quotation mark:

Who wrote, "What's in a name?"

> A new idea about the universe always prompts the scientist to ask, "What's the evidence for it?"
> Suddenly he bellowed, "Get out!"

10. A question mark or exclamation point that does not belong to the quotation goes outside the closing quotation mark:

> Should a 1 percent drop in unemployment be called "a decisive sign of recovery"?
> Though two hundred thousand workers have lost their jobs in the past year, one congressman calls the economy "robust"!

For advice on fitting quotations smoothly into your own sentences, see section 24.6.

29.4 QUOTING LONG PROSE PASSAGES

To quote more than four lines of prose, use indentation instead of quotation marks, and follow the format shown here:

```
Vicki Hearne invokes the idea of artistry to explain
why a horse is willing to jump a high fence:
            There are various ways to talk about what
        could possibly motivate a horse, or any
        animal, to such an effort. Fear certainly
        does not do it. Courage, joy, exaltation
        are more like it, but beyond that horses
        have, some of the time, a strong sense of
        artistry. . . . When I say artistry, I mean
        that the movements of a developed horse,
        the figures and leaps, mean something, and
        an artistic horse is one who is capable of
        wanting to mean the movements and the jump
        perfectly.  (43)
```

29.5

Keep the punctuation of the original. For use of the ellipsis dots, see section 29.6B. On citing sources at the end of quotations, see section 35.1A.

When quoting one or more paragraphs, follow this format:

> At the end of his Inaugural Address, John F. Kennedy
>
> declared:

<table>
<tr><td>Indent
13
spaces →</td><td>And so, my fellow Americans: ask not
what your country can do for you, ask what</td></tr>
<tr><td>Indent
10
spaces →</td><td>you can do for your country.
    My fellow citizens of the world: ask
not what America will do for you, but what
together we can do for the freedom of man.</td></tr>
</table>

29.5 QUOTING VERSE

1. Quotations of verse must look like verse, not prose. Keep all capital letters that you find at the beginning of lines, and if you quote more than a line, use a slash (/), with a space on each side, to show where one line ends and another begins:

> Elsewhere, Sylvia Plath writes: "Mother to myself, I
> wake swaddled in gauze, / Pink and smooth as a baby."
> This preoccupation with herself and her own body . . .

2. To quote more than three lines of verse, double-space them and indent each line ten spaces from the left margin:

> William Blake's "The Tyger" begins with the lines:
>
>   Tyger! Tyger! burning bright
>
>   In the forests of the night,
>
>   What immortal hand or eye
>
>   Could frame thy fearful symmetry?

If the lines are long, you may indent fewer than ten spaces. If a single line is long, let it run to the right-hand margin and put the overflow under the right-hand side:

```
Ruefully alluding to his own ill-fated marriage,

Byron rhetorically asks,

            I don't choose much to say upon this head

            I'm a plain man, and in a single station,

            But--Oh! ye lords of ladies intellectual,

            Inform us truly, have they not hen-peck'd

                                    you all?
```

For more on quoting verse, see section 35.2B, nos. 15–17.

29.6 USING BRACKETS AND ELLIPSIS DOTS TO MARK CHANGES IN A QUOTATION

To quote effectively, you must quote accurately, keeping every word of the original or plainly indicating any changes you have made. Use brackets to mark any words you have added, and ellipsis dots to show where you have left words out.

29.6A USING BRACKETS TO MARK WORDS ADDED TO A QUOTATION   [ ]

1. Use brackets to insert a clarifying detail, comment, or correction of your own into a quotation:

"In the presidential campaign of 1993 [1992], Bill Clinton defeated George Bush."

"When we last see Lady Macbeth [in the sleepwalking scene], she is obviously distraught."

"Most remarkably, the Motherhood Myth [the notion that having babies is instructive and enjoyable] persists in the face of the most overwhelming maternal unhappiness and incompetence."   —Betty Rollin

2. Use brackets to note a misspelling with the Latin word *sic* ("thus") or to correct the misspelling:

> "There were no pieces of strong [sic] around the boxes," one witness wrote.
>
> [or] "There were no pieces of strong [string] around the boxes," one witness wrote.

3. Do not use brackets when inserting comments into your own writing. Use parentheses or dashes. (See sections 30.1–30.3.)

29.6B USING ELLIPSIS DOTS (. . .) TO MARK WORDS LEFT OUT OF A QUOTATION

1. Use three spaced dots to signal the omission of a word or words from the middle of a quoted sentence:

> And so the writer . . . suffers, especially in the creative years of youth, every form of distraction and discouragement.
> —Virginia Woolf

In all cases, the material left out should be nonessential to the meaning of what is quoted. Here, for example, the words omitted are "Keats, Flaubert, and Carlyle."

In typing, leave one space before the first dot, between each pair of dots, and after the last one.

2. Use a period and three spaced dots:

a. To show that you are omitting the end of a quoted sentence:

> Thoreau wrote: "We must learn to reawaken and keep ourselves awake, not by mechanical aids, but by an infinite expectation of the dawn. . . ."

The period follows the last quoted word without a space, and the fourth dot comes before the closing quotation mark. Normally you may cut off the end of a quoted sentence in this way only if what remains makes a complete sentence.

b. To show that you have omitted one or more whole sentences:

> "In other words," as Percy Marks says, "the spirit of football is wrong. 'Win at any cost' is the slogan of most teams,

and the methods used to win are often abominable. . . . In nearly every scrimmage the roughest kind of unsportsmanlike play is indulged in, and the broken arms and ankles are often intentional rather than accidental."

3. Use an entire line of spaced dots to signal that a line (or more) of poetry has been omitted:

> Under the cooling shadow of a stately elm
> Close sat I by a goodly river's side,
> Where gliding streams the rocks did overwhelm;
>
> . . . .
>
> I once that loved the shady woods so well,
> Now thought the rivers did the trees excel.
> And if the sun would ever shine, there would I dwell.
>
> —Anne Bradstreet,
> "Contemplations," no. 21

29.7 SPECIAL USES OF QUOTATION MARKS

1. Use quotation marks to enclose certain titles, as explained in section 32.3.

2. Use quotation marks to define words:

> As a verb, *censure* generally means "find fault with" or "reprimand."

3. Use quotation marks to set off common words and phrases that you don't take at face value:

> When a man and woman decide to live together without being married, are they "living in sin"?

4. Use quotation marks to identify a word that you are treating as a word:

> In the America of the 1990s the word "liberal" has become a political insult.

You may also use italics or underlining for this purpose, as explained in section 32.2, no. 2, and as shown in no. 2, above.

29.8 MISUSING QUOTATION MARKS (" ")

1. Do not use quotation marks in the indirect reporting of discourse:

▶ The lieutenant said that /her platoon had finished ahead of schedule./

▶ Clients are asking /when the rates will go down./

For more on the indirect reporting of discourse, see sections 24.2 and 24.4.

2. Do not use quotation marks for emphasis:

*Joe's restaurant serves "fresh" seafood.

Quotation marks used in this way cast doubt on the truth of the word or words they enclose.

EXERCISE   PUNCTUATING WITH QUOTATION MARKS

Use quotation marks and any other punctuation needed in the following sentences.

EXAMPLE

"
We are all strong enough, wrote La Rochefoucauld, to
endure the misfortunes of others."

1. What writer asked, Who has deceived thee so oft as thyself

2. Did Ambrose Bierce define a bore as a person who talks when you wish him to listen.

3. Alexander Pope wrote, True wit is nature to advantage dressed, What oft was thought, but ne'er so well expressed

4. The history of the earth says Rachel Carson has been a history of interaction between living things and their surroundings.

5. *Continual* means going on with occasional slight interruptions. *Continuous* means going on with no interruption.

6. Perhaps the poet John Donne was right when he wrote: One short sleep past, we wake eternally / And Death shall be no more.

7. My roommate torments me by repeating trite sayings like better safe than sorry.

8. "This song, which was composed by Bailey in 1928 1930, reflects the influences of his five years in New Orleans." [The second date represents your correction of a mistake in a sentence written by someone else.]

9. "The most popular recording of the song featured Bix Dandy on the trumpit trumpet." [The second spelling represents your correction of a misspelling in a passage written by someone else.]

10. [The following sentence has been taken from George Orwell's "Politics and the English Language." Using ellipsis dots to mark the omission of words we have italicized, copy the sentence.] "Each of these passages has faults of its own, but, *quite apart from avoidable ugliness,* two qualities are common to all of them."

11. [The following sentences appear near the start of Orwell's essay. Select two successive sentences to copy, using ellipsis dots to mark the omission of words from the end of the first sentence you copy.] "Now, it is clear that the decline of a language must ultimately have political and economic causes; it is not due simply to the bad influence of this or that individual writer. But an effect can become a cause, reinforcing the original cause and producing the same effect in an intensified form, and so on indefinitely. A man may take to drink because he feels himself to be a failure, and then fail all the more completely because he drinks. It is rather the same thing that is happening to the English language."

30

The Dash, Parentheses, the Slash

30.1 USING THE DASH   —

1. Use a dash to introduce a word, phrase, or clause that summarizes or restates what comes just before:

> Terns, geese, and warblers—all migratory birds—fly hundreds of miles each year.
> But ideas—that is, opinions backed with genuine reasoning—are extremely difficult to develop.   —Wayne Booth

2. Use a dash to set off an interruption that is important to the meaning of the sentence but not grammatically part of it:

> It matters not where or how far you travel—the farther commonly the worse—but how much alive you are.
>
> —Henry David Thoreau

Less important interruptions may be set off by parentheses (as explained in section 30.3).

3. Use dashes to set off a series of specific items:

> The wings of the natural extant flying vertebrates—the birds and the bats—are direct modifications of the preexisting front limbs.   —Michael J. Katz

4. Use a dash in dialogue to indicate an unfinished remark:

> "You wouldn't dare to—" Mabel gasped in disbelief.
> "But I would," he said. "In fact, I—"
> "No!" she screamed.

When the dash is used to indicate an unfinished remark, it should be followed only by quotation marks, not by a comma or period.

5. If dashes set off a parenthetical remark that asks a question or makes an exclamation, put the question mark or the exclamation point before the second dash:

> During the American bicentennial of 1976, Canada's gift to the United States was a book of superb photographs of—what else?—scenery.   —June Callwood

6. In typing, make a dash with two hyphens (--) and leave no space on either side.

30.2 MISUSING THE DASH

The main misuse is overuse. Too many dashes can make your writing seem breathless or fragmented:

> Merryl's new designs look stunning—do they ever look otherwise?—with their bold colors and daring lines. She was cheered by all of the regulars—the regular staff, that is—who work in the art department. One of them—I think it was Harry—did a cartwheel—what a surprise that was!—and then shrieked till he was blue in the face. I thought Merryl would die of blushing—she's really modest, you know.

30.3 USING PARENTHESES   ( )

1. Use parentheses to enclose words, phrases, or complete sentences that offer a side comment or help to clarify a point:

> All this does not mean, what I should be the last man in the world to mean, that revolutionists should be ashamed of being revolutionists or (still more disgusting thought) that artists should be content with being artists.   —G. K. Chesterton

> Why would parents want to go to such expense (treatment with biosynthetic hGH costs roughly $10,000 a year), cause their children pain (the shots hurt a bit), and risk unknown long-term side effects?   —Thomas Murray

Parentheses placed *within* a sentence do not change any other punctuation, and a parenthesized sentence within a sentence (such as *the shots hurt a bit*) does not need a capital or a period. But a freestanding parenthetical sentence needs both:

> No Allied leader would have flinched at assassinating Hitler, had that been possible. (The Allies did assassinate Heydrich.)
> —Michael Levin

2. Use parentheses to enclose numerals or letters introducing the items of a list:

> Motherhood is in trouble, and it ought to be. A rude question is long overdue: Who needs it? The answer used to be (1) society and (2) women.
> —Betty Rollin

3. Use parentheses to enclose numerals clarifying or confirming a spelled-out number:

> The law permits individuals to give no more than one thousand dollars ($1,000) to any one candidate in a campaign.

Like material put between dashes, a parenthetical insertion interrupts the flow of a sentence. Parentheses make the interruption less emphatic than dashes do, but since they do in fact break up the sentence, you should use them sparingly.

30.4 USING THE SLASH   /

1. Use a slash, or virgule, to indicate alternative items:

> Every writer needs to know at least something about his/her audience.

Leave no space before or after a slash used in this way.

2. Use a slash to mark off lines of poetry when you run them on as if they were prose:

> Coleridge introduces the mariner in the very first stanza: "It is an ancient Mariner, / And he stoppeth one of three."

Leave one space before and after a slash used in this way.

3. Use a slash in typing a fraction that is not on the keyboard of your typewriter or computer:

2 1/2   5 7/8   15/16

> **EXERCISE   USING THE DASH, PARENTHESES, AND THE SLASH**
>
> Each of the following requires a dash or dashes, parentheses, or a slash. Using the comment in brackets as a guide, add the appropriate punctuation.
>
> EXAMPLE
>
>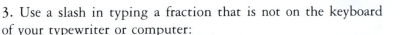
>
> The asking price for the clock a whopping $500,000 has not deterred some collectors from attending the auction. [The explanatory phrase is important to the meaning of the sentence.]
>
> 1. Somalia officially the Somali Democratic Republic is a country of about five million 5,000,000 people located on the east coast of Africa just south of the Arabian Peninsula. [The numerals clarify the spelled-out numbers.]
>
> 2. The country is made up of dry but varying terrain, with coastal lowlands rising to an inland plateau that is generally about 3,000 feet 910 meters high and reaches to the highlands in the north and west. [Feet and meters are alternative units of measurement.]
>
> 3. Herding of animals they include camel, sheep, goats, and cattle is the chief occupation. [The interruption is important to the rest of the sentence.]
>
> 4. Somalia chiefly exports live animals, hides, skins, and clarified butter it is known as ghee. [The last words are relatively unimportant to the rest of the statement.]
>
> 5. Somali they constitute more than 80 percent of the population are Sunni Muslims, and Islam is the state religion. [The interruption contains important information.]
>
> 6. In the nineteenth century, the region now known as Somalia was colonized by Italy and Britain, which conquered Italian Somaliland in World War II; renamed

Somalia, the former colony gained full independence in 1960 it had already gained internal autonomy in 1956. [The last words are relatively unimportant to the rest of the statement.]

7. In 1969, an army coup engineered by Major General Muhammad Siyad Barre led to a socialist government that was supported by the Soviet Union until 1977, when the Soviet advisors six thousand in all were expelled. [The interruption is important.]

8. In the late 1970s, the Somali army invaded the Ogaden region of Ethiopia it borders Somalia on the west but was driven back by Ethiopian forces. [The interruption offers a side comment.]

Spelling, Hyphen, Apostrophe

31.1 CHECKING YOUR SPELLING WITH A COMPUTER PROGRAM

If you're writing with a computer and have access to a spell-check program, use it. The program will check every word in your essay against the words in its own dictionary; it will list or "flag" every word of yours that its dictionary doesn't have; and in some cases, it will tell you which words in its dictionary resemble yours. If you've written *complament,* for instance, the program will furnish two correctly spelled alternatives: *compliment* and *complement.*

Spell-check programs, however, will not proofread your essay or correct your misspellings for you. The programs can merely tell you which of your words does not appear in the program dictionary, and suggest one or more similar words that do. Also, spell-check programs can seldom identify a word misspelled for its context. If you write a *peace of pie,* most programs will accept the phrase—simply because each of its words appears in the program dictionary. Likewise, when the program suggests *compliment* and *complement* as correctly spelled alternatives to *complament,* you must still choose between these alternatives. If you don't know what each means, you will need to consult a printed dictionary or our Glossary of Usage.

Spell-check programs can save you time and help you spot misspellings that you might have overlooked. But since no such program is foolproof, you should keep a good dictionary within easy reach of the computer screen. And to improve your spelling generally, you may also want to use one or more of the pre-electronic methods explained below.

31.2 LISTING YOUR SPELLING DEMONS

Keep an analytical list of your **spelling demons**—words you have trouble spelling. Beside each of the words, write out the correct spelling, as shown in your dictionary. Then, beside the correct spelling of the word, write the letter or letters involved in the error. Your list will look like this:

MISSPELLED	CORRECTLY SPELLED	ERROR
alot	a lot	al / a l
goverment	government	erm / ern
defensable	defensible	able / ible
imovable	immovable	im / imm
defenite	definite	en / in

31.3 LEARNING HOW TO ADD SUFFIXES

Learn how to add **suffixes**—extra letters at the end of a word.

1. Change final *y* to *i* before adding a suffix:

   beauty + ful = beautiful
   bury + ed = buried
   tricky + est = trickiest
   carry + es = carries

EXCEPTION: If *y* follows a vowel or if the suffix is *-ing*, keep the *y*:

   joy + ful = joyful
   carry + ing = carrying
   bury + ing = burying

2. Drop silent *e* before adding *-able* or *-ing:*

    love + able = lovable
    care + ing = caring
    restore + ing = restoring

If any other suffix is added, keep the *e:*

    care + ful = careful
    aware + ness = awareness

EXCEPTION: If the silent *e* follows *c* or *g,* keep the *e* before *-able:*

    change + able = changeable
    peace + able = peaceable

3. If the word ends in a single consonant after a single vowel *(forget)* and the accent is on the last syllable *(for get'),* double the consonant before adding *-ing, -ed, -or,* or *-er:*

    for get' + ing = forgetting
    re fer' + ed = referred
    bet' + or = bettor

If the accent is not on the last syllable, do not double the consonant:

    ham' mer + ing = hammering
    a ban' don + ed = abandoned
    al' ter + ing = altering

31.4 LEARNING HOW TO ADD PREFIXES

Learn how to add **prefixes**—extra letters at the beginning of a word. When adding a prefix, be careful to add all of its letters, and only those:

    dis + satisfaction = dissatisfaction
    mis + fire = misfire
    mis + spell = misspell
    un + necessary = unnecessary

31.5 RECOGNIZING HOMONYMS

1. Distinguish between **homonyms**—words that sound alike but have different meanings and different spellings, such as these:

bare	bear	
brake	break	
capital	capitol	
cite	site	sight
peace	piece	
principal	principle	
right	write	rite
there	their	they're

If you aren't sure how to spell a homonym, see your dictionary.

2. Distinguish between **partial homonyms**—words with syllables that sound alike but are spelled differently, such as these:

tole*r*ate   sep*a*rate
super*sede* ex*ceed* con*cede*
domin*ance* (think of domin*ate*)   exist*ence* (think of exist*ential*)
incred*ible* (think of cred*it*)   irrit*able* (think of irrit*ate*)

31.6 PLURALIZING SIMPLE NOUNS

1. Form the **plural** of most nouns by adding -*s*:

book, books

2. Form the plural of nouns ending in *ch, s, sh, x,* and *z* by adding -*es* (pronounced as a syllable):

church, churches   business, businesses   tax, taxes

EXCEPTIONS: crisis, crises; basis, bases; ox, oxen

3. Form the plural of nouns ending in *fe* by changing *f* to *v* before adding -*es*:

wife, wives   life, lives

4. Form the plural of nouns ending in *f* by changing the *f* to *v* and then adding *-es:*

> leaf, leaves   thief, thieves

EXCEPTION: Some nouns ending in *f* need only *-s* to become plural:

> chief, chiefs   belief, beliefs   proof, proofs

5. Form the plural of some nouns ending in *o* by adding *-es:*

> hero, heroes

Most nouns ending in *o* need only an *-s* to become plural:

> piano, pianos
> solo, solos
> mosquito, mosquitos (*or* mosquitoes)
> banjo, banjos (*or* banjoes)

6. Form the plural of words ending in a consonant plus *y* by changing the *y* to *-ies:*

> vacancy, vacancies   authority, authorities

Words ending in a vowel plus *y* need only an *-s* to become plural:

> day, days   attorney, attorneys

7. Form the plural of some nouns in special ways:

> datum, data   criterion, criteria   woman, women

The forms *data* and *criteria* reflect the derivation of the words from Latin and Greek respectively.

8. Form the plural of figures, numbers written as words, capitalized letters, undotted abbreviations, and isolated words by adding *-s* or an apostrophe plus *-s:*

> the 1990s / the 1990's
> three YMCAs / three YMCA's
> twos and threes / two's and three's
> four Cs / four C's
> no *ifs* or *buts* / no *if's* or *but's*

9. Form the plural of lowercase letters and dotted abbreviations by adding an apostrophe and -*s:*

> six *s*'s and five *m*'s   three M.A.'s   two c.o.d.'s

10. Some nouns are spelled the same in the plural as in the singular:

> deer, deer
> fish, fish
> barracks, barracks

31.7 PLURALIZING COMPOUND NOUNS

Compound nouns are written as separate words *(master chef)*, as words linked by a hyphen *(self-esteem)*, or as one word *(notebook)*. Here are guidelines.

1. If the compound is written as one word, pluralize the final word:

> notebook   notebooks
> blueberry   blueberries

EXCEPTION: passerby, passersby

2. If the compound is hyphenated or written as separate words, pluralize the major word:

> mother-in-law   mothers-in-law
> editor in chief   editors in chief

A few compounds have alternative plurals: *attorney general,* for instance, may be pluralized as *attorneys general* or *attorney generals.*

3. If the compound has no noun within it, pluralize the final word:

> also-ran   also-rans

4. If the compound ends in -*ful,* add *s:*

> mouthful   mouthfuls

> **EXERCISE 1** SPOTTING AND CORRECTING
> MISSPELLINGS

In the following passage by Andrew Evans, we have deliberately misspelled some words. Find these words and make the
necessary corrections.

Mr. Bunten's farm is sucessful largely because he has kept
the size within reason and because he is a skilful farmer. His
heard is relatively small, consistting of only thirty-five milkers
plus thirty more cows, including the heifers. When most
farmers in the region expanded there oparation after World 5
War II by building expensive silos and milking systemes, Mr.
Bunten kept his farm about the same size. Within a few years,
many of his neighbors had gone into debt, and some had failed
alltogether. It was a sad sceen for just about everybody.

We milk the cows both mourning and night. Mr. Bunten 10
gets up at 5:30, and I arive at 6 p.m. After geting down a
dozen bales of hey, I dash around, feeding the cows and pre-
pareing the milking machines. I literaly run to complete the
chores in the shortest time posible. He never askes me to do
them quickly; however, if I should be moveing slowly, he'll 15
exclaim, "Geeze, boy, what took ya!" Usualy he doesn't have
to say anything because he's the type of person one wants to
please—some one on the go all the time. For a man of sixty-
four Mr. Bunten has unbeleivable endurence. Viewing his
efforts as a challenge, I try to keep up and win his respect. 20
Fortunetely, he gives me the benifit of the doubt much of the
time.

31.8 USING THE HYPHEN   -

1. Use a hyphen to divide a long word at the end of a line:

   The long black centipede walked across the sand with an enormous limp.

Normally you divide a word at the end of a syllable. But do not
put syllables of one or two letters on either side of a hyphen, as
i-tem and *end-ed.* If you aren't sure what the syllables of a word
are, see your dictionary.

2. Use a hyphen to form a compound of three or more words:

> The older citizens don't want a Johnny-come-lately for mayor.
> But they don't want a stick-in-the-mud either.

3. Use a hyphen to form a compound adjective:

> Enrico Caruso was a world-famous tenor.
>
> I wouldn't touch cocaine with a ten-foot pole.
>
> Spike Lee is a well-known movie director.
>
> Twentieth-century writers include Faulkner and Hemingway.

4. Do not use a hyphen:

a. Between an adjective and a noun in a noun phrase:

> The twentieth century will soon come to an end.

b. In a compound predicate adjective:

> Spike Lee is *well known.*

c. In compounds made with an adverb ending in *-ly,* such as *widely held.*

31.8A FORMING COMPOUND NOUNS

Generally, use a hyphen in a compound noun when both items serve as nouns:

> city-state
>
> poet-critic
>
> teacher-scholar

Generally, use no hyphen when the first noun serves as an adjective modifying the second:

> stone wall
>
> city hall
>
> master chef
>
> police officer

EXCEPTIONS: Some compound nouns are made with neither a hyphen nor a space *(paintbrush, notebook),* and some make it hard to tell whether the first item is serving as an adjective or not *(beer drinker, cattle prod).* If in doubt about hyphenating a particular noun compound, see your dictionary.

31.8B ATTACHING PREFIXES

Use a hyphen to join a prefix to a *capitalized* word:

> un-American
> post-Renaissance
> pre-Reformation

Generally, use no hyphen to join a prefix to an *uncapitalized* word:

> deemphasize
> nonprofit
> antibodies

EXCEPTIONS: Some words made with prefixes may be written with or without hyphens, but the choice of one or the other affects the meaning of the word; *re-cover,* for instance, does not mean the same as *recover.* For words such as this, see your dictionary.

31.8C WRITING OUT NUMBERS

Use a hyphen in a number written as two words, provided it is below one hundred:

> Twenty-five applicants have requested interviews.
> Two-thirds of the trees had been cut.
> One-half of the design is complete.

Do not attach a hyphen to the word for any number over ninety-nine:

> Some suits now cost over three hundred dollars.
> Some of the new "economy" cars cost more than eight thousand dollars.
> Thirty-five thousand spectators watched the game.

Thirty-five, which is below one hundred, is hyphenated, but no hyphen is attached to *thousand.*

EXERCISE 2 USING THE HYPHEN

Each of the following may require the addition of one or more hyphens. Add one as needed. If an entry is correct as it stands, write *Correct*.

EXAMPLE

Running high‑speed trains between major cities would def-

initely reduce traffic on major highways.

1. The long distance runners looked buoyant as they passed the fifteen mile mark.

2. Organized by a well known sponsor, the race had attracted a number of world renowned athletes to compete before an all European audience.

3. Over three-quarters of the contestants were from Germany and Russia.

4. Many had come from medium sized towns with populations ranging from twenty one thousand to over fifty five thousand.

5. The front runners moved so fast that even spectators on ten speed bicycles had trouble keeping up with them.

6. After the race the winner told reporters of his long term plans for acquiring more trophies.

31.9 USING THE APOSTROPHE

1. To form the possessive of nouns and abbreviations that do not end in *s,* use an apostrophe plus *-s:*

a girl's hat	Bill's car	a team's mascot
NATO's future	the C.O.'s orders	Dr. T.'s patients
men's activities	children's toys	someone's coat

If a singular noun ends in *s* (as in *James*) you may form the possessive by adding an apostrophe plus *-s* (*James's apartment*) or by adding just the apostrophe (James' apartment). Custom calls for the latter form with Zeus, Moses, and Jesus: Zeus' thunderbolts, Moses' staff, Jesus' teachings.

2. To form the possessive of plural nouns ending in *s,* add just an apostrophe:

players	players' uniforms
animals	animals' eating habits
the Joneses	the Joneses' car

3. To indicate that two people possess something jointly, add an apostrophe, and -*s* if necessary, to the second of the two nouns:

Ann and James' apartment

Tim and Susan's wedding album

To indicate that two people possess two or more things separately, use the apostrophe, and -*s* if necessary, with both of the nouns:

Paul's and Marysa's cars

Kitty's and James' tests

4. To form the possessive with singular compound nouns, add an apostrophe plus -*s* to the last word:

my sister-in-law's career   the editor in chief's policy

5. To form the possessive of certain indefinite pronouns, add an apostrophe plus -*s:*

someone's coat   no one's fault   everybody else's jokes

With indefinite pronouns that do not take the apostrophe, form the possessive with *of: the plans of most, the hopes of many, the triumphs of few.*

6. Use the possessive case with nouns or pronouns followed by gerunds:

The *crowd's cheering* could be heard a mile away.

Everyone who hears the young violinist admires *her playing.*

For more on this point, see section 11.11.

7. Use an apostrophe, and *-s* when necessary, in common phrases of time and measurement:

four o'clock	five dollars' worth
two weeks' notice	a day's work
our money's worth	a stone's throw

8. Use an apostrophe plus *-s* to form the plurals shown above in section 31.6, nos. 8 and 9.

9. Use an apostrophe to mark the omission of a letter or letters in a contraction:

I have finished.	I've finished.
He is not here.	He's not here.
This does not work.	This doesn't work.
They will not stop.	They won't stop.
You should have written.	You should've written.

10. Use an apostrophe to mark the omission of numbers in dates:

the election of '92   the Great Crash of '29

31.10 MISUSING THE APOSTROPHE   Ⓥ

1. Do not use an apostrophe to form the plural of nouns:

▶ Five girl's went swimming.

▶ Two houses/ need paint.

2. Do not use an apostrophe with the possessive forms of the personal pronouns:

▶ This is our thermos; that one is their's.

▶ Ben's notes are incomplete; your's are thorough.

3. Do not confuse the possessive pronoun *its* with the contraction *it's* (for *it is*). Use *its* as you use *his;* use *it's* as you use *he's:*

his success   he's successful

its success   it's successful

4. Do not confuse the possessive *whose* with the contraction *who's* (for *who is*):

Whose notebook is this?

No one knows whose painting this is.

Who's going to the concert?

No one has heard of the pianist who's scheduled to play.

5. Do not use the apostrophe and *-s* to form a possessive when the construction would be cumbersome:

WEAK: Questions about the candidate's husband's financial dealings hurt her campaign.

EDITED: Questions about the financial dealings of the candidate's husband hurt her campaign.

> **EXERCISE 3 USING THE APOSTROPHE**
>
> Improve the punctuation in the following passage by adding or removing apostrophes wherever necessary. As you make these corrections, write out the entire passage.
>
> Everyones talking about Frank Smiths novel. Its plot seems to be based on something that happened to him during his freshman year. Its weird to read about characters youve seen in class or in the students lounge. I dont think there are many of his classmate's who wont be annoyed when they dis- 5 cover theyve been depicted as thugs' and moron's. Its as if Frank thought that his experiences were the same as everyones—Juanitas, Murrays, and Mikes. That kind of thinking can be overlooked in someone whos in his early teen's, but it isnt all right for someone in his twenties'.   10

Mechanics

Mechanics are conventional rules such as the one requiring capitalization for the first word of a sentence. You need to follow the conventions so that your writing will look the way formal writing is expected to look.

32.1 USING CAPITAL LETTERS   *cap*

1. Capitalize the first word of a sentence:

> The quick brown fox jumped over the lazy dog.
> Where do bears hibernate in the winter?

Here and elsewhere in the chapter, to **capitalize** a word means to capitalize its first letter.

2. Capitalize proper nouns and proper adjectives. Unlike a common noun, which names one or more in a class or group, a proper noun names a *particular* person, place, thing, or event. Proper adjectives are based on common nouns. Here are examples:

COMMON NOUNS	PROPER NOUNS	PROPER ADJECTIVES (also serve as proper nouns)
country	Canada	Canadian
person	Jefferson	Jeffersonian
state	Texas	Texan
river	Mississippi River	
revolution	the French Revolution	

COMMON NOUNS	PROPER NOUNS
party	the Republican Party
east (direction)	the East (particular region)
corporation	the Rand Corporation
economics	Economics 101
day	Wednesday

Do not capitalize words such as *a* and *the* when used with proper nouns, and do not capitalize the names of the seasons (*fall, winter, spring, summer*).

3. Capitalize a personal title when it is used before a name or when it denotes a particular position of high rank:

the president	President Clinton
	the President of the United States
	the Pope
the senator	Senator Nunn
the mayor	Mayor Young
the colonel	Colonel Templeton

4. Capitalize a term denoting kinship when it is used before a name:

my uncle	Uncle Bob

5. Capitalize titles as explained in section 32.3.

6. Always capitalize the pronoun *I:*

When I heard the news, I laughed.

EXERCISE 1 USING CAPITALS

Improve each of the following by capitalizing where necessary:

1. the grand canyon extends over 270 miles from east to west, measures 18 miles from rim to rim at its widest point, and reaches a depth of approximately 1 mile.

2. the canyon has been formed over billions of years by a combination of forces, including wind, erosion, and, in particular, the action of the mighty colorado river.

3. some of the canyon's most spectacular sights are to be found within grand canyon national park, which lies in northwestern arizona.

4. to protect the canyon from commercial development, president theodore roosevelt declared it a national monument in 1908; then, in 1919 the congress of the united states proclaimed it a national park.

5. today the park attracts visitors from all of the fifty states as well as from countries far and near, including japan, south korea, france, and canada; the tourists prefer to arrive in july and august.

6. all who view the canyon marvel at the extraordinary rock formations, many of which have impressive names like thor temple, dragon head, and cheops pyramid.

7. according to one report, the canyon received its present name from major john wesley powell, who in 1869 was the first to travel through the canyon by boat. a brave man, he had lost part of an arm in the civil war.

8. he began the journey in wyoming with nine companions and four boats; he ended the journey three months later at the virgin river near lake mead with only three boats and six men.

9. modern tourists have an easier time, hiking along well-marked trails or riding in automobiles to scenic spots like powell memorial and hopi point.

10. Like the other national parks in the united states, grand canyon national park is maintained by the national park service of the u.s. department of the interior.

32.2 USING ITALICS OR UNDERLINING
ital/und

Use **italics or underlining** as explained below. (If you're writing with a typewriter or word processor that can print *italic type like this,* use italics. Otherwise use underlining.)

1. Use italics or underlining to emphasize a word or phrase in a statement:

> If an inspired guess turns out to be correct, it is
> <u>not</u> reported as an inspired guess.   --Isaac Asimov

Use this kind of emphasis sparingly. When overused, it loses its punch. (If you add your own emphasis to any word in a passage you are quoting, you must say so; see p. 541.)

2. Use italics or underlining to identify a letter or a word treated as a word:

> Neither the term <u>sexism</u> nor the term <u>racism</u> existed
> fifty years ago.   --Casey Miller and Kate Swift

You may also use quotation marks to identify a word as such; see 29.7, no. 4.

3. Use italics or underlining to identify a foreign word or phrase not absorbed into English:

> <u>au courant</u>   <u>glasnost</u>   <u>Bildungsroman</u>   <u>jouissance</u>

4. Use italics or underlining to identify the name of a ship, an airplane, or the like:

> <u>Queen Elizabeth II</u> [ship]
> <u>Spirit of St. Louis</u> [airplane]
> <u>Apollo 2</u> [spaceship]

5. Use italics or underlining for titles as explained in section 32.3.

EXERCISE 2 USING UNDERLINING

Each of the following may require the addition or removal of underlining. Make any necessary changes. If an entry is correct as it stands, write *Correct*.

1. Carol and Alex have named their <u>motorboat</u> The Calex.

2. They wanted to call it Paradise, but couldn't agree whether the last consonant should be an s or a c.

3. They also argue about whether the <u>drink</u> known as a frappe is the same as the one called a <u>frost</u>.

4. But they do see eye to eye on some things, like <u>yoga</u> and <u>karate</u> classes, pasta and <u>pizza</u>, and the way to spell harass-ment.

5. When their first child was born, Alex gave Carol a dozen roses with a card explaining that the English word mother derives from the Middle English word moder and is akin to the Latin word mater.

6. Carol gave Alex a copy of the <u>first edition</u> of All Quiet on the Western Front.

32.3 TITLES   *title*

1. Capitalize the first and last word of a title, whatever they are. Also capitalize all the words in between except articles (such as *a* and *the*), prepositions (such as *for, among, between,* and *to*), and coordinating conjunctions (such as *and, but,* and *or*):

```
Zen and the Art of Motorcycle Maintenance [book]

"Ode on a Grecian Urn" [poem]
```

2. Use italics or underlining for the titles of books, scholarly journals, magazines, newspapers, government reports, plays, musicals, operas or other long musical compositions, films, tele-vision shows, radio programs, or long poems:

The Grapes of Wrath [book]

The American Scholar [journal]

Newsweek [magazine]

New York Times [newspaper]

Uniform Crime Reports for the United States

   [government publication]

Hamlet [play]

Oklahoma [musical]

The Barber of Seville [opera]

Star Wars [film]

Roseanne [television show]

Morning Pro Musica [radio program]

Song of Myself [long poem]

3. Use double quotation marks for titles of works like these:

"Seal Hunting in Alaska" [magazine article]

"Bullfighting in Hemingway's Fiction" [essay]

"The Tell-Tale Heart" [short story]

"Mending Wall" [short poem]

"Born in the U.S.A." [song]

"The American Scholar" [speech]

"Winning the West" [chapter in a book]

4. Change double to single quotation marks when the title appears within another title that needs quotation marks, or is mentioned within a quotation:

"Fences and Neighbors in Frost's 'Mending Wall' "

   [title of an essay on the poem]

"Frost's 'Mending Wall,' " said Professor Ainsley,

   "is a gently disarming poem."

5. Do not use both underlining and quotation marks unless the title *includes* an underlined title:

> "Experience" [essay]
>
> Gone with the Wind [novel]
>
> "On Sitting Down to Read King Lear Again" [poem]

6. Do not use italics or quotation marks in a title of your own unless it includes a reference to another title:

> What to Do with Nuclear Waste
>
> Bull-fighting in Hemingway's The Sun Also Rises
>
> Art and Sex in Pope's "Rape of the Lock"

EXERCISE 3 WRITING TITLES

Each of the following titles requires capitalization and may also require underlining or quotation marks. Make the necessary changes.

1. carmen [opera]
2. politics and leadership [speech]
3. my old kentucky home [song]
4. washington post [newspaper]
5. what freud forgot [essay]
6. 60 minutes [television show]
7. the will of zeus [history book]
8. john brown's body [long poem]
9. the mismatch between school and children [editorial]
10. natural history [magazine]
11. solutions to the energy problem [your report]
12. the role of fate in shakespeare's romeo and juliet [your essay]
13. imagery in the battle hymn of the republic [your essay]
14. barefoot in the park [play]
15. the age of innocence [novel]

32.4 USING ABBREVIATIONS *ab*

Writers differ about how they use **abbreviations,** but we recommend the following procedures:

1. Abbreviate most titles accompanying a name:

> Dr. Martha Peters
>
> Martha Peters, Ph.D.
>
> Robert Greene Jr.
>
> Ms. Elizabeth Fish
>
> Joseph Stevens, M.D.

But do not abbreviate when referring to people with religious, governmental, academic, and military titles:

> the Reverend Leonard Flischer
>
> Senator Nancy Kassebaum
>
> the Honorable Mario Cuomo, governor of New York
>
> Professor Pamela Pinckney
>
> General H. Norman Schwarzkopf

2. Abbreviate terms that help to specify a date or a time of day:

> 350 B.C.   8:30 A.M.
>
> A.D. 1776   2:15 P.M.

Note that A.D. precedes the date.

3. Abbreviate the *United States of America* as "U.S.A."

a. When abbreviating *United States* as an adjective, write "U.S." alone:

> the U.S. Supreme Court
>
> U.S. elections

b. In writing to a U.S. address from outside the country, or in writing your own return address on a letter going to another country, write "USA" (undotted) on a separate line:

> 28 Foster Street
>
> Cambridge MA 02138
>
> USA

4. Abbreviate the name of a state, province, or district when it forms part of an address:

> Austin TX
>
> Long Beach CA
>
> Washington DC
>
> Sherbrooke Que.

Abbreviate names of U.S. states, the District of Columbia, and Puerto Rico with just two capital letters and no periods. Here are standard abbreviations:

Alabama	AL	Kentucky	KY	North Dakota	ND
Alaska	AK	Louisiana	LA	Ohio	OH
Arizona	AZ	Maine	ME	Oklahoma	OK
Arkansas	AR	Maryland	MD	Oregon	OR
California	CA	Massachusetts	MA	Pennsylvania	PA
Colorado	CO	Michigan	MI	Puerto Rico	PR
Connecticut	CT	Minnesota	MN	Rhode Island	RI
Delaware	DE	Mississippi	MS	South Carolina	SC
District of		Missouri	MO	South Dakota	SD
Columbia	DC	Montana	MT	Tennessee	TN
Florida	FL	Nebraska	NE	Texas	TX
Georgia	GA	Nevada	NV	Utah	UT
Hawaii	HI	New		Vermont	VT
Idaho	ID	Hampshire	NH	Virginia	VA
Illinois	IL	New Jersey	NJ	Washington	WA
Indiana	IN	New Mexico	NM	West Virginia	WV
Iowa	IA	New York	NY	Wisconsin	WI
Kansas	KS	North Carolina	NC	Wyoming	WY

5. You may use undotted abbreviations in referring to well-known firms and other organizations:

> NBC   YMCA
>
> IBM   NAACP

6. If an abbreviation comes at the end of a declarative sentence, use the period marking the abbreviation as the period for the sentence:

> The rocket was launched at 11:30 P.M.

If an abbreviation ends a question, add a question mark:

Was the rocket launched at 11:30 P.M.?

7. Most abbreviations must be marked by periods, but you need no periods to abbreviate the names of U.S. states and of well-known organizations, as shown above, or to abbreviate well-known phrases:

mph   mpg

32.5 MISUSING ABBREVIATIONS

1. In formal writing, avoid using abbreviations for the days of the week and the months of the year:

Sunday   August

2. Avoid using abbreviations for the names of most geographical entities when they are not part of an address:

New England   the Snake River   Lake Avenue   Canada

You may, however, use *Mt.* before the name of a mountain, as in *Mt. McKinley,* and *St.* in the name of a place, as in *St. Louis.*

3. Avoid using abbreviations for the names of academic subjects and the subdivision of books:

French 205   biology   chapter 10   page 45

EXCEPTION: In parenthetical citations of books and articles, "page" is commonly abbreviated as "p." and "pages" as "pp."

4. Avoid using abbreviations for units of measurement (such as size and weight) unless the accompanying amounts are given in figures:

The new guard is six feet seven inches tall.
This box must weigh over fifty pounds.
A 50 lb. bag of fertilizer costs $24.50.

5. Avoid using any abbreviation that is not widely known without first explaining its meaning:

* The MISAA was passed in 1978.

EDITED: The Middle Income Student Assistance Act (MISAA) was passed in 1978.

After you have explained its meaning, you may use the abbreviation on its own. But beware of crowding too many abbreviations into a sentence or passage. If you don't keep them under control, your reader may end up drowning in alphabet soup:

* In 1971 Congress established the BEOG program, and the EOGs were renamed SEOGs.

EDITED: In 1972 Congress established the Basic Educational Opportunity Grant (BEOG) program, and the Educational Opportunity Grants (EOG) were renamed Supplemental Educational Opportunity Grants (SEOG).

If you aren't sure how to abbreviate a particular term, see your dictionary. If you don't know whether you should abbreviate a term at all, don't. In formal writing, most terms should be spelled out in full.

32.6 USING NUMBERS *num*

When you refer to a **number** in your writing, you have to decide whether to use a figure or to spell it out as a word. In much scientific and technical writing, figures predominate; in magazines and books of general interest, words are common, though figures are also used. In this section, we offer some guidelines for nontechnical writing.

1. Spell out a number when it begins a sentence:

Eighty-five dignitaries attended the opening ceremony.
Two hundred dignitaries had been invited.

Rearrange the sentence if spelling out the number would require more than two words:

The opening ceremony was attended by 157 dignitaries.
Invitations were sent to 218 dignitaries.

2. Spell out a number that can be written in one or two words, except as noted in no. 4, below:

> A batter is out after three strikes.
> The firefighters worked without relief for twenty-two hours.
> She owns seven hundred rare books.
> Twenty-five thousand people were evacuated.

A hyphenated number may be counted as one word.

3. Use numerals if spelling out a number would require more than two words:

> The stadium can hold 85,600 spectators.
> Attendance at last Saturday's game was 79,500.

4. Use numerals for addresses, dates, exact times of day, exact sums of money, and exact measurements such as miles per hour, scores of games, mathematical ratios, fractions, and page numbers:

> 22 East Main Street
> October 7, 1981
> 44 B.C.
> 11:15 A.M.
> $4.36
> 65 mph
> a ratio of 2 to 1
> 5⅞
> page 102

However, when a time of day or a sum of money is given as a round figure, spell it out:

> Uncle Ben always gets up at six.
> I reached the border at around eight o'clock.
> He used to earn two dollars for ten hours of work.
> It's hard to believe that fifty cents can no longer buy a cup of coffee.

EXERCISE 4 USING ABBREVIATIONS AND NUMBERS

Each of the following may include incorrectly written abbreviations and numbers. Make any necessary changes. If an entry is correct as it stands, write *Correct*.

> "Why," said the White Queen to Alice, "sometimes I've
> believed as many as ~~6~~ six impossible things before breakfast."
>
> —Adapted from Lewis Carroll

1. We plan to spend part of our vacation on a Miss. Riv. steamboat and the rest in the Cascade Mts.

2. 1st, however, we must attend a meeting of the Young Women's Christian Association that is expected to attract an audience of 25 hundred members in Alexandria, Virginia.

3. The Rev. Ann Proctor, Doctor of Divinity, will be one of the speakers; her talk is scheduled to begin at seven-fifteen P.M.

4. All of the speakers have said they will contribute ¾ of their honorarium to the Assoc.

5. The combined amounts should come to exactly seven hundred dollars and seventy-two cents.

6. Following the meeting, we will head west, doing our best to make time with a speed limit of sixty-five miles per hour.

7. If all goes well, we should arrive in St. Lou. on Fri., Aug. nine.

4

THE RESEARCH PAPER

33

Preparing the Research Paper

Writing a **library research paper** is much like writing an ordinary essay. Both involve choosing a topic, asking questions to define and develop it, gauging the audience, finding a thesis, outlining the paper, writing it, and revising it. What makes a research paper different is that much of its material comes not from your own head but from printed sources, chiefly books and periodicals. Collecting raw material—by reading and taking notes—corresponds to the process of pre-writing an ordinary essay.

Suppose, for instance, that you'd like to write about earthquakes but have no idea how to state the topic or what questions to ask about it. In that case, you might begin by reading an encyclopedia article, as explained in section 33.2D. That would help you to learn how to make the topic more specific (earthquakes in California, for instance) and might also provoke the kind of questions that could lead you to a thesis, or to further research that might help you discover one. But don't expect to find your thesis right away. Doing research—reading a variety of sources—is like listening to a long discussion and then suddenly realizing that you've formed an opinion of your own: that you know where you stand, that you're ready to speak. If you take this route to a thesis, you may be pleasantly surprised to see how much you have gathered along the way that will help you support it.

So treat the following sequence as flexible. If your topic is vague at the outset, let your research help you define it. If you can't think of a thesis, let your research help you discover one. Use whatever sequence works best for you.

33.1 CHOOSING A TOPIC

To choose a topic wisely, ask yourself these questions:

1. Why are you interested in this topic? Does it affect you personally? Does it raise questions you want to answer or problems you want to explore? The more you know about why the topic interests you, the more fascinating your research will be.

2. What do you already know about this topic? Take a few minutes to answer this question on paper. What you now know will be the starting point for what you will learn.

3. Where does your present knowledge come from? As soon as you ask yourself this question, you begin to think like a researcher. Suppose you "know," for instance, that AIDS can be transmitted by any kind of physical contact. But so far as you can recall, your source for this bit of information—actually misinformation—is a man you met at a party. Was he a specialist in AIDS research? If not, what was *his* source? To do research, one of the first things you need to know is that specific information on any topic is only as reliable as its source.

4. Can you find many sources of information on this topic? If only one or two sources are readily available, or none at all, you should rethink your topic or choose another.

5. Can you cut the topic down to manageable size? Be reasonable and realistic about what you can do in the time you have. If your general interest is the causes of the American Revolution, find something specific, such as the role of Patrick Henry or the harassment of loyalists after Watertown.

6. What questions does the topic provoke? Questions help you find a specific problem to investigate. Suppose you want to

write about sexual harassment. You could ask at least three or four pointed questions: Where does it occur? Who is responsible for it? What are its consequences? How does it affect the working relationships between men and women? A student named Rick Harris asked himself these questions as he started work on his research paper for a course taken in the spring of 1993. From time to time in this chapter and in chapters 34 and 36, we will follow his progress as he moves from these initial questions through the writing of his paper.

THINKING ABOUT YOUR RESEARCH TOPIC: IN BRIEF

- Why are you interested in this topic?
- What do you already know about it?
- Where does your present knowledge come from?
- Can you find many sources of information on it?
- Can you cut it to manageable size?
- What questions does it provoke?

EXERCISE 1 WRITING QUESTIONS ABOUT VARIOUS TOPICS

Choose five of the following topics, and write two questions on each of them. Make the questions as pointed and specific as possible.

1. Solar energy
2. Viking explorations in North America
3. Women in politics
4. French separatism in Quebec
5. Prayer in the public schools
6. Divorce
7. Sexual abuse of children
8. Violence on TV
9. Global warming
10. Prohibition
11. Date rape

33.2

12. Adult illiteracy

13. College athletics

EXERCISE 2 WRITING QUESTIONS ABOUT ONE TOPIC

Think of a research topic that interests you, or take a topic you have been assigned, and write at least three specific questions about it.

33.2 USING THE LIBRARY: THE REFERENCE SECTION

The best place to start working systematically on your research paper is the **reference section** of your college or university library. Whatever your subject, a computerized database or a reference book will tell what has been written about it. To find your way to either of these guides, ask the help of the reference librarian.

GUIDES TO SOURCES

- *Library of Congress Subject Headings* tells you what headings to use in looking for sources (33.2A)

- Bibliographies: guides to books and articles in a specified field (33.2B)

- Computerized indexes (databases) of sources in a specified field (33.2C)

- General encyclopedias (33.2D)

- Specialized encyclopedias (33.2E)

- Compilations of facts and statistics (33.2F)

- Biographical guides, containing brief lives of notable figures (33.2G)

- General indexes to periodicals (33.2H)

- Specialized indexes to periodicals (33.2I)

- Government publications (33.2J)

33.2A LEARNING WHAT YOUR TOPIC IS CALLED

If your library has an on-line catalog, it can give you a shortcut to some of the books on your topic. But to find any item in an on-line file, you must remember one thing: *computers don't understand any word that is misspelled.* If you're looking for sources on "sexual harassment" and you accidentally type *harrassment,* you'll be told there are 0 items in that file. So if any of your searches draws a blank in this way, make sure your search word or phrase is letter perfect before you give up.

If your search word or phrase is letter perfect and you're still not finding sources, you need to know what your topic is officially called. To learn this, ask the reference librarian or look up your subject in the set of volumes called *Library of Congress Subject Headings,* where you'll find entries like these:

This term is Used For these → **Sexual harassment**   *(May Subd Geog)* ← May be Subdivided Geographically
UF   Harassment, Sexual
BT   Child molesting
Related Term → RT   Sex role in the work environment
— **Investigation**
BT   Investigations
Boldface for recognized subject heading → **Sexual harassment in universities and colleges**
(May Subd Geog)
[LC212.86-LC212.863]
UF   Sexual harassment on campus ← Lightface for cross-references: use the boldface heading instead
BT   Universities and colleges
Sexual harassment of women
Broader Terms → *(May Subd Geog)*
UF   Harassment of women, Sexual ←
BT   Sex crimes
Sex discrimination against women
— **Law and legislation**   *(May Subd Geog)*
Use this term instead of the one above it → Sexual harassment on campus
USE   Sexual harassment in universities and colleges

Once you know the subject headings for your topic, you can start looking for sources on it. You'll usually find them listed in one or more of the following works.

33.2B A BOOK-AND-ARTICLE BIBLIOGRAPHY

Before you look anywhere else, find out if there's a **book-and-article bibliography** on your topic—a guide to both articles and books. To locate such a bibliography, check your subject heading in the on-line catalog or the card catalog (section 33.3B) or ask a reference librarian to help you. Here, for instance, is a sample of what can be found under "Euthanasia" in the annual *Bibliography of Bioethics,* which describes books and journal articles on ethical problems in medicine:

> **Crisp, Roger.** A good death: who best to bring it? *Bioethics.* 1987 Jan; 1(1): 74-79. 8 fn. BE22712.
> *active euthanasia; family members; living wills; nurses; *physician's role; physicians; psychological stress; terminal care; terminally ill; *voluntary euthanasia
>
> The author supports the right of persons to terminate their lives when it would be in their "best interests" to do so. He considers cases in which persons are unable to kill themselves and request euthanasia or have requested it beforehand in a living will. Crisp rejects relatives, friends, and most phsicians as the agents to carry out the request because of the emotional trauma to the agents and the damage to the image of physicians as savers of lives. He proposes that the practice of euthanasia be part of "telostrics," an area of medicine specialization in the care of the terminally ill, and that these "telostricians" should perform voluntary euthanasia.
>
> **Donahue, M. Patricia.** Euthanasia: an ethical uncertainty. In McCloskey , Joanne Comi; Grace, Helen Kennedy, eds. Current Issues in Nursing. Second Edition. Boston; Blackwell Scientific Publications; 1985: 1025- 1043. 26 refs. ISBN 0-86542-019-X. BE21569.
> *allowing to die; brain death; decision making; *ethical analysis; *euthanasia; extraordinary treatment; moral obligations; *moral policy; * nurses; *nursing ethics; *patient advocacy; prolongation of life; rights; self determination; *terminally ill; withholding treatment
>
> **Kuhse, Helga; Singer, Peter.** Should the Baby Live? The Problem of Handicapped Infants. New York: Oxford University Press; 1985 228 p. Includes references. ISBN 0-19-217745-1. BE22782.
> *active euthanasia; *allowing to die; case studies; *congenital defects; costs and benefits; cultural pluralism; *decision making; double effect

Unlike some bibliographies, which simply give titles and publication details, this one is *annotated,* which means that it offers notes on each source listed. The first entry summarizes an article that appeared in the January 1987 issue of *Bioethics;* the second identifies an essay that appears in a book, *Current Issues in Nursing;* the third identifies a book about handicapped infants. All three entries also cite the topics covered by each source, and the asterisk before a topic such as "active euthanasia" indicates that this is a subject heading for more entries elsewhere in the bibliography.

Many bibliographies are issued annually, so if you check the entries for your topic in the three or four most recent issues, you can quickly learn about all the most recently published sources on your topic.

33.2C A COMPUTERIZED INDEX

A **computerized index** (also called a **database**) is a computerized file of sources in a particular field. Dialog Information Services has many such indexes. To use one, you will normally need the help of a library technician and you may be asked to pay a small fee. But a computerized index can dramatically expedite your quest for sources because it's typically *cumulative,* covering all the years from a given year right up to the present one.

33.2D GENERAL ENCYCLOPEDIAS

These give you an overview of virtually any subject in language that a nonspecialist can understand, and many encyclopedia articles end with a short list of books recommended for further reading on the subject. For this reason, an **encyclopedia** is a good place to start your research, though you should not expect to use it or cite it as a major source in itself. General encyclopedias include the *Encyclopaedia Britannica,* the *Americana,* and the one-volume *Concise Columbia.* Some encyclopedias can be scanned by computer. The *Academic American Encyclopedia,* for instance, is available on-line from Grolier Electronic Publishing, with updates added each quarter.

33.2E SPECIALIZED ENCYCLOPEDIAS

These cover subjects in particular fields, such as art, education, history, literature, and psychology. To find the **specialized encyclopedia** for your subject, ask the reference librarian or see the *Guide to Reference Books* compiled by Eugene P. Sheehy, which lists specialized guides to research in all fields, such as the *Encyclopedia of World Art, The Encyclopedia of Education, The Canadian Encyclopedia,* and the *International Encyclopedia of the Social Sciences.* (Note, by the way, that "Encyclopedia" is sometimes spelled "Encyclopaedia.")

EXERCISE 3 USING ENCYCLOPEDIAS

Read an article in a standard encyclopedia about the research topic you used for exercise 2, and jot down any questions this article raises for you. Then find a specialized encyclopedia that contains an article on your topic. Explain how the second article differs from the first and whether or not the second answers all of the questions raised by the first.

33.2F COMPILATIONS OF FACTS AND STATISTICS

These include such works as *Facts on File* (1940–), a "weekly news digest with cumulative index," which summarizes current events, and *Statistical Abstract of the United States,* which offers statistics on many subjects.

EXERCISE 4 FINDING FACTS AND STATISTICS

Assume that you want to do research on oil spills at sea. Choose a six-month period from the past year, and check *Facts on File* and *Statistical Abstract of the United States* to see what you can learn about oil spills during this time.

33.2G BIOGRAPHICAL GUIDES

These give brief accounts of notable figures, sometimes with bibliographies. They include the following:

Chambers's Biographical Dictionary covers figures in all historical periods.

Who's Who covers living persons. Besides *Who's Who in the World,* there are national volumes such as *Who's Who in America, Who's Who in Canada,* and volumes devoted to categories such as black Americans, American women, and American politicians.

The *Dictionary of American Biography* covers deceased Americans.
The Dictionary of Canadian Biography covers deceased Canadians.
The *Dictionary of National Biography* covers deceased Britons.
Notable American Women, ed. Edward T. James and Janet W.
    James, covers American women from 1607 on.
Dictionary of American Negro Biography covers deceased African
    Americans.
Contemporary Authors covers chiefly living authors.

> **EXERCISE 5 USING BIOGRAPHICAL REFERENCE WORKS**
>
> If your topic concerns a particular person, consult one or more
> of the biographical dictionaries or *Who's Who* volumes men-
> tioned above. Jot down at least two questions about the per-
> son, and then search the computerized *Biography Index* (see
> section 33.2C) for the titles of two recent books or articles on
> your subject.

33.2H GENERAL INDEXES TO PERIODICALS

These include the following:

1. The *Readers' Guide to Periodical Literature,* issued every month
and cumulated quarterly as well as annually, is an author-and-
subject index to articles of general (rather than scholarly) interest published in over a hundred American magazines. Under
"Sexual harassment," the 1991 issue of the *Guide* lists these
items:

Author

Title of source → An all too common story. K. Marton. por *Newsweek* 118:8
O 21 '91 — Volume number
Cultural fascism. S. J. McCarthy. il por *Forbes* 148:116
D 9 '91
Date of issue (October 21, 1991) — Dealing with sexual harassment. A. Deutschman. il *Fortune* 124:145+ N 4 '91 — Page number
Ending sexual harassment: business is getting the message.
    M. Galen. il *Business Week* p98-100 Mr 18 '91
Everything but sex: the new office affair [platonic relationships]
    M. Dowd. il *Mademoiselle* 97:120-3 F '91
Getting reasonable about feelings [reasonable woman standard]
    J. Leo. il *U.S. News & World Report* 111:30 N 18 '91
Harassment: men on trial. T. Gest and A. Saltzman. il — Illustrated article
    U.S. News & World Report 111:38-40 O 21 '91
How to deal with sexual harassment. R. T. Gray. il *Nation's Business* 79:28+ D '91
Lust on the job. G. K. Brushaber. *Christianity Today* 35:21
D 16 '91 — Name of periodical
May I have the pleasure . . . [exaggerating problem of
    sexual harassment] G. Morgenson. il *National Review* 43:36-7+ N 18 '91

Moral, legal and media responsibility [union's responsibility in case of sexual harassment against black Ontario factory worker] G. Bain. il *Maclean's* 104:60 N 25 '91
My life as an office wife. J. L. Farbar. *Mademoiselle* 97:123+ F '91
The no-sex affair [platonic relationships] C. Botwin. il *Ladies' Home Journal* 108:126-7+ O '91
Office crimes. N. R. Gibbs. il *Time* 138:52-4+ O 21 '91
Out of the shadows: the Thomas hearings force business to confront an ugly reality [sexual harassment; special section] il *Business Week* p30-5 O 28 '91
The price of saying no [sexual harassment; special section] il *People Weekly* 36:44-9 O 28 '91
The principal ingredients of a sexual-harassment policy. D. H. Weiss. *Nation's Business* 79:31 D '91

Article starts on this page and continues on later pages

2. The *Magazine Index* lists chiefly by subject matter articles from over four hundred magazines. It's a microtext made to be used with a special viewer. The reference librarian will tell you if your library has one and where to find it.

3. The *New York Times Index* lists selected articles published in the *Times* from 1851 to 1912, and all articles published in the *Times* thereafter. Issued twice a month with quarterly cumulations and then bound into annual volumes, this index is a prime source of up-to-date information.

33.21 SPECIALIZED INDEXES TO PERIODICALS

These list articles in one or more specified fields. Ask the reference librarian to help you find an index on your topic. Here is a small selection from the many indexes available:

1. The *Environment Index* lists articles as well as books and technical reports under subject headings such as "Oil Spills." Many of the articles are briefly summarized in a companion volume, *Environment Abstracts.*

2. The *General Science Index* lists articles under subject headings in fields such as astronomy, botany, genetics, mathematics, physics, and oceanography.

3. The *Humanities Index* lists articles by author and subject in fields such as archaeology, folklore, history, language, literature, the performing arts, and philosophy.

4. The *Social Sciences Index* lists articles by author and subject in fields such as anthropology, economics, law, criminology, medical science, political science, and sociology.

5. The *Bulletin of the Public Affairs Information Service (PAIS)* covers articles on public affairs and public policy as well as government documents and books.

> EXERCISE 6 MAKING NOTES ON ARTICLES IN PERIODICALS
>
> Using a general or specialized index to periodicals, find out about two articles on your topic. Then fill out a source card on each one, following the model shown below in section 33.5B. (Leave out the library call number for now.)

33.2J GOVERNMENT PUBLICATIONS

The United States government produces a vast amount of printed matter on a wide range of subjects. Here is a sample of the guides to this material, which can often be found in the microfiche collections of many large libraries:

1. The *ASI (American Statistics Index)* consists of two volumes, *Index* and *Abstracts*. The first is a subject index to statistical documents produced by hundreds of government offices; the second describes the documents more fully.

2. The *CIS*, published by the Congressional Information Service, also consists of two volumes, *Index* and *Abstracts*. They index and describe working papers of Congress: reports, documents, and other special publications of nearly three hundred House, Senate, and joint committees and subcommittees.

3. The *Monthly Catalog of United States Government Publications*, indexed semiannually, lists government publications by author, title, and subject matter.

4. *Resources in Education (RIE)*, issued monthly and indexed semiannually by the Educational Resources Information Center (ERIC), lists books, pamphlets, and conference papers on educational topics under subject headings, author, and title, and also summarizes every document it lists. Though *RIE* does not list journal articles on education, you will find these in the *Current Index to Journals in Education (CIJE)*, also produced by ERIC.

33.3 Finding Books: The On-Line Catalog and the Card Catalog

33.3A Using the On-Line Catalog

The **on-line catalog** is a computerized file of a library's holdings. If your library has one, it's the best place to start your search for the books you need. (If your library doesn't have an on-line catalog, skip this section and go on to section 33.3B.) To use the on-line catalog, ask any librarian for the location of the nearest terminal and follow the instructions listed beside it. You can then call up a specific book by author or title, or ask the computer to search its file for books on a given topic. On the topic of "Sexual harassment," for instance, one library's computer came up with several books, including this one:

```
       Author:  Gutek, Barbara A.
        Title:  Sex and the workplace / Barbara A. Gutek. 1st ed.
    Collation:  xix, 216 p. ; 24 cm.
      Imprint:  San Francisco, Calif. : Jossey-Bass, c1985.
       Series:  Jossey-Bass management series.Jossey-Bass social and
                behavioral science series.
        Notes:  Bibliography: p. 203-210.
                Includes index.
                "The impact of sexual behavior and harassment on women, men,
                and organizations."
Material Type:  Book
     Language:  english
     Subjects:  Sexual harassment of women.
                Sex discrimination in employment.
                Organizational behavior.
 Other Titles:  Sex and the work place.
         LCCN:  85-45054
         RLIN:  85-B25452
         ISBN:  0875896561
     Location:  Bus-Engr HD/6060.3/G88/1985
```

Library call number indicates where you can find the book

If the computer terminal is connected to a printer, print out the information on any book that looks promising. If there's no printer handy, see section 33.5.

33.3B Using the Card Catalog

You will need the **card catalog** if your college library has no on-line catalog, and you may need it if the on-line catalog is incomplete.

Each book in the catalog is listed in three ways: by author, by title, and by subject. If you know the author of the book you want, check the author card. That will give you the title and a good deal more:

Library call number indicates where you can find the book

Place of publication, publisher, and date of publication

Number of pages

Author

The book has a bibliography

Tracings list the subject headings under which the book is catalogued

```
BUS ENGR Gutek, Barbara A.
HD          Sex and the workplace / Barbara A.
6060.3    Gutek. -- 1st ed. -- San Francisco,
.G88      Calif. : Jossey-Bass, c1985.
1985        xix, 216 p. ; 24 cm. -- (Jossey-Bass
          management series) (Jossey-Bass social
          and behavioral science series)

            Bibliography: p. 203-210.
            Includes index.
            "The impact of sexual behavior and
          harassment on women, men, and
          organizations."
            ISBN 0-87589-656-1

            1. Sexual harassment of women.  2.
          Sex discrimination in employment.  3.
          Organizational behavior.  I. Title.
          II. Title: Sex and the work place.
          III. Series.  IV. Series: Jossey-Bass
          social and behavioral science series.
```

If you know the title of the book you want, but aren't sure of the author, check the title card:

Title

```
            Sex and the work place.

BUS ENGR Gutek, Barbara A.
HD          Sex and the workplace / Barbara A.
6060.3    Gutek. -- 1st ed. -- San Francisco,
.G88      Calif. : Jossey-Bass, c1985.
1985        xix, 216 p. ; 24 cm. -- (Jossey-Bass
          management series) (Jossey-Bass social
          and behavioral science series)

            Bibliography: p. 203-210.
            Includes index.
            "The impact of sexual behavior and
          harassment on women, men, and
          organizations."
            ISBN 0-87589-656-1

            1. Sexual harassment of women.  2.
          Sex discrimination in employment.  3.
          Organizational behavior.  I. Title.
          II. Title: Sex and the work place.
          III. Series.  IV. Series: Jossey-Bass
          social and behavioral science series.
```

If you have only a subject, check the subject card:

Subject ————————→ heading

```
                        SEXUAL HARASSMENT OF WOMEN.

        BUS ENGR  Gutek, Barbara A.
        HD            Sex and the workplace / Barbara A.
        6060.3     Gutek. -- 1st ed. -- San Francisco,
        .G88       Calif. : Jossey-Bass, c1985.
        1985          xix, 216 p. ; 24 cm. -- (Jossey-Bass
                   management series) (Jossey-Bass social
                   and behavioral science series)

                      Bibliography: p. 203-210.
                      Includes index.
                      "The impact of sexual behavior and
                   harassment on women, men, and
                   organizations."
                      ISBN 0-87589-656-1

                      1. Sexual harassment of women.  2.
                   Sex discrimination in employment.  3.
                   Organizational behavior.  I. Title.
                   II. Title: Sex and the work place.
                   III. Series.  IV. Series: Jossey-Bass
                   social and behavioral science series.
```

33.3C GETTING BOOKS YOUR LIBRARY DOESN'T HAVE

If you can't find a book in the card catalog, see the person in charge of **interlibrary loan.** If you can wait at least a week, your library may be able to borrow the book for you from another library.

33.4 FINDING ARTICLES

Once you've identified **articles** on your topic, you need to locate them in your library.

If the article is in a book of articles or essays, find the call number of the book by looking up its title in the card catalog.

If the article appears in a periodical, ask the reference librarian where to find it. Some libraries list all periodicals under their titles (like book titles) in the card catalog; others list periodicals in a separate file, often called a "serials list."

If your library doesn't have the periodical, the librarian may be able to get a photocopy of the article from another library.

33.5 KEEPING TRACK OF YOUR SOURCES

As you learn about sources from reference books, record the authors, titles, and other information (such as names and dates of periodicals) so that you can find the sources in your library. The simplest way to keep track of books is to print information directly from an on-line catalog entry. But if you can't make printouts, fill out a 3-by-5-inch source card on each book you plan to consult. You'll also need a source card for each article you plan to see.

33.5A SOURCE CARD FOR A BOOK

KF
3467
.29
S49
1988

Library call number →

Deane, N., I. Shepard, H. Olsen, D. Rausch, and R. Mann

Name(s) of author(s), starting with last name of first author

Title and subtitle (if any) → Sexual Harassment Issues and Answers

Washington: College and University Personnel Association, 1986

Place of publication, publisher, and date of publication

33.5B SOURCE CARD FOR AN ARTICLE

Library call number of periodical containing the article → HF/I/N4

Author → R. Gray

Title of article → "How to Deal with Sexual Harassment"

Name of periodical → Nation's Business 79:28+ December 1991

Volume number   *Page number(s)*

Date of article

Once you actually get a particular source, make sure that the information on your source card is accurate and complete. Checking all this information now can save you trouble later, when you may not have the source in hand but will have to cite it fully and accurately.

> **EXERCISE 7 MAKING SOURCE CARDS**
>
> Using the card catalog and the list of serials, get the call numbers of one book and of one periodical containing an article that you would like to use in your research. Fill out a card for each source as shown above.

33.6 USING MICROTEXTS

Because of storage problems, libraries have increased their use of **microtexts**—printed material photographically reduced in size and readable only with the aid of mechanical viewers. Some excellent sources, such as complete files of major newspapers and magazines, may be available only in this form.

33.7 CONDUCTING AN INTERVIEW

An **interview** can enliven both the process of research and the finished product. Anyone with a special knowledge of your topic can be a living source of information that might not be readily available anywhere else. In addition, quotes and paraphrases from an interview can bring a special vitality to your paper.

To get as much as possible from an interview, we suggest you follow these steps:

1. Find the right person to interview. Ask your instructor or the reference librarian if anyone working on the college staff or living in your area specializes in your topic. When Rick Harris asked a reference librarian for help in finding sources on sexual harrassment, he was referred to the college's manager of personnel training and development.

2. Arrange the interview beforehand. Telephone the person to make an appointment. A face-to-face interview is best, but if that's not possible, make an appointment for a telephone interview. And however you conduct the interview, you should get advance permission if you plan to use a tape recorder.

3. Prepare your questions. A good interviewer comes prepared with some preliminary knowledge of the topic gleaned from printed sources, and—most important—with a list of productive questions. Productive questions generally call for more than a "yes" or "no" answer, and also for more than a simple expression of personal feeling. They call for information. Compare these questions:

a. How do you feel about smoking in restaurants?
b. Should smoking be banned in restaurants?
c. If all restaurants are required to maintain separate sections for smokers and nonsmokers, how will this requirement affect the restaurant business?

Question (a) invites a statement of personal feeling such as "I hate it," and question (b) invites a one-word answer: "yes" or "no." While such an answer can be helpful, only question (c) calls for the kind of information likely to enrich your paper.

Productive questions can be **open-ended** or **pinpointed**. An open-ended question stimulates a wide-ranging response, while a pinpointed question calls for a specific piece of information:

> OPEN-ENDED: How have tobacco companies responded to the growing body of evidence that links smoking to cancer?

> PINPOINTED: At what point—at what number of cigarettes a day—does smoking begin to pose a serious danger to health?

4. Ask follow-up questions whenever you need to clarify a point. Though you should come to the interview with a list of questions prepared in advance, you should also be ready for surprises. If your interviewee says something unexpected or puzzling, ask for clarification.

5. Take careful notes or tape the interview. The best way to record the whole interview is to get it on tape (with the per-

mission of the interviewee) and then transcribe it. But if you don't have or can't use a tape recorder, make sure your notes are accurate and thorough.

6. After the interview, check your quotations with the interviewee. Make sure they are accurate and consistent with the context from which you've taken them. It's also courteous to send the interviewee a note of thanks and a copy of your paper.

> **EXERCISE 8** **PREPARING AN INTERVIEW**
>
> Describe the kind of person you would most like to interview for your research paper and then make a list of at least six questions that you would ask.

CONDUCTING AN INTERVIEW: IN BRIEF

- Find out who at your college or in your area specializes in your topic.
- Arrange the interview beforehand.
- Prepare your questions.
- Ask follow-up questions whenever you need to clarify a point.
- Take careful notes or tape the interview.
- After the interview, check your quotations with the interviewee.

33.8 CHOOSING WHICH SOURCES TO CONSULT

As you work your way through reference books and catalogs, look for the following:

1. Works with obvious relevance to your topic. If your topic is whaling, you would certainly want to consult a book titled *Whale Hunt*, by Nelson Cole Haley. But if your topic is nineteenth-century exploration in the South Pacific, you can ignore this book, even though you may find it catalogued under the

subject heading "Voyages and Travels." Whaling and exploration are two different things, and the slim chance that Haley might have something to say about exploration doesn't justify a search for his book.

2. Works published recently. Most of the time you can safely assume that recently published works give you up-to-date information, which is valuable not just for current topics but for topics concerned with the past. Also, a recent book will usually cite most or all of the important books on its subject that came before it.

3. Works frequently cited. Any book or article cited frequently in other books or articles is probably important. To learn how often a particular source has been cited in a given year, see one of these three: the *Science Citation Index,* published bi-monthly and cumulated every five years; the *Social Science Citation Index,* published three times a year and cumulated annually; and the *Arts & Humanities Citation Index,* published in the same way.

4. Primary and secondary sources. *Primary* means "first," and a **primary source** is one on which later, or secondary, sources are based. Depending on the subject, primary sources may be more or less valuable than secondary ones.

There are two kinds of primary sources: informational and authorial. An **informational** primary source is any firsthand account of an experience or discovery—an interview, a survey, an Arctic explorer's diary of an expedition, a scientist's report on the results of an experiment, a news story on a disaster written by someone who has seen it. **Authorial** primary sources are the writings of the individual you are studying. If you were writing a paper on James Baldwin, for instance, Baldwin's novels, essays, and letters would be your primary sources, and the critical essays that have been written *about* Baldwin's work would be your secondary sources.

If you are investigating a particular author or thinker, you should normally start by reading at least some of what he or she has written. But if you are investigating a person's life, an event, or a problem not tied to any particular works of literature, you do best to start with **secondary sources** and let them lead you to the primary ones. Secondary sources are further than primary sources from what they describe, but for that reason, they may give you a more detached, objective point of view.

5. Books with bibliographies. As shown above (p. 519), the library catalogue tells you whether or not the book has a **bibliography**—a list of related books and articles.

> **SOURCES YOU SHOULD CONSULT: IN BRIEF**
>
> • Works with obvious relevance to your topic
> • Works published recently
> • Works frequently cited
> • Primary and secondary sources
> • Books with bibliographies

33.9 EXAMINING AND EVALUATING YOUR SOURCES

1. Organize your reading time. List in order of importance the books and articles you plan to consult, and set up a reading schedule. Plan to finish all your reading and note-taking at least a week before the paper is due.

2. Read selectively. If your source is a book, read the preface to get an idea of its scope and purpose. Then scan the table of contents and the index for specific discussions of your topic.

3. Read responsibly. Respect the context of what you quote. Reading selectively doesn't mean reading carelessly or lifting statements out of context. To understand what you are quoting and to judge it adequately, you may have to read a good part of the section or chapter in which it appears—enough, at least, to familiarize yourself with the context.

4. Read critically. If the writer gives opinions without facts to support them, or makes statements of "fact" without citing

sources, you should be suspicious. (For more on this point, see section 10.3E, "Judging the Supporting Points in an Essay.") You should also compare your sources. If you find one of them more reliable or more persuasive than another, you're already beginning to see how you will present them in your paper.

33.10 TAKING NOTES

33.10A IDENTIFYING YOUR SOURCES

Before photocopying or taking notes on any source, be sure you have a **source card** or **catalog printout** on it (see section 33.5). Then mark every copy or note with a short reference to the source and the pages you've used:

Author's last name ——→ Deutschman, "Dealing" 145 ←—— Page number(s) of material

First important word of title

Every note you take must be marked with this information. Without it, you won't be able to cite the source of the note, and if you use the material without citing the source, you will be guilty of **plagiarism** (see section 34.3).

33.10B PHOTOCOPYING

The simplest way to gather material for a research paper is to **photocopy** it. Copy completely any articles you plan to read. If you copy any pages from a book, be sure to mark them with a short reference to their source, as shown above. If you can't quickly decide what pages of a book you'll want to read, check it out of the library.

With all the convenience of photocopying, bear in mind that it's no substitute for reading, annotating, and highlighting or underlining the material you have thus gathered. Collecting source material is one thing; *digesting* it is another. To digest thoroughly each item you have photocopied, see our discussion of active reading in section 1.11.

33.10C Taking Notes with a Word Processor

Whether or not you have photocopied part or all the material you plan to read, you will need to break it up into chunks small enough to use in your paper. The simplest way of doing so is with a **word processor.** (If you don't have one, skip to section 33.10D.) Once you've typed a note into the word processor, you can call it up for use anywhere in your paper without retyping it. If you label each note with a headline, your notes will be much easier to arrange when you start writing:

```
NEED FOR FORMAL PROCEDURES  ◄─────────────────  Headline


                                                Quoted
                                                material
    "Employers need to consider formal as well as ◄
    informal complaint procedures, investigations,
    resolutions, sanctions or disciplinary action,
    reports of findings and record keeping."
                                                Short for et
 Short reference  ──────►  Deane et al., Sexual 17   alii, mean-
 to source                                          ing "and
                                                    others"

    Comment: Sounds like bureaucratic overkill. Will it   Student
    work?                                                  comment

    ------------------------------------------- ◄  Line of
                                                   dashes
                                                   divides the
                                                   notes
    POLICIES AND PROCEDURES CAN'T ELIMINATE INEQUALITY

    "Neither policies nor procedures can do much to
    weaken the structural roots of gender inequalities in
    organizations."
                            Riger, "Gender" 503


    Comment: So what can weaken these roots?


    - - - - - - - - - - - - - - - -
```

Each note is followed by a short reference to its source. If you add a comment of your own (which should be labeled as such to distinguish it from the quoted matter), you can turn the process of note-taking into active pre-writing. You can begin to think about how you will use the note in your paper.

Whether or not you add a comment, however, you must be *absolutely certain to record your source.* If you fail to do so, you may confuse the source material with your own words when you later call up the file for use in writing your paper.

You must also record the source of any material that you transfer to your computer electronically from a database. For such material you should create a separate file so that it cannot be confused with work of your own. Once this material is on your disk in a file of its own, you can easily transfer portions of it into your file of notes for the research paper, using headlines and short references just as if you were typing the passages from a printed text.

As you make your notes, you can add the information from each source card to a separate file called "Sources." Putting the author's last name first, enter each new item in alphabetical order:

```
Deane, N., I. Shephard, H. Olsen, D. Rausch, and R.

    Mann. Sexual Harassment Issues and Answers.

    Washington: College and University Personnel

    Association, 1986.

Deutschman, Alan. "Dealing with Sexual Harassment."

    Fortune 4 Nov. 1991: 145-48.

Riger, Stephanie. "Gender Dilemma in Sexual

    Harassment Policies and Procedures." American

    Psychologist May 1991: 497-503.
```

For detailed guidance on writing the list of your sources in the research paper itself, see chapter 35.

33.10D TAKING NOTES ON INDEX CARDS

If you don't have access to a word processor, the simplest way of taking notes is with a stack of index cards. Putting each note on a separate card considerably simplifies the task of arranging your notes when you start to organize your paper.

Use one whole card (4-by-6 or 5-by-7 inches) for each note. The larger size makes it easy to keep note cards separate from source cards and leaves room for comments of your own. (If a note is long, continue it on a second card, which can be stapled to the first.)

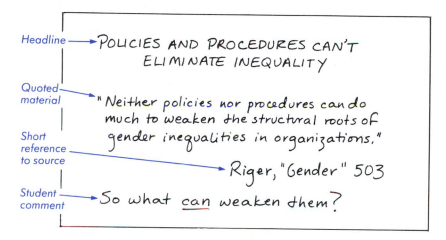

Headline ——▶ POLICIES AND PROCEDURES CAN'T
            ELIMINATE INEQUALITY

Quoted ——
material ——▶ " Neither policies nor procedures can do
            much to weaken the structural roots of
Short   gender inequalities in organizations."
reference ——
to source ——————————▶ Riger, "Gender" 503

Student —— So what can weaken them?
comment ——▶

33.11 FILLING GAPS IN YOUR RESEARCH

While you are rereading and sorting your notes, or even after you have decided what kind of paper you will write and what its thesis will be, you may discover that you need to know more about one or two things. You may suddenly realize that you have failed to consult an important source—one that several of your sources often refer to—or have failed to answer an important question. While sorting his own notes, for instance, Rick noticed that one of his sources cited a promising *Forbes* article on sexual harassment, but he had never seen the article itself. So he got a copy and made further notes before starting to write.

Writing the Research Paper

34.1 FORMULATING YOUR THESIS

The best way to **formulate a thesis** is to review all of your notes, especially if you've taken them with headlines and comments (see section 33.10). Rereading your notes gives you a concentrated view of all your research, and thus helps you decide—if you haven't already—what basic question you will try to answer. As Rick reread his cards, he found himself wondering about all the official steps taken against sexual harassment in the workplace. Just how effective, he asked himself, were all the training videos, the workshops, and the grievance procedures? Were they really striking at the root of the problem—or just swatting away at its branches? Some of his sources claimed that sexual harassment results from an imbalance of power between male and female workers. If so, mightn't that be the root of the problem? Could anything short of a new balance of power stop sexual harassment in the workplace? By raising and thinking about these questions, Rick came up with a working statement of thesis: To end sexual harassment in the workplace, companies must give more power to women.

34.2 MAKING AN OUTLINE

Once you have made a collection of notes and formulated a thesis, you may feel no strong need for an **outline**—especially if your notes are labeled with headlines for quick reference. But even though you may have plenty of clearly labeled notes, you must still decide how to organize the argument that will incorporate the material from those notes. In other words, you must still decide the order of your main points. This is what the making of an outline helps you to do.

To prepare yourself to make an outline, arrange your notes under separate headings. If your notes are in a computer file, print them up so that you can see what connections they have; then rearrange them on the screen so that notes about related points are grouped together. If your notes are on index cards, sort them into separate piles for each heading of your topic.

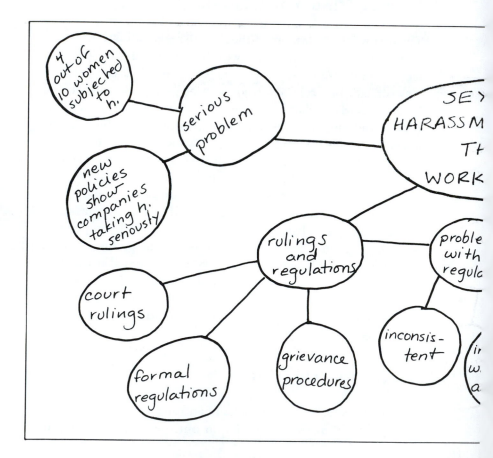

Once you have established your main headings, you must decide what arrangement of them will best serve to develop your thesis. To plot the arrangement, you can draft a branching diagram or a topic outline. Then, if you want to make your plan quite definite or if your teacher requires it, you can draft a full-sentence outline. We illustrate all three below, together with some revisions of the thesis and the adding of a conclusion in the sentence outline.

34.2A BRANCHING DIAGRAM

THESIS: To end sexual harassment in the workplace, companies must give more power to women.

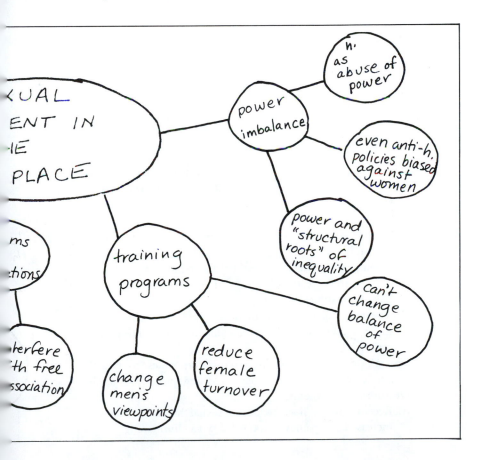

34.2B Topic Outline

THESIS: Sexual harassment will end in the workplace only when working women have as much power there as working men.

  I. Sexual harassment—widespread problem
     A. Four out of ten working women affected
     B. American companies taking problem seriously
 II. Rulings and procedures
     A. Recent court rulings
     B. Formal regulations, grievance procedures, etc.
     C. Problems with new regulations
        1. Inconsistent
        2. Interfere with free association
III. Training programs
     A. Change male perceptions
     B. Reduce female turnover
     C. But can't change balance of power
 IV. Power imbalance
     A. Harassment as a power play
     B. Even anti-harassment policies biased against women
     C. Power and "structural roots" of inequality

34.2C Full Sentence Outline

THESIS [REVISED]: Though new policies and programs have reduced sexual harassment in the workplace, it will end only when working women have as much power there as working men.

  I. Sexual harassment in the workplace is a serious and widespread problem.
     A. Though some men think sexual harassment is fantasy, surveys indicate that four out of ten working women have been subjected to it.
     B. The growing development of new policies on harassment shows that American companies are taking it seriously.
 II. Though legal pressures are forcing companies to take action against sexual harassment, the new procedures are creating new problems.
     A. Recent rulings have redefined sexual harassment and increased companies' responsibility to eliminate it.

B. In response, companies are adopting formal regulations, grievance procedures, and ways of dealing promptly with complaints.

C. But the new regulations are sometimes inconsistent and may infringe on the basic right of free association.

III. Sexual harassment cannot be ended by training programs.

A. Sexual harassment persists because many men do not see it as women do.

B. By helping men understand what sexual harassment is, training programs have lessened sexual harassment and thereby reduced the turnover of female employees.

C. But such programs do not change the balance of power between working men and women.

IV. So long as men hold most of the power in the workplace, sexual harassment will continue.

A. A man who harasses a woman in the workplace is typically using the power of his position over her.

B. Even the policies designed to stop sexual harassment reveal a bias in favor of the male viewpoint.

C. No number of rules and regulations can "weaken the structural roots" of inequality between working men and women.

V. CONCLUSION [ADDED]: Companies will eradicate sexual harassment altogether only when they decide to make men and women equal partners in running American business.

34.3 Avoiding Plagiarism

Plagiarism is presenting the words or thoughts of another writer as if they were your own. When you submit a paper that is wholly or partly plagiarized, you are taking credit—or asking your teacher to give you credit—for work done by someone else. This is fundamentally dishonest and therefore wrong.

You commit plagiarism whenever you use a source *in any way* without precisely acknowledging what you have taken from it. Consider first this passage:

If the waking world has certain advantages of solidity and continuity, its social opportunities are terribly restricted. In it we meet, as a rule, only the neighbors, whereas the dream world offers the chance of intercourse, however fugitive, with our distant friends, our dead, and our gods. For normal men it is the sole experience in which they escape the offensive and incomprehensible bondage of time and space.

—E. R. Dodds, *The Greeks and the Irrational*
(1951; Boston: Beacon, 1957) 102.

Following are four ways of plagiarizing from this passage, with plagiarized material appearing in bold print. After three of the plagiarized passages we show the same material with correct acknowledgment, using the parenthetical form of citation that is explained below in section 34.4B.

1. Word-for-word, continuous copying without quotation marks or mention of the author's name:

Dreams help us satisfy another important psychic need—our need to vary our social life. This need is regularly thwarted in our waking moments. **If the waking world has certain advantages of solidity and continuity, its social opportunities are terribly restricted. In it we meet, as a rule, only the neighbors, whereas the dream world offers the chance of intercourse, however fugitive, with our distant friends.** We awaken from such encounters feeling refreshed, the dream having liberated us from the here and now.

CORRECT ACKNOWLEDGMENT

Dreams help us satisfy another important psychic need—our need to vary our social life. This need is regularly thwarted in our waking moments. "If," as one critic observes, "the waking world has certain advantages of solidity and continuity, its social opportunities are terribly restricted. In it we meet, as a rule, only the neighbors, whereas the dream world offers the chance of intercourse, however fugitive, with our distant friends" (Dodds 102). We awaken from such encounters feeling refreshed, the dream having liberated us from the here and now.

2. Citing the author but copying many words and phrases without quotation marks, so that the reader has no way of knowing who has written what:

Dreams help us satisfy another important psychic need—our need to vary our social life. In **the waking world** our **social opportunities are terribly restricted. As a rule,** we usually encounter **only the neighbors.** In **the dream world,** on the other hand, we have a slight chance of meeting **our distant friends.** For most of us it is **the sole experience in which** we **escape the bondage of time and space** (Dodds 102).

We show no correct acknowledgment in this case because a passage stuffed with short quotations needs more than quotation marks. Such a passage needs rewriting to make the quotation more selective.

3. Paraphrasing the passage—expressing its meaning in your own words—without mention of the author's name:

Dreams help us satisfy another important psychic need—our need to vary our social life. **When awake, we are creatures of this time and this place. Those we meet are usually those we live near and work with. When dreaming, on the other hand, we can meet far-off friends.** We awaken refreshed by our flight from the here and now.

CORRECT ACKNOWLEDGMENT

Dreams help us satisfy another important psychic need—our need to vary our social life. E. R. Dodds observes that when we are awake, we are creatures of this time and this place. Those we meet are usually those we live near and work with. When dreaming, however, we can meet far-off friends (102). We awaken refreshed by our flight from the here and now.

4. Taking the author's idea without acknowledging the source:

Dreams help us satisfy another important psychic need—the need for a change. **They liberate us from the here and now, taking us out of the world we normally live in.**

CORRECT ACKNOWLEDGMENT

Dreams help us satisfy another important psychic need—the need for a change. According to E. R. Dodds, they liberate us from the here and now, taking us out of the world we normally live in (102).

34.3

This summary of Dodds's passage includes the word *world,* which also appears in the original. Generally, an individual word can be taken from the source without quotation marks unless the author of the source has coined it or used it in a special way. But any string of two or more words from the source must appear with quotation marks.

EXERCISE 1 RECOGNIZING PLAGIARISM

Read this two-paragraph passage. Then read the summary that follows, and indicate whether any part of the summary—aside from the word "motifs"—should be in quotation marks.

And, speaking more generally, it is plain foolishness to believe in ready-made systematic guides to dream interpretation, as if one could simply buy a reference book and look up a particular symbol. No dream symbol can be separated from the individual who dreams it, and there is no definite or 5 straightforward interpretation of any dream. Each individual varies so much in the way that his unconscious complements or compensates his conscious mind that it is impossible to be sure how far dreams and their symbols can be classified at all.

It is true that there are dreams and single symbols (I 10 should prefer to call them "motifs") that are typical and often occur. Among such motifs are falling, flying, being persecuted by dangerous animals or hostile men, being insufficiently or absurdly clothed in public places, being in a hurry or lost in a milling crowd, fighting with useless weapons or being wholly 15 defenseless, running hard yet getting nowhere. A typical infantile motif is the dream of growing infinitely small or infinitely big, or being transformed from one to the other—as you find it, for instance, in Lewis Carroll's *Alice in Wonderland.* But I must stress again that these are motifs that must be con- 20 sidered in the context of the dream itself, not as self-explanatory ciphers.   —Carl G. Jung, "Approaching the Unconscious,"
Man and His Symbols, ed. Jung and M.-L. von Franz
(Garden City: Doubleday, 1964) 53.

SUMMARY: According to Carl G. Jung in "Approaching the Unconscious," it would be just plain foolishness for anyone to think he or she could interpret dreams reliably by buying a ready-made reference book. No such guide has value because it is impossible to separate a dream symbol from the person who dreams it, and the unconscious of everyone is unique. Jung does admit that certain dreams and symbols come often to many. Calling these "motifs," he lists several, including falling, fighting with useless weapons, and running hard yet getting nowhere. But he emphasizes that even the motifs cannot be understood properly unless considered in the context of each dream itself.

34.4 SIGNALING USE OF A SOURCE

To avoid plagiarism, you must know how to mark the beginning and end of any material you have drawn from a source. This section explains how to do so.

34.4A INTRODUCING SOURCE MATERIAL

Whenever you use source material in any way, you must clearly signal just where the source material begins.

1. Use **quotation marks** to signal the beginning and end of any material you quote:

> As Carl Jung says, "One cannot afford to be naive in dealing with dreams."

2. Use the name or some other reference to the author to signal the beginning of any source material that you **summarize** or **paraphrase**—that is, restate in words of your own:

> **Carl Jung** warns that we should not think of dreams naively.
>
> As **one traffic specialist** observes, no police force can arrest everyone who violates a traffic law.
>
> According to **Senator Symms,** funds spent on the enforcement of the 55 mph limit in California could have been more effectively spent to reduce drunk driving.

NOTE: If the source material is anonymous or unsigned, use a phrase referring to the author or source:

> **A recent editorial** in the *Washington Post* complained that the end of the Cold War has not ended federal spending on the "Star Wars" defense system.

3. If you combine **paraphrase** with **quotation** of the exact words, use both signals in turn:

> According to **Senator Symms,** funds spent on the enforcement of the 55 mph limit in California could have been more effectively spent on "keeping drunk drivers off the road."

34.4B PARENTHETICAL CITING AFTER EACH USE

Cite each source parenthetically at the end of the source material used:

```
As one famous psychologist has written, "One cannot

afford to be naive in dealing with dreams" (Jung,

"Approaching" 62).
```
Author's last name

Page number(s)

First important word of title

```
According to Senator Symms, funds spent on the

enforcement of the 55 mph limit in California could

have been more effectively spent on "keeping drunk

drivers off the road" ("65 MPH" 27).
```
Author's name not used here because it's just been given here

```
As John A. Gardiner observes, no police force can

arrest everyone who violates a traffic law (5).
```
No title needed because paper cites only one work by this author

For more on parenthetical citing, see section 35.1A.

34.5 QUOTING

Observe the following guidelines:

1. Quote selectively. Quote source material when it concisely expresses a point important to your topic, when its language is notably vivid or eloquent, or when you plan to analyze it in detail.

As a rule, your commentary on anything you quote should be at least as long as the quotation itself. A long quotation followed by a single sentence of your own will often leave the reader wondering where *your* argument is going. Quote only as much as you need to make your points.

2. Quote accurately. Check each quotation carefully against the original to be sure you have copied it exactly.

3. Use ellipsis dots (. . .) to show that you have deliberately omitted words. You may omit words only when leaving them out does not change the basic meaning of the original:

> ORIGINAL: We must learn to reawaken and keep ourselves awake, not by mechanical aids, but by an infinite expectation of the dawn, which does not forsake us in our soundest sleep.   —Henry David Thoreau, *Walden,* ed. William Rossi, 2nd ed. (New York: Norton, 1992) 61.

> QUOTATION WITH BASIC MEANING UNCHANGED BY
> OMISSION OF NONESSENTIAL WORDS

> "We must learn to reawaken and keep ourselves awake, . . . by an infinite expectation of the dawn, which does not forsake us in our soundest sleep" (Thoreau 61).

> QUOTATION WITH BASIC MEANING CHANGED BY OMISSION
> OF ESSENTIAL WORDS

> "We must learn to reawaken and keep ourselves awake, . . . by mechanical aids . . ." (Thoreau 61).

For more on punctuating with ellipsis dots, see section 29.6B.

4. If you underline or italicize anything that is not underlined in the original, say so in parentheses:

> Jung finds something mysterious in dreams. "They originate," he writes, "in a spirit that is *not quite human*" ("Approaching" 53, emphasis added).

5. Use brackets to insert explanatory words:

> ORIGINAL: By the early seventies, most of the books [history schoolbooks] had been rewritten to include the history of blacks in America.

> —Frances FitzGerald, *America Revised: History Schoolbooks in the Twentieth Century* (Boston: Little, 1979) 84.

QUOTATION: "By the early seventies," writes Frances Fitz-Gerald, "most of the books [history schoolbooks] had been rewritten to include the history of blacks in America" (84).

For other uses of brackets in quoting, see section 29.6A.

6. Unless the quoted matter is perfectly clear by itself, explain its context as you introduce it:

Advising those who want to write, Annie Dillard says, "Appealing workplaces are to be avoided. One wants a room with no view, so imagination can meet memory in the dark" (26).

7. Whenever you quote less than a complete sentence, make it part of a complete one:

Annie Dillard advises writers to work in "a room with no view" (26).

For more on this point, see section 24.6.

34.6 SUMMARIZING AND PARAPHRASING

Though all research papers need some quotations, you don't need to quote all the source material you use. To keep the focus on your own argument, use **summary** and **paraphrase** as follows.

1. Summarize any long passage whose exact words are less important for your argument than its main idea:

ORIGINAL: It has been found that when desperate, unhappy youngsters are preparing to break away from a disordered, drug-ridden commune in which they have been living for months, they first gather together in one spot their few possessions and introduce a semblance of order among them. The need to define who you are by the place in which you live remains intact, even when that place is defined by a single object, like the small blue vase that used to mean home to one of my friends, the daughter of a widowed trained nurse who continually moved from one place to another. The Bushmen of the Kalahari Desert often build no walls when they camp in the desert. They simply hollow out a small space in the sand. But then they bend a slender sapling into an arch to make a doorway, an entrance to a dwelling as sacrosanct from invasion as the walled estates of the wealthy are or as Makati, in Manila, is, where watchmen guard the rich against the poor.

—Margaret Mead, *Blackberry Winter: My Earlier Years* (New York: Morrow, 1972) 12.

SUMMARY: According to Margaret Mead, all of us need to define ourselves by making some mark on the place we occupy, or by putting a special object there (12).

2. Whenever the exact words of a passage would needlessly break up your own writing, feel free to **paraphrase** the passage—that is, to express its meaning in your own words:

ORIGINAL: Wider variance in speed occurs at intersections, where the minimum speed is defined by the slower speed necessary for exiting and entering traffic.

—Edythe Traylor Crump, ed., *55: A Decade of Experience*, Transportation Research Board Special Report 204 (Washington: National Research Council, 1984) 241.

SENTENCE INCORPORATING PARAPHRASE: Higher speed limits inevitably increase the difference between cruising speed and speed at intersections, where—as Crump notes—drivers have to slow down to enter and exit (241).

3. Combine **paraphrase** and **quotation** to highlight a key phrase:

ORIGINAL: Neither policies nor procedures do much to weaken the structural roots of gender inequality.

—Stephanie Riger, "Gender Dilemma in Sexual Harassment Policies and Procedures," *American Psychologist* May 1991: 503.

PARAPHRASE AND QUOTATION COMBINED: As Riger observes, rules and regulations can scarcely "weaken the structural roots" of inequality between male and female employees (503).

34.7 COMPOSING THE PAPER AS A WHOLE

1. Introduce the paper by clearly announcing your topic and thesis. If the outline is not quite firm as you start to write, you can write the introduction *after* you've written the rest of the

paper—so that you know what you're introducing. But whenever you write it, the introduction should clearly establish your topic and thesis, and should also take note of possible objections to your line of argument:

<table>
<tr>
<td>

General knowledge: does not need documentation

</td>
<td>

In March 1974, a shortage of fuel precipitated by the Arab oil embargo led Congress to impose a temporary national speed limit of 55 miles per hour. When the number of highway fatalities dropped by some 9,100, from 55,511 in 1973 to 46,402 in 1974, the lifesaving benefits of the new speed limit became obvious, and Congress made it permanent (Crump 1, 15). But even though it came to be recognized as "the greatest traffic safety measure ever instituted in our history" (*National* 75), it did not last. Almost from the beginning, it provoked an opposition that steadily grew and that finally prevailed in March 1987, when Congress voted to let states raise the limit from 55 to 65 on rural interstates ("65 MPH" 12).

Critics of the 55 mph speed limit made many arguments against it. They claimed that speed was wrongly blamed for causing fatalities. They cited the millions of hours and dollars lost each year in extra time spent behind the wheel. Most of all, they argued that the law grew unenforceable because nearly everyone disobeyed it. But hard evidence shows that the 55 mph speed limit did save thousands of lives. In light of that crucial fact, what does repeal of the limit tell us? It tells me, I believe, that American motorists will sacrifice anything—including life itself—for the convenience and pleasure of driving faster than 55 miles per hour.

</td>
</tr>
</table>

—Robin Martinez, "What Happened to the 55 MPH National Speed Limit?"

2. Make the steps of your argument clear. A good research paper makes each of its points with the aid of evidence—facts and opinions cited from authoritative sources. It also uses careful transitions to move from one stage of the argument to the next. To see how one student writer constructed the steps of his argument, read the sample paper and marginal comments on pp. 567–78.

3. Use quotations sparingly. Don't let them crowd out your own words. If you offer the reader little more than a stack of quotations, you will bury the trail of your own argument.

Rather than quoting all the source materials you wish to use, summarize and paraphrase some of them. You will thus keep the reader's eye on your line of thought.

4. <u>Make your sources work together.</u> Writing the main part of a research paper is a process of building a coherent argument out of various source materials. When you summarize and paraphrase instead of quoting at length one source after another, you can show much more effectively how one source confirms or qualifies another, and how they work together to reinforce your argument:

> What finally brought repeal of the limit, however, was not so much the economic case against it as the argument that it could no longer be effectively enforced. A California writer tells us what happened in August 1985, when he drove a motorcycle for 30 miles in the slow right lane of a California freeway at exactly 55 mph. Thirty-seven vehicles came up from behind in that lane to go around him, and in nearby lanes he was passed by 170 cars before sheer boredom led him to stop counting ("Life" 18). What he saw typified American driving in 1985. Average speed on rural interstates in 1985 was 59.5 mph for the country as a whole, and over 60 mph in twenty-three states (Symms 27). "By actual measurement," according to one report, "75 percent of the vehicles on monitored stretches of rural interstate highways were exceeding the limit" that year (Martz 14).   —Robin Martinez

5. <u>End the paper by reaffirming your thesis and stating its implications:</u>

> It is not hard to see why American motorists generally disliked the national speed limit of 55 mph. We can readily imagine their resentment of a law that kept them in harness when they longed to gallop, to show what all of their horsepower could do. But if we are going to indulge this lust for speed, we should at least be honest enough to recognize what comes with it. After all the objections to the 55 mph speed limit have been studied, after all the arguments for higher limits have been weighed, we must face the hard and simple fact that higher speeds mean more fatalities. Human life is the price we have already begun to pay for repealing the national speed limit.   —Robin Martinez

35

Documenting the Research Paper

In the final draft of your research paper, you must clearly identify all the sources you have quoted from, summarized, or paraphrased. To do this you will need a **style of documentation.**

Styles of documentation are established by professional societies and journals to regularize the citing of sources in each field. Though each field has its own special requirements, scientists and social scientists generally cite their sources by parenthetical reference rather than numbered notes, and parenthetical citing has been adopted by many humanists also. This chapter explains just one kind of parenthetical citation; it offers a simplified version of the MLA style, which has been recommended by the Modern Language Association for research papers on literature, philosophy, art, and other subjects in the humanities. For brief remarks on styles of documentation in the social sciences and sciences, see sections 38.7 and 38.8.

35.1 THE MLA PARENTHETICAL STYLE: BASIC PROCEDURES

Complete information on the MLA style appears in the third edition of the *MLA Handbook for Writers of Research Papers,* by Joseph Gibaldi and Walter S. Achtert (New York: MLA, 1988). Here we explain briefly how to use the MLA style with the kinds of sources you are likely to cite in a research paper written for a college course.

Citing with parentheses calls for two steps: citing each source in parentheses as you use it, and making a list of Works Cited at the end of your paper—an alphabetical list of all the sources you have used. We treat each step in turn.

CITING AND LISTING SOURCES IN THE MLA PARENTHETICAL STYLE

- Parenthetical citing: basic procedures (35.1A)
- Listing the Works Cited: basic procedures (35.1B)
- Citing and listing various sources (35.2)
    1. Essay or any other short work in a book
    2. Article in a reference book
    3. Article in a monthly, weekly, or daily periodical
    4. Article in a journal
    5. Editorial
    6. Editor's introduction to a book
    7. Works by different authors cited from one book
    8. Multivolume work
    9. Anonymous work
    10. Material quoted by your source
    11. Two or three authors or editors
    12. More than three authors or editors
    13. Corporate author
    14. Play with act, scene, and line numbers
    15. Poem with numbered lines
    16. Poem with numbered sections and numbered lines
    17. Poem without numbered lines
    18. The Bible
    19. Translation
    20. Government publication
    21. Published interview
    22. Nonprint sources
        Computer program
        Film
        Interview conducted by the researcher
        Machine-readable document
        Performance
        Recording
        Television program
        Work of art

35.1

35.1A PARENTHETICAL CITING

1. Cite the source in parentheses immediately after the material used:

Page number(s)

First important word of title

> As one famous psychologist has written, "One cannot afford to be naive in dealing with dreams" (Jung, "Approaching" 52).

Author's last name

Period follows closing parenthesis

2. If the author of your source has written no other work cited in your paper, give just the author's name and the page number(s):

> As one traffic analyst observes, no police force can arrest everyone who violates a traffic law (Gardiner 5).

3. If you use the author's name to introduce the source, *do not repeat the name in parentheses.* Give just the page number(s):

> As Carl Jung says, "One cannot afford to be naive in dealing with dreams" (52).

But use a title word before the page number(s) if you are citing another work by the same author elsewhere in the paper:

> According to Margaret Mead, all of us need to define ourselves by making some mark on the place we occupy or putting a special object there (Blackberry 12).

4. When quoting a passage that must be indented from your text because it is more than four lines long, put the citation two spaces *after* the final punctuation mark:

> Virginia Woolf writes as follows about the role of women in literature and history:

> A very queer, composite being thus emerges.
> Imaginatively she is of the highest
> importance; practically she is completely
> insignificant. She pervades poetry from
> cover to cover; she is all but absent from
> history. She dominates the lives of kings
> and conquerors in fiction; in fact she was
> the slave of any boy whose parents forced a
> ring upon her finger. (60)

5. If all your quotations come from just one source, as in a paper written about a work of fiction, cite the source by page number(s) alone—*after* mentioning the author and title in your text:

> Meridel Le Sueur's "The Girl" is the story of
> what happens when a prim, unmarried, unnamed
> schoolteacher sets out to drive alone from Southern
> California to San Francisco. . . . But the story
> makes it clear that in rejecting his desires, she
> also stifles her own, dooming herself to a life of
> repressive order in which she will "never never
> change" (212).

For guidance in treating plays and poems, which are often *not* cited by page number(s), see section 35.2, items 14–17.

6. If your use of source material ends in the middle of a sentence, put the citation there:

> During the ride itself, neither her fear of being
> touched nor her annoyance at being flattered "just as
> if she were any common slut" (209) can altogether
> keep her from showing off.

35.1B LISTING THE WORKS CITED

Start the list on a separate page at the end of your paper. All the works you have cited should be listed alphabetically by the author's last name, or by the title if the source is unsigned:

Works Cited

Jameson, Frederic. _The Political Unconscious:_
Narrative as a Socially Symbolic Act. Ithaca:
Cornell UP, 1981.

Kermode, Frank. "Sensing Endings." _Nineteenth_
Century Fiction 33 (1978): 144-58.

Le Sueur, Meridel. "The Girl." _Ripening: Selected_
Work, 1927-1980. Ed. Elaine Hedges. Old
Westbury: The Feminist Press, 1982. 204-12.

Mead, Margaret. _Blackberry Winter_. New York:
Morrow, 1972.

Woolf, Virginia. _The Death of the Moth and Other_
Essays. New York: Harcourt, 1942.

---. _A Room of One's Own_. New York: Fountain, 1929.

Annotations (margin labels):
- Author's last name first, starting at margin
- Title of article in quotation marks
- Place of publication, publisher, date of publication
- Three hyphens plus a period signify another work by the same author.
- Book title and subtitle (if any) underlined
- Journal title underlined
- Volume and year of journal
- Edited by
- Page numbers of work in edited book
- Period ends each entry.

The simplest way to use parenthetical citation is to compile your Works Cited while making parenthetical references in your paper. Some software, such as _Norton Textra Writer,_ offers a special Works Cited function. With other software, you can create a "Workcit" file for your Works Cited. Then split the screen each time you make a parenthetical reference, switch to the "Workcit" file, and write the full reference there, as explained in the following sections. If you keep the alphabetical order as you insert each new entry in the "Workcit" file, your list of Works Cited will be ready to print just as soon as you've finished writing the paper.

If you aren't using a computer or can't split the computer screen, make a source card for each work you cite (as explained earlier in section 33.5). When you've finished the paper, alphabetize the cards and then write the list according to the instructions given here.

Following are guidelines for parenthetically citing and then listing various kinds of sources. Most of what you need to know is *illustrated* by examples rather than explained by detailed commentary, so you should study each example carefully.

35.2 CITING AND LISTING VARIOUS SOURCES

1. Essay or any other short work in a book

"Jefferson," writes Cox, "sees his life as a history
of himself" (133).

Hemingway's description of Macomber's death is coolly
technical. Firing a 6.5 Mannlicher, we are told,
Mrs. Macomber "hit her husband about two inches up
and a little to one side of the base of his skull"
(36).

                    Works Cited

Cox, James M. "Recovering Literature's Lost Ground

All lines
after the   Through Autobiography." <u>Autobiography: Essays</u>
first in each
entry are   <u>Theoretical and Critical</u>. Ed. James Olney.   — *University*
indented 5   *Press*
spaces   Princeton: Princeton UP, 1980. 123-45.

Hemingway, Ernest. "The Short Happy Life of Francis

                                                                   Double-
        Macomber." <u>The Short Stories of Ernest</u>   *space*
                                                                   between
        <u>Hemingway</u>. New York: Scribner's, 1938. 3-37.   *and within*
                                                                   entries

2. Article in a reference book

Anarchism seeks "the utmost possible freedom
compatible with social life" (Woodcock).

                    Works Cited

Woodcock, George. "Anarchism." <u>The Encyclopedia of</u>

        <u>Philosophy</u>. Ed. Paul Edwards. New York:

        Macmillan, 1967.

You don't need volume or page numbers if the articles are arranged in alphabetical order. If the article is unsigned, start with its title:

> "Pollution." <u>The Columbia Encyclopedia</u>. 1963 ed.

For general encyclopedias such as this one, which is named for the publisher (Columbia University Press), you need only the date of the edition.

3. Article in a periodical published monthly, weekly, or daily

> "In New York City," writes one observer, "black family median income is substantially higher than Puerto Rican, and is rising more rapidly" (Lehmann 97).
>
> According to David Rusk, "Most poor blacks and Hispanics are penned up in inner cities. They are surrounded by suburbs that are at least 90 percent white" (19).
>
> "Job insecurity," says one economist, "has been woven into daily life" (Wines 3).
>
> Works Cited
>
> Lehmann, Nicholas. "The Other Underclass." <u>The Atlantic</u> Dec. 1991: 96–110.
>
> Rusk, David. "America's Urban Apartheid." <u>New York Times</u> 21 May 1992: A19.
>
> Wines, Michael. "As Washington Lives on Credit, States Live on Gruel." <u>New York Times</u> 6 Sept. 1992, eastern ed., sec. 4: 1+.

Abbreviate month names when they are long

Article begins on page 1 of section 4 and continues on later pages

Special edition

If you're citing an issue with *lettered* sections (A, B, C, etc.), give the letter before the page number: A34, B16, C3.

4. Article in a journal

"Art history and museology," says one theorist, "both

work to legitimize their truths as original,

preconceived, and only recovered from the past"

(Preziosi, "Question" 383).

*Volume
number*

Works Cited

Preziosi, Donald. "The Question of Art History."

Critical Inquiry 18 (1992): 363-86.

Each *volume* of a periodical includes a full year of *issues*. If each
issue in the volume starts from page 1, give the volume number
and issue number with a period in between:

Posen, I. Sheldon, and Joseph Sciorra. "Brooklyn's

Dancing Tower." Natural History 92.6 (1983):

30-37.

*Volume
number*   *Issue
number*

5. Editorial

"Nature knows nothing of national boundaries. A

poisoned environment affects all living things on the

planet" ("Saving" 8).

Works Cited

"Saving the Cultural Environment." Editorial.

Christian Science Monitor 2 June 1992: 8.

Editorials should be labeled as such to distinguish them from
news stories.

6. Editor's introduction to a book

Kenneth Lynn writes: "In the slow, measured manner of

Hurstwood's preparation for suicide, Dreiser reveals

to us the essential dignity as well as the tragedy of

man" (xvi).

```
                        Works Cited

Lynn, Kenneth.  Introduction.  Sister Carrie.  By

    Theodore Dreiser.  New York: Rinehart, 1959.

    v-xvi.
```

If you're citing *both* the author's text *and* the editor's commentary, list the book under the author's name and use that for cross-reference:

```
Dreiser, Theodore.  Sister Carrie.  Ed. Kenneth Lynn.

    New York: Rinehart, 1959.

Lynn, Kenneth.  Introduction.  Dreiser v-xvi.
```

7. Works by different authors cited from one book

```
As St. John and Byce observe, the Department of

Education helps college students in two ways: through

Pell Grants and Guaranteed Student Loans (24).

According to one investigator, students are reluctant

to borrow because of "deep-seated fears about

excessive repayment burdens" (Hauptman 70).
```

List the book under the name of its editor, and use that for cross-reference:

```
                        Works Cited

Hauptman, Arthur M.   "Shaping Alternative Loan

        Programs."  Kramer 69-82.

Kramer, Martin, ed.  Meeting Student Aid Needs in a

        Period of Retrenchment.  New Directions for

        Higher Education 40.  San Francisco: Jossey-

        Bass, 1982.

St. John, Edward P., and Charles Byce.  "The Changing

        Federal Role in Student Aid."  Kramer 21-40.
```

8. Multivolume work

"Having witnessed the corruption of the English
government at first hand," Smith writes, colonists
who had visited England "were determined to preserve
America from exploitation and repression" (1: 151).

Works Cited

Smith, Page. <u>A New Age Now Begins</u>. 2 vols. New   *Volume*
    York: McGraw, 1976.   *number*

9. Anonymous work

Dupont and Corning, a recent article reports, have
led the way by implementing formal policies, training
programs, and grievance procedures ("Out" 30).

Works Cited

"Out of the Shadows: The Thomas Hearings Force
    Business to Confront an Ugly Reality." <u>Business
    Week</u> 28 Oct. 1991: 30-35.

10. Material quoted by your source

Robert G. Templin, Jr., Dean of Instruction at
Piedmont Community College in Virginia, says that
better-off students are "squeezing out the poor,
disadvantaged, and minority students who once called
the community college theirs" (qtd. in Watkins 1).

Works Cited

Watkins, Beverly T. "2-Year Colleges Told They're
    Becoming Institutions for Middle-Class
    Students." <u>Chronicle of Higher Education</u> 11
    Apr. 1984: 1.

11. Two or three authors or editors

One study found that commuting students are often poorer than residents and are generally forced to take on more outside work (Dickmeyer, Wessels, and Coldren 13).

Other names in normal order

Works Cited

Dickmeyer, Nathan, John Wessels, and Sharon L. Coldren. <u>Institutionally Funded Student Financial Aid</u>. Washington: American Council on Education, 1981.

Start with last name of first author listed

12. More than three authors or editors

The authors of a book on sexual harassment likewise urge a systematic response to allegations of misconduct:

> Employers need to consider formal as well as informal complaint procedures, investigations, resolutions, sanctions or disciplinary action, reports of findings and record keeping. (Deane et al. 17)

Works Cited

Deane, N., I. Shephard, H. Olsen, D. Rausch, and R. Mann. <u>Sexual Harassment Issues and Answers</u>. Washington: College and University Personnel Association, 1986.

Stands for et alii— "and others"

13. Corporate author

Many colleges still preserve "a vital commitment to equal access without regard to economic background" (Sloan, <u>Paying</u> 6).

```
                        Works Cited

   Sloan Study Consortium.  Paying for College:

        Financing Education at Nine Private

        Institutions.  Hanover: UP of New England, 1974.
```

14. Play with act, scene, and line numbers

Don't cite page numbers. Use arabic numerals with periods between them to indicate act, scene, and line number(s):

```
   In Shakespeare's Romeo and Juliet, Romeo sees Juliet

   as "the sun" of his universe (2.2.3).
```

If you're asked to cite plays with roman numerals, use uppercase for the act, lowercase for the scene, and arabic numeral(s) for the line number(s):

```
   Shakespeare's Romeo sees Juliet as "the sun" of his

   universe (II.ii.3).

                        Works Cited

   Shakespeare, William.  Romeo and Juliet.  Ed. John E.

        Hankins.  Baltimore: Penguin, 1970.
```

15. Poem with numbered lines

Cite it by the lines, not by page numbers:

```
   In Robert Frost's "Death of the Hired Man," one

   character speaks of home as "the place where, when

   you have to go there / They have to take you in"

   (lines 118-19).
```

Use the whole word "line" or "lines" in the first reference. Then just give the numbers:

```
   But his wife calls home "something you somehow

   haven't to deserve" (120).
```

Works Cited

Frost, Robert.   "The Death of the Hired Man."   <u>The</u>
<u>Poetry of Robert Frost</u>.   Ed. Edward Connery
Lathem.   New York: Holt, 1969.   34-40.

16. Poem with numbered sections and numbered lines

In Milton's <u>Paradise Lost</u>, the first sight of Adam
and Eve in their bliss moves Satan to cry out, "O
hell!" (4.358).

Works Cited

Milton, John.   <u>Paradise Lost</u>.   Ed. Scott Elledge.
2nd ed.   New York: Norton, 1993.

17. Poem without numbered lines

A poem without numbered lines may be cited by its title alone:

In "Cape Breton," Bishop speaks of mist hanging
in thin layers "like rotting snow-ice sucked away /
almost to spirit."

Works Cited

Bishop, Elizabeth.   "Cape Breton."   <u>The Complete</u>
<u>Poems</u>.   New York: Farrar, 1969.   75-77.

18. The Bible

When Jacob dreams, he hears the voice of God
promising to give him and his descendants "the land
whereon thou liest" (Genesis 28.12-13).

Cite biblical passages by giving the name of the biblical book
(without underlining or quotation marks) followed by the chapter
and verse numbers. If you *quote* from the Bible, list the version
or translation you have used.

Works Cited

The Bible. King James Version. Nashville: Thomas

    Nelson, 1972.

19. Translation

"It is the ridiculous and the shameful," writes

Rousseau, "not one's criminal actions, that it is

hardest to confess" (28).

Works Cited

Rousseau, Jean-Jacques. The Confessions. Trans.

    J. M. Cohen. Baltimore: Penguin, 1975.

20. Government publication

In any case, a census taken in 1982 showed that less

than half the working mothers of young children had

them supervised by a relative other than their father

(USBC 9-10).

Beyond such formalities and regulations, some

organizations require that managers set an example of

fairness in their own behavior. As one training

manual notes, their "doing" will be closely

scrutinized by employees sensitive to nonverbal

messages (USDI 38).

Works Cited

U.S. Bureau of Census [USBC]. Child-Care

Govern-
ment Print-   Arrangements of Working Mothers: June 1982.
ing Office

    Washington: GPO, 1983.

Your
abbrevia-
tion
noted here

U.S. Department of the Interior [USDI]. Training in

    the Prevention of Sexual Harassment. Rept. 637.

    Washington: GPO, 1987.

Numbered
report

21. Published interview

```
"I just think there's too much sleaze," the president
said (Bush 22).
                    Works Cited
Bush, George.  "Bush on the Record."  By Michael
        Kramer and Henry Muller.  Time 24 Aug. 1992:
        21-24.
```

List the interview by the name of the person interviewed.

22. Nonprint sources

Cite nonprint works by the title, by the name(s) of the persons chiefly responsible for the work cited, or both. Give pagination only for machine-readable documents.

Computer program

```
Computer programs such as Wayne Holder's The Word
Plus allow the writer to see exactly which of the
words in a computerized text may be misspelled.
                    Works Cited
Holder, Wayne.  The Word Plus.  Computer Software.
        Oasis Systems, 1982.  CP/M 2.2, disk.
```

Film

```
In Atlantic City, Guare exposes the tawdriness,
ruthlessness, and brutality that undermine the would-
be revival of a fabled sea resort.
                    Works Cited
Guare, John, screenwriter.  Atlantic City.  Dir.
        Louis Malle.  With Burt Lancaster, Kate Reid,
        and Susan Sarandon.  Paramount, 1980.
```

Interview conducted by the researcher

According to Captain Ernest Loomis of the New
Hampshire State Police, most drivers fail to adjust
their speed to changes in weather conditions.

Works Cited

Loomis, Ernest. Personal interview. 22 Apr. 1989.

Machine-readable document

"To err is human, and to write is to experience the
human inevitability of error" (Heffernan, Getting 4).

Works Cited

Heffernan, James A. W. Getting the Red Out: Grading
without Degrading. ERIC, 1983. ED 229 788.

Performance

A recent performance of Shakespeare's Much Ado about
Nothing once again demonstrated how much his language
can achieve theatrically without the aid of elaborate
sets.

Works Cited

Much Ado about Nothing. By William Shakespeare.
Dir. Terry Hands. With Derek Jacobi, Sinead
Cusack, and the Royal Shakespeare Company.
Gershwin Theatre, New York. 19 Oct. 1984.

Recording

Frost's own reading of "Birches" fully exploits the
resonance of its language.

Works Cited

Frost, Robert. "Birches." Robert Frost Reads His
Poetry. Caedmon, TC 1060, 1956.

Television program

"The Enlightened Machine" graphically revealed just
what happens to the brain during an epileptic
seizure.

Works Cited

"The Enlightened Machine." The Brain. Narr. George
    Page. PBS. WETK, Burlington, VT. 10 Oct.
    1984.

Work of art

The vortex that became Turner's trademark first
appeared in his Snow Storm: Hannibal and His Army
Crossing the Alps.

Works Cited

Turner, J. M. W. Snow Storm: Hannibal and His Army
    Crossing the Alps (1812). The Tate Gallery,
    London.

EXERCISE 1 CITING WITH PARENTHESES—MLA STYLE

Take the information given on each source, and use it to write
two entries in the MLA style: a parenthetical citation as it
would look in the text, and the entry as it would appear in a
list of Works Cited.

EXAMPLE

The source is a book by Paul Fussell entitled *The Great War
and Modern Memory*. It was published by the Oxford University
Press in 1975. The first place of publication listed is New
York. Your reference is to material on pages 96 and 97. In the
text you introduce the material without mentioning Fussell's
name. You are using no other book by him.

PARENTHETICAL CITATION

(Fussell 96-97)

IN WORKS CITED

Fussell, Paul.   The Great War and Modern Memory.

    New York: Oxford UP, 1975.

1. Your source is a book titled *A Literature of Their Own,* subtitled *British Women Novelists from Brontë to Lessing.* It was published in 1977 by Princeton University Press, which is located in Princeton, NJ. You refer to material on pages 121, 122, and 123, and you use the author's name (Elaine Showalter) to introduce the material.

2. The source is a book by Joseph Conrad entitled *Lord Jim.* It was edited by Thomas C. Moser and published by W. W. Norton & Company, Inc., in 1968. The place of publication is listed as New York. Your reference, a direct quotation, is to something the editor states in the preface on page vi, and you mention him by name when introducing the quotation. You are using no other work edited or written by Moser.

3. Your source is a book by Ngũgĩ wa Thiong'o. It is called *Decolonizing the Mind: The Politics of Language in African Literature.* It was published in 1986 by Heineman Educational Books, Inc., in London. You introduce the material without using the author's name, and the material comes from page 86.

4. The source is an essay by Stuart Levine entitled "Emerson and Modern Social Concepts." The essay is one of several essays by different authors in a book entitled *Emerson: Prospect and Retrospect.* The essay appears on pages 155 through 178 of the book. The editor of the book is Joel Porte. The book was published in 1982 by the Harvard University Press. The place of publication is Cambridge, Massachusetts. Your reference is to page 156 and you mention Levine by name in the text.

5. The source is an article by George F. Kennan entitled "America's Unstable Soviet Policy." It appears on pages 71 through 80 of *The Atlantic Monthly,* a monthly magazine published by The Atlantic Monthly Company. The place of publication is Boston, MA. Kennan's article is printed in the November 1982 issue. You quote two sentences from page 79, but do not mention Kennan. You are using another work by him, *The Nuclear Delusion.*

6. The source is Victor Hugo's *Les Misérables* in the translation by Norman Denny. The edition is in two volumes, each with its own pagination; that is, each begins with a page 1. The edition was first published by the Folio Press in 1976, then by Penguin Books in 1980. The place of publication of the Penguin edition, which is the one you are using, is listed as Harmondsworth, Middlesex, England. Your reference is to an episode Hugo presents on pages 210 through 214 of volume 2.

7. The source is an editorial printed on page 15 of *The Christian Science Monitor* dated November 9, 1984. The editorial is unsigned; its title is "Polling Power."

8. The source is a recording of a poem as read by the author, T. S. Eliot. The title of the poem is "The Love Song of J. Alfred Prufrock." It is one of several poems on a record entitled *T. S. Eliot Reading Poems and Choruses.* The manufacturer is Caedmon Records, Inc., of New York City. The catalog number is TC 1045. A note on the record states that the recording was made in 1955. Your reference is to Eliot's portrayal of Prufrock in the entire poem. Since no parenthetical citation is required for this type of source, write out just the reference that would appear in your list of Works Cited.

Preparing the Final Copy of the Research Paper

36.1 BASIC PROCEDURES

If your teacher has special requirements for the final copy of a research paper, you should of course follow those. Otherwise, we suggest you do as follows.

1. If you've written your paper with a word processor, be sure your hard copy is clear and readable, with page breaks inserted where you want them. If you're typing, use a fresh black ribbon on white, twenty-pound 8½-by-11-inch sheets. Don't submit your final copy on fanfold computer paper or erasable paper; make a photocopy on uncoated paper instead.

2. Use double-spacing throughout, leave one-inch margins all around the text (top, bottom, and both sides), and indent paragraphs as shown on p. 566.

3. Type on one side of the paper only.

4. If your instructor requires a title page, follow the format shown in section 5.7, p. 97. Otherwise follow the format shown on p. 566. Do not underline the title or put it in quotation marks.

5. On each page, give your last name and the page number at upper right, as shown on p. 566.

6. Always keep a copy of what you have submitted.

36.1

RESEARCH PAPER: FORMAT WITH TITLE ON FIRST PAGE OF TEXT

↑ ½"
Martinez 1
↓ ½"

Robin Martinez

Professor Sobel

←—— 1" ——→ English 2

8 May 1993

Whatever Happened to the 55 MPH National

Speed Limit?

⟩ Double-space

Indent 5 ——→ In March 1974, a shortage of fuel precipitated
spaces

by the Arab oil embargo led Congress to impose a

temporary national speed limit of 55 miles per hour.

When the number of highway fatalities dropped by some

9,100, from 55,511 in 1973 to 46,402 in 1974, the new

speed limit was widely credited with saving lives,

and Congress made it permanent (Crump 1, 15). But

RESEARCH PAPER: SECOND AND SUCCEEDING PAGES OF TEXT

↑ ½"
Martinez 2
↓ ½"

traffic safety measure ever instituted in our

←— 1" —→ history" (National 75), it did not last. Almost

from the beginning, it provoked an opposition that

steadily grew and that finally prevailed in March

1987, when Congress voted to let states raise the

limit from 55 to 65 on rural interstates ("65 MPH"

12).

As the following pages will show, critics of

the 55 mph speed limit made many arguments against

36.2 SAMPLE RESEARCH PAPER WITH MLA PARENTHETICAL STYLE

Harris 1

Rick Harris

Professor Frazer

English 1

14 December 1992

Sexual Harassment in the Workplace

In October 1991, television cameras showed the American public something it had never seen before: a tenured professor of law accusing a Supreme Court nominee of sexual harassment, with the nominee vehemently denying the charge and explicitly questioning the integrity of his accuser. The Clarence Thomas hearings turned the eyes of a nation on sexual harassment. In so doing, the hearings dramatically raised national consciousness of what Mark Garvey calls the "most widespread occupational hazard in the workplace today" (qtd. in Riger 497).

Opening paragraph highlights importance of the topic.

What is sexual harassment? According to the U.S. Equal Employment Opportunity Commission (EEOC), it is "verbal or physical contact of a sexual nature" that makes hiring or any other decision about workers depend on their sexual response, or that "creates a hostile working environment" (74677). But some men think sexual harassment is fantasy. In the wake of the Thomas hearings, the president of a New York real estate firm told a reporter, "Now you've got to be defensive as hell. . . . [Whatever you say], you get

Opposing views of topic: writer concedes that some think it's unimportant.

Harris 2

some screwball saying it's a sexist remark" (qtd. in "Men" A20). At its most extreme, this line of thought has led to the claim that sexual harassment is something fabricated by sexual harassment counselors in order to sell their services (Morgenson 71).

Statistics show that sexual harassment is a major problem.

Statistics disagree. In 1980, when the U.S. Merit Systems Protection Board surveyed over ten thousand women working for the federal government, four out of ten reported that they had been sexually harassed during the previous two years, and a similar study conducted in 1988 came up with almost identical results (Riger 497). In 1985, a survey of women working for private companies in Los Angeles revealed that half of them had been sexually harassed at least once (Gutek 46). More recent statistics confirm these earlier ones. According to the Rhode Island Commission for Human Rights, the complaints it hears about sex discrimination, including harassment, now outnumber complaints about racial discrimination ("Survey" 5).

In response to this evidence of widespread sexual harassment, some American corporations are working hard to eliminate it. Dupont and Corning, a recent article reports, have led the way by implementing formal policies, training programs, and grievance procedures ("Out" 30). These--particularly

Harris 3

the training programs--have already begun to bring
working women more respect. But they will not
command full respect so long as they lack access to
top positions. For this reason, I believe that
sexual harassment will end in the workplace only when
working women have as much power there as working
men.

Writer states thesis: only a redistribution of power can solve the problem.

    To see why nothing less than a redistribution of
power can end sexual harassment in the workplace, we
must first consider what steps have been proposed or
actually taken to combat it. Donald Weiss, program
manager for the Managing People Program at Citicorp
Executive Development Center in St. Louis, proposes
that all employees of a company should get three
things: a formal statement of company policy on
sexual harassment, an explanation of what their
responsibilities to each other are, and a list of the
sanctions that might result from the filing of a
complaint (31). The authors of a book on sexual
harassment likewise urge a systematic response to
allegations of misconduct:

> Employers need to consider formal as
> well as informal complaint procedures,
> investigations, resolutions, sanctions or
> disciplinary action, reports of findings
> and record keeping. (Deane et al. 17)

Writer considers another solution: formal procedures.

Harris 4

Beyond such formalities and regulations, some
organizations require that managers set an example of
fairness in their own behavior. As one training
manual notes, their "doing" will be closely
scrutinized by employees sensitive to nonverbal
messages (USDI 38). Furthermore, as Robert Gray
notes, all proposals and existing policies stress the
need for promptness in dealing with initial
complaints, for the speed of the company's response
largely determines its legal liability (28).

Writer con-
cedes that
legal rulings
force
companies
to take the
problem
seriously.

The specter of such liability has put new
pressure on companies. Garland and Segal note that
since the EEOC first defined sexual harassment in
1980, the courts have both redefined it and increased
companies' responsibility to eradicate it (32). In
1986, the Supreme Court upheld a lower court ruling
in the case of Meritor Savings Bank vs. Vinson.
Under this ruling, any kind of harassment that
creates a "hostile working environment" violates
Title VII of the Civil Rights Act (Deane et al. 6-7).
In 1991, in the case of Robinson vs. Jacksonville
Shipyards, a Florida court ruled that the question of
what makes a "hostile environment" must be referred
to the judgment of a "reasonable woman" as distinct
from a "reasonable person" (qtd. in Garland and Segal
32). These two rulings will surely influence future
verdicts. According to Stephen Bokat, vice president

Harris 5

and general counsel of the U.S. Chamber of Commerce,
the rulings will generate "tougher standards for
business and the likelihood that more allegations of
sexual harassment will be upheld" (qtd. in Gray 31).

In the scramble to adopt new policies and
procedures to cope with these new legal pressures,
however, companies are also generating new problems.
One new policy calls for two incompatible things:
complete confidentiality in the investigation of
complaints and the questioning of as many witnesses
as possible ("Out" 31-32). Greater problems arise
from any policy designed to regulate interpersonal
contact. Mary Rowe, for instance, argues that
companies can head off sexual harassment by banning
all sexual relations--whether consensual or not--
between employees at different levels of seniority
(46). But this sort of policy infringes on what many
workers see as their right to choose sexual partners.
Says construction manager Vincent del Nero, "I now
treat women less like friends. It means that the
workplace is basically less fun now" (qtd. in "Men"
A20).

This remark illustrates a further problem. By
implying that friendship between men and women must
always include the "fun" of sexual excitement, del
Nero exemplifies the very state of mind that makes
women feel uneasy. Sexual harassment persists

Writer shows how formal procedures generate new problems.

Harris 6

because many men simply do not see it as women do.
In 1985, Barbara Gutek found that "sexual touching"
was considered harassment by 85 percent of the women
she surveyed and only 58 percent of the men (43).
Likewise, while 24 percent of the women canvassed in
a 1990 survey thought that stares and visual "once-
overs" were harassment, just 8 percent of the men
thought so (Deutschman 148). What these surveys show
has been reaffirmed by Lauren Nile, a management
consultant. While a man, she says, tends to think of
sexual harassment as "blatant touching," a woman is
more likely "to consider the hostile work
environment--her chest being stared at or sexual
jokes" (qtd. in Garland 32).

To some extent, the gap between male and female
concepts of sexual harassment can be overcome by
training. According to one group of authors,
consistent and explicit training of employees "offers
a means of differentiating truly sexually harassing
activity from behavior that is not" (Deane et al.
19). Companies such as Dupont and Corning
wholeheartedly agree. Deutschman reports that
Dupont's training workshop, called "A Matter of
Respect," has been attended by over sixty-five
thousand employees and is used to introduce extended
sessions of employee role-playing (148). At Corning,
according to a recent article, an innovative training

They also fail to reconcile different views of sexual harass-ment.

Writer concedes that training programs can help solve the problem.

Harris 7

program combines workshops on sexual harassment with
a videotape showing reenactments of harassing
comments often heard in the lab ("Out" 32). This
program probably helps to explain why women employees
are now more willing to stay with Corning. The
article tells us that from 1987 to 1991, their rate
of attrition dropped from 16.2 percent to just over
2.6 percent (32).

Nevertheless, neither training programs nor
elaborate policies and procedures can touch the root
of sexual harassment in the workplace: the imbalance
of power between working men and working women. The
U.S. Department of Labor reports that although women
compose 45 percent of the workforce, they hold just
39.3 percent of managerial, executive, and
administrative jobs (1). Furthermore, according to a
study made by the University of California in 1990,
women hold only 2.6 percent of the senior executive
jobs--vice presidential level and above--in "Fortune
500" companies (Walters 4). In other words, while
the percentage of supervisory jobs held by women is
approaching the percentage of all jobs women hold,
the senior officers of American corporations remain
almost exclusively male.

How much does this imbalance of power block
efforts to eliminate sexual harassment? No other
obstacle comes close. The virtual exclusion of women

*But, he
argues,
they don't
give women
any more
power.*

Harris 8

from the highest levels of management means, quite
simply, that economic and political power in American
corporations is the property of men. Women in the
workplace, therefore, must depend for their
livelihood and well-being on those who all too often
see no compelling reason (outside of legal pressures)
to respect a woman's dignity--or her point of view.

Under these circumstances, many men feel free to
harass women. In two-thirds of the harassment cases
surveyed by the Connecticut Women's Education and
Legal Fund, the harasser was either the victim's
supervisor or a company VIP. "Clearly," the Fund
report concluded, "the common denominator of the
disparities between victims and harassers is power,
real and perceived" (qtd. in "Survey" 5). Patricia
Palmiotto, manager of personnel training and
development at Dartmouth College, emphatically

*Superior
power
licenses
men to
harass
women.*

agrees. "Sexual harassment," she told me, "<u>is</u> used
as a form of power, and it is the power issue which
is most prevalent." As one writer puts it, a man who
harasses a woman in the workplace typically uses the
power of his position as "a license for licentious-
ness" (Deutschman 145).

Beyond encouraging harassment, the imbalance of
power also constricts what companies are doing to
stop it. While some companies have reduced
harassment by means of training programs and formal

Harris 9

policies, as we have seen, the policies themselves
are often flawed by gender bias. As Riger argues,
"the way that policies define harassment and the
nature of dispute resolution may better fit male than
female perspectives" (497). For one thing, she
notes, the language of corporate policies is gender
neutral, ignoring the fact that women are sexually
harassed far more often than men are (498). She also
finds a male bias in the grievance procedures that
companies have established during the past ten years
(500). According to Carol Gilligan, men and women in
general experience conflict very differently: while
men seek justice and the recognition of their
individual rights, women are more likely to consider
their responsibility to others (16-17). This "care
perspective," Riger says, may lead women to reject
formal procedures that entail conflict and
retribution (500).

It also leads to policies that favor the male viewpoint.

     In response to this problem, companies might
well include informal as well as formal procedures
for dealing with cases of sexual harassment. They
might, for instance, encourage any woman who feels
harassed to tell the harasser why--in the presence of
another women. But any approach that leans entirely
on rules and procedures is doomed to fail. Says
Billie Wright Dziech, professor of English at the
University of Cincinnati:

Harris 10

We somehow have this concept that if we
have enough rules, enough laws, and enough
regulations, we'll be able to solve [the
problem of sexual harassment]. But I don't
think that is going to do it. (qtd. in
Leatherman A26)

Rules and regulations cannot stop sexual harassment
because they cannot get beneath it. As Riger
observes, they can scarcely "weaken the structural
roots" of inequality between male and female
employees (503).

So long as these "structural roots" remain in
place, working women will continue to undergo
harassment. If sexual harassment expresses power as
much as--or more than--desire, then corporations

Conclusion: To end sexual harassment, companies must equalize power between men and women.

should do everything possible to see that the power
within their ranks is evenly divided between men and
women. Companies with training programs and
carefully formulated policies on sexual harassment
have made impressive headway against it. But they
will eradicate it altogether only when they decide to
make men and women equal partners in the enterprise
of American business.

Harris 11

Works Cited

Deane, N., I. Shephard, H. Olsen, D. Rausch, and R.
     Mann. <u>Sexual Harassment Issues and Answers</u>.
     Washington: College and University Personnel
     Association, 1986.

Deutschman, Alan. "Dealing with Sexual Harassment."
     <u>Fortune</u> 4 Nov. 1991: 145-48.

Garland, Susan B., and Troy Segal. "Thomas v. Hill:
     The Lessons for Corporate America." <u>Business
     Week</u> 21 Oct. 1991: 32.

Gilligan, Carol. <u>In a Different Voice: Psychological
     Theory and Women's Development</u>. Cambridge:
     Harvard UP, 1982.

Gray, Robert T. "How to Deal with Sexual
     Harassment." <u>Nation's Business</u> Dec. 1991: 28-
     31.

Gutek, Barbara A. <u>Sex and the Workplace</u>. San
     Francisco: Jossey-Bass, 1985.

Leatherman, Courtney. "Colleges Seek New Ways to
     Deal with Sexual Harassment as Victims on
     Campuses Are Reluctant to File Complaints." <u>The
     Chronicle of Higher Education</u> 4 Dec. 1991: A1+.

"Men Say Worry about Harassment Leads Them to Tone
     Down Conduct." <u>New York Times</u> 7 Nov. 1991: A20.

Morgenson, G. "Watch that Leer, Stifle that Joke."
     <u>Forbes</u> May 1989: 69-72.

                                                    Harris 12

"Out of the Shadows: The Thomas Hearings Force

     Business to Confront an Ugly Reality." <u>Business</u>

     <u>Week</u> 28 Oct. 1991: 30-35.

Palmiotto, Patricia. Personal Interview. 7 Dec.

     1992.

Riger, Stephanie. "Gender Dilemma in Sexual

     Harassment Policies and Procedures." <u>American</u>

     <u>Psychologist</u> May 1991: 497-503.

Rowe, Mary P. "Dealing with Sexual Harassment."

     <u>Harvard Business Review</u> May-June 1981: 42-46.

"Survey Finds Workplace Remains Harassment Site."

     <u>New York Times</u> 22 March 1992, Connecticut ed.,

     sec. 8: 5.

U.S. Department of Labor [USDL]. <u>Facts on Working</u>

     <u>Women</u>. Rept. 89-4. Washington: GPO, 1989.

U.S. Equal Employment Opportunity Commission [EEOC].

     "Final Amendment to Guidelines on Discrimination

     Because of Sex Under Title VII of the Civil

     Rights Act of 1964." <u>Federal Register</u> Rept. 45.

     Washington: GPO, 1980. 74675-77.

U.S. Department of the Interior [USDI]. <u>Training in</u>

     <u>the Prevention of Sexual Harassment</u>. Rept. 637.

     Washington: GPO, 1987.

Walters, Donna K. H. "Pay Gap Narrows as Men Lose

     Ground." <u>Los Angeles Times</u> 14 Sept. 1992: 4.

Weiss, Donald H. "The Principal Ingredients of a

     Sexual Harassment Policy." <u>Nation's Business</u>

     Dec. 1991: 31.

Writing about Literature

37.1 THE LITERARY WORK AS A CREATED WORLD

Literature is writing that can be read in many ways. We can read it as a form of history, biography, or autobiography. We can read it as an example of linguistic structures or rhetorical conventions manipulated for special effect. We can view it as a material product of the culture that produced it. We can see it as an expression of the ideology—beliefs and values—of a particular class. We can also see a work of literature as a self-contained structure of words—as writing that calls attention to itself, to its own images and forms.

Viewed in this light, literature differs from the three other kinds of writing treated elsewhere in this book: expressive, persuasive, and expository. Expressive writing aims to express the feelings of the **writer;** persuasive writing seeks to influence the **reader;** expository writing tries to explain **the outside world.** By contrast, a work of literature creates a world of its own:

INFANT SORROW

My mother groaned! My father wept.
Into the dangerous world I leapt,
Helpless, naked, piping loud;
Like a fiend hid in a cloud.

Struggling in my father's hands,
Striving against my swaddling bands;
Bound and weary I thought best
To sulk upon my mother's breast.   —William Blake

The first thing we're likely to notice about this text is its form. Instead of running all the way from the left margin to the right one, like a block of prose, it is broken up into two sets of four short lines, and the end words rhyme: *wept, leapt, loud, cloud, hands, bands, best, breast.* Besides these formal features, the text offers us striking images, like that of the "fiend hid in the cloud."

Since such an image makes no reference to the outside world as we normally know it, this is not expository writing. Nor is it quite the same as persuasive writing. Though the poem works on us rhetorically by exciting our sympathy for the desperate and frustrated speaker, it makes no direct appeal to us as audience, no systematic effort to shape our opinions on a specified point. Furthermore, while it looks like expressive writing, the "I" speaking here is not the writer but an infant, a figure the writer has created or imagined. What we have, then, is an independent little world made of words: a world of forms, images, and sounds (groans and "piping loud" screams) that are all designed to work together.

This does not mean that works of literature have nothing to do with the outside world. On the contrary, Walt Whitman's poems often address the reader directly; Mark Twain's *Huckleberry Finn* has everything to do with the history of American slavery; and when Emily Dickinson writes, "I never hear the word 'escape' / Without a quicker blood," she is surely expressing her own feelings. The world of literature is watered by many streams—by the writer's feelings, by the writer's desire to stir the reader, and by the writer's consciousness of the outside world. But in a work of literature, all of these streams flow through a world the writer creates.

37.2 LITERARY GENRE: POETRY, FICTION, DRAMA

To write effectively about a literary work, you need to know something about its **genre**—about the *kind* of literary work it is. Works of literature generally come in one of three genres: poetry, fiction, and drama.

37.2A POETRY

Most people think of **poetry** as writing arranged into lines with a uniform number of syllables, a regular pattern of stresses (called *meter*), and rhyming words at the end. The Blake poem quoted just above fits this definition nicely. But many poems have neither meter nor rhyme, and some of them look just like prose on the printed page. So poetry cannot simply be defined by its formal features.

You may consider a poem as the concentrated expression of a moment of feeling, a moment of vision, or both. This definition obviously excludes long poetic narratives such as the ancient epics, but probably includes most if not all of the poems you may be asked to write about.

In studying a poem that you plan to write about, use the following questions as a guide:

1. Who is the speaker of the poem? Who is the "I"? Is it the poet or some character the poet has created? If the "I" is a created character, the title of the poem will often give you a clue to his or her identity. Blake's "Infant Sorrow," for instance, is spoken by an infant, and Langston Hughes's "Madam and the Phone Bill" is spoken by an angry woman talking to a telephone operator. But even if the speaker can be connected with the poet, the two are never identical. Wordsworth wrote his first-person "Tintern Abbey" while *walking* from the abbey to the city of Bristol; yet in the poem, he presents himself as *standing* on a riverbank a few miles north of the abbey. So we must ask ourselves why Wordsworth presents himself in this way and what sort of role he plays in the poem. Once you have identified the speaker, ask yourself what the poem tells us about his or her feelings and perceptions.

Poems such as Gwendolyn Brooks's "Mrs. Small" are spoken by a narrator who never becomes "I," a narrator speaking *about* someone or something in the third person. But even a third-person narrative can make us see a character or situation in a particular way—as "Mrs. Small" illustrates (see below, pp. 608–9).

2. <u>What is the dominant image?</u> An **image** is a word or phrase that calls to mind something we can experience with our senses, most often something we can imagine *seeing,* whether it is real or not. In Blake's "Infant Sorrow," the dominant image is that of the infant, who is first naked and then bound in "swaddling bands." The simile comparing the infant to "a fiend hid in a cloud" helps us to see infant energy trapped and smothered as if it were something diabolical—something threatening the established order.

3. <u>How does the dominant image express the **theme**?</u> The **theme** of a poem is the product of a reader's interpretation— the abstract meaning that a reader infers from particular details and images. As the examples just cited show, to explain the dominant image of a poem is to begin to formulate its theme. If we take the swaddled infant as the dominant image of "Infant Sorrow," we can infer that the poem's theme is the conflict between infant energy and adult constriction (swaddling) of that energy. In Emily's Dickinson's "I never hear the word 'escape,' " the dominant image is that of a prison, which plainly accentuates the urge to escape. In "Mrs. Small," the dominant image is hot coffee, a symbol of the warmth, domesticity, and hospitality that Mrs. Small herself personifies.

4. <u>How is the dominant image related to other images?</u> In "Mrs. Small," the title character splashes coffee on an insurance salesman's white shirt. As explained in Cirri Washington's essay on the poem (pp. 604–8), these two images—the coffee and the white shirt—help define the chief conflict between the poem's two characters.

5. <u>How does the poem develop its theme?</u> What sort of progression can you see as you move from the beginning to the end? Blake's "Infant Sorrow" consists of two verse paragraphs, or **stanzas.** The first reveals the primal energy of an infant leaping into life; the second shows weariness and resignation to confinement. The movement from one state to the other defines the speaker's state of mind.

6. How do rhyme and meter (if any) help to express meaning?
Meter is the pattern of stresses made by a line of poetry. The first line of Blake's poem, for instance, consists of eight syllables divided into four "iambic feet," each containing an unstressed syllable (da) followed by a stressed one (DUM):

> IAMBIC FOOT
> da-DUM   da-DUM   da-DUM   da-DUM
> My moth   er groaned!   My fa   ther wept.

The meter of this line—its pattern of stresses—helps to accentuate its two most important words—*groaned* and *wept.*

Rhyme highlights a relation between words. The rhyme of *wept* and *leapt* in the first stanza of Blake's poem underscores the paradox that the speaker's birth dismays the speaker's father; the rhyme between *hands* and *bands* in the second stanza helps us see that both are used to confine the speaker.

37.2B FICTION

Fiction includes short stories and novels. All fiction is imaginary **narrative,** telling a series of events in which one or more characters do or experience something that leaves them changed. In William Faulkner's short story "Dry September," the rumor that a black man has accosted a white woman leads to his being lynched, and a barber who tries to stop the lynching is forced to discover how brutal his fellow townsmen can be. In Ernest Hemingway's novel *A Farewell to Arms,* an American soldier wounded in Italy during the First World War falls in love with his nurse, recovers, and flees with her to neutral Switzerland; when she dies in childbirth, he is shattered.

In studying fiction, use the following questions as a guide:

1. What does the setting contribute? The **setting** of a piece of fiction—the place and time in which its central action originates—typically helps to explain how or why the action occurred. The setting is commonly established at the beginning, as in the opening sentences of Faulkner's "Dry September":

Through the bloody September twilight, aftermath of sixty-two rainless days, it had gone like a fire in dry grass—the rumor, the story, whatever it was. Something about Miss Minnie Cooper and a Negro. Attacked, insulted, frightened: none of them, gathered in the barber shop on that Saturday evening where the ceiling fan stirred, without freshening it, the vitiated air, sending back upon them, in recurrent surges of stale pomade and lotion, their own stale breath and odors, knew exactly what happened.

The dryness and stagnation of the air helps to explain how and why the rumor could ignite a lynching, acting "like a fire in dry grass."

2. What central conflict drives the plot? The **plot** of a fictional work is the sequence of events that it narrates. Typically the plot is driven by a **conflict** that is somehow resolved at the end. In "Dry September," for instance, a white barber who tries to use rational arguments on behalf of a black man is browbeaten and scorned by his enraged fellow whites, who end up lynching the man. Eudora Welty's "Why I Live at the P.O." is chiefly the tale of a young woman's feud with her sister, who has done everything possible to turn the rest of the family against her. But just as often the conflict takes place *within* the central character. In David Leavitt's "Territory," for example, the main character is a young man who has invited his male lover to accompany him on a visit to his mother's house in California. Though his mother knows he is gay, he is torn between the urge to be openly affectionate with his lover in her presence and the fear of antagonizing her by doing so.

3. How is the story told? By an **undramatized narrator** who plays no part in the story, by a **dramatized observer** (an "I") reporting largely the actions of others, or by a **narrator-agent** reporting his or her interaction with others? The story of Salinger's *Catcher in the Rye* is told by a narrator-agent named Holden Caulfield, the central figure in his own tale. Hawthorne's *Scarlet Letter* is told entirely by an undramatized narrator. Some stories combine different techniques of narration. Joseph Conrad's *Heart of Darkness,* for instance, is begun by a dramatized

observer and then largely taken over by a narrator-agent. In each case, the method of narration powerfully affects our experiences of the story. While an undramatized narrator often tells us what each of several characters thinks and feels, a narrator-agent makes us see the world of a story from his or her limited point of view. Thus we intimately share what one character does, suffers, and learns.

4. How does the story reveal its chief characters? Fictional **characters** are revealed by the way they appear, by what they say, by what they do, and by what others say about them. In *Heart of Darkness,* a man who enters an African jungle seeking ivory on behalf of a European company is described by another character as a messenger of "progress," and later he says of himself, "I had immense plans." But we also learn that he has presided over human sacrifice and that his own body has been wasted by disease. To understand fictional characters, weigh the words spoken by and about them along with their actions and appearance.

5. What changes does the story reveal? Plot requires not simply conflict but **development,** which usually means a change in one or more characters. Some characters change *for us* as we learn more about them; some change *in themselves* as they learn about themselves and the world around them; some do both. The would-be "emissary of pity . . . and progress" in *Heart of Darkness* changes for us when we learn how greedy and vicious he has become in the jungle; but he also changes in himself at the moment of his death, when he realizes the horror of what he has done.

6. How does the story develop its theme? Like the theme of a poem, the **theme** of a story is the product of a reader's interpretation: the general idea that a reader draws from the story as a whole. From "Dry September" we can draw the theme of racial hatred. The story develops this theme, we can say, by showing how blind and deaf such hatred can be to any voice of reason, and how murderous it finally becomes. This is a general statement about what the story *means.* But because a theme is the

product of interpretation, different readers may have different ways of stating the theme. Some readers might say, for instance, that the theme of "Dry September" is the force of rumor, and that the story develops this theme by showing how uncontrollable and destructive rumor can be. In either case, the resolution of the conflict between the barber and the other white characters completes the development of the theme.

37.2C DRAMA

Drama is a kind of writing designed to be spoken by one or more characters on a stage. In the script of a play, stage directions often describe the appearance of a character or set, and sometimes they say what a character does (slams the door, sits down, leaps up). But otherwise the only description or narration to be found in a play is spoken by the characters themselves. Essentially, then, a play consists of speeches—dialogues, monologues, or both.

Since plays are written to be seen and heard, reading a play can never substitute for seeing it performed. If you're writing about a play that you've never seen performed, try to see a video of a performance or hear a recording of it. If you can't do either of those things, read at least parts of the play aloud to yourself. Try as well as you can to imagine how the play might look and sound on a stage, and use the following questions as a guide to your study of the text:

1. Is the play a comedy or a tragedy? **Tragedy** ends in death or disaster for the main character(s), as in Shakespeare's *Romeo and Juliet*, where both the title characters die. **Comedy** ends by relieving the main characters of their problems, as in Eugene O'Neill's *Ah, Wilderness!*, where Richard finally overcomes the obstacles that stand between him and the young woman he loves. While some plays cannot readily be classified as either comic or tragic, this question can help you grasp the general shape of most plays.

2. What is the central conflict? All plays—whether comic or tragic—turn on some kind of **conflict**. In *Romeo and Juliet*, the love between Romeo and Juliet is thwarted by the feud between

their families. In *Hamlet,* Hamlet's urge to avenge the murder of his father must contend with all the power embodied in the murderer, King Claudius, as well as with Hamlet's own reluctance to strike. In *Ah, Wilderness!,* the lovesick Richard must contend with the suspicions of the father of the young woman he loves.

3. What sides of the conflict do the characters represent? Different characters in a play often stand for conflicting values, attitudes, or principles. In Ibsen's *Doll's House,* for instance, Torwald believes that his wife's duty is to obey him, amuse him, raise their children, and uphold his respectability. But she believes that her first duty is to herself as an independent human being.

4. How do the characters develop? While lesser characters may remain essentially the same, major characters often undergo a change. In the first act of *King Lear,* for instance, the king impulsively disowns his daughter Cordelia for refusing to express her love for him in extravagant superlatives; in the last act, her death leaves him grief-stricken just before he dies himself. Does this sequence of events tell us that Lear has fundamentally changed? If so, when and how? And what does he learn? These questions will prompt different answers from different readers (and viewers), but they are the kinds of questions that lead to the heart of a play.

5. What does the setting contribute? Though readers of older plays—Shakespeare's, for instance—must largely imagine the locale from hints in the dialogue, the scripts of modern plays usually include a detailed description of the set. *Where* the action occurs is often highly significant. In *Hamlet,* the shift from the dark night outside on the ramparts (where the ghost of Hamlet's father appears) to the bright inside light of Claudius's court symbolizes the contrast between dark vengeance and superficial gaiety. In Eugene O'Neill's *Long Day's Journey into Night,* the one living room where all the action takes place comes to epitomize the world in which all four major characters are trapped.

37.2

QUESTIONS TO GUIDE YOUR STUDY OF LITERATURE

QUESTIONS TO ASK ABOUT A POEM

Who is the speaker?

What is the dominant image?

How does the dominant image express the theme?

How is the dominant image related to other images?

How does the poem develop its theme?

How do rhyme and meter (if any) help to express the poem's meaning?

QUESTIONS TO ASK ABOUT A WORK OF FICTION (NOVEL OR SHORT STORY)

What does the setting contribute?

What central conflict drives the plot?

How is the story told? Is the narrator part of the action, or not?

How does the story reveal its chief characters?

What changes does the story reveal?

How does the story develop its theme?

QUESTIONS TO ASK ABOUT A PLAY

Is the play a comedy or a tragedy?

What is the central conflict?

What sides of the conflict do the characters represent?

How do the characters develop?

What does the setting contribute?

37.3 PRE-WRITING ABOUT LITERATURE

Pre-writing an essay about a work of literature is in some ways like pre-writing an essay on any other topic. But since writing about literature makes its own peculiar demands, you will do well to consider the following.

37.3A NOTING SIGNIFICANT DETAIL

Provided you own the text you're reading, you should feel free to mark it up and make it your own. Watch for **significant detail:** words, phrases, and images that tell you something revealing about the main character, the theme, or the central conflict in the work. Underline or highlight these items and write your comments in the margin, as illustrated by these comments on the opening paragraphs of a short story by Meridel Le Sueur:

THE GIRL

She was going the inland route because she had been twice on the coast route. She asked <u>three times</u> at the automobile club how far it was through the Tehachapi Mountains, and she <u>had the route marked</u> on the map in red pencil. The car was running like a T, the garage man told her. All her dresses were back from the cleaner's, and there remained only the lace collar to sew on her black crepe so that they would be all ready when she got to San Francisco.

wants to know exactly what's ahead of her — no surprises

She had read up on the <u>history</u> of the mountains and <u>listed all the Indian tribes</u> and marked the route of the Friars from the Sacramento Valley. She was glad now that Clara Robbins, the math teacher, was not going with her. <u>She liked to be alone</u>, to have everything <u>just the way she wanted it</u>, exactly. <u>There was nothing she wanted changed.</u> It was a remarkable pleasure to have everything just right, to get into her neat fine-looking little roadster, start out in the fine morning, with her map tucked into the seat, <u>every road marked</u>. She was lucky too, how lucky she was. She had her place <u>secure</u> at Central High, teaching history. On September 18, she knew she would be coming back to <u>the same room</u>, <u>to teach the same course in history</u>. It was a great pleasure. Driving along, she

a history buff?

a loner — and a perfectionist. liked her own way

loves security, sameness, predictability

might have known!

could see her lean face in the windshield. She couldn't help but think that she had no double chin, and her pride rode in her, a lean thing. She saw herself erect, a little caustic and severe, and the neat turn-over collar of her little blue suit. Her real lone self. This was what she wanted. Nothing messy. She had got herself up in the world. This was the first summer she had not taken a summer course, and she felt a little guilty; but she had had a good summer just being lazy, and now she was going to San Francisco to see her sister and would come back two days before school opened. She had thought in the spring that her skin was getting that papyrus look so many teachers had, and she had a little tired droop to her shoulders and was a little bit too thin. It was fine to be thin but not too thin. Now she looked better, brown, and she had got the habit of a little eye shadow, a little dry rouge, and just a touch of lipstick. It was really becoming.

Yes, everything was ideal.

37.3B RECORDING YOUR PERSONAL REACTIONS

It's often helpful to set down on paper your **first reactions** to a text: any thoughts or questions that occur to you as you read. Here, for instance, is what one student wrote after first reading the opening paragraphs of "The Girl":

> What to make of this "girl"? Something of a puzzle. Wants a little adventure, so she goes through the mountains, but has to be sure there'll be no surprises. So she's gotta know just how many miles it is and have the route marked in red, "every road marked," and learn all the history. Nuts about order—"nothing messy" in her life. Just imagine what she'd say if she saw my room! And you'd think she'd be looking forward to seeing San Francisco—the Golden Gate and all that—but no, she's looking forward to coming back—to teach the same course in the same room!
>
> A loner, too. Doesn't even want her girl friend with her, and no thoughts of a man in her head. But she likes her looks, likes looking at herself in the mirror. Does she unconsciously fantasize about some sort of romantic adventure?
>
> "Everything was ideal." Yeah—perfect. Too perfect. She must be headed for some sort of mess.

(Handwritten margin notes: "admires her own reflection"; "solitude again"; "something's bound to happen!"; "obsessed with order!"; "likes looking good—wants to attract men")

37.3C CHOOSING AND REFINING YOUR TOPIC

Choosing a topic for an essay about a work of literature begins with choosing the work itself. If you're given a choice among those you have read in a course, take the work you like best—the work you find most interesting. That's the one you're most likely to enjoy writing about. If you're assigned a specific work to analyze, of course, you can proceed at once to the task of defining your approach to it.

The longer the work, the greater the need to concentrate on a specific part or feature of it. If you're writing a short essay on *Moby-Dick,* for instance, you can't possibly treat the novel as a whole, or trace the full development of its major character. You need to focus on a chapter, on a minor character, or on some recurrent feature of the whaling voyage, such as the "gams"—the occasional meetings between ships at sea. Whatever you choose to examine closely, ask yourself how it helps to reveal the theme of the work—as you interpret it—or its major conflicts.

Suppose you decide to write about chapter 36 of *Moby-Dick,* in which Captain Ahab tells his crew that their whole purpose must be to hunt the great white whale. This chapter dramatizes a conflict that is central to the development of the novel: the conflict between Ahab and Starbuck, his first mate. Ahab's obsession with revenge at any cost collides with Starbuck's practical concern for safety and profit. So your topic (and a working title) might be "Revenge and Practicality in Chapter 36 of *Moby-Dick.*"

Another way of approaching the choice of a topic for an essay on a long work is to think of the general ideas you want to explore, and then choose a specific part or feature of the work to explore them in. Suppose, for instance, you want to analyze Ahab's defiance of warnings against his pursuit of revenge. If you anchor this general topic to one or more of the chapters about gams, your topic might then be "Warning and Defiance in the Gams of *Moby-Dick.*"

Besides looking for something specific to write about, look for something interestingly **problematic**: something that provokes a question you would really like to answer. If Ahab is obsessed with a purpose that is manifestly irrational and dangerous, how does he persuade the crew to follow him? If Starbuck makes good sense, why does he fail to match Ahab's influence on the crew? The search for answers to questions like these should lead you to a thesis that does far more than state the obvious. In fact, if such questions stir your own interest in the topic, you're much more likely to produce an essay that interests your reader.

If you're writing about a short story or short poem, you can certainly choose a topic that includes the whole work, but you will still need to identify the basic idea—or better still the basic conflict—that your paper will explore. After choosing Gwendolyn Brooks's poem "Mrs. Small" as the subject of her paper, a student named Cirri Washington was struck by the very last word of the poem—"business." Since this word was applied to what the woman was doing in her house when she was visited by a business*man*, Cirri decided to see how the poem presents the contrast between two different kinds of business—male and female.

CHOOSING AND REFINING A TOPIC FOR A PAPER ON A LITERARY WORK

If the work is long, identify a general issue or conflict that you can link to a specific part or feature of the text:

Ahab's obsession with revenge in chapter 36 of *Moby-Dick*

The cowardice of Falstaff in *1 Henry IV*, act 2, scene 4

Agamemnon's story of his bloody homecoming, in book 11 of *The Odyssey*

Public law and private duty in act 3 of *A Doll's House*

Enlightenment and destruction in the fire images of *Heart of Darkness*

If the work is short enough to be treated as a whole in a short paper, identify the basic idea or basic conflict your paper will explore:

Male and female business in Gwendolyn Brooks's "Mrs. Small"

Desire and repression in Meridel Le Sueur's "The Girl"

Racial hatred in Faulkner's "Dry September"

37.3D CONSULTING SECONDARY SOURCES

If you are writing a short paper on a work of literature, you may not be asked to use or cite any **secondary sources**—just to cite the work you are writing about. If you *are* asked to use secondary sources, the first place to look for them is the text in which the work appears. Many editions of literary works include—sometimes in headnotes, more often in the back of the book—a bibliography of critical studies of that particular work and its author. Some editions include critical essays or excerpts from them. The Norton Critical Edition of *Hamlet,* for instance, offers portions of fourteen modern essays on the play.

The next place to look for secondary sources is the card catalog or on-line catalog of your college library (see section 33.3). If you check the cards or computer listings under your author's name, you can readily find your way to all the books in the library written by or about your author.

For articles as well as books, see the *MLA International Bibliography* in the library reference room. Published annually, this is an author-and-subject index to books and journal articles on modern languages, literatures, folklore, and linguistics. In recent years, the annual issues have been put into a computerized index, so if your library has the MLA file on-line, you can call up just about everything published on the work of your author since 1980. (For guidance on finding articles in your library, see section 33.4.)

Once you've located a book about your author, check the table of contents and the index to find discussion of the work or topic you're writing about. By itself, the title of an article will often tell you whether or not the article is worth tracking down and reading in full.

37.3E FORMULATING A THESIS

A good thesis about a literary work makes an **arguable assertion** about its meaning, or the way that meaning is shaped. It must be more than an inarguable statement of fact or a statement of your topic:

STATEMENT OF FACT: In chapter 36 of *Moby-Dick*, Ahab goads his entire crew to swear vengeance on the great white whale.

STATEMENT OF TOPIC: Chapter 36 of *Moby-Dick* is about the conflict between Ahab's lust for revenge and Starbuck's concern with practicality.

STATEMENT OF THESIS: In chapter 36 of *Moby-Dick*, Ahab's refusal to heed Starbuck's warnings about the folly of pursuing a single whale shows the intensity of Ahab's obsession with revenge.

STATEMENT OF FACT: In Gwendolyn Brooks's "Mrs. Small," the title character has to pay an insurance premium.

STATEMENT OF TOPIC: Gwendolyn Brooks's "Mrs. Small" is about the difference between male and female business.

STATEMENT OF THESIS: In Gwendolyn Brooks's "Mrs. Small," the superficial contrast between a man's business and a woman's absentmindedness gives way to the point that this woman's business is crucial to human life.

37.4 SUMMARIZING AND INTERPRETING: KNOWING THE DIFFERENCE

To **summarize** a work of literature is to tell its plot—the sequence of actions that it represents. Summarizing, in fact, is one way of writing about literature, and a good way to test your understanding of what happens in a literary narrative. Summarizing a story also helps you to identify crucial moments in its development. A good plot summary of "Dry September," for instance, would include the fact that the barber jumps out of the car on the way to the site of the lynching.

But to **interpret** a work of literature, you need to do some jumping of your own. You need to jump off the track of chronological sequence—one thing after another—and consider the **meaning** of particular events. How does the barber's action affect the development of the story? If the black man would have been lynched anyway, what difference does it make that the barber jumps from the car? To answer this question, you must consider the role that the barber has played in the story up to now, and particularly the ways in which he has tried to combat the mindless rage of his fellow whites. In moving back to find examples of what the barber said to them, you would be gathering material for an interpretation, which is a *logical* rather than *chronological* way of writing about the story. That is, interpretation aims not to retell the plot of the story but to show what conclusions we can draw about its meaning.

Many good essays on a work of literature include summary—enough to situate the reader in the world of the text so that he or she can follow the writer's argument about it. The opening paragraph of the sample essay on pp. 599–603, for instance, summarizes Meridel Le Sueur's "The Girl" before stating a thesis about its meaning. But plot summary will not pass for interpretation. To see whether or not you're confusing the two as you write, check the first sentence of each of your paragraphs. If it merely states a fact about what happens in this story, you're falling into summary. Compare these openings:

> PLOT SUMMARY: After hearing that Catherine will accept Linton's proposal, Heathcliff runs away into the night.
>
> ANALYSIS: In running away after hearing that Catherine will accept Linton's proposal, Heathcliff reveals his bafflement and desperation.

> PLOT SUMMARY: En route to the site of the lynching, the barber jumps from the car.
>
> ANALYSIS: When the barber jumps from the car en route to the lynching, he shows us that hatred and fear have at last overpowered his rationality.

37.5 DEVELOPING YOUR INTERPRETATION: QUOTING AND CITING SOURCES

37.5A GIVING EVIDENCE

To make your points convincingly, you must support them with **evidence** from the text—references to specific incidents or images, quotations of particular words, phrases, or passages. In Meridel Le Sueur's "The Girl," a female schoolteacher sets out to drive alone from Southern California to San Francisco and reluctantly takes on a young male hitchhiker. In the following paragraph from an essay on this story, the author begins with an interpretative statement about the chief character and then develops it with significant detail:

> Her love of order goes hand in hand with an aversion to company. Initially, she is "glad" that Clara Robbins, the math teacher, is not with her, and she has no wish to take on anything or anyone else that might be "messy" (204). When she first sees the young man at the service station looking for a ride, she instantly decides that "she wouldn't pick him up, that was certain" (205). Even after the station owner tells her that he knows the young man's family and can "vouch for him," the sight of his smiling, eager face makes her feel only that he and the owner both "want something": something other than the "mite of education" that the owner "cunningly" suggests she could give the young man on the ride (207). "Men like that," she says to herself, "hate women with brains" (207). She trusts neither of them. Suddenly realizing "that she despised men and always had," she tells the station owner, "I don't like to drive with a strange man" (207).

The student author of this paragraph uses a series of brief quotations to develop the point made in the opening sentence. Here quotations and statements of fact about the story—such as the fact that the math teacher is not with the main character—constitute evidence for the author's interpretation. An effective interpretation combines evidence with interpretive points. Both are essential.

37.5B CITING SOURCES

Cite all sources in parentheses, observing these guidelines.

1. Cite secondary sources by the author's last name and the page number(s) of the material quoted:

```
One critic says of The Bean Eaters, "There is much
black womanness in this book" (Lee 20).
```

2. If you use the author's name in introducing the quoted material, give just the page number(s) in parentheses:

> As Maria Mootry notes, her very name--Mrs. Small--
> "conforms to the gender-based stereotype that women's
> lives are narrow and that women are preoccupied with
> unimportant matters" (181).

3. If you are writing about just one literary work, give the author's name and the title at the outset. You can then give just the page number(s) for each citation that follows:

> Meridel Le Sueur's "The Girl" is the story of what
> happens when a prim, unmarried, unnamed schoolteacher
> sets out to drive alone from Southern California to
> San Francisco on a bright, hot September day. . . .
> But the story makes it clear that in rejecting his
> desires, she also stifles her own, dooming herself to
> a life of repressive order in which she will "never
> never change" (212).

4. In quoting more than one item from the same page within the same sentence, give the page number(s) for all the quoted items at the end of the sentence:

> Initially, she is "glad" that Clara Robbins, the math
> teacher, is not with her, and she has no wish to take
> on anything or anyone else that might be "messy"
> (204).

5. In quoting plays and poems, follow the instructions given in section 35.2, items 14–17.

6. List all sources at the end of your paper under the heading "Works Cited":

Works Cited

Le Sueur, Meridel. "The Girl." <u>Ripening: Selected</u>
    <u>Work, 1927-1980</u>. Ed. Elaine Hedges. Old
    Westbury: The Feminist Press, 1982. 204-12.

Lee, Don L. Preface. <u>Report from Part One</u>. By
    Gwendolyn Brooks. Detroit: Broadside, 1972.
    13-30.

Mootry, Maria. "'Tell It Slant': Disguise and
    Discovery as Revisionist Poetic Discourse in <u>The</u>
    <u>Bean Eaters</u>." <u>A Life Distilled: Gwendolyn</u>
    <u>Brooks, Her Poetry and Fiction</u>. Ed. Maria K.
    Mootry and Gary Smith. Urbana: U of Illinois
    P, 1987. 177-92.

For detailed guidance on the format of the Works Cited list, see section 35.1B.

37.6 SAMPLE ESSAY ON A SHORT STORY: NO SECONDARY SOURCES

The following essay illustrates a method of critical analysis that focuses on the elements of the literary work itself. Specifically, the student author tries to show how the actions, descriptive detail, and dialogue of a short story all work together with the reported thoughts of the main character to reveal a central conflict within her. For another way of treating Le Sueur's story—an approach that connects the story to the author's life and historical circumstances—see section 37.8, where we explain how to link works of literature to the circumstances under which they are produced.

Garcia 1

Arturo Garcia

English 202

Professor Payne

26 October 1993

Desire and Repression in Le Sueur's "The Girl"

Meridel Le Sueur's "The Girl" is the story of
what happens when a prim, unmarried, unnamed
schoolteacher sets out to drive alone from Southern
California to San Francisco on a bright, hot
September day. Stopping for lunch at a service
station, she reluctantly takes on a passenger--a
muscular, sunburnt young farmhand who needs a lift to
a bridge some fifty miles up the road. His personal
remarks disturb and frighten her. When she stops the
car at one point and he suggests that they lie down
together in the shade, she silently refuses, drives
on until she drops him off, and continues her trip.
But the story makes it clear that in rejecting his
desires, she also stifles her own, dooming herself to
a life of repressive order in which she will "never
never change" (212).

Her love of order and predictability shows up at
once. Though taking the inland route in order to see
something new (she has taken the coast route twice
before), she has done everything she can to forestall
surprises. Her neat little roadster is "running like
a T" and her dresses are freshly cleaned. She has

Garcia 2

"asked three times at the automobile club how far it
was through the Tehachapi mountains," has carefully
marked on her map every road she will take, has
studied the history of the mountains and made a list
of its Indian tribes. Furthermore, rather than
looking forward to any new experience, she relishes
the thought that she will soon be returning to her
job, "coming back to the same room, to teach the same
course in history" at Central High (204).

    Her love of order goes hand in hand with an
aversion to company. Initially, she is "glad" that
Clara Robbins, the math teacher, is not with her, and
she has no wish to take on anything or anyone else
that might be "messy" (204). When she first sees the
young man at the service station looking for a ride,
she instantly decides that "she wouldn't pick him up,
that was certain" (205). Even after the station
owner tells her that he knows the young man's family
and can "vouch for him," the sight of his smiling,
eager face makes her feel only that he and the owner
both "want something": something other than the "mite
of education" that the owner "cunningly" suggests she
could give the young man on the ride (207). "Men like
that," she says to herself, "hate women with brains.
She trusts neither of them. Realizing "that she
despised men and always had," she tells the station
owner, "I don't like to drive with a strange man" (207).

Garcia 3

In taking the strange man on, however, she not
only yields to the station owner's urging. She also
reveals something she can hardly admit to herself,
let alone anyone else: a desire to attract men. We
get a hint of this earlier, when we learn that she
takes pride in her appearance. Looking at herself in
the windshield, she admires her own "lean" face ("no
double chin"), lightly tanned skin, and deftly
applied makeup: "a little eye shadow, a little dry
rouge, and just a touch of lipstick. It was really
becoming" (204). During the ride itself, neither her
fear of being touched nor her annoyance at being
flattered "just as if she were any common slut" (209)
can altogether keep her from showing herself off.
When she feels her passenger inching toward her "as
if about to touch her leg" (208), she shrinks away and
draws her skirt down sharply. But minutes later, "she
let her skirt slip up a little. She knew she had good
legs, tapering down swiftly to her ankles" (210).

The powerful appeal of sexuality in this story
is symbolized by the heat of the day and the
mountains, which are repeatedly described in terms
that suggest the human body. Before the woman has
even seen the young man, the sun shines "like a
golden body" and she looks "into the fold upon fold
of earth flesh lying clear to the horizon" (205).
Like the muscular, sunburnt man himself, the contours

Garcia 4

of the sun-baked land repel and arouse her by turns.
At first appalled by the "terrifying great mounds of
earth and the sun thrusting down like arrows" (205),
she is gradually entranced by "naked" mountains, by
"bare earth curves, tawny and rolling in the heat"
(208). At the same time, she feels the glowing
presence of the man like a force of nature, and she
tries to slow down on the curves "so that his big
body would not lounge down upon her like a mountain" (209).

As that passage suggests, he never overcomes her
fear. As long as he remains in the car, she feels
"frightened as if they were about to crack up in a
fearful accident" (209). Yet when she stops the car
and he invites her to lie down with him, she is
nearly overpowered by the combined effects of his
body and the sunburnt landscape, which have now
become virtually one:

> The rocks that skirted the road glistened
> like bone, . . . like the sheer precipice
> of his breast looming toward her so that
> she could feel the heat come from him and
> envelop her like fire, and she felt she was
> falling swiftly down the sides of him . . .
> and an ache, like lightning piercing stone,
> struck into her between her breasts. (211)

This moment leaves her to struggle with two
desires--the man's and her own. She thwarts his

Garcia 5

desire by simply pulling back from him "in hard resistance" (211). As soon as she does so, he withdraws
from her "completely" (212) and gets out of the car by
himself to catch a ride with a man driving a truckload
of melons. Yet the melon that he gives her as he says
good-bye symbolizes all he might have given her, and all
she has refused: "some sumptuous feast she had been unable
to partake of, the lush passional day, the wheaty boy,
some wonderful, wonderful fruit" (212). In rejecting
the fruit of passion, she stifles her own desire.

    As a result, she feels both "safe" and withered.
When she stops the car after dropping off the man,
she looks in the mirror and sees something quite
different from what she saw in the windshield at the
beginning of her trip. While she earlier admired her
lean, well-made-up face, now she feels "like a stick"
and looks "like a witch" (212). She is "safe--safe"
from violation (212), but she also realizes that she
is stuck in a life of sterility. In the end, the
prospect of order and sameness gives her only a grim
satisfaction: "She would never never change, pure and
inviolate forever; and she began to cry" (212).

Works Cited

Le Sueur, Meridel. "The Girl." <u>Ripening: Selected
    Work, 1927-1980</u>. Ed. Elaine Hedges. Old
    Westbury: The Feminist Press, 1982. 204-12.

37.7 SAMPLE ESSAY ON A POEM: SECONDARY SOURCES USED

Cirri Washington

Professor Porter

English 201

9 March 1993

Male and Female Business in Gwendolyn Brooks's

"Mrs. Small"

Gwendolyn Brooks's poem "Mrs. Small" captures a revealing moment in the life of a housewife and mother. Visited by an insurance man who has come to collect a premium, she goes to the kitchen for her pocketbook, absentmindedly returns with a steaming pot of coffee instead of the money, and accidentally splashes his shirt before she finally gets around to paying him. On the surface, the poem presents the conflict between a woman's absentmindedness and the business of a man. As Maria Mootry notes, her very name--Mrs. Small--"conforms to the gender-based stereotype that women's lives are narrow and that women are preoccupied with unimportant matters" (181). But by the time we reach the end of this poem about a woman named Small, we have learned just how crucial to human life is "her part / Of the world's business" (lines 55-56).

The opening stanza perfectly expresses her preoccupation with the business of hospitality.

Going off for her pocketbook, she returns "with a peculiar look / And the coffee pot" (2-3). The rhyming "look" takes the place of the pocketbook she has forgotten about, and the next two lines suggest that in the mind of the woman, "pocketbook" has also been replaced with a word that sounds like its first syllable, "pot." But her substitution of one for the other is not just an exercise in free association. Offering "a steaming coffee pot" is her instinctive way of treating a visitor "graciously" (15).

Coffee, however, is not what this particular visitor wants or expects. As a businessman with a busy schedule, he shows her a face that has "not . . . much time" for love "sublime" (8-9) or even for getting acquainted. He can't stop to savor the woman's company or sip her steaming brew, even if—as her husband says—it's "the best coffee in town" (27). Coffee has nothing to do with the money that the insurance man has come to collect. That is why she looks almost crazy to him, with her "half-open mouth and the half-mad eyes / And the smile half-human" (11-12).

From his point of view, her actions must seem as crazy—or at least as "peculiar"—as her look. Ironically, in coming "to her senses" (16) about her first mistake, she makes a second one: she jerks the pot and splashes coffee on the man. Thus she not

Washington 3

only forces him to take the coffee he didn't want;
she also stains the perfect whiteness of his shirt
"with a pair of brown / Spurts" (24-25). "There is
much black womanness in this book," says Don Lee of
The Bean Eaters, the volume containing this poem
(20). Symbolically, this "little plump tan woman"
(10) is disrupting the orderly world of white male
business, which is why her mistake is called
"unforgivable" (20).

But this word is ironic, for her mistake is
hardly unforgivable when we realize how trivial it
actually is and when we see it from her point of
view. She asks for no forgiveness. Though she says,
"I don't know where my mind is this morning" (34),
she knows her own mind. She scorns apologies because
she has no time to make them. Like the insurance
man, she is in a hurry, but she has more reason for
haste because she has more things to do than he does:
"such / Mountains of things, she'd never get anything
done / If she begged forgiveness for each one" (37-39).

We get a glimpse of those mountains when we
learn (near the end of the poem) that this woman is
the mother of ten children: six daughters scrambling
and yelling in the hall, and four sons who have run
off beyond earshot, who "could not be heard any more"
(44). The size of the woman's family explains why
she is even now planning to bake some apple pies. In

the face of this job--just one of many to be done
each day by this hard-working mother--the payment of
an insurance premium is a truly small matter,
something tersely set down in a stanza of just three
words: "she paid him" (40).

    In doing so with brisk efficiency, she is
anything but the absentminded or slightly crazy woman
the insurance man has seen. In the end, it's the
insurance man who glares "idiotically" (47), not she.
She knows how to cook and manage her children at the
same time, how to

              silence her six

        And mix

        Her spices and core

        And slice her apples, and find her four.

                              (51-54)

    The rhyming of "six" and "mix" and of "core" and
"four" shows just how she makes the parts of her
working day fit together, how she mixes cooking and
parenting, taking each in stride. This "little plump
tan woman" may look unimportant to the insurance man,
who symbolizes "the economic pressures of white
culture" (Melhem 120), and she may seem only an
absentminded hindrance to his business. But his
business finally proves far less important than hers.
In spite of her name, "her part / Of the world's
business" is demanding, essential, and big.

Washington 5

Works Cited

Brooks, Gwendolyn. "Mrs. Small." The Bean Eaters.

New York: Harper, 1960. 27-28.

Lee, Don L. Preface. Report from Part One. By

Gwendolyn Brooks. Detroit: Broadside, 1972. 13-30.

Melhem, D. H. Gwendolyn Brooks: Poetry and the

Voice. Lexington: UP of Kentucky, 1987.

Mootry, Maria. "'Tell It Slant': Disguise and

Discovery as Revisionist Poetic Discourse in

The Bean Eaters." A Life Distilled: Gwendolyn

Brooks, Her Poetry and Fiction. Ed. Maria K.

Mootry and Gary Smith. Urbana: U of Illinois P,

1987. 177-92.

MRS. SMALL

Mrs. Small went to the kitchen for her pocketbook
And came back to the living room with a peculiar look
And the coffee pot.
Pocketbook. Pot.
Pot. Pocketbook.   5

The insurance man was waiting there
With superb and cared-for hair.
His face did not have much time.
He did not glance with sublime
Love upon the little plump tan woman   10
With the half-open mouth and the half-mad eyes
And the smile half-human
Who stood in the middle of the living-room floor planning
   apple pies
And graciously offering him a steaming coffee pot.
Pocketbook. Pot.   15

"Oh!" Mrs. Small came to her senses,
Peered earnestly through thick lenses,
Jumped terribly. This, too, was a mistake,
Unforgivable no matter how much she had to bake.
For there can be no whiter whiteness than this one: 20
An insurance man's shirt on its morning run.
This Mrs. Small now soiled
With a pair of brown
Spurts (just recently boiled)
Of the "very best coffee in town."   25

"The best coffee in town is what *you* make, Delphine! There
     is none dandier!"
Those were the words of the pleased Jim Small—
Who was no bandier of words at all.
Jim Small was likely to give you a good swat
When he was *not*   30
Pleased. He was, absolutely, no bandier.
"I don't know where my mind is this morning,"
Said Mrs. Small, scorning
Apologies! For there was so much
For which to apologize! Oh such   35
Mountains of things, she'd never get anything done
If she begged forgiveness for each one.

She paid him.

But apologies and her hurry would not mix.
The six   40
Daughters were a-yell, a-scramble, in the hall. The four
Sons (horrors) could not be heard any more.

No.
The insurance man would have to glare
Idiotically into her own sterile stare   45
A moment—then depart,
Leaving her to release her heart
And dizziness
And silence her six
And mix   50
Her spices and core
And slice her apples, and find her four.
Continuing her part
Of the world's business.

                                   —Gwendolyn Brooks

37.8 LINKING LITERATURE TO HISTORY

A work of literature may be treated as a self-sufficient world—
something made of forms and images that can be wholly
explained in terms of their relation to each other. But since no
literary work is ever written in complete isolation from the material world, you can often enrich your study of a poem, play, or
work of fiction by linking it to history. You can link it to the
personal history of the author's own life or the historical period
in which it was written; you can consider the social, political,
cultural, or economic conditions that it may reflect.

Take, for example, Meridel Le Sueur's "The Girl." First published in 1936, this story of a woman who ends up feeling "like
a stick" because she rejected the advances of a hitchhiker may
seem peculiar to us now. Why should she be so repressed? Or
more to the point, why shouldn't she feel perfectly free to send
the randy hitchhiker packing *without* feeling like a stick?

Some knowledge of Meridel Le Sueur's early life helps to
answer these questions. Born in Nebraska in 1900, she grew up
in a suffocatingly repressive household. According to Elaine
Hedges, who has edited a volume of her writings, she inherited
from her grandmother in particular a sense of guilt and shame
about the human body. Against this repressive atmosphere she
soon rebelled, and it was chiefly her need to escape what she
called the "terrible purity" of her family background that
prompted her to write about the sexual experience of women
(qtd. in Hedges 6). In addition, at the time she wrote "The
Girl," she was deeply influenced by the novels of
D. H. Lawrence, which attack all forms of repression and glorify
sexual fulfillment as a way of uniting oneself with nature. Significantly, the hitchhiker in "The Girl" comes across as a force of
nature, and the contours of the mountainous landscape in the
story resemble those of the human body.

To bring biography or history into your paper, of course, you
will need to read some historical studies, consult secondary
sources, or both. But to illustrate what history can bring to the
analysis of literature, here is an excerpt from an essay on Jane
Austen's novel *Emma* by a student named Julie Cusick:

Cusick 2

The poor people mentioned just once in Emma are
not the only figures who live outside the comfortable
world of Highbury's landed gentry. Equally outcast--
and more threatening--are the gypsies. "Gypsies,"
writes David Simpson,

> had always been images as in a tense and
> contested relation to the rest of society.
> True gypsies had once been banned from
> Britain, by a statute of 1530, and . . .
> thirteen gypsies were executed under this
> law in the mid-seventeenth century. (44)

By the time Emma was written in the early nineteenth
century, gypsies were no longer banned. But as
Simpson notes, they were contemptuously classified
with beggars, vagrants, thieves, pickpockets, and
"the non-industrious poor" (44).

In Emma, gypsies appear only briefly--just long
enough to show how their wandering, unsettled way of
life can threaten the established order. When Emma's
friend Harriet Smith and another young woman are out
walking one day on the road from Highbury to
Richmond, they are suddenly accosted by a crowd of
gypsies. Though Harriet's companion scrambles away,
she herself cannot follow because her legs are
cramped from dancing at the ball. As a result,

> she was soon assailed by half a dozen
> children, headed by a stout woman, and a

> great boy, all clamorous, and impertinent
> in look, though not absolutely in word.
> More and more frightened, she immediately
> promised them money, and taking out her
> purse, gave them a shilling, and begged
> them not to want more, or to use her ill.
> She was then able to walk, though slowly,
> and was moving away--but her terror and her
> purse were too tempting; and she was
> followed, or rather surrounded, by the
> whole gang, demanding more. (305)

This is a fascinating passage, for it describes in
detail how gypsies strategically corner and attack
their prey. Significantly, the gypsies are tempted
quite as much by Harriet's "terror" as by her
"purse." To know something of how despised and
marginal they were in early nineteenth-century
England is to see why they would relish this moment
of power and control over one of their superiors in
rank and class. It is also to see how the novel
recognizes the social forces threatening the
apparently secure world of privilege in which Emma
lives.

Cusick 4

Works Cited

Austen, Jane. <u>Emma</u>. New York: Bantam, 1981.

Simpson, David. <u>Wordsworth's Historical Imagination:</u>

<u>The Poetry of Displacement</u>. New York: Methuen,

1987.

38

Writing and Research across the Curriculum

Good writing does not stop at the borders of the English department. College courses in many different subjects require written work, and many of the qualities that make an essay on Shakespeare effective can also enhance a paper on the biology of adaptation or the influence of urban environment on family life. Whatever its subject, a good piece of writing is grammatically correct, lucid, precise, coherent, well focused on its main point, and—just as importantly—well designed to meet the expectations of its readers, the audience for whom it is written.

But different disciplines (which is what academic subjects are called) require different kinds of writing. Even when a humanist, a social scientist, and a natural scientist examine the same object, they approach it from fundamentally different points of view. For this reason, a highly specialized study can sometimes seem to be written in a language of its own: a language that sounds strange and difficult to the nonspecialist reader.

So if you plan to write a paper in a specialized discipline, or even to read specialized books and articles, you will have to learn something about the methods, assumptions, and above all the language of that discipline. In what follows, we first consider the kind of writing specialists produce when they are writing for other specialists. Then we explain how you can begin to write in various disciplines yourself. Bear in mind, however, that only your instructor can tell you exactly what he or she requires.

38.1 THREE DISCIPLINES ILLUSTRATED: SPECIALISTS WRITING FOR SPECIALISTS

To see the difference between writing in the humanities, writing in the social sciences, and writing in the natural sciences, consider how specialists from each of these three different fields of study approach a common topic.

1. A literary critic writes about fictional treatments of cruelty to children:

> Any story will be unintelligible unless it includes, however subtly, the amount of telling necessary not only to make us aware of the value system which gives it its meaning but, more important, to make us willing to accept that value system, at least temporarily. It is true that the reader must suspend to some extent his own disbeliefs; he must be receptive, open, ready to receive the clues. But the work itself—any work not written by myself or by those who share my beliefs—must fill with its rhetoric the gap made by the suspension of my own beliefs.
>
> Even something as universally deplored as cruelty to children can be molded to radically different effects. When Huck's pap pursues him with the knife, or when the comic-strip father beats his child because he's had a bad day at the office; when Jim in "Haircut" and Jason in *The Sound and the Fury* disappoint the children about a circus; when Elizabeth Bowen's heroine experiences the death of the heart; when Saki's little pagan is punished by his aunt; when Medea kills her children; when Macbeth kills Lady Macduff's children; when Swift's Modest Proposer arranges to have the infants boiled and eaten; when Pip is trapped by Miss Havisham; when Farrington in Joyce's "Counterparts" beats his son; and, finally, when the child is beaten to death in *The Brothers Karamazov,* our reactions against the perpetrators range from unconcerned amusement to absolute horror, from pitying forgiveness to hatred, depending not primarily upon any natural relation between the bare events and our reaction but upon a judgment rendered by the author. —Wayne Booth, *The Rhetoric of Fiction*

Booth is writing for readers familiar with a wide variety of literary texts—with works ranging from *Huckleberry Finn* to *The*

Brothers Karamazov. His object of study is "the work itself." He treats the individual work of literature as the source of meaning and value, as something that can make us react in a variety of ways to any theme—even cruelty to children.

2. A sociologist writes about the family as a social group:

> The implications of conflict theory might best be considered from the perspective of an alternative theory. According to conflict theory, power pervades both the interactional and the societal levels of social life. Bierstedt (1974) elaborated on the theory of *social organization* by defining power as latent force, and identifying the sources of power as resources, numbers (especially majorities), and social organization (including authority, or institutionalized power). By implication, social organization must be triadic, because authority entails command, either by a person or by a norm, and obedience; this points to the consensus of a majority, and a majority cannot exist in a detached dyad. Resources *per se* cannot influence social life unless they are given social definition (Bierstedt, 1974). The conception of the family as an institution holds that normative structures have crescively developed to meet the functional requirements of men, women, and children joined by ties of kinship. Women give birth and are more nurturant, children require a long period of dependency, and males exhibit greater aggressiveness and dominance the world over (Maccoby and Jacklin, 1974). These universal features gave rise to the traditional consensus regarding family statuses and the norms attached to them, whether in the conjugal family today or in the patriarchal family of the past. In summary, the view we have outlined sees social organization as triadic and hierarchical, instead of dyadic and polarized, and points to the principle that each person acts where he or she is strong (Weaver, 1948).
>
> —Lawrence L. Shornack, "Conflict Theory and the Family"

Shornack writes for readers familiar with sociological terms such as *interactional* (relating to behavior between persons), *dyadic* (twofold), *triadic* (threefold), and *crescively* (increasingly). He distinguishes between two rival theories that could be used to explain the family: conflict theory, which treats all social structures in terms of a two-sided (dyadic) struggle between oppressive top dogs and powerless underdogs; and organizational theory, which treats social structures as triangular (triadic), with a peak of power resting on a base of majority consent. As a sociologist, Shornack focuses on social groups. While Booth describes the many different forms that child abuse can take in various fictional families, Shornack seeks to explain the social structure of *the* family—that is, the social structure common to all family groups.

3. A team of pediatricians and neurologists report on a study of children who suffered minor head injuries:

INTRODUCTION

Minor head injury is a common problem in the pediatric population. Yet, despite the relative frequency, it remains a source of concern often raising the spectra of serious sequelae and long-term neuropsychological problems. Relatively few data are available on the outcome of minor head trauma. Published studies have emphasized a substantial functional and behavioral morbidity and an increased incidence of headaches [1–6]. In general, however, these abnormalities have been established by comparing information obtained from individuals following head trauma with expected outcomes in healthy subjects.

The purpose of this study is to expand our knowledge of the physical and behavioral morbidity experienced by children with minor head injuries by comparing this population with individuals who had minor injuries to other parts of the body. All children were followed prospectively by telephone interviews. Our results have identified several short-term behavioral sequelae in a pediatric population treated in an emergency room for minor injuries, whether injuries affect the head or other body parts. Physician awareness of specific transient functional deficits following minor injuries can result in a reduction of parental anxiety.

—Mychelle Farmer et al., "Neurobehavioral Sequelae of Minor
Head Injuries in Children"

Farmer and her colleagues are writing for specialists in the fields of pediatrics and neurology—for readers familiar with terms such as *trauma* (wound), *morbidity* (illness), *sequelae* (abnormalities resulting from a wound), and *transient functional deficits* (short-term incapacities). They made their study to answer a specific question about a well-defined population: in children under thirteen, what special abnormalities can be expected to follow a minor head wound? To answer this question, they compared head-injured children with a "control group" of children suffering from other injuries. In this introduction to their report, they refer to what published studies have already shown; they explain the comparative method of their own study; and they note that what they have learned about minor head injuries can be used to reduce "parental anxiety."

Each of the three passages above considers children and the family—a topic everyone knows something about. Yet each is written to be read by specialists in a particular field. In addition, each also embodies a specialized way of thinking about its topic—a specialized kind of questioning.

38.2 ASKING THE QUESTION THAT FITS YOUR DISCIPLINE

The key to generating an effective piece of writing in any field is *to ask the kind of question that the field is organized to answer.* To learn what kind of question this is, consider the different things that humanists, social scientists, and natural scientists focus on when they write.

38.2A WRITING IN THE HUMANITIES: FOCUS ON THE WORK AND ITS CONTEXT

Specialists in philosophy and religion study what real people think and believe, but most other **humanists**—in spite of their generic name—do not study humans directly. They study works of literature, music, and visual art. In the process, they often try

THINKING LIKE A HUMANIST

Consider a work of literature, music, or visual art with questions such as these:

1. What kind of work is it?

2. How is it related to other works of its kind?

3. What is the relation of its parts to each other?

4. What does it tell us about the life and development of its creator?

5. How does it reflect the political, cultural, or socioeconomic conditions of the time and place in which it was created?

THINKING LIKE A SOCIAL SCIENTIST

Investigate social groups with questions such as these:

1. What is the correlation between event or condition X and event or condition Y within population Z?

2. What are the norms and values shared by a particular population?

3. What concept or theory will explain a particular form of behavior?

THINKING LIKE A SCIENTIST

Investigate the natural world with questions such as these:

1. What are the effects or causes of a particular physical condition or event?

2. What is the correlation between event or condition A and event or condition B?

3. If such a correlation may exist, what kind of experiment will confirm or disprove it?

to analyze the **form** of individual works or to explain how such works evoke the **historical context** in which they were produced.

To study the form of an individual work is to consider how its parts collaborate to make a whole: how the ending of a novel recalls its beginning, how the last movement of a sonata recapitulates its first one, how a dark tree in the foreground of a landscape painting can set off a sunlit mountain in the background. To study the form of a work is also to see what that work shares with other works like it: with other novels, other sonatas, other landscape paintings. Wayne Booth, for instance, treats all works of fiction as **rhetorical,** written to persuade us that we should judge their characters in a certain way. But this general theory of fiction helps to show what is distinctive about each fictional work. If the theme of cruelty to children can be "molded to radically different effects," made to enrage us in one work and to amuse us in another, what explains these differences? Only a detailed analysis of the rhetorical strategies used in particular works can answer the question. Even as he explains a general theory of fiction, therefore, Booth shows us how to discover the uniqueness of individual works, how to formulate the kinds of questions that can lead us to their meanings, such as "Why are we amused when Huck's pap pursues him with a knife?" or "What makes us sympathize with Medea even when she kills her own children?"

Besides analyzing the form of an individual work, humanists may consider it **biographically** or **historically.** They may ask what it tells us about the life and artistic development of its creator; they may also ask how it evokes or reflects the political, cultural, or socioeconomic conditions of the time and place in which it was created. They may ask, for instance, not only how Mark Twain's *Huckleberry Finn* recalls the structure of classical epic, but also how it uses the author's personal experience as a Mississippi riverboat pilot, or how it reflects the history of American debates about slavery and Reconstruction. Alternatively, looking at a sixteenth-century portrait of a married couple in Amsterdam, they may ask what the picture tells us about the status of women, marriage, and property rights in Holland or Europe at that time. (For further discussion of the historical approach to the study of literature, see section 37.8.)

Generally speaking, then, the humanities are organized to answer questions of this type about a work of music, literature, or art:

1. What kind of work is it?
2. How is it related to other works of its kind or other works by the same person?
3. How does it differ from other works like it?
4. What is the relation of any one of its parts to the whole?
5. How does it reflect the culture and ideas of the time and place in which it was produced?

38.2B WRITING IN THE SOCIAL SCIENCES: FOCUS ON SOCIAL GROUPS

While humanists often use categories and general terms to help them define something or someone unique, **social scientists** typically study groups. Shornack's approach to families differs from Booth's in two fundamental ways. He is not only writing about real families rather than fictional ones; he is also generalizing, as sociologists typically do, about *the* family. Even when he distinguishes "the conjugal family" of today from "the patriarchal family of the past," he is still dealing with groups, with social categories rather than individuals.

This generalizing viewpoint is particularly evident in the kind of essay he has written—a **review article** focusing on theories of the family rather than on any personal observation of actual families. In **case studies,** social scientists study individuals, and you may be asked to do the same. But you will study an individual as a **case**—that is, an example of a definable group, or of a particular stage of development. In a psychology course, for instance, you may be asked to observe a particular child at a daycare center in order to answer a question such as "What is the relation between language learning and socialization in three-year-olds?"

Professional social scientists use similar methods of investigation. A recent study of child development set out to explain the relation between child abuse and illness in children under three. By studying such a relationship in a randomly drawn sample of this population, investigators tried to learn whether illness is typically one of the causes or the effects of abuse.

The questions raised by social scientists, then, are designed to generate information about groups and recurrent situations. Typical studies seek to answer questions like these:

1. What is the correlation between event or condition X and event or condition Y within population Z?
2. What norms and values are shared by a particular population?
3. What concept or theory will explain a particular form of behavior?

38.2C WRITING IN THE NATURAL SCIENCES: FOCUS ON PHYSICAL PROPERTIES

When we turn from the social sciences to the **natural sciences,** the focus shifts from social groups to **physical properties.** While social scientists try to answer a question about a group of human beings by observing or interviewing sample members of the group, physical scientists try to answer a question about the human body or the physical properties of the natural world. The kind of question that a scientific researcher sets out to answer will call for observation, experiment, or both.

Suppose, for instance, that a biologist wants to know whether hair condition in humans tells anything about protein or calorie deficiencies. This is the kind of question that can be answered by observation and comparison—specifically by comparing hair samples taken from persons who don't have those deficiencies with hair samples taken from persons who do. Or suppose a neurologist wants to know whether or not minor head injuries in children produce any special long-term effects. This question too can be answered by observation and comparison, as shown by the article from which passage no. 3 is quoted above.

Like the authors of that article, physical scientists typically make **controlled comparisons.** To learn how one particular event or condition affects a certain population, they establish a control group that matches the group being tested in all but one respect—the one being studied. Controlled comparison allows researchers to focus on just one variable at a time and thus to see its effects clearly.

One other feature of this article about head injuries in children typifies scientific writing: the frequent use of the passive voice. It appears twice in the introductory passage we quote *(these abnormalities have been established, All children were followed prospectively by telephone interviews),* and often thereafter. Scientists use the passive voice in order to sound as objective as possible: to keep the focus on what was done rather than on who did it. (Even if the study was conducted by a team of researchers, reports do not usually say which member of a team did anything in particular.) Also, by separating the action from the agent, the passive voice underscores the point that scientific experiments and procedures are repeatable: anyone who is properly trained should be able to do them.

In general, then, physical scientists try to answer questions like these:

1. What are the effects or causes of a particular physical condition or event?
2. What is the correlation between event or condition A and event or condition B?
3. If such a correlation may exist, what kind of experiment will confirm or disprove it?

38.3 WRITING ON SPECIALIZED TOPICS FOR NONSPECIALISTS

Like good teachers, good **specialists** in any subject generally know how to explain it to **nonspecialists,** and—just as importantly—how to show why it matters to all of us. In the following paragraph, the author explains why some babies born with spina bifida (incomplete development of the vertebrae surrounding the spinal cord) are denied corrective surgery:

The single most common cause of mental retardation in children with spina bifida is infection of the brain: either infection of the chambers of the brain (ventriculitis) or of the linings and substance of the brain (meningoencephalitis). Such infection is most likely in those infants from whom corrective surgery is withheld. The parents of Baby Jane Doe, a child born with spina bifida, were told she would inevitably be severely retarded. For that reason they decided not to allow a surgeon to treat her. Because she was not treated, she acquired a brain infection, which means she is likely to be retarded. *This becomes a self-fulfilling prophecy.*

—David G. McLone, "The Diagnosis, Prognosis, and Outcome for
the Handicapped: A Neonatal View"

The author of this paragraph is a pediatric neurosurgeon who has treated hundreds of infants born with spina bifida. But since he is writing for a journal of general interest, he wants to reach more than just an audience of fellow specialists. So he explains such technical terms as *ventriculitis* and *meningoencephalitis.* He also explains—in language we can readily understand—exactly how the threat of retardation is used to justify the withholding of surgery from infants who need it.

This explanatory point serves a persuasive end. Elsewhere in his essay, McLone shows that no one can predict the life of an infant born with spina bifida until that infant has been treated. Here he shows what happens when a prediction of retardation is used to justify the withholding of corrective surgery: the withholding of surgery leads to infection and retardation, and the prediction becomes "self-fulfilling." Thus McLone converts his specialized knowledge into writing that can reach and persuade a general reader to accept his main point, which is that *all* infants born with spina bifida should be treated.

38.4 ORGANIZING A RESEARCH PAPER IN THE HUMANITIES

The essays given in sections 10.3F and 37.6 illustrate the organized analysis of a single work of literature. Likewise, the essay shown in section 37.7 illustrates how to use secondary sources in the analysis of a literary work. A research paper on one or more works of literature, art, music, or philosophy normally includes secondary as well as primary sources, and in general, you should organize this material as follows.

1. In the **introduction** you identify the particular work or works you will consider in the paper. You also formulate the question that you will try to answer: What do we learn about motherhood from Toni Morrison's *Beloved*—a novel about a black woman who kills her own infant daughter to save her from a life of slavery? How does J. D. Salinger's *Catcher in the Rye* represent the passage from innocence to experience? Why does Mary Wollstonecraft attack Rousseau in *Vindication of the Rights of Women*? Why does Velázquez's *Las Meninas* include a self-portrait of the artist himself at work? How does the hard-boiled hero of the American detective novel reflect American notions of heroism? Here, for instance, is the introduction to a research paper by a first-year college student:

> Individual identity is a cherished ideal, and when institutions threaten to deny it, they provoke resentment. Nevertheless, in order to function in a society, individuals must be willing to compromise their personal moralities and assume certain prescribed roles. This conflict between the rights of the individual and those of society produces a sense of frustration, creating the need for an outlet. Consequently, we look to heroes, to strong individuals who will never compromise their values or surrender their identities. To nineteenth-century individuals, America offered a vast and challenging frontier—a place where individuals could preserve their identities. The question I want to answer is how the values of these frontier heroes survive in the hard-boiled heroes of American detective novels. —Neil Okun, "Heroism in the American Detective Novel"

2. In the **body** of the paper, you develop an answer to the basic question in terms of individual works, supplemented by comments drawn from secondary sources. Secondary sources—books and articles—help you to clarify the meaning of the works you discuss, to explain the connections between them, and to

sharpen the edge of your argument. But the works themselves—not the secondary sources—should be the prime source of evidence for your argument:

> Dashiell Hammett's first novel, *Red Harvest,* pits the Continental Op against a town totally controlled by three mobs and a corrupt police force. As Robert Parker notes, Personville (pronounced "Poisonville") is the ultimate "symbol of the end of the frontier . . . a western city, sprung up on the prairie in the wake of the mines" (95). When the Op arrives in response to a call for his services, he discovers a dead client. At this point he could have left, since he had already received all the pay he would get. But in leaving, he would have sacrificed his heroic stature, so he stays to fight for what he sees as justice.
>
> He wins only a limited victory. Though he eventually cleans up the town by turning the various mobs against each other, the novel lets us see that evil will return. When the Op leaves, Personville is "nice and clean and ready to go to the dogs again" (178). Nevertheless, the detective has endured and upheld his own personal code of morality.   —Neil Okun

3. In the **conclusion** of the paper, you restate the main point of your argument and indicate what the argument contributes to our understanding of the works of literature you have discussed:

> The demand for an individual who will not compromise on questions of morality produced the wilderness hero, a man who fled the corrupting influence of society for the freedom and challenge of the frontier. When the frontier closed, this man no longer had a refuge; he was forced to fight to retain his individuality and preserve his moral integrity. With a value system rooted in the nineteenth-century frontier, the hero of the detective novel must often confront the twentieth-century city. The reaction is often violent, and the hero can never impose his values on society. Yet he is personally victorious, for he always leaves uncorrupted, and he continually restores our faith in what Sisk calls "the American as rugged individualist and shaper of his own destiny" (368).
>
> —Neil Okun

38.5 DOCUMENTING SOURCES IN THE HUMANITIES

The author of the paragraphs quoted above uses the MLA style of parenthetical citation. Chapter 35 explains this style, which is commonly used in research papers on humanistic subjects.

38.6 ORGANIZING RESEARCH PAPERS IN THE SOCIAL SCIENCES

Research papers in the social sciences are commonly based on the observation of particular cases or groups. If you are asked to write a case study or to report your findings on an assigned question, your most important primary source will be the record of your own observations, including the results of interviews you may conduct and questionnaires you may distribute. Together with published sources, these will provide the material for your paper.

A report of findings in the social sciences normally includes five parts:

1. The **introduction** states the question you propose to answer and explains how the methods of a particular social science can help you answer it. Suppose the question is "Do handicapped children gain more confidence from competitive sports (such as the Special Olympics) than from noncompetitive activities?" Having posed this question, the introduction explains how the methods of developmental psychology can help you find and interpret the data needed to answer it.

2. The **methods** section of the paper indicates how you gathered the data for your study. Here you describe the particular characteristics of the group you studied, your methods of study (observation, interview, questionnaire), the questions you asked, and the printed sources you consulted, such as previous studies of handicapped children engaged in competitive sports. You should describe your methods of gathering data in such a way that someone else can repeat your study and thus test its results.

3. The **results** section puts the raw data you have gathered into clearly organized form: into paragraphs, tabulated listings,

illustrations, or graphs. (On figures and tables, see section 38.10 below.)

4. The **discussion section** interprets the results of the study and explains its significance for an understanding of the topic as a whole. With reference to the sample question above, for instance, it could explain whether or not competitive sports actually benefit handicapped children. If competition threatens their confidence rather than strengthening it, then programs like the Special Olympics should be reevaluated.

5. The **conclusion** briefly summarizes what the study has found and states the implications of its findings, including points to be further explored.

In addition to the paper itself, you may be asked to furnish an abstract of it. If so, read on.

38.6A WRITING ABSTRACTS FOR SOCIAL SCIENCE PAPERS

The **abstract** of a social science paper normally appears at the beginning. It consists of a single paragraph that succinctly explains what your paper tries to show. Here, for instance, is an abstract of an article from the field of sociology:

> Pollution knows no frontiers: dirty or dangerous substances dumped in rivers or off the coast, or spewed into the atmosphere in one European country, have both direct and indirect harmful consequences for neighboring countries. Attempts by the capitalist democracies of Western Europe to clean up the local environment and avoid continental or even global ecological damage, have in the past been thwarted by the dirty, inefficient, and irresponsible modes of production adopted by the socialist countries of Eastern Europe. This was compounded by the political secrecy surrounding many of the polluting activities of the socialist military-industrial complex. Only recently, with the fall of socialism, has it been possible to envisage a full and free exchange of information about pollution and establish the basis for ecological cooperation throughout the entire continent.
>
> —Christie Davies, "The Need for Ecological Cooperation in Europe," *International Journal on the Unity of the Sciences* 4 (1991): 201–16.

This paragraph illustrates what every effective abstract should be: *succinct, informative, and comprehensive.*

First, the paragraph is succinct. Its first four words state one of the main points of the article: "Pollution knows no frontiers."

Second, the paragraph is informative. Using highly significant modifiers such as "dumped in rivers or off the coast" and "dirty, inefficient, and irresponsible," it tersely reveals how pollution moves from one country to another. Every sentence, in fact, is richly modified to deliver the maximum amount of information in a small number of words.

Third, the paragraph is comprehensive. It not only states the main point of the essay but shows how the point is developed. The recent history of pollution in Europe, we learn, is presented as a conflict between the cleanup efforts made by Western European democracies and the messes made by the socialist countries of Eastern Europe. Just as importantly, we learn what the article tells us about the latest development in this history: the fall of socialism may lead to full cooperation in the control of pollution throughout Western Europe.

38.7   DOCUMENTING SOURCES IN THE SOCIAL SCIENCES: THE APA PARENTHETICAL STYLE

The APA style of parenthetical citation is recommended by the American Psychological Association (APA) for research papers in the social sciences. Though some social scientists (such as Shornack, quoted above on p. 616) use a different style of parenthetical citation, the APA style is widely accepted for research papers in the social sciences. Complete information on this style appears in the *Publication Manual of the American Psychological Association,* 3rd ed. (Washington: APA, 1983). Here we briefly explain how to use the APA style with some of the sources you are likely to cite in a research paper written for a college course. Each source cited parenthetically in this section is also shown as it would appear in the list of References at the end of the paper. We explain how to write this list in section 38.7B.

38.7A WRITING APA PARENTHETICAL CITATIONS

1. Material introduced without the author's name
Give in parentheses the author's last name, the publication date, and—if you are citing one or more specific pages— "p." or "pp." with the page number(s):

> One researcher has found that "marriages in which the parents share responsibilities equally tend to be the happiest" (Levine, 1976, p. 176).
>
> References
>
> Levine, J. A. (1976). Who will raise the children? Philadelphia: Lippincott.

2. Material introduced with the author's name
Give only the date and page number(s) in parentheses:

> Kamerman (1983, p. 36) reports that from 1967 to 1980, kindergarten enrollment rose by about a third, and from 1969 to 1980, nursery school enrollment more than doubled.

References

Kamerman, S. B. (1983). Child-care services: A

national picture. <u>Monthly Labor Review</u>, <u>106</u> (12),

35-39.

3. A work with two authors
Give both names every time you cite the work:

> For all their efforts to generalize about child
>
> behavior, psychologists recognize that "no two
>
> children are exactly alike" (Gesell & Ilg, 1949, p.
>
> 68).

References

Gesell, A., & Ilg, F. L. (1949). <u>Child</u>

<u>development: An introduction to the study of human</u>

<u>growth</u>. New York: Harper.

4. A work with more than two authors
Give all the names in the first citation only:

FIRST CITATION: Miller, Dellefield, and Musso (1980)

have called for more effective advertising of

financial aid programs.

In later citations give just the first author's name followed by "et al.," which means "and others":

LATER CITATION: Miller et al. (1980) have studied the

institutional management of financial aid.

References

Miller, S., Dellefield, W., & Musso, T. (1980).

<u>A guide to selected financial aid management</u>

<u>practices</u>. Washington, DC: U.S. Department of

Education.

38.7B WRITING THE REFERENCE LIST: APA STYLE

Start the list on a separate sheet and alphabetize the entries by the authors' last names, with the date of publication immediately after each name. Use only initials for author's first and middle names. If you've cited two or more works by one author, list them chronologically by date of publication. If the works were published in the same year, list them alphabetically by title and use the letters a,b,c, etc., after the year, as shown below in the Astin entries.

```
                      References                        ⟵ Triple-
                                                          space

    Astin, A. W. (1975a). Financial aid and student

        persistence. Los Angeles: Higher Education

        Research Institute.
                                                         Double-
    Astin, A. W. (1975b). Preventing students from       space
                                                         between
        dropping out. San Francisco: Jossey-Bass.        and within
                                                         entries
    Cartwright, R. (1978, December). Happy endings

        for our dreams. Psychology Today, pp. 66-76.
```

All lines after the first in each entry are indented 3 spaces

1. A book with one author

Date of publication

```
    Erikson, E. H. (1964). Insight and responsibility:

        Lectures on the ethical implications of

        psychoanalytic insight. New York: Norton.
```

Capitalize only first word of title and subtitle

Place of publication and publisher

2. A book with two or more authors

```
    Hall, C. S., & Nordby, V. J. (1972). The individual

        and his dreams. New York: New American Library.
```

3. A book with an editor

```
    El-Khawas, E. (Ed.) (1980). Special policy issues in

        management of student aid. Washington, DC:

        American Council on Education.
```

4. An article in a journal

Volume number underlined

No quotation marks used with title of an article

Palvio, A. (1975). Perceptual comparisons through the mind's eye. <u>Memory & Cognition</u>, <u>3</u>, 635-647.

No "p." or "pp." for page numbers

If each issue in the volume starts from page 1, give the issue number in parentheses after the volume number:

Kamerman, S. B. (1983). Child-care services: A

national picture. <u>Monthly Labor Review</u>, <u>106</u> (12),

35-39.

Use "p." or "pp." with page numbers only when citing a newspaper or magazine (as in the Cartwright reference on p. 632).

38.8 ORGANIZING RESEARCH PAPERS IN THE NATURAL SCIENCES

Research papers in the natural sciences are generally of two kinds: **review papers,** which analyze the current state of knowledge on a specialized topic, and **laboratory reports,** which present the results of an actual experiment. Both kinds of papers normally begin with an **abstract:** a brief, one-paragraph summary of the paper's most important points. But the two kinds of papers differ in many respects.

The primary sources for a **review paper** are current articles in scientific journals, and the purpose of a review paper is not to make an argument or develop an original idea but to survey and explain what laboratory research has recently shown about the topic. A review paper normally does three things: (1) it introduces its topic by explaining why it is important and what questions about it have been raised by recent research; (2) it develops the topic by reviewing that research under a series of subheadings; and (3) it concludes by summarizing what has been discovered and stating what remains to be investigated.

A **laboratory report** explains how an experiment made in a natural science laboratory answers a question such as "How do changes in temperature affect the conductivity of copper?" Resembling in its format a report of findings in the social sciences, the lab report usually presents its materials as follows:

1. The *title* succinctly states what was tested. It might be, for instance, "The Effect of Temperature Changes on the Conductivity of Copper."

2. The *abstract* summarizes the report in about two hundred words.

3. The *introduction* explains the question that the lab test is designed to answer.

4. A section on *methods and materials* explains how the experiment was made, what apparatus was used, and how data were collected.

5. A section on *results* puts the data into clearly organized form, using graphs, tables, and illustrations where necessary. (See section 38.10 on the presentation of tables and figures.)

6. The *conclusion* explains the significance of the results.

7. A *reference list* gives any published sources used, including any manuals or textbooks.

38.9 DOCUMENTING SOURCES IN THE SCIENCES

Each subject in the sciences has its own style of documentation, which is explained in one of the following style manuals:

BIOLOGY
> Council of Biology Editors. Style Manual Committee. *Council of Biology Editors Style Manual: A Guide for Authors, Editors, and Publishers in the Biological Sciences.* 6th ed. Bethesda: Council of Biology Editors, 1993.

CHEMISTRY
> American Chemical Society. *Handbook for Authors of Papers in American Chemical Society Publications.* Washington: American Chemical Soc., 1978.

GEOLOGY

United States Geological Survey. *Suggestions to Authors of the Reports of the United States Geological Survey.* 6th ed. Washington: GPO, 1978.

LINGUISTICS

Linguistic Society of America. *LSA Bulletin,* Dec. issue, annually.

MATHEMATICS

American Mathematical Society. *A Manual for Authors of Mathematical Papers.* 7th ed. Providence: American Mathematical Soc., 1980.

MEDICINE

International Steering Committee of Medical Editors. "Uniform Requirements for Manuscripts Submitted to Biomedical Journals." *Annals of Internal Medicine* 90 (Jan. 1979): 95–99.

PHYSICS

American Institute of Physics. Publications Board. *Style Manual for Guidance in the Preparation of Papers.* 3rd ed. New York: American Inst. of Physics, 1978.

Your instructor will tell you which scientific style of documentation you are expected to use. What follows is a brief guide to the style recommended by the Council of Biology Editors (CBE). Complete information on this style will be found in the CBE manual cited above.

CITING SOURCES IN CBE STYLE

- Single author mentioned in text   636
- Two authors mentioned in text   636
- Three or more authors mentioned in text   636
- No author mentioned in text   636
- Specific page or pages cited   636
- Two or more sources cited in one reference   637

38.9A CITING SOURCES IN THE NATURAL SCIENCES: CBE STYLE

Cite each source with a superscript number that refers to a list of sources at the end of the paper. The form of citations varies, as shown here:

1. Single author mentioned in text

Superscript number goes inside punctuation

According to Nagle[1], sunburn affects reproductive success only in rare instances.

The reference comes immediately after the author's name.

2. Two authors mentioned in text

Weiss and Mann[2] have shown that folate deficiency retards growth, causes anemia, and inhibits fertility.

3. Three or more authors mentioned in text

Holick and others[3] exposed hypopigmented human skin to simulated solar ultraviolet radiation for various times and determined the photoproducts of 7-dehydrocholesterol.

4. No author mentioned in text

This theory implies that ultraviolet radiation can penetrate more easily into lightly pigmented skin and will result in a greater production of vitamin D than will a heavily melanated skin subjected to the same light[4].

5. Specific page or pages cited

It is reasonable to assume that dark pigmentation was prominent among the ancient human populations[5].

Page numbers appear in the list of references.

6. Two or more sources cited in one reference

> How is the distribution of skin color among
> indigenous populations to be explained? One
> hypothesis is that heavily melanated skin emerged in
> sundrenched countries as protection against
> sunburn[2,5].

38.9B WRITING THE REFERENCE LIST: CBE STYLE

Below is a reference list for all of the sources cited above in section 38.9A. Illustrating CBE style, the order of numbered sources follows the order in which they were first cited in the paper:

Use only initials (without space or punctuation between them) for first and middle names of authors

Double-space between and within entries

Capitalize first word of title only, with no underlining, italics, or quotation marks

Name of periodical, date, volume number, and pages of article

List of References

1. Nagle, JJ. Heredity and human affairs. St.
   Louis: Mosby; 1974. 337 p.

2. Weiss, MA, Mann, AE. Human biology and behaviour:
   an anthropological perspective: Boston: Little,
   Brown; 1985. 274 p.

3. Holick, MF, MacLaughlin, JA, Doppelt, SH.
   Regulation of cutaneous previtamin D3
   photosynthesis in man: skin pigment is not an
   essential regulator. Science 1981;211:589-95.

4. Loomis, WF. Skin-pigment regulation of vitamin-D
   biosynthesis in man. Science 1967;157:66-71.

5. Kottack, CP. Anthropology: the exploration of
   human diversity. New York: Random House; 1978.
   p. 62.

38.10 TABLES AND FIGURES IN RESEARCH PAPERS

Research papers in the social and physical sciences often require **tables** (tabular data) or **figures** (graphs and illustrations). Tables and figures should be numbered consecutively (Table 1, Table 2; Figure 1, Figure 2) and accompanied by a descriptive caption, as shown below.

38.10A PRESENTING TABLES

Put the caption for a table above it as a heading:

Table 1. Percent of Traffic Exceeding 55MPH

HIGHWAY SYSTEM	1980	1981	1982	1983	PERCENT CHANGE 1982–1983[a]
Urban Interstate	51.2	51.0	58.4	60.5	3.6
Rural Interstate	65.9	67.6	73.1	73.6	0.7
Other freeways	—[b]	47.1	53.8	56.6	5.2
Urban arterials	—[b]	30.2	32.4	34.3	5.8
Rural arterials	—[b]	43.2	46.2	47.5	2.8
Rural collectors	—[b]	32.7	34.8	36.6	5.2
All statewide highways polled at 55 mph	49.0	48.5	52.6	54.1	2.8

[a]Percentage change calculated for 1982-1983 because these are the only 2 years with consistent speed measurement in all states.

[b]Data not available.

Source: Crump, Edythe Traylor (Ed.) (1984). 55: A decade of experience. Transportation Research Board Special Rept. 204. Washington, DC: National Research Council.

Use lowercase letters (a,b,c) for footnotes to a table, and put the footnotes at the bottom of the table—not at the bottom of the page or the end of the paper. If the table is photocopied from a printed source, put a source note under it.

38.10B PRESENTING FIGURES

Put the caption for a figure—a graph or an illustration—just below the figure:

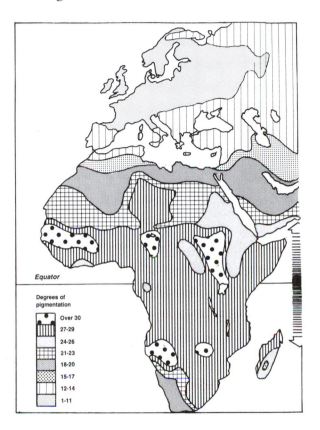

Figure 1. Map of Skin Color Distribution

Source: Weiss, ML, Mann, AE. Human biology and

behaviour: an anthropological perspective. Boston:

Little, Brown; 1985. p. 433.

The source note for a figure or table used in a paper on one of the sciences or social sciences may be written the same way as an entry in the reference list would be. (This note follows CBE style.)

GLOSSARIES

Glossary of Usage

a, an   Use *a* before a word starting with a consonant, and *an* before a word starting with a vowel.

> *A* fool and his money are soon parted
> *An* empty bag cannot stand upright.   —Ben Franklin

accept, except   *Accept* means "receive" or "agree to."

> Medical schools accept less than half the students who apply.

As a preposition, *except* means "other than."

> I can resist anything except temptation.   —Oscar Wilde

As a verb *except* means "exclude," "omit," "leave out."

> If you except Eisenhower and Reagan, no U.S. president since Roosevelt has served two full terms in office.

A.D., B.C., C.E., B.C.E   A.D. stands for *anno Domini,* "in the year of our Lord." It designates the period since the birth of Christ and precedes the year number.

> The emperor Claudius began the Roman conquest of England in A.D. 43.

B.C. designates the period before the birth of Christ and follows the year number. For this period, the lower the number, the more recent the year.

> Alexander the Great ruled Macedonia from 336 B.C. to his death in 323.

Instead of A.D., writers now often use C.E. (common era), and in place of B.C. they use B.C.E. (before the common era).

> Julius Caesar died in 44 B.C.E.

advice, advise   *Advice* is a noun meaning "guidance."

> When a man is too old to give bad examples, he gives good advice.
> —La Rochefoucauld

Advise is a verb meaning "counsel," "give advice to," "recommend," or "notify."

> Shortly before the stock market crash of 1929, Bernard Baruch advised investors to buy bonds.

affect, effect *Affect* is most often used as a verb meaning "change," "disturb," or "influence."

> The rising cost of health care has drastically affected the health of the American economy.

It can also mean "feign" or "pretend to feel."

> Though she knew exactly what the package contained, she affected surprise when she opened it.

As a noun, it can mean only "feeling."

> Her face was blank, with no sign of affect.

Effect is most often used as a noun meaning "result" or "impact."

> His appeal for mercy had no effect on the judge.

It may also be used as a verb meaning "bring about," "accomplish," or "perform."

> With dazzling skill, the gymnast effected a triple somersault.

afraid *See* frightened.

aggravate, irritate *Aggravate* means "make worse."

> The recent bombing of a school bus has aggravated racial hostilities.

Irritate means "annoy" or "bring discomfort to."

> His tuneless whistling began to irritate me.

all *See* almost.

all ready, already Use *all ready* when *all* refers to things or people.

> At noon the runners were all ready to start. [The meaning is that *all* of the runners were *ready*.]

Use *already* to mean "by this time" or "by that time."

> I reached the halfway mark, but the frontrunners had already crossed the finish line.

all right, *alright *All right* means "completely correct," "safe and sound," or "satisfactory."

> My answers on the quiz were all right. [The meaning is that *all* of the answers were *right*.]
> The car was demolished, but aside from a muscle bruise in my shoulder and a few minor cuts, I was all right.

In formal writing, do not use *all right* to mean "satisfactorily" or "well."

> * In spite of a bruised shoulder, Ashe played all right.
> EDITED: In spite of a bruised shoulder, Ashe played well.

In formal writing, do not use *all right* to mean "very good" or "excellent."

> * Her performance was all right.
> EDITED: Her performance was excellent.

Do not use *alright anywhere; it is a misspelling of *all right.*

all together, altogether   Use *all together* when *all* refers to things or people.

> The demonstrators stood all together at the gate of the nuclear power plant.

Use *altogether* to mean "entirely" or "wholly."

> Never put off till tomorrow what you can avoid altogether. (Preston's Axiom)

allude, refer   *Allude* means "call attention indirectly."

> When the speaker mentioned the "Watergate scandal," he alluded to a chain of events that led to the resignation of President Richard Nixon.

Refer means "call attention directly."

> In the Declaration of Independence, Jefferson refers many times to England's mistreatment of the American colonies.

allusion, delusion, illusion   An *allusion* is an indirect reference.

> Prufrock's vision of his own head "brought in upon a platter" is an allusion to John the Baptist, whose head was presented that way to Salome, Herod's daughter.

A *delusion* is a false opinion or belief, especially one that springs from self-deception or madness.

> A megalomaniac suffers from the delusion that he or she is fabulously rich and powerful.

An *illusion* is a false impression, especially one that springs from false perception (an optical illusion, for example) or from wishful thinking.

> The sight of palm trees on the horizon proved to be an illusion.
> The so-called "free gifts" offered in advertisements feed the illusion that you can get something for nothing.

almost, most, mostly, all, *most all   *Almost* means "nearly."

> By the time we reached the gas station, the tank was almost empty.
> Almost all the Republicans support the proposed amendment.

As an adjective or noun, *most* means "the greater part (of)" or "the majority (of)."

> Most birds migrate in the fall and spring.
> Most of the land has become a dust bowl.

As an adverb, *most* designates the superlative form of long adjectives and adverbs.

> Truman thought MacArthur the most egotistical man he ever knew.

Mostly means "chiefly," "primarily."

> Milk is mostly water.

All means "the whole amount," "the total number of," or "entirely."

> All art is useless.   —Oscar Wilde
> The manufacturer has recalled all (of) the new models.
> The new buildings are all finished.

In formal writing, do not use *most all. Use *almost all* or *most*.

> * Most all of the plants looked healthy, but two of the roses were dying.
> EDITED: Almost all of the plants looked healthy, but two of the roses were dying.

> * Most all of the refugees suffered from malnutrition.
> EDITED: Most of the refugees suffered from malnutrition.

a lot, *alot   *See* lots of.

already   *See* all ready.

* alright   *See* all right.

altogether   *See* all together.

alumnus, alumni; alumna, alumnae   Use *alumnus* for one male graduate of a school, college, or university, and *alumni* for two or more male graduates or for a predominantly male group of graduates.

> Dartmouth alumni are extraordinarily loyal to their college.

Use *alumna* for one female graduate, and *alumnae* for two or more female graduates or for a predominantly female group of graduates.

> Vassar's alumnae include Mary McCarthy and Meryl Streep.

If you can't cope with all those Latin endings, use *graduate* for an individual of either sex, and just remember that *alumni* designates a male group, *alumnae* a female group. Do not refer to any one person of either sex as an *alumni*.

> * He is an alumni of Florida State.
> EDITED: He is an alumnus [*or* a graduate] of Florida State.

among, between   Use *among* with three or more persons, things, or groups.

> There is no honor among thieves.

In general, use *between* with two persons, two things, or two groups.

> Political freedom in America means the right to choose between a Democrat and a Republican.

amoral, immoral   *Amoral* means "without morals or a code of behavior," "beyond or outside the moral sphere."

> Rich, riotous, and totally amoral, he lived for nothing but excitement and pleasure.

Immoral means "wicked."

> The Roman emperor Nero was so immoral that he once kicked a pregnant woman to death.

amount, number   Use *amount* when discussing uncountable things.

> No one knows the amount of damage that a nuclear war would do.

Use *number* when discussing countable things or persons.

> The store offered a prize to anyone who could guess the number of marbles in a large glass jug.

anxious, eager   *Anxious* means "worried" or "fearfully desirous."

> The long silence on the other end of the line made her anxious.
> He took the long street at a dead run, anxious to reach home before the midnight curfew began.

Eager means "strongly desirous."

> After all I had heard about it, I was eager to see what remained of the famous prison on Alcatraz Island.

anyone, any one   *Anyone* is an indefinite pronoun (like *everyone, everybody*).

> Anyone who hates dogs and children can't be all bad. —W. C. Fields

Any one means "any one of many."

> I felt wretched; I could not answer any one of the questions on the test.

apt   *See* likely.

as, as if, like   Use *as* or *as if* to introduce a subordinate clause.

> As I walked up the driveway, a huge dog suddenly leaped out at me.
> Susan looked as if she had just seen a ghost.

Use *like* as a preposition meaning "similar to."

> At first glance the organism looks like an amoeba.

Do not use *like* to mean "as if," "as," or "that."

> * Pat looked like he had just won the sweepstakes.
> EDITED: Pat looked as if he had just won the sweepstakes.

> * The hinge didn't work like the instructions said it would.
> EDITED: The hinge didn't work as the instructions said it would.

> * I felt like he resented me.
> EDITED: I felt that he resented me.

assure, ensure, insure *Assure* means "state with confidence to one or more persons."

> The builders of the *Titanic* assured everyone that it could not sink.

Ensure and *insure* mean "make sure" or "guarantee."

> There is no way to ensure (*or* insure) that every provision of the treaty will be honored.

Insure also means "make a contract for payment in the event of specified loss, damage, injury, or death."

> I insured the package for fifty dollars.

avenge, revenge *Avenge* is always a verb. It means "exact punishment on behalf of [someone] or in retaliation for [some wrong]."

> In slaying Claudius, Hamlet avenges his father.
> [or] In slaying Claudius, Hamlet avenges the murder of his father.

Revenge may be a verb or a noun. As a verb, it means "satisfy [oneself] by inflicting punishment on or upon [someone] who has injured [oneself]."

> In *Moby-Dick,* Ahab yearns to revenge himself upon the whale that has taken his leg.

As a noun, it means "retaliation."

> After Hindley beats him, Heathcliff grimly plans his revenge.

awfully *See* very.

bad, badly *Bad* is an adjective meaning "not good," "sick," or "sorry."

> We paid a lot for the meal, but it was bad.
> In spite of the medicine, I still felt bad.
> She felt bad about losing the ring.

Badly is an adverb meaning "not well."

> Anything that begins well ends badly. (Pudder's Law)

Used with *want* or *need, badly* means "very much."

> The fans badly wanted a victory.

Do not use *bad* as an adverb.

> * We played bad during the first half of the game.
> We played badly during the first half of the game.

B.C., B.C.E. *See* A.D.

because, since, *being that Use *since* and *because* to introduce clauses. Do not use **being that*.

> Since fossil fuels are becoming scarce, scientists are working to develop synthetic forms of energy.
> The soldiers could not advance because they had run out of ammunition.

because of *See* due to.

* being that *See* because.

beside, besides *Beside* means "next to."

> A little restaurant stood beside the wharf.

As a preposition, *besides* means "in addition to."

> Besides working with the sun and the wind, engineers are seeking to harness the power of tides.

As a conjunctive adverb, *besides* means "moreover" or "also."

> Randy's notion of bliss was a night at the disco, but discos made me dizzy; besides, he stepped on my toes whenever we danced.

between *See* among.

can hardly, *can't hardly *Can hardly* means virtually the same thing as *cannot* or *can't*. Do not use **can't hardly*.

> * We can't hardly cut taxes without increasing the deficit.
> EDITED: We can hardly cut taxes without increasing the deficit.

capital, capitol *Capital* means the seat of government of a country or state, the type of letter used at the beginning of a sentence, or a stock of accumulated wealth.

> Paris is the capital of France.
> This sentence begins with a capital *T*.
> What does capital consist of? It consists of money and commodities.
> —Karl Marx

Capitol means the building that houses the state or federal legislature. Remember that the *o* in *capitol* is like the *o* in the dome of a capitol.

> The governor delivered his first speech from the steps of the capitol.

C.E. *See* A.D.

censor, censure As a verb, *censor* means "expurgate."

Television networks usually censor X-rated movies before broadcasting them.

As a noun, *censor* means "one who censors."

Censors cut all of the nudity out of the film.

As a verb, *censure* means "find fault with" or "reprimand."

In the 1950s, Senator Joseph McCarthy was censured for publicly questioning the integrity of President Eisenhower.

As a noun, *censure* means "disapproval" or "blame."

Ridicule often hurts more than censure.

childish, childlike *Childish* means "disagreeably like a child."

The childish whining of a chronic complainer soon becomes an unbearable bore.

Childlike means "agreeably like a child."

Picasso's brilliant canvases express his childlike love of color.

cite *See* sight.

compare, comparison, contrast *Compare* means "bring together in order to note similarities and differences."

In *A Stillness at Appomattox,* Bruce Catton compares Lee and Grant not only to show the difference between a Virginia aristocrat and a rough-hewn frontiersman but also to show what these two men had in common.

Use *compare to* to stress similarities.

Lewis Thomas compares human societies to ant colonies, noting that individuals in each of these groups sometimes work together as if they were parts of a single organism.

Use *compare with* to stress differences.

Compared with Texas, Rhode Island is a postage stamp.

Comparison means "act of comparing."

Catton's comparison of Lee and Grant shows the difference between the South and the frontier.

In comparison with Texas, Rhode Island is a postage stamp.

As a transitive verb, *contrast* means "juxtapose to show one or more differences."

In *Huckleberry Finn,* Twain contrasts the peaceful, easy flow of life on the river with the tense and violent atmosphere of life on shore.

As an intransitive verb, *contrast* means "appear different in one or more ways."

> In *Huckleberry Finn,* the peaceful flow of life on the river contrasts vividly with the violent atmosphere of life on shore.

As a noun, *contrast* means "striking difference."

> To drive across America is to feel the contrast between the level plains of the Midwest and the towering peaks of the Rockies.

complement, compliment   As a verb, *complement* means "bring to perfect completion."

> A red silk scarf complemented her white dress.

As a noun, *complement* means "something that makes a whole when combined with something else" or "the total number of persons needed in a group or team."

> Experience is the complement of learning.
> Without a full complement of volunteers, a small-town fire department cannot do its job.

As a verb, *compliment* means "praise."

> The teacher complimented me on my handwriting but complained about everything else.

As a noun, *compliment* means "expression of praise."

> Cheryl's compliment made me tingle.

conscience, conscious   *Conscience* is a noun meaning "inner guide or voice in matters of right and wrong."

> A pacifist will not fight in any war because his or her conscience says that all killing is wrong.

Conscious is an adjective meaning "aware" or "able to perceive."

> Conscious of something on my leg, I looked down to see an ant crawling over my knee.
> I was conscious during the whole operation.

consul   *See* council.

continual, continuous   *Continual* means "going on with occasional slight interruptions."

> I grew up next to an airport. What I remember most from my childhood is the continual roaring of jet planes.

Continuous means "going on with no interruption."

> In some factories the assembly line never stops; production is continuous.

contrast *See* compare.

could care less, couldn't care less Don't use the first expression when you mean the second.

> *Carol likes hard rock and could care less about Beethoven and Brahms.
>
> EDITED: Carol likes hard rock and couldn't care less about Beethoven and Brahms.

council, counsel, consul *Council* means "a group of persons who discuss and decide certain matters."

> The city council often disagrees with the mayor.

As a verb, *counsel* means "advise."

> President John F. Kennedy was badly counseled when he approved the American attack on Cuba at the Bay of Pigs.

As a noun, *counsel* means "advice" or "lawyer."

> Camp counselors tend to give orders more often than counsel.
> When the prosecution showed a picture of the victim's mangled corpse, the defense counsel vigorously objected.

A *consul* is a government official working in a foreign country to protect the interests of his or her country's citizens there.

> If you lose your passport in a foreign country, you will need to see the American consul there.

credible, credulous *Credible* means "believable."

> A skillful liar can often sound highly credible.

Credulous means "overly ready to believe."

> Some people are credulous enough to believe anything they hear on television.

See also incredible, incredulous.

criterion, criteria A *criterion* is a standard by which someone or something is judged.

> In art, the only criterion of lasting value is lasting recognition.

Criteria is the plural of *criterion*.

> What criteria influence voters in judging a presidential candidate?

data *Data* is the plural of the Latin *datum*, meaning "something given"—a piece of information. *Data* should be treated as plural.

> The data transmitted by space satellites tell us much more about distant planets than we have ever known before.

delusion *See* allusion.

different from, *different than In formal writing do not use *than* after *different*. Use *from*.

> An adult's idea of a good time is often very different from a child's.

differ from, differ with *Differ from* means "be unlike."

> Black English differs from Standard English not only in its sounds but also in its structure. —Dorothy Z. Seymour

Differ with means "disagree with."

> Jung differed with Freud on the importance of the sex drive.

disinterested, uninterested *Disinterested* means "impartial," "unbiased," "objective."

> Lawyers respect Judge Brown for his disinterested handling of controversial cases.

Uninterested means "indifferent," "not interested."

> Some people are so uninterested in politics that they do not even bother to vote.

due to, because of *Due to* is adjectival and means "resulting from" or "the result of."

> Home-insurance policies sometimes fail to cover losses due to "acts of God," such as hurricanes and tornadoes.
> The senator's failure to win reelection was largely due to his lackluster campaigning.

Because of is adverbial and means "as a result of."

> Fighting persists in Northern Ireland because of animosities nearly three hundred years old.

Do not use *due to* to mean *because of*.

> * Due to a badly sprained ankle I had to drop out of the race.
> EDITED: Because of a badly sprained ankle I had to drop out of the race.

eager *See* anxious.

effect *See* affect.

emigrate *See* immigrate.

eminent, imminent, immanent *Eminent* means "distinguished," "prominent."

> An eminent biologist has recently redefined the concept of evolution.

Imminent means "about to happen."

> The leaden air and the black, heavy clouds told us that a thunderstorm was imminent.

Immanent means "inherent," "existing within."

> Pantheists believe that God is immanent in all things.

ensure *See* assure.

envelop, envelope *EnVELop* (second syllable accented) is a verb meaning "cover" or "enclose."

> Fog seemed to envelop the whole city.

Envelope (first syllable accented) is a noun meaning "container used for mailing."

> The small white envelope contained a big check.

* etc., et al. The abbreviation **etc.* stands for *et cetera,* "and other things." You should avoid it in formal writing. Instead, use *and so on,* or tell what the other things are.

> * Before setting out that morning, I put on my hat, mittens, etc.
> EDITED: Before setting out that morning, I put on my hat, mittens, scarf, and boots.

The abbreviation *et al.* stands for *et alii,* "and others." Use it only in a footnote or bibliography when citing a book with four or more authors or editors.

> Mack, Maynard, et al., eds. *World Masterpieces.* 6th ed. New York: Norton, 1992. 73–74.

everyday, every day *Everyday* means "ordinary" or "regular."

> The governor has a common touch; even in public speeches he likes to use everyday words.

Every day means "daily."

> While in training, Mary Thomas commonly runs at least ten miles every day.

except *See* accept.

factor *Factor* means "contributing element" or "partial cause." It can be used effectively, but far too often it simply clutters the sentence in which it appears. In general, you should avoid it.

> * One factor in the decay of the cities is the movement of middle-class families to the suburbs.
> EDITED: One reason for the decay of the cities is the movement of middle-class families to the surburbs.

farther, further   *Farther* means "a greater distance."

The trail went farther into the bush than the hunter had expected.

As an adjective, *further* means "more."

After high school, how many students really need further education?

As a conjunctive adverb, *further* means "besides."

Lincoln disliked slavery; further, he abhorred secession.

As a transitive verb, *further* means "promote" or "advance."

How much has the federal government done to further the development of solar energy?

fatal, fateful   *Fatal* means "sure to cause death" or "resulting in death."

Even a small dose of cyanide is fatal.
In a fruitless and fatal attempt to save the manuscript that he had spent ten years to produce, the novelist rushed back into the burning house.

Fateful means "momentous in effect" and can be used whether the outcome is good or bad.

In the end, Eisenhower made the fateful decision to land the Allies at Normandy.

few, little, less   Use *few* or *fewer* with countable nouns.

Few pianists even try to play the eerie music of George Crumb.

Use *little* (in the sense of "not much") or *less* with uncountable nouns.

A little honey on your hands can be a big sticky nuisance.
In spite of his grandiloquent title, the vice-president of the United States often has less power than a member of Congress.

flaunt, flout   Use *flaunt* to mean "exhibit openly" or "show off."

Stepping up to the crap table, the gambler flaunted a fat wad of bills.

Use *flout* to mean "defy" or "disobey."

Motorists who flout the law will be penalized.

former, formerly, formally   As an adjective, *former* means "previous."

When we moved in, the apartment was a mess. The former tenants had never even bothered to throw out the garbage.

As a noun, *former* refers to the first of two persons or things mentioned previously.

Muhammad Ali first fought Leon Spinks in February 1978. At the time, the former was an international celebrity, while the latter was a twenty-four-year-old unknown.

Formerly means "at an earlier time."

> Most of the men in the tribe were formerly hunters, not farmers.

Formally means "in a formal or ceremonious manner."

> The president is elected in November, but he does not formally take office until the following January.

frightened, afraid   *Frightened* is followed by *at* or *by*.

> Many people are frightened at the thought of dying.
> As I walked down the deserted road, I was frightened by a snarling wolfhound.

Afraid is followed by *of*.

> Afraid of heights, Scott would not go near the edge of the cliff.

fun   Use *fun* as a noun, but not (in formal writing) as an adjective before a noun.

> As soon as Mark arrived, the fun began.
> * We spent a fun afternoon at the zoo.
>   EDITED: We spent an enjoyable afternoon at the zoo.

further   *See* farther.

good, well   Use *good* as an adjective, but not as an adverb.

> The proposal to rebuild the chapel sounded good to many in the congregation.
> * She ran good for the first twenty miles, but then she collapsed.
>   EDITED: She ran well for the first twenty miles, but then she collapsed.

Use *well* as an adverb when you mean "in an effective manner" or "ably."

> Fenneman did so well in practice that the coach decided to put him in the starting lineup for the opening game.

Use *well* as an adjective when you mean "in good health."

> My grandfather hasn't looked well since his operation.

* got to   *See* has to.

hanged, hung   *Hanged* means "killed by hanging."

> The prisoner was hanged at dawn.
> The distraught man hanged himself.

Hung means "suspended" or "held oneself up."

> I hung my coat on the back of the door and sat down.
> I hung on the side of the cliff, frantically seeking a foothold.

has to, have to, *got to   In formal writing, do not use **got to* to denote an obligation. Use *have to, has to,* or *must.*

> * Anyone who wants to win the nomination has got to run in the primaries.
>
> EDITED: Anyone who wants to win the nomination has to run in the primaries.

hopefully   Use *hopefully* to modify a verb.

> As the ice-cream truck approached, the children looked hopefully at their parents. [*Hopefully* modifies *looked,* telling how the children looked.]

Do not use *hopefully* when you mean "I hope that," "we hope that," or the like.

> * Hopefully, the company will make a profit in the final quarter.
>
> EDITED: The stockholders hope that the company will make a profit in the final quarter.

human, humane   *Human* means "pertaining to human beings."

> To err is human.

Humane means "merciful," "kindhearted," or "considerate."

> To forgive is both divine and humane.

illusion   *See* allusion.

immanent, imminent   *See* eminent.

immigrate, emigrate   *Immigrate* means "enter a country in order to live there permanently."

> Professor Korowitz immigrated to the United States in 1955.

Emigrate means "leave one country in order to live in another."

> My great-great-grandfather emigrated from Ireland in 1848.

immoral   *See* amoral.

imply, infer   *Imply* means "suggest" or "hint at something."

> The manager implied that I could not be trusted with the job.

Infer means "reach a conclusion on the basis of evidence"; it is often used with *from.*

> From the manager's letter I inferred that my chances were nil.

in, into, in to   Use *in* when referring to a direction, location, or position.

> Easterners used to think that everyone in the West was a cowboy.

Use *into* to mean movement toward the inside.

> Before he started drilling, the dentist shot Novocain into my gum.

Use *in to* when the two words have separate functions.

> The museum was open, so I walked in to look at the paintings.

In formal writing, do not use *into* to mean "occupied with" or "studying."

> Brenda has been into ballet for the past year.
> EDITED: Brenda has been studying ballet for the past year.

incredible, incredulous   *Incredible* means "not believable."

> Since instrumental exploration of Mars has revealed no signs of life there, the idea that "Martians" could invade the earth is now incredible.

In formal writing, do not use *incredible* to mean "amazingly bad," "compelling," "brilliant," or "extraordinary." In speech, you can indicate the meaning of *incredible* by the way you say it, but in writing, this word may be ambiguous and confusing.

> * Marian gave an incredible performance. {The reader has no way of knowing just how good it was.}
> EDITED: Marian gave a brilliant performance.

Incredulous means "unbelieving" or "skeptical."

> When Columbus argued that his ship would not fall off the edge of the earth, many of his hearers were incredulous, for they believed the earth was flat.

infer   *See* imply.

inferior to, *inferior than   Use *to* after *inferior*, not *than*.

> * Are American automobiles still inferior than those made elsewhere?
> EDITED: Are American automobiles still inferior to those made elsewhere?

insure   *See* assure.

* irregardless   *See* regardless.

irritate   *See* aggravate.

its, it's   *Its* is the possessive form of *it*.

> We liked the house because of its appearance, its location, and its price.

It's means "it is."

> It's a pity that we seldom see ourselves as others see us.

kind of, sort of   In formal writing, do not use *kind of* or *sort of* to mean "somewhat" or "rather."

> * When I got off the roller coaster, I felt sort of sick.
> EDITED: When I got off the roller coaster, I felt rather sick.

later, latter   Use *later* when referring to time.

> Russia developed the atomic bomb later than the United States did.

Use *latter* when referring to the second of two persons or things mentioned previously.

> Muhammed Ali first fought Leon Spinks in February 1978. At the time, the former was an international celebrity, while the latter was a twenty-four-year-old unknown.

lay   *See* lie.

lead, led   *Lead* (rhymes with *seed*) is the present-tense and infinitive form of the verb meaning "cause," "guide," or "direct."

> Deficit spending leads to inflation.
> An effective president must be able to lead Congress without bullying it.

Led is the past-tense form and past participle of *lead*.

> During the Civil War, General Robert E. Lee led the Confederate forces.
> Some buyers are led astray by simple-minded slogans.

learn, teach   *Learn* means "gain knowledge, information, or skill." *Teach* means "give lessons or instructions."

> If you want to know how well you have learned something, teach it to someone else.

leave, let   *Leave* as a verb means "go away from" or "put in a place."

> I had to leave the house at 6:00 A.M. to catch the bus.
> I had to leave my suitcase at the bus station.

Leave as a noun means "permission," including permission to go away.

> After an hour, I asked leave to speak.
> The sailors were granted a leave of twenty-four hours.

Let means "permit," "allow."

> Some colleges let students take courses by mail.

led   *See* lead.

less   *See* few.

let   *See* leave.

let's, *let's us   Use *let's* before a verb. Do not follow *let's* with *us;* that would mean "let us us."

> * Let's us finish the job.
>> EDITED: Let's finish the job.

liable   *See* likely.

lie, lay   *Lie (lie, lying, lay, lain)* is an intransitive verb meaning "rest," "recline," or "stay."

> I love to lie on the sand in the hot sun.
> Lying on the sand, I watched the clouds and listened to the surf.
> After she lay in the sun for three hours, she looked like a boiled lobster.
> On April 26, 1952, workers digging peat near Grueballe, Denmark, found a well-preserved body that had lain in the bog for fifteen hundred years.

Lay (lay, laying, laid) is a transitive verb meaning "put in a certain position."

> The rebels were told to lay down their weapons.
> A good education lays the foundation for a good life.
> The workers were laying bricks when an earthquake struck.
> He laid the book on the counter and walked out of the library.
> The earthquake struck after the foundation had been laid.

like   *See* as.

likely, apt, liable   *Likely* indicates future probability.

> As gas becomes scarcer and more expensive, battery-powered cars are likely to become popular.

Apt indicates a usual or habitual tendency.

> Most cars are apt to rust after two or three years.

Liable indicates a risk or adverse possibility.

> Cars left unlocked are liable to be stolen.

little   *See* few.

loose, lose   *Loose* (rhymes with *moose*) means "free" or "not securely tied or fastened."

> The center grabbed the loose ball and ran for a touchdown.
> From the rattling of the door, I could tell that the catch was loose.

Lose (sounds like *Lou's*) means "fail to keep" or "fail to win."

> In some cultures, to lose face is to lose everything.
> The truth about sports is that when somebody wins, somebody else loses.

lots of, a lot of, *alot of   *A lot of* and *lots of* are colloquial and wordy. In formal writing, use *much* for "a great amount" and *many* for "a great number." Do not use **alot* anywhere; it is a misspelling of a *lot.*

> Lots of students come to college with no clear notion of what they want to do.
> BETTER: Many students come to college with no clear notion of what they want to do.

many, much, *muchly   Use *many* with countable nouns.

> Many hands make light work.

Use *much* with uncountable nouns.

> Much of the work has been done.

Use *much* or *very much*, not **muchly*, as an adverb.

> * The long sleep in the guest room left me muchly refreshed.
> EDITED: The long sleep in the guest room left me much [for "very much"] refreshed.

maybe, may be   *Maybe* means "perhaps."

> Maybe all cars will be electric by the year 2000.

May be is a verb phrase.

> By the year 2000, the president of the United States may be a woman.

might have, *might of   Use *might have*, not **might of.*

> * Oklahoma might of won the game if it had lasted just two minutes longer.
> EDITED: Oklahoma might have won the game if it had lasted just two minutes longer.

moral, morale   *MORal* (first syllable accented) is an adjective meaning "ethical" or "virtuous."

> To heed a cry for help is not a legal duty but a moral one.
> Piety and morality are two different things: a pious man can be immoral, and an impious man can be moral.

MoRALE (second syllable accented) is a noun meaning "spirit," "attitude."

> Eisenhower's habit of mixing with his troops before a battle kept up their morale.

most, mostly, *most all   *See* almost.

much, *muchly   *See* many.

not very, none too, *not too   In formal writing, use *not very* or *none too* instead of **not too.*

> * Not too pleased with the dull and droning lecture, the students filled the air with catcalls, spitballs, and paper planes.
> EDITED: None too pleased with the dull and droning lecture, the students filled the air with catcalls, spitballs, and paper planes.

nowhere, *nowheres   Use *nowhere,* not **nowheres.*

> * The child was nowheres to be seen.
> EDITED: The child was nowhere to be seen.

number   *See* amount.

OK, O.K., okay   Avoid all three in formal writing. In business letters or informal writing, you can use *OK* as a noun meaning "endorsement" or "approval," or *okay* as a verb meaning "endorse," "approve."

> The stockholders have given their OK.
> Union negotiators have okayed the company's latest offer.

only   Place *only* carefully. Usually, it belongs just before the word, phrase, or clause it modifies.

> * At most colleges, students only get their diplomas if they have paid all their bills.
> EDITED: At most colleges, students get their diplomas only if they have paid all their bills.

> * Some busy executives only relax on Sundays.
> EDITED: Some busy executives relax only on Sundays.

For more on the placement of *only,* see section 12.17.

ourselves, ourself   Use *ourselves* when the antecedent is plural.

> Nearly an hour after the frontrunners had come in, Sally and I dragged ourselves across the finish line.

Use *ourself* only on the rare occasion when the antecedent is a single person using the royal *we* in place of *I.*

> "Be as ourself in Denmark" (*Hamlet* 1.2.122).

passed, past   *Passed* means "went by" or "threw."

> The idiot passed me on the inside lane.
> Conversation ground to a painful halt, and minutes passed like hours.
> Seymour passed to Winowski, but the ball was intercepted.

As a noun, *past* means "a certain previous time" or "all previous time."

> Prehistoric monuments like Stonehenge speak to us of a past that we can only speculate about.

As an adjective, *past* means "connected with a certain previous time" or "connected with all previous time."

> Past experience never tells us everything we want to know about the future.

As a preposition, *past* means "beyond."

> The space probe *Pioneer 10* will eventually travel past the limits of the solar system.

persecute, prosecute   *Persecute* means "pester" or "harass."

> As Nero persecuted the Christians, Hitler persecuted the Jews.

Prosecute means "bring charges against someone in a formal, legal way."

> Al Capone ran his criminal empire so shrewdly that it was years before authorities were able to prosecute him.

personal, personnel   *PERsonal* (first syllable accented) is an adjective meaning "private" or "individual."

> In writing or speaking, you can sometimes use a personal experience to illustrate a general point.

PersonNEL (last syllable accented) is a noun meaning "persons in a firm or a military group."

> If you want a job with a big company, you normally have to see the director of personnel.

phenomenon, phenomena   *Phenomenon* means "something perceived by the senses" or "something extraordinary."

> A rainbow is a phenomenon caused by the separation of sunlight into various colors as it passes through raindrops.
> Old Barney is a phenomenon. At eighty years of age he still swims five miles every day.

Phenomena is the plural of *phenomenon*.

> The northern lights are among the most impressive phenomena in nature.

poor, poorly   Use *poor* as an adjective.

> The poor man stood waiting in the rain.

Use *poorly* as an adverb.

> Nearly half the applicants did poorly on the aptitude test.

Do not use *poor* as an adverb:

> * The car starts poor in cold weather.
> EDITED: The car starts poorly in cold weather.

Do not use *poorly* as an adjective.

> * Heather looked poorly after the operation.
> EDITED: Heather looked poor after the operation.

precede, proceed, proceeds, proceedings, procedure   To *precede* is "to come before or go before in place or time."

> A dead calm often precedes a hurricane.

To *proceed* is "to move forward or go on."

> With the bridge washed out, the bus could not proceed, so we had to get out and take a ferry across the river.
> The bishop proceeded toward the cathedral.
> After the judge silenced the uproar, he told the prosecutor to proceed with her questioning.

Proceeds are funds generated by a business deal or a money-raising event.

> The proceeds of the auction went to buy new furniture for the Student Center.

Proceedings are formal actions, especially in an official meeting.

> During a trial, a court stenographer takes down every word of the proceedings for the record.

A *procedure* is a standardized way of doing something.

> Anyone who wants to run a meeting effectively should know the rules of parliamentary procedure.

principal, principle   As a noun, *principal* means "administrator" or "sum of money."

> The school principal wanted all of us to think of him as a pal, but none of us did.
> The interest on the principal came to $550 a year.

As an adjective, *principal* means "most important."

> In most American households, television is the principal source of entertainment.

Principle means "rule of behavior," "basic truth," or "general law of nature."

> Whenever we officially recognize a government that abuses its own citizens, we are tacitly accepting the principle that might makes right.

proceed   *See* precede.

proceeds, proceedings, procedure   *See* precede.

prosecute   *See* persecute.

quote, quotation   *Quote* means "repeat the exact words of."

> In his "Letter from Birmingham Jail," Martin Luther King, Jr., quotes Lincoln: "This nation cannot survive half slave and half free."

Do not use *quote* to mean "refer to" or "paraphrase the view of." Use *cite*.

> In defense of his stand against segregation, King cites more than a dozen authorities, and he quotes Lincoln: "This nation cannot survive half slave and half free."

Do not use *quote* as a noun to mean "something quoted." Use *quotation*.

> * A sermon usually begins with a quote from Scripture.
> EDITED: A sermon usually begins with a quotation from Scripture.

Quotation means "something quoted," as in the preceding example. But you should not normally use it to mean something *you* are quoting.

> * In a quotation on the very first page of the book, Holden expresses his opinion of Hollywood. "If there's one thing I hate," he says, "it's the movies." [Holden is not quoting anybody. He is speaking for himself.]
> EDITED: Holden states his opinion of Hollywood on the very first page of the book: "If there's one thing I hate," he says, "it's the movies."

raise, rise   *Raise (raise, raising, raised, raised)* is a transitive verb—one followed by an object.

> Moments before his hanging, Dandy Tom raised his hat to the ladies.
> My grandmother has raised ten children.

Rise (rise, rising, rose, risen) is an intransitive verb—one that has no object.

> Puffs of smoke rose skyward.
> The farmhands rose at 5:00 A.M. Monday through Saturday.
> Have you ever risen early enough to see the sun rise?

rational, rationale, rationalize   *Rational* means "able to reason," "sensible," or "logical."

> Can a rational person ever commit suicide?
> Is there such a thing as a rational argument for nuclear warfare?

Rationale means "justification," "explanation," or "underlying reason."

> The rationale for the new bypass is that it will reduce the flow of traffic through the center of town.

Rationalize means "justify with one or more fake reasons."

> He rationalized his extravagance by saying that he was only doing his part to keep money in circulation.

real, really *Real* means "actual."

> The unicorn is an imaginary beast, but it is made up of features taken from real ones.

Really means "actually."

> Petrified wood looks like ordinary wood, but it is really stone.

In formal writing, do not use *real* to modify an adjective.

> * In parts of the country, synthetic fuels have met real strong resistance.
>
> EDITED: In parts of the country, synthetic fuels have met really strong resistance.
>
> FURTHER REVISED: In parts of the country, synthetic fuels have met strong resistance. [This version eliminates *really*, which—like *very*—often weakens rather than strengthens the word it modifies.]

reason . . . is that, *reason . . . is because Use *reason* with *that*, not with *because,* or use *because* by itself.

> * The reason many college freshmen have trouble with writing is because they did little or no writing in high school.
>
> EDITED: The reason many college freshmen have trouble with writing is that they did little or no writing in high school. [or] Many college freshmen have trouble with writing because they did little or no writing in high school.

refer *See* allude.

regardless, *irregardless Use *regardless,* not **irregardless.*

> * Irregardless of what happens to school systems and public services, some cities and towns have voted to cut property taxes substantially.
>
> EDITED: Regardless of what happens to school systems and public services, some cities and towns have voted to cut property taxes substantially.

respectively, respectfully, respectably *Respectively* means "in turn" or "in the order presented."

> The college presented honorary degrees to Harriet Brown and Emanuel Lee, who are, respectively, an Olympic medalist and a concert pianist.

Respectfully means "with respect."

> Parents who speak respectfully to their children are most likely to end up with children who speak respectfully to them.

Respectably means "presentably" or "in a manner deserving respect."

> She ran respectably but not quite successfully for the Senate.

revenge *See* avenge.

rise *See* raise.

set, sit *Set (set, setting, set, set)* means "put" or "place."

> I filled the kettle and set it on the range.
> When daylight saving changes to standard time, I can never remember whether to set my watch forward or back.

Sit (sit, sitting, sat, sat) means "place oneself in a sitting position."

> On clear summer nights I love to sit outside, listen to crickets, and look at the stars.
> Grandfather sat in an easy chair and smoked his pipe.

sight, cite, site As a verb, *sight* means "observe" or "perceive with the eyes."

> After twenty days on the open sea, the sailors sighted land.

As a noun, *sight* means "spectacle," "device for aiming," or "vision."

> Some travelers care only for the sights of a foreign country; they have no interest in its people.
> The deadliest weapon of all is a rifle with a telescopic sight.
> Most of us take the gift of sight for granted; only the blind know how much it is worth.

Cite means "refer to," "mention as an example or piece of evidence."

> Anyone opposed to nuclear power cites the case of Three Mile Island.

As a verb, *site* means "locate" or "place at a certain point."

> The architect sited the house on the side of a hill.

As a noun, *site* means "location" or "place," often the place where something has been or will be built.

> The site of the long-gone Globe Theatre, where Shakespeare himself once trod the boards, is now occupied by a reconstructed version of the Globe.

since *See* because.

sit *See* set.

site *See* sight.

so *See* very.

sometimes, sometime *Sometimes* means "occasionally."

> Sometimes I lie awake at night and wonder what I will do with my life.

As an adjective, *sometime* means "former."

> In the presidential campaigns of 1952 and 1956, Eisenhower twice defeated Adlai Stevenson, sometime governor of Illinois and later U.S. ambassador to the United Nations.

As an adverb, *sometime* means "at some point."

> Slot machine addicts invariably think that they will sometime hit the jackpot.

somewhere, *somewheres   Use *somewhere,* not **somewheres.*

> * Somewheres in that pile of junk was a diamond necklace.
> EDITED: Somewhere in that pile of junk was a diamond necklace.

sort of   *See* kind of.

stationary, stationery   *Stationary* means "not moving."

> Before you can expect to hit a moving target, you need to practice with a stationary one.

Stationery means "writing paper," "writing materials."

> Since my parents sent me off to college with a big box of personalized stationery, I feel obliged to write to them occasionally.

statue, statute   *Statue* means "sculpted figure."

> The Statue of Liberty in New York harbor was given to America by France.

Statute means "law passed by a governing body."

> Though the Supreme Court has ruled that abortion is legally permissible, some state legislatures have enacted statutes restricting the conditions under which it may be performed.

such a   Do not use *such a* as an intensifier unless you add a result clause beginning with *that.*

> WEAK: The commencement speech was such a bore.
> BETTER: The commencement speech was such a bore that I fell asleep after the first five minutes.

supposed to, *suppose to   Use *supposed to* when you mean "expected to" or "required to." Do not use **suppose to.*

> * Truman was suppose to lose when he ran against Dewey, but he surprised almost everyone by winning.
> EDITED: Truman was supposed to lose when he ran against Dewey, but he surprised almost everyone by winning.

teach   *See* learn.

than, then   Use *than* when writing comparisons.

> Many people spend money faster than they earn it.

Use *then* when referring to time.

> Lightning flashed, thunder cracked, and then the rain began.

that, which, who   Use *which* or *that* as the pronoun when the antecedent is a thing.

> There was nothing to drink but root beer, which I loathe.
> Any restaurant that doesn't serve grits ought to be closed.

Use *who* or *that* as the pronoun when the antecedent is a person or persons.

> I like people who can do things.   —R. W. Emerson
> Anyone that smokes a pack a day is living dangerously.

themselves, *theirselves, *theirself   Use *themselves,* not **theirselves* or **theirself.*

> * Fortunately, the children did not hurt theirselves when they fell out of the tree.
> EDITED: Fortunately, the children did not hurt themselves when they fell out of the tree.

then   *See* than.

there, their, they're   Use *there* to mean "in that place" or "to that place," and in the expressions *there is* and *there are.*

> I have always wanted to see Las Vegas, but I have never been there.
> There is nothing we can do to change the past, but there are many things we can do to improve the future.

There is and *there are* should be used sparingly, since most sentences are tighter and better without them.

> We can do nothing to change the past, but many things to improve the future.

Use *their* as the possessive form of *they.*

> The immigrants had to leave most of their possessions behind.

Use *they're* when you mean "they are."

> I like cats because they're sleek, quiet, and sly.

thus, therefore, *thusly   Use *thus* to mean "in that manner" or "by this means." In formal writing, do not use **thusly.*

> Carmichael bought a thousand shares of Microsoft when it was a brand-new company. Thus he became a millionaire.

Do not use *thus* to mean "therefore," "so," or "for this reason."

> A storm hit the mountain. *Thus the climbers had to take shelter.
> EDITED: A storm hit the mountain, so the climbers had to take shelter.

to, too Use *to* when writing about place, direction, or position, and with infinitives.

> We drove from Cleveland to Pittsburgh without stopping.
> Like many before him, Fenwick was determined to write the great American novel.

Use *too* when you mean "also" or "excessively."

> In spite of the cast on my foot, I too got up and danced.
> Some poems are too confusing to be enjoyable.

try to, *try and Use *try to,* not *try and.*

> * Whenever I feel depressed, I try and lose myself in science fiction.
> EDITED: Whenever I feel depressed, I try to lose myself in science fiction.

type Do not attach *-type* to the end of an adjective.

> * He had a psychosomatic-type illness.
> EDITED: He had a psychosomatic illness.

uninterested *See* disinterested.

unique *Unique* means "one of a kind."

> Among pop singers of the fifties, Elvis Presley was unique.

Do not use *unique* to mean "remarkable," "unusual," or "striking."

> * She wore a unique dress to the party.
> EDITED: She wore a striking dress to the party.

used to, *use to Write *used to,* not *use to,* when you mean "did regularly" or "was accustomed to."

> * She use to practice the flute every morning.
> EDITED: She used to practice the flute every morning.

very, awfully, so Use *very* sparingly, if at all. It can weaken the effect of potent modifiers.

> The very icy wind cut through us as we walked across the bridge.
> BETTER: The icy wind cut through us as we walked across the bridge.

Do not use *awfully* to mean "very."

> * We were awfully tired.
> EDITED: We were very tired.
> FURTHER REVISED: We were exhausted.

Do not use *so* as an intensifier unless you add a result clause beginning with *that*.

> * They were so tired.
> EDITED: They were so tired that they slept for ten hours.

wait for, wait on   To *wait for* means "to stay until someone arrives, something is provided, or something happens."

> The restaurant was so crowded that we had to wait half an hour for a table.

To *wait on* means "to serve."

> Monica waited on more than fifty people that night. When the restaurant closed, she could barely stand up.

way, ways   Use *way,* not *ways,* when writing about distance.

> * A short ways up the trail we found a dead rabbit.
> EDITED: A short way up the trail we found a dead rabbit.

well   *See* good.

were, we're   Use *were* as a verb or part of a verb phrase.

> The soldiers were a sorry sight.
> They were trudging across a wheat field.

Use *we're* when you mean "we are."

> We're trying to build a telescope for the observatory.
> Most Americans have lost the urge to roam. With television scanning the world for us, we're a nation of sitters.

which, who   *See* that.

whose, who's   *Whose,* meaning "of whom," is the possessive form of *who.*

> Whose property has been destroyed?

Who's means "who is."

> Who's deceived by such claims?

would have, *would of   Use *would have,* not **would of.*

> * Churchill said that he would of made a pact with the devil himself to defeat Hitler.
> EDITED: Churchill said that he would have made a pact with the devil himself to defeat Hitler.

Have, not *of,* is also customary after *may, might, must,* and *should.*

Glossary of Grammatical Terms

absolute phrase   A modifier usually made from a noun or noun phrase and a participle. It can modify a noun or pronoun or the whole of the base sentence to which it is attached.

> *Teeth chattering,* we waited for hours in the bitter cold.
> Who is the best person for the job, *all things considered?*

active voice   *See* voice.

adjective   A word that modifies a noun or pronoun, specifying such things as what kind, how many, and which one.

> For a *small* crime, he spent years in a *tiny* cell of the *old* prison.
> She is *funny.*

adjective phrase   A phrase that modifies a noun or pronoun.

> A *long, thin* scar was visible on his back.
> On the table was a vase *with red roses.*
> It was a *once-in-a-lifetime* opportunity.

adjective (relative) clause   A subordinate clause used as an adjective within a sentence. It normally begins with a relative pronoun—a word that relates the clause to a preceding word or phrase.

> Pablo Picasso, *who learned to paint by the age of twelve,* worked at his art for nearly eighty years.

adverb   A word that modifies a verb, an adjective, another adverb, or a clause. It tells such things as how, when, where, why, and for what purpose. It often ends in *-ly.*

> She *seldom* spoke.
> The road was *extremely* bumpy.
> The cyclists were breathing *very heavily.*
> *Fortunately,* no one was injured.

adverb clause   A subordinate clause used as an adverb within a sentence. It begins with a subordinator, a term like *because, if, when,* or *although.*

>We canceled the deal *because the buyer could not get a loan.*
>*If the temperature falls below freezing,* roads will become unsafe.
>Smiling *when the guests arrived,* she was miserable *when they left.*

adverb phrase   A phrase that modifies a verb, an adjective, another adverb, or a clause.

>The fox hid *under the hedge.*
>Wary *at first,* we approached *in silence.*
>The children were eager *to see the clowns.*

agent   The source of the action in a passive-voice construction.

>The preamble was written by *Alice Harvey.*
>The launching of the space shuttle will be viewed by *millions.*

agreement of pronoun and antecedent   Correspondence in gender and number between a pronoun and its antecedent.

>Nellie Bly, the American journalist, was noted for *her* daring. [*Her* is feminine and singular.]
>Ms. Sterns handed Mr. Nichols *his* briefcase. [*His* is masculine and singular.]
>You can't tell a book by *its* cover. [*Its* is neuter and singular.]
>The Andrews Sisters sang some of *their* best-known songs during World War II. [*Their* is plural and used for all genders.]

agreement of subject and verb   Correspondence in number between the form of a verb and its subject. In most cases, the subject affects the form of the verb only in the present tense; when the subject is a singular noun or a third-person singular pronoun, the present tense is made by the addition of *-s* or *-es* to the bare form.

>Jerry *paints* his houses.
>He *fishes* every summer.

When the subject is not a singular noun or a third-person singular pronoun, the present tense is normally the same as the bare form.

>I *paint* houses.
>The men *fish* every summer.

The verb *be* has special forms in the present and the past, as shown on p. 368.

antecedent   The word or word group that a pronoun refers to.

> A   P
> *Oliver* said that he could eat a whole pizza.

> A   P
> *The police,* who have surrounded the building, expect to free the hostages tonight.

> A   P
> A *snake* sheds its skin several times a year.

appositive   A noun, noun phrase, or series of nouns used to identify another noun, noun phrase, or a pronoun.

> The blackjack player, *an expert at counting cards in play,* was barred from the casino.
> They were denied their favorite foods—*ice cream, pizza, and peanut butter.*
> He and she—*brother and sister*—opened a record store.

article   A short word *(a, an,* or *the)* commonly used before a noun or noun equivalent.

> *The* bombing of *a* village provoked *an* outcry of protest.

See also determiner.

auxiliary (helping verb)   A verb used with a base verb to make a verb phrase.

> I *have* seen the Kennedy Library.
> It *was* designed by I. M. Pei.
> People *do* find it impressive.

bare form   The verb form used in the present tense with every subject except a singular noun and a third-person singular pronoun.

base (bare-bones) sentence   A sentence without modifiers.

> Prices rose.
> Orders dropped.
> Customers saved money.

base verb   The principal verb in a verb phrase made with an auxiliary.

> She has *earned* a promotion.
> She will be *supervising* all overseas operations.

case   The form that a noun or pronoun takes as determined by its role in a sentence. The **subject case** is used for a pronoun that is the subject of a verb.

> The dog was far from home, but *he* still wore a leather collar.

The **object case** is used for a pronoun that serves as an object (see object) or that immediately precedes an infinitive.

> I found *him* trailing a broken leash behind *him*.
> I wanted *him* to come home with *me*.

The **possessive case** of a noun or pronoun indicates ownership of something or close connection with it.

> The *dog's* hind feet were bleeding, and *his* coat was muddy.

The **reflexive/emphatic case** of a pronoun indicates a reflexive action—an action affecting the one who performs it. This case is also used for emphasis.

> The dog had hurt *himself*; as I tried to comfort him, the owner *herself* rushed up to me.

clause   A word group consisting of a subject and a predicate.

> S   P
> We / bought an old house. [one clause]

>   S   P   S   P
> After we / bought the house, we / found a crack in the foundation.
> [two clauses]

>   S   P   S   P
> Furthermore, the roof / leaked, the floors / sagged,

>   S   P
> and the furnace / was out of order. [three clauses]

collective noun   A noun naming a collection of people, animals, or things treated as an entity. Examples include *team, committee, herd, flock,* and *family*.

comma splice   The error of trying to link two independent clauses with nothing but a comma.

> * Sir Richard Burton failed to find the source of the Nile, John Hanning Speke discovered it in 1862.
> EDITED: Sir Richard Burton failed to find the source of the Nile; John Hanning Speke discovered it in 1862.

Separating the clauses with a period would give you two sentences.

common and progressive forms   Forms of the verb. The **common form** indicates an action that is habitual, completed, or to be completed.

> They *take* excursions on weekends.
> He *opened* the door and *entered* the room.
> She *will finish* by dark.

The **progressive form** indicates a continuing action or one that was in progress when something else occurred.

> They *are taking* an excursion right now.
> He *was opening* the door when the cat scratched him.
> She *will be working* on the design throughout the day.

The progressive consists of some form of the auxiliary *be* followed by a present particle—a verb with *-ing* on the end.

comparative, positive, and superlative　Forms of the adjective and adverb. The **positive** form describes a person or thing without drawing a comparison.

> This lemonade tastes *sour*.
> Ms. Berkle talks *loudly*.

The **comparative** is used to compare one person, thing, or group with another person, thing, or group.

> Los Angeles is *bigger* than Sacramento.
> Cal was *more ambitious* than his classmates.
> Sheila argued *less persuasively* than Susan did.
> In general, women live *longer* than men.

The **superlative** is used to compare one person, thing, or group with all others in its class.

> Joan's quilt was the *most colorful* one on display.
> Whales are the *largest* of all mammals.
> Gold is the *most eagerly* sought mineral in the world.

complete subject　See subject.

complex sentence　A sentence consisting of one independent clause and at least one subordinate clause. The independent clause in a complex sentence is usually called the main clause.

> Although Frank pleaded with Ida [subordinate clause], she would not give him any money [main clause].

compound-complex sentence　A sentence consisting of two or more independent clauses and one or more subordinate clauses.

> When I moved to Chicago [subordinate clause], I first applied for a job [main clause], and then I looked for an apartment [main clause].

compound phrase　Words or phrases joined by a conjunction, a comma, or both.

> The plan was *simple but shrewd*.
> We saw an *old, rough-skinned, enormous* elephant.

The kitten was *lively, friendly, and curious.*
You must *either pay your dues on time or turn in your membership card.*

compound sentence   A sentence consisting of two or more independent clauses.

Jill made the coffee, and Frank scrambled the eggs.
He practiced many hours each day, but he never learned to play the piano well.

conditional sentence   A sentence normally consisting of an *if* clause, which states a condition, and a result clause, which states the result of that condition.

If it rains on the Fourth of July, the fireworks will be canceled.
If Social Security were abolished, millions of retirees would be destitute.

conjunction (coordinating conjunction)   A word used to show a relation between words, phrases, or clauses. The conjunctions are *and, yet, or, but, nor,* and—for joining clauses only—*for* and *so.*

The tablecloth was red, white, *and* blue.
Small *but* sturdy, the cabin had withstood many winters.
Al *and* Joan walked to the meeting, *for* they liked exercise.

conjunctive adverb   A word or phrase used to show a relation between clauses or sentences. Conjunctive adverbs include *nevertheless, as a result, therefore, however,* and *likewise.*

The ship was supposed to be unsinkable; *nevertheless,* it did not survive its collision with an iceberg.
The lawyer spoke for an hour; the jury, *however,* was unimpressed.

coordinating conjunction   *See* conjunction.

coordination   An arrangement that makes two or more parts of a sentence equal in grammatical rank.

Martha *took the script* home and *read it* to her husband.
The fight ended, and *the crowd dispersed.*
A porcupine or *a raccoon* had raided the garbage can.

correlative   Words or phrases used in pairs to join words, phrases, or clauses. Correlatives include *both . . . and, not only . . . but also, either . . . or, neither . . . nor,* and *whether . . . or.*

He was *both* rich *and* handsome.
She *not only* got the part *but also* played it brilliantly.
Either they would visit us, *or* we would visit them.

dangling modifier   A modifier without a headword—a word or phrase that it can modify.

> * *Running angrily out the back way,* a couple of milk bottles were over-turned.
> EDITED: Running angrily out the back way, he overturned a couple of milk bottles.

declarative sentence   A sentence that makes a statement and ends with a period.

> The earth orbits around the sun.
> Americans spend millions of dollars on Japanese products every year.

definite pronouns   *See* pronoun.

dependent clause   *See* subordinate clause.

determiner   A modifier that always precedes a noun or noun equivalent and marks it as such. Determiners include articles (*a, an, the*), demonstratives (such as *this*), indefinites (such as *some*), possessives (such as *her*), ordinal numbers (such as *ten*), and cardinal numbers (such as *third*). Unlike adjectives (A), determiners cannot follow the nouns they modify and have no comparative or superlative forms.

> *The first ten* customers each got *a* box of popcorn.
>   A   A
> *The* manager, smiling and happy, greeted *every* customer.
>   A
> *His* smiling made them happier.

direct object   *See* object.

direct and indirect reporting   Two ways of reporting spoken or written statements and questions. A **direct report** reproduces within quotation marks the words someone spoke or wrote.

> "He that cannot obey, cannot command," writes Benjamin Franklin.

An **indirect report** turns the original statement into a subordinate clause usually starting with *that*.

> Franklin writes that anyone who cannot obey is unable to command.

double negative   The error of using two negative words to make one negative statement.

> * We *didn't* need *no* guide.
> EDITED: We *didn't* need a guide. [or] We needed *no* guide.

expletive   A word used before a linking verb when the subject follows it.

> *There* was no food in the house.
> *It* was exciting to see the bald eagles.

faulty comparison   The omission of one or more words needed to make a comparison clear.

> * The neighborhood is more violent than five years ago.
> EDITED: The neighborhood is more violent than it was five years ago.

faulty parallelism   A construction in which two or more elements are parallel in meaning but not in form.

> * He wants to write with clarity, power, and logically.
> EDITED: He wants to write *clearly, powerfully,* and *logically.*

faulty predication   Using words after a linking verb that are not compatible with the subject.

> * A necessary step in any campaign to lose weight is *eating habits.*
> EDITED: A necessary step in any campaign to lose weight is *to change one's eating habits.*

faulty shift in tense   An unjustified shift from one tense to another, or an inconsistency between the tense of a subordinate verb and the tense of the main verb.

> * I lit a candle, but the darkness *is* so thick I saw nothing.
> EDITED: I lit a candle, but the darkness was so thick I saw nothing.
> * Though the trumpeter *blows* as hard as he could, the drummer drowned him out.
> EDITED: Though the trumpeter blew as hard as he could, the drummer drowned him out.

fragment   *See* sentence fragment.

fused sentence   *See* run-on sentence.

future perfect tense   *See* tense.

future tense   *See* tense.

gender   The form of a pronoun as determined by the sex of its antecedent, which may be masculine, feminine, or neuter.

> Bill [antecedent] brought *his* fishing rod, and Sally [antecedent] brought *her* paints.
> The sun [antecedent] shed *its* rays over the lake.

gerund   A verbal noun made from the present participle.

> *Gambling* takes nerve.
> Fawn hated *washing dishes*.

headword (H)   A word or phrase modified (M) by another word, phrase, or clause.

>   M   H
> A black leather *wallet* was found in the men's room.
>
>   M   H
> Running for the elevator, *Pritchett* nearly knocked over Mr. Givens.
>
> M   H   M
> The *breeze* that refreshes us comes from the ocean.

helping verb   *See* auxiliary.

imperative   *See* mood.

indefinite pronoun   *See* pronoun.

independent clause   A clause that can stand by itself as a simple sentence.

> The roof leaks.

It can be combined with one or more independent clauses in a compound sentence.

> The roof leaks, and the floor sags.

And it can serve as the main clause in a complex sentence.

> Whenever it rains, the roof leaks.

indicative mood   *See* mood.

indirect object   *See* object.

indirect report   *See* direct and indirect reporting.

infinitive   A form usually made by the placing of *to* before the bare form of a verb.

> Some say that politicians are born *to run*.
> The prisoners of war refused to *continue* their forced march.

After some verbs the *to* in the infinitive is omitted. Compare:

> Jack wanted the little boy *to feed* the ducks.
> Jack watched the little boy *feed* the ducks.

infinitive phrase   A phrase formed by an infinitive and it object, its modifiers, or both.

She hates *to see horror movies.*
It was beginning *to rain furiously.*
I hope *to find a job soon.*

interrogative pronoun   A pronoun that begins a question.

What is making that noise?

interrogative sentence   A sentence that asks a question and ends with a question mark.

Do whales have lungs?

intransitive verb   *See* transitive and intransitive verbs.

irregular verb   *See* regular and irregular verbs.

linking verb   A verb followed by a word or word group that identifies or describes the subject.

This machine *is* a drill press.
I *feel* good today.
That perfume *smells* sweet.

main clause   The independent clause in a complex sentence.

Since the refrigerator was empty, *we went to a restaurant.*

main verb   The verb of the independent clause in a complex sentence.

I *cut* the grass before the storm came.
Since the store was closed, we *drove* away.

misplaced modifier   A modifier that does not clearly point to its headword—the word or phrase it modifies.

* Crawling slowly up the tree, the elderly Mrs. Cartwright spotted a
  bright green worm.
  EDITED: The elderly Mrs. Cartwright spotted a bright green worm
  crawling slowly up the tree.

mixed construction   Any combination of words that do not fit together grammatically or meaningfully.

* Fearful of punishment caused the boy to stutter.
  EDITED: Fear of punishment caused the boy to stutter.
  [or] Fearful of punishment, the boy stuttered.

modal auxiliary   A helping verb that indicates the subjunctive mood.

The children *should* be here on Father's Day this year.
I'm not so sure that the average citizen *can* fight City Hall.

Besides *should* and *can*, the modal auxiliaries include *would*, *could*, *may*, *might*, *must*, and *ought*.

modifier   A word or word group that describes, limits, or qualifies another word or word group in a sentence.

> Pat smiled *winningly*.
> I *rarely* travel *anymore*.
> The *big gray* cat seized *the little* mouse *as it ran up the stairs*.
> *Polished to a high gloss, the mahogany* table *immediately* drew *our* attention.

See also determiner.

mood   The form of a verb that indicates the writer's attitude toward a particular statement as it is made. The **indicative** is the mood used in statements of actuality or strong probability.

> He always *lingers* over his second cup of coffee.
> We *will* sleep well tonight.

The **imperative** is the mood of commands and requests made directly.

> *Be* quiet!
> Please *go* away.
> *Let us pray.*
> *Stop!*

The **subjunctive** is the mood used in statements of hypothetical conditions or of wishes, recommendations, requirements, demands, or suggestions. Normally the subjunctive requires either a modal auxiliary or a subjunctive verb form.

> I wish I *could go.* [modal auxiliary expressing a wish]
> I wish I *were* a rock star. [subjunctive verb form expressing a wish]
> Each member *must* pay her dues by December 1. [modal auxiliary expressing a requirement]
> The rules require that each member *pay* her dues by December 1. [subjunctive verb form expressing a requirement]

nonrestrictive modifier   *See* restrictive and nonrestrictive modifiers.

noun   A word that names a person, creature, place, thing, activity, condition, or idea.

noun clause   A subordinate clause that is used as a noun within a sentence. It serves as subject, object, predicate noun, or object of a preposition.

> *Whoever contributed to the office party* deserves many thanks.
> I said *that I was hungry.*
> You are *what you eat.*
> The station offered a prize to *whoever called first with the right answer.*

noun equivalent   A verbal noun or a noun clause.

noun marker   *See* determiner.

noun phrase   A phrase formed by a noun (N) and its modifiers (M).

M   N

She floated happily on a *big, fat, black inner tube.*

M   N

The *eighteenth-century building* was declared a landmark last week.

number   The form of a word as determined by the number of persons or things it refers to. Most nouns and many pronouns may be singular or plural.

> A *carpenter* [singular] works had.
> *Carpenters* [plural] work hard.
> Jeff said that *he* [singular] would give the party.
> All *his* [singular] friends said that *they* [plural] would come.

object   A word or word group naming a person or thing affected by the action that a verb, a participle, an infinitive, or a gerund specifies.

> I hit *the ball.*
> Sighting *the bear,* he started to aim *his rifle.*
> Splitting *wood* is hard work.

A **direct object** names the person or thing directly affected by the action specified.

> The accountant prepared *my tax return.*

An **indirect object** names the person or thing indirectly affected by the action specified.

> I gave *Joe* a bit of advice.
> She bought *her father* a shirt.

The **object of a preposition** is any word or word group that immediately follows a preposition.

> For *her,* the meeting was crucial.
> I found the sponge under *the kitchen sink.*

object case   *See* case.

object complement   A word or word group that immediately follows a direct object and identifies or describes it.

> I found the first chapter *fascinating.*
> Many sportswriters used to consider Greg Louganis *the best diver in the world.*

parallel construction   The arrangement of two or more elements of a sentence in grammatically equivalent patterns: noun lined up with noun, verb with verb, phrase with phrase, and clause with clause.

> *Sink or swim, live or die, survive or perish,* I give *my hand* and *my heart* to this vote.   —Daniel Webster

> We must *take the risk* or *lose our chance.*

> I'll take either *the chocolate cake* or *the coconut pie.*

particle   A preposition used as an adverb. Particles always follow a verb and strongly affect its meaning.

> I looked *up* the word in the dictionary.

> The rich sometimes look *down on* the poor.

participle   A term usually made by the addition of *-ing, -d,* or *-ed,* to the bare form of a verb.

| **present participle:** | calling | living | burning | lifting |
| **past participle:** | called | lived | burned | lifted |

A **perfect participle** is made by the combination of *having* or *having been* with the past participle.

> having called   having been lifted

participle phrase   A phrase formed by a participle and its object, its modifiers, or both. Usually a participle phrase modifies a noun or pronoun.

> *Screaming the lyrics of its hit song,* the rock group could hardly be heard above the cheers of the crowd.

> *Wearied after their long climb,* the hikers were glad to stop and make camp.

> She picked at the knot, *loosening it gradually.*

passive voice   *See* voice.

past participle   *See* participle.

past perfect tense   *See* tense.

past tense   *See* tense.

perfect infinitive   The form of the infinitive made with *have* and the past participle.

> I was glad *to have finished* the project by the deadline.

perfect participle   *See* participle.

person   In English grammar the term *person* designates the following system of classification.

	SINGULAR	PLURAL
FIRST PERSON	I, me, mine, my	we, us, ours, our
SECOND PERSON	you, yours, your	you, yours, your
THIRD PERSON	he, him, his	
	she, her, hers	they, them, theirs, their
	it, its	
	and singular nouns	*and* plural nouns

phrase   A sequence of two or more words that serves as a unit within or attached to a clause.

> *A bright red kimono* caught my eye.
> *Encouraged by her friends,* Helen bought the house.
> I hurried *to reach the post office.*

possessive case   *See* case.

predicate   A word or word group that normally follows the subject of a sentence and tells what it does, has, or is, or what is done to it.

> The strong man *can lift 450 pounds.*
> The pastry chef *makes doughnuts, napoleons, and éclairs.*
> Venice *is a golden city interlaced with canals.*

A **base predicate (simple predicate)** is a predict without its modifiers.

> Simon and Garfunkel *sang* for a crowd of almost half a million.
> The little boys *threw snowballs* at all of the passing cars.
> They *were* soon *punished.*

predeterminer   A word that precedes a determiner.

> *Half* the pie is yours.
> We met *both* the girls.

The main predeterminers are *all, both,* and *half.*

predicate adjective   An adjective or adjective phrase that follows a linking verb and describes the subject.

> Velvet feels *soft.*
> Henry seems *upset by the vote.*

predicate noun   A noun or noun phrase that follows a linking verb and identifies the subject.

> Time was our only *enemy.*
> J. D. Salinger is *a very reclusive writer.*

preposition   A word followed by its object—a noun, pronoun, or noun equivalent. A preposition shows the relation between its object and another word or word group in the sentence.

> The table was set *under* a tree.
> Hounded *by* his creditors, he finally declared himself bankrupt.

Besides *under* and *by*, prepositions include *with, at, of, in, from, over, after,* and *on.*

prepositional phrase   A phrase that starts with a preposition and ends with its object. Phrases of this type are regularly used as adjectives or adverbs.

> Helen admired women *with strong ambition.*
> Have you ridden *on the Ferris wheel?*
> I took the suitcase *from the woman / in the room / on the left.*

present participle   *See* participle.

present perfect tense   *See* tense.

present tense   *See* tense.

principal parts   The following parts of a verb.

PRESENT (BARE FORM)	PRESENT PARTICIPLE	PAST	PAST PARTICIPLE
see	seeing	saw	seen
work	working	worked	worked

progressive form   *See* common and progressive forms.

pronoun   A word that commonly takes the place of a noun or noun phrase. Pronouns may be definite or indefinite. A **definite pronoun** refers to an antecedent (A), a noun or noun phrase appearing before or shortly after the pronoun.

> A
> As soon as Grant saw the enemy, *he* ordered his men to fire.
>
> A
> Janis Joplin was only twenty-seven when *she* died.
>
> A
> Though *he* won the battle, Nelson did not live to savor the victory.

An **indefinite pronoun** refers to unspecified persons or things. It has no antecedent.

> *Everyone* likes Janet.
> Marvin will do *anything* to help a friend.

An **interrogative pronoun** introduces a question.

> *What* did the policeman say?
> *Who* is pitching for the Blue Jays tomorrow?

pronoun-antecedent agreement   *See* agreement of pronoun and antecedent.

reflexive/emphatic case   *See* case.

regular and irregular verbs   A **regular verb** is one for which the past tense and past participle are formed by the addition of *-d* or *-ed* to the present.

PRESENT (BARE FORM)	PAST	PAST PARTICIPLE
work	worked	worked
tickle	tickled	tickled
walk	walked	walked

An **irregular verb** is one for which the past, the past participle, or both are formed in other ways.

sew	sewed	sewn
have	had	had
eat	ate	eaten

relative clause   *See* adjective clause.

relative pronoun   A pronoun that introduces an adjective clause.

> Women *who* like engineering are hard to find.
> Some companies now make furnaces *that* burn wood as well as oil.
> I'm looking for someone *whose* degree is in economics.

The relative pronouns are *which, that, who, whom,* and *whose.*

restricter   An adverb that limits or restricts the meaning of the word immediately after it.

> On the first day, we hiked *nearly* thirty miles.
> Walking along the beach, she *almost* stepped on a crab.
> I ate *almost* all the turkey.

Restricters include *almost, hardly, just, only,* and *nearly.* When used at the end of a sentence, a restricter limits the meaning of the word just before it.

> Tickets were sold to adults *only.*

restrictive and nonrestrictive modifiers　A **restrictive** modifier restricts or limits the meaning of its headword.

> All taxpayers *who fail to file their returns by April 15* will be fined.

A restrictive modifier is essential to the meaning of a sentence. Without the modifier, the meaning of the sample sentence would be fundamentally different.

> All taxpayers will be fined.

A **nonrestrictive modifier** does not restrict or limit the meaning of its headword.

> Daphne, *who loves football*, cheered louder than anyone else.

A nonrestrictive modifier is not essential to the meaning of a sentence. Without the modifier, the meaning of the sample sentence remains basically the same.

> Daphne cheered louder than anyone else.

run-on sentence (fused sentence)　Two or more independent clauses run together with no punctuation or conjunction between them.

> * Mosquitoes arrived at dusk they whined about our ears as we huddled in our sleeping bags.
> EDITED: Mosquitoes arrived at dusk, and they whined about our ears as we huddled in our sleeping bags.

sentence　A word group consisting of at least one independent clause. A sentence begins with a capital letter and closes with a period, a question mark, or an exclamation point.

> The telephone was ringing.
> By the time I got out of the shower, the caller had hung up.
> I was furious!
> Was the call important?

sentence fragment　A part of a sentence punctuated as if it were a whole one.

> The plant drooped. *And died.*
> I could not get into the house. *Because I had forgotten my key.*

sequence of tenses　The relation between the tenses of the verbs in a sentence that contains more than one verb, or in a passage of several sentences.

> By the time I *arrived*, everyone else *had left*.
> When the parade *goes* through town, all the townspeople *come* to see it.

simple sentence   A sentence consisting of just one independent clause.

> The problem was complex.
> It challenged the skill of experts.
> For months there was no solution.
> Then a solution was found by two veterans in the decoding department.

simple subject   *See* subject.

split infinitive   An infinitive in which one or more words are wedged between *to* and the verb.

> The purchasing department is going *to carefully check* each new order.
> BETTER: The purchasing department is going to check each new order carefully.

squinting modifier   A modifier placed so that it could plausibly modify either the word(s) before it or the word(s) after it.

> * Cutting classes frequently leads to low grades.
> EDITED: Frequent cutting of classes leads to low grades.
> [or] Frequently, cutting classes leads to low grades.
> [or] Cutting classes leads frequently to low grades.

subject   A word or word group that tells who or what performs or undergoes the action named by a verb, or that is described or identified in a linking verb construction.

> *Gossip* fascinates me.
> *Morgan* hit one of Johnson's best pitches.
> *Piccadilly Circus* is the Times Square of London.
> Does *your allergy* cause a rash?
> *Jan and I* were pelted by the rain.
> There was *a snake* under the chair.

A **simple subject** is a subject without its modifiers.

> The old dusty *volumes* fell to the floor.

A **complete subject** is a subject with its modifiers.

> *The old dusty volumes* fell to the floor.

subject case   *See* case.

subject complement   A word or word group that immediately follows a linking verb and identifies or describes the subject:

> Blue is *my favorite color.*
> The house was *enormous.*

subject-verb agreement *See* agreement of subject and verb.

subjunctive mood *See* mood.

subordinate (dependent) clause A clause that normally begins with a subordinator or a relative pronoun. Such a clause cannot stand alone as a sentence. It must be connected to or included in a main clause.

> *Because Mrs. Braithwait was writing her memoirs,* she reviewed all her old diaries and correspondence.
> Has anyone ever seen the bullet *that killed John F. Kennedy?*
> I didn't know *where she had left the key.*

subordinate verb The verb of a subordinate clause in a complex sentence.

> I cut the grass before the storm *came.*
> Since the door *was* open, I walked in.

subordinating conjunction *See* subordinator.

subordination An arrangement that makes one or more parts of a sentence secondary to and dependent upon another part.

> WITHOUT SUBORDINATION: The dog ate lunch, and then he took a nap.
> WITH SUBORDINATION: *After the dog ate lunch,* he took a nap.

subordinator (subordinating conjunction) A word or phrase regularly used to introduce a subordinate clause.

> *Before* we left, I locked all the doors.
> They can do nothing *if* the drought continues.

superlative *See* comparative, positive, and superlative.

tense The form of a verb that helps to indicate the time of an action or condition.

> PRESENT: I jump.
> PAST: I jumped.
> FUTURE: I will jump.
> PRESENT PERFECT: I have jumped.
> PAST PERFECT: I had jumped.
> FUTURE PERFECT: I will have jumped.

transitive and intransitive verbs A **transitive verb** names an action that directly affects a person or thing specified in the predicate.

> He *struck* the gong.
> Water *erodes* even granite.
> Did you *mail* the letters?
> We *elected* Sloan.

An **intransitive verb** names an action that has no direct impact on anyone or anything specified in the predicate.

> Wilson *smiled* at the comedian's best efforts, but he did not *laugh*.

verb A word or phrase naming an action done by or to a subject, a state of being experienced by a subject, or an occurrence.

> My uncle was asleep when the hurricane *destroyed* his house.

verbal noun A word or phrase formed from a verb and used as a noun.

> *Hunting* was once the sport of kings.
> I want *to travel*.
> *Fixing bicycles* keeps me busy.
> *To sacrifice his rook* would have been Gilman's best move.

verb phrase A phrase formed by two or more verbs—a base verb and at least one auxiliary.

> Richard *may complete* his experiment by July.
> Alison *would have come* earlier if you *had called* her.

voice The aspect of a verb that indicates whether the subject acts or is acted upon. A verb is in the **active voice** when the subject performs the action named by the verb.

> The officer *told* me to leave.
> A famous surgeon *performed* the operation.

A verb is in the **passive voice** when the subject undergoes the action named by the verb.

> I *was told* to do it that way.
> The operation *was performed* by a famous surgeon.

APPENDICES

Appendix 1

Standard American English as a Second Language: A Brief Guide

A1.7 Using Participles (p. 721)

                                exciting.

The movie was very ~~excited.~~

A1.8 Using Progressive Forms of the Verb (p. 723)

                     have been

~~I am~~ living in San Diego for six months.

Following are notes on some features of American English that often cause trouble for students of English as a second language. This does not pretend to be a comprehensive guide. For further instruction, see any one of the following:

> *Collins COBUILD English Language Dictionary* (1989)
> Marcella Frank, *Modern English* (1972)
> Bruce Liles, *A Basic Grammar of Modern English,* 2nd ed. (1987)
> *Oxford Advanced Learner's Dictionary of Current English,* 4th ed. (1989)

A1.1 USING *A, AN, THE,* AND OTHER DETERMINERS

A1.1a DETERMINERS DEFINED

A **determiner** (D) is a type of modifier: a modifier that always precedes the noun (N) it modifies and marks it as such. Unlike adjectives (A), determiners cannot follow the nouns they modify, and they have no comparative or superlative forms:

        D   D   D   N   D N   D N

We spent *the first two* weeks of *our* trip in *a* village.

Though an adjective can follow the noun it modifies, a determiner must always precede it:

        D   A   N

It was *a* remote village.

        D   N   A   A

It was *a* village remote from modern development.

Unlike adjectives, determiners have no comparative (c) or superlative (s) forms:

        D   A   N   A(c)   D   D   N

It was also *a* poor village, poorer than *any other* village in the province.

D   A(S)   N
It was *the* poorest village I had ever seen.

A1.1b COUNTABLE AND UNCOUNTABLE NOUNS

To choose the right determiner, you must know whether the noun it modifies is *countable* or *uncountable*.

Countable nouns may be singular or plural:

car, cars
book, books
woman, women
course, courses

Uncountable nouns are normally singular. They include—

WORDS NAMING A MASS OF SOMETHING, SUCH AS	WORDS NAMING ABSTRACT IDEAS, SUCH AS
cement	fortune
wheat	luck
dirt	justice
rice	advice
mud	knowledge
air	cowardice
cotton	bravery

Some nouns are countable in one sense and uncountable in another:

We added *sand* [a mass] to the mixture.
The sands of time [individual grains] are running out.
Life is full of surprises.
What is the value of *a life?*

A1.1c USING A/AN

A and *an* are Group 1 determiners (see pp. 704–5). Use *a* or *an* before a noun that is singular, countable, and indefinite:

A man works from sun to sun; *a woman's work* is never done.
According to *an old story,* Sir Isaac Newton discovered the principle of gravity when *an apple* fell on his head.

If you refer again to a noun introduced by *a* or *an,* use *the:*

I have often wondered if Newton ever ate *the apple.*

The second sentence refers to something that has been made definite by the first one. *An* apple is now *the* apple *that fell on Newton's head.*

Use *a/an* in expressions of measurement where the meaning is "each":

> Swordfish now costs four dollars *a pound.*
> In my new job I work just four days *a week.*

In choosing between *a* and *an,* look only at the first letter of the next word.

Use *a* when the first letter of the next word is a consonant, including an *h* that is pronounced:

> a *c*ar
> a *b*ig apple
> a *b*ook
> a *g*reen umbrella
> a *w*oman
> a *h*acienda
> a *h*istory book

Use *an* when the first letter of the next word is a vowel or an unpronounced *h:*

> an *a*pple
> an *a*bsorbing book
> an *o*range car
> an *i*mbecile
> an *in*jured woman
> an *h*eir

A1.1d MISUSING OR MISTAKENLY OMITTING *A/AN*

Do not use *a/an* before an uncountable noun:

> ► I asked my uncle for ~~an~~ advice.
>
> ► The medal was awarded for ~~a~~ bravery.
>
> ► My question provoked ~~a~~ laughter.
>
> ► The room needs ~~a~~ new furniture.

Do not use *a/an* before any plural noun:

> ► ~~A~~ paperback books are cheaper than ~~a~~ hardbound books.
> ► ~~A~~ women generally earn less than ~~a~~ men.

Do not omit *a/an* before a singular, countable, definite noun:

> ► Marie Curie was $\overset{a}{\underset{\wedge}{}}$brilliant scientist.
> ► Every undergraduate studies $\overset{a}{\underset{\wedge}{}}$variety of subjects.

A1.1e USING *THE*

The is a Group 1 determiner (see pp. 704–5). Use *the* before a noun referring to one or more specific persons or things:

> *The first woman* in *the U.S. Senate* was Hattie Caraway of Arkansas, who served out her husband's term after his death in 1931. She gained *the seat* on her own in *the election of 1932.*

> In this instance, *the voters of Arkansas* were more progressive than *the voters of any northern state.*

> *The present form* of *the Great Wall of China* largely originated in *the Ming dynasty.*

> To commemorate *the American Revolution, the Statue of Liberty* was given to *the United States* by *the Franco-American Union* in 1886.

Use *the* with superlatives:

> When Jackie Joyner-Kersee won the seven-event heptathlon in the Summer Olympics of 1992, Bruce Jenner called her *"the greatest athlete* who has ever lived."

> Winning that event must have been *the most exciting moment* of her life.

Use *the* with any adjective or participle used as a noun:

> *The rich* cannot understand the misery of *the poor.*
> *The sick, the suffering,* and *the neglected* all need our help.
> *The real* and *the ideal* have little in common.
> What will happen to Hong Kong when *the British* transfer it to *the Chinese?*

A1.1f MISUSING *THE*

Do not use *the* before nouns used in a generalized sense. In the sample sentences below on the left, the italicized words particularize the nouns they modify; the sample sentences on the right contain no such particularizing words.

PARTICULAR	GENERAL
The men and the women *in my office* often have trouble understanding each other.	Men and women often have trouble understanding each other.

PARTICULAR	GENERAL
The dog *next door to me* barks at everyone.	When a dog is happy, it wags its tail.
The mistake *made by a ticket agent* cost me $250.00.	Scientists often make discoveries by making mistakes.

Some nouns follow neither *the* nor *a* when used in a general sense. They include *night, prison, school, court,* and the names of meals:

The breakfast *I had this morning* was nothing but coffee.	I take coffee with breakfast and wine with lunch and dinner.
I saw her on the night *before she left.*	She takes classes at night.
The school *I once attended* is now closed.	Most American children start going to school at the age of five.
The prison *on Alcatraz Island* is a ruin.	No one wants to go to prison.
Ellen never forgot the court *where she won her first case.*	In court judges wear black.

EXCEPTIONS:

Some nouns—such as *morning, afternoon, evening,* and *hospital*—regularly follow *the,* even when used in a generalized sense:

I take classes in *the morning* and work in *the afternoon.*
A night in *the hospital* can be very expensive.

When used as nouns, *left* and *right* follow *the* after *on,* but not after *at:*

At *left* stood the church; *at right* was the school.
On *the left* stood the church; *on the right* was the school.

A1.1g USING AND MISUSING *THE* WITH NAMES

Use *the* with names of the following:

POLITICAL/ECONOMIC UNIONS	RIVERS
the United States	the Mississippi River
the British Commonwealth	the Colorado River
the Common Market	the Amazon River

GEOGRAPHICAL REGIONS

the Arctic
the South Pole
the Canary Islands
the Southwest

OCEANS

the Pacific
the Atlantic
the Indian Ocean
the Mediterranean

MOUNTAIN RANGES

the Rocky Mountains
the Appalachians
the Himalayas
the Adirondacks

BUILDINGS AND MONUMENTS

the Empire State Building
the Washington Monument
the Eiffel Tower
the World Trade Center

Do not use *the* with names of persons, churches, languages, countries, political regions, lakes, or ponds:

▶ ~~The~~ Simón Bolívar liberated a great part of ~~the~~ Latin America from ~~the~~ Spain.

▶ In parts of San Francisco, ~~the~~ Chinese is spoken more often than ~~the~~ English.

▶ When recession struck ~~the~~ China, the Chinese government could not pay its debts.

▶ ~~The~~ Lake Michigan is much larger than ~~the~~ Walden Pond.

▶ The pastor of ~~the~~ Trinity Church was invited to deliver a sermon at ~~the~~ St. Patrick's Cathedral.

EXCEPTIONS:

Use *the* before *Church* when referring to a religious organization:

The Roman Catholic Church strongly opposes abortion.

Use *the* before *Church* or *Cathedral* when a name follows either of those words:

The Cathedral of St. John the Divine is in New York.

Use *the* before the name of a language when the word *language* follows the name:

The English language is widely spoken.

A1.1h USING *SOME, ANY, NO, AND NOT*

Some, any, no, and *not* are all Group 1 determiners (see pp. 704–5). *Some* denotes an unknown or unspecified amount or number. Use it in affirmative and imperative sentences:

> *Some people* are always lucky.
> Please give us *some help.*

Any denotes an unknown or unspecified small amount or number. Use it in sentences that are negative or express uncertainty:

> The box office did not have *any tickets.*
> I asked if there was *any standing room.*

Use *no* to negate a noun:

> *No tickets* were left.
> I saw *no animal* in the cage.

NOTE: Do not use *not* to negate a noun. Use it only to negate a verb:

> ▶ There was ~~not~~ solution [noun] to the problem.
>   *no*
> ▶ I could ~~no~~ solve [verb] the problem.
>   *not* ∧

A1.1i USING THE DEMONSTRATIVES *(THIS, THAT, THESE, THOSE)*

Demonstratives (Group 1 determiners, pp. 704–5) are words that point to one or more particular persons or things. Use them as follows:

Use *this* and *that* with singular nouns, whether countable or not. *This* suggests nearness *(this weekend, this room)* while *that* suggests distance in space or time *(that weekend, that room).*

Use *these* and *those* with plural countable nouns *(these men, those women).*

A1.1j USING THE POSSESSIVES

Possessives (Group 1 determiners, pp. 704–5) are pronouns in the possessive case, such as *my* and *your.* Use them as follows.

Use *my, your, his, her, its, ours,* and *their* before any noun:

my car	their properties	its roof
her job	our town	their courage
his letters	your house	her wisdom

Use the other possessives—*mine, yours, hers, ours,* and *theirs*—after any noun and a linking verb (LV):

LV
The house was *mine*.

LV
The car was *hers*.

On the possessive case of *nouns*, see *case* in the Glossary of Grammatical Terms and section 31.9.

A1.1k USING GROUP 2 DETERMINERS: ORDINAL NUMBERS

Ordinal numbers refer to the order of the items in a group (*first, second, third . . .*). Use the ordinals after a Group 1 word (see pp. 704–5) or by themselves:

> The *third chapter* of the novel describes the groom.
> Marilyn's story won *first prize*.

A1.1l USING GROUP 3 DETERMINERS: CARDINAL NUMBERS AND WORDS DENOTING QUANTITY

Cardinal numbers refer to the quantity of items in a group (*one, seven, forty-three, two hundred*, etc.); words denoting quantity include *many, much*, and *few*.

Use any of the above after words from Group 1 and Group 2 or by themselves before a noun:

> The first *three men* had visas.
> *Three men* were executed.
> Those *ten apples* all looked ripe.
> *Ten apples* filled the basket.
> His first *few mistakes* were minor.
> *Many mistakes* marred his performance.

Use *much* and *little* with uncountable nouns and singular countable nouns:

> much wisdom
> little creativity
> much land
> little industry

Use *few, several*, and *many* with plural countable nouns:

> few settlers
> several farms
> many animals

When *little* means "small in stature," it can be used with countable nouns: *little boys, little girls*.

A1

A1.1m *ALL. BOTH. HALF. AND OTHER PREDETERMINERS*

Predeterminers are words and phrases that can be used before some Group 1 determiners:

> 　　1　2　3
> *All* the first five runners beat the record.
> *Half* a　　　　　loaf is better than none.
> *Both* these　　　nations have suffered.

Both and *all* can also be used before a noun:

USING *A, AN, THE,* AND OTHER DETERMINERS: IN BRIEF

A **determiner** is a word marking a noun that follows it. Determiners come in three groups corresponding to the order in which they may be used:

> 1
> *Some* applicants had interviews.

> 1　　2
> *The first* applicants had interviews

> 1　　2　　3
> *The first five* applicants had interviews.

GROUP 1

a, an	with singular countable nouns: *a boy, a mistake, an orange*
the	with nouns referring to particular persons or things: *the Statue of Liberty, the owner of my apartment, the people of Nicaragua, the capital of Arkansas* with superlatives: *the greatest athlete in the world*
some	with nouns in affirmative sentences: *Some people are always lucky.*
any	with nouns in negative sentences: *I never have any luck.*
no	to negate any noun: *No tickets were left.*
this, that	with singular nouns, countable or not: *this college, this courage, that movie, that fear*
these, those	with plural countable nouns: *these men, those women*

Both women won congressional seats.

At night *all cats* are gray.

Some, any, none, and any Group 3 determiner may be used with *of* as a **predetermining phrase:**

None of the first five passengers had tickets.

Much of our confusion was due to inaccurate reports.

We did not hear *any of the latest news.*

Some of the food was missing.

Three of the women left the room.

my, your, his, her, its, our, their	with any noun: *my car, her job, his letter, their property, our town, your house, its roof*

GROUP 2

the ordinal numbers: first, second, third, etc.	after a Group 1 word or by themselves: 1 2 2 *the first chapter, first prize*

GROUP 3

the cardinal numbers: one, two, three, etc., and words denoting measurement	after words from Group 1 and Group 2 or by themselves with a noun: 1 2 3 3 *the first three men, three men* 1 2 3 3 *the last few sheep, few sheep*
much, little	with uncountable nouns: *much land, little industry*
few, several, many	with countable nouns: *few settlers, several farms, many animals*

PREDETERMINERS

all, both, half	before some Group 1 determiners:
	           1 1
	all the first five runners, half a loaf,
	      1
	both the women
	
	all and *both* may be used right before a noun:
	all runners, both women

EXERCISE 1 USING *A, AN,* AND *THE*

In the following passage, make an acceptable change wherever you find *a, an,* or *the* misused or needed. Write a clean copy of your version and give it to your instructor. We have edited the first mistake for you.

Three summers ago I became interested in ~~the~~ plants and the gardening. I began to plan garden. It would include three flower beds, small sundial, and stone wall. In center of garden, I wanted to put lily pool. By end of summer, I had constructed the pool and laid stone wall around it. Beyond wall were three flower beds, each of   5 which was shaped like a arc circling one part of pool. My sundial rested on top of large rock between two of flower beds. Because of drought, the soil was driest it had been in the ten years, so only few of plants grew well.

During the following winter, I had the many new ideas. I 10 taught myself about the gardening in general and a water gardening in particular by reading lots of the books. In spring I redid lily pool and three flower beds, adding waterfall, water lilies, and the many other aquatic plants, as well as stocking pool with the goldfish. I enlarged flower beds and fertilized soil with a compost, a peat, and a 15 manure, working material into soil with my hands and small trowel. During summer, which was wetter than one before, the every single plant quadrupled in size and stayed healthy.

EXERCISE 2 USING DETERMINERS

In the following passage, make an acceptable change wherever you find a determiner misused or needed. Write a clean copy of your version and give it to your instructor. We have edited the first mistake for you.

the
In evening of the April 18, 1775, any British troops occupying
 ^
the Boston prepared to make this surprise attack on the American colonists who lived in some nearby villages. As soon as the night fell, much small boats began to ferry British soldiers across Charles River from the Boston to the Cambridge. British believed that they were   5 acting in a secret. In reality, however, much agents of American patriots were watching all move of redcoats. On discovering enemy's

plan, agents dispatched several messengers, who hoped to warn villagers of threat to safety.

At the ten o'clock one of messengers, the Paul Revere by name, left his home and hastened to the Christ Church in the Boston. From there he hurried to Charles River, which he crossed in small rowboat using the muffled oars. Then he reported to another agent, who gave him horse and wished him a Godspeed. Although the Paul Revere was almost captured much times by these British patrols, he managed to elude his pursuers and to reach the Lexington shortly after the midnight. Shouting with many excitement, he warned any townspeople about British soldiers and then rode to the Concord, where he repeated message.

The Revere's work was well-done. As a result of now-famous ride in dark, these American colonists living in the Lexington were ready to defend themselves when British soldiers reached a village.

A1.2 USING GERUNDS AND INFINITIVES

A **gerund** (G) is a word or phrase made from a verb (V), ending in -*ing*, and used as a noun:

> V
> I run every day.

> G
> *Running* keeps me fit.

> V
> At night I play the piano.

> G
> I like *playing the piano.*

> G
> But my upstairs neighbor complains about *losing sleep.*

Words made from a verb and ending in -*ing* are gerunds only when they serve as nouns. A word made from a verb and ending in -*ing* may also be used as a **participle** (PART) modifying a noun and as part of a **verb phrase**:

>   VERB
>   PART   PHRASE
> For one *shining* moment, we *were basking* in the sun.

An **infinitive** (I) is a phrase made from a verb and starting with *to*. It is often used as a noun:

> V   V
> Some pray; others work.

> I   I
> *To work* is *to pray*.

> I
> Paula hopes *to publish* her poems.

A1.2a CHOOSING BETWEEN GERUNDS AND INFINITIVES

Use gerunds—*not* infinitives—as objects of prepositions (PREP):

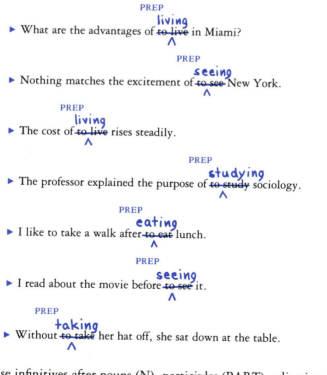

> PREP
> *living*
> ► What are the advantages of ~~to live~~ in Miami?
>   ∧

> PREP
> *seeing*
> ► Nothing matches the excitement of ~~to see~~ New York.
>   ∧

> PREP
> *living*
> ► The cost of ~~to live~~ rises steadily.
>   ∧

> PREP
> *studying*
> ► The professor explained the purpose of ~~to study~~ sociology.
>   ∧

> PREP
> *eating*
> ► I like to take a walk after ~~to eat~~ lunch.
>   ∧

> PREP
> *seeing*
> ► I read about the movie before ~~to see~~ it.
>   ∧

> PREP
> *taking*
> ► Without ~~to take~~ her hat off, she sat down at the table.
>   ∧

Use infinitives after nouns (N), participles (PART), adjectives (A), and most verbs (V):

> N
> I felt a desire *to roam*.

N
The urge *to wander* possessed me.

PART
I was determined *to travel*.

A
It was hard *to get* a passport.

A
It was easy *to buy* a plane ticket.

A
Eager *to see* the rest of the world, I boarded the plane.

PART
I was dismayed *to lose* my passport.

A
I was glad *to find* it.

V
I want *to explore* Latin America.

V
I hope *to become* a journalist.

N
My wish *to work* has been granted.

Some verbs may be followed by *either* a gerund *or* an infinitive:

I love *dancing*.
I love *to dance*.

I like *singing*.
I like *to sing*.

I hate *to wait*.
I hate *waiting*.

A few verbs may be followed by the gerund but *not* by the infinitive:

► I enjoy ~~to walk.~~ walking.

► I dislike ~~to jog.~~ jogging.

► She didn't mind ~~to work~~ working late.

► She finished ~~to write~~ writing the report at two in the morning.

Other verbs of this type are *avoid, delay, miss, practice, risk, resent,* and *suggest*.

EXERCISE 3 USING GERUNDS AND INFINITIVES

In the following sentences, choose between a gerund and an infinitive. In some sentences, only one of the two is correct. In other sentences, either one can be used. Write out each sentence with your choice included.

EXAMPLE

The cost of (to live, living) rises steadily.

The cost of living rises steadily.

1. Juanita usually exercises before (having, to have) supper.

2. She dislikes (to go, going) without a workout at the end of a day.

3. On weekends she often has an urge (taking, to take) a long hike.

4. After (to work, working) at the office all week, she enjoys (roaming, to roam).

5. She sometimes walks for hours without (to stop, stopping).

6. She likes (looking, to look) for elk and deer.

7. The thrill of (to see, seeing) wild birds and animals delights her.

8. Juanita's friends never grow tired of (to hear, hearing) her stories of life in the woods.

9. We are always ready (to hear, hearing) a new tale.

10. It is a pleasure (to know, knowing) her.

A1.3 MULTIWORD VERBS (VERB-PARTICLE COMBINATIONS)

A **multiword verb** is a single verb (V) followed by one or more **particles,** which are prepositions used as adverbs. Particles (PT) strongly affect the meaning of a verb. Compare:

    V   PT PT
We dropped in on [visited] Susan over the weekend.
I dropped out of [quit] Physics 102 last term.

Multiword verbs are usually less formal and more colloquial than single-word verbs, but they are commonly used in writing as well as speech.

A1.3a SEPARABLE MULTIWORD VERBS

Some multiword verbs may be separated to make way for a direct object (DO) of one or two words:

DO

After the party, he *cleaned* the kitchen *up*. (Also acceptable: . . . he cleaned up the kitchen.)

Whenever a separable multiword verb has a pronoun (PR) for its object, the pronoun goes between the verb and the particle:

PR

Since the kitchen was a mess, he *cleaned* it *up*.

PR

As soon as I got the application, I *filled* it *out*.

Some multiword verbs (such as *care about*) may not be separated by a noun or pronoun.

A1.3b COMMON MULTIWORD VERBS: A BRIEF LIST

Following is a list of common multiword verbs, with daggers marking those that should never be separated by a noun or pronoun:

agree

The negotiators have †*agreed to* [accepted] changes in the plan.
They have †*agreed with each other* [concurred] *on* some points.
Some shellfish †*doesn't agree with me* [makes me sick].

approve

The governor †*approved of* [accepted] the new proposal.

believe

Many people †*believe in* [accept the reality of] ghosts.
Magda was the only one who †*believed in* [accepted the value of] Jorge.

break

When she heard the news, she *broke down* [collapsed] and cried.
Finally, the relentless salesman *broke down* [overcame] my resistance.
In 1990, the Soviet Union *broke up* [disintegrated].
In the same year, Maria and Jose *broke up* [ended their relationship].

bring

I hated to *bring up* [raise for discussion] the question again.
Without help, how can a single parent *bring up* [nurture] a child?

burn

One night someone *burned down* [leveled by fire] the police station.

call

She was so sick that she decided to *call off* [cancel] the party.
She had to *call up* [telephone] all her friends.

care

He †*cared about* [loved/carefully considered] his family.
He often †*cared for* [tended] his children when they were sick.

clean

We *cleaned up* [cleaned thoroughly] the house before moving into it.

come

Rounding the bend, we †*came across* [encountered, found] a dog in the middle of the road.
I †*come from* [originate from] Costa Rica.

consist

My apartment †*consists of* [includes altogether] two bedrooms, a little kitchen, a bathroom, and a sitting area.

depend

I †*depend on* [need] my alarm clock to wake me each morning.

drop

On my way home. I †*dropped in on* [visited] my cousin.
I told her that I had decided not to †*drop out of* [quit] school.
Then I *dropped off* [left] my shirts at the laundry.

get

My sister and her husband try to †*get along* [subsist] on one salary.
People of different races often do not wish to †*get along with* [cooperate with, coexist with] each other.
Police say that the robbers †*got away with* [stole] a million dollars.
How many students †*get away with* [escape punishment for] cheating?
She *got up* [rose from bed] at 7:00 A.M.

give

The rebels refused to †*give in* [submit] or †*give up* [surrender].

keep

Whatever happens, I will †*keep on* [continue] trying.
I aim to *keep up* [maintain] my studies.

Can American companies †*keep up with* [compete effectively with] the Japanese?

I am trying to †*keep up with* [meet the requirements of] all my courses.

Some private clubs *keep out* [exclude] women.

look

My brother †*looked after* [tended] my apartment while I was away.

We †*looked at* [examined] many photographs.

We were †*looking for* [seeking] pictures of my grandfather.

Reporters are †*looking into* [investigating] the scandal.

Public radio †*looks to* [solicits] its listeners for financial support.

Egotists †*look down on* [despise] most other people.

While in the city, I *looked up* [arranged to meet] my cousin.

Children †*look up to* [admire] superstar athletes.

I †*looked over* [surveyed] the books quickly.

make

The ink was so blurred that I couldn't *make out* [understand] the words.

In spite of setbacks, she *made out* [succeeded] handsomely. (slang)

To celebrate, she *made over* [redecorated] her office.

Arriving hours late, he *made up* [invented] a ridiculous excuse.

After feuding for years, they *made up* [agreed to be friendly].

The five superstar players *made up* [constituted] a "dream team."

The professor let me *make up* [do at a time later than originally specified] the exam I had missed.

put

At the end of the day, the carpenter *put away* [stored] her tools.

She also *put back* [replaced] the broom she had taken from the closet.

The army soon *put down* [suppressed] the rebellion.

Whenever I say anything, he *puts* me *down* [criticizes me].

The committee voted to *put off* [postpone] a final decision.

The manager *put off* [dismissed] all my objections.

His indifference *put* me *off* [irritated me].

I felt thoroughly *put out* [annoyed].

Midnight was high time to *put out* [place outside] the cat.

The Acme Tire company *puts out* [produces] ten thousand tires a day.

When asked to serve a third time, she felt †*put upon* [overburdened].

There is no reason to †*put up with* [endure] bad service.

refer

In a lecture on civil disobedience, the professor †*referred to* [mentioned] Henry David Thoreau.

run

> While reading the paper, I †*ran across* [met by chance] a strange word.
> At the party she †*ran into* [met by chance] an old friend.
> While backing up the car, I *ran into* [collided with] a truck.
> I was afraid the gas would †*run out* [be wholly consumed].
> By noon the store had †*run out of* [exhausted its supply of] milk.
> Spending lavishly, he *ran up* [incurred] big debts.

take

> My sister and I sometimes †*take care of* [tend] my baby brother.
> The hot weather led me to *take off* [remove] my coat.
> Did you ever hear her *take off* [impersonate] the boss? (colloquial)

MULTIWORD VERBS (VERB-PARTICLE COMBINATIONS): IN BRIEF

A **multiword verb** is a single verb (V) combined with one or more *particles*. A particle (PT) is part of the verb and strongly affects its meaning, as in these two cases:

>   V   PT PT
> We *dropped in on* [visited] Susan over the weekend.
>   V   PT PT
> I *dropped out of* [quit] Physics 102 last term.

In a few cases, the same combination can produce different meanings in different sentences:

> He *made up* [invented] a ridiculous excuse.
> The five superstar players *made up* [constituted] a "dream team."

Some multiword verbs may be separated to make way for a word or short phrase (A1.3a). Whenever a separable multiword verb has a pronoun (PR) for its object, the pronoun goes between the verb and the particle:

>   PR
> Since the kitchen was a mess, he *cleaned it up*.

Some multiword verbs (such as *care about*) may not be separated.

For a brief list of common multiword verbs, see A1.3b.

After the meeting he *took* me *out* [escorted me] to dinner.
After just three months on the job, she was ready to *take over* [assume control or management of] the shipping room.

think

When asked to †*think about* [consider] the problem, she tried to †*think of* [devise] a solution.
What do you †*think of* [how do you judge] her proposal?
Do you need time to *think* it *over* [consider it]?

EXERCISE 4 USING MULTIWORD VERBS

Choose the correct particle or set of particles from those given in parentheses, and then write out the whole sentence.

EXAMPLE

All she cared (on, <u>about</u>) was her cat.

All she cared about was her cat.

1. Most corporations want their employees to get (along with, away with) each other.

2. Friendly employees help one another keep (on, up) working efficiently.

3. They even look (for, to) ways to reduce waste and increase production.

4. As a result, the corporations can keep (up, up with) their competitors.

5. No worker can be fully effective if he or she is made to put (down, up with) troublesome co-workers.

6. For this reason good managers regularly look (into, to) complaints whenever they are made to a supervisor.

7. Some companies devise training programs to break (up, down) hostility between workers.

8. Every month a few trainees drop (off, out of) the programs.

9. The dropouts cannot put (out, up with) the demands being placed upon them.

10. But most trainees learn to (keep out, keep up with) those demands.

A1.4 MAKING SENTENCES COMPLETE: SUBJECTS, LINKING VERBS, EXPLETIVES

A1.4a SUPPLYING A SUBJECT

In some languages the **subject** may be part of the **verb.** In Spanish, for instance, *vivo* means "I live," a complete sentence. But an English sentence normally requires a subject that is separate from the verb:

> *I* live in Miami.
> *She* works in Chinatown.
> *We* need jobs.
> *They* are scarce.
> *You* are thin.

EXCEPTION: Sentences that make commands omit the subject and start with the verb:

> *Watch* the conductor.
> *Lift* the handle.
> *Use* the seatbelt in your car.
> *Close* the door.

In sentences like these, the subject is understood as *you.*
For more on subjects, see section 11.4.

A1.4b USING LINKING VERBS *(IS, ARE, WAS, WERE)*

A **linking verb** (LV) is so called because it links the subject (S) to an adjective (A) or noun (N):

> S   LV   A
> The house is old.
> S   LV   N
> The men were thieves.

In some languages, the subject may be linked by position alone to a word that follows it (*My brother a police officer). In English the link must be made by a verb:

> ▶ The walk long.
>   **was**
>   ^
> ▶ The people tired and hungry.
>   **were**
>   ^
> ▶ My brother a police officer.
>   **is**
>   ^

A1.4c Using there and *It* (Expletives) to Start a
Sentence

An **expletive** (E) is a word typically used at the beginning of a sentence
whenever the subject (S) follows the verb:

> E   S
> *There* are alligators in the Florida everglades.
>
> E   S
> *It* is dangerous to skate on thin ice.

Normally, you must start with an expletive whenever the subject follows the verb:

>   **It is**
> ▸ ~~Is~~ hard to climb a mountain.
>   ^**There is**
> ▸ ~~Is~~ no fool like an old fool.
>   ^

When an opening *It* refers to the weather, the temperature, the date,
or the time, *It* is the subject:

> S
> *It* is always cold in the Arctic.
> *It* was Friday, July 2, when the earthquake struck.
> *It* was noon when I felt the first tremor.

> EXERCISE 5 Using Subjects, Linking Verbs, and
>   Expletives
>
> In the following passage, the writer omitted some subjects,
> linking verbs, and expletives. Provide these as needed, writing
> out the corrected passage in full. We have done the first bit of
> editing for you.
>
>   **is**
>   Electricity very important in our lives. Yet rarely think about
>   ^
> it. Take it for granted until something wrong. When is nothing we
> can do, we realize we helpless without its power. In the summer of
> 1959, everyone in New York City unhappy when the city's power
> plant broke down for many hours. Electric fans and air conditioners   5
> stopped working. Apartments and offices soon hot. Elevators
> motionless, and subways stopped on their tracks. That night, streets
> dark and gloomy. People scared. In the emergency, little the police
> could do. They helpless too. Then was a sudden change. Lights

shone again, trains began moving, and fans stirred the air in hot, 10
stuffy rooms. All of the people glad. They safe. Had their precious
electricity again.

A1.5 USING *DO* AND *DOES*

Do is used as a main verb and a helping (auxiliary) verb.

A1.5a *DO* AS A MAIN VERB

As a main verb, *do* takes the following forms:

	PRESENT	PRESENT PERFECT	PAST	PAST PERFECT	FUTURE	FUTURE PERFECT
you we they	do	have done				
			did	had done	will do	will have done
he she it	does	has done				

As a main verb, *do* can serve any one of the following purposes:

It can be a transitive verb:

> Carmen *does* many things.
> The storm *did* no damage to the house.

It can finish a comparison:

> Andrea speaks French better than Mark *does*.

It can take the place of a verb used in the preceding sentence:

> Carpenters recently renovated the cafeteria. They *did* it [the work] in
> just three weeks.

It can help to form an interrogative tag at the end of a statement:

> The soloist played well, *didn't* she?
> Guards never admit strangers, *do* they?

A1.5b *DO* AS A HELPING VERB

Use *do* as a helping verb in questions and negative statements:

Does money grow on trees?
Do jobs fall from the sky?

    does   **do**
▶ Money not grow on trees, and jobs not fall from the sky.
      ^   ^

You could also write *doesn't* and *don't,* which are both less formal than *does not* and *do not.*

A1.5c MISUSING *S* WITH *DOES*

When using *does* as a helping verb, never add *s* to the base form of the main verb (MV):

                  MV

▶ *Does* smoking causeſ cancer?

                  MV

▶ It certainly *does* not serveſ the cause of health.

EXERCISE 6 USING *DO* AND *DOES*

The following sentences may be flawed because a form of *do* is missing or a verb phrase is miswritten. Edit the mistakes and write out the new sentences. If a sentence is correct as it stands, write "correct."

EXAMPLE   **does**
    My uncle not phone me very often.
           ^
  My uncle does not phone me very often.

1. My basketball coach not look like a typical coach.

2. He is short and overweight, and he does not wears gym shoes or sneakers.

3. During practice he sometimes does not brings a ball, and he not have a whistle.

4. What we players think?

5. We not think that he is a good coach.

6. But we play hard for him, no matter what he do during practice.

A1

A1.6 AVOIDING REDUNDANT PRONOUNS

A **pronoun** (PR) is a word that takes the place of a noun. Usually the noun (N) comes before the pronoun referring to it:

N   PR

Arturo smiled when he recognized the old man.

You need a pronoun only when referring to a noun mentioned in a different clause:

CLAUSE 1   CLAUSE 2

Arturo smiled   when   he recognized the old man

Do not use a pronoun to refer to something already mentioned in the same clause:

► Arturo ~~he~~ smiled.

► The store ~~it~~ belongs to my grandfather.

Do not mistake the second half of an *interrupted* clause for a *new* clause:

CLAUSE 1

CLAUSE 2
► The store [that was burglarized] ~~it~~ belongs to my grandfather.

CLAUSE 1

CLAUSE 2
► The town [where I was born] ~~there~~ is near Cartagena.

Do not use two pronouns referring to the same noun as objects of one verb:

CLAUSE 1   CLAUSE 2

► Gabriella wore the kind of dress that I have always loved ~~it~~.

Since *that* and *it* both refer to *dress*, they cannot both be objects of *loved*.

EXERCISE 7 EDITING REDUNDANT PRONOUNS

The following sentences may or may not contain redundant pronouns. If you find any, remove them and write out the new sentences. If a sentence is correct as it stands, write "correct."

EXAMPLE

Peggy ~~she~~ laughed when she heard the joke.

Peggy laughed when she heard the joke.

1. Phillipa she wants to find a new apartment that it overlooks the city park.

2. Her present apartment, which she has rented it for two years, has too many drawbacks.

3. For one thing, the plumbing it keeps breaking down; for another thing, the landlords they keep raising the rent.

4. The rent that she now has to pay it comes to more than half of what she earns it at work.

5. With any luck, the new place it will cost her less money than she has to spend it on the old one, and the facilities they will function without a hitch.

A1.7 USING PARTICIPLES

A **participle** is a word made from a verb and ending in -*ing* or -*ed*. It can serve as part of a verb phrase and as a modifier. We treat each use in turn.

A1.7a USING PRESENT AND PAST PARTICIPLES IN VERB PHRASES

When you want to say how someone or something is, was, or will be act*ing,* use the present participle, which ends in -*ing:*

My cousin is *studying* economics.
He will be *taking* an exam next week.
Last week he was *preparing* for a sociology exam.
Next week he will be *visiting* me.

When you want to say how someone or something is, was, has been, had been, or will be act*ed upon,* use the past participle, which ends in -*ed, -d, -n,* or -*t:*

My car is *washed* once a week.
It was *washed* yesterday.

It has been *washed* regularly since I bought it.
Before then, it had never been *washed*.
It will be *washed* regularly as long as I own it.

The simple past (SP) of many verbs is the same in form as the past participle (PP):

> PP
> My car is *washed* once a week.
> SP
> I *washed* it yesterday.

For more on the use of participles in verb phrases, see chapters 20 and 22.

A1.7b USING PAST AND PRESENT PARTICIPLES AS MODIFIERS

Whenever a present participle is used to modify a noun, it tells what the noun is do*ing:*

> I woke up to the sound of *laughing* children.
> A *singing* waiter brought our food.

Whenever the past participle is used to modify a noun, it tells what has been *done to* the noun:

> Lincoln left behind a *stricken* nation, a people *divided* by civil war.
> After the long walk, Raul was *tired*.

For more on the use of participles as modifiers, see sections 12.9 and 12.10.

A1.7c PRESENT AND PAST PARTICIPLES COMMONLY CONFUSED

Confusion of past and present participles leads to sentences like these:

> ▸ The movie was ~~excited.~~ exciting.
> ▸ I was very ~~exciting~~ excited by it.

To avoid mistakes like these, you need to know the difference between present and past participles that are commonly confused.

NOUN/PRONOUN SAID TO BE ACT*ING*	NOUN/PRONOUN SAID TO BE ACTED UPON
N	PR
The mosquitos were annoy*ing*.	We were all annoy*ed* by them.

N
The bor*ing* speech lasted two hours.

N
The explanation was confu*sing.*

N
The news is often depres*sing.*

N
The song was exci*ting.*

N
An exhaus*ting* day began the week.

N
She told a fascina*ting* story.

N
The gunman was frighte*ning.*

N
We ate a satisf*ying* meal.

N
A surpri*sing* sight greeted us.

N
The bor*ed* listeners fell asleep.

N
It left the students confus*ed.*

N
The economy is often depress*ed.*

N
The crowd was exci*ted* by it.

PR
Exhaust*ed,* I crawled into bed.

N
Her fascinat*ed* listeners loved it.

N
The frighten*ed* onlookers froze.

PR
It made us all feel satisf*ied.*

N
A surpris*ed* raccoon sat on our porch.

A1.8 USING PROGRESSIVE FORMS OF THE VERB

The progressive form of the verb combines a form of *be* with the present participle.

A1.8a USING THE PROGRESSIVE FORMS

Use the <u>present</u> progressive to indicate—

• what is happening as you write:

  I *am* now *sitting* at my desk.

• what is in progress as you write, whether or not it is occurring at the moment of writing:

  The public school teachers in Los Angeles *are planning* a protest march.

Use the <u>present perfect</u> progressive to indicate what continues from the past into the present:

  They *have been planning* the march for several weeks.

On the progressive forms of other tenses, see sections 20.5–20.8.

A1

A1.8b MISUSING THE PROGRESSIVE FORMS

Do not use the present progressive with any phrase referring to past action that is continued up to the present. Use the perfect progressive:

have been
▶ I ~~am~~ living in San Diego for six months.

You can also use the simple perfect:

I have lived in San Diego for six months.

Do not use the present progressive for any action or condition that has become habitual and is likely to continue indefinitely. Use the simple present:

live
▶ I ~~am living~~ in San Diego.

work
▶ I ~~am working~~ for the telephone company

EXERCISE 8 EDITING MISTAKES IN THE USE OF PARTICIPLES

In the following sentences, correct every mistake in the use of a participle, writing out each sentence in full. The participle may be a part of a verb phrase or the modifier of a noun or pronoun. We have made the first correction for you.

wading
1. Children were ~~waded~~ in the cold water of a brook.

2. The water was swirling about in a small pool shaping by boulders from the ice age.

3. As the glacier covering the region was receded, it left behind a trail marking by boulders, sand beds, and narrow gorges.

4. The children, of course, were not thought of such things as they frolicked in water that only moments earlier had been tumbled down the mountainside.

5. They were wiggled their toes against moss-covering rocks and splashing friends with handfuls of sparkled water.

6. Squeals of laughter echoed in the clear air as busy hands scooping beneath the surface sent yet another shower cascaded into the sunlight.

7. Earlier that day the children had been hiked up a trail covering with roots, loose stones, and pine needles.

8. At first, they had been pleasing with the adventure and delighting to be carrying backpacks like the grownups.

9. But as the minutes passed and the sun's rays became hotter, they grew weary of the ever-risen trail.

10. The pool of cold water had appearing just in time to restore their flagged spirits and their pleasure in the day.

Appendix 2

Beyond Freshman English

WRITING EXAMINATIONS, APPLICATIONS, AND LETTERS

A2.1 WRITING EXAMINATION ESSAYS

The best way to start writing a good examination essay is to read the question carefully. On a final examination in a course on modern American history, for example, students were asked to "show how Lyndon Johnson's policies in Vietnam grew out of the policies pursued by his predecessors from 1941 on." The question was quite pointed. It asked not for general impressions of the Vietnam War but for a specific analysis of the succession of policies that led America into it.

After reading the question, one student made a single scratch outline inside the cover of his bluebook:

CONTAINMENT
1. FDR, Truman—Vietnam and Korea
2. Ike—1954, SEATO, South Vietnam
3. JFK—military buildup
Sum up Johnson's inheritance

With those few notes before him, the student then wrote the following essay:

> American involvement in the Vietnam War did not begin with
> Johnson, or even with Kennedy. Rather, it began during World War
> II and was developed considerably during the years of containment of
> the Truman administration. As Stephen Ambrose puts it in his book,

the U.S. was paying up on an insurance policy on containment that began with the Truman doctrine (1947), was extended to Korea (1950), and was applied finally to Vietnam (1954).

In 1941, Roosevelt supported the Vietnamese (specifically Ho Chi Minh), along with the French colonialists, against Japanese aggression. But after the Japanese were forced out, intense fighting broke out between the French and the Vietnamese, and in 1950 Truman signed a Mutual Defense Agreement with the French. From this point on, the U.S. had committed itself to support anyone against Ho Chi Minh and the communists of Hanoi. Truman was thus applying to Vietnam the containment policy he was also using in Korea. As in Korea, the U.S. aimed to halt the communism (in this case, of China) anywhere.

The next rung in the American ladder of involvement came in 1954. The Vietnamese defeat of the French at Dien Bien Phu signaled the end of French involvement and the official beginning of American involvement. In September 1954 the Eisenhower administration formed the Southeast Asia Treaty Organization (SEATO) and committed the United States to the defense of South Vietnam as a bulwark against the expansion of Communist China.

Kennedy inherited much of Eisenhower's policy toward Vietnam and added some of his own thinking, leaving Johnson an even larger legacy of involvement. While Kennedy did not commit troops, his military actions were significant. First, he increased dramatically (to 16,000) the number of American advisers in Vietnam. Second, he gave American air support to South Vietnam and allowed American advisers to shoot back if shot at. Third, he began military preparations within the Pentagon. As a result of all these actions, the first death of an American soldier occurred during Kennedy's first year in office, and American casualties increased considerably from that point on.

When Kennedy was assassinated in 1963, Johnson inherited the Vietnam quagmire, and his inheritance was a rich one. From Roosevelt, he got the beginning of a U.S. role in Vietnam. From Truman, the policy of containment—the pledge to stop communist expansion at the hands of Ho Chi Minh. From Eisenhower he got an official commitment to the defense of South Vietnam. And from Kennedy, finally, he got the beginnings of a substantial U.S military involvement there.

So Johnson's decision to send troops to Vietnam in 1965 simply capitalized on the military preparations that Kennedy had made. Though Johnson imposed his own personality on Vietnam policy, he was strongly influenced by what Truman, Eisenhower, and Kennedy gave him: the need to succeed in Vietnam—militarily—along the lines of containment.

Like most examination essays, this one shows some signs of haste, such as the sentence fragment in the next-to-last paragraph. But no one taking a one- or two-hour exam has much time to worry about the finer points of diction and sentence structure. What we do find here are the three things essential to a good examination essay: (1) a response focused sharply and consistently on the question, (2) a substantial quantity of specific detail, and (3) strong organization. Throughout the essay, the author keeps his eye on the task of answering the question: of explaining what Johnson received from his predecessors and how that inheritance shaped his actions in Vietnam.

Now consider what another student did with a question on a sociology exam. Asked to "define 'economic-opportunity structure' and describe its relation to the traditional nuclear family," the student wrote this:

> The "economic-opportunity structure" (EOS) refers to the "working world" and is most often associated with the practical aspect of marriage. Traditionally, males have had superior access to this structure and still do today.
>
> In the traditional nuclear family, the male is the mediator between the family and the EOS. Such a position gives him considerable "power" within the family unit. If members of a family are totally dependent on the man for economic survival, they must concede all power and authority to him. He is the "king of the family." He brings home the fruits of the EOS, the production (usually monetary), and the family consumes these products, investing in various material possessions which in turn give them social status and prestige.
>
> The man's degree of success in the EOS highly affects his relation to his wife and family. In the traditional family, if the man fulfills his "duty" as chief economic supporter, the wife "rewards" him with more attention to his needs and to her traditional duties— keeping a house and raising children. The husband then rewards her in various ways, with a car of her own, perhaps, or a fur coat, or a bigger house. It's an ongoing cycle. The higher-status wives are also more likely to concede that the husband should have the "upper hand" in the marriage.
>
> This whole cycle works in reverse in lower-status families where the husband is unsuccessful as a breadwinner, causing resentment among the wives and unwillingness to submit to his authority.
>
> If the wife in the traditional nuclear family decides to enter the EOS, her commitment to a career is usually far less than that of her husband. Her primary duty is still to her family and husband. The husband remains chief economic provider. But the woman gains

more marital power because now she actually brings income into the house. Her occupation gives her self-esteem, and the marriage moves toward an egalitarian relation.

All of these cases show how economic power outside the family affects the balance of power within it. A successful breadwinner is rewarded with attention; an unsuccessful one has to put up with resentment; and the status of a wife within the family improves when she takes a job. Thus the power of any one member of a nuclear family seems to depend a lot on his or her performance in the "economic-opportunity structure"—the working world.

The question calls for a definition of a phrase and an explanation of a relationship. The answer provides both. It defines the phrase and explains the relationship of the "EOS" to the traditional nuclear family, showing how the husband's power to make money affects his power within the family and how the status of the wife is affected by her decision to take a job. This essay has no introduction because it needs none; in effect, it is introduced by the question. But it does have a conclusion.

To write a good examination essay, then, you should go directly to the point of the question. You should deal with the question as specifically as possible, and you should keep it continually in sight. Finally, you should end by summarizing your chief points and reaffirming the main point of the essay as a whole.

A2.2 Applying for Admission to a School of Business, Law, Medicine, or Graduate Study: The Personal Statement

Applying for admission to any kind of graduate program takes more than simply filling out an application form. Most schools ask you to write a personal statement in which you explain why you plan to go into business, medicine, law, or an academic field. Your chances of getting admitted will of course depend considerably on your college grades, your letters of recommendation, and your performance on examinations like the LSAT. But a personal statement often tells more about you than anything else can.

What kind of statement do admissions officers want? They want to know as specifically as possible what has led you to choose a particular career, what you hope to accomplish in it, and what you have already done to prepare yourself for it. The more specific you can be about your motivation, your experience, and your long-range plans, the more persuasive your statement will be. Consider this statement made by an applicant to medical school:

A major turning point in my life occurred following my second year in college, when I was hired as a research assistant in pediatric hematology at the New England Medical Center. During the sixteen months I spent in Boston, I gained valuable insights into the practice of medicine and found that I had a special aptitude for research. I returned to college determined to become a doctor and quite motivated in my academic work.

At the New England Medical Center I worked with very little supervision and was expected to be resourceful and creative in carrying out my lab responsibilities. I found that I had a talent for working out technical problems and the intellectual ability to design my own procedures. In addition to my laboratory work, I took the initiative to learn about the various diseases seen by the pediatric hematology department and about the treatment programs that were employed.

I learned a great deal about terminal illness through my job, and also through the death, from leukemia, of the young son of close friends of mine. During the last months of this child's life, I spent a considerable amount of time with his family, helping them to cope with their impending loss. I found I was able to offer types of support other friends and family members could not. I matured and grew from this experience. I learned that I could be open and responsive when faced with difficult and painful situations. I also realized that a need existed for people who could assist the terminally ill and their families.

In January 1993 I joined Hospice of Santa Cruz, where I was trained as a volunteer visitor and was assigned to the family of a man with stomach cancer. I feel that my involvement with the family is of benefit both to them and to me. I can support them by serving as a catalyst to get feelings expressed, and from them I am learning to be a compassionate listener. I am convinced my experience with Hospice will help me, as a medical worker, to be understanding and open in dealing with death.

My academic work during the past two years has, for the most part, been of outstanding quality. I chose to complete a chemistry major, with emphasis in biochemistry, and will be graduating in December 1993. I have worked for the past year and a half on a senior research project in cryoenzymology. Laboratory work presents numerous technical and intellectual challenges, and I have become quite skilled and competent in approaching these problems. I have been attracted to research because it serves to ground the theory one learns in the classroom in practical day-to-day applications. Whereas I do not expect to pursue a career in research, my laboratory experience has given me a good perspective into the nature of scientific study, has helped me develop critical thinking skills, and has offered the pleasure and satisfaction that comes with the successful completion of a project.

This past academic year I have encountered for the first time the challenge of teaching. I have been a tutor in organic chemistry, introductory chemistry, and biochemistry. To be a good tutor one not only needs to have a solid command of the subject matter but must also look at the material from the student's perspective and seek creative methods to convey information in a way that can be grasped by the student. I have found that I can do this quite effectively, both at the very basic introductory level and at the more sophisticated level of biochemistry. Through tutoring I have discovered that I love teaching. I now realize that one of the compelling attractions that medicine offers me is the opportunity to be a teacher to all kinds of people, from patients to other physicians.

I am grateful to have had in these past five years a rich variety of experiences that have prepared me for the diversity I expect to encounter in a medical career. Research, teaching, the direct care of people who are sick, and encounters with death are all part of the practice of medicine. I have gained insights, limited though they may be, into all of these. As a result I am confident that I know what I will be facing as a doctor and that I have the skills and ability to be a creative and supportive physician.

This statement bristles with detail. It tells exactly how the writer discovered her interest in medicine and what she has already done to prepare herself for a career in it. By describing her experiences in laboratory research, college courses, teaching, and working with the families of the terminally ill, she shows that she has both the ability and the sensitivity to make a career in medicine.

Furthermore, this statement is well organized. Introduced with a paragraph on the particular experience that led the writer to a medical career, the statement concludes with a paragraph on the net effect of all her experiences. In between these two paragraphs, she tells in chronological order the story of her development, and each of her paragraphs is written to develop a specific point about what she learned. Altogether, it is not hard to see why this writer was admitted to medical school.

To see what a difference good writing makes, compare her statement with one made by an applicant to a graduate school of business:

Represented a Cable TV association in a twelve-million dollar public financing. Responsibilities included fostering a marketable image of our client and their objictives for the benifet of the underwriters and potential investors. This also involved making numerous decisions and analyses in regard to our interface with FCC requirements.

The more significint factors impacting my long-range development from this experience include that I learned the coordination of financing needs and federal requirements. Throughly mastered quality control. Discovered how to identify areas of agreement and difference among the participants. Who eventually reached agreement through my involvement. Developed methods of meeting and turning around objections. And developed the ability to state my opinions in spite of intense pressure from various individules in a high-demand environment situation.

The writer has obviously had a good deal of experience in business, but he has failed to describe it effectively. First of all, he has confused a personal statement with a resumé (see below, section A2.3). A personal statement requires complete sentences. The lack of subjects in the first two sentences of the opening paragraph and the vagueness of *This* in the third sentence make the paragraph incoherent. Instead of an organized summary of the writer's experience, we get a string of disconnected remarks.

Second, the language is at once pretentious and sloppy. The writer uses pretentious jargon in phrases like *fostering a marketable image, in regard to our interface,* and *impacting my long-range development.* At the same time, he makes a number of spelling errors; *objictives* for *objectives, benifet* for *benefit, significint* for *significant,* and *individules* for *individuals.* In the second paragraph the writer claims to have *throughly mastered quality control,* but he has not yet mastered the spelling of *thoroughly.*

These two examples show what makes the difference between a bad statement and a good one, or—to put it bluntly—between rejection and acceptance. If you want to be rejected, put a lot of high-sounding words and phrases together without bothering to check your organization, sentence construction, or spelling, and without bothering to provide any clear and telling detail about what you have done. If you want to be accepted, write clearly, honestly, and specifically about your own experience and goals; take the time to see that your statement is well organized, that every sentence is complete and correct, and that every word is spelled right.

A2.3 Applying for a Job: The Resumé and the Cover Letter

The most important thing you need when applying for a job is a resumé—a list of your achievements and qualifications. The resumé should give all the essential facts about the position you seek, the date of your availability, your education, your work experience (with informative details), your extracurricular activities, and your special interests. You may include personal data, but you do not have to. The resumé should also list the names and addresses of your references— persons who can write to a prospective employer on your behalf; before listing their names, of course, you should get their permission to do so. The sample resumé on p. 734 shows the format we recommend.

The resumé alone, however, will seldom get you a job or even an interview. With the resumé you must send what a hiring officer expects to see first: a cover letter. Since the resumé will list all the essential facts about you, the cover letter may be brief. But it should nonetheless be carefully written. If the letter makes a bad first impression, you will have one strike against you even before your résumé is seen. With some company offices getting over a thousand applications a month, you need to give yourself the best possible chance, and your cover letter can make a difference in the way your resumé is read.

What do hiring officers want in a cover letter? They look for a capsule summary of the resumé itself, and also for things that resumés don't often tell them: how much you know about the company you hope to work for, what kind of work you hope to do, where you want to work, and what special skills you may have that need to be emphasized. The resumé defines your past; the cover letter can define your future, indicating what you hope to do for the company if you are hired.

To see what a difference a cover letter can make, compare these two, both sent to the same company:

Dear Ms. ———:

In January 1993, you were interviewing at the ——— College campus. I was schedule to see you but I had just accepted a position with ——— Stores and canceled my interview.

At the present time I am working as an assistant buyer in Tulsa, Oklahoma. I have been commuting every two weeks to see my family in Chicago. I am seeking employment in the Chicago area.

Enclosed is my resumé for your consideration again. Thank you for your attention. I will look forward to hearing from you in the near future.

Sincerely,

A2

SAMPLE RESUMÉ

```
                      Harold B. Rivers
                      44 Buell Street
               Faribault, Minnesota 55021
                      (507) 555-6789


Job Objective          Marketing or advertising trainee
                       (Date available: July 1, 1993)


Education

   1989-93             Monmouth College, Monmouth, Illinois
                       Degree: B.A. (expected in June 1993)
                       Major: Business administration

   1985-89             Faribault Senior High School, Faribault,
                       Minnesota
                       Academic degree


Work Experience

   Summer 1992         Acting Assistant Manager, Brown's
                       Department Store, Faribault, Minnesota.
                       Responsibilities included checking
                       inventory, handling complaints, and
                       processing special orders.

   Summer 1991         Salesclerk, Brown's Department Store,
                       Faribault, Minnesota

   Summers 1989        Waiter, The Village Pub, Northfield,
   and 1990            Minnesota


Extracurricular        Undergraduate Council, Monmouth College
     Activities        Debate Forum (President, 1991-92),
                       Monmouth College
                       Drama Club (President, 1988-89),
                       Faribault Senior High School


Special Interests      Photography, public speaking, drama


References             For academic references:
                           Office of Student Placement
                           Monmouth College
                           Monmouth, Illinois 61462

                       For business references:
                           Mr. George C. Hazen
                           Manager, Brown's Department Store
                           300 Main Street
                           Faribault, Minnesota 55021

                           Mrs. Nancy Wright
                           Manager, The Village Pub
                           24 Harris Street
                           Northfield, Minnesota 55057
```

Dear Ms. ———:

I am seeking a challenging position in marketing and consumer relations with a company in the Chicago area. I am particularly drawn to your firm because it is a utility, and utilities must maintain a proper balance between serving the public and protecting their own corporate interests. The challenge of maintaining this balance strongly appeals to me.

I have studied both marketing and consumer relations. At Monmouth College, from which I will shortly receive a B.A. in business administration, I took courses in such subjects as Consumer Attitudes, Marketing Strategies, and Principles of Retail Management.

Along with my education, I have had job experience that has given me frequent contact with the public. Working in a small business for two summers, I learned firsthand how to deal with consumers, and in the second summer I was promoted from salesclerk to acting assistant manager.

I hope you will review the attached resumé. Although a position in my field of interest may not be open, I would appreciate your consideration for future management or marketing opportunities.

Yours truly,

These two letters make quite different impressions. The first writer opens by misspelling *scheduled* and by recalling that he once canceled an interview with the woman to whom he is now writing for a job; the second writer opens with a clear statement of her ambition. The first writer tells little about his interest in the company; the second tells exactly what makes the company appealing. The first writer asks to be hired because he wants to see more of his family; the second asks to be hired because her studies in marketing and consumer relations and her experience in selling will enable her to help the company. Which of these two applicants do you think the hiring officer will want to see?

(For the format of a cover letter, which is a kind of business letter, see the next section.)

A2.4 WRITING A BUSINESS LETTER: THE PROPER FORMAT

The cover letter that accompanies a resumé is just one example of a business letter—a letter designed to initiate or transact business. Such a letter should be concise and forthright. In relatively short paragraphs it should accurately state all the information that the writer needs to convey.

FORMAT OF A BUSINESS LETTER

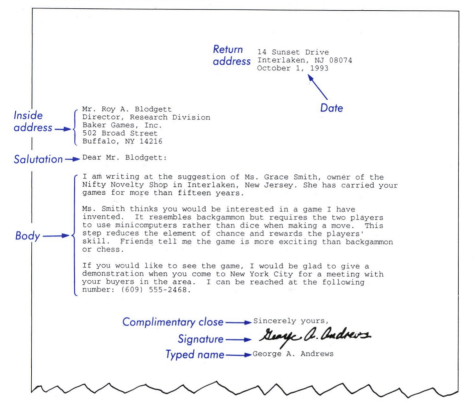

Return address   14 Sunset Drive
Interlaken, NJ 08074
October 1, 1993

Date

Inside address →   Mr. Roy A. Blodgett
Director, Research Division
Baker Games, Inc.
502 Broad Street
Buffalo, NY 14216

Salutation →   Dear Mr. Blodgett:

Body →

I am writing at the suggestion of Ms. Grace Smith, owner of the Nifty Novelty Shop in Interlaken, New Jersey. She has carried your games for more than fifteen years.

Ms. Smith thinks you would be interested in a game I have invented. It resembles backgammon but requires the two players to use minicomputers rather than dice when making a move. This step reduces the element of chance and rewards the players' skill. Friends tell me the game is more exciting than backgammon or chess.

If you would like to see the game, I would be glad to give a demonstration when you come to New York City for a meeting with your buyers in the area. I can be reached at the following number: (609) 555-2468.

Complimentary close → Sincerely yours,

Signature → George A. Andrews

Typed name → George A. Andrews

FORMAT OF A BUSINESS ENVELOPE

George A. Andrews
14 Sunset Drive
Interlaken NJ 08074

Mr. Roy A. Blodgett
Director, Research Division
Baker Games, Inc.
502 Broad Street
Buffalo NY 14216

The format of a business letter is shown on p. 736. For a business letter you normally use medium-weight typing paper or fanfold computer paper of standard size (8½ by 11 inches). Center the letter as well as you can, leaving side margins of at least 1½ inches. Unless the body of the letter is extremely short, use single-spacing and block form; indentation is optional, but if you type the paragraphs without it, separate one from the next by a double space. Also leave a double space between the inside address and the salutation, between the salutation and the body, and between the body and the complimentary close. Leave at least four spaces for your signature between the complimentary close and the typed name.

Fold the completed letter in two places—a third of the way down from the top and up from the bottom—and insert it in a business envelope (4⅛ by 9½ inches) addressed as shown on p. 736.

A2.5 WRITING FOR YOUR RIGHTS: THE LETTER OF PROTEST

We live in a world of huge and increasingly impersonal corporations. Most of the bills and probably most of the letters you get come not from human beings but from machines. Bills are processed automatically; letters are clacked out by computers that know your address, your date of birth, and your Social Security number and have been taught to use your name in every other sentence, but nonetheless have not the faintest idea who you are or what your specific problems might be. How do you shout back at all this machinery? When you have a problem that can't be solved by a computerized explanation, how do you make yourself heard?

In a word, write. Do not accept the words of a machine. If you think you have been overcharged or incorrectly billed or stuck with defective goods or shoddy service, don't keep silent. Fight back. Write a letter to the company or the institution, and demand to have your letter answered by a live human being. If the facts are on your side and you state them plainly, you may win your case without ever going to court or spending one cent for legal advice.

A friend of ours was billed $86.00 for an emergency service that he thought his medical insurance should cover. When the insurance company denied the claim, he phoned the company, got the name of the president, and wrote this letter directly to him:

Dear Sir:

In connection with the enclosed bill for emergency-room service provided to my son Andrew on October 15, I write to ask for an explanation for your company's refusal to pay for this service.

Your company's statement for October indicates that the charge for emergency-room service is not covered because "use of emergency room is covered when in connection with accident or minor surgery." Does this mean that use of the emergency room is covered *only* when in connection with accident or minor injury? Andrew had neither of these, but his condition was a genuine emergency, and I don't see why you refuse to cover treatment for it.

Andrew has asthma. He has long been treated for it by Dr. ————, who is an allergy specialist, but from time to time he has severe respiratory attacks that require emergency treatment—or rather, that require adrenalin, which is available *only* at the emergency room of ———— Hospital. If Andrew could have received adrenalin anywhere else, I could understand your denial of our claim, but so long as the hospital dispenses adrenalin *only* to emergency-room patients, we have to take him there. If we hadn't taken him there on October 15, he might have stopped breathing.

I can fully understand why you stop short of reimbursing all visits to the emergency room, since that would be an open invitation for your subscribers to use the emergency room for any and all ailments. But I believe you must distinguish between genuine emergencies and routine problems. I therefore expect your company to pay this particular bill in full.

Yours truly,

This letter got fast results. The president of the company referred it to the vice-president in charge of claims, and within a week the vice-president wrote to say that an asthma attack was indeed a genuine emergency, so the company would pay the bill in full. Thus the letter writer saved himself $86.00—not bad pay for the half hour he took to write the letter.

What writing ability finally gives you is the power to express yourself on paper for any purpose you choose. The more you write, the more you will discover what writing can do for you. If you care about your writing, you will continue to refine and develop it long after the composition course is over. Very few things that college can give you will be more important to you afterward than the ability to put your thoughts and feelings into words.

Index of Authors and Titles

Subject Index

Boldface page numbers point to definitions and major discussions of basic grammatical issues. "G" preceding a page number refers to a glossary entry. "(ESL)" following a page number refers to appendix 1. Page numbers of "In-Brief" boxes are followed by "(box)."

defined, **295**, G677
and run-on (fused) sentences, 304–5
semicolons in, 298
and subordination, 334–40
copying, as plagiarism, 536–37
corporate authors, 556–57
correlatives, 309, G677
could care less, couldn't care less, G652
council, counsel, consul, G652
countable nouns, 697(ESL), 699(ESL)
cover letters, 733–35
credible, credulous, G652
criterion, criteria, G652
critical reading, 222–24, 224(box)
cumulative index, 513
Current Index to Journals in Education (CIJE), 517
curriculum, writing and research across, 614–39

dangling modifiers, **291–92**, G678
dashes, 278, 474–75
data, G652
databases, 513
dates:
abbreviations with, 499, 501
apostrophes with, 490
commas with, 450, 451
numbers in, 503
declarative sentences, 460, G678
deduction, 142–50
and induction, 147–48
and persuasion, 144–45
syllogisms in, 143–44
and validity, 143–44
definite pronouns, 347, G686
definitions:
combining methods of, 121
and dictionary, 119, 197
as method of development, 119–21
degrees, academic, 450
delusion, allusion, illusion, G645
demonstratives, 702(ESL)
denotation, 200–201
dependent clauses, **315–16**, G690
description:
analytical, 104–5

defined, 103
as development method, 103–6
evocative, 105–6
external, 104
and narration, 109–10
technical, 104–5
and visualization, 104
detail, significant, 589–90
determiners, 493, G643, G674, G678, 696–707(ESL), 704–5(ESL)
development:
of characters, 587
of interpretation, 595–98
of plot, 585
development methods, 103–32, 131(box)
analogy, 112–14
combination of, 132
comparison and contrast, 114–19
definitions, 119–21
description, 103–6, 109–10
examples, 111–12
explaining by analyzing, 121–25
explaining cause and effect, 127–30
explaining processes, 125–26
narration, 106–10
dialectal mistakes, in agreement, 368–70
Dialog Information Services, 513
dialogue:
dashes with, 474
extended, 424
paragraphing of, 464
quotation marks with, 464–65
unfinished remarks in, 474–75
diction:
defined, 192
highly formal, 194–95
informal, 194
levels of, 192–96
middle level of, 192–93
mixed level of, 195
dictionary, 196–99
and abbreviations, 461, 502
and definitions, 119, 197
etymology in, 198–99
spelling in, 196–97

style, MLA parenthetical
style
partial homonyms, 482
participle phrases, 278, G684
participles, 278–80, 280(box), 721–
23(ESL)
defined, **278**, G684, 721(ESL)
past, 279, 280, G684
perfect, 279, G684
present, 278–79, G684
punctuation with, 279–80
tense and time with, 390–91
the with, 699(ESL)
particle, topic as, 20–21
particles, 209, G684, 710–14(ESL)
parts of speech, 197
passed, past, G662–63
passive voice:
agent in, 406
choosing, 409–10, 410(box)
defined, 258, **406**
formation of, 407–8
misuse of, 410
in natural sciences, 623
vs. progressive form, 408
and writing style, 433–34
past participles, 279, 280, G684
past perfect subjunctive mood, 420
past perfect tense, 382, 386–87,
398, G690
past progressive tense, 386
past subjunctive mood, 419
past tense, 382, 386, 398, G690
peer comments, on draft, 69–71
peer review questionnaire, 70
perfect infinitives, G684
perfect participles, 279, G684
perfect tense, with participles and
infinitives, 390–91
performance, in documentation, 561
periodicals:
in documentation, 552–53, 633
indexes to, 515–17
periods:
with abbreviations, 460–61, 500–
501
with acronyms, 460–61
and comma splices, 302–3
as end marks, 460–62
between independent clauses,

302–3, 304–5
in lists, 461
misuse of, 461–62
and quotation marks, 466
spacing with, 460
persecute, prosecute, G663
person, of nouns and pronouns,
G685
personal, personnel, G663
personal attack, 152
personal statements, in applications
for admission, 729–32
personal titles, 450, 493, 499
personal tone, 41
persuasion:
and advertising, 134
as aim, 33–34
and argument, 133–63
and deduction, 144–45
defined, 133–34
and explanatory points, 624
and feelings, 134
and power, 133–34
persuasive writing, 579
phenomenon, phenomena, G663
photocopying, 527, 565
phrases:
absolute, 285–86, G672
adjective, 272, G672
adverb, 274, G673
compound, 264–66, G676–77
defined, **G685**
infinitive, 283, G680–81
introductory, 465
noun, 260, 486, G683
participle, 278, G684
predetermining, 705(ESL)
prepositional, 218, G686
quotations of, 464
verb, 256, G691, 721–22(ESL)
physical properties, in natural sciences, 622–23
physics, style manual in, 635
pinpointed questions, 523
place, and subordinators, 327
placement:
of adverb clauses, 327–28
and emphasis, 334
of main point, 182–83
of modifiers, 286–92